SALLY E. STUART

CHRISTIAN WRITERS'

MARKET GUIDE

1998

Harold Shaw Publishers
Wheaton, Illinois

ISSN: 1080-3955

ISBN 0-87788-168-5

Cover design by David LaPlaca

00 99 98

3 2 1

CONTENTS

THE 1998 CHRISTIAN WRITERS' MARKET GUIDE

III. PERIODICALS

VII. INDEXES AND GLOSSARY

INTRODUCTION

It seems that each year as I prepare the new market guide, there is something different that defines it. This year there appears to be more than the usual number of basic changes—things like editors, addresses, phone, fax, etc. Also, with this 1998 edition, the thirteenth, we see an even greater move into the electronic age. We have a 30% increase in publishers on e-mail (484), and a 42% increase in those with their own Websites (272). If you are not already on the Internet, you will need to be soon, as visiting a publisher's Website will be one of the best ways to gain insight into what that publisher is all about, and what is wanted from you. Many of the sites include writer's guidelines and upcoming themes, which you can print out for an immediate copy of their needs. To help you access these Websites even more easily, I have put up my own page where you can connect directly to all the publishers with a Website or e-mail address. It may still be under construction, but visit us at: http://www.stuart-market.com.

In the current fluctuating—and often decreasing—market for freelance material, it has been an even greater challenge to find new publishers to add to what is already the largest listing of Christian publishers in existence. In fact, it is now the only such listing available. During the last year I have heard many writers lament that there is no market for their material anymore. It is true that many of the old stand-by markets have ceased publication or are no longer accepting freelance material, but there are a good number of new ones that have come along to take their place. I have been reminding writers throughout the year that what they need to do now is go back and research the market again to find the new publications or publishers they can write for. To help with that search, I have added 86 new periodicals and 32 new book publishers.

In addition, this is the most up-to-date guide ever, with 85% of the listings updated. Rather than making any major changes in format or adding a lot of new topics this year, I concentrated on getting responses from as many publishers as possibly, sending out over 2,000 questionnaires. When a publisher did not return their questionnaire, I continued to try to contact them by phone, fax, e-mail or even through their Website. Some still managed to elude our attempts to reach them, but we hope to track them down during the year. I have added a new topic listing for Online Magazines—one of the fasting growing segments of the market with about 14 included this year.

One of the other changes you will have already noticed is an increase in the price. We have managed to hold the line on the price the last few years, even while the guide increased in size each year, but as always, inflation wins out. It is still one of the best investments you can make in your future as a writer. No other resource will contribute nearly as much to your success.

The most exciting change will help you find the markets you are seeking more quickly or tell you why they are not listed. Instead of going to several different listings that tell which publishers are out of business, changed names or use no freelance, that information is now all available in the General Index. See the introduction to that index for a list of codes used. I would encourage you to make a habit of always looking up a market in the index first, as it will either give you the page number or tell you what has happened to that market.

Generally, I have continued to expand the market listings for greeting cards and specialty markets, groups, conferences, and editorial services. You will find some new agents listed, but we continue to lose about as many as we gain each year.

Many of the new markets seem to be a part of the explosion in publishing that came with the advent of desk-top publishing a few years ago. Many of those publications are small and pay little or nothing, but they still provide a good opportunity for the beginning writer to be published. My feeling is that writing and getting published, whether you are paid or not, is good for polishing your skills and may get you in on the ground floor of a new publication that may pay later. Good writing (no matter where it is found) will eventually gain the notice of the larger, paying markets. It can be a win-win situation for both the struggling new writer and the struggling new periodical.

It is a good idea each year to study the market analysis sections of this book for more insight into what's happening in the industry. As with any new reference book, I suggest you spend some quality time becoming familiar with its contents and structure. Discover the supplementary lists available throughout the book. Read through the glossary and spend a few minutes learning terms you are not familiar with. Review the lists of writer's groups and conferences and mark those you might be interested in pursuing during the coming months. The denominational listing will help you start making the important connection between periodicals and book publishers associated with different denominations, and the list I started last year will help you put the "families" of publishers together that are not denominational. With so many publishers being bought out or merging, it will help keep you up-to-date with the new members of these often growing families.

Be sure to carefully study the "How to Use This Book" section. It will save you a lot of time and frustration in trying to understand the meaning of all the notations in the primary listings, and it's full of helpful hints. Remember to send for sample copies (or catalog) and guidelines for any of these publishers or periodicals you are not familiar with. Then study those carefully before submitting anything to that publisher.

Editors tell me repeatedly that they are looking for writers who understand them, their periodical or publishing house, and most of all, their unique approach to the marketplace. One of the biggest complaints I've gotten from publishers over the years is that the material they receive routinely is not appropriate for their needs. I got fewer of those complaints this year. I hope that is an indication that you are all doing a better job of marketing. With a little time and effort, you can fulfill all their expectations, distinguish yourself as a professional, and sell what you write.

Again, I wish you well as you embark on this exciting road to publication, whether for the first time or as a long-time veteran. And as I remind you every year, each of you has been given a specific mission in the field of writing. You and I often feel inadequate to the task, but I learned a long time ago that the writing assignments

God has given me cannot be written quite as well by anyone else.

Sally E. Stuart
1647 SW Pheasant Dr.
Aloha, OR 97006
(503)642-9844 (Please call after 9 A.M. Pacific time.)
Fax (503)848-3658
E-mail: stuartcwmg@aol.com.
Website: http://www.stuartmarket.com

P.S. For information on how to receive the market guide automatically every year and freeze the price at $21.99 for future editions, or for information on getting the guide at a discounted group rate or getting books on consignment for your next seminar or conference, contact me at the address or numbers above.

HOW TO USE THIS BOOK

The purpose of this market guide is to make your marketing job easier and more targeted. However, it will serve you well only if you put some time and effort into studying its contents and using it as a springboard for discovering and becoming an expert on those publishers best suited to your writing topics and style.

Below you will find information on its general set-up and instructions for its use. In order to help you become more of an expert on marketing, I am including an explanation of each entry in the alphabetical listings for both the book section and the periodical section. Be sure to study these before trying to use this book.

1. Spend some time initially getting acquainted with the contents and set-up of this resource book. You cannot make the best use of it until you know exactly what it has to offer.

2. Study the Contents pages, where you will find listings of all the periodical and book topics. When selecting a topic, be sure to check related topics as well. Some cross-referencing will often be helpful. For example, if you have a novel that deals with doctor-assisted suicide, you might find the list for adult novels and the list for controversial issues and see which publishers are on both lists. Those would be good potential markets. In the topical sections you will find a letter "R" following publishers that accept reprints (pieces that have been printed in other publications, but for which you retain the rights).

3. The Primary/Alphabetical Listings for book and periodical publishers contain those publishers who answered the questionnaire and those who did not. The listings preceded by an asterisk (*) are those publishers who didn't respond and whose information I was unable to update from other sources. Those with a number symbol (#) were updated from their printed guidelines or other current sources. Since the information in those two groups was not verified by the publisher, you are encouraged to send for sample copies or catalogs and writer's guidelines before submitting to them.

4. In each **book publisher listing** you will find the following information (as available) in this format:

a) Name of publisher

b) Address, phone and fax numbers, e-mail address, Website

c) Denomination or affiliation

d) Name of editor—This may include the senior editor's name, followed by the name of another editor to whom submissions should be sent. In a few cases, several editors are named with the type of books each is responsible for. Address to appropriate editor.

e) Sometimes a statement of purpose

f) Sometimes a list of imprint names

g) Number of inspirational/religious titles published per year

h) Number of submissions received annually

i) Percentage of books from first-time authors

j) Those publishers who do not accept books through agents. If it says nothing about agents, you may assume they do accept books through agents.

k) The percentage of books from freelance authors they subsidy publish (if any).

This does not refer to percentage paid by author. If percentage of subsidy is over 50%, the publisher will be listed in a separate section under Subsidy Publishers.

l) Whether they reprint out-of-print books from other publishers

m) Preferred manuscript length in words or pages

n) Average amount of royalty, if provided. If royalty is a percentage of wholesale or net, it is based on price paid by bookstores or distributors. If it is on retail price, it is based on cover price of the book.

o) Average amount paid for advances—Whether a publisher pays an advance or not is noted in the listing; if they did not answer the question, there is no mention of it.

p) Whether they make any outright purchases and amount paid. In this kind of sale, an author is paid a flat fee and receives no royalties

q) Average first printing (number of books usually printed for a first-time author).

r) Average length of time between acceptance of a manuscript and publication of the work

s) Whether they consider simultaneous submissions. This means you can send a query or complete manuscript simultaneously to more than one publisher, as long as you advise everyone involved that you are doing so.

t) Length of time it should take them to respond to a query/proposal or to a complete manuscript (when two lengths of time are given, the first generally refers to a query and the latter to a complete manuscript). Give them a one-month grace period beyond that and then send a polite follow-up letter if you haven't heard from them.

u) Whether a publisher "Accepts," "Prefers," or "Requires" the submission of an ACCEPTED manuscript on disk. Most publishers now do accept or require that books be sent on a computer disk (usually along with a hard copy), but since each publisher's needs are different, that information will be supplied to you by the individual publisher when the time comes.

(v) Availability and cost for writer's guidelines and book catalogs—If the listing says "Guidelines," it means they are available for a #10 (business-sized) SASE with a first-class stamp. The cost of the catalog (if any), the size of envelope, and amount of postage are given, if specified (affix stamps to envelope; don't send loose). Tip: If postage required is more than $1.24, I suggest you put $1.24 in postage on the envelope and clearly mark it "Special Standard Mail." (That is enough for up to 1 pound). (Please note that if the postage rates increase this year, this amount may change. Check with your local Post Office.) If the listing says "free catalog," it means you need only request it; they do not ask for payment or SASE. Note: If sending for both guidelines and catalog, it is not necessary to send two envelopes; guidelines will be sent with catalog.

w) Nonfiction Section—Preference for query letter, book proposal, or complete manuscript, and if they accept phone, fax, or e-mail queries (if it does not say they accept them, assume they do not; this applies to fiction as well as nonfiction). If they want a query letter, send just a letter describing your project. If they want a query letter/proposal, you can add a chapter-by-chapter synopsis and the number of sample chapters indicated. If not specified, send one to three chapters. This is often followed by a quote from them about their needs or what they don't want to see.

x) Fiction Section—Same information as nonfiction section

y) Special Needs—If they have specific topics they need that are not included in the subject listings, they are indicated here.

z) Ethnic Books—Usually specifies which ethnic groups they target or any particular needs

aa) Also Does—Indicates which publishers also publish booklets, pamphlets or tracts.

bb) Tips—Specific tips provided by the editor/publisher

Note: At the end of some listings you will find an indication that the publisher receives mailings of book proposals from The Writer's Edge (see Editorial Services/Illinois for an explanation of that service).

5. In each **periodical listing** you will find the following information (as available) in this format:

a) Name of periodical

b) Address, phone, fax, and e-mail address, Website

c) Denomination or affiliation

d) Name of editor and editor to submit to (if different)

e) Theme of publication—This will help you understand their particular slant.

f) Format of publication, frequency of publication, number of pages and size of circulation—tells whether magazine, newsletter, journal, tabloid, newspaper, or take-home paper. Frequency of publication indicates quantity of material needed. Number of pages usually indicates how much material they can use. Circulation indicates the amount of exposure your material will receive and often indicates how well they might pay or the probability that they will stay in business.

g) Subscription rate—Amount given is for a one-year subscription in the country of origin. I suggest you subscribe to at least one of your primary markets every year to become better acquainted with its specific focus.

h) Date established—included only if 1994 or later

i) Openness to freelance; percentage freelance written. If they buy only a small percentage, it often means they are open but receive little that is appropriate. The percentage freelance written indicates how great your chances are of selling to them. When you have a choice, choose those with the higher percentage, but only if you have done your homework and know they are an appropriate market for your material.

j) Preference for query or complete manuscript tells if they want a cover letter with complete manuscripts and whether they will accept phone, fax, or e-mail queries. (If it does not mention cover letters or phone, fax, or e-mail queries, assume they do not accept them.)

k) Payment schedule, payment on acceptance (they pay when the piece is accepted) or publication (they pay when it is published), and rights purchased (see glossary for definitions of different rights)

l) If a publication does not pay, or pays in copies or subscription, that is indicated in bold, capital letters.

m) If a publication is not copyrighted, that is indicated. That means you should ask for your copyright notice to appear on your piece when they publish it, so your rights will be protected.

n) Preferred word lengths and average number of manuscripts purchased per year (in parentheses)

o) Response time—The time they usually take to respond to your query or manuscript submission (add at least two weeks for delays for mailing)

p) Seasonal material (also refers to holiday)—If sending holiday or seasonal material, it should reach them at least the specified length of time in advance.

q) Acceptance of simultaneous submissions and reprints—If they accept simultaneous submissions, it means they will look at submissions (usually timely topic or holiday material) sent simultaneously to several publishers. Best to send to non-overlapping markets (such as denominational), and be sure to always indicate that it is a simultaneous submission. Reprints are pieces you have sold previously, but to which you hold the rights (which means you sold only first or one-time rights to the original publisher and the rights reverted to you as soon as they were published).

r) If they accept, prefer or require submissions on disk, and whether there is extra compensation for that. Most of them seem to want a disk after the piece is accepted, but want a query or hard copy first. If it does not say they prefer or require disks, you should wait and see if they ask for them.

s) Average amount of kill fee, if they pay one (see glossary for definition).

t) Whether they use sidebars (see glossary for definition).

u) Their preferred Bible version is indicated. The most popular version is the NIV (New International Version). If no version is indicated, they usually have no preference. See glossary for Bible Versions list.

v) Availability and cost for writer's guidelines, theme list, and sample copies—If the listing says "Guidelines," it means they are available for a #10 SASE (business-sized) with a first-class stamp. The cost for a sample copy, the size of envelope, and number of stamps required are given, if specified (affix stamps to envelope; don't send loose). Tip: If postage required is more than $1.24, I suggest you put $1.24 in postage on the envelope and clearly mark it "Special Standard Mail." (That is enough for up to one pound). If the listing says "Free sample copy," it means you need only to request them; they do not ask for payment or SASE. Note: If sending for both guidelines and sample copy, it is not necessary to send two envelopes; guidelines will be sent with sample copy. If a listing doesn't mention guidelines or a catalog, they probably don't have them.

w) "Not in topical listings" means the publisher has not supplied a list of topics they are interested in.

x) Poetry—Name of poetry editor (if different). Average number of poems bought each year. Types of poetry; number of lines. Payment rate. Maximum number of poems you may submit at one time.

y) Fillers—Name of fillers editor (if different). Types of fillers accepted; word length. Payment rate.

z) Columns/Departments—Name of column editor. Names of columns in the periodical (information in parentheses gives focus of column); word length requirements; payment. Be sure to see sample before sending ms or query. Most columns require a query.

aa) Special Issues or Needs—Indicates topics of special issues they have planned for the year, or unique topics not included in regular subject listings

bb) Ethnic—Any involvement they have in the ethnic market

cc) Contest— Information on contests they sponsor or how to obtain that information

dd) Tips—Tips from the editor on how to break into this market or how to be successful as an author

ee) At the end of some listings you will find a notation as to where that particular periodical placed in the Top 50 Plus Christian Periodical list in 1997, and/or their place in previous years. This list is compiled annually to indicate the most writer-friendly publications. To receive a complete listing, plus a prepared analysis sheet and writer's guidelines for the top 50 of those markets, send $23 (includes postage) to: Sally Stuart, 1647 SW Pheasant Dr., Aloha OR 97006, or call (503)642-9844 for more information.

Some listings also include EPA winners. These awards are made annually by the Evangelical Press Association (a trade organization for Christian periodicals).

6. It is important that you adhere closely to the guidelines set out in these listings. If a publisher asks for a query only, do not send a complete manuscript. Following these guidelines will mark you as a professional.

7. If your manuscript is completed, select the proper topical listing and target audience, and make up a list of possible publishers. Check first to see which ones will accept a complete manuscript (if you want to send it to those that require a query, you will have to write a query letter or book proposal to send first). Please do not assume that your manuscript will be appropriate for all those on the list. Read the primary listing for each and if you are not familiar with a publisher, read their writer's guidelines and study one or more sample copies or book catalog. (The primary listings contain information on how to get these.) Be sure the slant of your manuscript fits the slant of the publisher.

8. If you have an idea for an article, short story, or book but you have not written it yet, a reading of the appropriate topical listing will help you decide on a possible slant or approach. Select some publishers to whom you might send a query about your idea. If your idea is for an article, do not overlook the possibility of writing on the same topic for a number of different periodicals listed under that topic, either with the same target audience or another from the list that indicates an interest. For example, you could write on money management for a general adult magazine, a teen magazine, a women's publication, or one for pastors. Each would require a different slant, but you would get a lot more mileage from that idea.

9. If you do not have an idea, simply start reading through the topical listings or the primary listings. They are sure to trigger any number of book or magazine ideas you could go to work on.

10. If you run into words or terms you are not familiar with, check the glossary at the back of the book for definitions.

11. If you need someone to look at your material to evaluate it or to give it a thorough editing, look up the section on Editorial Services and find someone to send it to for such help. That often will make the difference between success or failure in publishing.

12. If you are a published author with other books to your credit, you may be interested in finding an agent. Unpublished authors generally don't need or won't be able to find an agent. However, some agents will consider unpublished authors (their listing will indicate that), but you must have a completed manuscript before you approach an agent (see agent list). Christian agents are more at a premium than ever, so realize it will be extremely hard to find an agent unless you have had some success in book writing.

13. Check the group list to find a group to join in your area. Go to the conference list to find a conference you might attend this year. Attending a conference every year or two is almost essential to your success as a writer.

14. **ALWAYS SEND AN SASE WITH EVERY QUERY OR MANUSCRIPT.**

15. **DO NOT RELY SOLELY ON THE INFORMATION PROVIDED IN THIS MARKET GUIDE.** It is just that—a guide—and is not intended to be complete in itself. It is important to your success as a freelance writer that you learn how to use writer's guidelines and study book catalogs or sample copies before submitting to any publisher. Be a professional!

ADDITIONAL RESOURCES TO HELP WITH YOUR WRITING AND MARKETING

1. **1998 Top 50+ Christian Periodical Publishers Packet**—Includes a list of the Top 50+ "writer-friendly" periodicals, pre-prepared analysis sheets, and publisher's guidelines for each of the top 50, and a master form for analyzing your own favorite markets. Saves more than $40 in postage and 25-30 hours of work. $23, postpaid. New packet every year.

2. **The 1998 Christian Writers' Market Guide on computer disk** in ASCII Text on 3$\frac{1}{2}$" HD disk, for quick marketing reference. This is in text form as it appears in the book, not in a database. $29.50 postpaid.

3. **A Market Plan for More Sales**—A step-by-step plan to help you be successful in marketing. Includes 5 reproducible forms. $4.75 postpaid.

4. **The Complete Guide to Christian Writing and Speaking**—A how-to handbook for beginning and advanced writers and speakers written by the 19 members of the editorial staff of *The Christian Communicator*. $12, postpaid.

5. **Permissions Packet**—A compilation of over 16 pages of information directly from publishers on how and when to ask permission to quote from other people's material or from Bible paraphrases. Information not available elsewhere in printed form. $5, postpaid.

6. **The Christian Writer's Book**—Here's a new book that focuses on the writing and selling of Christian books. Many valuable sections, including what an editor does, a guided tour of the book contract, an extensive bibliography of writer's resources, and a style guide for authors and editors. $18 postpaid.

7. **Copyright Law, What You Don't Know Can Cost You**—Answers all the questions about rights and copyright law that affect you as a writer. Simple Q & A format followed by the actual wording of the law. Includes reproducible copyright forms & instructions. $17 postpaid.

8. **Write on Target,** A Five-Phase Program for Nonfiction Writers, by Dennis Hensley & Holly Miller—The craft of writing, the nuts and bolts, finding your niche, selling your manuscript, and mapping your future success as a writer. $14 postpaid.

9. **100 Plus Motivational Moments for Writers and Speakers**—A devotional book specifically for writers and speakers written by successful writers and speakers. $12 postpaid.

10. **You Can Do It! A Guide to Christian Self-Publishing,** by Athena Dean. Dean shares insider self-publishing secrets for the Christian market. Takes you step-by-step through the project, including actual budgets and current cost estimates. $10 postpaid.

11. **1998 Internet Directory of Christian Publishers**—A handy listing of over 485 Christian publishers who have e-mail addresses. Note: Since you can now access the Websites of all Christian publishers who have them through my Web page at http://www.stuartmarket.com, and because the list is growing daily, this directory now

includes e-mail addresses only. Also, if the list gets too long to maintain a booklet format, it may come on $8\frac{1}{2}$ x11sheets, three-hole punched to put in a notebook. This listing also indicated which of these publishers accept e-mail queries. New ones will be added as they become available. $5 postpaid.

12. The following resources are all 8-page, $8\frac{1}{2}$x 11 booklets on areas of specific interest, as indicated:

a. **Keeping Track of Your Periodical Manuscripts**—These pages can be duplicated to keep track of every step involved in sending out your periodical manuscripts to publishers. $4.75 postpaid.

b. **Keeping Track of Your Book Manuscripts**—A similar booklet summarizing the steps in tracking a book manuscript from idea to publication. $4.75 postpaid.

c. **How to Submit a Book Proposal to a Publisher**—Contains all you need to know to present a professional looking book proposal to a publishing house (includes a sample book proposal). $4.75 postpaid.

d. **How to Submit an Article or Story to a Publisher**—Shows how to write a query, prepare a professional-looking manuscript, and more. $4.75 postpaid.

e. **How to Write That Sure-Sell Magazine Article**—Contains a 3-step writing plan for articles, a list of article types, 12 evaluation questions, sample manuscript page, and more. $4.75 postpaid.

f. **How to Write a Picture Book**—An inside look at how to write, format, and lay out a children's picture book, with tips for those all-important finishing touches. $4.75 postpaid.

g. **How to Write Daily Devotionals That Inspire**—Includes the basic format and patterns for daily devotionals, marketing tips, 12 evaluation questions, and polishing. $4.75 postpaid.

13. The following resources are all $8\frac{1}{2}$ x $5\frac{1}{2}$ booklets, 12-20 pages, on areas of specific interest, as indicated:

a. **The Art of Researching the Professional Way.**—$4.75 postpaid.

b. **Interviewing the Professional Way.**—$4.75 postpaid.

c. **The Professional Way to Write Dialogue.**—$4.75 postpaid.

d. **The Professional Way to Create Characters.**—$4.75 postpaid.

e. **Writing Junior Books the Professional Way (for ages 8-12)**—$4.75 postpaid.

f. **Writing for Young Adults the Professional Way.**—$4.75 postpaid.

To order any of the above resources, send a list of what you want with your check or money order to: Sally E. Stuart, 1647 SW Pheasant Dr., Aloha OR 97006, (503)642-9844. Fax: (503)848-3658.

14. **The Writer's Edge**—A service that links book writers and Christian publishers. The writer fills out a book information form and sends that along with 3 sample chapters, a synopsis, and a check for $45. The writer receives a brief critique of the manuscript or, if the manuscript is accepted by The Writer's Edge, a synopsis of the manuscript will appear in a newsletter that goes to more than 40 Christian publishers who use The Writer's Edge as a screening tool for unsolicited manuscripts. *For further information, send an SASE to The Writer's Edge, PO Box 1266, Wheaton, IL 60189.*

RESOURCES FOR WRITERS

Below you will find a variety of resources that will help you as you carry out your training or work as a freelance writer. In addition to the resources here, also check out the separate listings for groups, conferences, editorial services, contests (see periodical topics). This is only a preliminary list of resources and will be added to each year as the writer's needs grow and expand.

CORRESPONDENCE COURSES

AT HOME WRITING WORKSHOPS. Director: Marlene Bagnull, Write His Answer Ministries, 316 Blanchard Rd., Drexel Hill PA 19026. E-mail: mbagnull@aol.com. Offers 3 courses of study with 6-10 study units in each. (1) Putting Your Best Foot Forward (lays foundation for your writing ministry), 6 units, $150; (2) Nonfiction (articles, tracts, curriculum, devotionals, how-tos, etc., plus planning a nonfiction book and book proposal), 10 units, $250; (3) Fiction, 10 units, $250. Also offers an easy payment plan of $30 per unit.

CHRISTIAN WRITERS GUILD. Director: Norman B. Rohrer, 260 Fern, Hume CA 93628. (209)335-2333. Offers a 3-year home study course: Discover Your Possibilities in Writing. Includes an introduction to writing, article writing, short inspirational pieces, and fiction, plus a number of additional benefits. Send for your free Starter Kit. Cost for 3-year course is $495. Offers several payment plans and a $75 discount for full payment up front. Special offer through the Christian Writers' Market Guide: Instead of paying $150 down payment, you may pay $25 down, plus $15/month for the next 27 months as you study. Ask about the CWMG special when you request your starter kit.

CHRISTIAN WRITERS INSTITUTE CORRESPONDENCE COURSES. Call or write for information: American Christian Writers, Reg Forder, PO Box 110390, Nashville TN 37222. (800)21-WRITE.

POETRY WRITING SESSION. Mary Sayler, instructor. PO Box 730, DeLand FL 32721-0730. (904)783-3388. Fax (904)738-0169. Seven units dealing specifically with poetry: purposes, content, language, meter, and much more. A unique poetry course with a Christian perspective. Cost $200.

WRITING CLASSES ON CASSETTE TAPES

CHRISTIAN WRITERS LEARNING CENTER. Hundreds of cassette tapes to choose from. Cost is $4-5 each, depending on quantity. Send SASE for list of topics to: American Christian Writers, Reg Forder, PO Box 110390, Nashville TN 37222. (800)21-WRITE.

CREATIVE CHRISTIAN MINISTRIES. Tapes on a variety of topics. $4.95 ea.; 3 or more $3.95 ea. Send SASE for list of topics: Creative Christian Ministries, PO Box 12644, Roanoke VA 24027. (703)432-7511. Also has a series called How to Turn Everyday Events into Personal Experience Articles, $19.95, plus $2.05 p/h. Request free writer's catalog.

WRITE HIS ANSWER MINISTRIES. Director: Marlene Bagnull, 316 Blanchard Rd., Drexel Hill PA 19026. E-mail: mbagnull@aol.com. Tapes on 20+ topics, $5 ea. Topics include: Taking the Pain Out of Marketing; Self-publishing; and Turning Personal Experience Into Print. Marlene's day-long seminars (four 90-minute sessions) are $18.95. All tapes include handouts. Also offers a Ministry/Marketing Packet with over 60 resources for $10; and an ABC's of Marketing Packet for $5.

GROUPS/ORGANIZATIONS OF INTEREST

AMERICAN CHRISTIAN WRITERS, PO Box 110390, Nashville TN 37222. (800)21-WRITE. Reg Forder, director.

THE AMY FOUNDATION. Sponsors two annual contests for prizes up to $10,000. One for publication in the secular media and the other for publication in the religious media. For details on both contests, and a copy of last year's winning entries, contact: The Amy Foundation, PO Box 16091, Lansing MI 48901-6091. (517)323-6233. Website: http://www.amyfound.org.

ASSOCIATED CHURCH PRESS, PO Box 30215, Phoenix AZ 85046-0215. (602)569-6371. John Stapert, executive director.

CHRISTIAN BOOKSELLERS ASSN., PO Box 200, Colorado Springs CO 80901-0200. (800)252-1950. Bill Anderson, president.

EVANGELICAL CHRISTIAN PUBLISHERS ASSN., 3225 S. Hardy Dr., Ste. 101, Tempe AZ 85282. (602)966-3998. Doug Ross, pres./CEO.

EVANGELICAL PRESS ASSN., 314 Dover Rd., Charlottesville VA 22901. (804)973-5941. Ronald E. Wilson, director.

INTERNATIONAL CHRISTIAN WRITERS GROUP. Stanley C. Baldwin, director, 12900 SE Nixon, Milwaukie OR 97222. E-mail: SCBaldwin@juno.com. A point of contact for writers around the world.

INTERNATIONAL SMALL PRESS PUBLISHING INSTITUTE. Sponsors 6-8 educational forums a year for publishers and authors. Contact: David Rattigan, director, at e-mail: d.rattigan@smallpress.com, or Theresa Nelson, Jenkins Group, Inc., 121 E. Front St., 4th Fl., Traverse City MI 49684. (616)933-0445. Fax (616)933-0448. E-mail: theresa.nelson@smallpress.com. Website: http://www.smallpress.com.

NATIONAL RELIGIOUS BROADCASTERS., 7839 Ashton Ave., Manassas VA 22110. (703)330-7000. Request information on the Directory of Religious Media.

RELIGION NEWS SERVICE, 1101 Connecticut Ave. NW, Ste 350, Washington DC 20036. (202)463-8777. Fax (202)463-0033. Dale Hanson Bourke, publisher.

RELIGIOUS NEWSWRITERS ASSN. An organization formed to advance the professional standards of religion reporting in the secular media. Joan Connell, Newhouse News Service, 200 Pennsylvania Ave., NW, Washington DC 20006. (202)785-0101.

ON THE INTERNET

CHRISTIAN WRITER'S WORKSHOP. This is an interactive Christian writer's group that meets once a week on the Internet for discussion and has a weekly newsletter that comes by e-mail. To find the club at 9:00 ET on Thursday nights, go to Key Word: Writers—Writer's Club—Chat rooms. Select the Writer's Workshop chat room. They will tell you how to sign up for the newsletter. Contact person is Bill Yates, e-mail: WTYates@aol.com.

CROSSSEARCH is an online directory that offers Internet users a search engine for Christian and religion-related resources. Includes links to nearly 40 ministries on Gospel Communications Network. Website: http://www.cross-search.com.

INTERNATIONAL@WRITERS CLUB. Provides writers worldwide with a host of services and opportunities with a base for networking, job opportunities, and invaluable writing resources. Membership is $35/year. For more information, visit their Website at: http://members.tripod.com/awriters/iwc.htm.

INTERNET FOR CHRISTIANS, a book by Quentin J. Schultze, Gospel Films, Inc., $12.95. Available at your local Christian bookstore. Author also offers a free newsletter, Internet for Christians. To subscribe send the message "SUBSCRIBE and your e-mail address" to: ifc-request@gospelcom.net. Website: http://www. gospelcom.net/ifc (includes hyperlinks to all listed sites).

JUNO OFFERS FREE E-MAIL SERVICE. This service is free and an easy solution for those who want an e-mail address and the ability to correspond with others by e-mail, but don't need or want additional access to the Internet. There is no obligation for requesting the software or trying it out. E-mail your request to: signup@juno.com, or call (800)654-5866. This service is advertiser supported, and membership is limited to the US for now (although you can communicate with e-mail users in other countries). Since they release a limited number of memberships a day, it may take 6-8 weeks to have your request fulfilled.

RESOURCES FOR THE CHRISTIAN WRITER is a part of the ACW Press Website. Go to: http://www.acwpress.com/links.htm. Links to lots of great resources.

RESOURCES FOR WRITERS ON THE WEB. Website: http://www.interlog. com/~ohi/www/writesource.html. To subscribe to Inklings, an electronic newsletter that covers online resources for writers, send e-mail to: majordomo@ samuri.com, with the message "subscribe inklings" in the message box.

WEBSITES OF INTEREST TO WRITERS

GENERAL:

CHRISTIAN BOOK DISTRIBUTORS (CBD): http://www.christianbook.com. Check out what's selling in the marketplace. Books can be found by publisher, author or subject.

WEB PAGE OF LINKS FOR CHRISTIAN WRITERS: http://users.aol.com/ kayhall/cwise.html. Maintained by Kay Hall.

INTERNET FOR CHRISTIANS: http://www.gospelcom.net/ifc/.

SPECIALTY TOPICS:

BIBLE PROPHECY: http://www.sel-mor.com/armageddon. Links to every Bible Prophecy site on the Web.

CHRISTIAN COMICS INTERNATIONAL: http://members.aol.com/ChriCom/ or, http://members.aol.com/ChriCat/. Nate Butler can be reached by e-mail at: ChrisCom@aol.com. Also a bimonthly newsletter for writers of Christian Comics is available: New Creation, Kevin Yong, PO Box 254, Dept. C, Temple City CA

91780, or e-mail: Densign888@aol.com. The first issue is free on request. Another contact person for writers interested in scripting a comic or other aspects of comic ministry is: Len Cowan, 519 - 164th Pl. SE, Bothell WA 98012, e-mail: clcowan@xc.org.

CHRISTIAN MUSIC SITES. Christian Music Online at http://www.cmo.com; Salt Inc. Music at http://saltinc.edumaster.net; and Steve Green Ministries at http://www.gocin.com/stevegreen.

CHRISTIAN SPOTLIGHT ON THE MOVIES, provides reviews of Christian films and mainstream movies from a Christian perspective. Find it at: http://www.ChristinAnswers/net/spotlight.

>**HOMESCHOOLING:** http://www.learnathome.com/. For writers in home schooling market.

>**PARENT SOUP:** http://www.parentsoup.com. For writers of parenting articles.

>**POETRY:** An online version of Poetry Update from London, England. Also sponsors contests with e-mail for information: info@poetry.co.uk. Website: http://www.poetry.co.uk. E-mail for Eric Goldsworthy, the editor/director, is: eric@poetry.co.uk.

SERVICES

CHRISTIAN INFORMATION MINISTRY/RESEARCH SERVICE. Provides fee-based custom research for authors, publishers, ministries, churches and individuals; primarily Bible, theology and Christian living. Basic research fee is $25/hr, plus expenses, such as photocopying. Cecil R. Price, TH.M., PO Box 141055, Dallas TX 75214. (214)827-0057.

CREATIVE RESOURCES: CONSULTING & MEDIA SERVICES. Don S. Otis, PO Box 1665, Sandpoint ID 83864. (208)263-8055. Fax (208)263-9055. E-mail: CMResources@aol.com. A publicist for Christian authors and para-church agencies.

INTERACTIVE DATA MANAGEMENT. David Gibby, 1786 NW Jay St., Roseburg OR 97470, (541)957-1786. Can help you develop a web page; design business logos or brochures; develop interactive CD magazines and books; put all your articles, artwork, or other data on a CD; plus much more. Call or write for information.

CORRESPONDENCE COURSE FOR MANUSCRIPT EDITING. The University of Wisconsin offers a correspondence course in manuscript editing for those wanting to do editing on a professional level or for writers wanting to improve their personal editing skills. Reasonable cost. Contact: U of Wisconsin Extension, 432 N. Lake St., Madison WI 53706. Ask about Manuscript Editing A52.

SOFTWARE

AMERICAN CHRISTIAN WRITERS SOFTWARE FOR WRITERS, PO Box 110390, Nashville TN 37222. (800)21-WRITE. Reg Forder, director. Send a #10 SASE/1 stamp for an 8-page catalog of software (mostly shareware) of special interest to writers.

BESTSELLER: A SUBMISSION TRACKING SOFTWARE FOR WRITERS.

For a demo copy send $12 US or $17.50 CAN; for complete program, send $73.95 US or $99.45 CAN (prices include postage) to: Salt Spring Island Software, 137 McPhillips Ave., Salt Spring Island BC, V8K 2T6 Canada. For more information call (604)537-4339.

WRITER'S PUBLICATIONS/SPECIALIZED

THE CHRISTIAN MUSIC DIRECTORY. Easy-to-use guide to the Christian music, film, and video business. James Lloyd Group, PO Box 448, Jacksonville OR 97530. (541)899-8888. Fax (541)488-0418. (Call for current price). Also has The Christian Artist Survival Guide, How to Produce, Manufacture, Distribute & Promote an Independent Christian Record., $33.45, incl. postage.

HEREIN IS LOVE. A bimonthly, 4-page newsletter for inspirational romance writers (those who write romance novels for the Christian market). $15/yr. Jane LaMunyon, 1943 Inyo St., Mojave CA 93501.

TAX TIPS FOR WRITERS. A book that deals with tax law and tax return preparation from a writer's standpoint. Cost is $8.95, plus $1.55 postage. Tower Enterprises, 2130 Sunset Dr., #47, Vista CA 92083. (619)941-9293.

TOPICAL/SUBJECT LISTINGS OF BOOK PUBLISHERS

One of the most difficult aspects of marketing is trying to determine which publishers might be interested in the book you want to write. This topical listing was designed to help you do just that.

First, look up your topic of interest in the following lists. If you don't find the specific topic, check the list of topics in the table of contents and find any related topics. Once you have discovered which publishers are interested in a particular topic, the next step is to secure writer's guidelines and book catalogs from those publishers. Don't assume, just because a particular publisher is listed under your topic, that it would automatically be interested in your book. It is your job to determine whether your approach to the subject will fit within the unique scope of that publisher's catalog. It is also helpful to visit a Christian bookstore to actually see some of the books produced by each publisher you are interested in pursuing.

Note, too, that the primary listings for each publisher indicate what the publisher prefers to see in the way of a query, book proposal, or complete manuscript.

R—Indicates which publishers reprint out-of-print books from other publishers.

APOLOGETICS

ACU Press
Baker Books—R
Bethany House
Black Forest—R
Brentwood—R
Bridge/Logos
Christendom Press—R
Christian Publications
Christian Univ. Press—R
College Press—R
Comments Publishing—R
Concordia
Cornerstone Press
Cornerstone Pub.
Cross Cultural
Crossway Books
CSS Publishing
Eerdmans Publishing—R
Evangel Publishing—R
Faith Publishing
FOG Publishing
Franciscan Univ. Press—R
Gospel Folio Press
Gospel Publishing House—R
HarperSanFrancisco
Harvard House
Hendrickson—R
Hensley, Virgil—R
InterVarsity Press
Kregel—R

Lightwave Publishing
Magnus Press—R
Master Books—R
Messianic Jewish—R
Morehouse—R
Our Sunday Visitor—R
Oxford University
Presbyterian & Reformed
Read 'N Run—R
Regnery Publishing—R
Revell, Fleming H.
Review & Herald—R
Rose Publishing
Son-Rise
Still Waters Revival—R
Sword of the Lord—R
Toccoa Falls
Trinity Foundation—R
Tyler Press—R
United Methodist—R
Vital Issues Press—R
WaterBrook Press
Zondervan/Trade—R
Zondervan/Academic

ARCHAEOLOGY

Baker Books—R
Black Forest—R
Brentwood—R
Christopher Publishing
College Press—R

Concordia
CSS Publishing
Doubleday
Eerdmans Publishing—R
Facts on File
HarperSanFrancisco
Hendrickson—R
Journey Books—R
Kregel—R
Monument Press
New Leaf Press—R
Oxford University
Ragged Edge—R
Read 'N Run—R
Review & Herald—R
Schocken Books—R
Trinity Press Intl.—R
Tyler Press—R
U of Ottawa Press
University Press/America—R
Westminster/John Knox
Winston-Derek—R
Yale Univ. Press—R
Zondervan/Trade—R
Zondervan/Academic

AUTOBIOGRAPHY

Bantam Books
Bethany House
Bethel Publishing—R
Black Forest—R

Blue Dolphin
Brannon & Baker
Brentwood—R
Bridge/Logos
Butterfly Press
Christopher Publishing
Cornerstone Pub.
CSS Publishing
Dabar Publishing—R
Daybreak Books—R
Doubleday
Eerdmans Publishing—R
Fairway Press—R
FOG Publishing
Friends United Press—R
Guernica Editions—R
HarperSanFrancisco
Hearth Publishing—R
Lydia Press—R
Messianic Jewish—R
Paraclete Press—R
Read 'N Run—R
Regnery Publishing—R
Schocken Books—R
Shaw Publishers, Harold—R
Son-Rise
Southern Baptist Press—R
Still Waters Revival—R
Sword of the Lord—R
Toccoa Falls
Tyler Press—R
VESTA—R
Vital Issues Press—R
Western Front—R
Westminster/John Knox
Zondervan/Trade—R

BIBLE/BIBLICAL STUDIES

Accent Publications
ACU Press
Alba House—R
Baker Books—R
Bantam Books
Bethany House
Black Forest—R
Brentwood—R
Bridge/Logos
Broadman & Holman
Brown-ROA
Butterfly Press
Chalice Press
Christian Ed Pub.
Christian Publications
Christopher Publishing
College Press—R
Concordia
Contemporary Drama Service

Continuum Publishing—R
Cornell Univ Press—R
Cornerstone Pub.
Creation House
Cross Cultural
CSS Publishing
Dabar Publishing—R
Daybreak Books—R
Doubleday
Eerdmans Publishing—R
Evangel Publishing—R
Fairway Press—R
FOG Publishing
Franciscan Univ. Press—R
Goetz Publishing, B.J.
Gospel Folio Press
Gospel Publishing House—R
GROUP Publishing—R
HarperSanFrancisco
Hendrickson—R
Hensley, Virgil—R
HI-TIME
Holy Cross—R
Innisfree Press
Intl. Awakening Press—R
InterVarsity Press
Judson Press—R
Kindred Productions
Kregel—R
Libros Liguori
Logion Press
Loizeaux (commentary)
Lydia Press—R
Magnus Press—R
Mercer University Press
Messianic Jewish—R
Morehouse—R
Mt. Olive College Press
New City Press—R
New Hope—R
Omega House
Our Sunday Visitor—R
Oxford University
Pastoral Press
Pauline Books
Paulist Press
Presbyterian & Reformed
Promise Publishing
Ragged Edge—R
Read 'N Run—R
Resource Publications
Revell, Fleming H.
Review & Herald—R
Royal Productions—R
Schocken Books—R
Seaside Press—R
Shaw Publishers, Harold—R
Sheed & Ward—R

Shining Star
Smyth & Helwys
Son-Rise
Southern Baptist Press—R
Starburst Publishers
Sword of the Lord—R
Toccoa Falls
Treasure Publishing—R
Trinity Press Intl.—R
Tyler Press—R
United Church Pub.
United Methodist—R
University Press/America—R
Upper Room Books—R
VESTA—R
Vital Issues Press—R
Wadsworth—R
Warner Press
WaterBrook Press
Wesleyan Publishing House
Westminster/John Knox
Woman's Miss. Union—R
Women of the Promise
Wood Lake Books
World Bible
Yale Univ. Press—R
Zondervan/Trade—R
Zondervan/Academic

BIOGRAPHY

Alba House—R
Alexander Books
Bantam Books
Barbour Publishing—R
Bethany House
Bethel Publishing—R
Black Forest—R
Blue Dolphin
Brannon & Baker
Brentwood—R
Bridge/Logos
Butterfly Press
Catholic Univ/America—R
Christian Publications
Christopher Publishing
College Press—R
Cornell Univ. Press—R
Cornerstone Pub.
CSS Publishing
Daybreak Books—R
Dimension Books—R
Doubleday
Eerdmans Publishing—R
Facts on File
Fairway Press—R
Faith Publishing
HarperSanFrancisco

Hearth Publishing—R
ICS Publications—R
Impact Christian Books
Intl. Awakening Press—R
Journey Books—R
Judson Press—R
Kaleidoscope Press—R
Kregel—R
Lifetime Book—R
Light and Life—R
Lydia Press—R
Messianic Jewish—R
Middle Atlantic—R
Morehouse—R
Morrow and Co., Wm
Mt. Olive College Press
New Hope—R
One World
Oxford University
Paraclete Press—R
G.P. Putnam's Sons
Read 'N Run—R
Regnery Publishing—R
Review & Herald—R
Royal Productions—R
St. Bede's—R
Schocken Books—R
Shaw Publishers, Harold—R
Son-Rise
Southern Baptist Press—R
Still Waters Revival—R
Sword of the Lord—R
Toccoa Falls
Tyler Press—R
University Press/America—R
Upper Room Books—R
VESTA—R
Vital Issues Press—R
Warner Press
Western Front—R
Westminster/John Knox
Windflower—R
Woman's Miss. Union—R
Yale Univ. Press—R
YWAM Publishing—R
Zondervan/Trade—R

BOOKLETS

Accent Books
Apologetics Press
Barbour Publishing—R
Barclay Press—R
Christendom Press—R
Christian Lit. Crusade—R
Christian Publications
Church Growth Inst.
Comments Publishing—R

Cornerstone Pub.
Cross Way Pub.
Dry Bones Press—R
Faith Publishing
Forward Movement—R
Franciscan Univ. Press—R
Good News Publishers
Gospel Folio Press
Gospel Publishing House—R
GROUP Publishing—R
Hearth Publishing—R
HI-TIME
Holy Cross—R
Image Press
Intl. Awakening Press—R
InterVarsity Press
Kindred Productions
Libros Liguori
Lightwave Publishing
Liguori Publications
Longwood—R
Master Books—R
Messianic Jewish—R
Middle Atlantic—R
Moody Press (series only)
Omega House
Our Sunday Visitor—R
Pacific Press—R
Paradise Research
Pauline Books
Pilgrim Press—R
Read 'N Run—R
Rose Publishing
Royal Productions—R
Shaw Publishers, Harold
Sword of the Lord—R
TEACH Services—R
Trinity Foundation—R
Tyler Press—R
United Methodist—R
Vital Issues Press—R
Wine Press Publishing
Woman's Miss. Union—R
Women of the Promise
Wood Lake Books

CANADIAN/FOREIGN

Cerdic Publications
Essence Publishing
Guernica Editions
Hunt and Thorpe
Inheritance Publications
Kindred Productions
Northstone
Still Waters
Summit Publishing
United Church Pub. Hs

Univ. of Ottawa Press
VESTA—R
Windflower—R
Wood Lake Books

CELEBRITY PROFILES

Blue Dolphin
Bridge/Logos
Christopher Publishing
Cross Cultural
Daybreak Books—R
Doubleday
Lifetime Books—R
New Leaf Press—R
G.P. Putnam's Sons
Read 'N Run—R
Royal Productions—R
Shaw Publishers, Harold—R
Sword of the Lord—R
Western Front—R
Zondervan/Trade—R

CHILDREN'S PICTURE BOOKS

Alba House—R
Art Can Drama—R
Bay Public., Mel—R
Black Forest—R
Brannon & Baker
Bridge/Logos
CEF Press
Chariot Books
Concordia
Cornerstone Pub.
CSS Publishing
Eerdmans Publishing—R
Fairway Press—R
Focus Publishing
Gold 'n' Honey Books
Hunt & Thorpe
Kaleidoscope Press—R
Lightwave Publishing
Lion Publishing
Living the Good News
Lydia Press—R
Messianic Jewish—R
Morehouse—R
Morris, Joshua
National Baptist—R
Pauline Books
Paulist Press
Pelican Publishing—R
Read 'N Run—R
Regina Press
Royal Productions—R
Son-Rise

Standard
Sword of the Lord—R
Tommy Nelson—R
Treasure Publishing—R
United Methodist—R
Vital Issues Press—R
WaterBrook Press
Woman's Miss. Union—R
Zondervan/Trade—R

CHRISTIAN EDUCATION

Accent Publications
ACU Press
Alba House—R
Baker Books—R
Bantam Books
Bethel Publishing—R
Black Forest—R
Brannon & Baker
Brentwood—R
Bristol House—R
Brown-ROA
Cerdic Publications
Chalice Press
Christendom Press—R
Christian Ed Pub.
Christopher Publishing
Concordia
Contemporary Drama Service
Cornerstone Pub.
CSS Publishing
Educational Ministries
Eerdmans Publishing—R
Fairway Press—R
Faith Publishing
Goetz Publishing, B.J.
Gospel Publishing House—R
GROUP Publishing—R
Hensley, Virgil—R
Hunt & Thorpe
Judson Press—R
Kregel—R
Liguori Publications
Lightwave Publishing
Liturgical Press
Logion Press
Master Books—R
Meriwether—R
Moody Press
Morehouse—R
National Baptist—R
New Canaan
New Hope—R
New Leaf Press—R
Omega House
Paraclete Press—R
Presbyterian & Reformed

Preservation Press
Ragged Edge—R
Rainbow/Legacy Press—R
Rainbow/Rainbow Books
Read 'N Run—R
Religious Education
Resource Publications
Review & Herald—R
Rose Publishing
Royal Productions—R
Scripture Press
Smyth & Helwys
Southern Baptist Press—R
Standard
Still Waters Revival—R
Sword of the Lord—R
Tabor Publishing
TEACH Services—R
Toccoa Falls
Treasure Publishing—R
Trinity Foundation—R
Tyler Press—R
United Church Press
United Methodist—R
Vital Issues Press—R
Warner Press
Westminster/John Knox
Windflower—R
Winston-Derek—R
Woman's Miss. Union—R
Women of the Promise
Wood Lake Books
Zondervan/Trade—R

CHRISTIAN HOME SCHOOLING

Art Can Drama—R
Baker Books—R
Bantam Books
Bay Public., Mel—R
Brannon & Baker
Brentwood—R
Bridge/Logos
Brown-ROA
Christian Publications
College Press—R
Cornerstone Pub.
Crossway Books
CSS Publishing
Eerdmans Publishing—R
Fairway Press—R
Faith Publishing
Focus Publishing
Hensley, Virgil—R
Hunt & Thorpe
Kaleidoscope Press—R
Morehouse—R

New Canaan
Omega House
Rainbow/Legacy Press—R
Rainbow/Rainbow Books
Rainbow's End
Read 'N Run—R
Review & Herald—R
Royal Productions—R
Shaw Publishers, Harold—R
Son-Rise
Standard
Still Waters Revival—R
Sword of the Lord—R
TEACH Services—R
Treasure Publishing—R
Trinity Foundation—R
Tyler Press—R
Vital Issues Press—R
Women of the Promise
YWAM Publishing—R
Zondervan/Trade

CHRISTIAN LIVING

ACTA Publications
Alba House—R
Albury Publishing—R
Baker Books—R
Bantam Books
Barbour Publishing—R
Barclay Press—R
Beacon Hill Press
Bethany House
Bethel Publishing—R
Black Forest—R
Brannon & Baker
Brentwood—R
Bridge/Logos
Bristol House—R
Broadman & Holman
Chalice Press
Chariot Victor Books
Chosen Books
Christian Lit. Crusade—R
Christian Publications
Christopher Publishing
College Press—R
Concordia
Cornerstone Pub.
Creation House
Cross Cultural
Crossway Books
CSS Publishing
Dabar Publishing—R
Daybreak Books—R
Destiny Image
Doubleday
Eerdmans Publishing—R

Element Books—R
Fairway Press—R
Faith Publishing
FOG Publishing
Forward Movement—R
Franciscan Univ. Press—R
Friends United Press—R
Good Book
Gospel Publishing House—R
HarperSanFrancisco
Haworth Press—R
Hearth Publishing—R
Hendrickson—R
Hensley, Virgil—R
HI-TIME
Holy Cross—R
Honor Books—R
Horizon House—R
Howard Publishing
Image Press
InterVarsity Press
Judson Press—R
Kregel—R
Libros Liguori
Life Cycle Books—R
Light and Life—R
Liguori Publications
Lion Publishing
Liturgical Press
Lydia Press—R
Magnus Press—R
Moody Press
Morehouse—R
Multnomah Publishers
Nelson, Thomas
New City Press—R
New Leaf Press—R
Omega House
Our Sunday Visitor—R
Pacific Press—R
Paraclete Press—R
Presbyterian & Reformed
Ragged Edge—R
Rainbow/Legacy Press—R
Read 'N Run—R
Resurrection Press—R
Revell, Fleming H.
Review & Herald—R
Royal Productions—R
St. Bede's—R
Shaw Publishers, Harold—R
Sheed & Ward—R
Shining Star
Small Helm Press—R
Smyth & Helwys
Son-Rise
Standard
Starburst Publishers

Still Waters Revival—R
TEACH Services—R
Toccoa Falls
Tyler Press—R
United Church Press
United Methodist—R
Upper Room Books—R
Vital Issues Press—R
Warner Press
WaterBrook Press
Wellness
Western Front—R
Westminster/John Knox
Woman's Miss. Union—R
Women of the Promise
Zondervan/Trade—R

CHRISTIAN SCHOOL BOOKS

Art Can Drama—R
Baker Books—R
Black Forest—R
Christian Publications
Concordia
Cornerstone Pub.
CSS Publishing
Fairway Press—R
Faith Publishing
Hensley, Virgil—R
Hunt & Thorpe
Kaleidoscope Press—R
Lightwave Publishing
Morehouse—R
New Canaan
Rainbow/Rainbow Books
Read 'N Run—R
Royal Productions—R
Son-Rise
Southern Baptist Press—R
Sword of the Lord—R
Tyler Press—R

CHURCH LIFE

ACTA Publications
ACU Press
Alban Institute
Albury Publishing—R
Art Can Drama—R
Baker Books—R
Bethany House
Bethel Publishing—R
Black Forest—R
Brentwood—R
Bridge/Logos
Bristol House—R
Chalice Press

Christendom Press—R
Christian Publications
Christopher Publishing
Church Growth Inst.
College Press—R
Concordia
Cornerstone Pub.
CSS Publishing
Destiny Image
Eerdmans Publishing—R
Fairway Press—R
Faith Publishing
Forward Movement—R
Friends United Press—R
Gospel Publishing House—R
GROUP Publishing—R
HarperSanFrancisco
Hendrickson—R
Hensley, Virgil—R
Holy Cross—R
Image Press
InterVarsity Press
Judson Press—R
Kregel—R
Libros Liguori
Light and Life—R
Liguori Publications
Moody Press
Morehouse—R
New Leaf Press—R
Pacific Press—R
Presbyterian & Reformed
Ragged Edge—R
Read 'N Run—R
Review & Herald—R
Shaw Publishers, Harold—R
Sheed & Ward—R
Smyth & Helwys
Sword of the Lord—R
Tyler Press—R
United Church Press
United Methodist—R
Upper Room Books—R
Vital Issues Press—R
Warner Press
WaterBrook Press
Wood Lake Books
Zondervan/Trade—R

CHURCH RENEWAL

ACTA Publications
Alban Institute
Baker Books—R
Barclay Press—R
Bethany House
Black Forest—R
Brentwood—R

Bridge/Logos
Bristol House—R
Chosen Books
Christian Publications
Church Growth Inst.
College Press—R
Concordia
Cross Cultural
Crossway Books
CSS Publishing
Dabar Publishing—R
Destiny Image
Dimension Books—R
Doubleday
Eerdmans Publishing—R
Evangel Publishing—R
Fairway Press—R
Faith Publishing
Franciscan Univ. Press—R
Gospel Publishing House—R
GROUP Publishing—R
HarperSanFrancisco
Hendrickson—R
Hensley, Virgil—R
Image Press
Intl. Awakening Press—R
InterVarsity Press
Judson Press—R
Libros Liguori
Light and Life—R
Middle Atlantic—R
Moody Press
Morehouse—R
Omega House
Pacific Press—R
Paraclete Press—R
Pastoral Press
Pastor's Choice
Presbyterian & Reformed
Ragged Edge—R
Read 'N Run—R
Royal Productions—R
Resurrection Press—R
Review & Herald—R
Royal Productions—R
Schocken Books—R
Sheed & Ward—R
Smyth & Helwys
Southern Baptist Press—R
Tyler Press—R
United Church Press
United Church Pub.
United Methodist—R
Upper Room Books—R
Vital Issues Press—R
WaterBrook Press
Westminster/John Knox
Wood Lake Books

Zondervan/Trade—R
Zondervan/Academic

CONTROVERSIAL ISSUES

Accent Books
Baker Books—R
Bantam Books
Black Forest—R
Blue Dolphin
Brentwood—R
Bridge/Logos
Chalice Press
Chosen Books
Christendom Press—R
Christian Publications
Comments Publishing—R
Continuum Publishing—R
Cross Cultural
CSS Publishing
Daybreak Books—R
Destiny Image
Doubleday
Dry Bones Press—R
Element Books—R
Faith Publishing
FOG Publishing
HarperSanFrancisco
Haworth Press—R
Hendrickson—R
InterVarsity Press
Kregel—R
Lifetime Books—R
Light and Life—R
Lydia Press—R
Magnus Press—R
Monument Press
Morehouse—R
Pilgrim Press—R
Presbyterian & Reformed
Read 'N Run—R
Regnery Publishing—R
Review & Herald—R
Schocken Books—R
Still Waters Revival—R
Sword of the Lord—R
Trinity Foundation—R
Tyler Press—R
United Church Pub.
United Methodist—R
U of Ottawa Press
University Press/America—R
Vital Issues Press—R
Winston-Derek—R
Wood Lake Books
Zondervan/Trade

COOKBOOKS

Bantam Books
Barbour Publishing—R
Brannon & Baker
Brentwood—R
Christopher Publishing
Daybreak Books—R
Doubleday
Fairway Press—R
Hearth Publishing—R
Morrow & Company, Wm.
Mt. Olive College Press
Omega House
One World
Read 'N Run—R
Royal Productions—R
Schocken Books—R
Son-Rise
Southern Baptist Press—R
Starburst Publishers
Tyler Press—R

COUNSELING AIDS

Accent Publications
Baker Books—R
Bethany House
Black Forest—R
Brannon & Baker
Brentwood—R
Bridge/Logos
Brown-ROA
Chosen Books
Christopher Publishing
College Press—R
Concordia
Continuum Publishing—R
Crossroad Publishing—R
CSS Publishing
Dimension Books—R
Eerdmans Publishing—R
Fairway Press—R
Gospel Publishing House—R
HarperSanFrancisco
Haworth Press—R
Hensley, Virgil—R
InterVarsity Press
Kaleidoscope Press—R
Kregel—R
Life Cycle Books—R
Liguori Publications
Morehouse—R
Neibauer Press—R
New Leaf Press—R
Pastor's Choice
Presbyterian & Reformed
Rainbow's End

Read 'N Run—R
Resource Publications
Resurrection Press—R
Review & Herald—R
Royal Productions—R
Shaw Publishers, Harold—R
Son-Rise
Southern Baptist Press—R
Tyler Press—R
United Methodist—R
Warner Press
Westminster/John Knox
Zondervan/Trade—R
Zondervan/Academic

CREATION SCIENCE

Albury Publishing—R
Black Forest—R
Bridge/Logos
Christopher Publishing
Hensley, Virgil—R
InterVarsity Press
Kaleidoscope Press—R
Lightwave Publishing
Magnus Press—R
Pacific Press—R
Presbyterian & Reformed
Rainbow's End
Read 'N Run—R
Rose Publishing
Sword of the Lord—R
TEACH Services—R
Zondervan/Trade

CULTS/OCCULT

Albury Publishing—R
Baker Books—R
Bantam Books
Bethany House
Black Forest—R
Bridge/Logos
Comments Publishing—R
Concordia
CSS Publishing
Faith Publishing
HarperSanFrancisco
Harvard House
Hendrickson—R
InterVarsity Press
Lydia Press—R
Monument Press
Moody Press
New Leaf Press—R
Open Court—R
Presbyterian & Reformed
Read 'N Run—R

Review & Herald—R
Rose Publishing
Schocken Books—R
Son-Rise
Tyler Press—R
University Press/America—R
Vital Issues Press—R
Zondervan/Trade—R
Zondervan/Academic

CURRENT/SOCIAL ISSUES

Accent Books
Alba House—R
Baker Books—R
Bantam Books
Barclay Press—R
Baylor University Press
Beacon Hill Press
Bethany House
Black Forest—R
Blue Dolphin
Brannon & Baker
Brentwood—R
Bridge/Logos
Bristol House—R
Chalice Press
Chosen Books
Christendom Press—R
Christian Media—R
Christian Publications
Christopher Publishing
College Press—R
Concordia
Continuum Publishing—R
Cornell Univ. Press—R
Cross Cultural
Crossroad Publishing—R
Crossway Books
CSS Publishing
Dabar Publishing—R
Eerdmans Publishing—R
Element Books—R
Fairway Press—R
Faith Publishing
FOG Publishing
Forward Movement—R
HarperSanFrancisco
Haworth Press—R
Hendrickson—R
Horizon House—R
Howard Publishing
InterVarsity Press
Judson Press—R
Kregel—R
Libros Liguori
Life Cycle Books—R
Lifetime Books—R

Liguori Publications
Living the Good News
Lydia Press—R
Moody Press
Morehouse—R
New Hope—R
Northstone
Oxford University
Paulist Press
PREP Publishing—R
Presbyterian & Reformed
Ragged Edge—R
Read 'N Run—R
Regnery Publishing—R
Resurrection Press—R
Review & Herald—R
Shaw Publishers, Harold—R
Small Helm Press—R
Smyth & Helwys
Son-Rise
Still Waters Revival—R
Sword of the Lord—R
Trinity Foundation—R
Tyler Press—R
United Church Pub.
United Methodist—R
U of Ottawa Press
University Press/America—R
VESTA—R
Vital Issues Press—R
Western Front—R
Westminster/John Knox
Woman's Miss. Union—R
Zondervan/Trade—R

CURRICULUM

Accent Bible Curric.
Art Can Drama—R (drama, arts)
Christian Ed Pub.
Church Growth Inst.
Concordia
CSS Publishing
Educational Ministries
Facts on File
Gospel Publishing House—R
GROUP Publishing—R
Group's Hands-On
Hensley, Virgil—R
Lydia Press—R
Master Books—R
Morehouse—R
Rainbow/Rainbow Books
Read 'N Run—R
Rose Publishing
Royal Productions—R
Scripture Press

Smyth & Helwys
Standard
Treasure Publishing—R
Tyler Press—R
United Church Press
United Methodist—R
University Press/America—R
Wellness
Wesleyan Publishing House
Winston-Derek—R
Wonder Time (mag.)

DEATH/DYING

ACTA Publications
Albury Publishing—R
Black Forest—R
Blue Dolphin
Bridge/Logos
Christopher Publishing
Conari Press—R
Continuum Publishing—R
Crossroad Publishing—R
CSS Publishing
Daybreak Books—R
Doubleday
Fairway Press—R
Forward Movement—R
Gilgal Publications
Haworth Press—R
InterVarsity Press
Kregel—R
Life Cycle Books—R
Liguori Publications
Liturgy Training
Morehouse—R
Northstone
Paraclete Press—R
Read 'N Run—R
Resurrection Press—R
Schocken Books—R
Shaw Publishers, Harold—R
Sheed & Ward—R
Smyth & Helwys
So. Methodist Univ.
United Church Press
United Methodist—R
U of Ottawa Press
University Press/America—R
Wood Lake Books
Zondervan/Trade

DEVOTIONAL BOOKS

ACU Press
Alba House—R
Albury Publishing—R
Barbour Publishing—R

Barclay Press—R
Bethel Publishing—R
Black Forest—R
Brentwood—R
Bridge/Logos
Broadman & Holman
Chariot Books
Chariot Victor Books
Chosen Books
Christian Publications
Christopher Publishing
Church Street Press
Concordia
Contemporary Drama Service
Continuum Publishing—R
Cornerstone Pub.
Crossroad Publishing—R
Crossway Books
CSS Publishing
Dabar Publishing—R
Daybreak Books—R
Doubleday
Dry Bones Press—R
Eerdmans Publishing—R
Fairway Press—R
Faith Publishing
FOG Publishing
Franciscan Univ. Press—R
Friends United Press—R
Gilgal Publications
Good Book
Gospel Folio Press
Gospel Publishing House—R
GROUP Publishing—R
HarperSanFrancisco
Hendrickson—R
Hensley, Virgil—R
Honor Books—R
Howard Publishing
Image Press
Jordan Publishing
Kindred Productions
Libros Liguori
Light and Life—R
Liguori Publications
Lion Publishing
Loyola Press—R
Lydia Press—R
Morehouse—R
Multnomah Publishers
Nelson, Thomas
New Leaf Press—R
Northstone
Pacific Press—R
Paraclete Press—R
Pauline Books
Promise Publishing
Rainbow/Legacy Press—R

Rainbow's End
Read 'N Run—R
Resurrection Press—R
Revell, Fleming H.
Review & Herald—R
St. Anthony Messenger—R
Schocken Books—R
Shaw Publishers, Harold—R
Sheed & Ward—R
Sheer Joy! Press
Smyth & Helwys
Son-Rise
Standard (for kids)
Starburst Publishers
TEACH Services—R
Toccoa Falls
Tyler Press—R
United Church Press
United Church Pub.
United Methodist—R
Upper Room Books—R
Warner Press
WaterBrook Press
Westminster/John Knox
Women of the Promise
World Bible
Zondervan/Trade—R

DISCIPLESHIP

Accent Publications
ACU Press
Albury Publishing—R
Baker Books—R
Barclay Press—R
Beacon Hill Press
Bethany House
Bethel Publishing—R
Black Forest—R
Brentwood—R
Bridge/Logos
Bristol House—R
Chalice Press
Chariot Victor Books
Chosen Books
Christian Lit. Crusade—
Christian Publications
Church Growth Inst.
College Press—R
Concordia
Creation House
Crossway Books
CSS Publishing
Dabar Publishing—R
Destiny Image
Eerdmans Publishing—R
Fairway Press—R
Faith Publishing

Gospel Publishing House—R
HarperSanFrancisco
Hendrickson—R
Hensley, Virgil—R
Horizon House—R
Howard Publishing
InterVarsity Press
Judson Press—R
Kregel—R
Libros Liguori
Light and Life—R
Loyola Press—R
Lydia Press
Magnus Press—R
Messianic Jewish—R
Middle Atlantic—R
Moody Press
Morehouse—R
Neibauer Press—R
New Hope—R
New Leaf Press—R
Omega House
Pacific Press—R
Paraclete Press—R
Presbyterian & Reformed
Rainbow/Legacy Press—R
Read 'N Run—R
Review & Herald—R
Schocken Books—R
Shaw Publishers, Harold—R
Sheed & Ward—R
Smyth & Helwys
Southern Baptist Press—R
Standard
Sword of the Lord—R
Toccoa Falls
Treasure Publishing—R
Tyler Press—R
United Methodist—R
Upper Room Books—R
Vital Issues Press—R
WaterBrook Press
Westminster/John Knox
Women of the Promise
YWAM Publishing—R
Zondervan/Trade—R

DIVORCE

ACTA Publications
Albury Publishing—R
Baker Books—R
Bantam Books
Bethany House
Black Forest—R
Brentwood—R
Bridge/Logos
Concordia

CSS Publishing
Forward Movement—R
Gilgal
HarperSanFrancisco
Haworth Press—R
Lydia Press
Monument Press
Morehouse—R
PREP Publishing—R
Presbyterian & Reformed
Read 'N Run—R
Regnery Publishing—R
Resurrection Press—R
Review & Herald—R
Schocken Books—R
Shaw Publishers, Harold—R
Sheer Joy! Press
Southern Baptist Press—R
Tyler Press—R
United Methodist—R
Vital Issues Press—R
Zondervan/Trade—R

DOCTRINAL

ACU Press
Albury Publishing—R
Baker Books—R
Beacon Hill Press
Bethany House
Brentwood—R
Broadman & Holman
Christendom Press—R
Christian Publications
Christian Univ. Press—R
Concordia
Doubleday
Eerdmans Publishing—R
Evangel Publishing—R
Fairway Press—R
Faith Publishing
Friends United Press—R
Gospel Folio Press
Gospel Publishing House—R
HarperSanFrancisco
Hearth Publishing—R
Hendrickson—R
Image Press
Intl. Awakening Press—R
InterVarsity Press
Kregel—R
Libros Liguori
Light and Life—R
Liturgical Press
Loizeaux
Magnus Press—R
Moody Press
Paulist Press

Pilgrim Press—R
Presbyterian & Reformed
Read 'N Run—R
Review & Herald—R
Royal Productions—R
St. Anthony Messenger—R
Shaw Publishers, Harold—R
Sheed & Ward—R
Southern Baptist Press—R
Still Waters Revival—R
Sword of the Lord—R
Toccoa Falls
Trinity Foundation—R
Tyler Press—R
United Methodist—R
Westminster/John Knox
Zondervan/Trade—R

DRAMA

Art Can Drama—R
Baker Books—R
Baker's Plays
Black Forest—R
Brentwood—R
Christian Media—R
Church Street Press
Concordia
Contemporary Drama Service
CSS Publishing
Eldridge Pub.
Fairway Press—R
Faith Publishing
GROUP Publishing—R
Judson Press—R
Lillenas
Meriwether—R
New Hope—R (missions)
Read 'N Run—R
Resource Publications
Sheer Joy! Press
Southern Baptist Press—R
So. Methodist Univ.
Standard
Tyler Press—R
United Methodist—R (juv)
Western Front—R
Windflower—R
Woman's Miss. Union—R
Women of the Promise
Zondervan/Trade

ECONOMICS

Brentwood—R
Bridge/Logos
Christopher Publishing
Concordia

Cross Cultural
Dimension Books—R
Eerdmans Publishing—R
FOG Publishing
HarperSanFrancisco
Haworth Press—R
Moody Press
Oxford University
Paulist Press
Pilgrim Press—R
Read 'N Run—R
Regnery Publishing—R
Review & Herald—R
Schocken Books—R
Trinity Foundation—R
Tyler Press—R
U of Ottawa Press
University Press/America—R
Vital Issues Press—R
Western Front—R

ENVIRONMENTAL ISSUES

Baker Books—R
Bantam Books
Blue Dolphin
Chalice Press
Christian Univ. Press—R
Christopher Publishing
Concordia
Continuum Publishing
Cross Cultural
Daybreak Books—R
Doubleday
Eerdmans Publishing—R
Element Books—R
Facts on File
Forward Movement—R
HarperSanFrancisco
Haworth Press—R
Hearth Publishing—R
HI-TIME
Holy Cross—R
Innisfree Press
Judson Press—R
Liturgy Training
Monument Press
Morehouse—R
Northstone
Oxford University
Paulist Press
Read 'N Run—R
Resurrection Press—R
Royal Productions—R
Schocken Books—R
Southern Baptist Press—R
So. Methodist Univ.
Trinity Foundation—R

Tyler Press—R
United Church Press
United Methodist—R
U of Ottawa Press
University Press/America—R
Vital Issues Press—R
Wood Lake Books
Zondervan/Trade—R

ETHICS

ACU Press
Alba House—R
Baker Books—R
Bantam Books
Baylor University Press
Bethany House
Black Forest—R
Brentwood—R
Chalice Press
Christian Publications
Christian Univ. Press—R
Christopher Publishing
College Press—R
Concordia
Cornell Univ. Press—R
Creation House
Crossroad Publishing—R
Crossway Books
CSS Publishing
Daybreak Books—R
Doubleday
Dry Bones Press—R
Eerdmans Publishing—R
Evangel Publishing—R
Faith Publishing
Forward Movement—R
Gospel Publishing House—R
HarperSanFrancisco
Haworth Press—R
Hearth Publishing—R
Holy Cross—R
Howard Publishing
InterVarsity Press
Kregel—R
Life Cycle Books—R
Lifetime Books—R
Logion Press
Magnus Press—R
Mercer University Press
Morehouse—R
New Leaf Press—R
Open Court—R
Oxford University
Paulist Press
Pilgrim Press—R
Presbyterian & Reformed
Read 'N Run—R

Regnery Publishing—R
Resource Publications
Review & Herald—R
Royal Productions—R
St. Anthony Messenger—R
Schocken Books—R
Sheed & Ward—R
Smyth & Helwys
So. Methodist Univ.
Still Waters Revival—R
Trinity Foundation—R
Trinity Press Intl.—R
Tyler Press—R
United Church Press
United Church Pub.
United Methodist—R
U of Ottawa Press
University Press/America—R
Upper Room Books—R
Vital Issues Press—R
Wadsworth—R
Westminster/John Knox
Yale Univ. Press—R
Zondervan/Trade—R
Zondervan/Academic

ETHNIC/CULTURAL

ACU Press
Baker Books—R
Bantam Books
Barclay Press—R
Beacon Hill Press
Black Forest—R
Broadman & Holman
Chalice Press
Christian Univ. Press—R
Christopher Publishing
College Press—R
Cornerstone Pub.
Cross Cultural
CSS Publishing
Dabar Publishing—R
Daybreak Books—R
Doubleday
Eerdmans Publishing—R
Evangel Publishing—R
Facts on File
Forward Movement—R
Franciscan Univ. Press—R
Friends United Press—R
Gospel Publishing House—R
Guernica Editions—R
Haworth Press—R
Hearth Publishing—R
Hensley, Virgil
Holy Cross —R
InterVarsity Press

Judson Press—R
Kaleidoscope Press—R
Kregel—R
Libros Liguori
Liguori Publications
Lydia Press—R
Messianic Jewish—R (Jewish only)
Middle Atlantic—R
Monument Press
Morehouse—R
National Baptist—R
Nelson, Thomas
One World
Pacific Press—R
Palisades
Pelican Publishing—R
Pilgrim Press—R
Read 'N Run—R
St. Anthony Messenger—R
Schocken Books—R
Shaw Publishers, Harold—R
So. Methodist Univ.
Standard (few)
United Church Press
United Methodist—R
U of Ottawa Press
University Press/America—R
VESTA—R
Winston-Derek—R
Woman's Miss. Union—R
World Bible
Zondervan/Trade

EVANGELISM/ WITNESSING

Accent Publications
ACU Press
Albury Publishing—R
Baker Books—R
Bethany House
Black Forest—R
Brentwood—R
Bridge/Logos
Bristol House—R
Broadman & Holman
Chosen Books
Christian Lit. Crusade—R
Christian Publications
Christopher Publishing
Church Growth Inst.
College Press—R
Concordia
Crossway Books
CSS Publishing
Doubleday
Eerdmans Publishing—R

Evangel Publishing—R
Fairway Press—R
Faith Publishing
Friends United Press—R
Gospel Folio Press
Gospel Publishing House—R
HarperSanFrancisco
Hensley, Virgil—R
Horizon House—R
Image Press
InterVarsity Press
Judson Press—R
Kregel—R
Langmarc
Light and Life—R
Messianic Jewish—R
Middle Atlantic—R
Moody Press
Morehouse—R
Multnomah Publishers
Neibauer Press—R
Nelson, Thomas
New Hope—R
New Leaf Press—R
Omega House
Pacific Press—R
Presbyterian & Reformed
Ragged Edge—R
Read 'N Run—R
Resurrection Press—R
Review & Herald—R
Rose Publishing
Royal Productions—R
Shaw Publishers, Harold—R
Sheer Joy! Press
Son-Rise
Southern Baptist Press—R
Still Waters Revival—R
Sword of the Lord—R
Toccoa Falls
Treasure Publishing—R
Tyler Press—R
United Church Press
United Methodist—R
Vital Issues Press—R
Warner Press
WaterBrook Press
Westminster/John Knox
Woman's Miss. Union—R
Women of the Promise
Wood Lake Books
YWAM Publishing—R
Zondervan/Trade—R
Zondervan/Academic

EXPOSÉS

Brentwood—R

Christian Publications
Faith Publishing
Lifetime Books—R
Open Court—R
Read 'N Run—R
Schocken Books—R
Southern Baptist Press—R
Sword of the Lord—R
Tyler Press—R
Vital Issues Press—R

FAMILY LIFE

ACTA Publications
ACU Press
Alba House—R
Albury Publishing—R
Baker Books—R
Bantam Books
Barclay Press—R
Beacon Hill Press
Bethany House
Bethel Publishing—R
Black Forest—R
Blue Dolphin
Brentwood—R
Bridge/Logos
Broadman & Holman
Chalice Press
Chariot Victor Books
Christian Publications
Christopher Publishing
Church Growth Inst.
College Press—R
Concordia
Continuum Publishing—R
Crossroad Publishing—R
Crossway Books
CSS Publishing
Daybreak Books—R
Eerdmans Publishing—R
Fairway Press—R
Faith Publishing
Focus Publishing
Gospel Publishing House—R
HarperSanFrancisco
Haworth Press—R
Hensley, Virgil—R
Holiday House
Honor Books —R
Howard Publishing
Image Press
Judson Press—R
Kindred Productions
Langmarc
Libros Liguori
Life Cycle Books—R
Light and Life—R

Lightwave Publishing
Liguori Publications
Lion Publishing
Moody Press
Morehouse—R
Multnomah Publishers
New City Press—R
New Hope—R
New Leaf Press—R
Northstone
Our Sunday Visitor—R
Pacific Press—R
Pauline Books
Pelican Publishing—R
Presbyterian & Reformed
Ragged Edge—R
Rainbow's End
Read 'N Run—R
Recovery Communications
Resurrection Press—R
Revell, Fleming H.
Review & Herald—R
Schocken Books—R
Seaside Press—R
Shaw Publishers, Harold—R
Son-Rise
Southern Baptist Press—R
So. Methodist Univ.
Sower's Press
Still Waters Revival—R
Sword of the Lord—R
TEACH Services—R
Tyler Press—R
United Methodist—R
Upper Room Books—R
Vital Issues Press—R
Warner Press
WaterBrook Press
Wellness
Western Front—R
Westminster/John Knox
Windflower—R
Women of the Promise
Zondervan/Trade—R

FICTION: ADULT/ RELIGIOUS

Alexander Books
Baker Books—R
Bantam Books
Barbour Publishing—R
Beacon Hill Press
Bethany House
Bethel Publishing—R
Black Forest—R
Blue Dolphin
Brannon & Baker

Broadman & Holman
Chariot Victor Books
Christian Publications
Christopher Publishing
Comments Publishing—R
Cornerstone Press
Cornerstone Pub.
Creation House
Crossway Books
CSS Publishing
Daybreak Books—R
Dry Bones Press—R
Eerdmans Publishing—R
Faith Publishing
Focus Publishing
Friends United Press—R
Guernica Editions—R
Heartsong Presents
Hearth Publishing—R
Horizon House—R
Image Press
Kregel—R
Lion Publishing
Messianic Jewish—R
Morrow & Company, Wm.
Mt. Olive College Press
Moonletters Press
Multnomah Publishers
Nelson, Thomas
Northstone
Pacific Press—R
Palisades
Pelican Publishing—R
PREP Publishing—R
G.P. Putnam's Sons
Rainbow's End
Read 'N Run—R
Recovery Communications
Revell, Fleming H.
Shaw Publishers, Harold—R
Sheer Joy! Press
So. Methodist Univ.
Starburst Publishers
WaterBrook Press
Western Front—R
Windflower—R
Wine Press—R
Women of the Promise
Wood Lake Books
Zondervan/Trade—R

FICTION: ADVENTURE

Bantam Books
Barbour Publishing—R
Bethany House
Bethel Publishing—R
Black Forest—R

Brannon & Baker
Brentwood—R
Broadman & Holman
Butterfly Press
Chariot Books
Christian Ed Pub.
Christian Publications
Christopher Publishing
Concordia
Cornerstone Pub.
Crossway Books
Dry Bones Press—R
Fairway Press—R
GROUP Publishing—R (juv/teen)
Hearth Publishing—R
Kaleidoscope Press—R (juv)
Morehouse—R
Morris, Joshua
Morrow & Co., Wm. (juv)
Multnomah Publishers
Nelson, Thomas
Palisades
G.P. Putnam's Sons
Read 'N Run—R
Revell, Fleming H.
Southern Baptist Press—R
Starburst Publishers
Sword of the Lord—R
Toccoa Falls
Tommy Nelson—R
WaterBrook Press
Windflower—R
Wine Press—R

FICTION: ALLEGORY

Black Forest—R
Brannon & Baker
Cornerstone Pub.
Creation House
CSS Publishing
Eerdmans Publishing—R
Fairway Press—R
GROUP Publishing—R
Morris, Joshua
Morehouse—R
Palisades
Read 'N Run—R
Sword of the Lord—R
Wine Press—R
Zondervan/Trade—R

FICTION: BIBLICAL

Black Forest—R
Brannon & Baker
Brentwood—R

Christopher Publishing
College Press—R
Concordia
Cornerstone Pub.
Creation House
CSS Publishing
Fairway Press—R
Faith Publishing
Friends United Press—R
GROUP Publishing—R
Kregel—R
Messianic Jewish—R
Middle Atlantic—R (juv)
Morehouse—R
Morris, Joshua
Multnomah Publishers
New Hope—R (juv)
Palisades
Pacific Press—R
Ragged Edge—R (juv)
Read 'N Run—R
Revell, Fleming H.
Sheer Joy! Press
Southern Baptist Press—R
Sword of the Lord—R
Toccoa Falls
Western Front—R
Windflower—R
Wine Press—R
Zondervan/Trade—R

FICTION: CONTEMPORARY

Baker Books—R
Bantam Books
Barbour Publishing—R
Bethany House
Bethel Publishing—R
Black Forest—R
Brannon & Baker
Brentwood—R
Broadman & Holman
Chariot Books
Chariot Victor Books
Christian Ed Pub.
Christian Publications
Christopher Publishing
Concordia
Cornerstone Press
Creation House
Crossway Books
CSS Publishing
Dry Bones Press—R
Eerdmans Publishing—R
Fairway Press—R
Guernica Editions—R
HarperSanFrancisco

Heartsong Presents
Journey Books—R
Kindred Productions
Lion Publishing
Middle Atlantic—R (juv)
Morehouse—R
Morris, Joshua
Mt. Olive College Press
National Baptist—R
Nelson, Thomas
One World
Palisades
Rainbow Books
Read 'N Run—R
Revell, Fleming H.
Shaw Publishers, Harold—R
Southern Baptist Press—R
So. Methodist Univ.
Starburst Publishers
Toccoa Falls
Tommy Nelson—R
WaterBrook Press
Western Front—R
Windflower—R
Wine Press—R
Zondervan/Trade—R

FICTION: ETHNIC

Baker Books—R
Black Forest—R
Blue Dolphin
Brannon & Baker
Cornerstone Pub.
CSS Publishing
Eerdmans Publishing—R
Guernica Editions—R
Kaleidoscope Press—R (juv)
Messianic Jewish—R
Palisades
Pelican Publishing—R
Shaw Publishers, Harold—R
WaterBrook Press
Wine Press—R

FICTION: FANTASY

Bantam Books
Black Forest—R
Brannon & Baker
CSS Publishing
Dry Bones Press—R
Eerdmans Publishing—R
Fairway Press—R
Palisades
Read 'N Run—R
Shaw Publishers, Harold—R
Wine Press—R

Zondervan/Trade—R

FICTION: FRONTIER

Bantam Books
Beacon Hill Press
Bethany House
Black Forest—R
Brannon & Baker
Brentwood—R
Broadman & Holman
Christian Publications
Christopher Publishing
CSS Publishing
Fairway Press—R
Hearth Publishing—R
Kaleidoscope Press—R (juv)
Multnomah Publishers
Nelson, Thomas
Palisades
Read 'N Run—R
Revell, Fleming H.
Southern Baptist Press—R
WaterBrook Press
Windflower—R
Wine Press—R

FICTION: FRONTIER/ROMANCE

Bantam Books
Barbour Publishing—R
Beacon Hill Press
Bethany House
Black Forest—R
Brannon & Baker
Brentwood—R
Christian Publications
Christopher Publishing
CSS Publishing
Fairway Press—R
Heartsong Presents
Hearth Publishing—R
Multnomah Publishers
Nelson, Thomas
Palisades
PREP Publishing—R
Proclaim Publishing
Read 'N Run—R
Revell, Fleming H.
Southern Baptist Press—R
WaterBrook Press
Wine Press—R
Zondervan/Trade—R

FICTION: HISTORICAL

Bantam Books

Beacon Hill Press
Bethany House
Bethel Publishing—R
Black Forest—R
Brannon & Baker
Brentwood—R
Broadman & Holman
Butterfly Press
Chariot Books
Chariot Victor Books
Christian Publications
Christopher Publishing
Cornerstone Press
Crossroad Publishing—R
Crossway Books
CSS Publishing
Dry Bones Press—R
Eerdmans Publishing—R
Fairway Press—R
Friends United Press—R
HarperSanFrancisco
Hearth Publishing—R
Holiday House
Horizon House—R
Journey Books—R
Kregel—R
Lion Publishing
Misty Hill Press
Morehouse—R
Morris, Joshua
Morrow & Company, Wm.
Mt. Olive College Press
Multnomah Publishers
Nelson, Thomas
One World
Palisades
PREP Publishing—R
Ragged Edge—R (juv)
Read 'N Run—R
Revell, Fleming H.
Son-Rise
Southern Baptist Press—R
So. Methodist Univ.
WaterBrook Press
Western Front—R
Windflower—R
Wine Press—R
YWAM Publishing—R
Zondervan/Trade—R

FICTION: HISTORICAL/ROMANCE

Bantam Books
Barbour Publishing—R
Beacon Hill Press
Bethany House
Black Forest—R

Brannon & Baker
Brentwood—R
Chariot Victor Books
Christian Publications
Christopher Publishing
Creation House
Crossway Books
Fairway Press—R
Heartsong Presents
Hearth Publishing—R
Horizon House—R
Kregel—R
Multnomah Publishers
Nelson, Thomas
Palisades
PREP Publishing—R
Read 'N Run—R
Revell, Fleming H.
Southern Baptist Press—R
WaterBrook Press
Wine Press—R
Zondervan/Trade—R

FICTION: HUMOR

Bantam Books
Black Forest—R
Brannon & Baker
Broadman & Holman
Chariot Books
Christian Publications
Christopher Publishing
Cornerstone Pub.
CSS Publishing
Fairway Press—R
Hearth Publishing—R
Holiday House
Journey Books—R
Kaleidoscope Press—R (juv)
Morehouse—R
Morris, Joshua
Multnomah Publishers
Nelson, Thomas
Northstone
Palisades
PREP Publishing—R
Rainbow Books
Read 'N Run—R
Shaw Publishers, Harold—R
Sheer Joy! Press
Sword of the Lord—R
WaterBrook Press
Wine Press—R

FICTION: JUVENILE (Ages 8-12)

Barbour Publishing—R

Bay Public., Mel—R
Bethany House
Bethel Publishing—R
Black Forest—R
Brannon & Baker
Broadman & Holman
Butterfly Press
CEF Press
Chariot Books
Christian Publications
Concordia
Cornerstone Press
Cornerstone Pub.
Crossway Books
CSS Publishing
Eerdmans Publishing—R
Fairway Press—R
Focus Publishing
Forward Movement—R
Friends United Press—R
Gold 'n' Honey
GROUP Publishing—R
Hearth Publishing—R
Holiday House
Horizon House—R
Journey Books—R
Kaleidoscope Press—R
Kindred Productions
Lightwave Publishing
Living the Good News
Lydia Press—R
Messianic Jewish—R
Misty Hill Press
Morehouse—R
Morris, Joshua
Mt. Olive College Press
Pacific Press—R
Pauline Books
Pelican Publishing—R
PREP Publishing—R
Read 'N Run—R
Revell, Fleming H.
Sheer Joy! Press
Sword of the Lord—R
Toccoa Falls
Tommy Nelson—R
Tyler Press—R
WaterBrook Press
Wine Press—R
Woman's Miss. Union—R
YWAM Publishing—R
Zondervan/Trade—R

FICTION: LITERARY

Baker Books—R
Black Forest—R
Brannon & Baker

Chariot Books
Christian Publications
CSS Publishing
Dry Bones Press—R
Eerdmans Publishing—R
FOG Publishing
Guernica Editions—R
Morrow & Company, Wm.
Mt. Olive College Press
Palisades
Read 'N Run—R
Shaw Publishers, Harold—R
So. Methodist Univ.
Wine Press—R

FICTION: MYSTERY

Baker Books—R
Bantam Books
Bethany House
Bethel Publishing—R
Black Forest—R
Brannon & Baker
Broadman & Holman
Christian Ed Pub.
Christian Publications
Concordia
Dry Bones Press—R
Eerdmans Publishing—R
Journey Books—R
Lion Publishing
Morehouse—R
Morrow & Company, Wm.
Multnomah Publishers
Nelson, Thomas
Palisades
PREP Publishing—R
Prescott Press—R
Rainbow Books
Read 'N Run—R
Revell, Fleming H.
Shaw Publishers, Harold—R
Sword of the Lord—R
Toccoa Falls
WaterBrook Press
Wine Press—R
Western Front—R
Zondervan/Trade—R

FICTION: MYSTERY/ROMANCE

Bantam Books
Barbour Publishing—R
Bethany House
Black Forest—R
Brannon & Baker
Brentwood—R

Chariot Victor Books
Christian Publications
Fairway Press—R
Heartsong Presents
Love Inspired
Multnomah Publishers
Nelson, Thomas
Palisades
PREP Publishing—R
Rainbow's End
Read 'N Run—R
Revell, Fleming H.
Shaw Publishers, Harold—R
Southern Baptist Press—R
Sword of the Lord—R
WaterBrook Press
Wine Press—R
Zondervan/Trade—R

FICTION: PLAYS

Baker's Plays
Bantam Books
Bay Public., Mel—R
Brentwood—R
Creatively Yours
CSS Publishing
Eldridge Pub. (& musicals)
Fairway Press—R
Lillenas
Meriwether—R
Mt. Olive College Press
National Baptist—R
Read 'N Run—R
Resource Publications
Sheer Joy! Press
Southern Baptist Press—R
So. Methodist Univ.

FICTION: ROMANCE

Bantam Books
Barbour Publishing—R
Beacon Hill Press
Bethany House
Black Forest—R
Brannon & Baker
Butterfly Press
Chariot Victor Books
Christian Publications
Fairway Press—R
Heartsong Presents
Hearth Publishing—R
Love Inspired
Morrow & Company, Wm.
Multnomah Publishers
Nelson, Thomas
Palisades

PREP Publishing—R
Read 'N Run—R
Revell, Fleming H.
Sheer Joy! Press
Sword of the Lord—R
WaterBrook Press
Wine Press—R

FICTION: SCIENCE FICTION

Bantam Books
Black Forest—R
Brannon & Baker
Dry Bones Press—R
GROUP Publishing—R
Morrow & Company, Wm.
Nelson, Thomas
Read 'N Run—R
Shaw Publishers, Harold—R
Skysong Press
Wine Press—R

FICTION: SHORT STORY COLLECTION

Black Forest—R
Christopher Publishing
Concordia
Fairway Press—R
GROUP Publishing—R
Hearth Publishing—R
Kaleidoscope Press—R (juv)
Morehouse—R
Mt. Olive College Press
National Baptist—R
Northstone
Read 'N Run—R
Revell, Fleming H.

FICTION: TEEN/YOUNG ADULT

Bay Public., Mel—R
Bethany House
Bethel Publishing—R
Black Forest—R
Brannon & Baker
Christian Publications
Comments Publishing—R
Cornerstone Pub.
CSS Publishing
Eerdmans Publishing—R
Fairway Press—R
Focus Publishing
Friends United Press—R
GROUP Publishing—R
Hearth Publishing—R

Horizon House—R
Journey Books—R
Living the Good News
Lydia Press—R
Messianic Jewish—R
Mt. Olive College Press
Palisades
PREP Publishing—R
Ragged Edge—R
Read 'N Run—R
St. Mary's Press
Sheer Joy! Press
Sword of the Lord—R
Toccoa Falls
Tommy Nelson—R (12-14)
Windflower—R
Wine Press—R
Women of the Promise
YWAM Publishing—R
Zondervan/Trade—R

GAMES/CRAFTS

Bay Public., Mel—R
Brown-ROA
CEF Press
Concordia
Contemporary Drama Service
CSS Publishing
Educational Ministries
Gospel Publishing House—R
GROUP Publishing—R
Hunt & Thorpe
Judson Press—R
Kaleidoscope Press—R
Lightwave Publishing (games)
Meriwether—R
Messianic Jewish—R
Morehouse—R
Pacific Press—R
Rainbow/Rainbow Books
Read 'N Run—R
Schocken Books—R
Shaw Publishers, Harold—R
Shining Star
Standard
Tyler Press—R
United Methodist—R
Women of the Promise
Zondervan/Trade—R

GIFT BOOKS

Albury Publishing—R
Baker Books—R
Barbour Publishing—R
Berrie, Russ
Black Forest—R

Bridge/Logos
Broadman & Holman
Calligraphy Collection
Chariot Victor Books
Christian Publications
Church Street Press
Conari Press—R
Contemporary Drama Service
Creation House
CSS Publishing
Daybreak Books—R
Eerdmans Publishing—R (art)
Element Books—R
HarperSanFrancisco
Hearth Publishing—R
Honor Books—R
Howard Publishing
Hunt & Thorpe
Image Craft
Judson Press—R
Kaleidoscope Press—R
Lion Publishing
Living the Good News
Manhattan Greeting Card
Morehouse—R.
Mt. Olive College Press
Multnomah Publishers
New Leaf Press—R
Painted Hearts & Friends
Palisades (romantic)
Preservation Press
Read 'N Run—R
Resurrection Press—R
Schocken Books—R
Shaw Publishers, Harold—R
Starburst Publishers
Sunrise Publications
United Methodist—R
Upper Room Books—R
Warner Press
WaterBrook Press
Western Front—R
Westminster/John Knox
Wine Press—R
Zondervan/Trade—R

GROUP STUDY BOOKS

Alban Institute
Baker Books—R
Brentwood—R
Bridge/Logos
Church Growth Inst.
College Press—R
Concordia
Dabar Publishing—R
Fairway Press—R
Faith Publishing

FOG Publishing
GROUP Publishing—R
HarperSanFrancisco
Hendrickson—R
Hensley, Virgil—R
Image Press
Innisfree Press
Judson Press—R
Langmarc
Morehouse—R
New Hope—R
New Leaf Press—R
Presbyterian & Reformed
Ragged Edge—R
Rainbow's End
Read 'N Run—R
Resource Publications
Review & Herald—R
Shaw Publishers, Harold—R
Sheed & Ward—R
Smyth & Helwys
Southern Baptist Press—R
Standard
Treasure Publishing—R
Tyler Press—R
United Methodist—R
Upper Room Books—R
Woman's Miss. Union—R
Women of the Promise
Zondervan/Trade—R

HEALING

Albury Publishing—R
Baker Books—R
Bantam Books
Bethany House
Black Forest—R
Blue Dolphin
Brannon & Baker
Brentwood—R
Bridge/Logos
Chosen Books
Christian Lit. Crusade—R
Christian Publications
Christopher Publishing
Conari Press—R
Concordia
Continuum Publishing—R
Cornerstone Pub.
Crossroad Publishing—R
CSS Publishing
Dabar Publishing—R
Daybreak Books—R
Destiny Image
Doubleday
Eerdmans Publishing—R
Elder Books—R

Element Books—R
Fairway Press—R
Faith Publishing
Gilgal
Gospel Publishing House—R
HarperSanFrancisco
Haworth Press—R
Hensley, Virgil—R
Image Press
Judson Press—R
Libros Liguori
Lifetime Books—R
Magnus Press—R
Middle Atlantic—R
Morehouse—R
Northstone
Omega House
Paraclete Press—R
Paradise Research
Read 'N Run—R
Recovery Communications
Resource Publications
Resurrection Press—R
Review & Herald—R
Schocken Books—R
Son-Rise
Southern Baptist Press—R
So. Methodist Univ.
Tyler Press—R
United Church Press
United Methodist—R
U of Ottawa Press
Upper Room Books—R
Western Front—R
Women of the Promise
Wood Lake Books
Zondervan/Trade

HEALTH

Accent Books
Alba House—R
Albury Publishing—R
Baker Books—R
Bantam Books
Bethany House
Black Forest—R
Blue Dolphin
Brannon & Baker
Brentwood—R
Bridge/Logos
Christopher Publishing
Concordia
Continuum Publishing—R
Crossroad Publishing—R
CSS Publishing
Daybreak Books—R
Destiny Image

Doubleday
Dry Bones Press—R
Eerdmans Publishing—R
Elder Books—R
Element Books—R
Facts on File
Fairway Press—R
Good Book
HarperSanFrancisco
Haworth Press—R
Hensley, Virgil—R
Journey Books—R
Kaleidoscope Press—R
Life Cycle Books—R
Lifetime Books—R
Morehouse—R
Northstone
Pacific Press—R
Paraclete Press—R
Paradise Research
Read 'N Run—R
Recovery Communications
Regnery Publishing—R
Review & Herald—R
Schocken Books—R
Shaw Publishers, Harold—R
Son-Rise
Southern Baptist Press—R
So. Methodist Univ.
Starburst Publishers
TEACH Services—R
Tyler Press—R
United Methodist—R
U of Ottawa Press
Upper Room Books—R
VESTA—R
Vital Issues Press—R
Wellness
Western Front—R
Wood Lake Books
Zondervan/Trade—R

HISTORICAL

Albury Publishing—R
Bantam Books
Baylor University Press
Bethany House
Black Forest—R
Brannon & Baker
Brentwood—R
Catholic Univ./America—R
Cerdic Publications
Christian Publications
Christian Univ. Press—R
Christopher Publishing
Cistercian Publications
College Press—R

Concordia
Continuum Publishing—R
Cornell Univ. Press—R
Cross Cultural
Crossroad Publishing—R
Custom Communications
Daybreak Books—R
Dimension Books—R
Doubleday
Eerdmans Publishing—R
Element Books—R
Evangel Publishing—R
Facts on File
Faith Publishing
Friends United Press—R
Good Book
HarperSanFrancisco
Hearth Publishing—R
Holiday House
Holy Cross—R
Intl. Awakening Press—R
InterVarsity Press
Journey Books—R
Kregel—R
Light and Life—R
Magnus Press—R
Mercer University Press
Middle Atlantic—R
Morehouse—R
Morrow & Company, Wm.
Our Sunday Visitor—R
Oxford University
Paradise Research
Ragged Edge—R
Read 'N Run—R
Regnery Publishing—R
Review & Herald—R
St. Anthony Messenger—R
St. Bede's—R
Schocken Books—R
Son-Rise
Southern Baptist Press—R
So. Methodist Univ.
Still Waters Revival—R
Trinity Foundation—R
Tyler Press—R
United Methodist—R
U of Ottawa Press
University Press/America—R
VESTA—R
Vital Issues Press—R
Western Front—R
Windflower—R
Winston-Derek—R
Zondervan/Academic

HOW-TO

Accent Books
Accent Publications
ACTA Publications
Alba House—R
Albury Publishing—R
Alexander Books
Baker Books—R
Bantam Books
Bethany House
Bethel Publishing—R
Black Forest—R
Blue Dolphin
Brannon & Baker
Brentwood—R
Bridge/Logos
Broadman & Holman
Brown-ROA
Chosen Books
Christian Publications
Christopher Publishing
Church Street Press
Concordia
Continuum Publishing—R
Cornerstone Pub.
Dabar Publishing—R
Elder Books—R
Element Books—R
Facts on File
Fairway Press—R
Faith Publishing
Gilgal
GROUP Publishing—R
HarperSanFrancisco
Hearth Publishing—R
Hensley, Virgil—R
Howard Publishing
Judson Press—R
Kaleidoscope Press—R
Lifetime Books—R
Living the Good News
Lydia Press—R
Meriwether—R
Morehouse—R
Morrow & Company, Wm.
Mt. Olive College Press
New City Press—R
New Leaf Press—R
Paradise Research
Pauline Books
PREP Publishing—R
Rainbow Books
Rainbow's End
Read 'N Run—R
Recovery Communications
Resource Publications
Review & Herald—R

Royal Productions—R
Schocken Books—R
Shaw Publishers, Harold—R
Sheed & Ward—R
Son-Rise
Southern Baptist Press—R
Standard
Starburst Publishers
Still Waters Revival—R
Tyler Press—R
Vital Issues Press—R
Westminster/John Knox

HUMOR

Albury Publishing—R
Bantam Books
Barbour Publishing—R
Black Forest—R
Blue Dolphin
Brannon & Baker
Brentwood—R
Bridge/Logos
Broadman & Holman
Christian Publications
Christopher Publishing
Concordia
Cornerstone Pub.
CSS Publishing
Daybreak Books—R
Dimension Books—R
Dry Bones Press—R
Fairway Press—R
Faith Publishing
Friends United Press—R
HarperSanFrancisco
Hearth Publishing—R
Holiday House
Honor Books—R
Howard Publishing
Journey Books—R
Judson Press—R
Kaleidoscope Press—R
Light and Life—R
Moody Press
Morehouse—R
New Leaf Press—R
Northstone
Omega House
Pacific Press—R
PREP Publishing—R
Read 'N Run—R
Regnery Publishing—R
Review & Herald—R
Schocken Books—R
Son-Rise
Southern Baptist Press—R
Tyler Press—R

United Methodist—R
Upper Room Books—R
Vital Issues Press—R
WaterBrook Press
Zondervan/Trade—R

INSPIRATIONAL

Accent Books
ACU Press
Albury Publishing—R
Baker Books—R
Bantam Books
Barbour Publishing—R
Beacon Hill Press
Bethany House
Bethel Publishing—R
Black Forest—R
Blue Dolphin
Brannon & Baker
Brentwood—R
Bridge/Logos
Broadman & Holman
Catholic Book Publishing
Chariot Victor Books
Christian Publications
Christopher Publishing
Conari Press—R
Concordia
Cornerstone Pub.
Cross Cultural
Crossroad Publishing—R
CSS Publishing
Dabar Publishing—R
Daybreak Books—R
Destiny Image
Doubleday
Elder Books—R
Element Books—R
Fairway Press—R
Faith Publishing
FOG Publishing
Franciscan Univ. Press—R
Friends United Press—R
Gilgal
Good Book
Gospel Publishing House—R
HarperSanFrancisco
Hearth Publishing—R
Hendrickson—R
Hensley, Virgil—R
Honor Books—R
Howard Publishing
ICS Publications—R
Image Press
Innisfree Press
Judson Press—R
Kaleidoscope Press—R

Kindred Productions
Langmarc
Libros Liguori
Lifetime Books—R
Light and Life—R
Lydia Press—R
Magnus Press—R
Middle Atlantic—R
Moody Press
Morehouse—R
Mt. Olive College Press
Multnomah Publishers
Nelson, Thomas
New Leaf Press—R
Northstone
Omega House
One World
Our Sunday Visitor—R
Pacific Press—R
Paradise Research
Pelican Publishing—R
PREP Publishing—R
G.P. Putnam's Sons
Ragged Edge—R
Read 'N Run—R
Resurrection Press—R
Review & Herald—R
St. Anthony Messenger—R
Schocken Books—R
Shaw Publishers, Harold—R
Sheed & Ward—R
Sheer Joy! Press
Smyth & Helwys
Son-Rise
Southern Baptist Press—R
Starburst Publishers
Sword of the Lord—R
TEACH Services—R
Toccoa Falls
Tyler Press—R
United Church Press
United Methodist—R
Upper Room Books—R
Vital Issues Press—R
WaterBrook Press
Wellness
Western Front—R
Westminster/John Knox
Winston-Derek—R
Women of the Promise
Wood Lake Books
World Bible
Zondervan/Trade—R

LEADERSHIP

ACU Press
Albury Publishing—R

Baker Books—R
Bantam Books
Beacon Hill Press
Bethel Publishing—R
Black Forest—R
Brannon & Baker
Bridge/Logos
Broadman & Holman
Chalice Press
Chariot Victor Books
Christian Publications
Christopher Publishing
Church Growth Inst.
College Press—R
Continuum Publishing—R
Cornerstone Pub.
Creation House
Crossway Books
CSS Publishing
Destiny Image
Faith Publishing
Gospel Publishing House—R
GROUP Publishing—R
Hensley, Virgil—R
Honor Books—R
Judson Press—R
Kregel—R
Lifetime Books—R
Light and Life—R
Middle Atlantic—R
Moody Press
Morehouse—R
New Leaf Press—R
Paulist Press
Read 'N Run—R
Schocken Books—R
Shaw Publishers, Harold—R
Standard
Tyler Press—R
United Church Press
United Methodist—R
Upper Room Books—R
Vital Issues Press—R
WaterBrook Press
Western Front—R
Wood Lake Books
Zondervan/Trade

LITURGICAL STUDIES

Alba House—R
American Cath. Press—R
Blue Dolphin
Brentwood—R
Catholic Book Publishing
Cerdic Publications
Chalice Press
Christendom Press—R

Christian Univ. Press—R
Christopher Publishing
Concordia
Cornell Univ. Press—R
CSS Publishing
Doubleday
Dry Bones Press—R
Eerdmans Publishing—R
Fairway Press—R
Faith Publishing
HarperSanFrancisco
Hendrickson—R
Holy Cross—R
InterVarsity Press
Judson Press—R
Liturgy Training
Morehouse—R
Oxford University
Pastoral Press
Paulist Press
Pelican Publishing—R
Presbyterian & Reformed
Ragged Edge—R
Read 'N Run—R
Resource Publications
St. Anthony Messenger—R
St. Bede's—R
Sheed & Ward—R
Southern Baptist Press—R
Trinity Press Intl.—R
Tyler Press—R
United Church Press
United Church Pub.
United Methodist—R
University Press/America—R
Upper Room Books—R
Westminster/John Knox
Wood Lake Books

MARRIAGE

ACTA Publications
Alba House—R
Albury Publishing—R
Baker Books—R
Bantam Books
Beacon Hill Press
Bethany House
Black Forest—R
Brannon & Baker
Brentwood—R
Bridge/Logos
Broadman & Holman
Cerdic Publications
Chalice Press
Chariot Victor Books
College Press—R
Concordia

Continuum Publishing—R
Cornerstone Pub.
Crossroad Publishing—R
Crossway Books
CSS Publishing
Dabar Publishing—R
Daybreak Books—R
Destiny Image
Doubleday
Eerdmans Publishing—R
Fairway Press—R
Faith Publishing
Focus on the Family
Focus Publishing
Forward Movement—R
HarperSanFrancisco
Haworth Press—R
Hensley, Virgil—R
Holy Cross—R
Honor Books—R
Howard Publishing
InterVarsity Press
Judson Press—R
Kregel—R
Libros Liguori
Lifetime Books—R
Logion Press
Liguori Publications
Lion Publishing
Meriwether—R
Messianic Jewish—R
Morehouse—R
Multnomah Publishers
New Leaf Press—R
Northstone
Omega House
Pacific Press—R
Pauline Books
PREP Publishing—R
Presbyterian & Reformed
Ragged Edge—R
Read 'N Run—R
Resource Publications
Resurrection Press—R
Revell, Fleming H.
Review & Herald—R
St. Anthony Messenger—R
Schocken Books—R
Shaw Publishers, Harold—R
Sheed & Ward—R
Sheer Joy! Press
Southern Baptist Press—R
Sower's Press
So. Methodist Univ.
Standard
Starburst Publishers
Still Waters Revival—R
Sword of the Lord—R

Tyler Press—R
United Methodist—R
Upper Room Books—R
Vital Issues Press—R
WaterBrook Press
Westminster/John Knox
Women of the Promise
Wood Lake Books
Zondervan/Trade—R

MEN'S BOOKS

ACTA Publications
Albury Publishing—R
Baker Books—R
Bantam Books
Beacon Hill Press
Bethany House
Black Forest—R
Blue Dolphin
Brannon & Baker
Bridge/Logos
Broadman & Holman
Chalice Press
Chariot Victor Books
Christian Publications
Concordia
Continuum Publishing
Cornerstone Pub.
Crossway Books
CSS Publishing
Daybreak Books—R
Destiny Image
Doubleday
Faith Publishing
Focus on the Family
Forward Movement—R
Gospel Publishing House—R
Hensley, Virgil—R
Honor Books—R
Judson Press—R
Kregel—R
Liguori Publications
Moody Press
Morehouse—R
Multnomah Publishers
New Leaf Press—R
Pacific Press—R
Pilgrim Press—R
Presbyterian & Reformed
Read 'N Run—R
Resource Publications
Resurrection Press—R
Schocken Books—R
Shaw Publishers, Harold—R
Son-Rise
Sword of the Lord—R
Tyler Press—R

United Church Press
United Methodist—R
Vital Issues Press—R
WaterBrook Press
Western Front—R
Winston-Derek—R
Wood Lake Books
Zondervan/Trade—R

MIRACLES

Albury Publishing—R
Baker Books—R
Black Forest—R
Brannon & Baker
Brentwood—R
Bridge/Logos
Chosen Books
Christian Publications
Cornerstone Pub.
CSS Publishing
Destiny Image
Fairway Press—R
Faith Publishing
FOG Publishing
Friends United Press—R
Gospel Publishing House—R
HarperSanFrancisco
Honor Books—R
Omega House
Paraclete Press—R
Read 'N Run—R
Review & Herald—R
Royal Productions—R
Schocken Books—R
Shaw Publishers, Harold—R
Southern Baptist Press—R
Toccoa Falls
Tyler Press—R
United Church Press
United Methodist—R
Upper Room Books—R
Zondervan/Trade—R

MISSIONARY

ACU Press
Albury Publishing—R
Barbour Publishing—R
Bethany House
Bethel Publishing—R
Black Forest—R
Brannon & Baker
Brentwood—R
Bridge/Logos
Chosen Books
Christian Lit. Crusade—R
Christian Publications

Christian Univ. Press—R
Christopher Publishing
Concordia
CSS Publishing
Eerdmans Publishing—R
Fairway Press—R
Faith Publishing
Friends United Press—R
Gospel Publishing House—R
HarperSanFrancisco
Horizon House—R
Journey Books—R
Messianic Jewish—R
Middle Atlantic—R
New Hope—R
Omega House
Promise Publishing
Read 'N Run—R
Review & Herald—R
Southern Baptist Press—R
Sword of the Lord—R
TEACH Services—R
Toccoa Falls
Tyler Press—R
United Methodist—R
University Press/America—R
Vital Issues Press—R
Westminster/John Knox
Woman's Miss. Union—R
YWAM Publishing—R
Zondervan/Academic

MONEY MANAGEMENT

Alban Institute
Baker Books—R
Bantam Books
Bethany House
Black Forest—R
Blue Dolphin
Brannon & Baker
Brentwood—R
Bridge/Logos
Broadman & Holman
Christopher Publishing
Church Growth Inst.
Concordia
Cornerstone Pub.
Facts on File
Fairway Press—R
HarperSanFrancisco
Hensley, Virgil—R
Howard Publishing
Lifetime Books—R
Lightwave Publishing
New Leaf Press—R
Read 'N Run—R
Regnery Publishing—R

Review & Herald—R
Schocken Books—R
Shaw Publishers, Harold—R
Southern Baptist Press—R
Tyler Press—R
United Methodist—R
Western Front—R
Winston-Derek—R
Women of the Promise
Zondervan/Trade—R

MUSIC-RELATED BOOKS

ACU Press
Albury Publishing—R
American Cath. Press—R
Bay Public., Mel—R
Brannon & Baker
Christian Media—R
Christopher Publishing
Church Street Press
Concordia
Contemporary Drama Service
Cornell Univ. Press—R
Cornerstone Press
Destiny Image
Dimension Books—R
GROUP Publishing—R
HarperSanFrancisco
Judson Press—R
Lifetime Books—R
Lillenas
Liturgy Training
Middle Atlantic—R
Morehouse—R
Paraclete Press—R
Pastoral Press
Ragged Edge—R
Read 'N Run—R
Standard
Tyler Press—R
United Methodist—R
Upper Room Books—R
Windflower—R
Zondervan/Trade—R

PAMPHLETS

American Cath. Press—R
Barclay Press—R
Cornerstone Pub.
Cross Way Pub.
Dry Bones Press—R
Faith Publishing (maybe)
Forward Movement—R
Franciscan Univ. Press—R
Gospel Folio Press
Hearth Publishing—R

HI-TIME
Image Press
Intl. Awakening Press—R
Kindred Productions
Libros Liguori
Life Cycle Books
Liguori Publications
Master Books—R
Messianic Jewish—R
Middle Atlantic—R
Neibauer Press—R
Omega House
Our Sunday Visitor—R
Pacific Press—R
Paradise Research
Pauline Books
Read 'N Run—R
Rose Publishing
Royal Productions—R
Shaw Publishing, Harold—R
Sword of the Lord—R
TEACH Services—R
Wine Press Publishing
Women of the Promise

PARENTING

ACTA Publications
ACU Press
Albury Publishing—R
Baker Books—R
Bantam Books
Beacon Hill Press
Bethany House
Bethel Publishing—R
Black Forest—R
Brannon & Baker
Brentwood—R
Bridge/Logos
Broadman & Holman
Chalice Press
Chariot Victor Books
Christian Publications
Christopher Publishing
Church Growth Inst.
College Press—R
Conari Press—R
Concordia
Cornerstone Pub.
Crossroad Publishing—R
Crossway Books
CSS Publishing
Dabar Publishing—R
Daybreak Books—R
Doubleday
Eerdmans Publishing—R
Facts on File
Fairway Press—R

Faith Publishing
Focus on the Family
Focus Publishing
Forward Movement—R
HarperSanFrancisco
Hensley, Virgil—R
Horizon House—R
Howard Publishing
Judson Press—R
Kaleidoscope Press—R
Kregel—R
Liguori Publications
Lightwave Publishing
Lion Publishing
Living the Good News
Morehouse—R
New Leaf Press—R
Northstone
Pacific Press—R
Pauline Books
Presbyterian & Reformed
Ragged Edge—R
Read 'N Run—R
Resurrection Press—R
Revell, Fleming H.
Review & Herald—R
St. Anthony Messenger—R
Schocken Books—R
Shaw Publishers, Harold—R
Sheed & Ward—R
Standard
Starburst Publishers
Still Waters Revival—R
Sword of the Lord—R
Tabor Publishing
Treasure Publishing—R
Tyler Press—R
United Church Press
United Methodist—R
Upper Room Books—R
Vital Issues Press—R
WaterBrook Press
Western Front—R
Westminster/John Knox
Women of the Promise
Wood Lake Books
Zondervan/Trade—R

PASTORS' HELPS

Accent Publications
ACTA Publications
Alba House—R
Alban Institute
Albury Publishing—R
Baker Books—R
Beacon Hill Press
Bethany House

Bethel Publishing—R
Brannon & Baker
Brentwood—R
Bristol House—R
Brown-ROA
Christian Lit. Crusade—R
Christian Publications
Christopher Publishing
Church Growth Inst.
College Press—R
Concordia
Cornerstone Pub.
CSS Publishing
Eerdmans Publishing—R
Evangel Publishing—R
Fairway Press—R
Gospel Publishing House—R
GROUP Publishing—R
HarperSanFrancisco
Haworth Press—R
Hendrickson—R
Hensley, Virgil—R
InterVarsity Press
Judson Press—R
Kregel—R
Langmarc
Liguori Publications
Morehouse—R
Neibauer Press—R
New Leaf Press—R
Pacific Press—R
Pastor's Choice
Paulist Press
Presbyterian & Reformed
Read 'N Run—R
Resurrection Press—R
Review & Herald—R
St. Anthony Messenger—R
Southern Baptist Press—R
Standard
Sword of the Lord—R
Toccoa Falls
Tyler Press—R
United Church Press
United Methodist—R
Vital Issues Press—R
Wellness
Wesleyan Publishing House
Westminster/John Knox
Wood Lake Books
Zondervan/Trade—R

PERSONAL EXPERIENCE

Bantam Books
Bethel Publishing—R
Black Forest—R
Brannon & Baker

Brentwood—R
Concordia
Cross Cultural
CSS Publishing
Dabar Publishing—R
Daybreak Books—R
Destiny Image
Dry Bones Press—R
Eerdmans Publishing—R
Fairway Press—R
Friends United Press—R
Gilgal
HarperSanFrancisco
Hensley, Virgil—R
Innisfree Press
Libros Liguori
Lydia Press—R
Magnus Press—R
Omega House
Pacific Press—R
Rainbow's End
Read 'N Run—R
Review & Herald—R
Schocken Books—R
Shaw Publishers, Harold—R
Son-Rise
Southern Baptist Press—R
Tyler Press—R
United Church Press
United Methodist—R
VESTA—R
Vital Issues Press—R
Windflower—R
Zondervan/Trade—R

PERSONAL RENEWAL

Baker Books—R
Barclay Press—R
Bethany House
Black Forest—R
Blue Dolphin
Brannon & Baker
Bridge/Logos
Broadman & Holman
Chosen Books
Christian Lit. Crusade—R
Christian Publications
Christopher Publishing
College Press—R
Creation House
Cross Cultural
CSS Publishing
Daybreak Books—R
Destiny Image
Eerdmans Publishing—R
Faith Publishing
Forward Movement—R

Friends United Press—R
Haworth Press—R
Hendrickson—R
Intl. Awakening Press—R
Libros Liguori
Lydia Press
Magnus Press—R
Middle Atlantic—R
Omega House
Read 'N Run—R
Schocken Books—R
Shaw Publishers, Harold—R
Tyler Press—R
United Methodist—R
WaterBrook Press
Women of the Promise
Wood Lake Books
Zondervan/Trade

PHILOSOPHY

ACU Press
Alba House—R
Bantam Books
Black Forest—R
Brannon & Baker
Brentwood—R
Catholic Univ./America—R
Cerdic Publications
Christendom Press—R
Christopher Publishing
Concordia
Continuum Publishing—R
Cornell Univ. Press—R
Cornerstone Press
Cross Cultural
Crossroad Publishing—R
Daybreak Books—R
Doubleday
Dry Bones Press—R
Eerdmans Publishing—R
Element Books—R
Fairway Press—R
Faith Publishing
Friends United Press—R
HarperSanFrancisco
Hendrickson—R
InterVarsity Press
Mercer University Press
Mt. Olive College Press
Open Court—R
Oxford University
Paulist Press
Read 'N Run—R
Regnery Publishing—R
Schocken Books—R
Still Waters Revival—R
Tabor Publishing

Trinity Foundation—R
United Methodist—R
U of Ottawa Press
University Press/America—R
VESTA—R
Vital Issues Press—R
Wadsworth—R
Western Front—R
Winston-Derek—R
Yale Univ. Press—R
Zondervan/Trade—R
Zondervan/Academic

POETRY

Black Forest—R
Brannon & Baker
Brentwood—R
Christopher Publishing
Cornerstone Press
Creatively Yours
Cross Way Pub.
CSS Publishing
Dry Bones Press—R
Fairway Press—R
Focus Publishing
Guernica Editions—R
HarperSanFrancisco—R
Image Books—R
Middle Atlantic—R
Moonletters Press
Morrow & Company, Wm.
Mt. Olive College Press
Omega House
Poets Cove Press
Rainbow's End
Read 'N Run—R
Shaw Publishing, Harold—R
Southern Baptist Press—R
Tyler Press—R
VESTA—R
Vital Issues Press—R
Westminster/John Knox
Windflower—R
Women of the Promise

POLITICAL THEORY

Bantam Books
Baylor University Press
Black Forest—R
Brannon & Baker
Brentwood—R
Catholic Univ./America—R
Christopher Publishing
Concordia
Daybreak Books—R
Doubleday

Faith Publishing
HarperSanFrancisco
Open Court—R
Pilgrim Press—R
Read 'N Run—R
Regnery Publishing—R
Schocken Books—R
Still Waters Revival—R
Trinity Foundation—R
Tyler Press—R
United Methodist—R
U of Ottawa Press
University Press/America—R
Vital Issues Press—R
Western Front—R
Zondervan/Trade

PRAYER

ACTA Publications
ACU Press
Alba House—R
Albury Publishing—R
Baker Books—R
Bantam Books
Barbour Publishing—R
Barclay Press—R
Beacon Hill Press
Bethany House
Bethel Publishing—R
Black Forest—R
Brannon & Baker
Brentwood—R
Bridge/Logos
Bristol House—R
Broadman & Holman
Brown-ROA
Catholic Book Publishing
Chariot Books
Chariot Victor Books
Chosen Books
Christian Lit. Crusade—R
Christian Publications
Concordia
Continuum Publishing
Creation House
Crossroad Publishing—R
CSS Publishing
Dabar Publishing—R
Daybreak Books—R
Destiny Image
Doubleday
Dry Bones Press—R
Eerdmans Publishing—R
Fairway Press—R
Faith Publishing
FOG Publishing
Forward Movement—R

Friends United Press—R
Good Book
Gospel Publishing House—R
HarperSanFrancisco
Hendrickson—R
Hensley, Virgil—R
Holy Cross—R
Howard Publishing
ICS Publications—R
Image Press
Innisfree Press
InterVarsity Press
Kregel—R
Libros Liguori
Light and Life—R
Lightwave Publishing
Liguori Publications
Lion Publishing
Liturgy Training
Living the Good News
Loyola Press—R
Lydia Press—R
Magnus Press—R
Middle Atlantic—R
Moody Press
Morehouse—R
Multnomah Publishers
Nelson, Thomas
New Hope—R
New Leaf Press—R
Northstone
Omega House
Our Sunday Visitor—R
Pacific Press—R
Paraclete Press—R
Pastoral Press
Pauline Books
Presbyterian & Reformed
Preservation Press
Rainbow/Legacy Press—R
Read 'N Run—R
Regina Press
Resource Publications
Resurrection Press—R
Revell, Fleming H.
Review & Herald—R
Rose Publishing
Royal Productions—R
St. Anthony Messenger—R
St. Bede's—R
Schocken Books—R
Shaw Publishers, Harold—R
Sheed & Ward—R
Smyth & Helwys
Southern Baptist Press—R
Standard
Still Waters Revival—R
Sword of the Lord—R

Toccoa Falls
Tyler Press—R
United Church Press
United Methodist—R
Upper Room Books—R
Vital Issues Press—R
Warner Press
WaterBrook Press
Westminster/John Knox
Winston-Derek—R
Woman's Miss. Union—R
Women of the Promise
Wood Lake Books
World Bible
Zondervan/Trade—R

PROPHECY

Albury Publishing—R
Black Forest—R
Blue Dolphin
Brannon & Baker
Brentwood—R
Bridge/Logos
Chosen Books
Creation House
CSS Publishing
Destiny Image
Element Books—R
Fairway Press—R
Faith Publishing
FOG Publishing
Gospel Publishing House—R
HarperSanFrancisco
Harvard House
Hendrickson—R
Hensley, Virgil—R
Image Press
Kregel—R
Messianic Jewish—R
Multnomah Publishers
New Leaf Press—R
Omega House
Read 'N Run—R
Rose Publishing
Schocken Books—R
Small Helm Press
Southern Baptist Press—R
Starburst Publishers
Still Waters Revival—R
Sword of the Lord—R
TEACH Services—R
Tyler Press—R
Vital Issues Press—R
Western Front—R
Zondervan/Trade—R

PSYCHOLOGY

Alba House—R
Baker Books—R
Bantam Books
Barclay Press—R
Bethany House
Black Forest—R
Blue Dolphin
Brannon & Baker
Brentwood—R
Broadman & Holman
Christopher Publishing
Conari Press—R
Concordia
Continuum Publishing
Cross Cultural
Crossroad Publishing—R
Daybreak Books—R
Dimension Books—R
Doubleday
Dry Bones Press—R
Eerdmans Publishing—R
Elder Books—R
Element Books—R
Fairway Press—R
Faith Publishing
Good Book
HarperSanFrancisco
Haworth Press—R
Innisfree Press
InterVarsity Press
Judson Press—R
Liguori Publications
Lydia Press—R
Morehouse—R
Open Court—R
Oxford University
PREP Publishing—R
Read 'N Run—R
Recovery Communications
Religious Education
Resurrection Press—R
Revell, Fleming H.
Review & Herald—R
Schocken Books—R
Shaw Publishers, Harold—R
Southern Baptist Press—R
Starburst Publishers
Tabor Publishing
Tyler Press—R
U of Ottawa Press
University Press/America—R
Vital Issues Press—R
Yale Univ. Press—R
Zondervan/Trade—R
Zondervan/Academic

RECOVERY BOOKS

Baker Books—R
Black Forest—R
Brannon & Baker
Christopher Publishing
Church Growth Inst.
Continuum Publishing—R
Crossroad Publishing—R
CSS Publishing
Daybreak Books—R
Elder Books—R
Forward Movement—R
Gilgal Publications
Good Book
HarperSanFrancisco
Haworth Press—R
Hensley, Virgil—R
Image Press
Libros Liguori
Liguori Publications
Lydia Press—R
Morehouse—R
Our Sunday Visitor—R
Paradise Research
PREP Publishing—R
Rainbow's End
Read 'N Run—R
Recovery Communications
Resource Publications
Rose Publishing
Schocken Books—R
Starburst Publishers
Tyler Press—R
United Methodist—R
Women of the Promise
Zondervan/Trade

REFERENCE BOOKS

Baker Books—R
Bantam Books
Baylor University Press
Bethany House
Brannon & Baker
Brentwood—R
Chariot Victor Books
Christian Univ. Press—R
Concordia
Continuum Publishing—R
Crossroad Publishing—R
CSS Publishing
Doubleday
Dry Bones Press—R
Eerdmans Publishing—R
Element Books—R
Evangel Publishing—R
Fairway Press—R

Good Book
HarperSanFrancisco
Hendrickson—R
Intl. Awakening Press—R
InterVarsity Press
Kaleidoscope Press—R
Kregel—R
Lifetime Books—R
Lightwave Publishing
Loizeaux
Middle Atlantic—R
Morehouse—R
Our Sunday Visitor—R
Oxford University
Presbyterian & Reformed
Ragged Edge—R
Read 'N Run—R
Religious Education
Review & Herald—R
Scarecrow Press
Schocken Books—R
Southern Baptist Press—R
Still Waters Revival—R
Sword of the Lord—R
Tyler Press—R
United Methodist—R
U of Ottawa Press
University Press/America—R
VESTA—R
Westminster/John Knox
World Bible
Zondervan/Academic
Zondervan/Trade—R

RELIGION

ACU Press
Alba House—R
Alexander Books
Baker Books—R
Bantam Books
Bethany House
Black Forest—R
Blue Dolphin
Brannon & Baker
Brentwood—R
Catholic Univ./America—R
Cerdic Publications
Christendom Press—R
Christian Lit. Crusade—R
Christian Publications
Christopher Publishing
Concordia
Continuum Publishing
Cornell Univ. Press—R
Cross Cultural
Crossroad Publishing—R
Crossway Books

CSS Publishing
Daybreak Books—R
Dimension Books—R
Doubleday
Dry Bones Press—R
Eerdmans Publishing—R
Element Books—R
Facts on File
Fairway Press—R
Faith Publishing
Focus Publishing
FOG Publishing
Forward Movement—R
Franciscan Univ. Press—R
Friends United Press—R
Good Book
HarperSanFrancisco
Hendrickson—R
Holy Cross—R
Image Press
InterVarsity Press
Kregel—R
Light and Life—R
Liguori Publications
Liturgy Training
Living the Good News
Magnus Press—R
Mercer University Press
Middle Atlantic—R
Morehouse—R
More Press, Thomas
Morrow & Co, Wm.
Mt. Olive College Press
Multnomah Publishers
New Hope—R
One World
Open Court—R
Oxford University
Paraclete Press—R
Paulist Press
Pilgrim Press—R
Presbyterian & Reformed
Preservation Press
G.P. Putnam's Sons
Ragged Edge—R
Read 'N Run—R
Regnery Publishing—R
Religious Education
Resurrection Press—R
Review & Herald—R
Rose Publishing
St. Bede's—R
Scarecrow Press
Schocken Books—R
Shaw Publishers, Harold—R
Sheed & Ward—R
Sheer Joy! Press
Smyth & Helwys

Southern Baptist Press—R
Still Waters Revival—R
Sword of the Lord—R
Tabor Publishing
Trinity Press Intl.—R
Tyler Press—R
United Church Press
United Church Pub.
United Methodist—R
U of Ottawa Press
University Press/America—R
VESTA—R
Vital Issues Press—R
Wadsworth Publishing
Westminster/John Knox
Wood Lake Books
Yale Univ. Press—R
Zondervan/Trade—R
Zondervan/Academic

RETIREMENT

ACTA Publications
Baker Books—R
Bethany House
Brannon & Baker
Broadman & Holman
Chalice Press
Christian Publications
College Press—R
Concordia
Elder Books—R
Fairway Press—R
HarperSanFrancisco
Judson Press—R
Liguori Publications
Read 'N Run—R
Regnery Publishing—R
Review & Herald—R
Schocken Books—R
Shaw Publishers, Harold—R
Southern Baptist Press—R
Tyler Press—R
United Methodist—R
Upper Room Books—R
Westminster/John Knox
Zondervan/Trade—R

SCHOLARLY

Baker Books—R
Baylor University Press
Brannon & Baker
Broadman & Holman
Continuum Publishing—R
Crossroad Publishing—R
Crossway Books
CSS Publishing

Dry Bones Press—R
Eerdmans Publishing—R
Evangel Publishing—R
Faith Publishing
Haworth Press—R
Hendrickson—R
Holy Cross—R
Intl. Awakening Press—R
InterVarsity Press
Logion Press
Messianic Jewish—R
Monument Press
Morehouse—R
Our Sunday Visitor—R
Oxford University
Paulist Press
Pilgrim Press—R
Presbyterian & Reformed
Ragged Edge—R
Read 'N Run—R
Religious Education
Royal Productions—R
St. Bede's—R
Scarecrow Press
Shaw Publishers, Harold—R
Smyth & Helwys
So. Methodist Univ.
Trinity Foundation—R
Trinity Press Intl.—R
Tyler Press—R
United Methodist—R
U of Ottawa Press
University Press/America—R
VESTA—R
Vital Issues Press—R
Zondervan/Trade

SCIENCE

Bantam Books
Black Forest—R
Brannon & Baker
Chariot Books
Christopher Publishing
Cornell Univ. Press—R
Crossroad Publishing—R
Dry Bones Press—R
Eerdmans Publishing—R
Facts on File
HarperSanFrancisco
Harvard House
InterVarsity Press
Journey Books—R
Kaleidoscope Press—R
Master Books—R
Open Court—R
Oxford University
Read 'N Run—R

Royal Productions—R
Regnery Publishing—R
Review & Herald—R
Schocken Books—R
Shaw Publishers, Harold—R
Trinity Foundation—R
Tyler Press—R
U of Ottawa Press
Vital Issues Press—R
Zondervan/Trade

SELF-HELP

Accent Books
Albury Publishing—R
Alexander Books
Black Forest—R
Blue Dolphin
Brannon & Baker
Broadman & Holman
Butterfly Press
Christian Publications
Christopher Publishing
Cornerstone Pub.
Crossroad Publishing—R
Daybreak Books—R
Destiny Image
Doubleday
Facts on File
Fairway Press—R
Good Book
Howard Publishing
Image Press
Innisfree Press
Libros Liguori
Liguori Publications
Living the Good News
Morehouse—R
Mt. Olive College Press
Nelson, Thomas
One World
Paradise Research
Preservation Press
G.P. Putnam's Sons
Ragged Edge—R
Rainbow Books
Rainbow's End
Read 'N Run—R
Resurrection Press—R
Review & Herald—R
Revell, Fleming H.
Schocken Books—R
Shaw Publishers, Harold—R
Sheed & Ward—R
Starburst Publishers
United Methodist—R
Western Front—R
Zondervan/Trade

SENIOR ADULT CONCERNS

ACTA Publications
Baker Books—R
Bethany House
Broadman & Holman
Chalice Press
Christian Publications
Christopher Publishing
Church Growth Inst.
Concordia
Facts on File
Fairway Press—R
Faith Publishing
Gospel Publishing House—R
GROUP Publishing—R
HarperSanFrancisco
Haworth Press—R
Hensley, Virgil—R
Horizon House—R
Howard Publishing
Judson Press—R
Langmarc
Liguori Publications
Morehouse—R
New Leaf Press—R
Read 'N Run—R
Review & Herald—R
Schocken Books—R
Shaw Publishers, Harold—R
Southern Baptist Press—R
Tyler Press—R
United Methodist—R
Westminster/John Knox
Woman's Miss. Union—R
Women of the Promise
Zondervan/Trade—R

SERMONS

Albury Publishing—R
Brentwood—R
Bridge/Logos
Concordia
CSS Publishing
Destiny Image
Doubleday
Eerdmans Publishing—R
Fairway Press—R
GROUP Publishing—R
HarperSanFrancisco
Kregel—R
Liguori Publications
Liturgical Press
Omega House
Pastor's Choice
Proclaim Publishing

Read 'N Run—R
Review & Herald—R
Southern Baptist Press—R
Still Waters Revival—R
Sword of the Lord—R
Tyler Press—R
United Church Press
United Methodist—R
Vital Issues Press—R
Wood Lake Books

SINGLES ISSUES

Albury Publishing—R
Baker Books—R
Bethany House
Brentwood—R
Broadman & Holman
Christian Publications
Church Growth Inst.
Concordia
CSS Publishing
Dabar Publishing—R
Destiny Image
Faith Publishing
Gospel Publishing House—R
HarperSanFrancisco
Hensley, Virgil—R
Horizon House—R
InterVarsity Press
Judson Press—R
Langmarc
Liguori Publications
Morehouse—R
New Leaf Press—R
Read 'N Run—R
Review & Herald—R
Schocken Books—R
Tyler Press—R
United Methodist—R
Vital Issues Press—R
WaterBrook Press
Women of the Promise
Zondervan/Trade—R

SOCIAL JUSTICE ISSUES

Alban Institute
Baker Books—R
Bantam Books
Barclay Press—R
Bethany House
Black Forest—R
Brannon & Baker
Brentwood—R
Chalice Press
Chosen Books
Concordia

Continuum Publishing—R
Cross Cultural
Crossway Books
Daybreak Books—R
Eerdmans Publishing—R
Faith Publishing
Forward Movement—R
HarperSanFrancisco
Haworth Press—R
Innisfree Press
InterVarsity Press
Judson Press—R
Libros Liguori
Life Cycle Books—R
Lifetime Books—R
Liguori Publications
Liturgy Training
Monument Press
Morehouse—R
Oxford University
Paulist Press
Pilgrim Press—R
Ragged Edge—R
Read 'N Run—R
Regnery Publishing—R
Resurrection Press—R
Review & Herald—R
Schocken Books—R
Shaw Publishers, Harold—R
Sheed & Ward—R
Still Waters Revival—R
Tyler Press—R
United Church Press
United Church Pub.
United Methodist—R
U of Ottawa Press
University Press/America—R
Vital Issues Press—R
Westminster/John Knox
Winston-Derek—R
Woman's Miss. Union—R
Wood Lake Books
Zondervan/Trade—R
Zondervan/Academic

SOCIOLOGY

Alba House—R
Baker Books—R
Bethany House
Black Forest—R
Brentwood—R
Cerdic Publications
Christopher Publishing
Continuum Publishing—R
Daybreak Books—R
Faith Publishing
HarperSanFrancisco

Haworth Press—R
InterVarsity Press
Oxford University
Paulist Press
Read 'N Run—R
Review & Herald—R
Schocken Books—R
Still Waters Revival—R
U of Ottawa Press
University Press/America—R
Vital Issues Press—R
Zondervan/Academic

SPIRITUALITY

ACTA Publications
ACU Press
Alba House—R
Alban Institute
Baker Books—R
Bantam Books
Barclay Press—R
Bethany House
Black Forest—R
Blue Dolphin
Brannon & Baker
Brentwood—R
Bridge/Logos
Broadman & Holman
Chalice Press
Chariot Victor Books
Chosen Books
Christian Publications
Christopher Publishing
Cistercian Publications
Conari Press—R
Continuum Publishing—R
Cornerstone Pub.
Crossroad Publishing—R
Crossway Books
CSS Publishing
Dabar Publishing—R
Daybreak Books—R
Dimension Books—R
Doubleday
Dry Bones Press—R
Eerdmans Publishing—R
Elder Books—R
Element Books—R
Fairway Press—R
Faith Publishing
Forward Movement—R
Franciscan Univ. Press—R
Friends United Press—R
Good Book
HarperSanFrancisco
Hendrickson—R
Hensley, Virgil—R

HI-TIME
Holy Cross—R
Honor Books—R
Image Press
Innisfree Press
InterVarsity Press
Kregel—R
Libros Liguori
Light and Life—R
Liguori Publications
Living the Good News
Loyola Press—R
Magnus Press—R
More Press, Thomas
Morehouse—R
Multnomah Publishers
Northstone
Omega House
Oxford University
Pacific Press—R
Paraclete Press—R
Paradise Research
Pastoral Press
Pauline Books
Pilgrim Press—R
PREP Publishing—R
Ragged Edge—R
Read 'N Run—R
Regnery Publishing—R
Resurrection Press—R
Review & Herald—R
St. Anthony Messenger—R
St. Bede's—R
Schocken Books—R
Shaw Publishers, Harold—R
Sheed & Ward—R
Smyth & Helwys
Southern Baptist Press—R
Sword of the Lord—R
Toccoa Falls
Tyler Press—R
United Church Press
United Church Pub.
United Methodist—R
U of Ottawa Press
Upper Room Books—R
Vital Issues Press—R
WaterBrook Press
Western Front—R
Westminster/John Knox
Winston-Derek—R
Women of the Promise
Wood Lake Books
Zondervan/Trade—R
Zondervan/Academic

SPIRITUAL WARFARE

Albury Publishing—R
Black Forest—R
Brannon & Baker
Bridge/Logos
Chosen Books
Christian Lit. Crusade—R
Christian Publications
Cornerstone Pub.
Creation House
CSS Publishing
Destiny Image
Faith Publishing
Gospel Publishing House—R
Hendrickson—R
Hensley, Virgil—R
Image Press
InterVarsity Press
Lydia Press—R
Multnomah Publishers
Omega House
Read 'N Run—R
Schocken Books—R
Shaw Publishers, Harold—R
Starburst Publishers
Sword of the Lord—R
WaterBrook Press
Women of the Promise
Zondervan/Trade

SPORTS/RECREATION

ACTA Publications
Bantam Books
Christopher Publishing
Cornerstone Pub.
Facts on File
Lifetime Books—R
Multnomah Publishers
New Leaf Press—R
Read 'N Run—R
Royal Productions—R
Schocken Books—R
Starburst Publishers
Tyler Press—R
Zondervan/Trade—R

STEWARDSHIP

Albury Publishing—R
Baker Books—R
Black Forest—R
Chalice Press
Christian Publications
Church Growth Inst.
Creation House
CSS Publishing

Eerdmans Publishing—R
Faith Publishing
Forward Movement—R
Gospel Publishing House—R
Hensley, Virgil—R
Judson Press—R
Kregel—R
Lightwave Publishing
Messianic Jewish—R
Morehouse—R
Neibauer Press
Northstone
Pacific Press—R
Presbyterian & Reformed
Read 'N Run—R
Schocken Books—R
Shaw Publishers, Harold—R
TEACH Services—R
Tyler Press—R
United Church Pub.
United Methodist—R
Upper Room Books—R
Vital Issues Press—R
Wood Lake Books
Zondervan/Trade

THEOLOGICAL

ACU Press
Alba House—R
Baker Books—R
Bethany House
Black Forest—R
Blue Dolphin
Brentwood—R
Bridge/Logos
Broadman & Holman
Butterfly Press
Catholic Univ./America—R
Cerdic Publications
Chalice Press
Christendom Press—R
Christian Publications
Christian Univ. Press—R
Christopher Publishing
Cistercian Publications
Concordia
Continuum Publishing—R
Crossroad Publishing—R
Crossway Books
CSS Publishing
Dimension Books—R
Doubleday
Dry Bones Press—R
Eerdmans Publishing—R
Evangel Publishing—R
Fairway Press—R
Faith Publishing

FOG Publishing
Friends United Press—R
HarperSanFrancisco
Hendrickson—R
Holy Cross—R
Image Press
Intl. Awakening Press—R
InterVarsity Press
Kregel—R
Light and Life—R
Liguori Publications
Liturgical Press
Liturgy Training
Loizeaux
Magnus Press—R
Mercer University Press
Messianic Jewish—R
Morehouse—R
Multnomah Publishers
New City Press—R
New Leaf Press—R
Open Court—R
Oxford University
Pastoral Press
Paulist Press
Pilgrim Press—R
Presbyterian & Reformed
Ragged Edge—R
Read 'N Run—R
Religious Education
Resurrection Press—R
Review & Herald—R
St. Anthony Messenger—R
St. Bede's—R
Schocken Books—R
Shaw Publishers, Harold—R
   (lay)
Sheed & Ward—R
Smyth & Helwys
Southern Baptist Press—R
So. Methodist Univ.
Still Waters Revival—R
Sword of the Lord—R
Toccoa Falls
Trinity Foundation—R
Trinity Press Intl.—R
Tyler Press—R
United Church Press
United Church Pub.
United Methodist—R
U of Ottawa Press
University Press/America—R
Vital Issues Press—R
WaterBrook Press
Westminster/John Knox
Wood Lake Books
Zondervan/Academic
Zondervan/Trade—R

TRACTS

American Tract Society
Apologetics Press
Cornerstone Pub.
Dry Bones Press—R
Faith, Prayer & Tract
Faith Publishing (maybe)
Forward Movement—R
Franciscan Univ. Press—R
Good News Publishers
Gospel Folio Press
Image Press
Impact Christian Books
Intl. Awakening Press—R
Liguori Publications
Messianic Jewish—R
Middle Atlantic—R
Neibauer Press—R
Omega House
Read 'N Run—R
Rose Publishing
Royal Productions—R
TEACH Services—R
Trinity Foundation—R
Woman's Miss. Union—R

TRAVEL

Accent Books
Brannon & Baker
Brentwood—R
Christopher Publishing
Doubleday
Eerdmans Publishing—R
Image Books—R
Journey Books—R
Morehouse—R
Mt. Olive College Press
Read 'N Run—R
Schocken Books—R

WOMEN'S ISSUES

Alban Institute
Albury Publishing—R
Baker Books—R
Bantam Books
Barbour Publishing—R
Baylor University Press
Beacon Hill Press
Bethany House
Black Forest—R
Blue Dolphin
Brannon & Baker
Bridge/Logos
Broadman & Holman
Cerdic Publications

Chalice Press
Christian Publications
Christopher Publishing
Conari Press—R
Concordia
Continuum Publishing
Cornell Univ. Press—R
Cornerstone Pub.
Creation House
Cross Cultural
Crossway Books
CSS Publishing
Dabar Publishing—R
Daybreak Books—R
Doubleday
Eerdmans Publishing—R
Elder Books—R
Element Books—R
Facts on File
Fairway Press—R
Faith Publishing
Focus Publishing
Forward Movement—R
Gospel Publishing House—R
Guernica Editions—R
HarperSanFrancisco
Haworth Press—R
Hearth Publishing—R
Hensley, Virgil—R
Honor Books—R
Horizon House—R
Howard Publishing
Innisfree Press
Judson Press—R
Kregel—R
Life Cycle Books—R
Liguori Publications
Monument Press
Moody Press
Morehouse—R
Multnomah Publishers
New Hope—R
New Leaf Press—R
Northstone
Pacific Press—R
Pastoral Press
Pelican Publishing—R
Pilgrim Press—R
PREP Publishing—R
Read 'N Run—R
Resurrection Press—R
Revell, Fleming H.
Review & Herald—R
St. Anthony Messenger—R
Schocken Books—R
Shaw Publishers, Harold—R
Sheed & Ward—R
Son-Rise

Southern Baptist Press—R
Starburst Publishers
Still Waters Revival—R
Tyler Press—R
United Church Press
United Church Pub.
United Methodist—R
U of Ottawa Press
University Press/America—R
Vital Issues Press—R
WaterBrook Press
Westminster/John Knox
Winston-Derek—R
Woman's Miss. Union—R
Women of the Promise
Wood Lake Books
Zondervan/Academic
Zondervan/Trade—R

WORLD ISSUES

Baker Books—R
Bantam Books
Barclay Press—R
Bethany House
Black Forest—R
Blue Dolphin
Brannon & Baker
William Carey Library
Chalice Press
Christopher Publishing
Cross Cultural
Crossway Books
CSS Publishing
Daybreak Books—R
Faith Publishing
Guernica Editions—R
HarperSanFrancisco
Liguori Publications
Morehouse—R
New Leaf Press—R
Orbis Books
Pilgrim Press—R
Read 'N Run—R
Regnery Publishing—R
Schocken Books—R
Shaw Publishers, Harold—R
Still Waters Revival—R
Trinity Foundation—R
Tyler Press—R
United Methodist—R
University Press/America—R
VESTA—R
Vital Issues Press—R
Zondervan/Trade—R

WORSHIP RESOURCES

Art Can Drama—R
Baker Books—R
Barclay Press—R
Bethany House
Catholic Book Publishing
Chalice Press
Christian Publications
Church Growth Inst.
Church Street Press
Concordia
CSS Publishing
Destiny Image
Educational Ministries
Eerdmans Publishing—R
Fairway Press—R
Forward Movement—R
GROUP Publishing—R
HarperSanFrancisco
Hendrickson—R
Image Press
Judson Press—R
Kregel—R
Liturgical Press
Liturgy Training
Morehouse—R
Pastoral Press
Read 'N Run—R
Royal Productions—R
St. Anthony Messenger—R
Sheed & Ward—R
Smyth & Helwys
Standard
Tyler Press—R
United Church Press
United Church Pub.
United Methodist—R
Vital Issues Press—R
Westminster/John Knox
Women of the Promise
Wood Lake Books
Zondervan/Trade—R

WRITING HOW-TO

Black Forest—R
Bridge/Logos
Cornerstone Pub.
Fairway Press—R
Promise Publishing
Schocken Books—R
Sheed & Ward—R

YOUTH BOOKS
(Nonfiction)

Note: Listing denotes books

for 8- to 12-year-olds, junior highs or senior highs. If all three, it will say "all."

Albury Publishing—R (all)
Art Can Drama—R (all)
Baker Books—R (all)
Barbour Publishing—R (8-12)
Bethany House (all)
Bethel Publishing—R (8-12)
Black Forest—R (8-12)
Brannon & Baker (all)
Broadman & Holman (all)
Butterfly Press (8-12)
CEF Press (8-12)
Cerdic Publications
Christian Ed Pub. (8-12)
Christian Lit. Crusade—R (Jr High)
Christian Publications (Jr/Sr High)
Concordia (all)
Contemporary Drama Service
Cornerstone Pub. (all)
Creation House (Sr High)
Crossway Books (8-12)
CSS Publishing (all)
Eerdmans Publishing—R (8-12/Jr High)
Facts on File (all)
Fairway Press—R (all)
Faith Publishing (Sr high)
Friends United Press—R (Jr High)
Gospel Publishing House—R
Horizon House—R (Jr/Sr High)
Journey Books—R (all)
Judson Press—R
Kaleidoscope Press—R (8-12)
Langmarc (Jr/Sr High)
Libros Liguori (all)
Lightwave Publishing (8-12)
Liguori Publications (all)
Lion Publishing (8-12)
Living the Good News
Lydia Press—R (Sr High)
Morehouse—R (all)
Morris, Joshua (all)
New Canaan (all)
New Hope—R (8-12)
Pacific Press—R (8-12)
Pauline Books—R (all)
Pelican Publishing—R (8-12)
Ragged Edge—R (8-12)
Rainbow/Legacy Press—R (8-12)
Read 'N Run (all)
Royal Productions—R (8-12)
Resurrection Press—R
Review & Herald—R (all)
St. Anthony Messenger—R (all)
Shining Star (8-12)
Son-Rise (all)
So. Baptist Press—R (all)
Still Waters Revival—R (all)
Sword of the Lord—R (all)
TEACH Services—R (8-12/Jr High)
Tommy Nelson—R (8-12, Jr High)
Treasure Publishing—R (all)
Tyler Press—R (all)
United Methodist—R (all)
Upper Room Books—R
Vital Issues Press—R
Windflower—R (all)
Woman's Miss. Union—R
Women of the Promise—(all-girls)
World Bible (all)
Zondervan/Trade—R (all)

YOUTH PROGRAMS

Baker Books—R
Church Growth Inst.
Concordia
Contemporary Drama Service
Cornerstone Pub.
Educational Ministries
Fairway Press—R
GROUP Publishing—R
Hensley, Virgil—R
Judson Press—R
Langmarc
Liguori Publications
Morehouse—R
Read 'N Run—R
Resurrection Press—R
St. Anthony Messenger—R
Sheer Joy! Press
Standard
Vital Issues Press—R
Zondervan/Trade

ALPHABETICAL LISTINGS OF BOOK PUBLISHERS

(*) An asterisk before a listing indicates no or unconfirmed information update.
(#) A number symbol before a listing indicates it was updated from their guidelines or other current sources.
(+) A plus sign before a listing indicates it is a new listing this year and was not included last year.

If you do not find the publisher you are looking for, look in the General Index. See the introduction of that index for the codes used to identify the current status of each unlisted publisher.

ABINGDON PRESS—See **The United Methodist Publishing House**.

ACCENT BIBLE CURRICULUM, PO Box 36640, Colorado Springs CO 80936-3664. (719)536-0100. Cook Communications Ministries. Mary B. Nelson, mng. ed. Buys all rts as work for hire of assigned projects. Writers must be Baptist or baptistic. Submit query letter explaining qualifications to write curriculum; experience; published works. No freelance submissions.

    Special Needs: Writers for kindergarten, junior and adult.

+ACCENT BOOKS & VIDEOS, PO Box 700, Bloomington IL 61702. (309)378-8296. Fax (309)378-4420. E-mail: acntlug@aol.com. Website: http://www.blvd.com/blvd. Cheever Publishing. Betty Garee, ed. Information for the mobility impaired. Publishes 1-2 titles/yr (mostly how-to books). Receives 15-20 submissions annually. 85% of books from first-time authors. No mss through agents. Prefers 64 pgs (max.). Outright purchases. Average first printing 300. Publication within 6 mos. Considers simultaneous submissions. Responds in 2 wks. Accepts disk. Guidelines; catalog $3.50.

    Nonfiction: Query only first; phone/fax/e-mail query OK.

    Also Does: Booklets.

#ACCENT PUBLICATIONS, PO Box 36640, Colorado Springs CO 80936-3664. (719)536-0100x3337. Imprint of Cook Communications Ministries. Mary B. Nelson, mng. ed. Publishes 6-8 titles/yr. Receives 500 submissions annually. 90% of books from first-time authors. No mss through agents. Royalty on retail or outright purchase; no advance. Publication within 1 yr. Considers simultaneous submissions. Responds in 13 wks. Guidelines; catalog for 9x12 SAE/3 stamps.

    Nonfiction: Query letter only; no phone query. "Looking for church resource products that promote the work of the local church in any ministry aspect; also series ideas for Bible studies/group study books."

    Tips: "Be fresh, creative, and in tune with the needs and ministries of the local church's Christian education programs."

ACTA PUBLICATIONS, 4848 N. Clark St., Chicago IL 60640-4711. (312)271-7399. E-mail: acta@one.org. Catholic. Gregory F. Augustine Pierce, co-pub. Resources for the "end-user" of the Christian faith. Imprints: Buckley Publications; National Center for the Laity. Publishes 10 titles/yr. Receives 200 submissions annually. 20% of books from first-time authors. Prefers 150-200 pgs. Royalty 10% of net; no advance. Average first printing 3,000. Publication within 1 yr. Disk accepted. Responds in 4 wks. Guidelines; catalog for 9x12 SAE/2 stamps.

Nonfiction: Query or proposal/1 chapter; no phone/e-mail query.

Tips: "Most open to books that are useful to a large number of average Christians. Read our catalog and one of our books first."

ACU PRESS, 1648 Campus Ct., Abilene TX 79601. (915)674-2720. Fax (915)674-6471. E-mail: LEMMONST@acuprs.acu.edu. Church of Christ/Abilene Christian University. Thom Lemmons, ed. Guidance in the religious life for members and leaders of the denomination. Publishes 10 titles/yr. Receives 100 submissions annually. 10% of books from first-time authors. Royalty 10%. Average first printing 5,000. Publication within 3 mos. Considers simultaneous submissions. Responds in 1 mo. Catalog.

Nonfiction: Proposal/3 chapters.

#ALBA HOUSE, 2187 Victory Blvd., Staten Island NY 10314-6603. (718)761-0047. Fax (718)761-0057. Catholic/Society of St. Paul. Edmund C. Lane, S.S.P., ed. Publishes 24 titles/yr. Receives 450 submissions annually. 20% of books from first-time authors. No mss through agents. Reprints books. Royalty 7-10% on retail; no advance. Publication within 9 mos. Responds in 1-2 mos. Free guidelines/catalog.

Nonfiction: Query.

*THE ALBAN INSTITUTE, INC., 4550 Montgomery Ave., Ste. 433N, Bethesda MD 20814-3341. (301)718-4407. Fax (301)718-1958. Episcopal Church. Celia A. Hahn, ed-in-chief. Publishes 10 titles/yr. Receives 100 submissions annually. No mss through agents. Prefers 100 pgs. Royalty 7-10% of net; outright purchases for $50-100 for 450-2,000 wd articles on congregational life; advance $100. Publication within 1 yr. Responds in 4 mos. Guidelines; catalog for 9x12 SAE/3 stamps.

Nonfiction: Proposal only first. Books for clergy and laity.

Tips: "Books on congregational issues: problems and opportunities in congregational life; the clergy role and career; the ministry of the laity in church and world." Intelligent/liberal audience.

ALBURY PUBLISHING, PO Box 470406, Tulsa OK 74147-0406. (800)811-3921 or (918)496-2200. Fax (918)496-7702. Website: http://www.alburypublishing.com. Elizabeth Sherman, ed. mng. Charismatic Christian lifestyle and doctrinal issues. Publishes 12 titles/yr. Receives 96 submissions annually. 2% of books from first-time authors. Reprints books. Prefers 192 pgs. Royalty; advance. Average first printing 10,000. Publication within 10 mos. No simultaneous submissions. Responds in 3 mos. Guidelines; catalog for 9x12 SAE/2 stamps.

Nonfiction: Query only. "Want well-written and compelling content, whether the topic has to do with personal or corporate Christian experience."

+ALEXANDER BOOKS, 65 Macedonia Rd., Alexander NC 28701. (704)252-9515. Vivian Terrell, exec. ed. Imprint: Farthest Star. Publishes 8-10 titles/yr. Receives 300 submissions annually. 10% of books from first-time authors. Royalty 12-15% on net; few advances. Publication within 1 yr. Considers simultaneous submissions. Responds in 1-3 mos. Guidelines; catalog for #10 SAE/2 stamps.

Nonfiction: Query or proposal/3 chapters. "Subjects include religion."

Fiction: Query or proposal/3 chapters. Adult.

Tips: "Know your market and send a professionally prepared manuscript."

+ALPHA PUBLISHERS, 15430 Herring Rd., Colorado Springs CO 80908. (719)495-8845. Fax (719)495-2348. Sherif Michael, ed. New publisher; plans 9-10 titles in 1998.

Nonfiction: Complete ms. "Looking for health, success, revelation, and dynamic trends in world politics and belief."

Fiction: Complete ms. "Looking for fantasy, suspense, mystery, drama, and science fiction (from a Christian perspective)."

#AMERICAN CATHOLIC PRESS, 16565 State St., South Holland IL 60473-2025. (708)331-5485. Catholic worship resources. Father Michael Gilligan, ed. dir. Publishes 4 titles/yr. Reprints books. Pays $25-100 for outright purchases only. Average first printing 3,000. Publication within 1 yr. Considers simultaneous submissions. Responds in 2 mos. Catalog for SASE.

Nonfiction: Query first.

Tips: "We publish only materials on the Roman Catholic liturgy. Especially interested in new music for church services."

+APOLOGETICS PRESS, 230 Landmark Dr., Montgomery AL 36117. (800)234-8558 or (334)272-8558. Fax (800)234-2882 or (334)270-2002. Website: http://www.ApologeticsPress.org. Publishes books, tracts and booklets for self study, group study, or evangelistic purposes. Catalog. Incomplete topical listings.

*ART CAN DRAMA RESOURCES, Promise Productions Inc., PO Box 927, Glen Rose TX 76043. (800)687-2661. Fax (817)897-3388. Travis Tyre, dir. Supplies Christian schools, churches, and home schools with drama study materials. Publishes 2-3 titles/yr. Receives 50-100 submissions annually. 10% of books from first-time authors. Reprints books. Prefers 150-250 pgs. Royalty 5-10% on retail; $250-500 advance. Average first printing 500-1,000. Publication within 3-6 mos. No simultaneous submissions. Responds in 1-3 mos. Requires disk. Free guidelines/catalog.

Nonfiction: Proposal/1chapter. Fax query OK.

Special Needs: Stage or radio playscripts. Youth plays (contemporary comedies); children's plays (short sketches), creation dramatics (how-to).

Tips: "Most open to books on the arts in a Christian context; playscripts which have been produced, won awards, and explore the Christian experience."

#ASLAN PUBLISHING, 3595 Webb Bridge Rd., Alpharetta GA 30202. (770)442-1500. Website: http://www.aslangroup.com. The Aslan Group. Publishes books by individuals deemed to have a message worthy of publication based upon their own personal experiences with the Lord Jesus Christ; focus is on experiencing Christ in the marketplace. Not in topical listings.

Nonfiction: Query with a short proposal. "Books on business and work from a biblical basis will be considered."

AUGSBURG BOOKS, 426 S. 5th St., Box 1209, Minneapolis MN 55440. (612)330-3300. Fax (612)330-3215. No longer accepting freelance submissions.

**Note: This publisher serviced by The Writer's Edge.

BAKER BOOKS, Box 6287, Grand Rapids MI 49516-6287. (616)676-9185. Fax (616)676-9573. Website: http://www.bakerbooks.com. Evangelical. Allan Fisher, dir. of publications; submit to Jane Schrier, asst. Imprint: Raven's Ridge. Publishes 120 titles/yr. Receives 2,000 submissions annually. 10% of books from first-time authors. Reprints books. Prefers 150-300 pgs. Royalty 14% of net; some advances. Average first printing 5,000. Publication within 1 yr. Considers simultaneous submissions. Responds in 3 mos. No disk. Guidelines (on Website); catalog for 9x12 SAE/6 stamps.

> **Nonfiction:** Proposal/3 chapters; no e-mail query. "Request our brochure on how to prepare a proposal."
>
> **Fiction:** Query. "We are interested in mysteries and contemporary women's fiction from a Christian world view without being preachy. Our fiction is more literary than popular. Request summary of contemporary women's fiction."
>
> **Ethnic Books:** Would be interested in publishing specifically for the African-American market; also multicultural fiction.
>
> **Tips:** "Please prepare a complete, well-organized proposal. Request our guidelines for guidance."
>
> ****Note:** This publisher serviced by The Writer's Edge.

BAKER'S PLAYS, 100 Chauncy St., Boston MA 02111-1783. (617)482-1280. Fax (617)482-7613. E-mail: info@BakersPlays.com. Website: http://www.Bakers Plays.com. Raymond Pape, assoc. ed. Publishes 3-4 plays/yr. Receives 100-150 submissions annually. 40% of plays from first-time authors. Production royalty varies; no advance. Average first printing 1,000. Publication within 3-4 mos. Considers simultaneous submissions. Requires disk. Responds in 2-3 mos. Free guidelines/catalog.

> **Plays:** Complete ms; fax/e-mail query OK.
>
> **Tips:** "We currently publish full-length or one-act plays, theater texts and musicals, with a separate division which publishes plays for religious institutions. The ideal time to submit work is from September to April."

#BALLANTINE BOOKS, 201 E. 50th St., New York NY 10022. (212)572-4910. Fax (212)572-4912. A Division of Random House. Joanne Wycoff, religion ed. General publisher that does a few religious books. No guidelines or catalog. Not in topical listings.

> **Nonfiction & Fiction:** Proposal/100 pages of manuscript.

#BANTAM BOOKS, 1540 Broadway, New York NY 10036. (212)354-6500. General trade publisher with a religious/inspirational list. Thomas Cahill, dir. Accepts mss only through agents. Prefers at least 80,000-100,000 wds. Royalty 4-15%; advance. Publication within 8 mos. Considers simultaneous submissions from agents. Responds in 1 mo. Catalog for SASE.

> **Nonfiction:** Proposal/2-3 chapters. "Want all types of religious/inspirational books." No humor, no triumph over tragedy unless subject is well known or a celebrity.
>
> **Fiction:** Proposal/2-3 chapters. "Books must cross over into the trade market."
>
> **Tips:** "We want books that appeal to a large, general audience and fresh ideas. Be sure to investigate the competition and include an author bio. The

author's relevant experience and authority is very important to us."

#BARBOUR PUBLISHING, INC., 1810 Barbour Dr., PO Box 719, Uhrichsville OH 44683. (614)922-6045. Fax (614)922-5948. E-mail: booksbarbour@ tusco.net. Website: http://www.barbourbooks.com. Susan Johnson, mng ed. Imprints: Barbour Books (nonfiction) and Heartsong Presents (fiction—see separate listing); Inspirational Library. Publishes 75 titles/yr. Receives 450 submissions annually. 40% of books from first-time authors. No mss through agents. Reprints books. Prefers 50,000-60,000 wds or 300 pgs. Outright purchases $750-2,500; advance is half of outright purchase. Average first printing 15,000-20,000. Publication within 1 yr. Considers simultaneous submissions. Responds in 9-12 wks. No disk. Guidelines; catalog $2.

> **Nonfiction:** Query; no phone/fax/e-mail query.
>
> **Fiction:** Proposal/2 chapters to Rebecca Germany, fiction ed. "We are interested in a mystery/romance series." See separate listing for Heartsong Presents.
>
> **Also Does:** Booklets.
>
> **Tips:** "A great idea is more important than a great agent here."

BARCLAY PRESS, 110 S. Elliott Rd., Newberg OR 97132-2120. (503)538-7345. Fax (503)538-7033. E-mail: info@barclaypress.com. Website: http://www.barclay press.com. Friends/Quaker. Dan McCracken, general manager. Books dealing with Christian spirituality and contemporary issues that Christians should address. Publishes 1-5 titles/yr. Receives 40-50 submissions annually. 1% of books from first-time authors. No mss through agents. Reprints books. Prefers 100-200 pgs. Royalty 10% on net; no advance. Average first printing 1,500. Publication within 1 yr. Considers simultaneous submissions. Responds in 6 wks. Prefers disk. No guidelines; free book list.

> **Nonfiction:** Query only; fax/e-mail query OK. "Looking for books on spirituality and current social issues."
>
> **Also Does:** Booklets and pamphlets.
>
> ****Note:** This publisher serviced by The Writer's Edge.

MEL BAY PUBLICATIONS, INC., #4 Industrial Dr., Pacific MO 63069. (314)257-3970. Fax (314)257-5062. E-mail: email@melbay.com. Website: http://www. melbay.com. William Bay, VP; submit to Review Committee. Imprints: Cathedral Music Press; Creative Keyboard Publications. Publishes 25 inspirational/religious titles/yr. Reprints books. Royalty 10% on retail; no advance. Publication within 6-9 mos. Responds in 1-6 wks. Free guidelines/catalog.

> **Nonfiction:** Complete ms or proposal/3-4 chapters (photocopy only); no fax/e-mail query.
>
> **Fiction:** Complete ms or proposal. Children's picture books, juvenile, plays.
>
> **Tips:** Specializes in music books. "In case of musical submissions, we appreciate a demo tape, if available."

#BAYLOR UNIVERSITY PRESS, PO Box 97363, Waco TX 76798-7363. (817)755-3164. Baptist. Janet L. Burton, ed. Imprint: Markham Press Fund. Academic press producing scholarly books on religion and social sciences; separation of church and state. Publishes 2 titles/yr. Receives 120 submissions annually. Royalty 10% of net; no advance. Average first printing 1,000. Publication within 6 mos. Responds in 2 mos. Free catalog.

Nonfiction: Proposal/1-3 chapters; no phone query.

BEACON HILL PRESS OF KANSAS CITY, PO Box 419527, Kansas City MO 64141. (816)931-1900. Fax (816)753-4071. E-mail: bhp@nph.com. Website: http://www.nphdirect.com. Nazarene Publishing House/Church of the Nazarene. Bonnie Perry, mng. ed. A Christ-centered publisher that provides authentically Christian resources that are faithful to God's Word and relevant to life. Imprint: Beacon Hill Books. Publishes 35 titles/yr. Receives 1,000 submissions annually. 10% of books from first-time authors. No mss through agents. Prefers 250 pgs. Royalty 12-18% of net; advance. Average first printing 5,000. Publication within 1 yr. Considers simultaneous submissions. Responds in 3 mos. Free guidelines/catalog.

> **Nonfiction:** Query or Proposal/2-3 chapters; no phone/fax query. "Looking for applied Christianity, spiritual formation, and leadership resources."
>
> **Fiction:** Proposal/2-3 chapters. For adults. "Must be wholesome, Christian fiction."
>
> **Ethnic Books:** Spanish division—Casa Nazarena De Publicaciones. Publishes in several languages.

#BETHANY HOUSE PUBLISHERS, 11300 Hampshire Ave. S, Minneapolis MN 55438. (612)829-2500. Fax (612)829-2768. A ministry of Bethany Fellowship, Inc. Cindy M. Alewine, ms review ed. To publish information that communicates biblical truth and assists people in both spiritual and practical areas of life. Imprint: Portraits (Barbara Lilland, ed). Publishes 120-150 titles/yr. Receives 3,000 submissions annually. 2% of books from first-time authors. Negotiable royalty on net & advance. Publication within 1 yr. Considers simultaneous submissions. Responds in 3 mos. Guidelines for fiction/nonfiction/juvenile; catalog for 9x12 SAE/5 stamps.

> **Nonfiction:** Cover letter, synopsis, 3 chapters; no phone/fax query. "Seeking well-planned and developed books in the following categories: personal growth, devotional, contemporary issues, marriage & family, reference, applied theology and inspirational."
>
> **Fiction:** Cover letter/synopsis/3 chapters. "PORTRAITS is our new contemporary fiction line. We also publish adult historical fiction, teen/young adult fiction, and children's fiction series (7-12 yrs; no picture books). Send SASE for guidelines."
>
> **Tips:** "Seeking high quality fiction and nonfiction that will inspire and challenge our audience—the man and woman in the pew. "
>
> ****Note:** This publisher serviced by The Writer's Edge.

BETHEL PUBLISHING, 1819 S. Main, Elkhart IN 46516. (800)348-7657 or (219)293-8585. Fax (800)230-8271 or (219)522-5670. Missionary Church. Pam Merillat, publishing mngr; submit to Larry Avery. Publishes resources to help people meet Jesus, know Jesus, and serve just like Jesus. Publishes 5-8 titles/yr. Receives 600 submissions annually. 50% of books from first-time authors. Subsidy publishes 1%. Reprints books. Prefers 35,000-70,000 wds. Royalty10% of net; no advance. Average first printing 5,000. Publication within 8 mos. Considers simultaneous submissions. Responds in 9-12 wks. Accepts disk. Free guidelines/catalog.

> **Nonfiction:** Complete ms; fax query OK.

Fiction: Complete ms. For all ages.

Also Does: Board games.

BLUE DOLPHIN PUBLISHING, INC., PO Box 8, Nevada City CA 95959. (916)265-6925. Fax (916)265-0787. E-mail: Bdolphin@netshel.net. Website: http://www.bluedolphinpublishing.com. Paul M. Clemens, pub. Imprint: Pelican Pond. Books that help people grow in their social and spiritual awareness. Publishes 12-15 titles/yr. Receives 4,000 submissions annually. 90% of books from first-time authors. Prefers about 60,000 wds or 200 pgs. Royalty 10-15% of net; no advance. Average first printing 3,000-5,000. Publication within 10 mos. Considers simultaneous submissions. No disk until contract. Responds in 1-3 mos. Guidelines; catalog for 6x9 SAE/2 stamps.

> **Nonfiction:** Proposal/1 chapter; e-mail query OK: "Looking for books on interspecies and relationships."
>
> **Fiction:** Query/2-pg synopsis.
>
> **Tips:** "We look for topics that would appeal to the general market, are interesting, different and that will aid in the growth and development of humanity."

BRIDGE/LOGOS, 1300 Airport Rd. #E, North Brunswick NJ 08902-1700. (732)435-8700. Fax (732)435-8701. E-mail: BLOGOS@aol.com. Harold Chadwick, ed. dir.; submit to Kitty Morrell. Purpose is to clearly define God's changeless Word to a changing world. Imprints: Logos, Bridge. Publishes 25 titles/yr. Receives 370 submissions annually. 20% of books from first-time authors. **SUBSIDY PUBLISHES 12%.** Prefers 180 pgs. Royalty 6-25% of net; some advances, $1,000-$10,000. Average first printing 5,000. Publication within 6 mos. Considers simultaneous submissions. Responds in 6 wks. No disk. Guidelines; catalog for 9x12 SAE/4 stamps.

> **Nonfiction:** Query only; phone query OK. "Most open to evangelism, spiritual growth, self-help and education."
>
> **Tips:** "Have a great message, a well-written manuscript, and a willingness, as well as ways, to market your book. "

BRISTOL HOUSE, LTD., PO Box 4020, Anderson IN 46013-0020. (765)644-0856. Fax (765)622-1045. Sara Anderson, sr. ed. Imprint: Bristol Books. Publishes 4 titles/yr. Receives 35-55 submissions annually. Few books from first-time authors. Reprints books. **SOME SUBSIDY.** Prefers 160-240 pgs. Royalty 14% of net; no advance. Average first printing 1,000. Publication within 6-9 mos. Responds in 4 mos. Requires disk. Catalog for 9x12 SAE/2 stamps.

> **Nonfiction:** Proposal/2 chapters; fax/e-mail query OK. "Looking for books on renewal. Most of our books are Methodist/Wesleyan in emphasis."

BROADMAN & HOLMAN PUBLISHERS, 127 9th Ave. N, Nashville TN 37234. (615)251-3638. Fax (615)251-3752. Southern Baptist. Richard P. Rosenbaum, Jr., ed. Publishes 60 titles/yr. Receives 1,800 submissions annually. 10% of books from first-time authors. Prefers 60,000-80,000 wds. Variable royalty on net; advance. Average first printing 5,000. Publication within 12-18 mos. Considers simultaneous submissions. Responds in 8 wks. Guidelines; no catalog.

> **Nonfiction:** Query only; no phone/fax query.
>
> **Ethnic:** Spanish translations.
>
> **Tips:** "Follow guidelines when submitting. Be informed about the market in

general and specifically related to the book you want to write."

**Note: This publisher serviced by The Writer's Edge.

BROWN-ROA (formerly **BROWN PUBLISHING-ROA MEDIA**), 1665 Embassy West Dr., Ste. 200, Dubuque IA 52002-2259. (800)922-7696. Fax (319)557-3720. Catholic. Marge Krawczuk, ed. Publishes 50-100 titles/yr. Receives 100-300 submissions annually. Variable royalty or outright purchase; rarely pays advance. Average first printing 1,000-3,000. Publication within 1 yr. Considers simultaneous submissions. Responds in 2 mos. Free catalog.

> **Nonfiction:** Complete ms. "Looking primarily for school and parish text books and easy-to-use help books."

*WILLIAM CAREY LIBRARY, 1705 N. Sierra Bonita Ave., Pasadena CA 91104. (818)798-4067. Fax (818)794-0477. David Shaver, gen. mgr. Publishes 10-15 titles/yr. Not in topical listings.

> **Nonfiction:** Query only. "As a specialized publisher, we do only books and studies of church growth and world missions. "

CATHOLIC BOOK PUBLISHING CORP., 77 West End Rd., Totowa NJ 07512. (973)890-2400. Fax (973)890-2410. Website: http://www.catholicbookpub.com. Catholic. Anthony Buono, mng. ed. Inspirational books for Catholic Christians. Publishes 15-20 titles/yr. Receives 75 submissions annually. 30% of books from first-time authors. No mss through agents. Variable royalty or outright purchases; no advance. Average first printing 3,000. Publication within 12-15 mos. No simultaneous submissions. Responds in 2-3 mos. Catalog for 9x12 SAE/5 stamps.

> **Nonfiction:** Query letter only; no phone/fax query.
>
> **Tips:** "We publish mainly Liturgical books, Bibles, Missals, and prayer books. Most of the books are composed in-house or by direct commission with particular guidelines. We strongly prefer query letters in place of full manuscripts."

THE CATHOLIC UNIVERSITY OF AMERICA PRESS, 620 Michigan Ave. NE, Washington DC 20064. (202)319-5052. Fax (202)319-4985. E-mail: cua-press@ cua.edu. Website: http://www.cua.edu/www/cupr. Catholic. Dr. David L. McGonagle, dir. Publishes 6 titles/yr. Receives 100 submissions annually. 75% of books from first-time authors. No mss through agents. Reprints books. Prefers 400 pgs. Variable royalty on net; no advance. Average first printing 750. Publication within 6 mos. Considers simultaneous submissions. Responds in 2 wks. Accepts disk. Guidelines; catalog for 9x12 SASE.

> **Nonfiction:** Query first; phone/fax/e-mail query OK. "Looking for history, literature, philosophy, political theory and theology."
>
> **Tips:** "We publish only works of original scholarship of interest to practicing scholars and academic libraries; works that are aimed at college and university classrooms. We do not publish for the popular religious audience."

CEF PRESS, PO Box 348, Warrenton MO 63383-0348. (314)456-4321. Fax (314)456-2078. Betty Johnson, ed. Produces evangelizing resources for teachers, leaders and evangelists of children. Publishes 40+ titles/yr. 5% of books from first-time authors. Prefers 200 pgs. Royalty; no advance. Average first printing 5,000. Publication within 4 mos. Accepts disks. No guidelines or catalog.

> **Nonfiction:** Query only; fax query OK.
>
> **Fiction:** Query only. For children.

Also Does: Pamphlets, booklets and tracts.

CERDIC PUBLICATIONS, PJR-RIC, 11, rue Jean Sturm, 67520 Nordheim, France. Phone (03)88.87.71.07. Fax (03)88.87.71.25. Marie Zimmerman, dir. Publishes 3-5 titles/yr. All books from first-time authors. Prefers 230 pgs. The first print run in the field of law in religion does not make money. Average first printing 2,200. Publication within 3 mos. Considers simultaneous submissions. Responds in 4 wks. No guidelines; free catalog.

> **Nonfiction:** Complete ms; phone/fax query OK. "Looking for books on law and religion. All topics checked in topical listings must relate to the law."
>
> **Tips:** "We publish original studies in law of religion (any) with preference for young, beginning authors; in French only."

CHALICE PRESS, Box 179, St. Louis MO 63166-0179. (314)231-8500. Fax (314)231-8524. E-mail: chalice@cbp21mail.com. Website: http://www.chalicepress. com. Christian Church (Disciples of Christ). Dr. David P. Polk, ed-in-chief. Books for a thinking, caring church. Publishes 25-40 titles/yr. Receives 400+ submissions annually. 10% of books from first-time authors. No mss through agents. Prefers 144 pgs. Royalty 12-14% of net; no advance. Average first printing 2,500-3,000. Publication within 1 yr. Disk required on acceptance. Responds in 1-3 mos. Guidelines; catalog for 9x12 SAE/2 stamps.

> **Nonfiction:** Proposal/2 chapters; fax/e-mail query OK. "Looking for books that treat current issues perceptively, especially from a moderate-to-liberal perspective."
>
> **Ethnic Books:** African American & Hispanic.

CHARIOT PUBLISHING, 4050 Lee Vance View, Colorado Springs CO 80918. (719)536-3271. Fax (719)536-3269. E-mail: chariotpub@aol.com. Website: http://www.chariotvictor.com. Cook Communications Ministries. Imprints: Chariot Books (children). Liz Duckworth, ed. Provides the best in spiritual growth products for children. Publishes 30 titles/yr. Receives 2,500 submissions annually. 16% of books from first-time authors. Royalty .05-20% on net; advance. Average first printing 7,500-12,500. Publication within 12-18 mos. Considers simultaneous submissions. Responds in 3 mos. Guidelines; catalog for SAE/2 stamps.

> **Nonfiction:** Query only; no phone/fax/e-mail query.
>
> **Fiction:** Query only. Children's picture books and novels for 8-12 year olds.
>
> **Tips:** "We look for books with strong biblical and Christian values that are integral to the characters' lives."
>
> ****Note:** This publisher serviced by The Writer's Edge.

CHARIOT VICTOR BOOKS, 4050 Lee Vance View, Colorado Springs CO 80918. (719)536-3271. Fax (719)536-3269. E-mail: chariotpub@aol.com. Website: http://www.chariotvictor.com. Cook Communications Ministries. Greg Clouse, exec. ed; submit to Lee Hough. Leading the way with spiritual growth products. Publishes 45-50 titles/yr. Receives 1,200 submissions annually. 15% of books from first-time authors. Royalty .05-20% on net; advance $8,750; outright purchases for $500-5,000. Average first printing 7,500-10,000. Publication within 18-24 mos. Considers simultaneous submissions. Responds in 4-6 wks. Guidelines; catalog for 9x12 SAE/2 stamps.

> **Nonfiction:** Query, then proposal/2 chapters; no phone/fax/e-mail query.
>
> **Fiction:** Query, then proposal/2 chapters. For adults.

**Note: This publisher serviced by The Writer's Edge.

CHOSEN BOOKS, Division of Baker Book House, 3985 Bradwater St., Fairfax VA 22031-3702. (703)764-8250. Fax (703)764-3995. E-mail: JECampbell@aol.com. Website: http://www.bakerbooks.com. Charismatic. Jane Campbell, ed. Books that recognize the gifts and ministry of the Holy Spirit and help the reader live a more empowered and effective life for Christ. Publishes 8 titles/yr. Receives 300 submissions annually. 10% of books from first-time authors. Prefers 60,000 wds or 200 pgs. Royalty on net; advance. Average first printing 5,000-7,500. Publication within 18 mos. Considers simultaneous submissions. Responds in 2-3 mos. Requires disk. Guidelines; no catalog.

> **Nonfiction:** Query or proposal/2 chapters (summary, outline, author resume); e-mail query OK. "Looking for books that help the reader live a more empowered and effective life for Jesus Christ."
>
> **Tips:** "State your theme clearly in your cover letter, along with your qualifications for writing on that subject, and be sure to enclose an SASE."
>
> ****Note:** This publisher serviced by The Writer's Edge.

CHRISTENDOM PRESS, 134 Christendom Dr., Front Royal VA 22630. (540)636-2900. Fax (540)636-1655. E-mail: press@christendom.edu. Christendom College/Catholic. John Janaro, dir. Publishes important works of Catholic scholarship and commentary. Publishes 4 titles/yr. Receives 100 submissions annually. **LESS THAN 10% SUBSIDY.** Reprints books. Prefers 62,500 wds or 250 pgs. Royalty 20% on net (after production costs); no advance. Average first printing 1,000. Publication within 24 mos. Responds in 6-8 mos. Free catalog.

> **Nonfiction:** Complete ms.
>
> **Special Needs:** Catholic theology faithful to Catholic church's magisterium; philosophy (especially Thomism); history, political science, literary criticism, and educational theory from a Catholic point of view.
>
> **Tips:** "Most open to a book that provides intelligent, firm and well-balanced reflection in liberal arts, from an unashamedly Catholic point of view. We want books by responsible Catholic scholars and thinkers."

*CHRISTIAN ED. PUBLISHERS, Box 26639, San Diego CA 92196. (619)578-4700. Carol Rogers, mng. ed. An evangelical publisher of Bible Club materials for ages two through high school. Publishes 80 titles/yr. Receives 120 submissions annually. 10% of books from first-time authors. No mss through agents. Outright purchases for .03/wd; no advance. Publication within 1 yr. Considers simultaneous submissions. Responds in 1-2 mos. Guidelines; catalog for 9x12 SAE/4 stamps.

> **Nonfiction:** Query first. Bible studies, curriculum and take-home papers.
>
> **Fiction:** Query first. Juvenile fiction for take-home papers. "Each story is about 1,000 wds. Write for an application."
>
> **Tips:** "All writing done on assignment. Need Bible-teaching ideas for preschool through sixth grade. Also publishes Bible stories for primary take-home papers, 300 wds."

CHRISTIAN LITERATURE CRUSADE, 701 Pennsylvania Ave., Fort Washington PA 19034. (215)542-1242. Fax (215)542-2580. E-mail: 76043.3053@ compuserve. com or CLCBooks@juno.com. Willard Stone, publications coordinator. Publishes 6-8 titles/yr. Receives 100+ submissions annually. Most books from first-time authors. No mss through agents. Reprints books. Prefers 120 pgs & up. Royalty 10-15% on retail; no advance. Average first printing 2,500-5,000. Publication within 6-8 mos. Considers simultaneous submissions. Responds in 1-3 mos. Free guidelines/catalog.

Nonfiction: Proposal/3 chapters; fax query OK. Missions oriented or deeper life.

Also Does: Booklets.

CHRISTIAN MEDIA, Box 448, Jacksonville OR 97530. (541)899-8888. Fax on request. James Lloyd, ed/pub. Publishes 5 titles/yr. Receives 12 submissions annually. Most books from first-time authors. Would consider reprints. Prefers 200 pgs. Royalty on net; no advance. Considers simultaneous submissions. Responds in 3 wks. Catalog for 9x12 SAE/2 stamps.

Nonfiction: Query; phone query OK. Works dealing with the internal workings of the media industry; publishing, broadcasting, records, etc.

Tips: "Produces manuals, instructional or otherwise. Exposés; also books of prophetic interpretation, end times, eschatology, interpolations of political events, etc."

CHRISTIAN PUBLICATIONS, 3825 Hartzdale Dr., Camp Hill PA 17011. (717)761-7044. Fax (717)761-7273. E-mail: editor@cpi-horizon.com. Website: http://www.cpi-horizon.com. Christian and Missionary Alliance. David E. Fessenden, mng. ed. Publishes books which emphasize Christ as Savior, Sanctified, Healer, and Coming King. Imprint: Horizon Books. Publishes 40 titles/yr. Receives 1,200-1,500 submissions annually. 20% of books from first-time authors. Prefers 150-300 pgs. Royalty 5-10% of retail or net; outright purchases $100-400 (booklets); advance $1,000. Average first printing 3,000-5,000. Publication within 12 mos. Considers simultaneous submissions on full proposals. Disk required. Responds in 1-2 mos. Guidelines; no catalog.

Nonfiction: Query/proposal/2 chapters (include 1st); one-page fax/e-mail query OK. "Looking for books on applying the power of the Spirit to practical, daily life."

Also Does: Booklets, 10-32 pages.

Tips: "Looking for anything that encourages a deeper walk with God and a practical application of taking up your cross . Proposals must be complete and fine-tuned."

**Note: This publisher serviced by The Writer's Edge.

CHRISTIAN UNIVERSITIES PRESS, 7831 Woodmont #345, Bethesda MD 20814. (301)654-7414. Fax (301)654-7336. E-mail: AUSTINISP1@aol.com. An imprint of International Scholar's Publications. Dr. Robert West, ed-in-chief. The best obtainable projects in evangelical/Christian research. Publishes 100+ titles/yr. Receives 250+ submissions annually. 60% of books from first-time authors. No mss through agents. Reprints books. Prefers 264 pgs. Royalty 8-12% of net; no advance. Average first printing 500+. Publication within 8 mos. Considers simultaneous submissions. Responds in 1 mo. No disk. Guidelines; free catalog.

Nonfiction: Proposal/2 chapters; fax/e-mail query OK. "Looking for history and theology."

Ethnic Books: Hispanic (Latin America) or (West)African.

Tips: "Most open to scholarly monograph/dissertation, non-fiction research; New Testament."

THE CHRISTOPHER PUBLISHING HOUSE, 24 Rockland St., Hanover MA 02339. (781)826-7474. Fax (781)826-5556. Nancy A. Lucas, mng. ed. Publishes 6-8 titles/yr. Receives 200+ submissions annually. 90% of books from first-time authors. **SUBSIDY PUBLISHES 8-10%.** Prefers 100+ pgs. Prefers 120 pgs. Royalty 5-30% of net; no advance. Average first printing 2,000. Publication within 12-14 mos. Considers simultaneous submissions. Responds in 6-8 wks. Accepts disk. Guidelines; catalog for #10 SAE/2 stamps.

Nonfiction: Complete ms. Most topics; no juvenile material.

Fiction: Complete ms. Adult only. About 100 pgs.

CHURCH & SYNAGOGUE LIBRARY ASSN., PO Box 19357, Portland OR 97280-0357. (503)244-6919. Fax (503)977-3734. E-mail: csla@worldaccessnet. com. Website: http://www.worldaccessnet.com/~csla. Karen Bota, ed. An interfaith group set up to help librarians set up and organize/reorganize their religious libraries. Publishes 6 titles/yr. No mss through agents. Advance. Average first printing 750. Catalog.

#CHURCH GROWTH INSTITUTE, PO Box 7000, Forest VA 24551. (804)525-0022. Fax (804)525-0608. Ephesians Four Ministries. Cindy G. Spear, ed. Publishes 10 titles/yr. Receives 52 submissions annually. 7% of books from first-time authors. No mss through agents. Prefers 64-160 pgs. Royalty 5% on retail or outright purchase; no advance. Average first printing 500. Publication within 1 yr. Considers simultaneous submissions. Responds in 3 mos. Requires disk. Guidelines; catalog for 9x12 SAE/4 stamps.

Nonfiction: Proposal/1 chapter; fax query OK. "We prefer our writers to be experienced in what they write about, to be experts in the field."

Special Needs: Topics that help churches grow spiritually and numerically; leadership training; attendance & stewardship programs; new or unique ministries (how-to).

Tips: "Most open to a practical manual or complete resource packet for the pastor or other church leaders. Write with a conservative Christian slant; be very practical. "

*CHURCH STREET PRESS, 127 Ninth Ave. N., Nashville TN 37234. (800)436-3689. Genevox Music Group. Does music, academic, how-to, drama, and coffeetable books.

CISTERCIAN PUBLICATIONS, INC., Wallwood Hall, WMU Station, Kalamazoo MI 49008. (616)387-8920. Fax (616)387-8921. St. Joseph's Abbey/Catholic/Order of Cistercians of the Strict Observance. Dr. E. Rozanne Elder. ed. dir. Publishes 8-14 titles/yr. Receives 30 submissions annually. 50% of books from first-time authors. No mss through agents. Prefers 204-286 pgs. Variable payment. Average first printing 1,500. Publication within 2-10 yrs. Free style sheet/catalog.

Nonfiction: Proposal/1 chapter. History, spirituality and theology.

Tips: "We publish only on the Christian Monastic Tradition."

COLLEGE PRESS PUBLISHING CO., INC., 223 W. Third St. (94801), Box 1132, Joplin MO 64802. (417)623-6280. Fax (417)623-8250. E-mail: collegepress @collegepress.com. Website: http://www.collegepress.com. Christian Church/ Church of Christ. John M. Hunter, ed. Imprint: Forerunner Books. Christian materials that will help fulfill the Great Commission and promote unity on the basis of biblical truth and intent. Publishes 30 titles/yr. Receives 400+ submissions annually. 1-5% of books from first-time authors. Reprints books. Prefers 250-300 pgs (paperback) or 300-600 pgs (hardback). Royalty 10% of net; no advance. Average first printing 2,000. Publication within 6 mos. Considers simultaneous submissions. Responds in 2-3 mos. Guidelines; catalog for 9x12 SAE/5 stamps.

Nonfiction: Query only, then proposal/2-3 chapters; no phone/fax/e-mail query. "Looking for apologetics and preparation for life in the 21st century."

Ethnic Books: Reprints their own books in Spanish.

Tips: "Most open to conservative, biblical exposition with an 'Armenian' view and/or 'amillennial' slant."

#CONARI PRESS, 2550 - 9th St., Ste. 101, Berkeley CA 94710-2551. (510)649-7175. Fax (510)649-7190. E-mail: conaripub@aol.com. Website: http://www.readersndex.com/conari. Mary Jane Ryan, exec. ed; Claudia Schaab, ed. assoc. Focus is on the human experience. Publishes 26 titles/yr. Receives 1,000 submissions annually. 50% of books from first-time authors. Reprints bks. Royalty 7.5-15%; $2,000 advance. Average first printing 10,000. Publication within 1-3 yrs. Considers simultaneous submissions. Responds in 3 mos. Guidelines; catalog for 7x10 SAE/3 stamps.

Nonfiction: Proposal/3 chapters; no phone/fax query.

CONCORDIA PUBLISHING HOUSE, 3558 S. Jefferson Ave., St. Louis MO 63118-3968. (314)268-1000. Fax (314)268-1329. Website: http://www.cph.org. Lutheran Church/Missouri Synod. Dawn Weinstock, mng. ed. Publishes 80 titles/yr. Receives 2,500 submissions annually. 10% of books from first-time authors. Royalty 3-12% on retail; some outright purchases. Publication within 2 yrs. Considers simultaneous submissions. Responds in 3 mos. Prefers disk. Guidelines.

Nonfiction: Proposal/2 chapters.

Fiction: Proposal/2 chapters; no fax query. For children (5-8, 6-9, or 8-12; series only); also picture books. Fiction guidelines available on request. Christian fiction only.

Christian Drama: Individual scripts and collections; seasonal and topical. Fee based; some royalty. Write for guidelines, attn: Rachel Hoyer.

Tips: "Most open to family, inspirational/devotional, children's, and teachers' resource books."

**Note: This publisher serviced by The Writer's Edge.

CONTEMPORARY DRAMA SERVICE—See MERIWETHER PUBLISHING, LTD.

THE CONTINUUM PUBLISHING COMPANY, 370 Lexington Ave., Ste. 1700, New York NY 10017-6503. (212)953-5858. Fax (212)953-5944. E-mail: contin@tiac.net. Website: http://www.continuum-books.com. Frank Oveis, ed. dir. Publishes 30 titles/yr. Receives 150 submissions annually. 40-50% of books from first-time authors. Reprints books. Prefers 160-200 pgs. Royalty 6-15% on retail or net; advance. Average first printing 2,500-3,500. Publication within 1 yr. Some simultaneous submissions. Responds in 4-6 wks. Disk required. Free guidelines/catalog.

Nonfiction: Proposal/1 chapter; phone/fax/e-mail query OK.

COOK COMMUNICATIONS MINISTRIES—See CHARIOT PUBLISHING, Chariot Victor Books.

DAVID C. COOK PUBLISHING CO.—See CHARIOT PUBLISHING, Chariot Victor Books.

CORNELL UNIVERSITY PRESS, Sage House, 512 E. State St., Ithaca NY 14853. (607)277-2338. Nondenominational. Frances Benson, ed-in-chief; Kay Scheuer, mng. ed. Publishes 6-8 titles/yr. Receives 20 submissions annually. 50% of books from first-time authors. Reprints books. Prefers 100,000 wds. Royalty 5-10%; rarely pays advance. Average first printing 1,250. Publication within 1 yr. May consider simultaneous submission. Responds in 3 mos. Free guidelines/catalog.

    Nonfiction: Query first. "Looking for historical (esp. medieval and early modern) and philosophical books."

*CORNERSTONE PRESS, 939 W. Wilson Ave., Ste. 202C, Chicago IL 60640. (773)561-2450. Fax (773)989-2076. Jane Hertenstein, ed. Imprint: Mere Bones. Publishes 4 titles/yr. Receives 60 submissions annually. Prefers 200-250 pgs. Royalty 12%. Average first printing 2,000-3,000. Publication within 1 yr. Considers simultaneous submissions. Catalog for SASE.

    Nonfiction: Proposal/1 chapter.

    Fiction: Proposal/1 chapter. Children, teen, adults.

#CREATION HOUSE, 600 Rinehart Rd., Lake Mary FL 32746-4872. (407)333-3132. Fax (407)333-7100. Website: http://www.creationhouse.com. Strang Communications. Alyse Lounsberry, ed. dir.; Ginger Schmaus, acq. ed, To provide the charismatic market with books on Spirit-led living. Publishes 25-30 titles/yr. Receives 700 submissions annually. 2% of books from first-time authors. Prefers 40,000 wds or 200 pgs. Royalty 4-18% on retail; advance $1,500-5,000. Average first printing 5,000. Publication within 9 mos. Considers simultaneous submissions. Responds in 2-3 mos. No disk. Free guidelines; no catalog.

    Nonfiction: Proposal/3 chapters; fax query OK. "Looking for books of Spirit-filled interest, devotional life, practical Christian living, and Bible study/foundational."

    **Note: This publisher serviced by The Writer's Edge.

CREATIVELY YOURS, 2906 W. 64th Pl., Tulsa OK 74132. Phone/fax (918)446-2424. Creatively Yours Puppetry. Jill Morris, pub. Publishes individual scripts and books of plays, poems, and related material; general religious. Send complete ms. Responds in 2 mos or less. Pays $25 for plays; $5 for poems (4-20 lines/action), and $10 for choral readings. Buys all rts. Guidelines/brochure for SASE.

    Tips: "Try the material on children—if they don't like it, don't send it to us. Use humor whenever possible. The plays we publish can be used with puppets or children, so don't overload on characters, props, or setting—keep it simple."

    Note: Since this publisher wants individual plays or poems, it is listed in the topical section for periodicals.

CROSS CULTURAL PUBLICATIONS, INC., PO Box 506, Notre Dame IN 46556. (800)561-6526 or (219)272-0889. Fax (219)273-5973. E-mail: crosscult@ aol.com.Website: http://www.bookworld.com/cross-cultural-religion. Cyriac K.

Pullapilly, gen. ed. Promotes intercultural and interfaith understanding. Imprint: CrossRoads Books. Publishes 5-8 titles/yr. Receives 2,000-3,000 submissions annually. 75% of books from first-time authors. Prefers 200-250 pgs. Royalty 5-10% of net; no advance. Average first printing 1,000-1,500. Publication within 5-12 mos. Considers simultaneous submissions. Requires disk. Responds in 2-3 mos. Free catalog.

Nonfiction: Query first; no phone/fax/e-mail query.

Ethnic Books: Seeks to serve the cross cultural, intercultural, and multicultural aspects of religious traditions.

Tips: "Most open to solidly researched, well-written books on serious issues. Do a thorough job of writing/editing, etc."

THE CROSSROAD PUBLISHING CO., 370 Lexington Ave., New York NY 10017. (212)532-3650. Fax (212)532-4922. Michael Leach, pub. Books on religion, spirituality, and personal growth that speak to the diversity of backgrounds and beliefs; books that inform, enlighten, and heal. Publishes 50 titles/yr. Receives 1,000 submissions annually. 10% of books from first-time authors. Rarely subsidy publishes (5%). Reprints books. Prefers 50,000-60,000 wds or 160 pgs. Royalty 6-15% of net; advance $1,000 (more for established authors). Average first printing 5,000. Publication within 6-8 mos. Considers simultaneous submissions. Responds in 3 mos. Accepts disk. Free catalog.

Nonfiction: Proposal/2 chapters or complete ms; fax query OK.

Fiction: Proposal/2 chapters or complete ms. Prefers historical fiction that focuses on important figures or periods in the history of Christianity.

CROSSWAY BOOKS, 1300 Crescent St., Wheaton IL 60187. (630)682-4300. Fax (630)682-4785. E-mail: goodnewsz@aol.com. A division of Good News Publishers. Ted Griffin, sr. ed.; submit to Jill Carter, ed. asst. Publishes books that combine the truth of God's Word with a passion to live it out; with unique and compelling Christian content. Publishes 50 titles/yr. Receives 2,500 submissions annually. 2% of books from first-time authors. Prefers 25,000 wds & up. Royalty 15-21% on net; advance varies. Average first printing 5,000-10,000. Publication within 18 mos. Considers simultaneous submissions. Requires disk (compatible with Macintosh and Microsoft Word). Responds in 6-8 wks. Guidelines; catalog for 9x12 SAE/6 stamps.

Nonfiction: Query only, then proposal/2 chapters; fax query OK.

Fiction: Query first/proposal/2 chapters. Adult; children's books for 8-12 year olds, series only.

Also Does: Tracts. See Good News Publishers.

Tips: "Most open to books that are consistent with what the Bible teaches and stand within the stream of historic Christian truth; books that give a clear sense that the author is a genuine Christian seeking to live a consistent Christian life." Not seeking new projects until winter of 1997.

**Note: This publisher serviced by The Writer's Edge.

+CROSS WAY PUBLICATIONS, 1351 Morgan Ave., Williamsport PA 17701-2849. (717)323-3921. E-mail: crosspub@mail.microserve.net. Website: http://www. microserve.net/~crosspub/Crossway.html. Jerry Hoffman, ed. Produces poetry books which proclaim Christ as King. Publishes 2 titles/yr. Receives 15 submissions annually. 100% of books from first-time authors. No mss through agents.

Prefers 75-100 pgs. No royalty/advance. Does all pre- and post-press preparation at no cost. Printing is done out of house. All copies are shipped to author. Also does web advertising for free. Average first printing 1,000. Publication within 6 mos. No simultaneous submissions. Responds in 2 wks. Requires disk (.txt format desired). No guidelines/catalog.

> **Nonfiction:** Complete ms; e-mail query OK. "We accept only Christian poetry. Although we accept all forms, ideas must be clearly stated and openly point to Christ. Not interested in vague ideas which leave the reader wondering."
>
> **Also Does:** Pamphlets; booklets.

C.S.S. PUBLISHING CO., PO Box 4503, 517 S. Main St., Lima OH 45802-4503. (419)227-1818. Fax (419)228-9184. E-mail: Tom@csspub.com. Website: http://www.csspub.com. Terry Rhoads, ed; Tom Lentz, acq. ed. A clearing house for the promotion and exchange of creative ideas used in ministry. Publishes 200 titles/yr. Receives 1,200-1,500 submissions annually. 50% of books from first-time authors. **SUBSIDY PUBLISHES 40%** through Fairway Press. Prefers 100-125 pgs. Royalty 3-7% or outright purchases for $25-400. Average first printing 1,000. Publication within 6-10 mos. Considers simultaneous submissions. Responds in 3-4 mos. Accepts disk. Free guidelines/catalog.

> **Nonfiction:** Complete ms; fax/e-mail query OK. "Looking for clergy resources for special seasons, Lent/Easter or Advent/Christmas."
>
> **Fiction:** Complete ms. For all ages. Inspirational; plays (Advent/Christmas); short story collections. Children's books, 6-12 years, series or single books.

CUSTOM COMMUNICATIONS SERVICES, INC./SHEPHERD PRESS/CUS-TOMBOOK, 77 Main St., Tappan NJ 10983. (914)365-0414. Norman Shaifer, pres. Publishes 50-75 titles/yr. 50% of books from first-time authors. No mss through agents. Royalty on net; some outright purchases for specific assignments. Publication within 6 mos. Responds in 1 month. Guidelines.

> **Nonfiction:** Query/proposal/chapters. "Histories of individual congregations, denominations, or districts."
>
> **Tips:** "Find stories of larger congregations (750 or more households) who have played a role in the historic growth and development of the community or region."

*DABAR PUBLISHING CO., PO Box 35377, Detroit MI 48235. (313)531-7534. Fax (313)531-7660. U. Francis Osaigbovo, acq. ed. Books for African-American Christian women. Publishes 2-5 titles/yr. Receives 30-40 submissions annually. 75% of books from first-time authors. Reprints books. Prefers 200-250 pgs. Outright purchase of $3,000-5,000 (plus additional royalties based on sales); $500 advance. Average first printing 4,000. Publication within 6-9 mos. Considers simultaneous submissions. Responds in 1 mo, if interested; rejected mss not returned. Guidelines.

> **Nonfiction:** Proposal/3 chapters; phone/fax query OK (leave your phone #).
>
> **Ethnic Books:** "Books that will help African-American Christian women face day-to-day personal/family relationships, community, economic, health, spiritual growth and maturity."
>
> **Tips:** "We're small, so author will have to be willing to be involved in many phases, including promotion. Author does not have to be an African-American woman, but the message should be one that will be of interest to this

group. Established speakers among African-American female audiences are especially desired."

+DAYBREAK BOOKS/RODALE, 733 Third Ave., New York NY 10017. (212)573-0250. Fax (212)682-0665. E-mail: karchar@aol.com. Website: http://www. rodalepress.com. Karen Kelly, ed. dir. Publishes books that empower and enlighten. Publishes 12 inspirational titles/yr. Receives 100+ submissions annually. 50% of books from first-time authors. Some reprints. Prefers 35,000-50,000 pgs. Royalty 6-15% on retail; advance $10,000 & up. Average first printing 12,000. Publication within 12-18 mos. Considers simultaneous submissions. Responds in 6-8 wks. Requires disk. No guidelines; free catalog.

Nonfiction: Query first; fax/e-mail query OK. "Looking for books of personal stories, work, and ethics."

Fiction: Query first. For adults. "We want non-genre fiction of a spiritual, not religious, nature."

Tips: "An expert writing in their area, or a professional with some credentials in the area they are writing about, has the best chance of succeeding."

DESTINY IMAGE PUBLISHERS, INC., 167 Walnut Bottom Rd., PO Box 310, Shippenburg PA 17257. (717)532-3040. Fax (717)532-9291. E-mail: dlm@ reapernet.com. Website: http://www.reapernet.com.Charismatic/Pentecostal. Don Milam, ed; submit to Phillip Zook. Publishes books that will give direction and purpose to the church. Imprints: Revival Press, Treasure House & Destiny Image. Publishes 60-70 titles/yr. Receives 1,000 submissions annually. 80% of books from first-time authors. No mss through agents. Prefers 182 pgs. Royalty 10-20% on net; no advance. Average first printing 5,000-10,000. Publication within 5 mos. No simultaneous submissions. Responds in 2 wks. Free guidelines & catalog.

Nonfiction: Query only; phone/fax/e-mail query OK.

Special Needs: Revival/renewal books.

Also Does: Video/audio tapes; provides Internet services.

*DIMENSION BOOKS, INC., Box 811, Denville NJ 07835. (201)627-4334. Catholic. Thomas P. Coffey, ed. Publishes 12 titles/yr. Receives 800 submissions annually. 2% of books from first-time authors. Reprints books. Prefers 200 pgs. Royalty 10-15% on retail; advance. Average first printing 6,000-20,000. Publication within 6 mos. Considers simultaneous submissions. Responds in 2-5 wks. Catalog for #10 SAE/1 stamp.

Nonfiction: Query. Christian spirituality, music, biography and psychology.

DIMENSIONS FOR LIVING—See THE UNITED METHODIST PUBLISHING HOUSE.

*DISCOVERY PUBLISHING HOUSE, Box 3566, Grand Rapids MI 49501. E-mail: cholquist@rbc.org. Radio Bible Class. Robert DeVries, pub.; submit to Carol Holquist, assoc. pub. Guidelines. Not in topical listings.

**Note: This publisher serviced by The Writer's Edge.

DOUBLEDAY PUBLISHERS, 1540 Broadway, New York NY 10036. (212)354-6500. Fax (212)782-8911. E-mail: webmaster@bdd.com. Website: http://www. bdd.com. Bantam Doubleday Dell. Eric Major. VP of Religion; submit to Mark Fretz or Trace Murphy. Imprints: Image, Galilee, Doubleday Hardcover, Anchor Bible Commentaries. Publishes 30 titles/yr. Receives 400 submissions annually. 5% of books from first-time authors. Accepts mss only through agents. Royalty

6-15% on retail; advance. Average first printing varies. Publication within 1 yr. Considers simultaneous submissions. Responds in 30 days. No disk. No guidelines; free catalog.

Nonfiction: Accepts mss ONLY through agents.

Ethnic Books: African American.

Also Does: CD-ROM reference.

Tips: "Most open to a book that has a big and well-defined audience. Have a clear proposal, lucid thesis and specified audience."

DRY BONES PRESS, 655 Sutter St. Ste. 401, San Francisco CA 94102. (415)292-7371. Fax (415)292-7314. E-mail: jrankin@drybones.com. Website: http://www.drybones.com/. Jim Rankin, ed/pub. Nursing and specialty books. Publishes 2-3 titles/yr. Receives 10 submissions annually. 90% of books from first-time authors. Open to subsidy publishing. Reprints books. Prefers 50-200 pgs (unless poetry, special topic or tract). Royalty 6-10% on retail or as per arrangement; no advance. Average first printing 1,000. Publication within 18-24 mos. Considers simultaneous submissions. Requires disk. Responds in 1-2 mos. No guidelines; catalog for 6x9 SAE/3 stamps.

Nonfiction: Proposal/table of contents & chapters 1-3; fax/e-mail query OK. "Looking for books written by patients about their experience of illness."

Fiction: Proposal/1-3 chapters. Adults.

Also Does: Pamphlets, booklets, tracts.

Tips: "Most open to liturgical books, e.g. psalter; poetry, if not overly trite or sentimental; patient experiences, if well-told and suitable to examination along with professional literature."

EDEN PUBLISHING, 1665 Dixon St. NE, Keizer OR 97303-2214. (503)390-9013. Fax (503)390-9068. Nondenominational. Barbara Griffin, ed. Concerned with covering areas often neglected by more commercially oriented publishing houses. Note: This publisher is not accepting submissions during 1998.

EDITORIAL CARIBE, 9300 S. Dadeland Blvd. Ste. 203, Miami FL 33156. (800)322-7423. Subsidiary of Thomas Nelson. Targets the needs and wants of the Hispanic community.

EDITORIAL PORTAVOZ, PO Box 2607, Grand Rapids MI 49333. (616)451-4775. (800)733-2607. Fax (616)451-9330. Website: http://www.portavoz.com. Spanish Division of Kregel Publishing.

WM B. EERDMANS PUBLISHING CO., 255 Jefferson Ave. SE, Grand Rapids MI 49503. (616)459-4591. Fax (616)459-6540. Protestant/Academic/Theological. Jon Pott, ed-in-chief; Judy Zylstra, children's ed. Publishes 140 titles/yr. Receives 2,000 submissions annually. 5% of books from first-time authors. Reprints books. Royalty 7-10% on retail; occasional negotiable advance. Average first printing 4,000. Publication within 1 yr. Considers simultaneous submissions. Accepts disk. Responds in 3-4 wks Guidelines; free catalog.

Nonfiction: Proposal/2 chapters; fax query OK. "Looking for religious approaches to contemporary issues; spiritual growth; scholarly works; biography for middle readers through young adults; children's picture books expressing positive family values."

Fiction: Query letter only. Children/teen/adult. "We are looking for adult novels with high literary merit. For our children's program we look for manuscripts that help a child explore life in God's world, and to foster a child's exploration of her or his faith."

Ethnic Books: Spanish imprint is Nueva Creacion.

Tips: "Most open to material with general appeal, but well researched, cutting-edge material that bridges the gap between evangelical and mainline worlds."

**Note: This publisher serviced by The Writer's Edge.

ELDER BOOKS, PO Box 490, Forest Knolls CA 94933. (415)488-9002. Carmel Sheridan, dir. Publishes 6-10 titles/yr. Receives 250 submissions annually. 50% of books from first-time authors. Reprints books. Prefers 130 pgs. Royalty 7% of retail; no advance. Average first printing 3,000. Publication within 9 months. Responds in 3 mos.

> **Nonfiction:** Proposal/2 chapters. "Most open to parenting, health, women's or seniors' issues."

ELDRIDGE PUBLISHING CO., INC., PO Box 1595, Venice FL 34284. (800)95-CHURCH. Fax (800)453-5179. E-mail: info@95church.com. Website: http://www.95church.com. Independent Christian drama publisher. Dottie Dunham, religion ed. To provide superior religious drama to enhance preaching and teaching, whatever your Christian faith. Publishes 35 plays/yr. Receives 350-400 plays annually. 75% of plays from first-time authors. One-act to full-length plays. Outright purchases of $100-500; royalty for full-length plays; no advance. Publication within 1 yr. Considers simultaneous submissions. Responds in 1-3 mos. Requires disk. Free guidelines/ catalog.

> **Plays:** Complete ms; e-mail query OK. For children, teens and adults.

> **Special Needs:** Always looking for high quality Christmas and Easter plays but open to other holiday and "anytime" Christian plays too. Can be biblical or current day, for performance by all ages, children through adult.

> **Tips:** "Have play produced at your church and others prior to submission, to get out the bugs. At least try a stage reading. T-shirts, posters and sound effects tapes accompany our dramas."

ELEMENT BOOKS, 21 Broadway, Rockport MA 01966. (978)546-1040. Fax (978)546-9882. E-mail: element@cove.com. Website: http://www.eastwest.com/ Element. Roberta Scimone, acq. ed. Books for broad religious market. Publishes 100 titles/yr. Receives hundreds of submissions annually. 15% of books from first-time authors. Reprints books. Prefers 125-250 pgs. Variable royalty & advance. Average first printing 3,000-5,000. Publication within 18 mos. Considers simultaneous submissions. Responds in 6-8 wks. Free guidelines & catalog.

> **Nonfiction:** Query only.

> **Tips:** "Try to reach a broad-based market—no books on very scholarly or limited-interest subjects."

EVANGEL PUBLISHING HOUSE, 2000 Evangel Way, PO Box 189, Nappanee IN 46550. (219)773-3164. Fax (219)773-5934. E-mail: eph@tln.net. Brethren in Christ Church. Glen Pierce, ed. Provides resources helpful in biblical and theological foundations for Christian ministry, with emphasis on books for use in Christian college and seminary classes. Publishes 15 titles/yr. Receives 25 submissions annually. 0% from first-time authors. **SUBSIDY PUBLISHES 25%.** Reprints books. Royalty 8-12% on retail; no advance. Average first printing

2,000. Publication within 6 mos. Considers simultaneous submissions. Guidelines; catalog for 3 stamps.

Nonfiction: Proposal/2-3 chapters. "Looking for resources for ministry; biblical studies, theology and biblical theology."

Ethnic: Hispanic.

Tips: "Authors should have excellent credentials/experience to give credibility to work. Ph.D. preferred, but not required. Generally books must be suitable for use as texts in college or seminary classes."

+FACTS ON FILE, 11 Penn Plaza, New York NY 10001. (212)967-8800. Website: http://factsonfile.com. Infobase Holdings. Laurie Likoff, ed. School and library reference and trade books tied to curriculum and areas of cross-cultural studies, including religion. Publishes 3-5 titles/yr. Receives 10-20 submissions annually. 2% of books from first-time authors. Prefers 224-480 pgs. Royalty 8-15% on retail; outright purchases of $2,000-10,000; advance $5,000. Some work for hire. Average first printing 5,000. Publication within 9-12 mos. Considers simultaneous submissions. Responds in 4-6 wks. Requires disk. Free guidelines/catalog.

Nonfiction: Query or proposal/2 chapters; fax/e-mail query OK.

*FAITH PUBLISHING CO., PO Box 237, Milford OH 45150-0237. (513)576-6400. Fax (513)576-0022. Catholic. Bill Reck, pres. Publishes 6-12 titles/yr. 50% of books from first-time authors. No mss through agents. Prefers 100-300 pgs. Negotiable terms; no advance. Average first printing 5,000-7,000. Publication within 1-3 mos. Considers simultaneous submissions. Responds in 3-6 mos. Prefers disk. Free guidelines/catalog.

Nonfiction: Complete ms; fax query OK.

Fiction: Complete ms. Biblical/religious only. "Fiction must draw the reader to a deeper knowledge of and devotion to God."

Also Does: Booklets; would consider pamphlets or tracts.

+FOCUS PUBLISHING, 1375 Washington Ave. S., Bemidji MN 56601. (218)759-9817. Website: http://www.paulbunyan.net/focus. Jan Haley, V.P. Does both Christian and secular books geared toward children and homeschooling families. Publishes 4-6 titles/yr. Receives 20 submissions annually. 90% of books from first-time authors. No mss through agents. Reprints books. Royalty 7-10% on retail; advance. Publication within 1 yr. Responds in 2 mos. Free catalog.

Nonfiction: Proposal. Children's or women's (religious) books.

Fiction: Query with synopsis. "Need Christian fiction for children, men, and young adults."

Tips: "Include your target market with proposals, and send SASE."

FOCUS ON THE FAMILY PUBLISHERS, 8605 Explorer Dr., Colorado Springs CO 80920-1051. (719)531-3496. Fax (719)531-3484. Larry Weeden, mng. ed. Dedicated to the preservation of marriage and the family. Publishes 15-20 titles/yr. Receives 2,000 submissions annually. Prefers 200 pgs. Average first printing 25,000. Publication within 1 yr. Considers simultaneous submissions. Responds in 6-8 wks. Free guidelines.

Nonfiction: Submit ONLY a 1-pg query letter.

Tips: "Need highly practical books—tell how to do something and don't make it too complicated. Also looking for writers who are verbal and can do a good, lively interview."

**Note: This publisher serviced by The Writer's Edge.

*FOG (FRIENDS OF GOD) PUBLISHING HOUSE, PO Box 2703, Houston TX 77252-2703. (713)759-0207. Submit to The Editor. To be a servant of God, so that all will boast in the Lord and know His grace. Publishes 5+ titles/yr. Receives 200 submissions annually. 20% of books from first-time authors. Negotiated royalty; no advance. Average first printing 5,000. Publication within 8 mos. Considers simultaneous submissions. Requires disk on request. Responds in 2 mos. Guidelines; no catalog.

> **Nonfiction:** Complete ms only; no phone query.
>
> **Fiction:** Complete ms only. "Must be classic/timeless stories stressing values gained through learned experience "
>
> **Special Needs:** Will consider computer games, especially if created for MACINTOSH.
>
> **Tips:** "Must be extremely well researched and well written. We toss anything remotely unprofessional." Does not return manuscripts.

FORWARD MOVEMENT PUBLICATIONS, 412 Sycamore St., Cincinnati OH 45202. (513)721-6659. Fax (513)721-0729. E-mail: forward.movement@ ecunet.org. Website: http://www.dfms.org/forward-movement. Episcopal. Edward S. Gleason, ed/dir. Publishes 12 titles/yr. Receives 50 submissions annually. 50% of books from first-time authors. No mss through agents. Rarely reprints books. Prefers 150 pgs. One-time honorarium; no advance. Average first printing 5,000. Publication within 9 mos. Reluctantly considers simultaneous submissions. Responds in 1-2 mos. Guidelines; catalog for 9x12 SAE/6 stamps.

> **Nonfiction:** Query for book, complete ms if short; fax/e-mail query OK.
>
> **Fiction:** "We publish almost no fiction, but will look at fiction for children."
>
> **Ethnic Books:** Pamphlets in Spanish.
>
> **Also Does:** Booklets, 4-32 pgs; and pamphlets 4-8 pgs.
>
> **Tips:** "We sell primarily to a mainline Protestant audience."

#FRANCISCAN UNIVERSITY PRESS, University Blvd., Steubenville OH 43952. (614)283-6357. Fax (614)283-6427. E-mail: FUSPRESS@aol.com. Website: http://www.esoptron.umd.edu/fusfolder/press.html. Catholic/Franciscan University of Steubenville. James Fox, exec. dir. To provide literature to inform and inspire readers on their pilgrimage of faith. Publishes 7 titles/yr. Receives 50 submissions annually. 5% of books from first-time authors. No mss through agents. Reprints books. Prefers 300 pgs. Royalty 5-15% on retail; no advance. Average first printing 3,000. Publication within 1 yr. Considers simultaneous submissions. Prefers disk. Responds 3 mos. Free guidelines/catalog.

> **Nonfiction:** Proposal/3 chapters. "Looking for Catholic apologetic/catechetical books in a popular vein."
>
> **Ethnic Books:** "Spanish translations of our best-selling devotional works."
>
> **Also Does:** Pamphlets, booklets, tracts.
>
> **Tips:** "Most of our books are solicited from university professors and associates."

FRIENDS UNITED PRESS, 101 Quaker Hill Dr., Richmond IN 47374. (765)962-7573. Fax (765)966-1293. Friends United Meeting (Quaker). Ardith Talbot, ed. To gather persons into a fellowship where Jesus Christ is known as Lord and Teacher. Publishes 4-6 titles/yr. Receives 50-75 submissions annually. 90% of books from first-time authors. No mss through agents. Rarely does subsidy, 5%. Reprints books. Prefers 200 pgs. Royalty 7.5% of net; no advance. Average first printing 1,000. Publication within 1 yr. Considers simultaneous submissions. Responds in 4-6 mos. Disk required. Guidelines; free catalog.

Nonfiction: Query or complete ms; phone/fax query OK.

Fiction: Query or complete ms. For all ages. Must have Quaker tie-in.

Ethnic Books: Howard Thurman Books (African American).

Tips: "Most open to Quaker-related spirituality; Quaker authors."

GILGAL PUBLICATIONS, Box 3399, Sunriver OR 97707. (541)593-8418. Fax (541)593-5604. Judy Osgood, exec. ed. Focuses on collections of meditations on specific themes. Publishes 1 title/yr. Receives 100+ submissions annually. 25-30% of submissions from first-time authors. No mss through agents. Pays $25/meditation on acceptance, plus 2 copies of the book. Average first printing 3,000. Publication time varies. Responds in 1-2 mos. No disk. Guidelines (required).

Nonfiction: Complete ms (after reading guidelines); fax query OK. "Our books are all anthologies on coping with stress and resolving grief. Not interested in other book mss. Currently interested in meditations on bereavement of various kinds."

*B.J. GOETZ PUBLISHING CO., 3055 W. John Beers Rd., Stevensville MI 49127. (616)429-6442. Fax (616)429-5353. B.J. Goetz, pub. Specializes in materials to enhance Christian education programs; experiential/environmental concepts. Publishes 1 title/yr. Receives 12 submissions annually. 100% of books from first-time authors. Variable payment for outright purchase. Average first printing 1,000. Responds in 1-3 mos. Catalog.

Nonfiction: Proposal or complete ms. "We need an interdenominational approach in Christian education programs or Bible studies for children 5-12."

GOLD 'N' HONEY BOOKS/MULTNOMAH. Children's books. See **MULTNOMAH PUBLISHERS**.

GOOD BOOK PUBLISHING COMPANY, PO Box 959, Kihei HI 96753-0959. Phone/fax (808)874-4876. E-mail: dickb@dickb.com. Website: http://www.dickb.com. Christian/Protestant Bible Fellowship. Ken Burns, pres. Researches and publishes books on the biblical/Christian roots of Alcoholics Anonymous. Publishes 3 titles/yr. Receives 5 submissions annually. 80% of books from first-time authors. No mss through agents. Prefers 250 pgs. Royalty 10%; no advance. Average first printing 3,000. Publication within 3 mos. Considers simultaneous submission. Responds in 1 wk. No disk. No guidelines; free catalog.

Nonfiction: Proposal; no phone/fax/e-mail query. Books on the spiritual history and success of A.A.; 12-step spiritual roots.

Also Does: Pamphlets & booklets.

GOOD NEWS PUBLISHERS, 1300 Crescent St., Wheaton IL 60187. (630)682-4300x308. Fax (630)682-4785. E-mail: gdennis@goodnews-crossway.org. Geoffrey Dennis, mngr. Tracts only; publishing the gospel message in an attractive and relevant format. Publishes 30 tracts/yr. Receives 500 submissions annually. 2% of tracts from first-time authors. Prefers 650-800 wds. Pays about $150 or a quantity of tracts. Average first printing 250,000. Publication within 8 mos. Considers simultaneous submissions. Responds in 6 wks. Guidelines; free tract catalog.

Tracts: Complete ms.

Also Does: Booklets.

#GOSPEL FOLIO PRESS, PO Box 2041, Grand Rapids MI 49501-2041. (616)456-9166. Fax (616)456-5522. E-mail: gospelfoli@aol.com. Website: http://www.uplook.org. Uplook Ministries. J.B. Nicholson, Jr., ed; submit to Caroline Cairns. To build up the saints with clear, scriptural teaching. Publishes 6-10 titles/yr. Receives 20 submissions annually. Up to 1% of books from first-time authors. No mss through agents. Reprints books. Prefers 160 pgs. Often our authors donate their work. Average first printing 3,000. Publication within 3-6 mos. Considers simultaneous submissions. Responds in 1 mo. No guidelines; free catalog.

> **Nonfiction:** Proposal/3 chapters; fax/e-mail query OK. "Virtually all our books are solicited mss or prearranged with the author."
>
> **Also Does:** Pamphlets, booklets, tracts.
>
> **Tips:** "Almost all our writers are Plymouth Brethren. We are a conservative, fundamental, evangelical organization. Books must be clearly presented and doctrinally sound according to our beliefs."

GOSPEL LIGHT PUBLICATIONS—See **REGAL BOOKS**.

+GOSPEL PUBLISHING HOUSE, 1445 Boonville Ave., Springfield MO 65802. (417)862-2781. Glen Ellard, sr. book ed. Supports the pastors and churches of the Assemblies of God. Publishes 3-5 nondepartmental & 7-9 departmental titles/yr. Receives 260 submissions annually. 33-50% of books from first-time authors. Reprints books. Prefers 50,000 wds or 160 pgs. Royalty on net; no advance. Average first printing 5,000. Publication within 12-18 mos. Considers simultaneous submissions. Responds in 4 wks. Requires disk. Guidelines.

> **Nonfiction:** Query only; no phone query.
>
> **Special Needs:** Books on Pentecostal and pastoral leadership; Holy Spirit; deaf culture ministries.
>
> **Ethnic Books:** Hispanic.
>
> **Also Does:** Booklets.
>
> **Tips:** "Any books related to departmental ministries would require the interest and support of the corresponding department (such as Christian education or youth)."

GROUP PUBLISHING, INC., Box 481, Loveland CO 80539. (970)669-3836. Fax (970)669-1994. E-mail: GREditor@aol.com. Website: http://www.grouppublishing. com. Kerry Nance, ed. asst. Imprints: Group Books and Vital Ministry. Encourages Christian growth in children, youth and adults. Publishes 40-50 titles/yr. Receives 300-400 submissions annually. 5% of books from first-time authors. No mss through agents. Reprints books. Royalty 0% of net; some outright purchases or work-for-hire; $1,000 advance. Average first printing 5,000. Publication within 12-18 mos. Considers simultaneous submissions. Responds in 3 mos. Requires disk. Writer test; catalog for 9x12 SAE/2 stamps.

> **Nonfiction:** Proposal/2-3 chapters; phone/fax/e-mail query OK. "Most open to practical ministry tools for pastors, youth workers, C.E. directors, and teachers with an emphasis on active learning. Read *Why Nobody Learns Much of Anything at Church: And How to Fix It* by Thom & Joani Schultz."
>
> **Also Does:** Booklets.

GROUP'S HANDS-ON BIBLE CURRICULUM, Box 481, Loveland CO 80539.

(970)669-3836x4243. Fax (970)669-3269. E-mail: kloesche@grouppublishing. com. Website: http://www.grouppublishing.com. Kerri Loesche, ed. asst. Publishes 24 titles/yr. Receives 200 submissions annually. 40% of books from first-time authors. No mss through agents. Outright purchase. Publication within 12-18 mos. Considers simultaneous submissions. Responds in 3-6 mos. Accepts disk. Trial assignment guidelines/catalog for 9x12 SAE/2 stamps.

>**Nonfiction:** Query requesting a trial assignment; phone/fax query OK. Produces curriculum for preschoolers, 1st-2nd, 3rd-4th, 5th-6th graders; junior highs and senior highs. Submissions received are only kept on file for 30 days.

GUERNICA EDITIONS, PO Box 117, Stn. P, Toronto ON M5S 2S6 Canada. Phone/fax (416)658-9888. Fax (416)657-8885. Toward creating an essential library. Antonio D'Alfonso, ed. Publishes 1 religious title/yr. Receives 50 submissions annually. 10% of books from first-time authors. No mss through agents. Reprints books. Prefers 128 pgs. Royalty 7-10% of net; advance $1,000. Average first printing 1,000. Publication within 18-24 mos. Responds in 1 mo. Requires disk. For catalog send money order for stamps (if from US).

>**Nonfiction:** Query first; no phone query. "Looking for books on world issues."

>**Fiction:** Query first. Interested in ethnic and translations.

>**Ethnic Books:** Concentration on Italian culture. "We are involved in translations and ethnic issues."

#HARPERSANFRANCISCO, 353 Sacramento St. #500, San Francisco CA 94111-1213. (415)477-4400. Fax (415)477-4444. E-mail: hcsanfrancisco@harpercollins. com. Website: http://www.harpercollins.com. Imprint of HarperCollins. Patricia S. Klein, ed. Publishes 36-46 titles/yr. Receives 200-300 submissions annually. 98% of books from first-time authors. Prefers 160-256 ms pgs. Royalty 10-15% on cloth, 7.5% on paperback, on retail; advance. Average first printing 7,500-10,000. Publication within 8-12 mos. Considers simultaneous submissions. Responds in 3-4 mos. Requires disk. Free guidelines.

>**Nonfiction:** Proposal/2 chapters; fax query OK.

>****Note:** This publisher serviced by The Writer's Edge.

HARRISON HOUSE PUBLISHERS, Box 35035, Tulsa OK 74153. (918)494-5944. Evangelical/Charismatic. This company is booked up for the next 4-5 years.

HARVEST HOUSE PUBLISHERS, 1075 Arrowsmith, Eugene OR 97402. (541)343-0123. Fax (541)342-6410. E-mail: macgregorc@harvesthousepubl. com. Website: http://www.harvesthousepubl.com. Evangelical. Carolyn McCready, ed. dir.; submit to Manuscript Coordinator. Books that help the hurts of people. Publishes 100 titles/yr. No longer accepting unsolicited submissions, proposals, queries, etc. Catalog for 9x12 SAE/8 stamps.

>****Note:** This publisher serviced by The Writer's Edge and ECPA First Edition Website.

#THE HAWORTH PASTORAL PRESS, An imprint of The Haworth Press, 10 Alice St., Binghamton NY 13904-1580. (607)722-5857. Fax (607)722-6362. Bill Palmer, mng ed. Publishes 10 titles/yr. Receives 100 submissions annually. 50% of books from first-time authors. Reprints books. Prefers up to 250 pgs. Royalty 7 1/2-15% of net; advance $500-1,000. Average first printing 1,500. Publication within 1 yr. Requires disk. Responds in 2 mos. Guidelines; free catalog.

Nonfiction: Proposal/3 chapters; no phone/fax query. "Looking for books on psychology/social work, etc., with a pastoral perspective."

+HEALTH COMMUNICATIONS, 3201 S. 15th St., Deerfield Beach FL 33442. (954)360-0909. Fax (954)472-7288. Submit to Editorial Committee. Nonfiction that emphasizes self-improvement, personal motivation, psychological health and overall wellness; recovery/addiction, self-help/psychology, health/wellness, soul/spirituality, inspiration, women's issues, relationships and family. Negotiable royalty. Responds in 2 mos. Must get & follow guidelines for submission. Not in topical listings.

Nonfiction: Proposal/2 chapters; no phone query.

HEARTH PUBLISHING, 212 N. Ash, Hillsboro KS 67063. (316)947-3966. Fax (316)947-3392. Stan Thiessen, ed/dir. Wholesome literature of a classic nature, not necessarily religious. Publishes 4-6 titles/yr. Receives 600 submissions annually. 80+% of books from first-time authors. No mss through agents. Reprints books. Prefers 96-224 pgs (poetry 96 pgs). Negotiable royalty and advance. Average first printing 1,500-20,000. Publication within 8+ mos. Considers simultaneous submissions. Responds in 1-3 mos. Requires disk. Guidelines; no catalog.

Nonfiction: Proposal/3-4 chapters; no phone/fax query. "Any topic, including genealogy and cookbooks."

Fiction: Proposal/3-4 chapters. "Looking for juvenile and young adult (7-12) series or single books, classic adventure, fun to read; should fit secular markets as well as religious. Call about ongoing anthologies."

Also Does: Booklets and chapbooks.

Tips: "Most open to books espousing Christian ethics but not necessarily religious. Good, wholesome adventure of any kind. Specialty cookbooks."

HEARTSONG PRESENTS, Imprint of Barbour Publishing, Inc., PO Box 719, 1810 Barbour Dr., Uhrichsville, OH 44683. (614)922-6045. Fax (614)922-5948. E-mail: heartsong@barbourbooks.com. Website: http://www.barbourbooks.com. Rebecca Germany, ed. Produces affordable, wholesome entertainment through a book club that also helps to enhance and spread the Gospel. Publishes 52 titles/yr. Receives 700+ submissions annually. 25-35% of books from first-time authors. Prefers 50,000 wds. Outright purchases $2,000-2,500; rare advance. Average first printing 20,000. Publication within 6-9 months. Considers simultaneous submissions. Responds in 6-9 wks. Requires disk. Guidelines; no catalog.

Fiction: Proposal/3-4 chapters; fax/e-mail query OK. "We publish 2 contemporary and 2 historical romances every 4 weeks. We cover all topics and settings. Specific guidelines available."

Tips: "Most open to romance with a strong conservative-Christian theme."

HENDRICKSON PUBLISHERS, 140 Summit St., PO Box 3473, Peabody MA 01961. (508)532-2248. Fax (508)532-8248. E-mail: DPenwell@hendrickson. com. Dan Penwell, mngr. of trade products. To provide biblically oriented books for reference, learning and personal growth. Publishes 15-20 titles/yr. Receives 100-150 submissions annually. 25% of books from first-time authors. No mss through agents. Reprints books. Prefers 200-500 pgs. Royalty 10-14% of net; some advances. Average first printing 2,500. Publication within 9-12 mos. Considers simultaneous submissions. Responds in 1-2 mos. Requires disk. Follow *Chicago Manual of Style* guidelines; catalog for 9x12 SAE/6 stamps.

Nonfiction: Query/summary or sample chapters; fax/e-mail query OK.

Special Needs: Books that help the reader's confrontation and interaction with Scripture, leading to a positive change in thought and action; books that give a hunger to studying, understanding and applying Scripture; books that encourage and facilitate personal growth in such areas as personal devotions and a skillful use of the Bible.

Tips: "A well-organized, thought-provoking, clear, and accurate proposal has the best chance of being read and accepted."

**Note: This publisher serviced by The Writer's Edge.

#VIRGIL HENSLEY PUBLISHING, 6116 E. 32nd St., Tulsa OK 74135. (918)664-8520. Terri Kalfas, ed. To edify and challenge the readers to a higher level of spiritual maturity in their Christian walk. Publishes 5-10 titles/yr. Receives 800 submissions annually. 50% of books from first-time authors. Reprints books. Prefers up to 250 pgs. Royalty 5% on net; some outright purchases of $250 & up; no advance. Average first printing 5,000. Publication within 18 mos. Considers simultaneous submissions. Disk required in MAC format. Responds in 2 mos. Guidelines; catalog for 9x12 SAE/3 stamps.

Nonfiction: Query or proposal/3 consecutive chapters, or complete ms; no phone query. "If it's good we'll consider it even if it doesn't fit the categories we've indicated. Target a broad market, not a narrow one."

Ethnic Books: Will have a limited number of titles available this year.

Tips: "Most open to a Bible study that can be used by anyone; no denominational influences."

#HI-TIME PUBLISHING CORP., 12040-L W. Feerick St., PO Box 13337, Milwaukee WI 53222-2136. (414)466-2420. Catholic. Lorraine Kukulski, sr. ed. Sound, contemporary resources to help Catholic teens and adults live out and develop their faith. Publishes 3 titles/yr. Receives 15-20 submissions annually. 50% of books from first-time authors. Negotiates royalty or outright purchase; negotiable advance. Publication within 6 mos. Responds in 2-5 wks. Free guidelines/catalog.

Nonfiction: Query or proposal/1 chapter; phone query OK.

Also Does: Pamphlets & booklets.

HOLY CROSS ORTHODOX PRESS, 50 Goddard Ave., Brookline MA 02146. (617)731-3500. Fax (617)566-9075. Greek Orthodox. Anton C. Vrame, mng. ed. Academic and general works of interest to Orthodox Christians in church history, worship, spirituality and life. Publishes 8-10 titles/yr. Receives 15-20 submissions annually. 50% of books from first-time authors. No mss through agents. Reprints bks. Prefers 200-300 pgs. Royalty 8-12% on retail; no advance. Average first printing 750-1,000. Publication within 12-18 mos. Considers simultaneous submissions. Requires disk (MAC). Responds in 3-4 mos. Free catalog.

Nonfiction: Complete ms. Also open to saints and iconography. "Most open to a book on historic Orthodox Christianity with a sound theological basis."

Ethnic Books: Greek (orthodox).

HONOR BOOKS, 2448 E. 81st St., Ste. 4800, PO Box 55388, Tulsa OK 74155. (918)496-9007. Fax (918)496-3588. Website: http://www.HonorBooks.com. Inspirational/devotional. Mark K. Gilroy, ed. dir. Sue Rhodes Sesso, acq. ed. Publishes 60 titles/yr. Receives 1,500 submissions annually. Few books from first-time authors. Reprints books. Prefers 160+ pgs. Royalty 5-15% on net or outright purchase; advance. Publication within 1 yr. Considers simultaneous submissions. Responds in 1-3 mos. Guidelines.

Nonfiction: Proposal/2 chapters.

Special Needs: Seasonal gift books; third-person stories reflecting God's wisdom applied to everyday life, in a devotional format.

Tips: "We do 85% of our titles on assignment to work-for-hire writers. Show us writing samples if you are interested in researching, writing, or compiling our own creative ideas."

HOWARD PUBLISHING CO., INC., 3117 N. 7th St., West Monroe LA 71291. (318)396-3122 Fax (318)397-1882. E-mail: Info@howardpublishing.com. John Howard, pres.; submit to Denny Boultinghouse. Christian publisher. Publishes 12-18 titles/yr. Receives 100 submissions annually. 20% of books from first-time authors. Prefers 200-250 pgs. Negotiable royalty & advance. Average first printing 5,000. Publication within 1 yr. Considers simultaneous submissions. Responds in 4-6 wks. No disk. Free guidelines/catalog.

Nonfiction: Proposal/3 chapters; phone query OK.

Tips: "Our authors must first be Christ-centered in their lives and writing, then qualified to write on the subject of choice. Public name recognition is a plus. Authors who are also public speakers usually have a ready-made audience."

HUNT AND THORPE, Laurel House, Station Approach, New Alresford Hants, UK S024 95H. (01962) 735320. John Hunt, ed. Children's books for the international Christian market. Publishes 25 titles/yr. Receives 100 submissions annually. 1% of books from first-time authors. Prefers 1,000 wds or 10 pgs for color books. Royalty 5-10% on net; advance $500. Average first printing 20,000. Publication within 2 yrs. No simultaneous submissions. Responds in 1 mo. No disk. Free catalog.

Nonfiction: Proposal/1 chapter; no phone query.

Fiction: For young teens to age 20. No children's fiction.

#ICS PUBLICATIONS, 2131 Lincoln Rd NE, Washington DC 20002. (202)832-8489. Fax (202)832-8967. Website: http://www.ocd.or.at/ics. Catholic/Institute of Carmelite Studies. Steven Payne, OCD, ed. dir. For those interested in the Carmelite tradition with focus on prayer and spirituality. Publishes 8 titles/yr. Receives 30 submissions annually. 10% of books from first-time authors. Reprints books. Prefers 200 pgs. Royalty 2-6% on retail; some outright purchases; advance $500. Average first printing 3,000-7,000. Publication within 2 yrs. Considers simultaneous submissions. Responds in 2 mos. Guidelines; catalog for 7x10 SAE/2 stamps.

Nonfiction: Query or outline/1 chapter; phone query OK. "Most open to translation of Carmelite classics; popular introductions to Carmelite themes which show a solid grasp of the tradition."

IGNATIUS PRESS, 2515 McAllister St., San Francisco CA 94118. (415)387-2324 or (800)651-1531. Fax (415)387-0896. E-mail: info@ignatius.com. Website: http://www.ignatius.com. Catholic. Joseph Fessio, ed. Publishes 40 titles/yr. Query. Books for children & youth, catechisms and teaching aids.

*INHERITANCE PUBLICATIONS, Box 154, Neerlandia AB T0G 1R0 Canada. (403)674-3949.

INNISFREE PRESS, 136 Roumfort Rd., Philadelphia PA 19119-1632. (215)247-4085. Fax (215)247-2343. E-mail: InnisfreeP@aol.com. Marcia Broucek, ed-in-chief. Specializes in books that go beyond traditional boundaries to investigate all aspects of spirituality. Publishes 8 titles/yr. Receives 500 submissions annually. 60% of books from first-time authors. Prefers 40,000-50,000 wds. Royalty 10% of net; advance $500. Average first printing 5,000. Publication within 1 yr. Considers simultaneous submissions. Responds in 6 wks. Requires disk. Free guidelines/catalog.

> **Nonfiction:** Proposal/2 chapters; no phone/fax/e-mail query. "Looking for books with a spiritual perspective on everyday living in the workplace, in relationships, in personal growth."
>
> **Tips:** "Looking for books that match our company's byline, 'A Call to the Deep Heart's Core.'" Books with personal experience and women's perspective are of special interest.

INTERNATIONAL AWAKENING PRESS, 139 N. Washington, PO Box 232, Wheaton IL 60189. Phone/fax (630)653-8616. Intl. Awakening Ministries, Inc. Richard Owen Robbers, pres. Scholarly books on religious awakenings or revivals. Publishes 4 titles/yr. Receives 12 submissions annually. Reprints books. Royalty 10% on retail; no advance. Average first printing 3,000. Publication within 6 mos. Responds in 3 mos. Requires disk. No guidelines; free catalog.

> **Nonfiction:** Query only; no phone/fax query. "Looking for books on revival."
>
> **Also Does:** Booklets, pamphlets, tracts.

INTERVARSITY PRESS, Box 1400, Downers Grove IL 60515. (630)887-2500. Fax (630)887-2520. E-mail: mail@ivpress.com. Website: http://www.ivpress.com. InterVarsity Christian Fellowship. Andrew T. LePeau, ed. dir.; submit to Rodney Clapp or Cindy Bunch Hotaling. To communicate the Lordship of Christ in all of life through a serious-minded approach to Scripture, the church and the world. Imprints: Ediciones Certeza; LifeGuide Bible Studies; Saltshaker Books. Publishes 70 titles/yr. Receives 450 submissions annually. 35% of books from first-time authors. Prefers 50,000 wds or 200 pgs. Negotiable royalty on retail; negotiable advance. Average first printing 5,500. Publication within 10 mos. Considers simultaneous submissions. Requires disk. Responds in 8-10 wks. Guidelines; catalog for 9x12 SAE/5 stamps.

> **Nonfiction:** All unsolicited mss (from people they have had no previous contact with) are referred to The Writer's Edge (see their listing under Editorial Services—IL); fax/e-mail query OK. "Looking for academic and reference books."
>
> **Ethnic Books:** Black, Hispanic, Asian.
>
> **Also Does:** Booklets.
>
> **Tips:** "We look for a thoughtful approach. We shy away from black and white treatments. Writers who are nuanced, subtle, discerning and perceptive will get farther at IVP."
>
> ****Note:** This publisher serviced by The Writer's Edge.

+JORDAN PUBLISHING, PO Box 67, Jenison MI 49429-0067. (616)457-3300.

Fax (616)457-6662. E-mail: JordanPub@aol.com. Website: http://members.aol. com/JordanPub. Evangelical/Wesleyan. Joseph Allison, pub. To sustain the people of God by producing innovative Christian resources for study and service. New publishers; first titles to be released in fall 1998. Royalty. Guidelines. Not in topical listings.

Nonfiction: Query. "We are specializing in quick-reference books for laypeople and pastors."

Special Needs: Aids for study; tools for ministry; resources for dialogue. Devotional books in innovative formats.

Tips: "Our goal is to serve the needs of the church and make reference material more accessible to people who might not have seminary training or who are pressed for time. We will also do devotional books on tape for shut-ins, hospital patients, and the terminally ill."

#JOSSEY-BASS INC., PUBLISHERS/RELIGION IN PRACTICE, 350 Sansome St., San Francisco CA 94104. (415)433-1740. Fax (415)433-0499. Simon & Shuster, Inc. Sara Polster, ed. Royalty 10%. Publication within 1 yr. Considers simultaneous submissions. Responds in 1-2 mos.

Nonfiction: Query. "We are starting a new line of books for religious professionals (called Religion in Practice) that will address the issues of leadership and empowerment, similar to those we deal with in our secular lines."

JOURNEY BOOKS (formerly **BOB JONES UNIVERSITY PRESS**), 1700 Wade Hampton Blvd., Greenville SC 29614. (864)242-5100x4353. Fax (864)298-0268. E-mail: grepp@wpo.bju.edu. Bob Jones University Press. Gloria Repp, acq. ed. Imprints: Light Line and Pennant Books. Goal is to publish books for children that excel in both literary and moral content. Publishes 10-12 titles/yr. Receives 500 submissions annually. 30% of books from first-time authors. Reprints books. Prefers up to 10,000 wds (depends on age group). Royalty on net; outright purchases of $1,000 (for first-time authors); advance $1,000. Average first printing 5,000. Publication within 12-18 months. Considers simultaneous submissions. Accepts disks. Responds in 2 mos. Guidelines; catalog for 9x12 SAE/2 stamps.

Nonfiction: Biography only.

Fiction: Proposal/5 chapters or complete ms. For children and teens. "Looking for humor or mystery; problem realism; historical fiction."

Also Does: Story cassettes and book sets.

Tips: "Most open to realistic or historical fiction for upper elementary through teens; biography with a good moral tine; or easy readers with satisfying content."

JUDSON PRESS, Box 851, Valley Forge PA 19482-0851. (610)768-2109. Fax (610)768-2441. Website: http://www.judsonpress.com. American Baptist Churches USA. Randy Frame, acq. ed. Publishes 16 titles/yr. Receives 500 submissions annually. 50% of books from first-time authors. Reprints books. Prefers 180-200 pgs. Royalty 5-10% on retail; some work-for-hire agreements; advance $300. Average first printing 2,000. Publication within 9-18 mos. Considers simultaneous submissions. Responds in 2-3 mos. Requires disk. Free guidelines/catalog.

Nonfiction: Proposal/2 chapters; phone query OK.

Ethnic Books: African-American.

Tips: "Authors should avoid books based primarily on their own experiences and personal reflections. Writing style must be engaging and the writer should be well qualified to address the topic."

**Note: This publisher serviced by The Writer's Edge.

KALEIDOSCOPE PRESS, 2507—94th Ave. E., Edgewood WA 98371. Phone/fax (206)848-1116. Penny Lent, ed/pub. Providing tools for growth and enrichment that are unavailable. Publishes 7 titles/yr. Receives 175 submissions annually. 90% of books from first-time authors. No mss through agents. Reprints books. Variable length. Royalty 10% on retail; no advance. Average first printing 2,000. Publication within 1 yr. Considers simultaneous submissions. Responds in 2 mos. Requires disk. Guidelines; catalog for #10 SAE/1 stamp.

> **Nonfiction:** Query letter only; no phone/fax query. "Actively seeking submissions of inspiration, short poetry, anecdotes, humor, short poetry, quips & quotes, and bizarre rejections from/about writers for a book in progress."
>
> **Fiction:** For children only; also picture books. Query only. "Show us in your query how the piece is unique or needed in the marketplace."
>
> **Tips:** "Most open to nonfiction that fills a need. Do and show your market research. Grab our interest."

KINDRED PRODUCTIONS, 169 Riverton Ave., Winnipeg MB R2L 2E5 Canada. (204)669-6575. Fax (204)654-1865. E-mail: kindred@cdnmbconf.ca. Website: http://www.mbconf.org/mbc/kp/kindred.htm. Mennonite Brethren. Marilyn Hudson, mngr. To resource the churches within the denomination (Anabaptist perspective). Publishes 3-4 titles/yr. Receives 60 submissions annually. 90% of books from first-time authors. **SUBSIDY PUBLISHES 5%.** Prefers 200-250 pgs. Royalty 10-15% on retail; no advance. Average first printing 1,000-2,000. Publication within 9-12 mos. Considers simultaneous submissions. Responds within 4-5 mos. Requires disk. Free guidelines/catalog.

> **Nonfiction:** Proposal/2 chapters; fax/e-mail query OK. Also does pamphlets & booklets. "Looking for inspirational books, story-based."

KREGEL PUBLICATIONS, PO Box 2607, Grand Rapids MI 49501. (616)451-4775. Fax (616)451-9330. E-mail: Editorial@kregel.com. Website: http://www.kregel.com. Evangelical/Conservative. Dennis R. Hillman, pub. To provide tools for ministry and Christian growth from a conservative, evangelical perspective. Publishes 60 titles/yr. Receives 250+ submissions annually. 20% of books from first-time authors. Reprints books. Royalty 8-16% of net; some outright purchases; $1,000-2,000 advance. Average first printing 5,000. Publication within 16 mos. Considers simultaneous submissions. Requires disk. Responds in 1-2 mos. Guidelines; catalog for 9x12 SAE/3 stamps.

> **Nonfiction:** Query only; fax/e-mail query OK.
>
> **Fiction:** Query only. Looking for biblical/historical fiction with strong Christian themes and characters.
>
> **Ethnic Books:** Spanish division: Editorial Portaroz.
>
> **Tips:** "Most open to biblically based books of practical Christian teaching or books of interest to the vocational Christian worker. Take the time to study our line of books and tell us how your book meets our needs."
>
> ****Note:** This publisher serviced by The Writer's Edge.

*LANGMARC PUBLISHING, PO Box 33817, San Antonio TX 78265. (210)822-2521. Fax (210)822-5014. Lutheran. Lois Qualben, pub. Focuses on spiritual growth of readers. Publishes 4 titles/yr. Receives 200 submissions annually. 50% of books from first-time authors. No mss through agents. Prefers 150-300 pgs. Royalty 8-10% on retail; no advance. Average first printing 1,500. Publication usually within 1 yr. Considers simultaneous submissions. Responds in 2-4 mos. Requires disk. Catalog for SASE.

> **Nonfiction:** Proposal/3 chapters; phone query OK. "Most open to inspirational, congregational leadership, or materials for teens."
>
> **Fiction:** Does some.

LIBROS LIGUORI, 1 Liguori Dr., Liguori MO 63125. (314)464-2500. Fax (314)464-8449. E-mail: LibrosLiguori@compuserve.com. Website: http://www. Liguori.org. Spanish division of Liguori Publications. Vincent Hamon-Enriquez, ed. To spread the gospel in the Hispanic community by means of low-cost publications. Publishes 15 titles/yr. Receives 6-8 submissions annually. 5% of books from first-time authors. Prefers up to 30,000 wds. Royalty 4-12% of net or outright purchases of $400 (book and booklet authors get royalties; pamphlet authors get $400 on acceptance and royalties thereafter); advance. Average first printing 3,500-5,000. Publication within 18 mos. No simultaneous submissions. Requires disk. Responds in 4-8 wks. Free guidelines/catalog.

> **Nonfiction:** Query first; fax/e-mail query OK. "Looking for issues families face today—substance abuse, unwanted pregnancies, etc.; family relations; religion's role in immigrant's experiences."
>
> **Ethnic Books:** Focuses on Spanish-language products.
>
> **Also Does:** Pamphlets and booklets; PC software, and clip art.
>
> **Tips:** "Needs books on the Hispanic experience in the U.S. Keep it concise; avoid academic/theological jargon; and stick to the tenets of the Catholic faith—avoid abstract arguments."

*LIFE CYCLE BOOKS, Box 420, Lewiston NY 14092. (416) 690-8532. Fax (416)690-5860. E-mail: pbroughton@lcbooks.com. Website: http://www. lcbooks.com. Paul Broughton, gen. mgr. Publishes 1-3 pro-life titles/yr. Receives 50 submissions annually. 50% of books from first-time authors. Reprints books. Royalty 8% of net; outright purchase of brochure material, $250+; advance $100-300. **SUBSIDY PUBLISHES 10%.** Publication within 10 mos. Responds in 6 wks. Free catalog.

> **Nonfiction:** Query or complete ms. "Our emphasis is on pro-life and pro-family titles."
>
> **Tips:** "We are most involved in publishing leaflets of about 1,500 wds, and welcome submissions of mss of this length."

LIFETIME BOOKS, 2131 Hollywood Blvd., Hollywood FL 33020. (954)925-5242x13. Fax (954)925-5244. E-mail: lifetime@shadow.net. Website: http://www. lifetimebooks.com. Callie Rucker, sr. ed. General publisher that publishes 2-4 religious titles/yr. Receives 100 submissions annually. 60% of books from first-time authors. Reprints books. Prefers 60,000 wds or 250-300 pgs. Royalty 6-15% on retail; advance of $500-10,000. Average first printing 10,000. Publication within 9 mos. Considers simultaneous submissions. Responds in 1-2 mos. Guidelines; catalog for 9x12 SAE/5 stamps.

Nonfiction: Proposal/1 chapter; fax query OK. Include a clear marketing and promotional strategy.

Tips: "Spirituality, optimism, and a positive attitude have international appeal. Steer clear of doom and gloom; less sadness and more gladness benefits all."

LIGHT AND LIFE COMMUNICATIONS, PO Box 535002, Indianapolis IN 46253-5002. Free Methodist. Submit to The Editor. Denominational publisher; publishes books that minister. Publishes 30 titles/yr. Receives 60 submissions annually. 33% of books from first-time authors. Reprints books. Royalty & advance negotiable. Publication within 6-12 mos. Reluctantly accepts simultaneous submissions. Responds in 6 wks. (or after next acquisitions committee meeting). Requires disk. Guidelines.

Nonfiction: Proposal/3 chapters.

Tips: "Most open to books that have obvious marketability; and books that speak more to the heart than to the head."

+LIGHTWAVE PUBLISHING, INC., Box 160, Maple Ridge BC V2X 7G1 Canada. (604)462-7890. Fax (604)462-8208. E-mail: wave@lightwavepublishing.com. Website: http://www.lightwavepublishing.com. Christie Bowler, ed. To help children understand the basics of the Christian faith, and to help parents pass these values on to their children. Publishes 24 titles/yr. No mss through agents. Royalty on net; outright purchases or work for hire (pays an hourly or per-project rate, amount depends on project size; wages up front, on delivery of manuscript). Publication within 4-8 mos. Considers simultaneous submissions. Responds in 1 mo (if requested). Guidelines; no catalog.

Nonfiction: Query only to inquire about work-for-hire and send resume; fax/e-mail query OK.

Fiction: Query only. "We do very little fiction, and only as related to teaching children about prayer, stewardship, general Bible knowledge, or creation science."

Special Needs: Books related to children and parenting issues from a variety of angles.

Also Does: Some booklets.

Tips: "We usually come up with book ideas, then hire a writer/researcher, with expertise in that particular field, to write it."

**Note: This publisher serviced by The Writer's Edge.

LIGUORI PUBLICATIONS, 1 Liguori Dr., Liguori MO 63125. (314)464-2500. Fax (314)464-8449. Website: http://www.Liguori.org. Catholic/Redemptorists. Publishes 50 titles/yr. Prefers 2,800-35,000 wds. Royalty 9-11% on retail; outright purchase of 24-page pamphlets for $400; no advance. Average first printing 3,500-5,000 on books & booklets, 10,000 on pamphlets. Accepts disks. Responds in 10-15 wks.

Nonfiction: Proposal/2 chapters (complete ms for pamphlets). "Looking for books on teen issues."

Fiction: Complete ms. "Generally we don't do fiction, but will consider children's picture books, allegory or biblical books for children."

Ethnic Books: Publishes books in Spanish. See separate listing for Libros Liguori.

Also Does: Booklets, pamphlets & tracts; computer games and screen savers.

Tips: "Manuscripts accepted by us must have a strong, practical application."

LILLENAS PUBLISHING CO., Program Builder Series and Other Drama Resources, Box 419527, Kansas City MO 64141-6527. (816)931-1900. Fax (816)753-4071. E-mail: drama@lillenas.com. Paul M. Miller, ed. Publishes 15 drama resource books and 3 program builders/yr. Royalty 10% for drama resources; outright purchase of program builder material; no advance. No simultaneous submissions. Responds in 3 mos. Guidelines; catalog.

> **Drama Resources:** Query or complete ms.; phone/fax/e-mail queries OK. Accepts readings, one-act and full-length plays, puppet scripts, program and service features, monologues, and sketch collections.
>
> **Tips:** "We have added a new line of full-length plays for use in schools and dinner theater that are wholesome but not specifically religious."

#LION PUBLISHING, 4050 Lee Vance View, Colorado Springs CO 80918-7102. (719)536-3271. Cook Communications. Liz Duckworth, mng ed (children's); Greg Clouse, exec. ed. (adult). Books suitable for a general (crossover) market, not specifically a Christian market. Publishes 10 titles/yr. 5% of books from first-time authors. Royalty on net; advance. Average first printing 7,500. Publication within 18 mos. Considers simultaneous submissions. Responds in 3 mos. Guidelines.

> **Nonfiction & Fiction:** Query or proposal/1 chapter; no phone query.
>
> **Tips:** "When writing for Lion, assume the reader has no knowledge of or background in Christianity."

THE LITURGICAL PRESS, PO Box 7500, St. John's Abbey, Collegeville MN 56321. (320)363-2213. Fax (800)445-5899. E-mail: mtwomey@osb.org. Website: http://www.litpress.org/edit.html. St. John's Abbey (a Benedictine group). Imprints: Michael Glazier Books and Pueblo Books. Mark Twomey, mng ed. Academic manuscripts to Linda Maloney, E-mail: lmmaloney@osb.org. Publishes 100 titles/yr. Prefers 100-600 pgs. Royalty 10% of net; some outright purchases; no advance. Responds in 2 mos. Guidelines; free catalog.

> **Nonfiction:** Query/proposal. Adult only.
>
> **Tips:** "We publish liturgical, scriptural, and pastoral resources."

*LITURGY TRAINING PUBLICATIONS, Office of Divine Worship, 1800 N. Hermitage Ave., Chicago IL 60622-1101. (773)486-8970. Fax (773)486-7094. E-mail: editors@LTP.org. Catholic/Archdiocese of Chicago. Victoria Tufano, sr. acq. ed. Resources for liturgy in Christian life. Publishes 25 titles/yr. Receives 150 submissions annually. 50% of books from first-time authors. Variable royalty. Average first printing 2,000-5,000. Publication within 1 yr. Considers simultaneous submissions. Responds in 2-10 wks. Requires disk. Catalog.

> **Nonfiction:** Proposal/1 chapter; phone/fax/e-mail query OK.

LIVING THE GOOD NEWS, 600 Grant St., Ste. 400, Denver CO 80203. Fax (303)832-4971. Division of the Morehouse Group. Liz Riggleman, ed. admin. Publishes 15 titles/yr. Royalty. Publication within 2 yrs. Considers simultaneous submissions. Responds in 2 mos. Guidelines; catalog for 9x12 SAE/4 stamps.

> **Nonfiction:** Query or proposal/1 chapter. "Seeking books on practical, personal, spiritual growth for all ages."

Fiction: Query with synopsis. For children and teens; also picture books.

Special Needs: Grandparenting and storytelling; youth resources.

Tips: "Readers are mainly from liturgical and mainline church backgrounds. Seeking creative ways to connect with self, others, God and the earth."

+LOGION PRESS, 1445 Boonville Ave., Springfield MO 65802. (417)862-2781. Assemblies of God. Dr. Stanley Horton, ed. Academic Line of Gospel Publishing House; primarily college textbooks. Publishes 2 titles/yr. Receives 5 submissions annually. 20% of books from first-time authors. No mss through agents. Prefers up to 185,000 words. Royalty on retail; no advance. Average first printing 3,500. Publication within 1 yr. No simultaneous submissions. Responds in 3 mos. Requires disk. Free guidelines/catalog.

Nonfiction: Proposal/1-2 chapters.

Tips: "Books must not contradict our statement of Fundamental Truths that all our ministers must sign annually."

LOIZEAUX, PO Box 277, Neptune NJ 07754-0277. (732)922-6665. Fax (732)922-9487. Website: http://www.biblecompanionsoftware.com. Evangelical. Marjorie Carlson, mng. ed. Publishes 15-20 titles/yr. Receives 50 submissions annually. 5% of books from first-time authors. No mss through agents. Negotiable royalty on net; no advance. Average first printing 4,000. Publication within 24 mos. No simultaneous submissions. Responds in 2-3 wks. No guidelines; free catalog.

Nonfiction: Query only; no phone/fax query. Looking for Bible commentaries.

LOVE INSPIRED/STEEPLE HILL, 300 E. 42nd St., New York NY 10017. (212)682-6080. Fax (212)682-4539. Harlequin Enterprises. Christian romance imprint. Isabel Swift, ed. dir.; Tara Gavin, sr. ed.; Anne Canedeo, freelance ed.; Melissa Jeglinski, ed. Publishes 36 titles/yr. 10% of books from first-time authors. Rarely reprints books. Prefers 75,000-80,000 wds or 300-320 pgs. Royalty on net; advance. Publication within 12-24 mos. Responds in 4-6 wks. No disk. Guidelines.

Fiction: Query letter or 3 chapters and up to 5-page synopsis. Contemporary romance. "Portray Christian characters learning an important lesson about the powers of truth and faith. Include humor, drama, and the many challenges of life and faith."

LOYOLA PRESS, 3441 N. Ashland Ave., Chicago IL 60657-1397. (773)281-1818. Fax (773)281-0885. Catholic. LaVonne Neff, sr. acq. ed. Books that contribute to the Catholic faith formation. Publishes 12 titles/yr. Receives 400 submissions annually. 20% of books from first-time authors. Usually no mss through agents. Reprints books. Prefers 60,000-80,000 wds or 200-250 pgs. Variable royalty on net; occasional advance. Average first printing 3,000-5,000. Publication within 1 yr. Considers simultaneous submissions. Responds in 9 wks. Requires disk. Guidelines; catalog for 6x9 SAE/3 stamps.

Nonfiction: Query; fax query OK. "Most open to professionally written mss, more or less in the Catholic tradition (but not conservative), written out of solid field training and experience."

*LYDIA PRESS, PO Box 417, Galloway OH 43119-0417. Phone/fax (614)851-9448. Nondenominational. Alaine Pakkala, pres.; submit to Carolyn Reynolds. Specializes in discipleship and encouragement materials to rebuild shattered lives.

Publishes 10-15 titles/yr. 60% of books from first-time authors. **SUBSIDY PUB-LISHES 2%.** Reprints books. Prefers 200 pgs. Royalty 25-50% on net; no advance. Average first printing 2,000. Publication within 10 mos. Considers simultaneous submissions. Responds in 4 wks. Guidelines.

Nonfiction: Query; phone/fax query OK.

Fiction: Query. For children & teens; also picture books.

Ethnic Books: Encouragement and discipleship for black youth.

Also Does: CD-ROM discipleship materials for teens.

MAGNUS PRESS, PO Box 41157, San Jose CA 95160. Fax (408)226-8638. Fax (408)226-2334. Warren Angel, ed. dir. To publish biblical studies which are written for the average person and which minister life to Christ's Church. Publishes 6 titles/yr. Receives 60 submissions annually. 50% of books from first-time authors. Reprints books. Prefers 125-375 pgs. Graduated royalty on retail; no advance. Average first printing 10,000. Publication within 7 mos. Considers simultaneous submissions. No disks. Responds in 1 mo. Guidelines; no catalog.

Nonfiction: Proposal/2-3 chapters; fax query OK. "Looking for biblical studies, any subject, including apologetics and controversial issues."

Tips: "Our writers need solid knowledge of the Bible, and a mature spirituality which reflects a profound relationship with Jesus Christ."

MASTER BOOKS, PO Box 726, Green Forest AR 72638-0726. (870)438-5288. Fax (870)438-5120. E-mail: mbnlp@cswnet.com. Website: http://www.master/newleaf.com. New Leaf Press. Jim Fletcher, ed. Publishes 8-10 titles/yr. Receives 100 submissions annually. 10% of books from first-time authors. No mss through agents. **SUBSIDY PUBLISHES 5-15%.** Reprints books. Royalty 10-15% of net; no advance. Average first printing 5,000. Publication within 6 mos. Considers simultaneous submissions. Responds in 7-10 days. Free catalog.

Nonfiction: Query. "Looking for biblical creationism; biblical science; creation/evolution debate material."

Also Does: Pamphlets and booklets; computer games.

*MERCER UNIVERSITY PRESS, 1400 Coleman Ave., Macon GA 31207. (912)752-2880. Fax (912)752-2264. Edd Rowell, dir.

Nonfiction: Proposal/chapters."We are looking for books on history, philosophy, theology and religion, including history of religion, philosophy of religion, Bible studies and ethics."

MERIWETHER PUBLISHING LTD., 885 Elkton Dr., Colorado Springs CO 80907-3557. (719)594-4422. Fax (719)594-9916. E-mail: MeriwthPub@aol.com. Primarily a publisher of plays for Christian and secular; must be acceptable for use in a wide variety of Christian denominations. Arthur L. Zapel, ed.; submit to Rhonda Wray. Publishes 2-3 titles/yr.; 25-30 plays/yr. Receives 800 submissions annually (mostly plays). 50% of books from first-time authors. Reprints books. Prefers 200 pgs & up. Royalty 10% on net or retail; no advance. Average first printing of books 2,500, plays 500. Publication within 1 yr. Considers simultaneous submissions. Accepts disk. Responds in 2-8 wks. Guidelines; catalog $1/9x12 SAE/3 stamps.

Nonfiction: Query letter only; fax query OK. "Looking for creative worship books, i.e., drama, using the arts in worship, how-to books with ideas for Christian education."

Fiction: Plays only. Always looking for Christmas and Easter plays. Send complete ms.

Tips: "Our books are on drama or any creative, artistic area that can be a part of worship."

+MESSIANIC JEWISH PUBLISHERS, The Lederer Foundation, 6204 Park Heights Ave., Baltimore MD 21215. (410)358-6471. Fax (410)764-1376. E-mail: ledmessmin@aol.com. Website: http://www.goshen.net/lederer. Alan J. Tannenbaum, ed. Books that witness to the unsaved Jewish person or teach the Christian about the Jewish roots of Christianity. Publishes 6-12 titles/yr. Receives 50 submissions annually. 50% of books from first-time authors. No mss through agents. **SUBSIDY PUBLISHES 10%.** Reprints books. Prefers 150-250 pgs. Royalty 7-14% on net; no advance. Average first printing 2,000-3,000. Publication within 6-9 mos. No simultaneous submissions. Responds in 3-6 mos. Requires disk. No guidelines; free catalog.

Nonfiction: Proposal/2-3 chapters; no phone/fax/e-mail query.

Fiction: Proposal/2-3 chapters. All ages. "Need Jewish themes."

Ethnic Books: Jewish.

Also Does: Booklets, pamphlets and tracts. Children's curriculum.

*MIDDLE ATLANTIC REGIONAL PRESS, 100 Bryant St. NW, Washington DC 20001. (202)265-7609. Middle Atlantic Regional Gospel Ministries. Myron Noble, pres. Helps publish works of unpublished African American authors. Publishes 1-3 titles/yr. Receives 8-12 submissions annually. 75% of books from first-time authors. **SUBSIDY PUBLISHES 20%.** Reprints books. Prefers 80-125 pgs. Royalty 10-15% of net; no advance. Average first printing 5,000. Publication within 6-18 mos. Considers simultaneous submissions. Responds in 3-6 mos. No disk. Guidelines; free catalog.

Nonfiction: Proposal/3 chapters or complete ms; phone query OK.

Fiction: Query.

Ethnic Books: African American.

Also Does: Pamphlets, booklets, tracts.

*MISTY HILL PRESS, 5024 Turner Rd., Sebastopol CA 95472. (707)823-7437. Small press that does some religious titles. Sally C. Karste, ed. Publishes 1 title/yr. Negotiable royalty. Responds in 1 week. Guidelines; catalog for 9x12 SAE/2 stamps.

Fiction: Query first. Historical fiction for children.

*MONUMENT PRESS, PO Box 140361, Irving TX 75014-0361. Phone/fax (972)686-5332. Member of the consortium Publishers Associates (8 publishers). Belinda Buxjom, sr. ed.; submit to Mary Markal. Publishes only scholarly books. Other imprints: Ide House and Tangelwuld. Publishes 10 titles/yr. Receives 240 submissions annually. 70% of books from first-time authors. No mss through agents. Any length. Royalty 2-8% on retail; no advance. Average first printing 3,000. Publication within 24 mos. No simultaneous submissions. Prefers disk. Responds in 4 mos (goes to all houses in the consortium). Guidelines.

Nonfiction: Query only; no phone/fax query.

Ethnic: Publishes for all ethnic groups.

#MOODY PRESS, 820 N. LaSalle Blvd., Chicago IL 60610. (312)329-2101. Fax (312)329-2144. Website: http://www.moody.edu. Imprint: Northfield Publishing.

Julie-Allyson Ieron, mng ed. To provide books that evangelize, edify the believer, and educate concerning the Christian life. Publishes 65-70 titles/yr. Receives 3,500 submissions annually. 1% of books from first-time authors. Occasionally reprints books. Royalty on net; advance $500-50,000. Average first printing 10,000. Publication within 1 yr. Considers simultaneous submissions. Responds in 8-12 wks. Guidelines; catalog for 9x12 SAE.

Nonfiction: Proposal/3 chapters; no phone/fax query.

Also Does: Booklets in series only.

Tips: "Most open to books where the writer is a recognized expert and already has a platform to promote the book. Not currently accepting fiction."

**Note: This publisher serviced by The Writer's Edge.

THOMAS MORE PRESS, 200 E. Bethany Dr., Allen TX 75002. (972)390-6300. Fax (800)688-8356. Website: http://www.rclweb.com/. Catholic/Tabor Publishing. Submit to Acquisitions Dept. Publishes 6-10 titles/yr. Receives 150 submissions annually. 100% of books from first-time authors. Prefers 40,000 wds. Royalty 7.5% on retail; advance. Average first printing 2,500-25,000. Publication within 1 yr. Considers simultaneous submissions. Responds in 6-9 wks. Guidelines; free catalog.

Nonfiction: Proposal/1 chapter. Religion and spirituality.

Tips: "Looking for books on theology, commentary, reflection, spirituality and reference—for the serious, but non-scholarly reader."

#MOREHOUSE PUBLISHING CO., 4775 Linglestown Rd., Harrisburg PA 17112. E-mail: eakelley@aol.com. Episcopal/ecumenical. Deborah Grahame-Smith, sr. ed.; Ken Quigley, ed. Academic, devotional, reference, and Bible study materials for Christians of all denominations. Publishes 15 titles/yr. Receives 500 submissions annually. 40% of books from first-time authors. Reprints books. Prefers 80-150 pgs. Royalty 7-10% on net; advance $500-1,000. Average first printing 2,500-3,500. Publication within 8 mos. Considers simultaneous submissions. Responds in 4 mos. Guidelines; catalog for 9x12 SAE/4 stamps (#10 SAE if children's catalog only). Outside US, include one IRC for each ounce.

Nonfiction: Proposal/1-2 chapters; no phone/fax query. "Looking for books on marriage, parenting skills, single parenting, relations, marriage counseling helps for clergy, stewardship, Bible studies, dealing with grief/loss, and current social issues."

Fiction: Proposal/2 chapters. For children/teens.

Tips: "Most open to a book aimed at a specific market/readership, which has perhaps evolved from a workshop or study program (field-tested and fine-tuned by interested Christians); a book that answers a specific need or fills a specific gap in the bookstores."

*MORNING STAR PUBLICATIONS, 16000 Lancaster Hwy., Charlotte NC 28277-2061. Rick Joyner, ed.

JOSHUA MORRIS PUBLISHING, 355 Riverside Ave., Westport CT 06880-4810. (203)341-4000. Fax (203)341-4385. Anglican/Evangelical. Beverly Larson, ed. To create unique novelty-type books that bring the stories and truth of the Bible to life for young children. Imprint: Reader's Digest Young Families. Publishes 60 titles/yr. Receives 200 submissions annually. 5% of books from first-time authors. Makes outright purchases. Average first printing 25,000. Publication within 9 mos. Considers simultaneous submissions. Responds in 2-3 mos. No guidelines/catalog.

Nonfiction: Proposal/1 chapter.

Fiction: Proposal/1 chapter. Children's picture books.

Special Needs: Produces board games and all kinds of novelty books for children.

Tips: "We are looking for writers who are excellent at rhyming and can write for preschoolers particularly. We commission authors to write books that we have come up with. Authors should send samples of their best work, rather than sending a specific proposal."

#WILLIAM MORROW AND CO., 1350 Avenue of the Americas, New York NY 10019. (212)261-6500. Fax (212)261-6595. General trade publisher that does a few religious titles. Debbie Mercer-Sullivan, mng. ed. Publishes 5 religious titles/yr. Receives 10,000 submissions annually. 30% of books from first-time authors. Accepts most mss through agents. Prefers 50,000-100,000 wds. Standard royalty on retail; advance varies. Publication within 2 yrs. Considers simultaneous submissions. Responds in 3 mos.

Nonfiction & Fiction: Query only; mss and proposals accepted only through an agent.

Note: Morrow Junior Books accepts no unsolicited manuscripts.

MOUNT OLIVE COLLEGE PRESS, 634 Henderson St., Mount Olive NC 28365. (919)658-2502. Dr. Pepper Worthington, ed. Publishes 5 titles/yr. Receives 250 submissions annually. 85% of books from first-time authors. Prefers 220 pgs. Negotiated royalty. Average first printing 500. Publication within 12-18 mos. No simultaneous submissions. Responds in 6-12 mos. No disk. Free guidelines/catalog.

Nonfiction: Proposal/3 chapters; no phone query. Religion. For poetry submit 6 sample poems.

Fiction: Proposal/3 chapters. Religious.

MULTNOMAH PUBLISHERS (formerly **QUESTAR PUBLISHERS**), Box 1720, Sisters OR 97759. (541)549-1144. Fax (541)549-2044. Donald Jacobson, pub. Imprint information listed below. Publishes 120 titles/yr. Receives 2,400 submissions annually. 5% of books from first-time authors. Length depends on project. Negotiable royalty and advance. Average first printing 12,500. Publication within 12-24 mos. Considers simultaneous submissions. Responds in 3-6 mos. Requires disk. Guidelines; catalog for 9x12 SAE/7 stamps.

Multnomah Books: Christian living, theology and sports books. Submit to: Editorial Dept.

Gold 'n' Honey: Children's books. Cover letter and complete ms. Submit to: Editorial Dept.

Multnomah Fiction: Message-driven, clean, moral, uplifting fiction, not necessarily religious. Cover letter, synopsis and 3 chapters. Submit to Rod Morris.

Palisades & Alabaster: Contemporary (pure) romance (Palisades) and women's fiction (Alabaster). For Alabaster, looking for longer, more developed stories within a variety of genres: stand alone, comedy, cozy mystery and suspense, all with a thread of romance. Cover letter, synopsis and 3 chapters. Submit to Karen Ball.

Multnomah Gift Books: Looking for proposals on substantive topics with beautiful, lyrical writing. Cover letter, synopsis and 2-3 chapters. Submit to Editorial Dept.

**Note: This publisher serviced by The Writer's Edge.

NATIONAL BAPTIST PUBLISHING BOARD, 6717 Centennial Blvd., Nashville TN 37209. (615)350-8000. Fax (615)350-9018. E-mail: nbpb@nbpb.org. Website: http://www.nbpb.org. National Missionary Baptist Convention of America. Rev. Willie N. Paul, dir. of publications. To provide quality Christian education resources to be used by African-American churches. Receives 200 submissions annually. 30% of books from first-time authors. Reprints books. Prefers 130 pgs. Outright purchases; advance. Average first printing 20,000. Publication within 1 yr.

> **Nonfiction:** Complete ms; phone query OK.
>
> **Fiction:** Complete ms. "We need biblically based fiction for children."
>
> **Ethnic Books:** African-American publisher.
>
> **Tips:** "Most open to religious books that can be used for Christian education."

NAVPRESS/PIÑON PRESS, Box 35001, Colorado Springs CO 80935. (719)548-9222. Website: http://www.navpress.org or http://www.gospelcom.net/navs/NP. "We are no longer accepting any unsolicited submissions, proposals, queries, etc."

> ****Note:** This publisher serviced by The Writer's Edge.

NAZARENE PUBLISHING HOUSE—See BEACON HILL PRESS OF KANSAS CITY

NEIBAUER PRESS, 20 Industrial Dr., Warminster PA 18974. (215)322-6200. Fax (215)322-2495. E-mail: Nathan@Neibauer.com. Website: http://www.nathan@Neibauer.com. Evangelical/Protestant clergy and church leaders. Nathan Neibauer, ed. Publishes 8 titles/yr. Receives 100 submissions annually. 5% of books from first-time authors. No mss through agents. Reprints books. Prefers 200 pgs. Royalty on net; some outright purchases. **SOME SUBSIDY.** Publication within 6 mos. Considers simultaneous submissions. Responds in 2 wks. Requires disk. Catalog for 9x12 SAE.

> **Nonfiction:** E-mail query OK.
>
> **Also Does:** Pamphlets & tracts.
>
> **Tips:** "Publishes only religious books on stewardship and church enrollment, stewardship and tithing, and church enrollment tracts."

THOMAS NELSON PUBLISHERS, Nashville TN. Corporate address does not accept unsolicited manuscripts. No phone queries. Send one page query letter via fax to one of the following: fax (770)391-9784 or fax (803)548-2684; for Biblical Reference Books and Electronic Products send fax to (615)391-5225. Publishes 150-200 titles/yr. Publication within 1-2 yrs.

> **Nonfiction:** Fax (see above). "Looking for inspirational, motivational, devotional, self-help, Christian living, prayer and evangelism."
>
> **Fiction:** Fax (see above). "Seeking successfully published commercial fiction authors who write for adults from a Christian perspective."
>
> ****Note:** This publisher serviced by The Writer's Edge.

+TOMMY NELSON, a division of Thomas Nelson, Inc., 404 BNA Dr., Ste. 508, Nashville TN 37217. (615)889-9000. Laura Minchew, ed. Publishes 65 titles/yr. Receives 2,400 submissions annually. 5% of books from first-time authors. Reprints books. Length varies with product. Royalty on net, outright purchase, or work-for-hire (flat fee); advance. Average first printing 35,000. Publication within 9 mos. Considers simultaneous submissions. Responds in 3 mos. Requires disk. Guidelines; free catalog.

Nonfiction: Query or proposal/1 chapter; no phone query.

Fiction: Complete ms for picture books; proposal/1 chapter for juvenile novel. For children and young teens through age 14.

Special Needs: Beginning to explore specialty products.

Tips: "All proposals must have a spiritual take-away, but must not be authoritarian or preachy; Christian values, not just general values."

**Note: This publisher serviced by The Writer's Edge.

+NEW CANAAN PUBLISHING CO., INC., PO Box 752, New Canaan CT 06840. Phone/fax (203)966-3408. E-mail: newcan@sprynet.com. Website: http://ourworld. compuseve.com/homepages/new_canaan. Kathy Mittelstadt, ed. Publishes 1-2 titles/yr. Receives 100 submissions annually. 50% of books from first-time authors. Prefers 20,000 wds or 140 pgs. Royalty 8-12 % on net; no advance. Average first printing 500-5,000. Publication within 6-8 mos. No simultaneous submissions. Responds in 2-3 mos. Requires disk. Guidelines; free catalog.

Nonfiction: Query letter; proposal/2-3 chapters; e-mail query OK.

Fiction: Complete ms. For children and teens.

Special Needs: Middle-school-level educational books.

*NEW CITY PRESS, 202 Cardinal Rd., Hyde Park NY 12538. (914)229-0335. Fax (914)229-0351. E-mail: PATNCP@aol.com. Catholic. Pat Markey, ed. Focus is on Christian living and unity. Publishes 12 titles/yr. Receives 60 submissions annually. 5% of books from first-time authors. Reprints books. Prefers 56,000 wds. Royalty 10% on net; no advance. Average first printing 5,000. Publication with 16 mos. Considers simultaneous submissions. Responds in 3 mos. Requires disk. Free catalog.

Nonfiction: Query only; fax/e-mail query OK. "Looking for how-to and family topics."

NEW HOPE, Box 12065, Birmingham AL 35202-2065. (205)991-8100. Fax (205)995-4841. E-mail: new_hope@wmu.org. Website: http://www.wmu.com/ wmu. Imprint of Woman's Missionary Union; Auxiliary to Southern Baptist Convention. Cindy McClain, acq. ed. Publishes 10-12 titles/yr. Receives 80-100 submissions annually. 10-15% of books from first-time authors. Rarely reprints books. Prefers 150-250 pgs. Royalty on retail or outright purchases; no advance. Average first printing 5,000-10,000. Publication within 18 mos. Considers simultaneous submissions. Responds in 6 mos. Requires disk. Guidelines; catalog for 9x12 SAE/4 stamps.

Nonfiction: Complete ms or proposal/3-4 chapters; no phone/fax/e-mail query. "All that we publish must have a missions/ministry emphasis."

Fiction: Complete ms or proposal/3-4 chapters. For preschoolers and children only. Children's picture books or storybooks, especially with a multicultural aspect.

Tips: "Most open to books which lead to spiritual growth toward a missions lifestyle; books that address ministry issues or social/moral issues; books that lead to involvement in missions or support of missions; books that teach appreciation for other cultures and people groups. Follow guidelines."

#NEW LEAF PRESS, PO Box 726, Green Forest AR 72638-0726. (870)438-5288. Fax (870)438-5120. Pentecostal/Charismatic. Jim Fletcher, ed. Imprint: Master Books. Publishes 15-20 titles/yr. Receives 500 submissions annually. 15% of books from first-time authors. Reprints books. Prefers 100-400 pgs. Royalty 10% on net; no advance. Average first printing 10,000. Publication within 10 mos. Considers simultaneous submissions. Responds in 3 mos. Guidelines; catalog for 9x12 SAE/5 stamps.

Nonfiction: Complete ms; phone/fax query OK. "Looking for devotional, gift books and Christian living."

Tips: "Tell us why this book is marketable and why it will be a blessing and fulfill the needs of others."

NORTHSTONE PUBLISHING, INC., 330 - 1980 Cooper Rd., Kelowna BC V1Y 9G8 Canada. (250)766-2926. Fax (250)766-1201. E-mail: info@northstone.com. Website: http://www.northstone.com. Michael Schwartzentruber, ed. To provide high quality products promoting positive social and spiritual values. Publishes 12-14 titles/yr. Receives 100 submissions annually. 40% of books from first-time authors. Prefers 244 pgs. Royalty 8-12% on retail; some advances $1,500. Average first printing 4,000. Publication within 9 mos. Considers simultaneous submissions. Responds in 6 wks. Requires disk. Free guidelines/catalog.

Nonfiction: Proposal/2 chapters; fax/e-mail query OK.

Fiction: Proposal/2 chapters. Adult; humorous, and spirituality themes.

Tips: "Although we publish from a Christian perspective, we seek to attract a general audience. Our target audience is interested in spirituality and values, but may not even attend church (nor do we assume that they should)."

+OMEGA HOUSE PUBLISHING, PO Box 68, Three Rivers MI 49093. (616)278-3075. Fax (616)273-7026. Non-denominational. Zendra Manley, ed. To distribute and increase knowledge in the body of Christ (Hosea 4:6). Publishes 5 titles/yr. 75% of books from first-time authors. No mss through agents. Prefers 80-250 pgs. Royalty 8-10% of net; no advance. Average first printing 2,000-5,000. Publication within 6 mos. Considers simultaneous submissions. Responds in 2 wks. No disk. Guidelines; no catalog

Nonfiction: Query only; fax query OK.

Special Needs: Renewal, inspirational, healing.

Also Does: Booklets, pamphlets & tracts.

Tips: "We prefer small booklets. Develop a proposal that will grab our interest."

+ONE WORLD, 201 E. 50th St., New York NY 10022. (212)572-2620. Fax (212)940-7539. Website: http://www.randomhouse.com. Imprint of Ballantine Books. Cheryl Woodruff, assoc. pub.; submit to Gary Brozek, assoc. ed. Books that are written by and focus on African Americans, Native Americans, Asian Americans and Latino Americans; but from an American multicultural perspective. Publishes 8-10 titles/yr. Receives 1,200 submissions annually. 25% of books from first-time authors. Reprints books. Royalty 8-12% on retail; variable advance. Publication within 2 yrs. Considers simultaneous submissions. Responds in 4 mos. Guidelines/catalog for #10 SASE.

Nonfiction: Query or proposal with 100 pgs. "Religious/inspirational books for Americans of color."

Fiction: Query or proposal/3 chapters. "Looking for contemporary or historical."

Ethnic Books: All are ethnic books.

*OPEN COURT PUBLISHING CO., 332 S. Michigan Ave., Ste. 2000, Chicago IL 60604-9968. David Ramsey Steele, ed. dir. Publishes 4 religious titles/yr. Receives 600 submissions annually. 20% of books from first-time authors. Reprints books. Prefers 350-400 pgs. Royalty 5-12% of net; advance $1,000-2,000. Average first printing 500 (cloth), 1,500 (paperback). Publication within 1-3 yrs. Considers simultaneous submissions. Responds in 6 mos. Free catalog.

Nonfiction: Proposal/2 chapters. "We're looking for works of high intellectual quality for a scholarly or general readership on comparative religion, philosophy of religion, and religious issues."

ORBIS BOOKS, PO Box 308, Maryknoll NY 10545-0308. (914)941-7590. Fax (914)945-0670. E-mail: orbisbooks@aol.com. Catholic Foreign Mission Society. Robert Ellsberg, ed. Publishes 50-55 titles/yr. Receives 2,200 submissions annually. 2% of books from first-time authors. Accepts few mss through agents. Prefers 250-350 pgs. Royalty 10-15% of net; advance $500-3,000. Publication within 15 mos. Responds in 2 mos. Free guidelines/catalog.

Nonfiction: Proposal/1 chapter. "Global justice and peace; religious development in Asia, Africa, and Latin America; Christianity and world religions."

OUR SUNDAY VISITOR, INC., 200 Noll Plaza, Huntington IN 46750-4303. (219)356-8400. Fax (219)359-9117. E-mail: Jmanney@aol.com. Catholic. Greg Erlandson, ed; submit to James Manney, acq. ed. To assist Catholics to be more aware and secure in their faith and capable of relating their faith to others. Publishes 30 titles/yr. Receives 100+ submissions annually. 10% of books from first-time authors. Reprints books. Royalty 10-13% on net; advance $2,000. Average first printing 5,000. Publication within 1 yr. Considers simultaneous submissions. Responds in 6 wks. Requires disk. Free guidelines/catalog.

Nonfiction: Proposal/2 chapters; phone/fax/e-mail query OK. "Most open to devotional books (not 1st person), church histories, heritage & saints, the parish, prayer and family."

Also Does: Pamphlets & booklets.

Tips: "All books published must relate to the Catholic Church. Give as much background information as possible on why the topic was chosen. Follow our guidelines."

OXFORD UNIVERSITY PRESS, 198 Madison Ave., New York NY 10016-4314. (212)679-7300. Website: http://www.oup-usa.org/. Academic press. Laura Brown, trade ed. Service to academic community. Imprint: Clarendon Press. Publishes 60+ titles/yr. Receives hundreds of submissions annually. 40% of books from first-time authors. Prefers 300 pgs. Royalty 0-15% on net or retail; advances $0-40,000. Average first printing 1,500. Publication within 10 mos. Considers simultaneous submissions. Responds in 3 mos. Free catalog.

Nonfiction: Proposal/2 chapters. "Most open to academic books."

PACIFIC PRESS PUBLISHING ASSN., Box 5353, Nampa ID 83653-5353. (208)465-2511. Fax (208)465-2531. E-mail: jertho@pacificpress.com. Website: http://www.pacificpress.com. Seventh-day Adventist. Kenneth Wade, acq. ed.; submit to Jerry Thomas. Primary market is to their denomination, with some sales to general Christian market. Publishes 30 titles/yr. Receives 900 submissions annually. 30% of books from first-time authors. Prefers 40,000-70,000 wds or 128-256 pgs. Royalty 12-15% of net; advance $1,500. Average first printing 6,000. Publication within 10 mos. Considers simultaneous submissions. Responds in 3 mos. Requires disk. Guidelines.

> **Nonfiction:** Query or proposal/2 chapters; fax/e-mail query OK.
>
> **Fiction:** Adults and children (7-12 years old), series or single books. Query or proposal. "Must be true-to-life. No talking animals."
>
> **Ethnic Books:** Occasionally publishes for ethnic market.
>
> **Tips:** "Our Website has the most up-to-date information, including samples of recent publications. Do not send full manuscript unless we request it after reviewing your proposal."

PALISADES/MULTNOMAH. Pure romance novels. See Multnomah Publishers.

PARACLETE PRESS, PO Box 1568, Orleans MA 02653. (508)255-4685. Fax (508)255-5705. E-mail: mail@paraclete-press.com. Website: http://www. paralete-press.com. Ecumenical. Lillian Miao, sr. ed. Publishes 10 titles/yr. Receives 160 submissions annually. Few books from first-time authors. Reprints few books. Prefers 200 pgs. Royalty 10-12% on retail or net; no advance. Average first printing 3,000-5,000. Publication within 6-12 mos. Responds in 3-4 wks. Requires disk. Guidelines; catalog for 9x12 SAE/3 stamps.

> **Nonfiction:** Proposal/1 chapter; phone/fax/e-mail query OK. "Looking for books on deeper spirituality that appeal to all denominations."
>
> **Tips:** Vision statement: "In all times, in different branches of the Christian family, there are people who have written, sung, or spoken things that encouraged us to give our lives to God and to listen to His voice. We gather and share these treasures."

PARADISE RESEARCH PUBLICATIONS, PO Box 959, Kihei HI 96753-0959. Phone/fax (808)874-4876. E-mail: dickb@dickb.com. Website: http://www. dickb.com. Imprint of Good Book Publishing Co. Ken Burns, ed. Publishes 5 titles/yr. Receives 5 submissions annually. 80% of books from first-time authors. No mss through agents. Prefers 250 pgs. Royalty 10% on retail; no advance. Average first printing 3,000. Publication within 2 mos. Considers simultaneous submission. Responds in 2 wks. No disk. No guidelines; free catalog.

> **Nonfiction:** Proposal/2 chapters; no phone/fax/e-mail query. Books on the spiritual history and success of Alcoholics Anonymous; 12-step biblical roots.
>
> **Also Does:** Pamphlets & booklets.

*THE PASTORAL PRESS, PO Box 1470, Laurel MD 20725. (800)976-9669. Fax (800)979-9669. Catholic/National Assn. of Pastoral Musicians. Lawrence Johnson, dir. Publishes 16 titles/yr. Receives 12 submissions annually. 60% of books from first-time authors. Prefers 250 pgs. Royalty 10% of net; no advance. Publication within 10 mos. Considers simultaneous submissions. Responds in 2 mos. Free catalog.

Nonfiction: Complete ms.

Tips: "Most open to theology and planning of Roman Catholic liturgies."

PAULINE BOOKS & MEDIA, 50 St. Paul's Ave., Boston MA 02130. (617)522-8911. Fax (617)541-9805. E-mail: pbm_edit@psinet.com. Website: http://www.pauline.org. Catholic. Sr. Mary Mark Vickenheiser, F.S.P., acq. ed. To help clarify Catholic belief and practice for the average reader. Publishes 25-35 titles/yr. Receives 1,300 submissions annually. 75% of books from first-time authors. No ms through agents. Royalty 8-12% of net; advance $200. Average first printing 3,000. Publication within 2-3 yrs. Responds in 3 mos. No disk. Guidelines; catalog for 9x12 SAE/4 stamps.

> **Nonfiction:** Query only, fax query OK. "Looking for books on faith and moral values, spiritual growth and development, and Christian formation for families."
>
> **Fiction:** Query only. Children's picture books, 150-500 wds; easy-to-read, 750-1,500 wds; and middle reader, 15,000-25,000 wds. No adult fiction.
>
> **Tips:** "Open to religion teacher's resources and adult catechetics. No biographical or autobiographical material."

PAULIST PRESS, 997 Macarthur Blvd., Mahwah NJ 07430. (201)825-7300. Fax (201)825-8345. Catholic. Donald Brophy, mng. ed; Karen Scialabba, children's book ed. Imprints: Newman Press; Stimulus Books. Publishes 90-100 titles/yr. Receives 500 submissions annually. 5-8% of books from first-time authors. Prefers 100-400 pgs. Royalty 10% on retail; advance $500. Average first printing 3,500. Publication within 10 mos. Responds in 2 mos. Guidelines.

> **Nonfiction:** Proposal/2 chapters. "Looking for theology (Catholic and ecumenical Christian), popular spirituality, liturgy, and religious education texts." Children's books for 5-7 years or 8-10 years; complete ms.
>
> **Tips:** "Most open to progressive, world-affirming, theologically sophisticated, growth-oriented, well-written books. Have strong convictions but don't be pious. Stay well-read. Pay attention to contemporary social needs."

PELICAN PUBLISHING CO., INC., PO Box 3110, Gretna LA 70054-3110. (504)368-1175. Website: http://www.pelicanpub.com/. Nina Kooij, ed. Imprints: Creager Publishing; Hope Publishing; Marmac. Publishes 5 titles/yr. Receives 500 submissions annually. 20% of books from first-time authors. Reprints books. Prefers 200+ pgs. Royalty 10%; some advances. Average first printing 6,000. Publication within 9-18 mos. Responds in 1 mo. Disk on request. Guidelines; catalog for 9x12 SAE/7 stamps.

> **Nonfiction:** Proposal/2 chapters; no phone query.
>
> **Fiction:** Proposal/2 chapters. Children's. Picture books, juvenile novels, and holiday topics.
>
> **Ethnic Books:** Fiction for blacks, Hispanics, Native Americans, Asian Americans, etc. Ethnic history for above groups.
>
> **Tips:** "On inspirational titles we need a high-profile author who already has an established speaking circuit so books can be sold at these appearances. Travel guides and picture books must have a specific target audience."

PILGRIM PRESS, 700 Prospect Ave. E., Cleveland OH 44115-1100. (216)736-3700. Fax (216)736-3703. E-mail: stavet@ucc.org. Website: http://www. pilgrimpress. com. United Church of Christ. Timothy G. Staveteig, ed. Scholarly and trade books on social issues and the moral life. Publishes 30 titles/yr. Receives 500 submissions annually. 50% of books from first-time authors. Reprints books. Prefers 65,000 wds. Royalty 8% of net; negotiable advance. Publication within 1 yr. Might consider simultaneous submissions. Disk required. Responds in 12 wks. Free guidelines/catalog.

Nonfiction: Query only; phone/fax/e-mail query OK.

Ethnic Books: Black, Hispanic and Asian. Always interested in books on pluralism and multiculturalism.

Also Does: Booklets; journal/calendar for women.

Tips: "Looking for a timely topic with a fresh thesis."

PREP PUBLISHING, 1110 1/2 Hay St., Fayetteville NC 28305. (910)483-6611. Website: http://www.prep-pub.com. PREP, Inc. Anne McKinney, mng ed. Books to enrich people's lives and help them find joy in human experience. Publishes 5 titles/yr. Receives 1,500+ submissions annually. 85% of books from first-time authors. Reprints books. Prefers 250 pgs. Royalty 10% on retail; advance. Average first printing 3,000-5,000. Publication within 18 mos. Considers simultaneous submissions. Responds in 1 mo. Guidelines/catalog for #10 SAE/1 stamp.

Nonfiction: Query only; no phone query.

Fiction: Query only. All ages. Prefers mystery/romance.

PRESBYTERIAN AND REFORMED (P & R) PUBLISHING CO., Box 817, Phillipsburg NJ 08865. (908)454-0505. Fax (908)859-2390. Not a denominational house. Thom E. Notaro, ed. All books must be consistent with the Westminster Confession of Faith. Imprints: Craig Press; Evangelical Press. Publishes 8-10 titles/yr. Receives 200 submissions annually. 20% of books from first-time authors. Prefers 140-240 pgs. Royalty 5-14% of net; no advance. Average first printing 3,000. Publication within 8-10 mos. Considers simultaneous submissions. Disk required. Responds in 1-3 mos. Free guidelines/catalog.

Nonfiction: Proposal/3 chapters; fax query OK.

Tips: "Clear, engaging, and insightful applications of reformed theology to life. Offer us fully developed proposals and polished sample chapters."

#PRESERVATION PRESS, PO Box 612, 25 Russell Mill Rd., Swedesboro NJ 08085. (609)467-8902. Fax (609)467-3183. Website: http://www.preservationpress. com. Norma J. Del Viscio, pres. Seeks to release titles that speak to the restoration of the orthodox faith. Est. 1994. Publishes 16 titles/yr. Receives 80 submissions annually. 33% of books from first-time authors. No mss through agents. Royalty 15% of net; no advance. Publication within 1 yr. Considers simultaneous submissions. Responds in 1-3 mos. Free guidelines/catalog.

Nonfiction: Query or proposal/2-3 chapters; phone query OK.

+G.P. PUTNAM'S SONS, 200 Madison Ave., New York NY 10016. (212)951-8405. Fax (212)951-8694. Website: http://www.putnam.com. Imprint of Penguin Putnam. David Briggs, mng ed.; submit to Mayo Rao, ed. asst. 5% of books from first-time authors. Accepts mss through agents only. Variable royalty on retail; variable advance. Considers simultaneous submissions. Responds in 6 mos. Guidelines.

Nonfiction: Query only. "We publish some religious/inspirational books."

Fiction: Adult.

Tips: "We prefer agented submissions."

QUESTAR PUBLISHERS—Now **MULTNOMAH PUBLISHERS**.

*RAGGED EDGE, 353 Ragged Edge Rd., Chambersburg PA 17201. (717)263-5132. Fax (717)532-7704. White Mane Publishing Co., Inc. Harold E. Collier, acq. ed. Christian, social science and self-help books; to make a difference in people's lives. Publishes 10-15 titles/yr. Receives 50-75 submissions annually. 50% of books from first-time authors. **SUBSIDY PUBLISHES 20%.** Reprints books. Prefers 200 pgs. Variable royalty on net; advance. Average first printing 3,000. Publication within 1 yr. Considers simultaneous submissions. Responds in 60 days. Free guidelines/ catalog.

> **Nonfiction:** Query only; fax query OK.
> **Fiction:** Query only. For children (8-12) or teens (12-17).
> **Tips:** "Most open to a Protestant book in the middle of the spectrum."

RAINBOW BOOKS, PO Box 430, Highland City FL 33846-0430. Phone/fax (941)648-4420. E-mail: naip@aol.com. Betsy A. Lampe, sr. ed. To provide solutions to real problems on an ethical level. Publishes 5 titles/yr. Receives 600 submissions annually. 90% of books from first-time authors. Minimum 15,000 wds. Royalty 6-10% on retail; variable advance. Average first printing 5,000. Publication within 10 mos. Considers simultaneous submissions. Disk on request. Responds in 8-10 wks. Guidelines; free copy.

> **Nonfiction:** Query only; no phone/fax/e-mail query. Looking for self-help/how-to books from authors with credentials on their subject matter. Wants something refreshing from the religious left; nothing from the religious right.
> **Fiction:** Query only. For adults. No graphic violence or sex; good taste must prevail.
> **Tips:** "We want to see books that deal with real world problems and provide solutions on a very ethical level."

+RAINBOW PUBLISHERS/LEGACY PRESS, PO Box 261129, San Diego CA 92196. (619)271-7600. Fax (619)578-4795. Christy Allen, ed. Books that promote biblical growth and development in children and adults. Publishes 6-10 titles/yr. Receives 250 submissions annually. 50% of books from first-time authors. No mss through agents. Reprints books. Prefers 150 pgs & up. Royalty 4% on net; advance. Average first printing 2,500. Publication within 1 yr. Considers simultaneous submissions. Responds in 6 wks. Prefers disk. Guidelines; catalog for 9x12 SAE/2 stamps.

> **Nonfiction:** Proposal/5 chapters; no phone/fax query. "Looking for fresh devotional ideas for children and adults; ministry resources for kids. "
> **Tips:** "Please study the market first. We are looking for writers who can present Bible-teaching materials or resources in an interesting way. Check out our *Dickens Family Gospel* or our children's book, *My Prayer Journal,* for example."

RAINBOW PUBLISHERS/RAINBOW BOOKS, Box 261129, San Diego CA 92196. (619)271-7600. Fax (612)578-4795. Christy Allen, ed. Publishes teacher-friendly books that help kids learn biblical concepts. Publishes 12-20 titles/yr. Receives 500 submissions annually. 50% of books from first-time authors. No mss through agents. Prefers 64 pgs & up. Outright purchases $640. Average first printing 2,500. Publication within 1 yr. Considers simultaneous submissions.

Responds in 6 wks. Prefers disk. Guidelines; catalog for 9x12 SAE/2 stamps.

Nonfiction: Proposal/5 chapters; no phone/fax query. "Looking for fun and easy ways to teach Bible concepts to kids, ages 2-12."

Tips: "If you were a kid, what would capture your attention in Bible learning? Creative, fresh games. Fun and attractive crafts. Interactive lessons. That's what we want!"

RAINBOW'S END CO., 354 Golden Grove Rd., Baden PA 15005. Phone/fax (412)266-4997. E-mail: Btucker833@aol.com. Website: http://adpages.com/ REBOOKS. Wayne P. Brumagin, ed.; Bettie Tucker, dir. of publications. To reach out in Christ and impact lives. Publishes 2-4 titles/yr. Receives 100 submissions annually. 100% of books from first-time authors. No longer a subsidy/cooperative publisher. Prefers 150-200 pgs. Royalty 12-14% on retail; advance $250. Average first printing 1,000-3,000. Publication within 12-15 mos. Considers simultaneous submissions. Responds in 4-12 wks. Prefers disk. Guidelines; catalog for 9x12 SAE.

Nonfiction: Complete ms; e-mail query OK. "Looking for recovery books, self-help and how-to."

Fiction: Complete ms. "Self-help fiction based on reality."

*READ 'N RUN BOOKS, PO Box 294, Rhododendron OR 97049. (503)622-4798. Crumb Elbow Publishing. Michael P. Jones, pub. Books of lasting interest. Publishes 6 titles/yr. Receives 25 submissions annually. 100% of books from first-time authors. Reprints books. Royalty on net or copies; no advance; **SOME COOPERATIVE PUBLISHING**. Average first printing 1,000. Publication within 6 mos. Considers simultaneous submissions. Responds in 2 mos. Guidelines; catalog $3.

Nonfiction: Complete ms; no phone query. "Looking for historical (particularly Old West); the Pacific Northwest; missionary work among American Indians; fur trade and environmental."

Fiction: Complete ms. Any type; any age. "Historical fiction would be great, especially if it involves the Old West or the Pacific NW."

Ethnic Books: Open to.

Tips: "We're really interested in NW books, but are open to reading about anything."

REGAL BOOKS, 2300 Knoll Dr., Ventura CA 93003. Does not accept unsolicited manuscripts.

THE REGINA PRESS, 10 Hub Dr., Melville NY 11747-3503. (516)694-8600. Fax (516)694-2205. Catholic/Christian. George Malhame, juvenile ed. Publishes 5-10 titles/yr. Royalty on net; some outright purchases; some advances. Sometimes sends free catalog.

Fiction: Query/proposal. Children's picture books for ages 3-8; coloring books.

#REGNERY PUBLISHING, 422 1st St. SE, #300, Washington DC 20003-1803. (202)546-5005. Fax (202)546-8759. Trade publisher that does scholarly Catholic books and evangelical Protestant books. Richard Vigilante, exec. ed; submit to Submissions Editor. Imprint: Gateway Editions. Publishes 2-4 religious titles/yr. Receives 30-50 submissions annually. Few books from first-time authors. Reprints books. Prefers 250-500 pgs. Royalty 8-15% on retail; advances to $50,000.

Average first printing 5,000. Publication within 1 yr. Considers simultaneous submissions. Responds in 6 mos. Free catalog.

Nonfiction: Proposal/1-3 chapters. Looking for history, popular biography and popular history.

Tips: "Religious books should relate to politics, history, current affairs, biography, and public policy. Most open to a book that deals with a topical issue from a conservative point of view—something that points out a need for spiritual renewal; or a how-to book on finding spiritual renewal."

RELIGIOUS EDUCATION PRESS, 5316 Meadow Brook Rd., Birmingham AL 35242-3315. (205)991-1000. Fax (205)991-9669. E-mail: releduc@ix.netcom. com. Website: http://www.bham.net/releduc/. Nancy J. Vickers, mng ed. Imprint: Doxa Books. Mission is specifically directed toward helping fulfill, in an inter-faith and ecumenical way, the Great Commission. Publishes 4-5 titles/yr. Receives 300+ submissions annually. 30% of books from first-time authors. No books through agents (generally). Prefers 300 pgs & up. Royalty 10% on net; no advance. Average first printing 2,000. Publication within 6-9 mos. Disk required. Responds in 30 days. Guidelines; free catalog for 9x12 SAE/2 stamps.

Nonfiction: Proposal/1 chapter & resume; fax/e-mail query OK (if one page). Also publishes books on religious psychology and pastoral care.

Tips: "We publish serious, scholarly books written on a professional level in the field of religious education and closely related subject areas. Our books are intentionally multifaith, written for an ecumenical audience."

*RENLOW PUBLISHING, PO Box 951, Middletown OH 45042. A general publisher that does a few inspirational or religious titles. D.E. Margerum, ed/pub. Send proposal/sample chapters. Not in topical listings.

RESOURCE PUBLICATIONS, INC., Ste. 290, 160 E. Virginia St., San Jose CA 95112. (408)286-8505. Fax (408)287-8748. E-mail: editor@rpinet.com. Website: http://www.rpinet.com. Nick Wagner, ed. dir. Publishes 20 titles/yr. Receives 450 submissions annually. 20% of books from first-time authors. Prefers 50,000 wds. Royalty 8% of net: no advance. Average first printing 3,000. Publication within 1 yr. Considers simultaneous submissions. Responds in 1-3 mos. Prefers disk. Guidelines; catalog for 9x12 SAE/2 stamps.

Nonfiction: Proposal/1 chapter; phone/fax/e-mail query OK.

Fiction: Query. Adult/teen/children. Only short skits or read-aloud stories for storytellers. "Must be useful in ministerial, counseling, or educational settings."

Also Does: Computer programs; aids to ministry or education.

Tips: "Know our market. We cater to ministers in Catholic and mainstream Protestant settings. We are not an evangelical house or general interest publisher."

RESURRECTION PRESS LTD, PO Box 248, Williston Park NY 11596. (516)742-5686. Fax (516)746-6872. Http://www.catholicity.cm/market/rpress. Catholic. Imprint: Spirit Life Series. Emilie Cerar, sr. ed. Publishes 8 titles/yr. Receives 200 submissions annually. 20% of books from first-time authors. No mss through agents. Reprints books. Prefers 200 pgs. Royalty 5-10% on retail; advance $250-2,000. Average first printing 3,000. Publication within 1 yr. Considers simultaneous submissions. Responds in 1-2 mos. Free guidelines & catalog.

Nonfiction: Proposal/2 chapters; fax query OK. "Most open to pastoral resources, self-help, and spirituality for the active Christian."

FLEMING H. REVELL CO., Box 6287, Grand Rapids MI 49516. (616)676-9185. Fax (616)676-9573. E-mail: lholland@bakerbooks.com. Website: http://www. bakerbooks.com. Subsidiary of Baker Book House. Imprints: Revell, Chosen, Spire, Paver Books. Linda Holland, ed. dir; submit to Sheila Ingram. Publishes 60 titles/yr. Receives 1,000 submissions annually. 10% of books from first-time authors. Prefers 60,000 wds. Royalty 10-14% on net; advance. Average first printing 5,000. Publication within 1 yr. Considers simultaneous submissions. Responds in 3 mos. Requires disk. Free guidelines/catalog.

    Nonfiction: Proposal/2 chapters; no phone/fax/e-mail query.

    Fiction: Proposal/2 chapters. Adult.

    Tips: "Research the market for what's needed; maintain excellence; address a felt need; use good clarity and focus on topic."

    **Note: This publisher serviced by The Writer's Edge.

*REVIEW AND HERALD PUBLISHING ASSN., 55 W. Oak Ridge Dr., Hagerstown MD 21740-7390. (301)791-7000. Fax (301)790-9734. Seventh-Day Adventist. Jeannette Johnson, acq. ed. Publishes 40-50 titles/yr. Receives 500 submissions annually. 2-3% of books from first-time authors. Reprints books. Prefers 128-160 pgs. or 45,000 wds. Royalty 12-16% of net; advance $500+. Average first printing 3,500. Publication within 12-18 mos. Considers simultaneous submissions. Responds in 3 mos. Requires disk. Guidelines; catalog $3.

    Nonfiction: Proposal/2-3 chapters or complete ms; fax/e-mail query OK.

ROSE PUBLISHING, 4455 Torrance Blvd. #259, Torrance CA 90503. (310)316-4780. Fax (310)316-4401. E-mail: rosepubl@aol.com. Website: http://members. aol.com/rosepublis. Nondenominational. Carol Witte, mng ed. Publishes only large Sunday school charts and teaching materials. Publishes 5 titles/yr. Receives 1-2 submissions annually. 5% of books from first-time authors. Outright purchases. Publication within 6-12 mos. Free catalog.

    Special Needs: Query with sketch of proposed chart (non-returnable); fax query OK. Large teaching charts for Sunday schools; church history time lines; charts for children & youth. Also books on the Trinity, creation vs. evolution, Christian history, how we got the Bible, Ten Commandments, and the Lord's Prayer.

    Tips: "Now accepting more freelance submissions. Material for children, youth, Bible study charts and study guides, pamphlets, maps, timelines."

ROYAL PRODUCTIONS, 7127 Little River Turnpike, Ste. 205, Annandale VA 22003. (703)750-3078. Fax (703)916-7773. E-mail: TWMgroup@ipo.net. Nondenominational Christian & educational publisher. Fidelis Iyebote, mng ed. Publishes 8 titles/yr. 50% of books from first-time authors. Reprints books. Prefers 200 pgs. Royalty on net; no advance. Average first printing 5,000. Publication within 6 mos. Responds in 3 mos. Guidelines/catalog.

    Nonfiction: Query only. Looking for Christian school books, celebrity profiles, environmental issues, ethics and sports, biographies/autobiographies of Christian music, entertainment or sports stars.

    Fiction: Children's picture books.

    Special Needs: Considering ideas for production of educational audio and video films, instructional and study aid material for math, biology, chemistry, physics, French & Spanish, and Christian education.

ST. ANTHONY MESSENGER PRESS, 1615 Republic St., Cincinnati OH 45210. (513)241-5615. (800)488-0488. Fax (513)241-0399 or 241-1197. E-mail: StAnthony @AmericanCatholic.org. Website: http://www.AmericanCatholic.org. Catholic. Lisa Biedenbach, mng. ed. Seeks to publish affordable resources for living a Catholic-Christian lifestyle. Imprint: Franciscan Communications. Publishes 18-20 titles/yr. Receives 240 submissions annually. 5% of books from first-time authors. No mss through agent. Reprints books. Prefers 25,000-50,000 wds or 100-200 pgs. Royalty 10-12% of net; advance $1,000. Average first printing 5,000. Publication within 12-18 mos. Responds in 2 mos. Accepts disk. Guidelines; catalog for 9x12 SAE/4 stamps.

> **Nonfiction:** Query only; fax/e-mail query OK. "Looking for resources for prayer & liturgy, and Catholic identity, "
>
> **Ethnic Books:** Hispanic, occasionally.
>
> **Also Does:** Pamphlets & booklets.
>
> **Tips:** "Books should be written in popular (not academic) style, use anecdotes or stories liberally to illumine your points or thesis, and reflect the best of modern Catholic teaching."

ST. BEDE'S PUBLICATIONS, Box 545, Petersham MA 01366-0545. (978)724-3407. Fax (978)724-3574. Website: http://www.stbedes.org. Catholic. Sr. Mary Joseph, OSB, ed. Publishes 8-12 titles/yr. Receives 100 submissions annually. 30-40% of books from first-time authors. Reprints books. Prefers 150-200 pgs. Royalty 5-10% on net or retail; no advance. Average first printing 500-1,500. Publication within 2 yrs. Accepts simultaneous submissions. Responds in 2 mos. Prefers disk. Guidelines; catalog for 9x12 SAE/2 stamps.

> **Nonfiction:** Query or proposal/chapters. E-mail query OK.
>
> **Tips:** "Just state what you've got simply without gimmicks or attention-getting ploys that usually turn off editors before they've even read your proposal. If your work is worthy of publication, it will stand on its own."

ST. MARY'S PRESS, 702 Terrace Heights, Winona MN 55987-1320. (507)457-7900. (800)533-8095. Fax (507)457-7990. E-mail: yanovel@smp.org. Website: http://www.smp.org. Catholic. Steve Nagel, ed-in-chief. Fiction for teens, ages 14-17. Prefers up to 40,000 wds. Royalty. Accepts simultaneous submissions. Guidelines.

> **Fiction:** Query/outline & chapters; e-mail query OK.
>
> **Tips:** "Books that give insight into the struggle of teens to become healthy, hopeful adults and also shed light on Catholic experience, history or cultures."

+SCARECROW PRESS, 4720 Boston Wy., Lanham MD 20706. (301)459-3366. Fax (301)459-2118. Website: http://www.scarecrowpress.com. University Press of America. Shirley Lambert, ed. dir.; submit to Amanda Irwin, asst. ed. Publishes 5-15 titles/yr. Receives 50 submissions annually. 35% of books from first-time authors. Prefers 250-350 pgs. Royalty 10-15% of net; no advance. Average first printing 525. Publication within 8-12 mos. Considers simultaneous submissions. Responds in 2-4 mos. Requires disk. Free guidelines/catalog.

> **Nonfiction:** Proposal/2-3 chapters; phone/fax/e-mail query OK. "Looking

for reference, religion and scholarly books."

SCHOCKEN BOOKS, INC., 201 E. 50th St., New York NY 10022. (212)572-2559. Fax (212)572-6030. Website: http://www.Randomhouse.com. Religious imprint of Random House. Arthur Samuelson, ed. dir. Publishes trade nonfiction in a variety of areas that have potential for substantial backlist life. Publishes 4 religious titles/yr. Receives 1,000 submissions annually. 5% of books from first-time authors. Reprints books. Royalty; advance. Average first printing 10,000. Publication within 1 yr. Considers simultaneous submissions. Responds in 4-6 wks. No disk. No guidelines; free catalog.

> **Nonfiction:** Send query, proposal or complete ms; fax query OK. "Looking for general non-fiction."

SCRIPTURE PRESS—See VICTOR BOOKS.

#SEASIDE PRESS, 1506 Capitol Ave. #101, Plano TX 75074. (972)423-0092. Fax (972)881-9147. E-mail: sales@wordware.com. Website: http://www.wordware. com. Imprint of Wordware Publishing, Inc. Russell A. Stultz, pub; Mary Goldman, mng. ed. Publishes 2 titles/yr. Receives 75 submissions annually. 40% of books from first-time authors. **SUBSIDY PUBLISHES 5%** Reprints books. Prefers 150 pgs. Royalty 8-10% of net; no advance. Average first printing 5,000. Publication within 6 mos. No simultaneous submissions. Requires disk. Responds in 3 wks. Free guidelines/catalog.

> **Nonfiction:** Query only; fax/e-mail query OK. Bible studies or family life.
> **Tips:** Not presently publishing many religious books.

HAROLD SHAW PUBLISHERS, Box 567, Wheaton IL 60189. (630)665-6700. Fax (630)665-6793. E-mail: shawpub@compuserve.com. Joan Guest, ed. dir; Mary Horner Collins, Bible study ed; Lil Copan, literary series. Publishes a "full circle," broad range of books on topics relevant to Christians of all types. Imprints: Wheaton Literary Series, North Wind. Publishes 40-45 titles/yr. Receives 800 submissions annually. 10-20% of books from first-time authors. Reprints books. Royalty on retail; outright purchases $375-2,000 (for Bible study guides and compilations); advance. Average first printing 5,000. Publication within 9-18 mos. Prefers no simultaneous submissions. Responds in 12-18 wks. Guidelines; catalog for 9x12 SAE/5 stamps.

> **Nonfiction:** Proposal/3 chapters; no phone/fax/e-mail query. "Looking for stellar books on felt need just developing in the marketplace."
> **Fiction:** Proposal/3 chapters. Prefers high-quality, literary fiction; no phone/fax/e-mail query.
> **Tips:** "Most open to well-written, practical books from evangelical worldview. Avoid sensational or highly sectarian topics. Interested in mental health issues and books that fill a void in the marketplace."
> ****Note:** This publisher serviced by The Writer's Edge.

*SHEED & WARD, Box 419492, Kansas City MO 64141. (816)531-0538. Fax (816)968-2280. E-mail: NCR@aol.com. National Catholic Reporter Publishing Co. Robert Heyer, ed-in-chief. Publishes 30 titles/yr. Receives 200 submissions annually. 10% of books from first-time authors. No mss through agents. **SUBSIDY PUBLISHES 2%.** Reprints books. Prefers 100-200 pgs. Royalty 6/8/10% on retail; some work-for-hire; flexible advance. Average first printing 2,000. Publication within 6 mos. Responds in 3 mos. Requires disk. Guidelines; catalog for 7x11 SAE/2 stamps.

Nonfiction: Complete ms; phone/fax/e-mail query OK. "Looking for parish ministry (euthanasia, health care, spirituality, leadership, sacraments, small group or priestless parish facilitating books)."

Tips: "Be in touch with needs of progressive/changing parishes."

SHINING STAR PUBLICATIONS, 1204 Buchanan St., Carthage IL 62321. (217)357-6093. Fax (217)357-6095. Division of Frank Schaffer Publications. Mary Tucker, ed. Publishes 20 titles/yr. Receives 30-40 submissions annually. 25% of books from first-time authors. No mss through agents. Prefers 48-96 pgs. Outright purchases $20/pg.; no advance. Average first printing 3,000. Publication within 12 mos. No simultaneous submissions. Prefers disk. Responds in 2 mos. Guidelines; free catalog.

Nonfiction: Query first; phone/fax query OK. "We need reproducible workbooks to teach Scriptures and Christian values; Bible activities; Bible story crafts; skits and songs with a Christian emphasis."

Tips: "We publish only Bible activity books with reproducible pages for teachers and parents to use in home or church teaching situations; no picture books or children's novels."

+SKYSONG PRESS, 35 Peter St. S., Orillia ON L3V 5A8 Canada. Website: http://www.bconnex.net/~skysong. Steve Stanton, ed. Guidelines on Website.

Fiction: Christian science-fiction only. "New authors should not submit novel manuscripts. Send us something for Dreams & Visions (see periodical section) first."

SMALL HELM PRESS, 622 Baker St., Petaluma CA 94952-2525. (707)763-5757. E-mail: smllhelm@sonic.net. Website: http://www.sonic.net/~smllhelm. Alice Pearl Evans, pub. Interprets direction in contemporary life. Publishes 1 title/yr. Receives few submissions. Reprints books. Prefers 96-224 printed pgs. Outright purchase, negotiable. Average first printing 1,000-2,000. Considers simultaneous submissions. Responds in 2-4 wks. Catalog for 9x12 SAE/3 stamps.

Nonfiction: Query, proposal or complete ms; prefers phone query.

Tips: "Most open to nonfiction of interest to general public and based on cultural or philosophical issues with a Christian worldview. Write with conviction and credibility."

SMYTH & HELWYS PUBLISHING, INC., 6316 Peake Rd., Macon GA 31210-3960. (912)752-2217. Fax (912)752-2264. E-mail: shelwys@mindspring.com. Website: http://www.helwys.com. Susan Webb, ed. Quality resources for the church and individual Christians that are nurtured by faith and informed by scholarship. Imprint: Peake Road. Publishes 35 titles/yr. Receives 600 submissions annually. 25% of books from first-time authors. Prefers 144 pgs. Royalty 10% of net; advance $500. Average first printing 3,000. Publication within 1 yr. Considers simultaneous submissions. Responds in 3 mos. Free guidelines/catalog.

Nonfiction: Query only; fax/e-mail query OK." Looking for books for group study."

Tips: "Most open to books with a strong secondary or special market beyond the trade."

SOUTHERN METHODIST UNIVERSITY PRESS, PO Box 415, Dallas TX

75275. (214)768-1433. Fax (214)768-1428. Southern Methodist. Kathryn Lang, sr. ed. Publishes nonfiction and literary fiction. Publishes 10-15 titles/yr. Receives 1,000 submissions annually. 75% of books from first-time authors. Royalty 8-10% of net; $500 advance. Average first printing 2,000. Publication within 1 yr. Responds in 2 wks. to a query, 6-12 mos to complete ms. No disk. Catalog.

> **Nonfiction:** Proposal/3 chapters. "We publish nonfiction in the following areas: human values, medical ethics, death & dying; film/theater; Southwest studies; and theological studies."
>
> **Fiction:** Query/synopsis, chapters and author bio. No genre fiction, poetry, sci-fi, romance; stay away from experimental fiction. Adult only.
>
> **Tips:** "Pay attention to our stated areas of interest."

*SOWER'S PRESS, PO Box 666306, Marietta GA 30066. (770)565-8202. Fax (770)977-3784. Jamey Wood, ed. Books to further establish the ministries of speakers and teachers. Publishes 2-3 titles/yr. Responds in 1 mo.

> **Nonfiction:** Proposal/chapters. Marriage & family books.

STANDARD PUBLISHING, 8121 Hamilton Ave., Cincinnati OH 45231. (513)931-4050. Fax (513)931-0950. E-mail: standardpub@attmail.com. Standex Intl. Corp. Diane Stortz, dir. of new product development. An evangelical Christian publisher of curriculum, classroom resources, teen resources, children's books, and drama. Publishes 150 titles/yr. Receives 1,500 submissions annually. 25% of books from first-time authors. Royalty 4-10% of net; outright purchases $500-2,000 (if work-for-hire); advance. Average first printing 20,000 (depends on product). Publication within 12-18 mos. Considers simultaneous submissions. Responds in 2 mos. Prefers disk. Guidelines; catalog $2.

> **Nonfiction:** Send complete proposal, including sample chapters, to Christian Education Team, Children's Editor, Teen Editor, Drama Team, or Adult Editor.
>
> **Tips:** "Many titles developed by in-house staff or on assignment. Most open now to teacher's helps and ideas for ages 8-12."
>
> ****Note:** This publisher serviced by The Writer's Edge.

STARBURST PUBLISHERS, PO Box 4123, Lancaster PA 17604. (717)293-0939. Evangelical. Ellen Hake, ed. dir. A Christian publisher having success with cross-over books. Publishes 10 titles/yr. Receives 1,000 submissions annually. 50% of books from first-time authors. Prefers 200-300 pgs. Royalty 6-15% of net; some advances. Average first printing 5,000-10,000. Publication within 12-18 mos. Considers simultaneous submissions. No disks. Responds in 2-4 wks. Guidelines; catalog for 9x12 SAE/4 stamps.

> **Nonfiction:** Proposal/3 chapters; no phone query.
>
> **Fiction:** Proposal/3 chapters. Adult. "We are looking for good, wholesome fiction. Inspirational self-help."
>
> **Tips:** "Most open to nonfiction that can be sold in both Christian and general markets."

*STILL WATERS REVIVAL BOOKS, 4710-37A Ave., Edmonton AB T6L 3T5 Canada. (403)450-3730. Reformed Church. Reg Barrow, pres. Publishes 15 titles/yr. Receives few submissions. Very few books from first-time authors. Reprints books. Prefers 128-160 pgs. Negotiated royalty or outright purchase. Considers simultaneous submissions. Catalog for 9x12 SAE/2 stamps.

Nonfiction: Proposal/2 chapters. "Reformed and Reconstructionistic books of scholarly value, for the use of educated laymen." No non-Reformed or premillennial.

Tips: "Most open to books based on the system of doctrine found in the Westminster confession of faith, as it applies to our contemporary setting."

*SUMMIT PUBLISHING, LTD., Denvigh House, Denvigh Rd., Milton Keynes MK1 1YP, England. Charismatic. Noel Halsey, pres. Send query with a summary, table of contents, and excerpts from the manuscript.

SWORD OF THE LORD PUBLISHERS, PO Box 1099, Murfreesboro TN 37133. (615)893-6700. Fax (615)895-7447. E-mail: sword@edge.net. Independent Baptist. Guy King, dir. Publishes 24 titles/yr. Receives 60-75 submissions annually. 20% of books from first-time authors. No mss through agents. Reprints books. Royalty 5-10% on net or retail; no advance. Average first printing 7,500. Publication within 6-12 mos. Considers simultaneous submissions. Disk OK. Responds in 6-9 mos. Prefers KJV. Free guidelines/catalog.

> **Nonfiction:** Complete ms; no phone/fax/e-mail query.
>
> **Fiction:** Complete ms. For all ages, including picture books.
>
> **Also Does:** Booklets, pamphlets.
>
> **Tips:** "Check spelling and grammar. Have professionally edited. "

+TABOR PUBLISHING, PO Box 7000, Allen TX 75002. (972)390-6300. Fax (800)688-8356. Website: http://www.rclweb.com/. Catholic. Submit to Acquisitions Dept. Publishes 6-10 titles/yr. Receives 150 submissions annually. 100% of books from first-time authors. Prefers 40,000 wds. Royalty 7.5% on retail; advance. Average first printing 2,500-25,000. Publication within 1 yr. Considers simultaneous submissions. Responds in 6-9 wks. Guidelines; free catalog. Not in topical listings.

> **Nonfiction:** Proposal/1 chapter. Resources for the educational community, catechists, and youth.

TOCCOA FALLS COLLEGE PRESS, Toccoa Falls College, PO Box 800067, Toccoa Falls GA 30598. (706)886-6831. (706)886-0210. Marcille P. Jordan, ed. Publishes quality Christian material for the church and academic community that would otherwise go unpublished. Publishes 4 titles/yr. Receives 7 submissions annually. 25% of books from first-time authors. Very limited subsidy. Prefers 150-250 pgs. Royalty 10% of retail; no advance. Average first printing 1,500-3,000. Publication within 3 mos. Considers simultaneous submissions. Responds ASAP. No guidelines.

> **Nonfiction:** Query, proposal or complete ms; phone/fax query OK.
>
> **Fiction:** Query, proposal, or complete ms. For children or teens.
>
> **Tips:** "We are looking for material that is biblical, practical and well written."

*TOUCH PUBLICATIONS, PO Box 19888, Houston TX 77079. (281)497-7901. Fax (281)497-0904. Touch Outreach Ministries. Jim Egli, dir. of new products. To awaken the church in North America to dynamic life and outreach so more brought to Christ through cell churches. Publishes 8 titles/yr. Receives 25 submissions annually. 40% of books from first-time authors. Reprints books. Prefers 75-200 pgs. Royalty 10-15% of net; no advance. Average first printing 2,000. Not in topical listings.

Nonfiction: Query only. "Must relate to cell church life."

Tips: "Our market is extremely focused. We publish books, resources and discipleship tools for churches, using a cell group strategy."

TREASURE PUBLISHING, 1133 Riverside Ave., Fort Collins CO 80524. (970)484-8483. Fax (970)495-6700. E-mail: treasure@webaccess.net. Website: http://www.treasurepub.com. Treasure Learning Systems. Mark Steiner, sr. ed. To assist the church in fulfilling the Great Commission. Publishes 10 titles/yr. Receives 100 submissions annually. 80% of books from first-time authors. Reprints books. Prefers 1,200 wds or 32 pgs. Royalty 5-10% of net; outright purchases of $1,000-5,000; advance. Publication within 1 yr. Considers simultaneous submissions. Responds in 4 wks. Accepts disk. Free guidelines; catalog for SAE/2 stamps.

> **Nonfiction:** Proposal/2 chapters. Children's picture books or topical and exegetical Bible study resources for adults.
>
> **Tips:** "We need Bible-based material and curriculum writers for children, teens and adults."

THE TRINITY FOUNDATION, PO Box 1666, Hobbs NM 88240. Phone/fax (505)392-8584. Fax (505)392-7274. Website: http://members.tripod.com/~trinity foundation/books.html. John W. Robbins, pres. To promote the logical system of truth found in the Bible. Publishes 6 titles/yr. Receives 12 submissions annually. No books from first-time authors. No mss through agents. Reprints books. Prefers 200 pgs. Outright purchase; free books; no advance. Average first printing 3,000. Publication within 9 mos. No simultaneous submissions. Responds in 2 mos. Catalog for #10 SAE/1 stamp.

> **Nonfiction:** Query letter only. Most open to Calvinist/Clarkian books.
>
> **Also Does:** Booklets & tracts.
>
> **Tips:** "Most open to well-written, Calvinist, biblical books. Read Gordon Clark first."

TRINITY PRESS INTERNATIONAL, PO Box 1321, Harrisburg PA 17105. (717)541-8130. Fax (717)541-8131. E-mail: hrast@morehousegroup.com. Website: http://www.morehousegroup.com. Dr. Harold W. Rast, dir. A nondenominational, academic religious publisher. Publishes 35 titles/yr. Receives 150-200 submissions annually. 3% of books from first-time authors. Reprints books. Royalty 10% on net; advance $500 & up. Average first printing 2,000. Publication within 8-12 mos. Responds in 3-6 mos. Guidelines; free catalog.

> **Nonfiction:** Complete ms or proposal/3 chapters. "Religious material only in the area of Bible studies, theology, ethics, etc." No dissertations or essays.
>
> **Tips:** "Most open to a book that is academic, to be used in undergraduate biblical studies, theology or religious studies program."

TYNDALE HOUSE PUBLISHERS, 351 Executive Dr., Box 80, Wheaton IL 60189-0080. (630)668-8300. Fax (630)668-6885. Website: http://www.tyndale. com. Ronald Beers, VP editorial. Imprints: Living Books; Pocket Guides. Publishes 100 titles/yr. 5-10% of books from first-time authors. Reprints books. Royalty; outright purchase of some children's books. Average first printing 5,000-10,000. Publication within 12-18 mos. No unsolicited mss. Guidelines (separate guidelines for children's books—request specifically); catalog for 9x12 SAE/9 stamps.

Note: This publisher serviced by The Writer's Edge.

UNITED CHURCH PRESS, 700 Prospect Ave. E., Cleveland OH 44115-1100. (216)736-3704. Fax (216)736-3703. E-mail: sadlerk@ucc.org. Website: http://www. pilgrimpress.com. United Church of Christ/Board for Homeland Missions. Kim M. Sadler, ed. Publishes 15-25 titles/yr. Receives 50+ submissions annually. 50% of books from first-time authors. Royalty 8% of net; work for hire, one-time fee; advance $1,500. Average first printing 3,000. Publication within 9-12 mos. Considers simultaneous submissions. Responds in 6-8 wks. Requires disk. Free guidelines/catalog.

Nonfiction: Proposal/2 chapters or complete ms; e-mail query OK.

Special Needs: Children's sermons, worship resources, youth materials, religious materials for ethnic groups.

Ethnic Books: African-American, Native-American, Asian-American, Pacific Islanders, and Hispanic.

Tips: "Most open to well-written mss that are United Church of Christ specific and/or religious topics that cross denominations. Use inclusive language and follow the *Chicago Manual of Style*."

THE UNITED CHURCH PUBLISHING HOUSE, 3250 Bloor St. W., 4th floor, Toronto ON M8X 2Y4 Canada. (416)231-5931. Fax (416)232-6004. E-mail: bparker@uccan.org. Website: http://www.uccan.ucph.org. The United Church of Canada. Submit to Managing Editor. Publishes 10 titles/yr. Receives 75 submissions annually. 60% of books from first-time authors. No mss through agents. Prefers 150-200 pgs. Royalty 10% of net; advance $100. Average first printing 1,500. Publication within 6 mos. considers simultaneous submissions. Responds in 4-8 wks. Disk required. Guidelines; free catalog.

Nonfiction: Proposal/1-2 chapters; phone/e-mail query OK. Publishes Canadian authors only.

Tips: "We publish books in the areas of Christian education; resources for church, worship, music; social issues; United Church History and leaders; and women and religion. Liberal viewpoints and theology."

*UNITED METHODIST PUBLISHING HOUSE, Box 801, Nashville TN 37202-0801. (615)749-6301. Fax (615)748-6512. United Methodist. Imprints: Abingdon Press, Dimensions for Living (Sally Sharpe, ed.), Kingswood Books, and Parthenon Press. Neil M. Alexander, pub. To provide resources that help others know, love and serve God and neighbor. Publishes 130 titles/yr. Receives 2,500 submissions annually. Few books from first-time authors. No mss through agents. Reprints books. Prefers 32-300 pgs. Negotiable royalty; advance 25% of expected first-year royalty. Average first printing 4,000-5,000. Publication within 24 mos. Responds in 3 mos. Guidelines; free catalog.

Nonfiction: Proposal/2 chapters; fax query OK.

Fiction: Children's picture books.

Ethnic Books: African-American, Korean, and Hispanic.

Also Does: Booklets.

Tips: "Most open to books different from similar books in the market. Include detailed information in the proposal regarding competitive books and what sets yours apart."

UNIVERSITY OF OTTAWA PRESS, 542 King Edward Ave., Ottawa ON K1N 6N5

Canada. (613)562-5246. Fax (613)562-5247. E-mail: press@uottawa.ca. Dr. V. Bennett, ed-in-chief. Promotes scholarly, academic publications. Publishes 2-4 titles/yr. Receives 300 submissions annually. No mss through agents. Prefers 250-300 pgs. Royalty 8-10% on net; no advance. Average first printing 800. Publication within 10-12 mos. Accepts simultaneous submissions. Responds in 2 wks. Accepts disk. Free guidelines/catalog.

Nonfiction: Query/proposal/at least 2 chapters; fax/e-mail query OK. Scholarly books only (peer reviewed). Social scientific study of religion.

UNIVERSITY PRESS OF AMERICA, 4720 Boston Way, Lanham MD 20706. (301)459-3366. Fax (301)459-2118. E-mail: nulrich@univpress.com. Website: http://www.univpress.com. Academic press. Nancy J. Ulrich, acq. ed. Publishes scholarly works in the social sciences and humanities. Publishes 60 religious titles/yr. Receives 100 submissions annually. 75% of books from first-time authors. Reprints books. Prefers 200 pgs. Royalty to 12% of net; no advance. Average first printing 500. Publication within 6 mos. Considers simultaneous submissions. Responds in 1-2 mos. Requires disk. Free guidelines/catalog.

Nonfiction: Complete ms/resume; phone/fax/e-mail query OK. "Looking for scholarly manuscripts."

Ethnic Books: African studies; Black studies.

Tips: "We publish academic and scholarly books only. Authors should have strong academic background in religious studies."

UPPER ROOM BOOKS, 1908 Grand Ave., Box 189, Nashville TN 37202-0189. (615)340-7256. Fax (615)340-7006. Website: http://www.upperroom.org. United Methodist. George Donigian, leadership & group resources; JoAnn Miller, laity & family resources. Provides resources for individuals and congregations to encourage and support spiritual growth. Publishes 25-30 titles/yr. Receives 150-200 submissions annually. 50% of books from first-time authors. Reprints books. Prefers 40,000-60,000 wds. Royalty on net; some work for hire; $1,000 advance. Average first printing 5,000. Publication within 1 yr. Responds in 6-8 wks. Free guidelines.

Nonfiction: Query letter or proposal; fax query OK.

Tips: "Wants books that focus less on the intimate individual experience and more on that which relates to the concerns of all disciples."

#VICTOR BOOKS, 4050 Lee Vance View, Colorado Springs CO 80918. Fax (719)536-3269. Adult imprint of Chariot Victor Publishing/Cook Communications Ministries. Greg Clouse, ed. dir. Publishes 40-50 titles/yr. Receives 1,200 submissions annually. 5-10% of books from first-time authors. Variable length. Royalty on net; occasional outright purchase; advance $2,000-3,000. Average first printing 7,500. Publication within 9-12 mos. Considers simultaneous submissions. Responds in 1 mo. Requires disk. Guidelines; no catalog.

Nonfiction: Query letter only; no phone query. "Most open to fresh, marketable concepts; well-thought-out and well-written books."

Fiction: Query letter only. Children/adult; picture books.

**Note: This publisher serviced by The Writer's Edge.

*VICTORY HOUSE, INC., Box 700238, Tulsa OK 74170. (918)747-5009. Fax (918)747-1970. Lloyd B. Hildebrand, mng. ed. To edify the body of Christ. Publishes 4-5 titles/yr. Not accepting unsolicited mss at this time. No mss through agents. No guidelines; catalog for #10 SAE/1 stamp.

*VITAL ISSUES PRESS, Box 53788, Lafayette LA 70505-3788. (319)237-7049. Mark Anthony, ed-in-chief. Focus is on educating readers on current events. Publishes 25-30 titles/yr. Receives 1,500 submissions annually. 25% of books from first-time authors. Reprints books. Prefers 50,000-60,000 wds or 208-224 pgs. Royalty 10% on net; negotiable advance. Average first printing 5,000-10,000. Publication within 1 yr. Considers simultaneous submissions. Responds in 4 mos. Free guidelines/catalog.

Nonfiction: Query/outline.

#WADSWORTH PUBLISHING COMPANY, 10 Davis Dr., Belmont CA 94002. (415)595-2350. Fax (415)637-7544. E-mail: peter_adams@wadsworth.com. Website: http://www.thomson.com/wadsworth.html. Division of International Thomson Publishing, Inc.; secular publisher that does some religious books. Mr. Robin Zwettler, ed. dir. Publishes 5-10 higher education religious textbooks/yr. Receives 200 submissions annually. 35% of books from first-time authors. No mss through agents. Reprints books. Royalty 5-15% on net; few advances. Average first printing 5,000. Publication within 1 yr. Considers simultaneous submissions. Responds in 1 mo. Free guidelines/catalog (by subject area).

Nonfiction: Query or proposal/chapters; fax/e-mail query OK. "Looking for college textbooks, especially on world religions; anthologies."

WARNER PRESS, Box 2499, Anderson IN 46018-2499. (765)644-7721. Church of God. David C. Schultz, ed-in-chief; Dan Harman, book ed. Publishes 10-15 titles/yr. Receives 200 submissions annually. 5% of books by first-time authors. Prefers 120 pgs. Royalty 15% of net; seldom makes advances. Average first printing 5,000. Publication within 8 mos. Responds in 2 wks. Free catalog.

Nonfiction: Query only.

WATERBROOK PRESS, 5446 N. Academy Blvd., Colorado Springs CO 80918. (719)590-4999. Fax (719)590-8977. Autonomous subsidiary of Bantam Doubleday Dell Publishing Group. Daniel P. Rich, pres.; Thomas Womack, children; Lisa Bergren, fiction; Liz Heaney, nonfiction. Publishes 60 titles/yr. Receives 300 submissions annually. 5% of books from first-time authors. Length depends on category (see guidelines). Royalty on net; advance. Average first printing 12,500-15,000. Publication within 9 mos. Considers simultaneous submissions. Responds in 3-4 mos. Requires disk. Guidelines.

Nonfiction: Query only; no phone/fax/e-mail queries

Fiction: Proposal/3 chapters; no phone/fax/e-mail queries. For children and adults. "Actively acquiring women's fiction of 100,000-120,000 wds."

Tips: "Most open to books that have a unique slant, are marketable, and well-written."

**Note: This publisher serviced by The Writer's Edge.

+WESLEYAN PUBLISHING HOUSE, Box 50434, Indianapolis IN 46250. (317)570-5300. Fax (317)570-5370. E-mail: publisher@wesleyan.org. The Wesleyan Church. Nathan Birky, pub. Denominational publisher. Does full royalty publishing, printing, and helps authors with self-publishing. Royalty. Requires disk. Guidelines. Incomplete topical listings.

Nonfiction: Proposal/1 chapter.

Tips: "We provide Christian curriculum and ministry resources, Bible study materials and books of general interest to Wesleyans. While membership in the Wesleyan Church is not required of our writers, we carefully examine manuscripts for such things as doctrinal compatibility and biblical interpretation."

+WESTERN FRONT, LTD., 2132 Century Park Ln. #216, Los Angeles CA 90067. (310)284-9092. Fax (310)552-2935. E-mail: rkcwfl@earthlink.net. Rachel Condino, ed. Publishes 4 titles/yr. Receives 30 submissions annually. 10% of books from first-time authors. No mss through agents. Reprints books. Prefers 320 pgs. Royalty 13-18% of net; no advance. Average first printing 15,000. Publication within 1 yr. No simultaneous submissions. Responds in 2-3 mos. Guidelines; no catalog.

Nonfiction: Query only; phone/e-mail query OK.

Fiction: Query only. For adults.

WESTMINSTER JOHN KNOX PRESS, 100 Witherspoon St., Louisville KY 40202-1396. (502)569-5043. Fax (502)569-5113. Website: http://www. pcusa.org/ppc. Presbyterian Church (USA). Dr. Richard E. Brown, dir.; Stephanie Egnotovich, mng. ed.; G. Nick Street, Mark Ledbetter, and Cynthia Thompson, eds. Publishes 80-100 titles/yr. Prefers 200 pgs. Royalty 7-10%; negotiable advance. Responds in 2-3 mos. Requires disk. Guidelines; free catalog.

Nonfiction: Proposal/chapters; fax query OK. Emphasizes Bible, ethics, spirituality, inspiration, biography, and theology.

+WINGS OF EAGLES PRESS, PO Box 81665, San Diego CA 92138. (619)238-5790. Fax (619)702-5662. E-mail: wings@eagle-nest.com. Website: http://www. eagle-nest.com/wings/index.htm.

WOMAN'S MISSIONARY UNION, PO Box 830010, Birmingham AL 35283-0010. (205)991-8100. Fax (205)995-4841. Website: http://www.wmu.com/wmu. Southern Baptist. Carol Causey, ed. dir. A missions publisher. Publishes 15-25 titles/yr. (many of which are works for hire). Receives 20-30 submissions annually. 25% of books from first-time authors. Rarely reprints books. Prefers 150-250 pgs. Royalty on retail or outright purchase; no advance. Average first printing 5,000-10,000. Publication within 18 mos. Considers simultaneous submissions. Responds in 6 mos. Requires disk. Guidelines; copy for 9x12 SAE/4 stamps.

Nonfiction: Complete ms or proposal/3-4 chapters; no phone/fax query. (Mss considered in the spring and fall only.) "All that we produce must have a missions/ministry emphasis."

Fiction: Complete ms or proposal/3-4 chapters. Children's picture books or storybooks, particularly with a multicultural aspect.

Ethnic Books: Hispanic.

Tips: "Most open to how-to for missions involvement or books that address involvement in missions or lead persons into involvement."

**Note: This publisher serviced by The Writer's Edge.

+WOMEN OF THE PROMISE, INC., 5620 Hummer Lake Rd., Oxford MI 48371-2814. Phone/fax (248)628-5953. E-mail: AdamRibU@aol.com. Website: http://www.crossplaza.com/wotp. Non-denominational. Gina Lawton, ed; submit to Penny Griffiths. Encouragement resources for Christian women. Publishes 2-4 titles/yr. No mss through agents. Prefers 40-60 pgs. No advance. Average first printing 250. Publication within 8 mos. Considers simultaneous submissions. Responds in 6-8 wks. Accepts disk. Free guidelines/brochure.

Nonfiction: Complete ms; phone/fax/e-mail query OK. "Looking for Bible studies and women's issues."

Fiction: Complete ms. "We accepts fiction only of interest to women or teen girls."

Also Does: Pamphlets & booklets; T-shirts; prayer journals.

Tips: "Most open to Bible studies that encourage women. Please note that most of our material is on a publication basis, not a paid basis."

WOOD LAKE BOOKS, INC., 10162 Newene Rd., Winfield BC V4V 1R2 Canada. (250)766-2778. Fax (250)766-2736. E-mail: info@woodlake.com. Ecumenical/mainline. Cheryl Perry, ed. Publishes quality resources that respond to the needs of the ecumenical church and promote spiritual growth and commitment to God. Publishes 6 titles/yr. Receives 200 submissions annually. 50% of books from first-time authors. Prefers 200-250 pgs. Royalty on retail; some advances $1,000-1,500. Average first printing 4,000. Publication within 2 yrs. Considers simultaneous submissions. Requires disk. Responds in 6 wks. Free guidelines/catalog.

Nonfiction: Query or proposal/2 chapters; fax/e-mail query OK. "Books with inclusive language and mainline, Protestant interest."

Fiction: Query or proposal/2 chapters. Adult.

Tips: "We publish Canadian authors only."

WORD PUBLISHING, 545 Marriott Dr., Ste 750, PO Box 141000, Nashville TN 37214. Does not accept unsolicited manuscripts.

**Note: This publisher serviced by The Writer's Edge.

WORLD BIBLE PUBLISHERS, 2976 Ivanrest Ave., Grandville MI 49418. (616)531-9110. Fax (616)531-9120. E-mail: WorldPub@aol.com. Riverside Book & Bible (Jordan Industries). Shari TeSlaa. ed.; submit to Carol Ochs, pub. asst. Publishes Bibles and Bible-related products. Imprints: World & World Audio. Publishes 15-20 titles/yr. Receives 500-600 submissions annually. 1% of books from first-time authors. Prefers 200-375 pgs. Royalty 5-12% of net; advance $1,000. Average first printing 5,000-10,000. Publication within 18 mos. Considers simultaneous submissions. Responds in 3 mos. Requires disk. Guidelines; catalog for 9x12 SAE/5 stamps.

Nonfiction: Proposal/3 chapters; no phone/fax/e-mail query. "Looking for devotional/inspirational books with a unique approach that are well-written."

Ethnic Books: African-American.

Tips: "Most open to books that are Bible-based; non-technical reference; devotional; books that can incorporate God's Word translation."

**Note: This publisher serviced by The Writer's Edge.

#YALE UNIVERSITY PRESS, 302 Temple St., New Haven CT 06520. (203)432-0960. Fax (203)432-0948. Website: http//www.yale.edu/yup. Charles Grench, ed-in-chief. Publishes 10 religious titles/yr. Receives 175 submissions annually. 15% of books from first-time authors. Reprints books. Prefers up to 100,000 wds or 400 pgs. Royalty to 15% on net; advance $500-30,000. Average first printing

1,500. Publication within 1 yr. Considers simultaneous submissions. Responds in 1-3 mos. Free guidelines/catalog.

Nonfiction: Query only. "Excellent and salable scholarly books."

YOUNG READER'S CHRISTIAN LIBRARY, 1810 Barbour Dr., PO Box 719, Uhrichsville OH 44683. (614)922-6045. Fax (614)922-5948. E-mail: info@ barbourbooks.com. Website: http://www.barbourbooks.com. Susan Johnson, mng ed. Children's imprint of Barbour Publishing, Inc. 90% of books from first-time authors. No mss through agents. Reprints books. Prefers about 16,000 wds. Makes outright purchases $1,000. Publication within 2 yrs. Considers simultaneous submissions. Responds in 10 wks. Guidelines; catalog for 9x12 SAE/4 stamps.

Nonfiction & Fiction: Proposal/3-4 chapters.

Tips: "We prefer action-oriented, fast-paced style at a sixth-grade reading level. The subject of the manuscript can be contemporary (post-World War II to today), a Bible character, or an historical figure."

YWAM PUBLISHING, PO Box 55787, Seattle WA 98155. (425)771-1153. Fax (425)775-2383. E-mail: 75701.2772@compuserve.com. James Drake, sr. ed. Provides missions-based materials to assist the Body of Christ worldwide in fulfilling the great commission. Publishes 12 titles/yr. Receives 100 submissions annually. 30% of books from first-time authors. Reprints books. Prefers 190 pgs. Royalty on net; advance. Average first printing 10,000. Publication within 4 mos . Considers simultaneous submissions. Responds in 3 mos. Accepts disk. Guidelines; free catalog.

Nonfiction: Query only; e-mail query OK."Needs non-fiction missionary stories from different countries."

Fiction: Query only. For children & teens."Especially missions stories with evangelism themes."

Also Does: Personal prayer diary—daily planner.

ZONDERVAN PUBLISHING HOUSE, General Trade Books; Academic and professional Books, 5300 Patterson SE, Grand Rapids MI 49530-0002. (616)698-6900. Fax (616)698-3454. E-mail: zpub@zph.com. Website: http://www. zondervan.com. HarperCollins. Submit to Trade Manuscript Review Editor (A-1). Seeks to meet the needs of people with resources that glorify Jesus Christ and promote biblical principles. Publishes 150 trade titles/yr. Receives about 2,000 submissions annually. 1% of books from first-time authors. Prefers 50,000 wds. Royalty on net; variable advance. Publication within 1 yr. Considers simultaneous submissions. Responds in 8-12 wks. Prefers NIV. Prefers disk. Free guidelines (also on Website at http://www.zondervan.com/subguide.htm) and catalog.

Nonfiction: Query only; no phone/fax/e-mail query.

Fiction: Query only.

Ethnic Books: Vida Publishers division: Spanish, Portuguese, and French.

Tips: "Absolutely stellar prose that meets demonstrated needs of our market always receives a fair and sympathetic hearing."

**Note: This publisher serviced by The Writer's Edge.

BOOK PUBLISHERS NOT INCLUDED
This information is now included in the General Index. See introduction to that section.

SUBSIDY PUBLISHERS

WHAT YOU NEED TO KNOW ABOUT SUBSIDY PUBLISHERS

Again this year, I am listing here any publishers who do 50% or more subsidy publishing. For our purposes here, I am defining a subsidy publisher as any publisher that requires the author to pay for any part of the publishing costs. They may call themselves by a variety of names, such as a book packager, a cooperative publisher, self-publisher, or simply someone who helps authors get their books published. Note that some of these also do at least some royalty publishing.

In the last couple of years, with the refinement of desk-top publishing, more subsidy publishers have sprung up, and there has been an increase in confusion over who or what type of subsidy publishing is legitimate, and what publishers fall in with what we call "vanity publishers." As many of the legitimate publishers (and even some questionable ones) try to distance themselves from the notoriety of the vanity publisher, they have come up with a variety of names to try to form definite lines of distinction. Unfortunately, it has only served to confuse the authors who might use their services. It is my hope in offering this separate listing that I can help you understand what this side of publishing entails, what to look for in a subsidy publisher, as well as what to look out for. To my knowledge the following publishers are legitimate subsidy publishers and are not vanity publishers. It is important that as a writer you understand that any time you are asked to send money for any part of the production of your book, you are entering into a non-traditional relationship with a publisher. In this constantly changing field it becomes a matter of buyer beware.

Realize, too, that some of these publishers will publish any book, as long as the author can afford to pay for it. Others are as selective about what they publish as a royalty publisher would be, or they publish only certain types of books. Many will do only nonfiction, no novels or children's books. These distinctions will be important as you seek the right publisher for your project.

Because there is so much confusion about subsidy publishing, with many authors going into agreements with these publishers having little or no knowledge of what to expect or even what is typical in this situation, many have come away unhappy or disillusioned. For that reason I frequently get complaints from authors who feel they have been cheated or taken advantage of. (Of course, I often get similar complaints about the royalty publishers listed in this book.) Each complaint brings with it an expectation that I should drop that publisher from the book. Although I am sensitive to their complaints, I also have come to the realization that I am not in a position to pass judgment on which publishers should be dropped. It has been my experience in publishing that for every complaint I get on a publisher, I can usually find several other authors who will sing the praises of the same publisher. For that reason, I feel I can serve the needs of authors better by giving them some insight into what to expect from a subsidy publisher and that kinds of terms should send up a red flag.

Because I am not an expert in this field, and because of space limitations, I will keep this brief and to the point. Let me clarify first that unless you know your book has a limited audience or you have your own method of distribution (such as being a speaker who can sell your own books when you speak), I recommend that you try all the appropriate royalty publishers first. If you are unsuccessful with the royalty publishers, but feel strongly about seeing your book published and have the financial resources to do so (or have your own distribution), one of the publishers listed below may be able to help you.

You can go to a local printer and take your book through all the necessary steps yourself, but a legitimate subsidy publisher has the contacts, know-how and resources to make the task easier and often less expensive. It is always good to get more than one bid to determine whether the terms you are being offered are fair and competitive with other such publishers.

There is not currently any kind of watchdog organization for subsidy publishers, but one is in the works. Until that group is in place, and since I do not have direct knowledge about all of the publishers listed below, I would recommend that no matter who makes you a first offer, you get a second one from Wine Press Publishing, Longwood Communications, or ACW Press (ones I can personally recommend).

As with any contract, have someone review it before signing anything. I do such reviews, as do a number of others listed in the Editorial Services section of this book. Be sure that any terms agreed upon are IN WRITING. Verbal agreements won't be binding. A legitimate subsidy publisher will be happy to provide you with a list of former clients as references (if they aren't, watch out). Don't just ask for that list; follow through and contact more than one of those references. Get a catalog of their books or a list of books they have published and try to find them or ask them to send you a review copy of one or two books they have published. Use those to check the quality of their work, the bindings, etc. Get answers to all your questions before you commit yourself to anything.

Keep in mind that the more copies of a book that are printed, the lower the cost per copy, but never let a publisher talk you into publishing more (or fewer) copies than you think is reasonable. Also find out up front, and have included in the contract, whether and how much promotion the publisher is going to do. Some will do as much as a royalty publisher; others do none at all. If they are not doing promotion, and you don't have any means of distribution yourself, it may not be a good idea to pursue publication. You don't want to end up with a garage full of books you can't sell. At the end of this section I am including the names and addresses of some of the main Christian book distributors. I don't know which ones will consider distributing a subsidy published book, so you will want to contact them to find out before you sign a contract.

LISTING OF SUBSIDY PUBLISHERS

Below is a listing of any publishers that do 50% or more subsidy publishing (where author pays some or all of the production costs). Before entering into dealings with any of these publishers, be sure to read the preceding section on what you need to know.

(*) An asterisk before a listing indicates no or unconfirmed information update.
(#) A number symbol before a listing indicates it was updated from their guidelines or

other current sources.

(+) A plus sign before a listing indicates it is a new listing this year or was not included last year.

ACW PRESS, 5501 N. 7th Ave., Ste. 502, Phoenix AZ 85013. (800)931-BOOK. (602)530-2230. E-mail: acwpress@aol.com. Website: http://www.acwpress.com. Steven R. Laube, exec. ed. Est. 1997. A self-publishing book packager. Publishes 12-18 titles/yr. Reprints books. **SUBSIDY PUBLISHES 95%.** Average first printing 500 minimum. Responds in 1 wk. Guideline booklet. Not in topical listings; will consider any topic.

> **Tips:** "We offer a high quality publishing alternative to help Christian authors get their material into print. High standards, high quality."

+AMBASSADOR HOUSE, PO Box 1153, Westminster CO 80030. (303)469-4056. Sandra Myers, pub. "Our goal is to help individuals with important messages self-publish their books, and get the marketing, public relations and distribution they need. We will strive to insure that bookstores, and ultimately bookstore customers, know that these crucial books exist. " Not in topical listings.

BLACK FOREST PRESS , 539 Telegraph Canyon Rd. #521, Chula Vista CA 91910. (619)656-8048. Fax (619)482-8704. E-mail: bfp@flash.net. Website: http://www. flash.net/~dbk. Keith Pearson, acq. ed. A self-publishing company. Imprints: Kinder Books (children's); Dichter Books (black & Hispanic); Arbentener Books. Publishes 10-15 titles/yr. Receives 1,000+ submissions annually. 95% of books from first-time authors. **SUBSIDY PUBLISHES 100%** (helps people get published). Reprints books. Prefers 75+ pgs. Average first printing 2,000-3,000. Publication within 5-6 months. Considers simultaneous submissions. Disk on request. Responds in 2-3 wks. Free guidelines/catalog.

> **Nonfiction:** Complete ms; phone/e-mail query OK. "Looking for true testimonials."
>
> **Fiction:** Complete manuscript. "Looking for Christian novels and prophecy novels; 150-350 pages."
>
> **Ethnic Books:** Publishes in Spanish, Tagalog, Russian and Japanese.
>
> **Tips:** "Looking for books on vital Christian issues; books with literary merit and significant lessons for life."

+BRANNON & BAKER PUBLISHING, 1082 Wellington Way, Lexington KY 40513. (606)296-9780. Fax (606)223-3744. E-mail: brannonbkr@aol.com. Larry V. Franklin, ed. Publishes 20-30 titles/yr (projected). Receives 60 submissions annually. 40% of books from first-time authors. **SUBSIDY PUBLISHES 50%.** Prefers 75-120,000 wds. Royalty 10-40% on net; advance $10,000 (to published authors). Average first printing 5,000. Publication within 1 yr. Considers simultaneous submissions. Responds in 3 mos. No guidelines/catalog at this time.

> **Nonfiction:** Complete ms; no phone/fax/e-mail query. "Looking for self-help books."
>
> **Fiction:** Complete ms. All types for all ages.

BRENTWOOD CHRISTIAN PRESS, 4000 Beallwood Ave., Columbus GA 31904. (404)576-5787. Website: http://www.goshen.net/bcp. Mainline. Jerry L. Luquire, exec. ed. Publishes 267 titles/yr. Receives 2,000 submissions annually. Reprints books. **SUBSIDY PUBLISHES 95%.** Prefers 120 pgs. Average first printing

500. Publication within 2 mos. Considers simultaneous submissions. Responds in 2 days. Guidelines.

Nonfiction: Complete ms. "Collection of sermons on family topics; poetry; relation of Bible to current day."

Fiction: Complete ms. "Stories that show how faith helps overcome small, day-to-day problems. Prefer under 200 pgs."

Tips: "Keep it short; support facts with reference." This publisher specializes in small print runs of 300-1,000.

COMMENTS PUBLISHING, PO Box 819, Assonet MA 02702. (508)763-8050. E-mail: comments@abaweb.com. Website: http://www.webshowplace.com/CommentsPublishing. David A. Reed, ed. A Christian outreach to Jehovah's Witnesses; cult exposés. Imprint: Access Publishing. Publishes 1 title/yr. Receives 3 submissions annually. 33% of books from first-time authors. **SUBSIDY PUBLISHES 100%.** Reprints books. Prefers 40,000 wds or 150 pgs. In most cases author pays for books; average cost $2-4/bk. Average first printing 1,000. Publication within 2 mos. Considers simultaneous submissions. Responds in 1 mo. No guidelines; catalog for #10 SAE/2 stamps.

Nonfiction: Query only first. E-mail query OK.

Fiction: Query only. For teens and adults.

Also Does: Booklets on Jehovah's Witnesses, 40-60 pages. Publisher pays for production and royalties.

Tips: "Our marketing and distribution are limited; we sell mostly via direct mail-order to evangelicals in counter-cult work. Authors in other fields should plan to distribute most of their own books."

CORNERSTONE PUBLISHING, INC., PO Box 7972, Louisville KY 40257. (888)442-6096 or (812)544-2577. Fax (802)896-4594. E-mail: CornerstonePub@worldnet.att.net. Website: http://www.CornerstonePub.com. Wendy O'Rourke, ed.; submit to Marie Gates. A major provider of resources for writers; multicultural books; and resources that motivate, educate and inspire. Publishes 7 titles/yr. Receives 1,700 submissions annually. 70% of books from first-time authors. No mss through agents. **SUBSIDY PUBLISHES 50%.** Prefers 25,000 wds or 200 pgs. Royalty 10-40% on net; no advance. Average first printing 1,500. Publication within 7 mos. Considers simultaneous submissions. Responds in 2-4 mos. Requires disk. Guidelines; free catalog.

Nonfiction: Proposal/3 chapters; fax/e-mail query OK. "Looking for books on angels, miracles and dynamic testimonies; how to live the Christian life in the 21st century; humor."

Fiction: Proposal/3 chapters. All ages. "Looking for multicultural novels."

Ethnic Books: Books for all ethnic markets.

Also Does: Booklets, pamphlets, tracts.

ESSENCE PUBLISHING CO., INC., 44 Moira St. W., Belleville ON K8P 1S3 Canada. (800)236-6376. (613)962-3294. Fax (613)962-3055. E-mail: info@essence.on.ca. Website: http://www.essence.on.ca. Essence, Inc. Bonnie Visser, ed. Provides affordable, short-run book publishing to the Christian community. Publishes 60 titles/yr. Receives 100+ submissions annually. 85% of books from first-time authors. **SUBSIDY PUBLISHES 90%.** Reprints books. Prefers 80-400 pgs. Average first printing 250-1,000. Publication within 3-4 mos. Considers simultaneous submissions. Responds in 2-4 wks. Accepts disk. Free guidelines/catalog. Not in topical listings; almost any topic.

Nonfiction & Fiction: Complete ms; phone/fax/e-mail query OK.

Also Does: Pamphlets, booklets and tracts.

FAIRWAY PRESS, Subsidy Division for C.S.S. Publishing Company, 517 S. Main St., Box 4503, Lima OH 45802-4503. (419)227-1818. Fax (419)228-9184. E-mail: csspub@csspub.com. Website: http://www.csspub.com. Teresa Rhoads, ed; submit to Ruth Ann Baker. Publishes 100 titles/yr. Receives 200-300 submissions annually. 80% of books from first-time authors. Reprints books. **SUBSIDY PUBLISHES 100%.** Royalty to 50%; no advance. Average first printing 500-1,000. Publication within 6-9 mos. Considers simultaneous submissions. Responds in up to 1 month. Prefers disk. Free guidelines/catalog for 9x12 SAE.

Nonfiction: Complete ms; phone/fax/e-mail query OK. "Looking for mss with a Christian theme, and seasonal material."

Fiction: Complete ms. For adults, teens, or children; all types.

FAME PUBLISHING, INC., 820 S. MacArthur Blvd., Ste. 105-220, Coppell TX 75019. (214)393-1467. Fax (214)462-9350. E-mail: FamePub@aol.com. Nondenominational. Margaret J. Kinney, pres. Publishes 3-5 titles/yr. **SUBSIDY PUBLISHER.** Not in topical listings.

Nonfiction & Fiction: Proposal/chapters.

+GESHER, PO Box 33373, Philadelphia PA 19142-3373. (215)365-3350. Fax (215)365-3325. E-mail: info@gesher.org. Website: http://www.gesher.org. Helping people walk in all that God intends for them. Robert Winer, pres. New publisher; plans 4 titles in 1998. Primarily a subsidy publisher; does some royalty projects.

Nonfiction: "Looking for books on spirituality, issues of reconciliation, gifts of the Spirit, and spiritual warfare."

*HARVARD HOUSE, PO Box 5172, Golden CO 80401. (303)378-3813. Fax (707)434-0850. Donald Webster, ed. Publishes 1-2 titles/yr. Receives 30 submissions annually. All books from first-time authors. No mss through agents. **SUBSIDY PUBLISHES 100%.** Prefers 80-200 pgs. Average first printing 1,000. Publication within 6 mos. Considers simultaneous submissions. Responds in 1-2 mos. Guidelines; catalog $1.

Nonfiction: Proposal/up to 5 chapters or complete ms; fax query OK. "Looking for apologetics, prophecy, science/religion interface that appeals to both religious and secular. Must be marketable to secular talk shows."

Tips: "Author must be capable/willing to do radio/TV interviews."

IMAGE PRESS, INC., 247 N. Broadway, Edmond OK 73034. (405)844-6007. Fax (405)348-5577. M.M. Yeager, ed; submit to S.G. Shelton. Publishes 3-10 titles/yr. 80% of books from first-time authors. **SUBSIDY PUBLISHES 100%.** Might reprints books. Prefers 200-250 pgs. Royalty on retail; no advance. Average first printing 1,000+. Publication within 3-4 mos. Considers simultaneous submissions. Responds in 3-4 wks. Prefers disk. No guidelines or catalog.

Nonfiction: Complete ms; phone/fax query OK.

Fiction: Complete ms.

Also Does: Pamphlets, booklets and tracts.

Tips: "We offer the good and relevant author, who has been turned down by major publishers, an opportunity to publish and have exposure to a national market, at about 50% less than vanity publishers."

IMPACT CHRISTIAN BOOKS, INC., 332 Leffingwell Ave. Ste. 101, Kirkwood MO 63122. (314)822-3309. William D. Banks, pres. Publishes 20+ titles/yr. Receives 20-50 submissions annually. 50-70% of books from first-time authors. No mss through agents. **SUBSIDY PUBLISHES 50-70%.** Reprints books. Average first printing 5,000. Publication within 2 mos. Considers simultaneous submissions. Responds by prior arrangement in 30 days. Accepts disk. Guidelines; catalog for 9x12 SAE/5 stamps. Not in topical listings.

> **Nonfiction:** Tracts, outstanding personal testimonies, and Christ-centered books.

LONGWOOD COMMUNICATIONS, 397 Kingslake Dr., DeBary FL 32713. (904)774-1991. Fax (904)774-8181. E-mail: longwood@totcon.com. Murray Fisher, VP. A service for authors who cannot get their books accepted by a traditional house. Publishes 8-12 titles/yr. Receives 80 submissions annually. 85% of books from first-time authors. No mss through agents. **100% SUBSIDY.** Reprints books. Average first printing 5,000. Publication within 3-5 mos. Considers simultaneous submissions. Responds in 1-2 wks. Requires disk. No guidelines; catalog for 2 stamps.

> **Nonfiction:** Complete ms; phone query OK. Any topic as long as it's Christian. Also does booklets. Not in topical listings.
>
> **Fiction:** Complete ms. For all ages. Any genre.
>
> **Tips:** Looking for basic Christian books.

+MOONLETTERS PRESS, 7210 W. 57th Pl., Summit IL 60501. E-mail: ShaunaSkye@aol.com. Website: http://members.aol.com/ShaunaSkye/index. html. Shauna Skye, ed. Publishes mostly chapbooks. Guidelines; catalog.

> **Nonfiction:** Small poetry chapbooks. Send completed poems.
>
> **Fiction:** Small fiction chapbooks; 8,000 wds total (one story or several short ones).
>
> **Tips:** "Author will receive 10 copies of their chapbook, plus 25% off additional copies. Chapbooks will also be made available through our catalog."

PARTNERSHIP BOOK SERVICES, 212 N. Ash, Hillsboro KS 67063. (316)947-3966. Fax (316)947-3392. Hearth Publishing, Inc. Stan Thiessen, ed. Publishes 12 religious titles/yr (70 total). Receives 400 submissions annually. 85% of books from first-time authors. No mss through agents. **100% SUBSIDY.** Reprints books. Prefers 20,000-150,000 wds or 96-352 pgs. Average first printing 100-20,000. Publication within 6 mos. Considers simultaneous submissions. Responds in 2 wks-3 mos. No disk. Guidelines; no catalog. Not included in topical listings; considers any topic.

> **Nonfiction/Fiction:** Proposal/3-4 chapters; no phone/fax query. Send $35/SASE for manuscript evaluation. "Response includes suggestions for improvement."
>
> **Also Does:** Booklets, pamphlets, tracts and chapbooks.
>
> **Tips:** "PBS services include evaluation, editing, cover design, formatting, disk to film, printing, promotions and marketing."

PASTOR'S CHOICE PRESS, 4000 Beallwood Ave., Columbus GA 31904. (404/706)576-5787. Website: http://www.goshen.net/bcp. Subsidiary of Brentwood Publishers Group. Jerry Luquire, exec. dir. **SUBSIDY OR CUSTOM**

PUBLISHES 100%. Focus is on sermon notes, outlines, illustrations, plus news that pastors would find interesting. Publishes 300-500 copies. Cost of about $3-4/book. Publication in 45 days. Same day response.

POET'S COVE PRESS, 4000 Beallwood Ave., Columbus GA 31904. (404/706)576-5787. Website: http://www.goshen.net/bcp. Subsidiary of Brentwood Publishers Group. Jerry Luquire, exec. dir. Publishes 125 titles/yr. **SUBSIDY OR CUSTOM PUBLISHES 100%.** Specializes in self-publishing books of religious or inspirational poetry, in small press runs of under 500 copies. Publication in 45 days. Same day response.

> **Tips:** "Type one poem per page; include short bio and photo with first submission."

PROMISE PUBLISHING, 2324 N. Batavia #105, Orange CA 92665. (714)282-1199. Fax (714)997-5545. E-mail: ed_mary@ix.netcom.com. M.B. Steele, ed./V.P. Publishes 6 titles/yr. 50% of books from first-time authors. **100% COOPERATIVE PUBLISHING** in support of ministry organizations. Royalty 10% on retail (negotiable); no advance. Average first printing 5,000. Publication within 6 mos. Considers simultaneous submissions. Pre-acceptance talks determine acceptance. Prefers disk.

> **Nonfiction:** Proposal/3 chapters; phone/fax/e-mail query OK.

> **Special Needs:** "We are interested in whatever topics fall within the parameters of our 'cooperative publishing' approach, if it is not contradictory to the Bible. Not in topical listings.

RECOVERY COMMUNICATIONS, INC., PO Box 19910, Baltimore MD 21211. Fax (410)243-8558. Toby R. Drews, ed. Publishes 4-6 titles/yr. No mss through agents. **SUBSIDY PUBLISHER.** Prefers 110 pgs. Co-op projects; no royalty or advance. Average first printing 5,000. Publication within 11 mos. Excellent nationwide distribution and marketing in book stores.

> **Nonfiction or Fiction:** Query only.

SHEER JOY! PRESS/PROMOTIONS, 5502 Murphy Rd., Pink Hill NC 28572. (919)568-6101. Fax (919)568-4171. Protestant. James R. Adams, pres.; submit to Patricia Adams, ed. Publishes 1-2 titles/yr. Receives 5-10 submissions annually. No mss through agents. **SUBSIDY PUBLISHES 85%.** Prefers 20,000-30,000 wds (200 pgs). Royalty on retail; no advance. Average first printing 1,000. Publication within 6 mos. Considers simultaneous submissions. Responds in 3-4 wks.

> **Nonfiction:** Complete ms. "Need Bible-based dramatic readings."

> **Fiction:** Complete ms. "Need Bible-based puppet skits."

> **Tips:** "Be very illustrative and forceful in writing Christian drama." Note: This publisher is recovering from hurricane damage and will not be open to submissions until mid to late 1998.

SON-RISE PUBLICATIONS, 143 Greenfield Rd., New Wilmington PA 16142. (800)358-0777. Fax (412)946-8700. Florence W. Biros, acq. ed. Publishes 5-6 titles/yr. Receives 20 submissions annually. 50% of books from first-time authors. **SUBSIDY PUBLISHES 50%.** Prefers 25,000-40,000 wds or 90-196 pgs. Royalty 7.5-10% on retail; no advance. Average first printing 3,000. Publication within 8-9 mos. Responds ASAP.

> **Nonfiction:** Query. "Most open to Christian teaching and testimony combined."

Fiction: Query only; overstocked.

Tips: "We are overstocked with royalty manuscripts. The only ones I can consider for now are subsidy manuscripts."

SOUTHERN BAPTIST PRESS, 4000 Beallwood, Columbus GA 31904. (404)576-5787. Jerry L. Luquire, exec. ed. Publishes 42 books/yr. Receives 600 submissions annually. Reprints books. **SUBSIDY OR CUSTOM PUBLISHES 95%.** Prefers 120 pgs. Average first printing 500. Publication within 2 mos. Considers simultaneous submissions. Responds in 1 week. Guidelines.

Nonfiction: Complete ms. "Collections of sermons on family topics; poetry; relation of Bible to current day."

Fiction: Complete ms. "Stories that show how faith helps overcome small, day-to-day problems. Prefers under 200 wds."

Tips: "Keep it short; support facts with reference."

+STONE RIVER PUBLISHING, INC., 4135 Hemlock Ln., Titusville FL 32780. (888)426-7100. Fax (407)264-7424. E-mail: dwilson@digital.net. **SUBSIDY PUBLISHES 100%.** Printings of 500-10,000. Considers simultaneous submissions. Guidelines. Not in topical listings.

Nonfiction & Fiction: Complete ms.

TEACH SERVICES, INC., RR 1, Box 182, Brushton NY 12916. (518)358-2125. Fax (518)358-3028. Timothy Hullquist, pres.; submit to Wayne Reid, acq. ed. To publish uplifting books for the lowest price. Publishes 70-75 titles/yr. Receives 130 submissions annually. 35% of books from first-time authors. No mss through agents. **SUBSIDY PUBLISHES 50%** (author has to pay for first printing, then publisher keeps it in print). Reprints books. Prefers 45,000 wds or 96 pgs. Royalty 10% on retail; no advance. Average first printing 2,000. Publication within 4 mos. Disk required. Responds in 2 wks. Guidelines; no catalog.

Nonfiction: Query only; no phone/fax query. "Looking for books on nutrition."

Also Does: Pamphlets, booklets and tracts. IBM (music typesetting).

TYLER PRESS, 1221 W.S.W. Loop 323, Tyler TX 75701. (903)581-2255. Fax (903)581-7841. E-mail: tylerpress@electro-image.com. J. A. Johnson, sr. ed. A self-publisher's service bureau that will lend its imprint to selected titles. Publishes 20 titles/yr. Receives 250+ submissions annually. 80% of books from first-time authors. **SUBSIDY PUBLISHES 100%.** Reprints books. Prefers 204 pgs & up. Provides full editing and design services, if needed. Average first printing 500-5,000. Publication within 2 mos. Considers simultaneous submissions. Responds in 1 wk.

Nonfiction: Query; fax query OK. "We enthusiastically promote self-help/how-to, historical, creation science, current social and political issues, biographies, autobiographies, marriage and family, and women's issues."

Fiction: Query. For children only.

Also Does: Booklets.

VESTA PUBLICATIONS, LTD., Box 1641, Cornwall ON K6H 5V6 Canada. (613)932-2135. Fax (613)932-7735. E-mail: sg@glen-net.ca. General trade publisher that does a few religious titles; focus is on world peace. Stephen Gill, ed. Publishes 4 titles/yr. Receives 20-60 submissions annually. 95% of books from first-time authors. No mss through agents. **SUBSIDY PUBLISHES 90%** (author pays about 50% of cost). Reprints books. Any length. Royalty 15% of net; no advance. Average first printing 1,500. Publication within 3 mos. No simultaneous submissions. Responds in 4-7 wks. Requires disk. Catalog for SAE/IRCs.

Nonfiction: Proposal/1 chapter; phone query OK.

Tips: "Most open to scholarly/religious books."

*WELLNESS PUBLICATIONS, Box 2397, Holland MI 49423. (616)335-5553 or (800)543-0815. Darrell Franken, pres. Specializes in health and faith books. Publishes 3 titles/yr. Receives 200 submissions annually. All books from first-time authors. **100% SUBSIDY.** Prefers 250 pgs. Royalty 10% on retail; no advance; minimum subsidy $3,000. Average first printing 2,000. Publication within 6 mos. Considers simultaneous submissions. Responds in 2-4 wks. Free catalog.

Nonfiction: Complete ms.

Tips: "Most open to health/healing, stress management and psychological concerns."

WINDFLOWER COMMUNICATIONS, 844-K McLeod Ave., Winnipeg MB R2G 2T7 Canada. (204)668-7475. Fax (204)661-8530. E-mail: windflower@brandt family.com. Website: http://www.infobahn.mb.ca/brandtfamily. Brandt Family Enterprises. Gilbert Brandt, pres. Publishes quality, wholesome literature for family reading, pleasure and learning. Publishes 4-6 titles/yr. Receives 200 sub-missions annually. 90% of books from first-time authors. **SUBSIDY PUBLISH-ES 80%.** Reprints books. Prefers 200 pgs. Royalty 10-20% on net; no advance. Average first printing 2,500. Publication within 10 mos. Considers simultaneous submissions. Responds in 6 mos. Prefers disk. Free guidelines/catalog.

Nonfiction: Query or proposal/1-2 chapters; fax/e-mail query OK.

Fiction: Proposal/1-2 chapters. All ages.

Tips: "We are currently focusing on historical fiction."

WINE PRESS PUBLISHING, 12108 Mukilteo Speedway, PO Box 1406, Mukilteo WA 98275. (800)326-4674. Fax (206)353-4402. E-mail: BOOKS4HIM@ aol.com. Website: http://www.winepresspub.com. Vic Lipsey, ed; submit to Athena Dean. Publishes 100+ titles/yr. Receives 500+ submissions annually. 70% of books from first-time authors. No mss through agents. **BOOK PACKAGERS 85%.** Reprints books. Prefers 40,000 wds or 150 pgs. Author pays production costs, keeps all income from sales. Average first printing 1,000-2,500. Publication in 3 mos. Considers simultaneous submissions. Responds in 48-72 hrs. Accepts disk. Free guidelines/catalog. Not included in topical listings because they con-sider any topic or genre.

Nonfiction: Complete ms; phone/fax/e-mail query OK. Publishes any topic as long as it's biblical or glorifies God.

Fiction: Complete ms. All ages and all genres.

Also Does: Booklets, gift books, calendars.

Tips: "We offer professional, yet affordable, book packaging for Christian writers, with unique marketing, distribution and fulfillment services available for qualifying projects. We don't purchase rights to books, but we still turn down manuscripts that don't glorify God or have a reasonably good chance of selling at least 1,000 copies."

LISTING OF CHRISTIAN BOOK DISTRIBUTORS

APPALACHIAN, INC., PO Box 1573, 506 Princeton Rd., Johnson City TN 37601. (800)289-2772.

+BEACON DISTRIBUTING/COOK COMMUNICATIONS CANADA, http://www.cook.ca/.

INGRAM BOOK COMPANY, 1125 Heil Quaker Rd., Nashville TN 37217. (615)793-5000.

R.G. MICHELL, 565 Gordon Baker Rd., Willowdale ON M2H 2W2, Canada.

+MISSION PUBLISHING, 2824 Madrona Beach Rd. NW, Olympia WA 98502. Submit to Artist Relations. Distributes Christian music and drama on the Internet. Website: http://www.pacificnet.net/mpub. Details on Website.

NEW DAY CHRISTIAN DISTRIBUTORS, 126 Shivel Dr., Hendersonville TN 37075. (800)251-3633.

QUALITY BOOKS, 1003 W. Pines Rd., Oregon IL 61061. (815)732-4450. Distributes to secular libraries.

RIVERSIDE BOOK AND BIBLE, PO Box 370, Iowa Falls IA 50126-0370. (515)648-4271.

SLEEPER, DICK, DISTRIBUTION, 18680-B Langensand Rd., Sandy OR 97055-9427. (503)668-3454. Fax (503)668-5314. Represents small press authors.

SPRING ARBOR DISTRIBUTORS, 10885 Textile Rd., Belleville MI 48111. (313)481-0900. (800)395-5599. Fax (800)395-2682. Website: http://www.springarbor.com/index.htm.

STAR SONG DISTRIBUTION GROUP, PO Box 150009, Nashville TN 37215.

WARNER CHRISTIAN DISTRIBUTION, 24 Music Square East, Nashville TN 37203. (615)248-3300. Distributes records.

WHITAKER DISTRIBUTORS, 30 Hunt Valley Cir., New Kinsington PA 15068. (412)334-7000.

MARKET ANALYSIS

ALL PUBLISHERS IN ORDER OF MOST BOOKS PUBLISHED PER YEAR

CSS Publishing 200
Thomas Nelson 150-200
Standard Publishing 150
Zondervan 150
Wm. B. Eerdmans 140
United Methodist 130
Bethany House 120-150
Baker Books 120
Multnomah 120
Christian Univ Press 100
Element Books 100
Harvest House 100
Liturgical Press 100
Tyndale House 100
Paulist Press 90-100
Westmin./John Knox 80-100
Christian Ed Publishers 80
Concordia 80
Barbour Publishing 75
InterVarsity Press 70
Winston-Derek 70
Moody Press 65-70
Tommy Nelson 65
Destiny Image 60-70
Oxford University 60
Broadman & Holman 60
Honor Books 60
Kregel 60
Joshua Morris 60
Fleming H. Revell 60
Univ. Press of America 60
WaterBrook Press 60
Heartsong Presents 52
Brown/ROA 50-100
Custom Commun. 50-75
Orbis Books 50-55
Crossroad Publishing 50
Crossway 50
Liguori Publications 50
Chariot Victor Books 45-50
GROUP Publishing 40-50
Review and Herald 40-50
Victor Books 40-50
Harold Shaw 40-45
Zondervan/Academic 40-45
CEF Press 40
Christian Publications 40
Ignatius Press 40
HarperSanFrancisco 36-46

Love Inspired 36
Beacon Hill Press 35
Eldridge 35 (plays)
Smyth & Helwys 35
Trinity Press Intl. 35
Chariot Publishing 30
College Press 30
Continuum 30
Doubleday 30
Good News Publishers 30
   (tracts)
Light and Life 30
Our Sunday Visitor 30
Pacific Press 30
Pilgrim Press 30
Sheed & Ward 30
Conari Press 26
Chalice Press 25-40
Pauline Books 25-35
Creation House 25-30
Meriwether 25-30 (plays)
Upper Room Books 25-30
Vital Issues Press 25-30
Mel Bay Publications 25
Bridge/Logos 25
Hunt and Thorpe 25
Liturgy Training 25
Alba House 24
Group's Hands-On 24
Lightwave Publishing 24
Sword Of The Lord 24
Gold 'n' Honey 20
Resource Publications 20
Shining Star 20
Sovereign/Appaloosa 20
St. Anthony Mess. Press 18-20
Lillenas 18
Judson Press 16
Pastoral Press 16
Preservation Press 16
United Church Press 15-25
Woman's Mission. Union
   15-25
Catholic Book Publishing
   15-20
Focus on the Family 15-20
Hendrickson 15-20
Loizeaux 15-20
New Leaf Press 15-20

World Bible 15-20
Evangel Pub. House 15
Libros Liguori 15
Living the Good News 15
Morehouse Publishing 15
Paraclete Press 15
Still Waters 15
Palisades 14
Rainbow Pub/Rainbow Books
   (CA)12-20
Howard Publishing 12-18
Blue Dolphin 12-15
Northstone Publishing 12-14
Albury Publishing 12
Daybreak Books/Rodale 12
Dimension Books 12
Forward Movement 12
Loyola Press 12
New City Press 12
YWAM Publishing 12
Carey Library, Wm. 10-15
Lydia Press 10-15
Ragged Edge 10-15
Southern Methodist 10-15
Warner Press 10-15
Gospel Publishing House 10-14
Journey Books 10-12
New Hope 10-12
ACTA Publications 10
ACU Press 10
Alban Institute 10
Church Growth Institute 10
Haworth Press 10
Lion Publishing 10
Monument Press 10
Starburst Publishers 10
Treasure Publishing 10
United Church Publishing 10
Yale University Press 10
Cistercian Publications 8-14
St. Bede's Publications 8-12
Alexander Books 8-10
Holy Cross Orthodox 8-10
Master Books 8-10
One World 8-10
Presbyterian/Reformed 8-10
Chosen Books 8
ICS Publications 8
Innisfree Press 8

Neibauer Press 8
Resurrection Press 8
Royal Productions 8
Touch Publications 8
Franciscan Univ Press 7
Kaleidoscope Press 7
Faith Publishing 6-12
Messianic Jewish Publishers
    6-12
Elder Books 6-10
Gospel Folio Press 6-10
Thomas More Press 6-10
Rainbow Pub/Legacy Press
    6-10
Accent Publications 6-8
Christian Literature Crusade
    6-8
Christopher Pub Hs 6-8
Cornell University Press 6-8
Catholic Univ of America 6
Church & Synagogue
    Libraries 6
Magnus Press 6
Read 'N Run Books 6
Trinity Foundation 6
Wood Lake Books 6
Scarecrow Press 5-15
Hensley, Virgil 5-10
Regina Press 5-10
Wadsworth Publishing 5-10
Bethel Publishing 5-8
Cross Cultural 5-8
FOG Publishing 5
Christian Media 5
Wm. Morrow 5
Mt. Olive College Press 5
Omega House 5
Paradise Research 5
Pelican Publishing 5
PREP Publishing 5
Rainbow Books (FL) 5

Rose Publishing 5
Focus Publishing 4-6
Friends United Press 4-6
Hearth Publishing 4-6
Religious Education Press 4-5
Victory House 4-5
American Catholic Press 4
Bristol House 4
Christendom Press 4
Cornerstone Press 4
Intl. Awakening Press 4
Langmarc Publishing 4
Open Court 4
Schocken Books 4
Toccoa Falls College Press 4
Western Front 4
Cerdic Publications 3-5
Facts on File 3-5
Baker's Plays 3-4 (plays)
Kindred Productions 3-4
Good Book 3
Hi-Time Publishing 3
Art Can Drama 2-5
Dabar Publishers 2-5
Women of the Promise 2-5
Lifetime Books 2-4
Rainbow's End 2-4
Regnery Publishing 2-4
Univ. of Ottawa Press 2-4
Dry Bones Press 2-3
Meriwether 2-3 (books)
Sower's Press 2-3
Baylor Univ. Press 2
Cross Way Publications 2
Logion Press 2
Seaside Press 2
Barclay Press 1-5
Life Cycle Books 1-3
Middle Atlantic 1-3
Accent Books & Video 1-2
Gilgal Publications 1

B.J. Goetz 1
Guernica Editions 1
Misty Hill Press 1
Small Helm Press 1

SUBSIDY PUBLISHERS:

Brentwood 267
Poet's Cove 125
Wine Press 100
Fairway Press 100
TEACH Services 70-75
Essence Publishing 60
Southern Baptist Press 42
Impact Books 20
Brannon & Baker 20-30
Tyler Press 20
ACW Press 12-18
Partnership Book Services 12
Black Forest Press 10-15
Longwood Communications
    8-12
Cornerstone Publishing 7
Promise Publishing 6
Son-Rise 5-6
Recovery Communications
    4-6
Windflower Communications
    4-6
VESTA Publications 4
Image Press 3-10
Fame Publishing 3-5
Wellness Publications 3
Harvard House 1-2
New Canaan 1-2
Sheer Joy! Press 1-2
Comments Publishing 1

BOOK PUBLISHERS WITH THE MOST BOOKS ON THE BESTSELLER LIST FOR THE LAST YEAR

Note: This tally is based on actual sales in Christian bookstores for October 1996-September 1997 (most recent information available). The list is broken down by types of books, i.e., children's, teen, fiction, nonfiction in paperback and cloth, mass-market paperbacks, and a new one this year, theology books. Numbers behind the names indicate the number of titles each publisher had on that bestseller list during the year. The combined list indicates the total number a particular publisher had on all the lists combined. If a particular publisher has more than one imprint listed, they are usually combined for these totals. It is interesting to note that each year the number of publishers appearing on the list has increased—26 publishers in 1993; 35 publishers in 1994; 43 in 1995, and 60 in 1996 until this year when it has dropped back to 48.

FICTION BOOKS

1. Bethany House 23

2. Tyndale House 7
3. Harvest House 6

4. Multnomah 5
5. Thomas Nelson 5

6. Zondervan 5
7. Crossway 4
8. Word 4
9. Palisades (Multnomah) 3
10. Doubleday 2
11. Barbour 1
12. Broadman & Holman 1
13. Chariot Victor 1
14. Simon & Schuster 1
15. Western Front 1

NONFICTION—CLOTH

1. Word 19
2. Thomas Nelson 9
3. Zondervan 7
4. Focus on the Family 3
5. Harrison House 3
6. J. Countryman 2
7. Discovery House (Nelson) 2
8. Honor Books 2
9. Tyndale House 2
10. Albury 1
11. Barbour 1
12. Broadman & Holman 1
13. Creation House 1
14. Doubleday 1
15. HarperCollins 1
16. Harvest House 1
17. Howard Publishing 1
18. Inspirational Press 1
19. Moody Press 1
20. Regal Books 1
21. Revell 1
22. Servant Publications 1

NONFICTION— PAPERBACK

1. Creation House 7
2. Honor Books 6
3. Multnomah 5
4. Thomas Nelson 5
5. Albury 3
6. Harrison House 3
7. Moody Press 3
8. NavPress 3
9. Frontier Research 2
10. Harvest House 2
11. Whitaker House 2
12. Chariot Victor 1
13. Destiny Image 1
14. Discovery House 1
15. Focus on the Family 1
16. HarperSanFrancisco 1
17. Regal Books 1
18. Regal/Tyndale 1
19. Standard 1

20. Tyndale House 1
21. Western Front 1

MASS-MARKET PAPERBACKS

1. Barbour Books 16
2. Tyndale House 7
3. J. Countryman/Word 5
4. Zondervan 4
5. Creation House 3
6. Thomas Nelson 3
7. Simon & Schuster 3
8. Avon 1
9. Bethany House 1
10. Broadman & Holman 1
11. Focus on the Family 1
12. Fortress Press 1
13. Harrison House 1
14. Harvest House 1
15. Hendrickson Publishers 1
16. InterVarsity 1
17. Pocket Books 1
18. Regal 1
19. Word 1
20. World Publishers 1

CHILDREN'S BOOKS

1. Tommy Nelson 18
2. Chariot 6
3. Gold 'n' Honey/Questar 5
4. Concordia 4
5. Crossway Books 4
6. Random House 4
7. Standard Publishing 4
8. Tyndale House 4
9. HarperCollins 2
10. Word 2
11. Zondervan 2
12. Baker Books 1
13. Barbour 1
14. Bethany House 1
15. Firefly 1
16. Honor Books 1
17. InterVarsity Press 1
18. Lion 1
19. Sparrow 1
20. Oliver-Nelson 1
21. Questar (Multnomah) 1
22. Regina Press 1
23. Star Song 1
24. World Bible 1

YOUTH/TEEN BOOKS

1. Bethany House 4
2. Focus on the Family 3
3. Standard Publishing 2
4. Baker Books 1

5. Harrison House 1
6. Honor Books 1
7. Regal Books 1
8. Harold Shaw 1

THEOLOGY BOOKS

1. Chariot Victor 3
2. InterVarsity Press 3
3. Zondervan 3
4. HarperCollins 2
5. Moody Press 2
6. Thomas Nelson 2
7. Simon & Schuster 2
8. Christian Publications 1
9. Concordia 1
10. Doubleday 1
11. Hendrickson 1
12. Liguori 1
13. NavPress 1
14. Revell 1
15. Walker 1
16. Word 1

Combined Bestseller Lists (Combination of seven lists above)

1. Word 38
2. Bethany House 29
3. Thomas Nelson 28
4. Tyndale House 22
5. Zondervan 21
6. Barbour 19
7. Multnomah 19
8. Tommy Nelson 18
9. Chariot Victor 12
10. Creation House 11
11. Harvest House 10
12. Honor Books 10
13. Crossway Books 8
14. Focus on the Family 8
15. Standard 7
16. HarperCollins & SF 6
17. Moody 6
18. Simon & Schuster 6
19. Concordia 5
20. Harrison House 5
21. Regal Books 5
22. Albury 4
23. Doubleday 4
24. InterVarsity Press 4
25. NavPress 4
26. Random House 4
27. Broadman & Holman 3
28. Baker Books 2
29. Frontier Research 2
30. Hendrickson 2
31. Inspirational Press 2

32. Revell 2	38. Destiny Image 1	44. Regina Press 1
33. Western Front 2	39. Firefly 1	45. Servant 1
34. Whitaker House 2	40. Fortress Press 1	46. Harold Shaw 1
35. World Bible 2	41. Howard Publishing 1	47. Star Song 1
36. Avon 1	42. Liguori 1	48. Walker 1
37. Christian Publications 1	43. Pocket Books 1	

BOOK TOPICS MOST POPULAR WITH PUBLISHERS

Note: The numbers following the topics indicate how many publishers said they were interested in seeing a book on that topic. To find the list of publishers interested in each topic, go to the Topical Listings for books (see Table of Contents).

1. Prayer 112
2. Christian Living 108
3. Bible/Biblical Studies 104
4. Inspirational 103
5. Religion 99
6. Spirituality 98
7. Marriage 91
8. Women's Issues 90
9. Devotional Books 89
10. Family Life 89
11. Theological 87
12. Current/Social Issues 80
13. Parenting 80
14. Christian Education 79
15. Evangelism/Witnessing 75
16. Discipleship 74
17. Biography 73
18. Ethics 72
19. Historical 69
20. Youth books 69
21. How-To 68
22. Church Renewal 67
23. Ethnic/Cultural 63
24. Healing 62
25. Church Life 61
26. Fiction: Adult/Religious 60
27. Health 59
28. Pastor's Helps 59
29. Booklets 55
30. Psychology 55
31. Social Justice Issues 55
32. Apologetics 54
33. Fiction: Juvenile 54
34. Men's Books 54
35. Controversial Issues 51
36. Reference 51
37. Doctrinal 50
38. Fiction: Contemporary 50
39. Gift Books 50

40. Fiction: Historical 49
41. Leadership 49
42. Philosophy 49
43. Humor 48
44. Counseling Aids 47
45. Liturgical Studies 46
46. Self-Help 45
47. Scholarly 44
48. Environmental Issues 43
49. Missionary 43
50. Christian
   Home-Schooling 42
51. Autobiography 41
52. Children's Picture Books
   41
53. Worship Resources 41
54. Group Study Books 40
55. Personal Renewal 39
56. Personal Experience 38
57. Prophecy 38
58. Death/Dying 37
59. Fiction: Adventure 37
60. Fiction: Teen/Young Adult
   36
61. Recovery 35
62. Senior-Adult Concerns 35
63. Money Management 34
64. Pamphlets 34
65. World Issues 34
66. Fiction: Biblical 33
67. Stewardship 33
68. Miracles 32
69. Music-Related Books 32
70. Curriculum 31
71. Divorce 31
72. Fiction: Mystery 31
73. Singles Issues 31
74. Archaeology 30
75. Cults/Occult 30

76. Drama 30
77. Poetry 30
78. Science 30
79. Fiction: Historical
   Romance 28
80. Fiction: Humorous 28
81. Spiritual Warfare 28
82. Sermons 27
83. Games/Crafts 26
84. Political Theory 26
85. Retirement 25
86. Economics 24
87. Fiction: Frontier
   Romance 24
88. Fiction: Mystery
   romance 24
89. Tracts 24
90. Fiction: Romance 23
91. Christian School Books
   22
92. Fiction: Frontier 22
93. Sociology 22
94. Cookbooks 20
95. Creation Science 17
96. Fiction: Literary 17
97. Fiction: Plays 17
98. Celebrity Profiles 16
99. Fiction: Allegory 16
100. Fiction: Ethnic 15
101. Fiction: Short-Story
    Collection 14
102. Sports/Recreation 14
103. Fiction: Fantasy 12
104. Travel 12
105. Exposés 11
106. Fiction: Science Fiction
    1
107. Youth Programs 10
108. Writing How-Tos 7

Comments:

If you are a fiction writer, you are more likely to sell adult fiction (60 possible publishers—2 less than last year) than you are juvenile fiction (54 publishers—8 more than last year) or teen fiction (36 publishers—3 more than last year). These figures indicate that fiction has leveled off or dropped for adults, but is improving for children and teens.

The most popular fiction genres with publishers are (1) Contemporary Fiction, 50 markets (went ahead of Historical Fiction again since last year), (2) Historical Fiction, 49 markets, (3) Adventure Fiction, 37 markets, (4) Biblical Fiction, 33 markets, (5) Mystery, 31 markets, and (6) Historical/Romance, 28 markets. All the numbers above show a decrease in actual markets for each genre, and this is exactly the same order as last year.

Last year the book market for poets increased by one, this year it dropped by three, putting us back to 30. That compares to only 14 in 1993, more than doubling the market in the last five years. Even though the market is improving, many will still want to consider self-publishing (look for subsidy publishers listed in another section of this book), or sell to periodicals. Go to the periodical topical listings in this book to find 246 markets for poetry.

Compared to last year, Prayer and Christian Living have switched places, putting Prayer at the top of the list for the first time. Inspirational has jumped 5 places to 4th place, and marriage has moved up 4 places to #7. Family life has dropped 6 places to #10. It is unusual to see such big steps up or down among the top 10. However, we find the same topics among the top 10, except for Current/Social Issues which dropped out to 12th place, and Marriage which moved back in at 7th place. Among the next 10 topics, the only changes were that Youth Books moved up two places to #20, and How-To Books dropped six places to #21.

In a general comparison to last year, the following topics showed a significant increase or decrease in interest among the publishers. The topics are listed under each heading with those making the greatest change in position at the top. The numbers indicate the number of places that topic moved up or down on the list since last year. An asterisk (*) before a topic indicates that the increase or decrease has continued from last year.

DECREASED IN INTEREST:
*Cult/Occult—down 21
Sociology—down 21
World Issues—down 20
*Divorce—down 16
*Group Study Books—down 14
Senior Adult Issues—down 13
Archaeology—down 12
*Youth Programs—down 12
*Singles Issues—down 11
Counseling Aids—down 10
Fiction: Biblical—down 10
Humor—down 10
Miracles—down 8

Fiction: Adventure—down 7
Fiction: Short Story Collection—down 7
Family Life—down 6
How-To—down 6
Political—down 6
Social Justice—down 6

INCREASED IN INTEREST:
Self-Help—up 19
Recovery—up 17
Fiction: Teen/Young Adult—up 16
Personal Renewal—up 14
Missionary—up 12
Personal Experience—up 12

*Curriculum—up 11
Christian Home-Schooling—up 9
*Booklets—up 8
Christian School Books—up 8
Prophecy—up 9
Ethnic/Cultural—up 8
Reference Books—up 8
Autobiography—up 7
Fiction: Ethnic—up 7
Science—up 7
Cookbooks—up 6
Creation Science—up 6
Games/Crafts—up 6
Stewardship—up 6

Comments:
Referring to the topics showing a decrease for more than one year, there are no significant trends, except that Divorce, Singles Issues, and Youth Programs are on the list for at least the third year in a row (Singles for a fourth year).

We have five topics that were down last year, but up this year: Fiction: Teen/Young Adult, Missionary, Christian School Books, Autobiography, and Cookbooks.

On the increased interest list, Curriculum appears for the second year, and Booklets for the third. Personal topics such as Self-Help, Recovery, Personal Renewal and Personal Experience appear to be growing trends. Teen fiction is continuing its regular pattern of being up one year and down the next.

The only topics that were up last year, but down this year are Sociology and Short Story Collections.

SUMMARY OF INFORMATION ON CHRISTIAN BOOK PUBLISHERS FOUND IN THE ALPHABETICAL LISTINGS

Note: The following numbers are based on the maximum total estimate for each company. For example, if a company gave a range of 5-10, the averages were based on the higher number, 10. This information will be valuable in determining if the contract offered by your publisher is in line with other publishers in some of these areas. For further help, check the section on editorial services to find those who offer contract evaluations, which are most valuable.

TOTAL MANUSCRIPTS RECEIVED:
Two hundred sixteen publishers indicated they received a combined total of over 124,360 manuscripts during the year. That is an average of 576 manuscripts per editor, per year, an increase over last year. That number had dropped the last two years, so it is interesting to note that it has gone up this year. The actual number of manuscripts received ranged from 2 to 10,000 per editor.

NUMBER OF BOOKS PUBLISHED:
Two hundred fifty-three publishers reported that they will publish a combined total of 7,175 titles during the coming year. That is an average of nearly 28 books per publisher (just slightly more per publisher than last year). The actual number per publisher ranges from 1 to 267. Of those who responded to the question this year, 37% will publish more books than last, 38% will publish about the same number, and 25% will publish fewer. If each publisher actually publishes his maximum estimate of books for the year, between 5% & 6% of the manuscripts submitted will be published (up slightly from last year).

AVERAGE FIRST PRINT RUN:
Based on 209 book publishers who indicated their average first print run, the average first printing of a book for a new author is about 6,700 books. That's an increase of more than 13% over last year. Actual print runs ranged from 300 to 250,000 copies.

ROYALTIES:
Of the 151 publishers who reported actual amounts that they paid for royalties, 59 (39%) pay on the retail price; 92 (61%) pay on the wholesale price or net. The average royalty based on the retail price of the book was 7.8% to 11.3% (up from 7.6% to 11% last year). Actual royalties varied from 2% to 15%. The average royalty based on net varied from 6.7% to 13.4%, down from the 10% to 14% last year. (Actual royalties varied from 0% to 50%.) The recommended royalty based on net is 18%, but only 12% of the Christian publishers counted here are paying 18% or higher (that is down 2% from last year).

ADVANCES:
Two hundred one publishers responded to the question about whether or not they paid advances. Of those, 116 paid advances and 85 did not—which means those who do have moved ahead of those who don't in just the last two years. Of those who pay advances, only 24% (49 publishers) gave a specific amount. The average advance for those 49 was $1,455-4,590 (about a 34% increase over last year). This large an increase after an 11% drop last year is encouraging, and an indication that advances are improving in the Christian market. The actual range is still from $100 to $50,000, so ask for the amount that you need or deserve based on past publishing history. Most publishers pay more for established authors or potentially best-selling books. It is not unusual for a first-time author to get no advance or a small one. Once you have one or more books published, feel free to ask for an advance, and raise the amount for each book. Don't be afraid to ask for an advance, even on a first book, if you need the money to support you while you finish the manuscript. Although more publishers are saying they don't give an advance or

are reluctant to name an amount, the truth is many publishers do give advances when warranted but are reluctant to advertise that fact or to divulge an amount.

REPORTING TIME:

Waiting for a response from an editor is often the hardest part of the writing business. Of the 234 editors who indicated how long you should have to wait for a response from them, the average time was just under 10 weeks (about the same as the last two years). However, since the times they actually gave ranged from 1 to 34 weeks, be sure to check the listing for the publisher you are interested in. Give them a 2-week grace period; then feel free to write a polite letter asking about the current status of your manuscript. Give them another month to respond, and if you don't hear anything, you can call as a last resort.

E-MAIL AND WEBSITES:

As expected, the number of publishers with e-mail and Websites has skyrocketed. Of the 286 book editors listed this year, 131 have e-mail addresses (almost twice as many as last year) and 60 (nearly half) will accept e-mail queries; 123 have Websites (more than three times as many as last year). To connect to any of their Websites, visit my Website at http://www.stuartmarket.com.

TOPICAL LISTINGS OF PERIODICALS

As soon as you have an article or story idea, look up that topic in the following topical listings (see Table of Contents for a full list of topics). Study the appropriate periodicals in the primary/alphabetical listings (as well as their writers' guidelines and sample copies), and select those that are most likely targets for the piece you are writing.

Note that most ideas can be written for more than one periodical if you slant them to the needs of different audiences; for example, current events for teens, or pastors, or women. Have a target periodical and audience in mind before you start writing. Each topic is divided by age group/audience, so you can pick appropriate markets for your particular slant.

If the magazine prefers or requires a query letter, be sure to write that letter first, and then follow any guidelines or suggestions they make if they give you a go-ahead.

R—Takes reprints.
(*)—Indicates new topic this year.

BIBLE STUDIES

ADULT/GENERAL
America
Annals of St. Anne
Arlington Catholic
Atlantic Baptist
Banner, The
Baptist Informer
Believer, The—R
Bible Advocate—R
Bible Today
Biblical Reflections—R
Bread of Life—R
Canadian Catholic
Catholic Digest—R
Catholic Rural Life
Catholic Twin Circle—R
Celebrate Life—R
Christian Computing
   (MO)—R
Christian Motorsports
Christian Ranchman
Christian Standard—R
Christianity Today—R
Church Advocate—R
Church Herald/Holiness—R
Compass
Connecting Point—R
Culture Wars—R
Discipleship Journal
Emphasis/Faith & Living—R
Evangelical Baptist—R

Fellowship Link—R
Family Network—R
First Things
Foursquare World—R
God's Revivalist
Good News Journal—R
Grail
Green Cross—R
Hallelujah! (CAN)—R
Head to Head—R
Healing Inn—R
Hearing Hearts
Heartlight Internet—R
Indian Life—R
Inspirer, The—R
Island Christian—R
John Milton—R
Life Gate—R
Liguorian
Lutheran, The—R
Lutheran Digest—R
Lutheran Journal
Lutheran Witness—R
Mennonite, The—R
MESSAGE/Open Bible—R
Messenger/St. Anthony
North American Voice
Our Family—R
Our Sunday Visitor
Perspectives
Plain Truth—R
Pourastan—R
PrayerWorks—R

Presbyterian Outlook
Presbyterian Record—R
Presbyterians Today—R
Preserving Christian
   Homes—R
St. Anthony Messenger
St. Willibrord Journal
Signs of the Times—R
Silver Wings—R
Sojourners
Spiritual Life
Stand Firm—R
Star of Zion
Today's Christian Senior—R
Trumpeter, The
U.S. Catholic
War Cry—R
Watchman, The
Way of St. Francis—R
Weavings—R
Wesleyan Advocate—R

CHILDREN
Discovery (NY)—R
R-A-D-A-R—R

CHRISTIAN EDUCATION/LIBRARY
Children's Ministry
CE Connection—R
Christian School
Church & Synagogue Lib.
Church Educator—R

GROUP
Leader/Church School
   Today—R
Religion Teacher's Journal
Shining Star
Teacher's Interaction

MISSIONS
Missiology
Quiet Hour Echoes
Urban Mission—R

PASTORS/LEADERS
Bibliotheca Sacra
Catholic Servant
Celebration
Emmanuel
Five Stones, The—R
GROUP's Jr. High
Journal/Christian Healing—R
Let's Worship
Liturgy—R
Ministries Today
Preacher's Magazine—R
Priest, The
PROCLAIM—R
Quarterly Review
Single Ad. Ministries Jour.
Today's Christian
   Preacher—R
Vital Issues
Word & World

TEEN/YOUNG ADULT
Alive!
Challenge (GA)
Conqueror—R
Cross Walk
Devo'Zine—R
Insight—R
Student Leadership—R
Teen Life (AG)—R
Teens on Target—R
YOU!—R
Young Adult Today
Young Salvationist—R
Youth Challenge—R
With—R

WOMEN
Adam's Rib—R
Church Woman
Handmaiden, The—R
Joyful Woman—R
Just Between Us—R
Lutheran Woman Today
Proverbs 31 Homemaker—R

Woman's Touch—R

BOOK EXCERPTS

ADULT/GENERAL
AXIOS—R
Bible Advocate—R
Biblical Reflections—R
Canadian Catholic
Catholic Digest—R
Celebrate Life—R
Charisma/Christian Life
Christian Arts Review
Christian Chronicle—R
Christian Edge—R
Christian Motorsports
Christian Reader—R
Comments from the
   Friends—R
Cornerstone—R
Covenant Companion—R
Culture Wars—R
Door, The
Emphasis/Faith & Living—R
Family Network—R
Fellowship Link—R
Hearing Hearts
Home Times—R
Indian Life—R
Jewel Among Jewels—R
Living—R
Mennonite, The—R
MESSAGE/Open Bible—R
Messenger, The (MI)—R
Metro Voice—R
Michigan Christian
New Covenant
New Heart, A—R
Perspectives
Plus—R
Power for Living—R
Presbyterian Outlook
Presbyterian Record—R
Prism—R
Religious Broadcasting—R
SCP Journal—R
Signs of the Times—R
Sojourners
Standard, The—R
Stand Firm—R
Star of Zion
Sursum Corda!—R
TEAK Roundup—R
Together—R
Upscale Magazine
U.S. Catholic
War Cry—R
Watchman, The

Weavings—R

CHRISTIAN
EDUCATION/LIBRARY
CE Connection—R
CE Leadership—R
Christian School

MISSIONS
Areopagus—R
East-West Church
Intl. Journal/Frontier—R
Missiology

PASTORS/LEADERS
Christian Century
Church Bytes—R
Ivy Jungle Report—R
Journal/Christian Healing—R
Ministries Today
Modern Liturgy—R
Networks—R
Preacher, The—R
Single Ad. Ministries Jour.
Voice of the Vineyard —R
Worldwide Challenge
Youthworker—R

TEEN/YOUNG ADULTS
Breakaway—R
Challenge (GA)
Teen Life (AG)—R
Teens on Target—R
YOU!—R
Youth Challenge—R

WOMEN
Conscience—R
Handmaiden, The—R
Horizons—R
Joyful Woman—R
Link & Visitor—R
Woman's Touch—R

WRITERS
Writers Connection—R

BOOK REVIEWS

ADULT/GENERAL
AGAIN—R
Anglican Journal—R
Arkansas Catholic
Arlington Catholic
AXIOS—R
Believer, The—R

Biblical Reflections—R
Burning Light—R
Canadian Catholic
Cathedral Age
Catholic Insight
Catholic Rural Life
Catholic Twin Circle—R
CBA Marketplace
Celebrate Life—R
Charisma/Christian Life
Christian Advocate—R
Christian Arts Review
Christian Century
Christian Chronicle—R
Christian Computing
   (MO)—R
Christian Courier (CAN)—R
Christian Edge—R
Christian Media—R
Christian Motorsports
Christian Ranchman
Christian Renewal—R
Christian Research
Christian Single—R
Christianity/Arts
Christianity Today—R
Christians in Business
Church Advocate—R
Comments /Friends—R
Commonweal
Compass
Connecting Point—R
Cornerstone—R
Cresset
Culture Wars—R
Disciple's Journal—R
Discovery—R
Dovetail—R
Evangelical Baptist—R
Expression Christian
Family Network—R
Fellowship Link—R
First Things
Gadfly—R
Good News Journal
Grail
Green Cross—R
Head to Head—R
Hearing Hearts
Heavenly Thoughts—R
Home Times—R
Impact Magazine—R
Inland NW Christian
Interim—R
Island Christian—R
Jewel Among Jewels—R
Joyful Noise
Life Gate—R

Living Light News—R
Mennonite Historian—R
Methodist History
Michigan Christian
Minnesota Christian—R
MovieGuide
National Catholic
New Creation
New Trumpet—R
No-Debt Living—R
Parent Paper, The
Perspectives
Poetry Forum—R
Poet's Park—R
Pourastan—R
Prairie Messenger—R
Presbyterian Layman
Presbyterian Outlook
Presbyterian Record—R
Presbyterians Today—R
Prism—R
ProLife News—R
Ratio
Religious Education
Sacred Journey—R
SCP Journal—R
Second Stone
Single Connection—R
Smart Dads
Smart Families
Social Justice
Sojourners
Something Better—R
Spiritual Life
Stand Firm—R
Star of Zion
TEAK Roundup—R
Touchstone—R
United Church Observer
Upscale Magazine
Upsouth—R
War Cry—R
Watchman, The
Weavings—R

CHILDREN
Skipping Stones

*CHRISTIAN
EDUCATION/LIBRARY*
Caravan
Christian Librarian—R
Christian Library Jour.—R
Christian School
Church & Synagogue Lib.
Church Libraries—R
Journal/Adventist Educ.—R
Leader/Church School

Today—R
Religion Teacher's Journal
Vision—R

MISSIONS
Areopagus—R
East-West Church
Evangelical Missions—R
Intl. Journal/Frontier—R
Missiology
World Christian—R
World Vision—R

MUSIC
CCM Magazine

PASTORS/LEADERS
Catechumenate
Christian Century
Christian Management—R
Christian Sentinel
Church Bytes—R
Church Growth Network—R
Diocesan Dialogue—R
Enrichment—R
Five Stones, The—R
Ivy Jungle Report—R
Journal/Christian Healing—R
Journal/Pastoral Care
Jour/Amer Soc/Chur
   Growth—R
Lutheran Partners—R
Ministries Today
Networks—R
Preacher, The—R
Preacher's Magazine—R
Resource—R
Sermon Notes
Single Ad. Ministries Jour.
Theology Today (rarely)
Voice of the Vineyard —R
WCA Monthly—R
Word & World
Worship Leader

TEEN/YOUNG ADULT
Challenge (GA)
Christteen—R
Student Leadership—R
Teen Power—R
Young Christian—R
Youth 98

WOMEN
Anna's Journal—R
Conscience—R
Esprit—R

Handmaiden, The—R
Horizons—R
Just Between Us—R
Kansas City Woman
Proverbs 31 Homemaker—R
Tea and Sunshine
Virtuous Woman
Wesleyan Woman
Woman's Touch—R

WRITERS
Advanced Chris. Writer—R
Canadian Writer's Jour—R
Cross & Quill—R
Fellowscript—R
Gotta Write
Inklings
W.I.N. Informer
Writer's Exchange—R
Writer's Ink—R
Southwestern Writers—R
Tickled by Thunder
VA Christian Writer—R
Writers Connection
Writer's Nook News

CANADIAN/FOREIGN MARKETS

ADULT/GENERAL
Anglican Journal
Annals of St. Anne
Atlantic Baptist
BC Catholic
Believer, The
Bread of Life
Canada Lutheran
Canadian Baptist
Canadian Catholic Review
Canadian Mennonite
Catholic Insight
Christian Courier
Companion
Compass
Crossway/Newsline
Dreams & Visions
Evangelical Baptist
Faith Today
Fellowship Link
Fellowship Today
Grail
Hallelujah!
Impact
Indian Life
Insights
Interim
Island Christian Info

Living Light News
Mennonite Brethren Herald
Mennonite Historian
Messenger of the Sacred
   Heart
Messenger of St. Anthony
Our Family
Pentecostal Testimony
Plowman, The
Pourastan
Prairie Messenger
Presbyterian Record
ProLife News
Revelation Post
River, The
Shantyman, The
TEAK Roundup
Time for Rhyme
United Church Observer

CHRISTIAN EDUCATION/LIBRARY
Caravan
Christian Librarian
Reaching Children at Risk

DAILY DEVOTIONALS
Words of Life

MISSIONS
Areopagus

PASTORS/LEADERS
Cell Life FORUM
Technologies for Worship
Resource

WOMEN
Esprit
Link & Visitor

WRITERS
Canadian Writer's Journal
Exchange
Fellowscript
Tickled by Thunder
Writer's Lifeline

CELEBRITY PIECES

ADULT/GENERAL
American Tract Soc.—R
Angels on Earth
Arlington Catholic
AXIOS—R
Canada Lutheran—R

Canadian Catholic
Catholic Digest—R
Catholic Twin Circle—R
CBA Frontline
Celebrate Life—R
Charisma/Christian Life
Christian Advocate—R
Christian Arts Review
Christian Chronicle—R
Christian Edge—R
Christian Motorsports
Christian Ranchman
Christian Reader—R
Columbia
Companion
Cornerstone—R
Disciple's Journal—R
Door, The
Emphasis/Faith & Living—R
E Street—R
Expression Christian
Family Journal—R
Fellowship Link—R
Focus on the Family
Good News (AL)—R
Good News, Etc—R
Good News Journal—R
Gospel Today
Guideposts
Head to Head—R
Hearing Hearts
Heartlight Internet—R
Heavenly Thoughts—R
Home Times—R
Indian Life—R
Inside Journal—R
Insights—R
Life Gate—R
Living—R
Living Light News—R
Living with Teenagers—R
Lutheran Parent
Marriage Partnership
Messenger/St. Anthony
Metro Voice—R
Michigan Christian
Minnesota Christian—R
New Writing—R
Our Sunday Visitor
ParentLife—R
Pentecostal Testimony—R
Plain Truth—R
Plus—R
Power for Living—R
PrayerWorks—R
Presbyterian Record—R
Prism—R
ProLife News—R

Pursuit—R
Religious Broadcasting—R
Revelation Post—R
Signs of the Times—R
Single Connection—R
Sports Spectrum
Standard—R
Standard, The—R
Stand Firm—R
Table Talk—R
Vibrant Life—R
War Cry—R

CHILDREN
Counselor—R
Guideposts for Kids
Live Wire—R
Touch—R

MISSIONS
Save Our World—R
Teachers in Focus—R
Worldwide Challenge

MUSIC
Christian Country—R
Gospel Industry Today

PASTORS/LEADERS
Catholic Servant
Christian Camp—R

TEEN/YOUNG ADULT
Breakaway—R
Brio
Challenge (GA)
Christteen—R
Listen—R
Sharing the VICTORY
    (sports) —R
Spirit
Straight—R
Teen Life (AG)—R
YOU!—R
Young Salvationist—R
Youth 98

WOMEN
Aspire
Ishshah—R
Today's Christian Woman
Virtue—R

WRITERS
Christian Communicator—R
Gotta Write
W.I.N. Informer

CHRISTIAN BUSINESS

ADULT/GENERAL
Angels on Earth
Annals of St. Anne
AXIOS—R
Banner, The
Believer, The—R
Biblical Reflections—R
Canada Lutheran—R
Catholic Sentinel—R
Catholic Twin Circle—R
CBA Marketplace
Christian Advocate—R
Christian Chronicle—R
Christian Courier (CAN)—R
Christian Edge—R
Christian Living—R
Christian News NW—R
Christian Motorsports
Christian Ranchman
Christian Edge—R
Christians in Business
Disciple's Journal—R
Discovery—R
Emphasis/Faith & Living—R
Evangel—R
Evangelical Visitor—R
Expression Christian
Faith Today
Family Network—R
Good News (AL)—R
Good News Journal—R
Gospel Today
Grail
Guideposts
Heartlight Internet—R
Home Times—R
Indian Life—R
Insights—R
Island Christian
John Milton—R
Life Gate—R
Living—R
Lutheran Journal
Mennonite, The—R
MESSAGE
Metro Voice
Michigan Christian
Minnesota Christian—R
New Covenant
Power for Living—R
PrayerWorks—R
Presbyterian Record—R
Preserving Christian
    Homes—R
Prism—R
Religious Broadcasting—R

Single Connection—R
Social Justice
Something Better—R
Standard, The—R
Stand Firm—R
Star of Zion
Today's Christian Senior—R
Together—R
Trumpeter, The
2-Soar—R
United Church Observer

MISSIONS
Worldwide Challenge

PASTORS/LEADERS
Catholic Servant
Christian Management—R
Clergy Journal—R
Preacher, The—R
Preacher's Magazine—R
Today's Christian
    Preacher—R
Today's Parish
Your Church—R

TEEN/YOUNG ADULT
Challenge (GA)
Young Christian—R

WOMEN
Aspire
Ishshah—R
Lutheran Woman Today
Proverbs 31 Homemaker—R

CHRISTIAN EDUCATION

ADULT/GENERAL
America
Anglican Journal—R
Annals of St. Anne
Arkansas Catholic
Arlington Catholic
Atlantic Baptist
AXIOS—R
Banner, The
Baptist Informer
B.C. Catholic—R
Believer, The—R
Bible Advocate—R
Biblical Reflections—R
Canada Lutheran—R
Canadian Baptist
Canadian Catholic
Catholic Digest—R
Catholic Parent

Catholic Sentinel—R
Catholic Twin Circle—R
Christian Advocate—R
Christian C.L. RECORD—R
Christian Courier (CAN)—R
Christian Edge—R
Christian Home & School
Christian Motorsports
Christian Ranchman
Church Advocate—R
Church Herald/Holiness—R
Columbia
Compass
Covenant Companion—R
Culture Wars—R
Disciple's Journal—R
Discovery—R
Emphasis/Faith & Living—R
Evangel—R
Evangelical Baptist—R
Evangelical Visitor—R
Expression Christian
Faith Today
Family Network—R
Focus on the Family
Foursquare World—R
God's Revivalist
Good News (AL)—R
Good News, Etc—R
Gospel Today
Grail
Hearing Hearts
Heartlight Internet—R
Home Times—R
Inland NW Christian
Interchange
Island Christian—R
John Milton—R
Joyful Noise
Life Gate—R
Liguorian
Living Church
Living Light News—R
Living with Teenagers—R
Lutheran Digest—R
Lutheran Journal
Mennonite, The—R
Mennonite Brethren—R
Messenger/St. Anthony
Messenger of the Sacred
    Heart
Metro Voice—R
Michigan Christian
Minnesota Christian—R
New Covenant
North American Voice
NW Christian Journal—R
Our Family—R

Our Sunday Visitor
Perspectives
Plain Truth—R
Pourastan—R
PrayerWorks—R
Presbyterian Layman
Presbyterian Outlook
Presbyterian Record—R
Preserving Christian
    Homes—R
Prism—R
Religious Education
SCP Journal—R
Single Connection—R
Social Justice
Something Better—R
Standard, The—R
Stand Firm—R
Star of Zion
Table Talk—R
Together—R
United Church Observer
U.S. Catholic
Way of St. Francis—R

CHILDREN
Discovery (NY)—R
My Friend
Together Time

*CHRISTIAN
EDUCATION/LIBRARY*
(See alphabetical listings)

MISSIONS
East-West Church
Save Our World—R

PASTORS/LEADERS
Art+Plus
Catholic Servant
Christian Ministry
Church Administration
Church Bytes—R
Clergy Journal—R
Enrichment—R
GROUP's Jr High
Lutheran Partners—R
Ministries Today
Modern Liturgy—R
Networks—R
Preacher's Magazine—R
Pulpit Helps—R
Resource—R
Sabbath School Leadership
Theology Today
Today's Christian

Preacher—R
Today's Parish
Vital Issues
Word & World
Youthworker—R

TEEN/YOUNG ADULT
Challenge (GA)
Christteen—R
Conqueror—R
Cross Walk
YOU!—R
Young Christian—R

WOMEN
Adam's Rib—R
Esprit—R
Handmaiden, The—R
Horizons—R
Ishshah—R
Just Between Us—R
Lutheran Woman Today
Proverbs 31 Homemaker—R

CHRISTIAN LIVING

ADULT/GENERAL
Advent Christian Witness—R
Alive!—R
alive now!
America
American Tract Soc.—R
Angels on Earth
Annals of St. Anne
Arkansas Catholic
Arlington Catholic
At Ease—R
AXIOS—R
Banner, The
B.C. Catholic—R
Believer, The—R
Bible Advocate—R
Bible Advocate Online—R
Biblical Reflections—R
Bread of Life—R
Brethren Evangelist
Canada Lutheran—R
Canadian Baptist
Canadian Catholic
Catholic Digest—R
Catholic New York
Catholic Parent
Catholic Rural Life
Catholic Sentinel—R
Catholic Twin Circle—R
Charisma/Christian Life
Christian Century

Christian Chronicle—R
Christian Courier (WI)—R
Christian Courier (CAN)—R
Christian Edge—R
Christian Home & School
Christian Living—R
Christian Motorsports
Christian Ranchman
Christian Reader—R
Christian Renewal—R
Christian Single—R
Christian Standard—R
Christianity Today—R
Church Advocate—R
Church Herald/Holiness—R
Church of God
    EVANGEL—R
Columbia
Commonweal
Companion
Companions—R
Connecting Point—R
Conquest
Cornerstone—R
Covenant Companion—R
Crossway/Newsline—R
Culture Wars—R
Decision
Disciple's Journal—R
Discipleship Journal
Emphasis/Faith & Living—R
Evangel—R
Evangelical Baptist—R
Evangelical Visitor—R
Family Digest
Family Network—R
Fellowship Link—R
Fellowship Today—R
Focus on the Family
Foursquare World—R
Gem, The—R
God's Revivalist
Good News (AL)—R
Good News(KY)—R
Good News, Etc—R
Gospel Tidings—R
Gospel Today
Grail
Guideposts
Hallelujah! (CAN)—R
Head to Head—R
Healing Inn—R
Hearing Hearts
Heartlight Internet—R
Heavenly Thoughts—R
Highway News—R
Home Times—R
Impact Magazine—R

Indian Life—R
Inland NW Christian
Insights—R
Inspirer, The—R
Interim—R
Island Christian—R
Jewel Among Jewels—R
John Milton—R
Jour/Christian Nursing—R
Life Gate—R
Lifeglow—R
Light and Life
Liguorian
Live—R
Living—R
Living with Teenagers—R
Lookout—R
Lutheran, The—R
Lutheran Digest—R
Lutheran Journal
Lutheran Parent
Marian Helpers—R
Marriage Partnership
Mature Years—R
Mennonite, The—R
Mennonite Brethren—R
MESSAGE
MESSAGE/Open Bible—R
Messenger, The (MI)—R
Messenger/St. Anthony
Messenger of the Sacred
    Heart
Metro Voice—R
Michigan Christian
Montana Catholic—R
Moody—R
New Covenant
New Oxford Review
North American Voice
Northwestern Lutheran—R
Our Family—R
Our Sunday Visitor
ParentLife—R
Pentecostal Evangel—R
Pentecostal Testimony—R
Physician
Plain Truth—R
Plus—R
Poet's Park—R
Pourastan—R
Power for Living—R
PrayerWorks—R
Presbyterian Layman
Presbyterian Record—R
Presbyterians Today—R
Preserving Christian
    Homes—R
Progress—R

Purpose—R
Religious Broadcasting—R
SCP Journal—R
Seek—R
Signs of the Times—R
Single Connection—R
Social Justice
Something Better—R
Spiritual Life
Standard—R
Standard, The—R
Stand Firm—R
Table Talk—R
TEAK Roundup—R
Time of Singing—R
Today's Christian Senior—R
Together—R
United Church Observer
U.S. Catholic
Upsouth—R
Vision, The—R
Voice, The—R
War Cry—R
Way of St. Francis—R
Weavings—R
Wesleyan Advocate—R

CHILDREN
Club Connection—R
CLUBHOUSE—R
Courage
Crusader (TN)
Discovery (NY)—R
GUIDE—R
High Adventure—R
Junior Trails—R
Lad
My Friend
Partners—R
Touch—R
Wonder Time

CHRISTIAN
EDUCATION/LIBRARY
Brigade Leader—R
Children's Ministry
Church & Synagogue Lib.
Church Educator—R
GROUP
Leader/Church School
    Today—R
Religion Teacher's Journal
Resource—R
Shining Star
Teacher's Interaction

MISSIONS
American Horizon—R
Quiet Hour Echoes
Worldwide Challenge

MUSIC
Christian Country—R

PASTORS/LEADERS
Art+Plus
Catholic Servant
Cell Church—R
Cell Life FORUM
Christian Management—R
Emmanuel
Eucharistic Minister—R
GROUP's Jr. High
Journal/Christian Healing—R
Minister's Family
Pastor's Family
Preacher, The—R
Preacher's Illus. Service—R
Preacher's Magazine—R
Pulpit Helps—R
Review for Religious
Today's Christian
     Preacher—R
Vital Issues
Word & World

TEEN/YOUNG ADULT
Alive!
Certainty
Challenge (GA)
Challenge (IL)
Christteen—R
Conqueror—R
Devo'Zine—R
Straight—R
Student Leadership—R
Teen Life (AG)—R
Teen Power—R
Teens on Target—R
Today's Christian Teen—R
With—R
YOU!—R
Young Adult Today
Young & Alive—R
Young Christian—R
Young Salvationist—R
Youth Challenge—R
Youth 98
Youth World—R

WOMEN
Adam's Rib—R
Aspire

CoLaborer—R
DOMESTIQUE—R
Esprit—R
Handmaiden, The—R
Helping Hand—R
Horizons—R
Ishshah—R
Journey—R
Joyful Woman—R
Just Between Us—R
Link & Visitor—R
Lutheran Woman Today
Lutheran Woman's Quar.
Proverbs 31 Homemaker—R
Sisters Today
Tea and Sunshine
Today's Christian Woman
Virtue—R
Wesleyan Woman—R
Woman's Touch—R

CHURCH GROWTH

ADULT/GENERAL
Annals of St. Anne
Banner, The
Believer, The—R
Bible Advocate—R
Canadian Baptist
Charisma/Christian Life
Christian Edge—R
Christian Motorsports
Christian Single—R
Christianity Today—R
Church Advocate—R
Church Herald/Holiness—R
Church of God
     EVANGEL—R
Covenant Companion—R
Culture Wars—R
Disciple's Journal—R
Fellowship Link—R
Good News(KY)—R
Good News, Etc—R
Gospel Tidings—R
Gospel Today
Grail
Hallelujah! (CAN)—R
Inside Journal—R
Insights—R
Interchange
Island Christian—R
John Milton—R
Liguorian
Lutheran Journal—R
Mennonite, The—R
Mennonite Brethren—R
MESSAGE/Open Bible—R

Messenger of the Sacred
     Heart
Michigan Christian
Pentecostal Evangel—R
Plain Truth—R
Presbyterian Layman
Presbyterian Outlook
Presbyterian Record—R
Star of Zion
Together—R
United Church Observer
Upsouth—R
Watchman, The

*CHRISTIAN
EDUCATION/LIBRARY*
CE Leadership—R
Children's Ministry
Church & Synagogue Lib.
GROUP
Leader/Church School
     Today—R
Resource—R

MISSIONS
Evangelical Missions—R
Missiology
P.I.M.E. World

PASTORS/LEADERS
Art+Plus
Catholic Servant
Cell Life FORUM—R
Church Growth Network—R
Creator—R
Emmanuel
Enrichment—R
GROUP's Jr. High
Jour/Amer Soc/Chur
     Growth —R
Five Stones, The—R
Leadership Journal—R
Lutheran Forum—R
Ministries Today
Ministry
Modern Liturgy—R
Preacher, The—R
Preacher's Magazine—R
Pulpit Helps—R
Sermon Notes
Technologies/Worship—R
Theology Today
Today's Christian
     Preacher—R
Vital Issues
Voice of the Vineyard —R
WCA Monthly—R

Worship Leader
Your Church—R

TEEN/YOUNG ADULT
Challenge (GA)
YOU!—R

WOMEN
DOMESTIQUE—R
Horizons—R
Joyful Woman—R
Just Between Us—R
Sisters Today

CHURCH LIFE

ADULT/GENERAL
Annals of St. Anne
Arkansas Catholic
Banner, The
Believer, The—R
Bible Advocate—R
Bread of Life—R
Brethren Evangelist
Canadian Baptist
Catholic Courier
Catholic Digest—R
Christian Edge—R
Christian Living—R
Christian Motorsports
Christian News NW—R
Christian Single—R
Church Herald/Holiness—R
Church of God
    EVANGEL—R
Companion
Conquest
Covenant Companion—R
Decision
Disciple's Journal—R
Discovery—R
Evangel—R
Family Digest
Family Journal—R
Family Network—R
Gem, The—R
Good News(KY)—R
Good News, Etc.—R
Gospel Tidings—R
Gospel Today
Grail
Heavenly Thoughts—R
Insights—R
Island Christian—R
John Milton—R
Living Church
Lookout—R

Lutheran Digest—R
Lutheran Journal—R
Lutheran Parent
Marriage Partnership
Mennonite, The—R
Mennonite Brethren—R
Messenger/St. Anthony
Michigan Christian
Moody—R
New Writing—R
North American Voice
Our Family—R
Pentecostal Testimony—R
Presbyterian Outlook
St. Anthony Messenger
Star of Zion
Today's Christian Senior—R
United Church Observer
Upsouth—R
Watchman, The
Way of St. Francis—R
Weavings—R

*CHRISTIAN
EDUCATION/LIBRARY*
CE Leadership—R
Children's Ministry
Church Educator—R
GROUP

MISSIONS
Quiet Hour Echoes

PASTORS/LEADERS
Catholic Servant
Cell Church—R
Christian Ministry
Church Growth Network—R
Clergy Journal—R
Enrichment—R
Five Stones, The—R
GROUP's Jr. High
Leadership Journal—R
Minister's Family
Ministry
Modern Liturgy—R
Pastor's Family
Preacher's Magazine—R
Pulpit Helps—R
Review for Religious
Sabbath School Leadership
Technologies/Worship—R
Theology Today
Today's Christian
    Preacher—R
Vital Issues
Voice of the Vineyard —R

TEEN/YOUNG ADULT
Challenge (GA)

WOMEN
Esprit—R
Helping Hand—R
Horizons—R
Joyful Woman—R
Wesleyan Woman—R

CHURCH MANAGEMENT

ADULT/GENERAL
AXIOS—R
Banner, The
Believer, The—R
Biblical Reflections—R
Canada Lutheran—R
Canadian Catholic
Christian Computing
    (MO)—R
Christian Edge—R
Christian News NW—R
Church Herald/Holiness—R
Church of God
    EVANGEL—R
Covenant Companion—R
Culture Wars—R
Disciple's Journal—R
Emphasis/Faith & Living—R
Evangelical Baptist—R
Expression Christian
Good News, Etc—R
Gospel Tidings—R
Gospel Today
Grail
Hearing Hearts
Island Christian—R
Joyful Noise
Living Church
Lutheran Digest—R
Lutheran Journal
MESSAGE/Open Bible—R
Metro Voice—R
Michigan Christian
Star of Zion
U.S. Catholic
Our Sunday Visitor
Pentecostal Testimony—R
Presbyterian Layman
Presbyterian Outlook
Wesleyan Advocate—R

*CHRISTIAN
EDUCATION/LIBRARY*
CE Connection—R
CE Counselor—R

CE Leadership—R
Children's Ministry
Church Educator—R
GROUP
Resource—R

PASTORS/LEADERS
Catholic Servant
Celebration
Christian Management—R
Christian Ministry .
Church Bytes—R
Church Growth Network—R
Clergy Journal—R
Enrichment—R
Five Stones, The—R
GROUP's Jr. High
Journal/Pastoral Care
Jour/Amer Soc/Chur
   Growth—R
Leadership Journal—R
Lutheran Forum—R
Lutheran Partners—R
Ministries Today
Ministry
Pastoral Life
Preacher's Magazine—R
Priest, The
Pulpit Helps—R
Resource—R
Technologies/Worship—R
Theology Today
Today's Christian
   Preacher—R
Vital Issues
Voice of the Vineyard —R
WCA Monthly—R
Word & World
Worship Leader
Your Church—R
Youthworker—R

WOMEN
Just Between Us—R

CHURCH OUTREACH

ADULT/GENERAL
Alive!—R
America
Annals of St. Anne
Arkansas Catholic
At Ease—R
AXIOS—R
Banner, The
Baptist Informer
Believer, The—R

Bible Advocate—R
Bread of Life—R
Brethren Evangelist
Canada Lutheran—R
Canadian Baptist
Canadian Catholic
Canadian Mennonite
Cathedral Age
Catholic Digest—R
Catholic Rural Life
Catholic Sentinel—R
Catholic Twin Circle—R
Charisma/Christian Life
Christian Edge—R
Christian Motorsports
Christian Reader—R
Christian Single—R
Church Advocate—R
Church Herald/Holiness—R
Church of God
   EVANGEL—R
Companion
Conquest
Cornerstone—R
Covenant Companion—R
Culture Wars—R
Decision
Disciple's Journal—R
Emphasis/Faith & Living—R
Episcopal Life—R
Evangel—R
Evangelical Baptist—R
Evangelical Visitor—R
Family Network—R
Fellowship Today—R
Gem, The—R
God's Revivalist
Good News(KY)—R
Good News, Etc—R
Gospel Tidings—R
Grail
Heavenly Thoughts—R
Indian Life—R
Insights—R
Inspirer, The—R
Island Christian—R
John Milton—R
Liguorian
Living Church
Lookout—R
Lutheran, The—R
Lutheran Digest—R
Lutheran Journal—R
Mature Years—R
MESSAGE/Open Bible—R
Metro Voice—R
Michigan Christian
Moody—R

New Covenant
New Oxford Review
North American Voice
Northwestern Lutheran—
   R
Our Family—R
Our Sunday Visitor
Pentecostal Evangel—R
Pentecostal Testimony—R
Plain Truth—R
Presbyterian Layman
Presbyterian Outlook
Presbyterian Record—R
Presbyterians Today—R
Prism—R
Purpose—R
Religious Education
Revelation Post—R
St. Joseph's Messenger—R
SCP Journal—R
Seek—R
Single Connection—R
Social Justice
Something Better—R
Standard, The—R
Stand Firm—R
TEAK Roundup—R
2-Soar—R
United Church Observer
U.S. Catholic
Watchman, The
Wesleyan Advocate—R

CHILDREN
Focus/Clubhouse
Kids' Ministry Ideas—R

*CHRISTIAN
EDUCATION/LIBRARY*
Brigade Leader—R
Caravan
CE Connection—R
CE Counselor—R
CE Leadership—R
Children's Ministry
Church Educator—R
GROUP
Insight—R
Journal/Adventist Educ.—R
Perspective—R
Religion Teacher's Journal
Resource—R

MISSIONS
American Horizon—R
Catholic Near East
East-West Church

Urban Mission—R
World Vision—R
Worldwide Challenge

PASTORS/LEADERS
Catholic Servant
Cell Church—R
Cell Life FORUM—R
Christian Management—R
Christian Ministry
Church Administration
Church Growth Network—R
Clergy Journal—R
Enrichment—R
Evangelism USA
Five Stones, The—R
GROUP's Jr. High
Jour/Amer Soc/Chur
   Growth—R
Lutheran Forum—R
Lutheran Partners—R
Ministries Today
Ministry
Modern Liturgy—R
Pastoral Life
Preacher's Magazine—R
Priest, The
Resource—R
Single Ad. Ministries Jour.
Technologies/Worship—R
Theology Today
Today's Christian
   Preacher—R
Today's Parish
Vital Issues
Word & World
Worship Leader
Your Church—R

TEEN/YOUNG ADULT
Challenge (GA)
YOU!—R
Young Adult Today
Young Christian—R

WOMEN
Esprit—R
Horizons—R
Joyful Woman—R
Just Between Us—R
Lutheran Woman Today
Wesleyan Woman

CONTESTS

Alberta Christian Writers
   (Canadian group)

Assn. of Christian Writers
   (UK group)
Blue Mountain Arts (cards)
Butterfly Press (books)
Byline
Cameron Press
Canadian Writer's Jour
CEHUC Spanish Group (CA)
Celebration
Christian Arts Review
Christian Ministry
Christian Reader
Co-Laborer
Columbus Christian Writers
   (OH)
Common Boundary
CWI Florida Conference
Disciple's Journal
Faith Today
Fatted Calf Forum
Fellowscript
FOF Clubhouse
Frontiers in Writing (TX
   conf.)
Greater Philadelphia Chr.
   Writ. (group)
Guideposts
Home Times
Housewife-Writer
Insight (teen)
Inspirational Writers Alive!
   (TX group)
Intl. Black Writers (IL group)
Intl. Network (conf./ID)
Jour/Christian Nursing
Kansas City Chris. Writers
   (KS/MO)
Maine Fellowship (group)
MESSAGE
MN Christian Writers (group)
Modern Liturgy
Moon Maid Press
New Writing
NE Georgia Writers Group
Pacific NW Writers (WA conf.)
Plowman, The
Pockets
Poetry Connection
Poetry Forum
Poets' Paper
Presbyterian Writers
Read 'N Run Books
Silver Wings
Skipping Stones
Smile
S.O.N. Writers (group/VA)
Southwest Writers Wkshp
   (NM)

State of Maine Conference
TEAK Roundup
Tickled by Thunder
Time of Singing
Today's Christian Teen
2-Soar
United Church Observer
   (seldom)
With (for teens)
Writer's Digest—R
Writer's Exchange
Writer's Ink
Writers' Intl. Forum
Writers' Intl. Forum/Young
Writer's Journal
Writing World
Young Christian
Young Salvationist

CONTROVERSIAL ISSUES

ADULT/GENERAL
American Tract Soc.—R
At Ease—R
AXIOS—R
Believer, The—R
Bible Advocate—R
Bible Advocate Online—R
Biblical Reflections—R
Canada Lutheran—R
Canadian Baptist
Canadian Catholic
Catholic Insight
Catholic Rural Life
Celebrate Life—R
Charisma/Christian Life
Christian Advocate—R
Christian Arts Review
Christian Century
Christian Chronicle—R
Christian Courier (CAN)—R
Christian Living—R
Christian Media—R
Christian Motorsports
Christian Reader—R
Christian Research
Christian Single—R
Christian Social Action—R
Christianity Today—R
Church Advocate—R
Church of God
   EVANGEL—R
Comments/Friends—R
Commonweal
Compass
Cornerstone—R
Covenant Companion—R
Cresset

Culture Wars—R
Disciple's Journal—R
Door, The
Episcopal Life—R
Evangel—R
Evangelical Baptist—R
Expression Christian
Faith Today
Family Network—R
Fatted Calf Forum—R
Gadfly—R
Gem, The—R
Good News(KY)—R
Good News, Etc—R
Good News Journal—R
Grail
Hallelujah! (CAN)—R
Head to Head—R
Healing Inn—R
Hearing Hearts
Highway News—R
Home Times—R
Indian Life—R
Insights—R
Island Christian—R
John Milton—R
Jour/Christian Nursing—R
Joyful Noise
Light and Life
Living—R
Living Church
Living with Teenagers—R
Lutheran, The—R
Lutheran Parent
Lutheran Witness—R
MESSAGE (limited)
Messenger/St. Anthony
Metro Voice—R
Michigan Christian
Minnesota Christian—R
Moody—R
MovieGuide
New Oxford Review
Newsline—R
New Trumpet—R
New Writing—R
Our Family—R
Perspectives
Prairie Messenger—R
Presbyterian Layman
Presbyterian Outlook
Presbyterian Record—R
Presbyterians Today—R
Preserving Christian
    Homes—R
Prism—R
ProLife News—R
Religious Education

Religious Broadcasting—R
St. Anthony Messenger
SCP Journal—R
Second Stone
Seek—R
Single Connection—R
Social Justice
Something Better—R
Standard, The—R
Stand Firm—R
Table Talk—R
TEAK Roundup—R
United Church Observer
Upsouth—R
U.S. Catholic
War Cry—R
Watchman, The
Way of St. Francis—R
Wesleyan Advocate—R

CHILDREN
Writers' Intl. Forum/Young

*CHRISTIAN
EDUCATION/LIBRARY*
Children's Ministry
CE Connection—R
CE Counselor—R
Church Educator—R
GROUP
Today's Catholic Teacher—R

MISSIONS
American Horizon—R
Save Our World—R
Worldwide Challenge

PASTORS/LEADERS
Art+Plus
Christian Century
Christian Sentinel
Cross Currents—R
GROUP's Jr. High
Lutheran Forum—R
Lutheran Partners—R
Ministries Today
Modern Liturgy—R
Networks—R
Preacher, The—R
Single Ad. Ministries Jour.
Vital Issues
Word & World
Youthworker—R

TEEN/YOUNG ADULT
Alive! (maybe)
Brio

Challenge (GA)
Christteen—R
Conqueror—R
Student Leadership—R
Teen Life (AG)—R
YOU!—R
Young Adult Today
Young Christian—R
Young Salvationist—R

WOMEN
Aspire
Conscience—R
Handmaiden, The—R
Horizons—R
Ishshah—R
Virtue—R

WRITERS
Christian Response—R
Writers' Intl. Forum

CREATION SCIENCE

ADULT/GENERAL
Banner, The
Bible Advocate—R
Christian Advocate—R
Christian Chronicle—R
Companions—R
Conquest
Cornerstone—R
Chrysalis Reader
Creation Spirituality
Faith Today
Fatted Calf Forum—R
Gospel Today
Hallelujah! (CAN)—R
Live—R
Living—R
MovieGuide
Pentecostal Evangel—R
Plain Truth—R
PrayerWorks—R
Something Better—R
Upsouth—R
War Cry—R

CHILDREN
Courage
Nature Friend—R
Partners—R
Primary Pal (IL)
R-A-D-A-R—R

CHRISTIAN
EDUCATION/LIBRARY
Journal/Adventist Educ.—R

PASTORS/LEADERS
Pulpit Helps—R

TEEN/YOUNG ADULT
Certainty
Challenge (IL)
Straight—R
Teen Life (AG)—R
Teens on Target—R
Youth Challenge—R

CULTS/OCCULT

ADULT/GENERAL
America
American Tract Soc.—R
AXIOS—R
Banner, The
Bible Advocate—R
Bible Advocate Online—R
Biblical Reflections—R
Canada Lutheran—R
Catholic Twin Circle—R
CBA Marketplace
Charisma/Christian Life
Christian Advocate—R
Christian Chronicle—R
Christian Edge—R
Christian Ranchman
Christian Research
Christian Single—R
Church Advocate—R
Church of God
    EVANGEL—R
Comments from the
    Friends—R
Conquest
Cornerstone—R
Culture Wars—R
Disciple's Journal—R
Evangelical Baptist—R
God's Revivalist
Good News, Etc—R
Good News Journal—R
Grail
Healing Inn—R
Heavenly Thoughts—R
Indian Life—R
Insights—R
Jour/Christian Nursing—R
Liguorian
Live—R
Living with Teenagers—R

Lutheran Digest—R
Lutheran Parent
MESSAGE/Open Bible—R
Metro Voice—R
Michigan Christian
Minnesota Christian—R
New Heart, A—R
New Oxford Review
New Trumpet—R
New Writing—R
Our Sunday Visitor
Plain Truth—R
SCP Journal—R
Social Justice
Something Better—R
Table Talk—R
United Church Observer
Watchman, The

CHILDREN
High Adventure—R

CHRISTIAN
EDUCATION/LIBRARY
Children's Ministry
GROUP
Team—R

MISSIONS
American Horizon—R
Areopagus—R
East-West Church
World Christian—R

PASTORS/LEADERS
Christian Sentinel
GROUP's Jr. High
Journal/Christian Healing—R
Journal/Pastoral Care
Ministries Today
Preacher, The—R
Today's Christian
    Preacher—R
Vital Issues
Word & World

TEEN/YOUNG ADULT
Brio
Certainty
Challenge (GA)
Christteen—R
Straight—R
Teenage Christian—R
Teen Life (AG)—R
Teens on Target—R
YOU!—R
Young Adult Today

Young Christian—R
Youth Challenge—R
Youth Update

WOMEN
Ishshah—R

CURRENT/SOCIAL ISSUES

ADULT/GENERAL
AGAIN—R
Alive!—R
alive now!
America
American Tract Soc.—R
Anglican Journal—R
Arlington Catholic
Atlantic Baptist
AXIOS—R
Banner, The
Baptist Informer
B.C. Catholic—R
Believer, The—R
Bible Advocate—R
Bible Advocate Online—R
Biblical Reflections—R
Brethren Evangelist
Canada Lutheran—R
Canadian Baptist
Canadian Catholic
Canadian Mennonite
Catholic Courier
Catholic Digest—R
Catholic Insight
Catholic New York
Catholic Rural Life
Catholic Sentinel—R
Catholic Twin Circle—R
CBA Marketplace
Celebrate Life—R
Charisma/Christian Life
Christian Advocate—R
Christian American
Christian Arts Review
Christian Chronicle—R
Christian Courier (WI)—R
Christian Courier (CAN)—R
Christian Crusade
Christian Edge—R
Christian Home & School
Christian Living—R
Christian Motorsports
Christian News NW—R
Christian Ranchman
Christian Reader—R
Christian Renewal—R
Christian Single—R
Christian Social Action—R

Christian Standard—R
Christianity Today—R
Church Advocate—R
Church & State—R
Church of God
    EVANGEL—R
Columbia
Commonweal
Compass
Cornerstone—R
Covenant Companion—R
Cresset
Chrysalis Reader
Culture Wars—R
Disciple's Journal—R
Door, The
Dovetail—R
Emphasis/Faith & Living—R
Episcopal Life—R
Evangel—R
Evangelical Baptist—R
Evangelical Visitor—R
Faith Today
Fellowship Link—R
Fellowship Today—R
First Things
Focus on the Family
Foursquare World—R
Gadfly—R
Gem, The—R
Good News(KY)—R
Good News, Etc—R
Good News Journal—R
Gospel Tidings—R
Grail
Hallelujah! (CAN)—R
Head to Head—R
Healing Inn—R
Hearing Hearts
Heartlight Internet—R
Heavenly Thoughts—R
Highway News—R
Home Times—R
Impact Magazine—R
Indian Life—R
Inland NW Christian
Insights—R
Interim—R
Island Christian—R
Jewel Among Jewels—R
John Milton—R
Jour/Christian Nursing—R
Journal of Church & State
Liberty—R
Life Gate—R
Light and Life
Liguorian
Live—R

Living—R
Living Church
Living with Teenagers—R
Lookout—R
Lutheran, The—R
Lutheran Journal
Lutheran Parent
Marian Helpers Bulletin
Marriage Partnership
Mature Living
Mennonite Brethren—R
MESSAGE
MESSAGE/Open Bible—R
Messenger, The (MI)—R
Messenger/St. Anthony
Metro Voice—R
Michigan Christian
Minnesota Christian—R
Moody—R
New Covenant
New Heart, A—R
New Oxford Review
New Trumpet—R
North American Voice
New Writing—R
Our Family—R
Our Sunday Visitor
Pentecostal Evangel—R
Pentecostal Testimony—R
Perspectives
Plain Truth—R
PrayerWorks—R
Presbyterian Layman
Presbyterian Outlook
Presbyterian Record—R
Presbyterians Today—R
Prism—R
ProLife News—R
Purpose—R
Quiet Revolution—R
Religious Broadcasting—R
Religious Education
St. Joseph's Messenger—R
SCP Journal—R
Seek—R
Signs of the Times—R
Single Connection—R
Social Justice
Sojourners
Something Better—R
Standard—R
Stand Firm—R
TEAK Roundup—R
Touchstone—R
Together—R
2-Soar—R
United Church Observer
Upsouth—R

War Cry—R
Watchman, The
Way of St. Francis—R
Wesleyan Advocate—R

CHILDREN
Club Connection—R
Discovery(NY)—R
God's World Today
High Adventure—R
On the Line—R
Skipping Stones
Writers' Intl. Forum/Young

*CHRISTIAN
EDUCATION/LIBRARY*
Catechist
Children's Ministry
CE Connection—R
CE Counselor—R
CE Leadership—R
Church Educator—R
GROUP
Team—R
Today's Catholic Teacher—R
Vision—R

MISSIONS
American Horizon—R
Areopagus—R
East-West Church
New World Outlook
Urban Mission—R
World Christian—R
World Vision—R
Worldwide Challenge

MUSIC
CCM Magazine

PASTORS/LEADERS
Art+Plus
Catholic Servant
Christian Century
Cross Currents—R
GROUP's Jr. High
Ivy Jungle Report—R
Journal/Pastoral Care
Liturgy
Lutheran Forum—R
Lutheran Partners—R
Ministries Today
Pastoral Life
Quarterly Review
Resource—R
Single Ad. Ministries Jour.
Vital Issues

Word & World
Youthworker—R

TEEN/YOUNG ADULT
Alive!
Brio
Challenge (GA)
Christteen—R
Conqueror—R
Devo'Zine—R
Insight—R
Listen—R
Straight—R
Student Leadership—R
Teenage Christian—R
Teen Life (AG)—R
Teen Power—R
Teens on Target—R
Today's Christian Teen—R
YOU!—R
Young Adult Today
Young Christian—R
Young Salvationist—R
Youth Challenge—R
Youth 98
Youth Update

WOMEN
Aspire
Conscience—R
DOMESTIQUE—R
Esprit—R
Handmaiden, The—R
Horizons—R
Ishshah—R
Jour/Women's Ministries
Journey—R
Lutheran Woman Today
Sisters Today
Today's Christian Woman
Virtue—R
Wesleyan Woman
Woman's Touch—R

WRITERS
Writers' Intl. Forum

DEATH/DYING

ADULT/GENERAL
Alive!—R
Arlington Catholic
Banner, The
Bible Advocate—R
Bible Advocate Online—R
Bread of Life—R
Catholic Courier

Catholic Digest—R
Christian Advocate—R
Christian Living—R
Christian Single—R
Christianity Today—R
Church of God
    EVANGEL—R
Columbia
Cornerstone—R
Covenant Companion—R
Family Digest
Family Network—R
Fellowship Link—R
Grail
Guideposts
Heartlight Internet—R
Heavenly Thoughts—R
Home Times—R
Insights—R
John Milton—R
Jour/Christian Nursing—R
Live—R
Lutheran Journal—R
Lutheran Parent
Mennonite, The—R
MESSAGE
Messenger, The (MI)—R
Messenger/St. Anthony
Messenger of the Sacred
    Heart
Michigan Christian
New Writing—R
Pentecostal Evangel
Physician
Plain Truth—R
Presbyterian Outlook
Prism—R
ProLife News—R
Remembrance—R
Sacred Journey—R
St. Anthony Messenger
Social Justice
Something Better—R
Star of Zion
Table Talk—R
Today's Christian Senior—R
United Church Observer
Upsouth—R
Way of St. Francis—R

CHILDREN
Skipping Stones

*CHRISTIAN
EDUCATION/LIBRARY*
Church Educator—R
Leader/Church School
    Today—R

PASTORS/LEADERS
Catholic Servant
Celebration
Journal/Pastoral Care
Lutheran Partners—R
Pastoral Life
Preacher's Magazine—R
Today's Christian
    Preacher—R

TEEN/YOUNG ADULT
Challenge (GA)
Devo'Zine—R
Straight—R
Teen Life (AG)—R
Today's Christian Teen—R
With—R

WOMEN
Aspire
Esprit—R
Handmaiden, The—R
Horizons—R

DEVOTIONALS/
MEDITATIONS

ADULT/GENERAL
alive now!
Arlington Catholic
At Ease—R
Banner, The
Baptist Informer
Believer, The—R
Bread of Life—R
Broken Streets
Canadian Baptist
Canadian Catholic
Catholic Rural Life
Catholic Twin Circle—R
Celebrate Life—R
Charisma/Christian Life
Christian Century
Christian Motorsports
Christian Renewal—R
Christianity Today—R
Church Advocate—R
Church Herald/Holiness—R
Church of God
    EVANGEL—R
Companion
Companions—R
Conquest (meditations)
Covenant Companion—R
Emphasis/Faith & Living—R
Evangel—R
Evangelical Baptist—R

Family Digest
Family Network—R
Fellowship Link—R
Fellowship Today—R
Foursquare World—R
Gem, The—R
God's Revivalist
Good News(KY)—R
Good News Journal—R
Green Cross—R
Head to Head—R
Healing Inn—R
Hearing Hearts
Heartlight Internet—R
Heavenly Thoughts—R
Highway News—R
Ideals—R
Indian Life—R
Insights—R
Inspirer, The—R
Island Christian—R
Jewel Among Jewels—R
John Milton—R
Keys to Living
Life Gate—R
Lifeglow—R
Light and Life
Liguorian
Living—R
Living Church
Lutheran Journal—R
Lutheran Parent
Lutheran Parent's Wellspring
Lutheran Witness—R
Mature Years—R
Mennonite Brethren—R
MESSAGE/Open Bible—R
Messenger/Sacred Heart
Messenger/St. Anthony
Metro Voice—R
Montana Catholic—R
New Covenant
New Heart, A—R
New Trumpet—R
North American Voice
Our Sunday Visitor
Perspectives
Plain Truth—R
Plowman, The—R
Pourastan—R
PrayerWorks—R
Presbyterian Outlook
Presbyterian Record—R
Presbyterians Today—R
Preserving Christian
    Homes—R
Prism—R
Progress—R (meditations)

Revelation Post—R
Sacred Journey—R
St. Anthony Messenger
Seek—R
Silver Wings—R
Single Connection—R
Smile—R
Sojourners
Standard—R
Stand Firm—R
Star of Zion
TEAK Roundup—R
Today's Christian Senior—R
Together—R
Upsouth—R
U.S. Catholic
War Cry—R
Way of St. Francis—R
Weavings—R

CHILDREN
Club Connection—R
Courage
Discovery (NY)—R
High Adventure—R
Keys for Kids—R
Partners—R
Pockets—R
Power & Light—R
Primary Pal (IL)
Touch—R

*CHRISTIAN
EDUCATION/LIBRARY*
Children's Ministry
Church & Synagogue Lib.
Church Educator—R
Church Worship
GROUP
Leader/Church School
    Today—R
Religion Teacher's Journal
Shining Star
Teacher's Interaction
Today's Catholic Teacher—R

DAILY DEVOTIONAL
(See alphabetical list)

MISSIONS
Areopagus—R
Quiet Hour Echoes
Save Our World—R

PASTORS/LEADERS
Art+Plus
Catholic Servant

Christian Century
Clergy Journal—R
Emmanuel
GROUP's Jr. High
Journal/Christian Healing—R
Minister's Family
Priest, The
Pulpit Helps—R
Today's Christian
    Preacher—R
Vital Issues
Voice of the Vineyard —R

TEEN/YOUNG ADULT
Alive!
Breakaway—R
Brio
Certainty
Challenge (GA)
Challenge (IL)
Conqueror—R
Cross Walk
Devo'Zine—R
Take Five
Teens on Target—R
Today's Christian Teen—R
With—R
YOU!—R
Young Adult Today
Young Christian—R
Young Salvationist—R
Youth Challenge—R

WOMEN
Adam's Rib—R
DOMESTIQUE—R
Esprit—R
Handmaiden, The—R
Helping Hand—R
Horizons—R
Jour/Women's Ministries
Joyful Woman—R
Just Between Us—R
Lutheran Woman Today
Proverbs 31 Homemaker—R
Tea and Sunshine
Woman's Touch—R

WRITERS
Cross & Quill—R
Fellowscript—R

DISCIPLESHIP

ADULT/GENERAL
Advent Christian Witness—R
American Tract Soc.—R

At Ease—R
Arlington Catholic
Atlantic Baptist
Banner, The
Bible Advocate—R
Bread of Life—R
Brethren Evangelist
Canada Lutheran—R
Canadian Baptist
Canadian Catholic
Catholic Digest—R
Charisma/Christian Life
Christian Century
Christian Living—R
Christian Motorsports
Christian Parenting—R
Christian Ranchman
Christian Reader—R
Christian Single—R
Christianity Today—R
Church Advocate—R
Church Herald/Holiness—R
Church of God
    EVANGEL—R
Companion
Companions—R
Conquest
Cornerstone—R
Covenant Companion—R
Cresset
Decision
Discipleship Journal
Disciple's Journal—R
Emphasis/Faith & Living—R
Evangel—R
Evangelical Baptist—R
Family Network—R
Focus on the Family
Gem, The—R
Good News(KY)—R
Good News, Etc—R
Gospel Tidings—R
Green Cross—R
Hallelujah! (CAN)—R
Head to Head—R
Healing Inn—R
Hearing Hearts
Heartlight Internet—R
Heavenly Thoughts—R
Highway News—R
Inland NW Christian
Insights—R
Inspirer, The—R
Island Christian—R
John Milton—R
Life Gate—R
Light and Life
Liguorian

Live—R
Living with Teenagers—R
Lookout—R
Lutheran Digest—R
Lutheran Journal—R
Lutheran Parent
Mature Years—R
Mennonite, The—R
Mennonite Brethren—R
MESSAGE/Open Bible—R
Metro Voice—R
Michigan Christian
Montana Catholic—R
Moody—R
New Covenant
New Oxford Review
North American Voice
Our Family—R
Pentecostal Evangel—R
Pentecostal Testimony—R
Plain Truth—R
PrayerWorks—R
Presbyterian Layman
Presbyterian Outlook
Prism—R
Purpose—R
Religious Education
St. Joseph's Messenger—R
Seek—R
Silver Wings—R
Sojourners
Standard—R
Standard, The—R
Stand Firm—R
Upsouth—R
U.S. Catholic
Vision, The—R
War Cry—R
Watchman, The
Way of St. Francis—R
Wesleyan Advocate—R

CHILDREN
BREAD/God's Children—R
Club Connection—R
Courage
Evangelizing Today's
    Child—R

CHRISTIAN
EDUCATION/LIBRARY
Brigade Leader—R
Caravan
CE Connection—R
CE Counselor—R
CE Leadership—R
Children's Ministry
Christian School

Church Educator—R
Evangelizing Today's
    Child—R
GROUP
Leader/Church School
    Today—R
Teacher's Interaction
Team—R

MISSIONS
American Horizon—R
Urban Mission—R
Worldwide Challenge

PASTORS/LEADERS
Art+Plus
Catholic Servant
Cell Church—R
Cell Life FORUM—R
Christian Camp—R
Christian Century
Christian Management—R
Emmanuel
Enrichment—R
GROUP's Jr. High
Ivy Jungle Report—R
Journal/Christian Healing—R
Jour/Amer Soc/Chur
    Growth—R
Lutheran Forum—R
Lutheran Partners—R
Ministries Today
Ministry
Modern Liturgy—R
Preacher, The—R
Preacher's Magazine—R
PROCLAIM—R
Pulpit Helps—R
Review for Religious
Today's Christian
    Preacher—R
Vital Issues
Word & World
Youthworker—R

TEEN/YOUNG ADULT
Alive!
Certainty
Challenge (GA)
Challenge (IL)
Conqueror—R
Straight—R
Student Leadership—R
Teenage Christian—R
Teen Life (AG)—R
Teen Power—R
Teens on Target—R

Today's Christian Teen—R
With—R
YOU!—R
Young Salvationist—R
Youth Challenge—R

WOMEN
Adam's Rib—R
CoLaborer—R
Esprit—R
Handmaiden, The—R
Helping Hand—R
Horizons—R
Ishshah—R
Journey—R
Joyful Woman—R
Just Between Us—R
Link & Visitor—R
Sisters Today
Today's Christian Woman
Virtue—R
Virtuous Woman
Wesleyan Woman—R
Woman's Touch—R

DIVORCE

ADULT/GENERAL
America
Angels on Earth
Arlington Catholic
At Ease—R
Banner, The
Believer, The—R
Bible Advocate—R
Bible Advocate Online—R
Canada Lutheran—R
Canadian Baptist
Catholic Digest—R
Catholic Twin Circle—R
Charisma/Christian Life
Christian Advocate—R
Christian Chronicle—R
Christian Edge—R
Christian Home & School
Christian Living—R
Christian Motorsports
Christian Parenting—R
Christian Ranchman
Christian Single—R
Church Advocate—R
Church of God EVANGEL—R
Cornerstone—R
Culture Wars—R
Disciple's Journal—R
Evangelical Baptist—R
Expression Christian
Faith Today

Focus on the Family
Good News, Etc—R
Good News Journal—R
Guideposts
Highway News—R
Home Times—R
Impact Magazine—R
Insights—R
Island Christian—R
John Milton—R
Life Gate—R
Liguorian
Living—R
Lutheran Digest—R
Lutheran Journal
Lutheran Parent
MESSAGE
MESSAGE/Open Bible—R
Metro Voice—R
Michigan Christian
Minnesota Christian—R
New Covenant
New Heart, A—R
New Trumpet—R
New Writing—R
Our Family—R
Physician
Plain Truth—R
PrayerWorks—R
Presbyterian Outlook
Presbyterian Record—R
Presbyterians Today—R
Preserving Christian
    Homes—R
Prism—R
Purpose—R
Seek—R
Signs of the Times—R
Single Connection—R
Single-Parent Family
Social Justice
Standard—R
Standard, The—R
Stand Firm—R
Star of Zion
Table Talk—R
2-Soar—R
United Church Observer
Upsouth—R
U.S. Catholic
War Cry—R

CHILDREN
Touch—R

CHRISTIAN
EDUCATION/LIBRARY
Leader/Church School

Today—R

MISSIONS
Worldwide Challenge

PASTORS/LEADERS
Art+Plus
Journal/Pastoral Care
Lutheran Partners—R
Ministries Today
Ministry
Pastoral Life
Pastor's Family
PROCLAIM—R
Pulpit Helps—R
Single Ad. Ministries Jour.
Word & World

TEEN/YOUNG ADULT
Challenge (GA)
Straight—R
Teenage Christian—R
With—R
Young Adult Today
Young Christian—R
Youth 98
Youth Update

WOMEN
Aspire
Esprit—R
Handmaiden, The—R
Horizons—R
Ishshah—R
Journey—R
Lutheran Woman Today
Virtuous Woman
Woman's Touch—R

DOCTRINAL

ADULT/GENERAL
America
Anglican Journal—R
At Ease—R
Banner, The
Baptist Informer
B.C. Catholic—R
Bible Advocate—R
Biblical Reflections—R
Bread of Life—R
Canadian Baptist
Canadian Catholic
Catholic Digest—R
Catholic Insight
Charisma/Christian Life
Christian Century

Christian Media—R
Christian Motorsports
Christian Renewal—R
Christianity Today—R
Church of God
   EVANGEL—R
Comments/Friends—R
Companions—R
Compass
Conquest
Cornerstone—R
Cresset
Culture Wars—R
Emphasis/Faith & Living—R
Evangelical Baptist—R
Evangelical Visitor—R
Fellowship Link—R
Gospel Today
Hallelujah! (CAN)—R
Hearing Hearts
Indian Life—R
Insights—R
Interim—R
John Milton—R
Lutheran Parent
Lutheran Witness—R
MESSAGE
Metro Voice—R
New Writing—R
North American Voice
Our Family—R
Our Sunday Visitor
Perspectives
Plain Truth—R
PrayerWorks—R
Presbyterian Layman
Presbyterian Outlook
Presbyterian Record—R
Presbyterians Today—R
Queen of All Hearts
St. Willibrord Journal
SCP Journal—R
Signs of the Times—R
Silver Wings—R
Social Justice
Standard, The—R
Star of Zion
This Rock
United Church Observer
U.S. Catholic
Upsouth—R
Watchman, The

CHILDREN
R-A-D-A-R—R

CHRISTIAN
EDUCATION/LIBRARY
Catechist
CE Counselor—R
Teacher's Interaction

MISSION
Intl Jour/Frontier—R
Quiet Hour Echoes
Urban Mission—R
Worldwide Challenge

PASTORS/LEADERS
Bibliotheca Sacra
Catholic Servant
Christian Century
Emmanuel
Enrichment—R
Jour/Amer Soc/Chur
   Growth—R
Lutheran Partners—R
Ministries Today
Ministry
Preacher, The—R
Preacher's Magazine—R
Priest, The
PROCLAIM—R
Pulpit Helps—R
Quarterly Review
Theology Today
Today's Christian
   Preacher—R
Word & World

TEEN/YOUNG ADULT
Certainty
Challenge (GA)
Teenage Christian—R
YOU!—R
Young Adult Today
Youth Update

WOMEN
Handmaiden, The—R
Ishshah—R
Lutheran Woman Today

ECONOMICS

ADULT/GENERAL
America
AXIOS—R
Banner, The
Believer, The—R
Biblical Reflections—R
Canadian Catholic
Catholic Digest—R

Catholic Rural Life
Catholic Twin Circle—R
CBA Marketplace
Christian C.L. RECORD—R
Christian Century
Christian Courier (CAN)—R
Christian Motorsports
Christian Ranchman
Christian Social Action—R
Christianity Today—R
Christians in Business
Compass
Covenant Companion—R
Cresset
Culture Wars—R
Disciple's Journal—R
Discovery—R
Faith Today
Family Network—R
First Things
Good News, Etc—R
Good News Journal—R
Home Times—R
Insights—R
Island Christian—R
Life Gate—R
Lutheran Parent
Messenger, The (MI)—R
Metro Voice—R
Michigan Christian
Minnesota Christian—R
MovieGuide
No-Debt Living—R
Our Sunday Visitor
Perspectives
Prairie Messenger—R
Presbyterian Layman
Preserving Christian
   Homes—R
Prism—R
Quiet Revolution—R
SCP Journal—R
Single Connection—R
Single-Parent Family
Social Justice
Sojourners
Something Better—R
Standard, The—R
Stand Firm—R
Table Talk—R
Today's Christian Senior—R
2-Soar—R
U.S. Catholic

MISSIONS
Urban Mission—R
World Vision—R

PASTORS/LEADERS
Christian Century
Lutheran Partners—R
Technologies/Worship—R
Today's Christian
    Preacher—R
Today's Parish
Word & World
Your Church—R

TEEN/YOUNG ADULT
Challenge (GA)
Christteen—R
Young Adult Today
Youth Update

WOMEN
Esprit—R

WRITERS
Writer's Nook News

ENVIRONMENTAL ISSUES

ADULT/GENERAL
Anglican Journal—R
AXIOS—R
Banner, The
Bible Advocate—R
Bible Advocate Online—R
Biblical Reflections—R
Brethren Evangelist
Canada Lutheran—R
Canadian Catholic
Catholic Digest—R
Catholic Forester—R
Catholic Rural Life
Catholic Sentinel—R
Celebrate Life—R
Christian Century
Christian Courier (CAN)—R
Christian Living—R
Christian Motorsports
Christian Single—R
Christian Social Action—R
Christianity Today—R
Chrysalis Reader
Church of God
    EVANGEL—R
Commonweal
Companion
Compass
Covenant Companion—R
Cresset
Disciple's Journal—R
Emphasis/Faith & Living—R
Faith Today

Fellowship Link—R
Good News Journal—R
Grail
Green Cross—R
Heavenly Thoughts—R
Home Times—R
Insights—R
John Milton—R
Keys to Living
Liguorian
Lutheran, The—R
Lutheran Digest—R
Lutheran Parent
Mennonite, The—R
Messenger/St. Anthony
Metro Voice—R
Michigan Christian
Minnesota Christian—R
NW Christian Journal—R
Our Family—R
Our Sunday Visitor
Pegasus Review—R
Pentecostal Testimony—R
Perspectives
Plain Truth—R
PrayerWorks—R
Presbyterian Layman
Presbyterian Outlook
Presbyterian Record—R
Presbyterians Today—R
Prism—R
Purpose—R
SCP Journal—R
Signs of the Times—R
Sojourners
Something Better—R
Standard, The—R
Star of Zion
Table Talk—R
TEAK Roundup—R
Time of Singing—R
Total Health
United Church Observer
Upsouth—R
War Cry—R
Way of St. Francis—R

CHILDREN
Discovery (NY)—R
Focus/Clubhouse
Live Wire—R
My Friend
On the Line—R
Pockets—R
R-A-D-A-R—R
Skipping Stones

CHRISTIAN
EDUCATION/LIBRARY
Christian School

MISSIONS
World Vision—R

PASTORS/LEADERS
Christian Camp—R
Christian Century
Christian Ministry
Cross Currents—R
Lutheran Partners—R
Pulpit Helps—R
Word & World
World Vision—R

TEEN/YOUNG ADULT
Challenge (GA)
Devo'Zine—R
Listen—R
Student Leadership—R
Teen Life (AG)—R
Teen Power—R
With—R
YOU!—R
Young Adult Today
Young Christian—R
Youth 98
Youth Update

WOMEN
Aspire
Esprit—R
Horizons—R
Sisters Today

ESSAYS

ADULT/GENERAL
alive now!
Arlington Catholic
AXIOS—R
Banner, The
Biblical Reflections—R
Burning Light—R
Catholic Answer
Catholic Insight
Catholic Parent
Catholic Twin Circle
Christian Arts Review
Christian Century
Christian Motorsports
Christian Traveler—R
Christianity/Arts
Chrysalis Reader
Church & State—R

Church of God
   EVANGEL—R
Commonweal
Compass
Covenant Companion—R
Cresset
Chrysalis Reader
Culture Wars—R
Discipleship Journal
Door, The—R
Emphasis/Faith & Living—R
E Street—R
Evangelical Visitor—R
Family Journal—R
Fatted Calf Forum—R
First Things
Good News (AL)—R
Grail
Green Cross—R
Head to Head—R
Healing Inn—R
Heavenly Thoughts—R
Home Times—R
Inspirer, The—R
Liguorian
Lutheran Parent
Marriage Partnership
Messenger/St. Anthony
Metro Voice—R
Michigan Christian
National Catholic
New Oxford Review
New Writing—R
Pegasus Review—R
Perspectives
Plenty Good Room
Poetry Forum—R
Poet's Park—R
PrayerWorks—R
Presbyterian Outlook
Presbyterians Today—R
Prism—R
Ratio
Religious Education
Remembrance—R
Rosebud
SCP Journal—R
Second Stone
Smile—R
Sojourners
Spiritual Life
TEAK Roundup—R
Touchstone—R
Upsouth—R
Visitation
Weavings—R

CHILDREN
Nature Friend—R
Writers' Intl. Forum/Young

MISSIONS
Areopagus—R
Catholic Near East
PFI World Report—R

MUSIC
Creator—R

PASTORS/LEADERS
Catholic Servant
Christian Century
Church Bytes—R
Journal/Pastoral Care
Word & World
Youthworker—R

TEEN/YOUNG ADULT
Challenge (GA)
Christteen—R
Student Leadership—R
YOU!—R
Young Adult Today

WOMEN
Anna's Journal—R
Aspire
DOMESTIQUE—R
Esprit—R
Handmaiden, The—R
Horizons—R
Lutheran Woman Today
Proverbs 31 Homemaker—R
Tea and Sunshine

WRITERS
Byline
Canadian Writer's Jour—R
Inklings
Once Upon a Time—R
Writer's Digest—R
Writer's Ink—R
Writers' Intl. Forum
Writer's Nook News

ETHICS

ADULT/GENERAL
Angels on Earth
At Ease—R
Atlantic Baptist
AXIOS—R
Banner, The

Bible Advocate—R
Bible Advocate Online—R
Biblical Reflections—R
Canadian Catholic
Catholic Digest—R
Catholic Insight
Catholic Parent
Catholic Rural Life
Celebrate Life—R
Christian Century
Christian Courier (CAN)—R
Christian Edge—R
Christian Media—R
Christian Motorsports
Christian Research
Christian Single—R
Christianity Today—R
Christians in Business
Chrysalis Reader
Church Advocate—R
Church Herald/Holiness—R
Church of God
   EVANGEL—R
Columbia
Commonweal
Companions—R
Compass
Conquest
Cornerstone—R
Covenant Companion—R
Culture Wars—R
Emphasis/Faith & Living—R
Evangelical Baptist—R
Faith Today
Family Journal—R
Fellowship Link—R
First Things
Good News (AL)—R
Good News, Etc—R
Gospel Tidings—R
Grail
Head to Head—R
Heavenly Thoughts—R
Home Times—R
Impact Magazine—R
Indian Life—R
Insights—R
John Milton—R
Jour/Christian Nursing—R
Journal of Church & State
Liguorian
Live—R
Lutheran Journal
Lutheran Parent
MESSAGE/Open Bible—R
Messenger, The (MI)—R
Messenger/St. Anthony
Metro Voice—R

Michigan Christian
Minnesota Christian—R
Moody—R
New Covenant
New Heart, A—R
New Oxford Review
Our Family—R
Our Sunday Visitor
Pegasus Review—R
Pentecostal Testimony—R
Perspectives
Physician
Pourastan—R
Prairie Messenger—R
PrayerWorks—R
Presbyterian Layman
Presbyterian Outlook
Prism—R
ProLife News—R
Purpose—R
Religious Broadcasting—R
Religious Education
Sacred Journey—R
St. Anthony Messenger
Seek—R
Social Justice
Sojourners
Something Better—R
Standard, The—R
Stand Firm—R
2-Soar—R
Touchstone—R
United Church Observer
Upsouth—R

CHILDREN
BREAD/God's Children—R
CLUBHOUSE—R
High Adventure—R
Skipping Stones
Wonder Time

*CHRISTIAN
EDUCATION/LIBRARY*
CE Connection—R
Vision—R

MISSIONS
Areopagus—R
East-West Church
Teacher's Interaction
Urban Mission—R
Worldwide Challenge

PASTORS/LEADERS
Art+Plus
Christian Century

Christian Management—R
Church Bytes—R
Cross Currents—R
Ivy Jungle Report—R
Journal/Christian Healing—R
Journal/Pastoral Care
Lutheran Partners—R
Priest, The
PROCLAIM—R
Pulpit Helps—R
Resource—R
Theology Today
Today's Christian
    Preacher—R
Word & World
Youthworker—R

TEEN/YOUNG ADULT
Certainty
Challenge (GA)
Christteen—R
Conqueror—R
Student Leadership—R
Teenage Christian—R
YOU!—R
Youth Update

WOMEN
Adam's Rib—R
Aspire
Conscience—R
Esprit—R
Handmaiden, The—R
Horizons—R
Ishshah—R
Wesleyan Woman—R

WRITERS
Canadian Writer's Jour—R

ETHNIC/CULTURAL
PIECES

ADULT/GENERAL
Arlington Catholic
Banner, The
Baptist Informer
Bible Advocate—R
Canadian Baptist
Catholic Digest—R
Catholic Insight
CBA Marketplace
Christian Advocate—R
Christian Century
Christian Edge—R
Christian Living—R
Christian Motorsports

Christian News NW—R
Christian Ranchman
Christian Single—R
Christian Social Action—R
Christianity Today—R
Church of God
    EVANGEL—R
Common Boundary
Cornerstone—R
Dovetail—R
Evangelical Baptist
Fellowship Link—R
First Things
Foursquare World—R
Gadfly—R
Good News(KY)—R
Good News, Etc.—R
Gospel Today
Grail
Green Cross—R
Hallelujah! (CAN)—R
Healing Inn—R
Home Times—R
Impact Magazine—R
Indian Life—R
Insights—R
John Milton—R
Jour/Christian Nursing—R
Journal of Church & State
Live—R
Living—R
Lookout—R
Joyful Noise
Living with Teenagers—R
Lutheran Parent
Mennonite Historian—R
MESSAGE
MESSAGE/Open Bible—R
Messenger/St. Anthony
Michigan Christian
Moody—R
New Writing—R
Northwestern Lutheran—R
Pentecostal Testimony—R
Perspectives
Plenty Good Room
PrayerWorks—R
Presbyterian Outlook
Preserving Christian
    Homes—R
Prism—R
Purpose—R
Religious Broadcasting—R
Sacred Journey—R
Sojourners
Something Better—R
Standard, The—R
Table Talk—R

TEAK Roundup—R
Together—R
Touchstone—R
Trumpeter, The
2-Soar—R
United Church Observer
Upscale Magazine
Upsouth—R
War Cry—R
Watchman, The
Way of St. Francis—R

CHILDREN
Discovery(NY)—R
On the Line—R
Skipping Stones
Story Friends—R

CHRISTIAN
EDUCATION/LIBRARY
Catechist
Leader/Church School
    Today—R
Vision—R

MISSIONS
Urban Mission
World Vision—R

PASTORS/LEADERS
Cell Life FORUM—R
Christian Ministry
Clergy Journal—R
Jour/Amer Soc/Chur
    Growth—R
Journal/Pastoral Care—R
Lutheran Partners—R
Ministries Today
Quarterly Review

TEEN/YOUNG ADULT
Certainty
Challenge (GA)
Christteen—R
Devo'Zine—R
Rock, The
Student Leadership—R
Take Five (photos)
Teen Life (AG)—R
Young Adult Today
Young Christian—R
Young Salvationist—R

WOMEN
Aspire
Esprit—R
Horizons—R

Ishshah—R
Sisters Today
Today's Christian Woman
Virtue—R

EVANGELISM/
WITNESSING

ADULT/GENERAL
Alive!—R
American Tract Soc.—R
Anglican Journal—R
Annals of St. Anne
At Ease—R
Atlantic Baptist
Banner, The
Baptist Informer
Bible Advocate—R
Bible Advocate Online—R
Bread of Life—R
Brethren Evangelist
Canadian Baptist
Canadian Catholic
Canadian Lutheran—R
Catholic Digest—R
Catholic Insight
Charisma/Christian Life
Christian Century
Christian Courier (WI)—R
Christian Edge—R
Christian Motorsports
Christian Ranchman
Christian Reader—R
Christian Research
Christian Single—R
Christianity Today—R
Church Advocate—R
Church Herald/Holiness—R
Church of God
    EVANGEL—R
Comments/Friends—R
Companion
Conquest
Cornerstone—R
Covenant Companion—R
Crossway/Newsline—R
Decision
Discipleship Journal
Disciple's Journal—R
Emphasis/Faith & Living—R
Evangel—R
Evangelical Baptist—R
Evangelical Visitor—R
Faith Today
Fellowship Link—R
God's Revivalist
Good News(KY)—R
Good News, Etc—R

Good News Journal—R
Gospel Tidings—R
Gospel Today
Green Cross—R
Hallelujah! (CAN)—R
Healing Inn—R
Hearing Hearts
Heavenly Thoughts—R
Highway News—R
Indian Life—R
Inland NW Christian
Insights—R
Inspirer, The—R
Island Christian—R
John Milton—R
Journal/Christian Nursing—R
Life Gate—R
Light and Life
Liguorian
Live—R
Living Light News—R
Lutheran, The—R
Lutheran Digest—R
Lutheran Journal
Lutheran Parent
Lutheran Witness—R
Marriage Partnership
MESSAGE/Open Bible—R
Metro Voice—R
Michigan Christian
Moody—R
New Covenant
New Heart, A—R
New Oxford Review
New Writing—R
Northwestern Lutheran—R
Our Family—R
Pentecostal Evangel—R
Pentecostal Testimony—R
Plain Truth—R
Poet's Park—R
Power for Living—R
PrayerWorks—R
Presbyterian Layman
Presbyterian Record—R
Presbyterians Today—R
Prism—R
Purpose—R
Pursuit—R
Queen of All Hearts
Religious Education
Revelation Post—R
St. Anthony Messenger
SCP Journal—R
Seek—R
Shantyman, The—R
Sharing—R
Silver Wings—R

Sojourners
Something Better—R
Standard—R
Standard, The—R
Stand Firm—R
This Rock
Trumpeter, The
United Church Observer
Upsouth—R
U.S. Catholic
Vision—R
Vision, The—R
Voice, The—R
War Cry—R
Watchman, The
Way of St. Francis—R
Wesleyan Advocate—R

CHILDREN
Club Connection—R
Counselor—R
Courage
Kids' Ministry Ideas—R
Live Wire—R
Primary Pal (IL)
R-A-D-A-R—R
Touch—R

CHRISTIAN
EDUCATION/LIBRARY
Brigade Leader—R
Children's Ministry
CE Connection—R
CE Counselor—R
Churcn Educator—R
Church Media Library—R
Evangelizing Today's
    Child—R
GROUP
Leader/Church School
    Today—R
Resource—R
Shining Star—R
Teacher's Interaction

MISSIONS
American Horizon—R
Evangelical Missions—R
Intl Jour/Frontier—R
Leaders for Today
Message of the Cross—R
Missiology
Quiet Hour Echoes
Save Our World—R
Urban Mission—R
World Christian—R
World Pulse—R

World Vision—R
Worldwide Challenge

MUSIC
Quest—R

PASTORS/LEADERS
Art+Plus
Cell Church—R
Cell Life FORUM—R
Christian Camp—R
Christian Recreation
Church Administration
Church Growth Network—R
Clergy Journal—R
Emmanuel
Enrichment—R
Eucharistic Minister—R
Evangelism USA
Five Stones, The—R
GROUP's Jr. High
Jour/Amer Soc/Chur
    Growth—R
Journal/Christian Healing—R
Let's Worship
Lutheran Forum—R
Lutheran Partners—R
Ministries Today
Networks—R
Preacher, The—R
Preacher's Magazine—R
Priest, The
PROCLAIM—R
Pulpit Helps—R
Resource—R
Review for Religious
Sermon Notes
Today's Christian
    Preacher—R
Vital Issues
Voice of the Vineyard —R
Youthworker—R

TEEN/YOUNG ADULT
Alive!
Certainty
Challenge (GA)
Challenge (IL)
Christteen—R
Conqueror—R
Devo'Zine—R
Insight—R
Straight—R
Student Leadership—R
Teenage Christian—R
Teen Life (AG)—R
Teen Power—R

Teens on Target—R
Today's Christian Teen—R
With—R
YOU!—R
Young Adult Today
Young Christian—R
Youth Challenge—R

WOMEN
Adam's Rib—R
Aspire
CoLaborer—R
Esprit—R
Handmaiden, The—R
Helping Hand—R
Horizons—R
Ishshah—R
Just Between Us—R
Link & Visitor—R
Lutheran Woman Today
Proverbs 31 Homemaker—R
Sisters Today
Today's Christian Woman
Wesleyan Woman—R
Woman's Touch—R

FAMILY LIFE

ADULT/GENERAL
Alive!—R
America
American Tract Soc.—R
Angels on Earth
Annals of St. Anne
Arlington Catholic
At Ease—R
Atlantic Baptist
AXIOS—R
Banner, The
Baptist Informer
B.C. Catholic—R
Bible Advocate—R
Biblical Reflections—R
Bread of Life—R
Brethren Evangelist
Canada Lutheran—R
Canadian Baptist
Canadian Catholic
Catholic Digest—R
Catholic Forester—R
Catholic Insight
Catholic Parent
Catholic Twin Circle—R
Celebrate Life—R
Charisma/Christian Life
Chesapeake Citizen
Christian Advocate—R
Christian C.L. RECORD—R

Christian Courier (WI)—R
Christian Courier (CAN)—R
Christian Edge—R
Christian Home & School
Christian Living—R
Christian Motorsports
Christian Parenting—R
Christian Ranchman
Christian Reader—R
Christian Renewal—R
Christian Single—R
Christian Social Action—R
Church Advocate—R
Church of God
    EVANGEL—R
Columbia
Companion
Companions—R
Connecting Point—R
Conquest
Covenant Companion—R
Culture Wars—R
Disciple's Journal—R
Decision
Dovetail—R
Emphasis/Faith & Living—R
Evangel—R
Evangelical Baptist—R
Evangelical Visitor—R
Expression Christian
Family Digest
Family Journal—R
Family Network—R
Fellowship Link—R
Fellowship Today—R
Focus on the Family
Foursquare World—R
Gem, The—R
God's Revivalist
Good News (AL)—R
Good News, Etc—R
Good News Journal
Good Shepherd
Gospel Tidings—R
Guideposts
Head to Head—R
Healing Inn—R
Hearing Hearts
Heartlight Internet—R
Heavenly Thoughts—R
Highway News—R
Homeschooling Today
Home Times—R
Ideals—R
Impact Magazine—R
Indian Life—R
Inland NW Christian
Insights—R

Interim—R
Island Christian—R
John Milton—R
Keys to Living
LA Catholic Agitator
Life Gate—R
Light and Life
Liguorian
Live—R
Living—R
Living with Teenagers—R
Lookout—R
Lutheran, The—R
Lutheran Digest—R
Lutheran Journal—R
Lutheran Parent
Lutheran Witness—R
Marriage Partnership
Mature Years—R
Mennonite, The—R
Mennonite Brethren—R
MESSAGE
MESSAGE/Open Bible—R
Messenger
Messenger, The (MI)—R
Messenger/St. Anthony
Metro Voice—R
Michigan Christian
Minnesota Christian—R
Moody—R
New Oxford Review
North American Voice
Northwestern Lutheran—R
Our Family—R
Our Sunday Visitor
ParentLife—R
Parent Paper, The
Pegasus Review—R
Pentecostal Evangel—R
Pentecostal Testimony—R
Physician
Plain Truth—R
Plus—R
Pourastan—R
Power for Living—R
Prairie Messenger—R
PrayerWorks—R
Presbyterian Layman
Presbyterian Record—R
Presbyterians Today—R
Preserving Christian
    Homes—R
Progress—R
Purpose—R
Religious Education
Remembrance—R
Sacred Journey—R
St. Anthony Messenger

Seek—R
Signs of the Times—R
Smart Dads
Smart Families
Social Justice
Sojourners
Something Better—R
Standard—R
Standard, The—R
Stand Firm—R
Star of Zion
Table Talk—R
TEAK Roundup—R
Time of Singing—R
Today's Christian Senior—R
    (grandparenting)
Together—R
Trumpeter, The
United Church Observer
Upsouth—R
U.S. Catholic
Vibrant Life—R
Vision, The—R
War Cry—R
Way of St. Francis—R
Wesleyan Advocate—R

CHILDREN
BREAD/God's Children—R
Club Connection—R
CLUBHOUSE—R
Courage
Discovery (NY)—R
Focus/Clubhouse
High Adventure—R
Junior Trails—R
My Friend
R-A-D-A-R—R
Skipping Stones
Touch—R
Wonder Time

CHRISTIAN
EDUCATION/LIBRARY
Caravan
CE Connection—R
CE Counselor—R
Children's Ministry
Church Educator—R
GROUP
Leader/Church School
    Today—R
Shining Star
Teacher's Interaction

MISSIONS
American Horizon—R

Quiet Hour Echoes
World Christian—R
Worldwide Challenge

MUSIC
Tradition—R

PASTORS/LEADERS
Art+Plus
Catholic Servant
Cell Life FORUM—R
Christian Camp—R
Christian Recreation
GROUP's Jr. High
Journal/Christian Healing—R
Leadership Journal—R
Lutheran Partners—R
Minister's Family
Ministries Today
Networks—R
Pastor's Family
Preacher's Illus. Service—R
PROCLAIM—R
Pulpit Helps—R
Today's Christian
    Preacher—R
Today's Parish
Vital Issues
Voice of the Vineyard —R
Word & World
Youthworker—R

TEEN/YOUNG ADULT
Breakaway—R
Certainty
Challenge (IL)
Christteen—R
Conqueror—R
Devo'Zine—R
Straight—R
Teens on Target—R
Today's Christian Teen—R
With—R
YOU!—R
Young Adult Today
Young Christian—R
Young Salvationist—R
Youth Challenge—R
Youth 98

WOMEN
Adam's Rib—R
Aspire
DOMESTIQUE—R
Esprit—R
Handmaiden, The—R
Helping Hand—R

Horizons—R
Ishshah—R
Journey—R
Kansas City Woman
Just Between Us—R
Link & Visitor—R
Lutheran Woman's Quar.
Lutheran Woman Today
Proverbs 31 Homemaker—R
Tea and Sunshine
Today's Christian Woman
Virtue—R
Virtuous Woman
Welcome Home
Wesleyan Woman—R
Woman's Touch—R

WRITERS
Housewife-Writer—R

FILLERS: ANECDOTES

ADULT/GENERAL
Alive!—R
Angels on Earth
AXIOS—R
Bible Advocate Online—R
Catholic Digest—R
CBA Frontline
CBA Marketplace
Christian Arts Review
Christian Chronicle—R
Christian Courier (WI)—R
Christian Edge—R
Christian Motorsports
Christian Ranchman
Christian Reader—R
Christian Traveler—R
Church Herald/Holiness—R
Church of God
    EVANGEL—R
Companion
Companions—R
Conquest
Decision
Disciple's Journal—R
Family Digest
Family Network—R
Foursquare World—R
Gem, The—R
Good News (AL)—R
Good News - Salem
Guideposts
Head to Head—R
Healing Inn—R
Heartlight Internet—R
Heavenly Thoughts—R
Home Times—R

Impact Magazine—R
Insights—R
Inspirer, The—R
Island Christian—R
Jewel Among Jewels—R
John Milton—R
Life Gate—R
Liguorian
Live—R
Living—R
Lutheran Digest—R
Lutheran Journal—R
Mature Living
Mennonite, The—R
Messenger/St. Anthony
Metro Voice—R
MovieGuide
New Heart, A—R
New Trumpet—R
Our Family—R
ParentLife—R
Pourastan—R
Presbyterian Record—R
Presbyterians Today—R
Purpose—R
Smile—R
Table Talk—R
TEAK Roundup—R
Visitation
Way of St. Francis—R

CHILDREN
Club Connection—R
CLUBHOUSE—R
Discovery (NY)—R
High Adventure—R
Skipping Stones

*CHRISTIAN
EDUCATION/LIBRARY*
Christian School
Christian Librarian—R
Religion Teacher's Journal
Shining Star
Teachers in Focus—R
Vision—R

MUSIC
Church Pianist, etc.
Creator—R
Tradition

PASTORS/LEADERS
Art+Plus
Cell Life FORUM—R
Christian Management—R
Christian Ministry

Eucharistic Minister—R
Five Stones, The—R
Ivy Jungle Report—R
Journal/Christian Healing—R
Joyful Noiseletter
Leadership Journal—R
Pastor's Family
Preacher's Magazine—R
Pulpit Helps—R
Resource—R
Voice of the Vineyard —R
Worship Leader—R

TEEN/YOUNG ADULT
Christteen—R
Young Christian—R
Young Salvationist—R
Youth 98

WOMEN
Anna's Journal—R
CoLaborer—R
DOMESTIQUE—R
Esprit—R
Just Between Us—R
Proverbs 31 Homemaker—R
Today's Christian Woman
Virtuous Woman
Wesleyan Woman—R
Woman's Touch—R

WRITERS
Byline
Cross & Quill—R
Canadian Writer's Jour—R
Christian Response—R
Fellowscript—R
Housewife-Writer—R
Once Upon a Time—R
Southwestern Writers—R
Tickled by Thunder
Writer's Digest—R
Writer's Exchange—R
Write Touch—R

FILLERS: CARTOONS

ADULT/GENERAL
Alive!—R
alive now!
Angels on Earth
At Ease—R
AXIOS—R
Banner, The
Catholic Digest—R
Catholic Forester—R
CBA Frontline

CBA Marketplace
Christian Chronicle—R
Christian Computing
  (MO)—R
Christian Edge—R
Christian Motorsports
Christian Ranchman
Church Herald/Holiness—R
Commonweal
Companion
Computing Today
Connecting Point—R
Cornerstone—R
Covenant Companion—R
Culture Wars—R
Disciple's Journal—R
Door, The
E Street—R
Evangel—R
Expression Christian
Faith Today
Family Network—R
Foursquare World—R
Gem, The—R
Good News (AL)—R
Good News Journal—R
Good News - Salem
Green Cross—R
Head to Head—R
Hearing Hearts
Heartlight Internet—R
Home Times—R
Impact Magazine—R
Inside Journal
Insights—R
Inspirer, The—R
Jewel Among Jewels—R
John Milton—R
Keys to Living
Lookout—R
Lutheran, The—R
Lutheran Digest—R
Lutheran Journal—R
Lutheran Witness—R
Marriage Partnership
Mature Living
Mature Years—R
Mennonite, The—R
MESSAGE/Open Bible—R
Messenger, The (MI)—R
Messenger/St. Anthony
Metro Voice—R
Michigan Christian
MovieGuide
New Creation
New Heart, A—R
New Trumpet—R
NW Christian Journal—R

Our Family—R
Pegasus Review—R
Physician
Power for Living—R
Presbyterian Record—R
Presbyterians Today—R
Purpose—R
Pursuit—R
Single Connection—R
Smile—R
Sojourners
Standard, The—R
Table Talk—R
TEAK Roundup—R
Today's Christian Senior—R
Way of St. Francis—R

CHILDREN
Club Connection—R
CLUBHOUSE—R
Counselor—R
Crusader—R
Discoveries—R
Focus/Clubhouse Jr
High Adventure—R
My Friend
On the Line—R
R-A-D-A-R—R
Skipping Stones
Story Friends—R

*CHRISTIAN
EDUCATION/LIBRARY*
Baptist Leader—R
CE Counselor—R
Children's Ministry
Christian Librarian—R
GROUP
Journal/Adventist Educ.—R
Team—R
Today's Catholic Teacher—R
Vision—R

MUSIC
Christian Country—R
Church Pianist, etc.
Creator—R
Glory Songs—R
Senior Musician—R

PASTORS/LEADERS
Art+Plus
Catholic Servant
Cell Life FORUM—R
Christian Century
Christian Management—R
Christian Ministry

Christian Sentinel
Clergy Journal—R
Diocesan Dialogue—R
Eucharistic Minister—R
Five Stones, The—R
GROUP's Jr. High
Ivy Jungle Report—R
Joyful Noiseletter
Leadership Journal—R
Lutheran Partners—R
Pastor's Family
Preacher's Magazine—R
Preaching
Priest, The
Reformed Worship
Resource—R
Sermon Notes
Vital Issues
Voice of the Vineyard—R
WCA Monthly—R
Your Church—R

TEEN/YOUNG ADULT
Breakaway—R
Brio
Campus Life—R
Christteen—R
Listen—R
Teen Life (AG)—R
Teen Power—R
With—R
YOU!—R
Young Christian—R
Young Salvationist—R

WOMEN
Esprit—R
Handmaiden, The—R
Horizons—R
Ishshah—R
Joyful Woman—R
Just Between Us—R
Proverbs 31 Homemaker—R
Today's Christian Woman
Virtuous Woman
Wesleyan Woman—R
Women Alive!—R

WRITERS
Byline
Canadian Writer's Jour—R
Cross & Quill—R
Fellowscript—R
Heaven—R
Housewife-Writer—R
NW Christian Author—R
Once Upon a Time—R

Writer's Exchange—R

FILLERS: FACTS

ADULT/GENERAL
Alive!—R
Angels on Earth
AXIOS—R
Bible Advocate—R
Bible Advocate Online—R
Bread of Life—R
Catholic Digest—R
CBA Frontline
CBA Marketplace
Christian Arts Review
Christian Chronicle—R
Christian Courier (WI)—R
Christian Edge—R
Christian Motorsports
Christian Ranchman
Christian Reader—R
Christian Single—R
Christian Traveler—R
Church Herald/Holiness—R
Disciple's Journal—R
Family Network—R
God's Revivalist
Good News (AL)—R
Good News - Salem
Hallelujah! (CAN)—R
Head to Head—R
Healing Inn—R
Insights—R
Inspirer, The—R
Jewel Among Jewels—R
John Milton—R
Life Gate—R
Live—R
Lutheran Digest—R
Lutheran Journal—R
Mature Living
Mennonite, The—R
MESSAGE
MESSAGE/Open Bible—R
Messenger/St. Anthony
MovieGuide
New Trumpet—R
PrayerWorks—R
Presbyterian Record—R
Revelation Post—R
Single Connection—R
Standard, The—R
Visitation
Way of St. Francis—R

CHILDREN
Club Connection—R
Guideposts for Kids

High Adventure—R
Junior Trails—R
Live Wire—R
On the Line—R
R-A-D-A-R—R

*CHRISTIAN
EDUCATION/LIBRARY*
Shining Star
Today's Catholic Teacher—R
Vision—R

MISSIONS
Save Our World—R

PASTORS/LEADERS
Christian Ministry
Church Management—R
Ivy Jungle Report—R
Journal/Christian Healing—R
Single Ad. Ministries Jour.
Voice of the Vineyard—R

TEEN/YOUNG ADULT
Breakaway—R
Brio
Campus Life—R
Certainty
Christteen—R
Student Leadership—R
Teen Life (AG)—R
Young Christian—R
Young Salvationist—R
Youth 98

WOMEN
Anna's Journal—R
DOMESTIQUE—R
Esprit—R
Ishshah—R

WRITERS
Christian Response—R
Fellowscript—R
Gotta Write
Writers Connection
Writer's Exchange—R
Writer's Nook News
Write Touch—R

FILLERS: GAMES

ADULT/GENERAL
Alive!—R
Angels on Earth
Catholic Digest—R

Catholic Forester—R
Christian Edge—R
Christian Motorsports
Christian Ranchman
Christian Recreation
Connecting Point—R
Disciple's Journal—R
Family Network—R
Good News Journal—R
Good News - Salem
Head to Head—R
Healing Inn—R
Hearing Hearts
Heartlight Internet—R
Inspirer, The—R
Keys to Living
Lutheran Journal
Mature Living
MESSAGE
MovieGuide
ParentLife—R
Smart Dads
Smart Families
Table Talk—R

CHILDREN
Club Connection—R
CLUBHOUSE—R
Courage
Discoveries—R
Discovery (NY)—R
Focus/Clubhouse
Focus/Clubhouse Jr
GUIDE—R
Guideposts for Kids
High Adventure—R
Listen
Live Wire—R
On the Line—R
Pockets—R
Primary Pal (IL)
R-A-D-A-R—R
Together Time
Touch—R

CHRISTIAN
EDUCATION/LIBRARY
Children's Ministry
CE Counselor—R
GROUP
Perspective—R
Religion Teacher's Journal
Shining Star
Voice of the Vineyard —R

PASTORS/LEADERS
GROUP's Jr. High

Vital Issues

TEEN/YOUNG ADULT
Challenge (IL)
Conqueror—R
Listen—R
Minister's Family
Student Leadership—R
YOU!—R
Young Salvationist—R

FILLERS: IDEAS

ADULT/GENERAL
Angels on Earth
Catholic Parent
CBA Frontline
CBA Marketplace
Christian Chronicle—R
Christian Edge—R
Christian Home & School
Christian Motorsports
Christian Ranchman
Christian Traveler—R
Church of God
   EVANGEL—R
Conquest
Disciple's Journal—R
Family Network—R
God's Revivalist
Good News (AL)—R
Good News - Salem
Head to Head—R
Healing Inn—R
Hearing Hearts
Heartlight Internet—R
Inspirer, The—R
Jewel Among Jewels—R
John Milton—R
Messenger/St. Anthony
Metro Voice—R
MovieGuide
Moonletters—R
New Trumpet—R
ParentLife—R
Pourastan—R
Presbyterian Record—R
St. Joseph's Messenger—R
Seek—R
Smart Dads
Smart Families
Standard, The—R
Table Talk—R
TEAK Roundup—R

CHILDREN
Club Connection—R

Discovery (NY)—R
High Adventure—R
Listen
Live Wire—R
Pockets—R
Together Time

CHRISTIAN
EDUCATION/LIBRARY
Children's Ministry
CE Counselor—R
Church Worship
GROUP
Parish Teacher—R
Religion Teacher's Journal
Shining Star
Teacher's Interaction
Team—R
Vision—R

MUSIC
Creator—R
Glory Songs—R
Senior Musician—R

PASTORS/LEADERS
Cell Life FORUM—R
Enrichment—R
Five Stones, The—R
GROUP's Jr. High
Journal/Christian Healing—R
Leadership Journal—R
Lutheran Partners—R
Minister's Family
Pray!—R
Preacher's Illus. Service—R
Preacher's Magazine—R
Single Ad. Ministries Jour.
Vital Issues
Voice of the Vineyard —R
WCA Monthly—R

TEEN/YOUNG ADULT
Brio
Campus Life—R
Certainty
Christteen—R
Young Christian—R

WOMEN
Proverbs 31 Homemaker—R
Wesleyan Woman—R
Woman's Touch—R

WRITERS
Fellowscript—R
Just Between Us—R

Housewife-Writer—R
Tickled by Thunder
VA Christian Writer—R
Writers Connection (tips)
Writer's Exchange—R
Writer's Ink—R
Write Touch—R

FILLERS: JOKES

ADULT/GENERAL
Angels on Earth
Catholic Digest—R
Christian Motorsports
Christian Ranchman
Disciple's Journal—R
Family Network—R
Good News (AL)—R
Good News - Salem
Healing Inn—R
Heartlight Internet—R
Home Times—R
Impact Magazine—R
Insights—R
Inspirer, The—R
Keys to Living
Liguorian
Lutheran, The—R
Lutheran Digest—R
Mature Years—R
Moonletters—R
MovieGuide
New Heart, A—R
New Trumpet—R
Our Family—R
PrayerWorks—R
Seek—R
Single Connection—R
Smile—R
Standard, The—R
Today's Christian Senior—R

CHILDREN
Club Connection—R
CLUBHOUSE—R
Discovery (NY)—R
Guideposts for Kids
High Adventure—R
Live Wire—R
My Friend
On the Line—R
Pockets—R (& riddles)
R-A-D-A-R—R

*CHRISTIAN
EDUCATION/LIBRARY*
Baptist Leader—R

MUSIC
Creator—R
Tradition

PASTORS/LEADERS
Cell Life FORUM—R
Five Stones, The—R
Ivy Jungle Report—R
Journal/Christian Healing—R
Joyful Noiseletter
Preacher's Illus. Service—R
Voice of the Vineyard —R

TEEN/YOUNG ADULT
Christteen—R
Teen Power—R
YOU!—R

WOMEN
DOMESTIQUE—R
Ishshah—R
Joyful Woman—R

WRITERS
Housewife-Writer—R
Writer's Exchange—R

FILLERS: NEWSBREAKS

ADULT/GENERAL
Angels on Earth
Anglican Journal—R
Arkansas Catholic
B.C. Catholic—R
Canada Lutheran—R
Catholic Telegraph
CBA Frontline
CBA Marketplace
Celebrate Life—R
Christian Arts Review
Christian Courier (WI)—R
Christian Edge—R
Christian Living—R
Christian Motorsports
Christian Ranchman
Christian Renewal—R
Christian Traveler—R
Common Boundary
Disciple's Journal—R
Family Network—R
Good News - Salem
Hallelujah! (CAN)—R
Head to Head—R
Healing Inn—R
Heartlight Internet—R
Home Times—R
Indian Life—R

Insights—R
Inspirer, The—R
Interim—R
Jewel Among Jewels—R
Mennonite Weekly
Metro Voice—R
MovieGuide
Religious Broadcasting—R
Second Stone
Standard, The—R
TEAK Roundup—R

CHILDREN
Club Connection—R

*CHRISTIAN
EDUCATION/LIBRARY*
Christian Librarian—R
Vision—R

MISSIONS
Save Our World—R

PASTORS/LEADERS
Christian Management—R
Christian Ministry, The
Ivy Jungle Report—R
Journal/Christian Healing—R
Preacher's Illus. Service—R
Single Ad. Ministries Jour.
Voice of the Vineyard —R

TEEN/YOUNG ADULT
Certainty
Teen Life (AG)—R
Young Christian—R

WOMEN
Anna's Journal—R
Conscience—R
Handmaiden, The—R
Joyful Woman—R

WRITERS
Gotta Write
Writers Connection
Writer's Exchange—R
Writer's Ink—R
Writer's Nook News

FILLERS: PARTY IDEAS

ADULT/GENERAL
Christian Ranchman
Disciple's Journal—R
Family Network—R

Head to Head—R
Hearing Hearts
Living with Teenagers—R
MovieGuide
ParentLife—R
Single Connection—R
Standard, The—R
TEAK Roundup—R

CHILDREN
Club Connection—R
Focus/Clubhouse
Live Wire—R
On the Line—R
Young Christian—R

**CHRISTIAN
EDUCATION/LIBRARY**
Perspective—R
Team—R

MUSIC
Creator—R
Glory Songs
Senior Musician—R

TEEN/YOUNG ADULT
Conqueror—R
Student Leadership—R
Young Christian—R

WOMEN
CoLaborer—R
Proverbs 31 Homemaker—R
Wesleyan Woman—R

FILLERS: PRAYERS

ADULT/GENERAL
alive now!
Angels on Earth
Christian Living—R
Christian Motorsports
Christian Ranchman
Cornerstone—R
Disciple's Journal—R
Family Network—R
Good News - Salem
Green Cross—R
Head to Head—R
Healing Inn—R
Heartlight Internet—R
Heavenly Thoughts—R
Insights—R
Inspirer, The—R
Jewel Among Jewels—R
John Milton—R

Liguorian
Mature Years—R
MovieGuide
New Trumpet—R
Plowman, The—R
Pourastan—R
PrayerWorks—R
Presbyterian Record—R
Way of St. Francis—R

CHILDREN
Pockets—R
Primary Pal (IL)
Touch—R

**CHRISTIAN
EDUCATION/LIBRARY**
Baptist Leader—R
Religion Teacher's Journal
Teacher's Interaction
Vision—R

PASTORS/LEADERS
Church Management—R
Clergy Journal—R
Preacher, The—R
Reformed Worship

TEEN/YOUNG ADULT
Christteen—R
Straight—R
YOU!—R
Young Christian—R
Young Salvationist—R

WOMEN
Anna's Journal—R
Esprit—R
Handmaiden, The—R
Horizons—R
Journey—R
Joyful Woman—R
Just Between Us—R
Proverbs 31 Homemaker—R
Virtuous Woman

WRITERS
Cross & Quill—R
Southwestern Writers—R
W.I.N. Informer

FILLERS: PROSE

ADULT/GENERAL
Angels on Earth
Bible Advocate—R

Bible Advocate Online—R
Bread of Life—R
Broken Streets—R
Christian Motorsports
Christian Ranchman
Christian Single—R
Church Herald/Holiness—R
Companions—R
Conquest
Decision
Disciple's Journal—R
Discovery—R
E Street—R
Family Network—R
Gem, The—R
God's Revivalist
Good News - Salem
Hallelujah! (CAN)—R
Head to Head—R
Healing Inn—R
Heartlight Internet—R
Heavenly Thoughts—R
Insights—R
Inspirer, The—R
Jewel Among Jewels—R
John Milton—R
Liguorian
Live—R
Lutheran Journal
Moonletters—R
MovieGuide
New Trumpet—R
Pegasus Review—R
Pentecostal Evangel—R
Plowman, The—R
Presbyterian Record—R
Presbyterians Today—R
Standard, The—R
TEAK Roundup—R
Way of St. Francis—R
Wesleyan Advocate—R

CHILDREN
CLUBHOUSE—R
Courage

**CHRISTIAN
EDUCATION/LIBRARY**
Vision—R

PASTORS/LEADERS
Church Management—R
Preacher's Illus. Service—R
Pulpit Helps—R

TEEN/YOUNG ADULT
Brio

Certainty
Christteen—R
Conqueror—R
Teen Power—R

WOMEN
Anna's Journal—R
DOMESTIQUE—R
Proverbs 31 Homemaker—R
Tea and Sunshine
Today's Christian Woman
Virtuous Woman

WRITERS
Chip Off Writer's Block—R
Once Upon a Time—R
The Writer
Writer's Exchange—R
Write Touch—R

FILLERS: QUIZZES

ADULT/GENERAL
Alive!—R
Angels on Earth
Catholic Digest—R
Christian Motorsports
Christian Ranchman
Christian Traveler—R
Door, The
Disciple's Journal—R
Family Network—R
Good News (AL)—R
Good News Journal—R
Good News - Salem
Healing Inn—R
Hearing Hearts
Impact Magazine—R
Insights—R
Inspirer, The—R
Jewel Among Jewels—R
Keys to Living
Lutheran Journal
Mature Living
MESSAGE
MovieGuide
New Trumpet—R
St. Willibrord Journal
Single Connection—R
Today's Christian Senior—R

CHILDREN
Club Connection—R
Counselor—R
Crusader—R
Discoveries—R
Discovery (NY)—R

Focus/Clubhouse
GUIDE—R
Guideposts for Kids
High Adventure—R
Nature Friend—R
On the Line—R
Partners—R
R-A-D-A-R—R
Skipping Stones
Story Mates—R
Touch—R
Young Christian—R

**CHRISTIAN
EDUCATION/LIBRARY**
CE Counselor—R

MUSIC
Glory Songs—R
Senior Musician—R

PASTORS/LEADERS
Ivy Jungle Report—R
Voice of the Vineyard —R

TEEN/YOUNG ADULT
Breakaway—R
Brio
Certainty
Conqueror—R
Listen—R
Student Leadership—R
Teen Power—R
Teens on Target—R
YOU!—R
Young Christian—R
Young Salvationist—R
Youth Challenge—R

WOMEN
Anna's Journal—R
Esprit—R
Virtuous Woman

WRITERS
Fellowscript—R
Once Upon a Time—R
W.I.N. Informer
Writer's Ink—R

FILLERS: QUOTES

ADULT/GENERAL
Angels on Earth
Bible Advocate—R
Bible Advocate Online—R

Bread of Life—R
Catholic Digest—R
Christian Arts Review
Christian Chronicle—R
Christian Edge—R
Christian Motorsports
Christian Ranchman
Christian Single—R
Christian Traveler—R
Church Herald/Holiness—R
Companion
Companions—R
Culture Wars—R
Disciple's Journal—R
Family Network—R
Good News (AL)—R
Good News Journal—R
Good News - Salem
Guideposts
Hallelujah! (CAN)—R
Head to Head—R
Healing Inn—R
Heartlight Internet—R
Home Times—R
Insights—R
Inspirer, The—R
Jewel Among Jewels—R
John Milton—R
Keys to Living
Lutheran Journal—R
MESSAGE/Open Bible—R
Messenger, The (MI)—R
Messenger/St. Anthony
Metro Voice—R
MovieGuide
New Trumpet—R
Pegasus Review—R
Poets' Paper—R
Pourastan—R
PrayerWorks—R
Revelation Post—R
Seek—R
Smart Dads
Smart Families
Smile—R

CHILDREN
Discovery (NY)—R
Live Wire—R
Skipping Stones

**CHRISTIAN
EDUCATION/LIBRARY**
Christian Library Jour.—R
Shining Star

PASTORS/LEADERS
Christian Management—R
Ivy Jungle Report—R
Journal/Christian Healing—R
Pastor's Family
Pulpit Helps—R
Single Adult Min Journal
Voice of the Vineyard —R
Worship Leader

TEENS/YOUNG ADULTS
Christteen—R
YOU!—R
Young Christian—R

WOMEN
Anna's Journal—R
Handmaiden, The—R
Ishshah—R
Joyful Woman—R
Just Between Us—R
Proverbs 31 Homemaker—R
Virtuous Woman
Wesleyan Woman—R

WRITERS
Christian Response—R
Southwestern Writers—R
W.I.N. Informer
Writer's Exchange—R
Writer's Ink—R

FILLERS: SHORT HUMOR

ADULT/GENERAL
Alive!—R
Angels on Earth
Catholic Digest—R
CBA Frontline
CBA Marketplace
Christian Chronicle—R
Christian Edge—R
Christian Motorsports
Christian Ranchman
Christian Reader—R
Christian Single—R
Christian Traveler—R
Church Herald/Holiness—R
Companion
Covenant Companion—R
Disciple's Journal—R
Door, The
E Street—R
Evangel—R
Evangelical Baptist
Family Network—R
Gem, The

God's Revivalist
Good News (AL)—R
Good News - Salem
Green Cross—R
Guideposts
Head to Head—R
Healing Inn—R
Highway News—R
Heartlight Internet—R
Home Times—R
Impact Magazine—R
Insights—R
Inspirer, The—R
Jewel Among Jewels—R
John Milton—R
Keys to Living
Liguorian
Live—R
Living—R
Living with Teenagers—R
Lutheran, The—R
Lutheran Digest—R
Lutheran Journal—R
Lutheran Witness—R
Mature Living
MESSAGE/Open Bible—R
Metro Voice—R
MovieGuide
New Heart, A—R
New Trumpet—R
Our Family—R
Pourastan—R
PrayerWorks—R
Presbyterian Record—R
Presbyterians Today—R
Purpose—R
St. Willibrord Journal
Seek—R
Single Connection—R
Smile—R
Standard, The—R
Star of Zion
TEAK Roundup—R
Visitation

CHILDREN
Club Connection—R
Discovery (NY)—R
Guideposts for Kids
Junior Trails—R
Touch—R

CHRISTIAN EDUCATION/LIBRARY
Christian Librarian—R
Teachers in Focus
Team—R

MUSIC
Christian Country—R
Creator—R
Glory Songs—R
Senior Musician—R

PASTORS/LEADERS
Catholic Servant
Christian Management—R
Enrichment—R
Eucharistic Minister—R
Five Stones, The—R
Ivy Jungle Report—R
Journal/Christian Healing—R
Joyful Noiseletter
Leadership Journal—R
Preacher's Illus. Service—R
Resource—R
Sermon Notes
Voice of the Vineyard —R

TEEN/YOUNG ADULT
Brio
Campus Life—R
Certainty
Christteen—R
Straight—R
Teen Power—R
Young Christian—R
Young Salvationist—R

WOMEN
DOMESTIQUE—R
Esprit—R
Ishshah—R
Journey—R
Joyful Woman—R
Just Between Us—R
Proverbs 31 Homemaker—R
Tea and Sunshine
Wesleyan Woman—R

WRITERS
Byline
Housewife-Writer—R
Once Upon a Time—R
Tickled by Thunder
Writer's Digest—R
Writer's Exchange—R
Write Touch—R

FILLERS: WORD PUZZLES

ADULT/GENERAL
Alive!—R
Christian Edge—R
Christian Ranchman

Companion
Connecting Point—R
Conquest
Disciple's Journal—R
Family Network—R
Good News (AL)—R
Good News Journal—R
Good News - Salem
Head to Head—R
Healing Inn—R
Hearing Hearts
Heartlight Internet—R
Impact Magazine—R
Inspirer, The—R
Jewel Among Jewels—R
Mature Living
Mature Years—R
MESSAGE
Michigan Christian
MovieGuide
Power for Living—R
Single Connection—R
Smile—R
Standard—R
Today's Christian Senior—R

CHILDREN
Club Connection—R
CLUBHOUSE—R
Counselor—R
Courage
Crusader—R
Discovery (NY)—R
Focus/Clubhouse
Focus/Clubhouse Jr
GUIDE—R
Guideposts for Kids
High Adventure—R
Live Wire—R
Nature Friend—R
On the Line—R
Our Little Friend—R
Partners—R
Pockets—R
Primary Pal (IL)
R-A-D-A-R—R
Skipping Stones
Story Friends—R
Story Mates—R
Young Christian—R

CHRISTIAN EDUCATION/LIBRARY
Parish Teacher—R
Shining Star
Voice of the Vineyard —R

TEEN/YOUNG ADULT
Certainty
Challenge (IL)
Conqueror—R
Listen—R
Teen Power—R
Teens on Target—R
YOU!—R
Young Christian—R
Young Salvationist—R
Youth Challenge—R

WRITERS
Heaven—R

FOOD/RECIPES

ADULT/GENERAL
AXIOS—R
Catholic Digest—R
Catholic Forester—R
Catholic Parent
Christian C.L. RECORD—R
Disciple's Journal—R
Dovetail—R
E Street—R
Family Network—R
Fellowship Link—R
Healing Inn—R
Home Times—R
Ideals—R
Living—R
Lutheran Digest—R
Lutheran Journal—R
Mature Living
MESSAGE
ParentLife—R
Parent Paper, The
Poetry Forum—R
Progress—R
Single Connection—R
Standard, The—R
Table Talk—R
Today's Christian Senior—R
Vibrant Life—R

CHILDREN
Club Connection—R
CLUBHOUSE—R
Discovery (NY)—R
Focus/Clubhouse
Focus/Clubhouse Jr.
Listen
Live Wire—R
On the Line—R
Pockets—R (recipes)
Skipping Stones

Together Time
Touch—R

MISSIONS
World Mission People—R
Young Christian—R

PASTORS/LEADERS
Minister's Family

WOMEN
Aspire
DOMESTIQUE—R
Helping Hand—R
Ishshah—R
Kansas City Woman
Proverbs 31 Homemaker—R
Virtue—R
Welcome Home

HEALING

ADULT/GENERAL
Angels on Earth
At Ease—R
Banner, The
Bible Advocate—R
Bible Advocate Online—R
Biblical Reflections—R
Bread of Life—R
Canadian Baptist
Catholic Digest—R
Catholic Twin Circle—R
Charisma/Christian Life
Christian Chronicle—R
Christian Motorsports
Christian Ranchman
Christian Single—R
Chrysalis Reader
Church of God
   EVANGEL—R
Common Boundary
Connecting Point—R
Covenant Companion—R
Disciple's Journal—R
Evangelical Baptist—R
Family Network—R
Foursquare World—R
Good News(KY)—R
Good News, Etc—R
Good News Journal—R
Guideposts
Head to Head—R
Healing Inn—R
Insights—R
Island Christian—R
John Milton—R

Jour/Christian Nursing—R
Life Gate—R
Liguorian
Live—R
Lutheran Digest—R
Mennonite, The—R
MESSAGE/Open Bible—R
Messenger, The (MI)—R
Metro Voice—R
Michigan Christian
New Covenant
New Heart, A—R
New Oxford Review
New Writing—R
Our Family—R
Pentecostal Testimony—R
PrayerWorks—R
Presbyterian Record—R
Presbyterians Today—R
Purpose—R
Remembrance—R
SCP Journal—R
Sharing—R
Single Connection—R
Smile—R
Sojourners
Something Better—R
Spiritual Life
Total Health
United Church Observer
Upsouth—R
Vision, The—R
Voice, The—R
Watchman, The
Way of St. Francis—R

CHILDREN
BREAD/God's Children—R
Discovery (NY)—R
High Adventure—R

MISSIONS
American Horizon—R
Areopagus—R

PASTORS/LEADERS
Art+Plus
Eucharistic Minister—R
Journal/Christian Healing—R
Journal/Pastoral Care
Lutheran Partners—R
Ministries Today
Ministry
Networks—R
Priest, The
Voice of the Vineyard—R
Word & World

TEEN/YOUNG ADULT
Conqueror—R
Devo'Zine—R
Teen Life (AG)—R
Young Adult Today
Young Christian—R

WOMEN
Adam's Rib—R
Aspire
Handmaiden, The—R
Helping Hand—R
Horizons—R
Lutheran Woman Today
Virtuous Woman
Woman's Touch—R

HEALTH

ADULT/GENERAL
Alive!—R
Angels on Earth
Anglican Journal—R
Banner, The
B.C. Catholic—R
Bible Advocate—R
Biblical Reflections—R
Canada Lutheran—R
Catholic Digest—R
Catholic Forester—R
Catholic Twin Circle—R
Charisma/Christian Life
Christian Chronicle—R
Christian Courier (WI)—R
Christian Courier (CAN)—R
Christian Living—R
Christian Motorsports
Christian Ranchman
Christian Single—R
Christian Social Action—R
Companion
Covenant Companion—R
Disciple's Journal—R
Discovery—R
Expression Christian
Family Network—R
Fellowship Link—R
Good News Journal—R
Gospel Today
Green Cross—R
Guideposts
Head to Head—R
Healing Inn—R
Home Times—R
Inland NW Christian
Inside Journal—R
Interim—R

Island Christian—R
John Milton—R
Jour/Christian Nursing—R
Lifeglow—R
Living—R
Living with Teenagers—R
Lutheran Digest—R
Lutheran Journal—R
Lutheran Parent
Lutheran Witness—R
Marriage Partnership
MESSAGE
MESSAGE/Open Bible—R
Messenger, The (MI)—R
Metro Voice—R
Michigan Christian
Montana Catholic—R
New Heart, A—R
No-Debt Living—R
ParentLife—R
Parent Paper, The
Physician
Plus—R
Poetry Forum—R
Pourastan—R
PrayerWorks—R
SCP Journal—R
Single Connection—R
Single-Parent Family
Something Better—R
Standard, The—R
Stand Firm—R
Table Talk—R
TEAK Roundup—R
Today's Christian Senior—R
Total Health
Trumpeter, The
Upscale Magazine
Upsouth—R
Vibrant Life—R
War Cry—R

CHILDREN
BREAD/God's Children—R
Club Connection—R
Focus/Clubhouse Jr
High Adventure—R
Live Wire—R
Skipping Stones
Touch—R
Young Christian—R

*CHRISTIAN
EDUCATION/LIBRARY*
CE Connection—R

MISSIONS
Areopagus—R
Missiology
Quiet Hour Echoes

PASTORS/LEADERS
Christian Camp—R
Christian Recreation
Journal/Christian Healing—R
Journal/Pastoral Care
Lutheran Partners—R
Minister's Family
Ministries Today
Word & World

TEEN/YOUNG ADULT
Challenge (GA)
Christteen—R
Conqueror—R
Today's Christian Teen—R
Young Adult Today
Young & Alive—R
Young Christian—R

WOMEN
Adam's Rib—R
Aspire
Esprit—R
Helping Hand—R
Horizons—R
Ishshah—R
Journey—R
Joyful Woman—R
Lutheran Woman's Quar.
Lutheran Woman Today
Proverbs 31 Homemaker—R
Today's Christian Woman
Virtue—R
Virtuous Woman
Welcome Home
Woman's Touch—R

HISTORICAL

ADULT/GENERAL
AGAIN—R
America
Angels on Earth
Arlington Catholic
At Ease—R
AXIOS—R
Banner, The
Baptist History
Canadian Catholic
Cathedral Age
Catholic Answer
Catholic Digest—R

Catholic Dossier
Catholic Heritage—R
Catholic Insight
Catholic Sentinel—R
Catholic Twin Circle—R
Celebrate Life—R
Christian Advocate—R
Christian C.L. RECORD—R
Christian Courier (CAN)—R
Christian History—R
Christian Motorsports
Christian Ranchman
Christian Reader—R
Christian Renewal—R
Christianity Today—R
Chrysalis Reader
Church & State—R
Columbia
Comments/Friends—R
Companions—R (church)
Compass
Conquest
Covenant Companion—R
Cresset
Dallas/Ft. Worth Heritage
Disciple's Journal—R
E Street—R
Evangelical Baptist—R
Faith Today
Family Digest
Fellowship Link—R
Good News, Etc—R
Gospel Today
Healing Inn—R
Heavenly Thoughts—R
Home Times—R
Indian Life—R
Island Christian—R
John Milton—R
Jour/Christian Nursing—R
Journal of Church & State
Lifeglow—R
Live—R
Lutheran Digest—R
Lutheran Journal—R
Lutheran Parent
Lutheran Witness—R
Mennonite Historian—R
Messenger/St. Anthony
Methodist History
Michigan Christian
Minnesota Christian—R
Our Sunday Visitor
Pentecostal Testimony—R
Presbyterian Layman
Presbyterian Outlook
Presbyterian Record—R
Presbyterians Today—R

Pourastan—R
Power for Living—R
PrayerWorks—R
Purpose—R
Religious Education
SCP Journal—R
Sharing—R
Single Connection—R
Social Justice
Something Better—R
Standard, The—R
TEAK Roundup—R
Today's Christian Senior—R
Touchstone—R
Upscale Magazine
Upsouth—R

CHILDREN
Courage
Junior Trails—R
My Friend
On the Line—R
Partners—R
Power & Light—R
Young Christian—R

CHRISTIAN EDUCATION/LIBRARY
Vision—R

MISSIONS
American Horizon—R
Areopagus—R
Catholic Near East
East-West Church
Missiology
Save Our World—R
Urban Mission—R
Worldwide Challenge

MUSIC
Church Pianist, etc.
Creator—R
Tradition—R

PASTORS/LEADERS
Journal/Christian Healing—R
Lutheran Partners—R
Ministry
Preacher's Magazine—R
Pulpit Helps—R
Today's Parish—R
Word & World

TEEN/YOUNG ADULT
Certainty
Challenge (GA)

Challenge (IL)
Listen—R
Student Leadership—R
Young Adult Today
Young & Alive—R
Young Christian—R

WOMEN
Esprit—R
Horizons—R
Just Between Us—R

WRITERS
Inklings

HOLIDAY/SEASONAL

ADULT/GENERAL
Advent Christian Witness—R
Alive!—R
alive now!
American Tract Soc.—R
Angels on Earth
Arlington Catholic
At Ease—R
AXIOS—R
Banner, The
Bible Advocate—R
Bible Advocate Online—R
Bread of Life—R
Canada Lutheran—R
Canadian Baptist
Canadian Catholic
Cathedral Age
Catholic Digest—R
Catholic Forester—R
Catholic New York
Catholic Parent
Catholic Sentinel—R
Catholic Twin Circle—R
Charisma/Christian Life
Christian Century
Christian Chronicle—R
Christian C.L. RECORD—R
Christian Courier (WI)—R
Christian Edge—R
Christian Home & School
Christian Living—R
Christian Motorsports
Christian Parenting—R
Christian Ranchman
Christian Reader—R
Christian Single—R
Christian Standard—R
Christian Traveler—R
Christianity Today—R
Christmas—R

Church Advocate—R
Church Herald/Holiness—R
Church of God
    EVANGEL—R
Connecting Point—R
Conquest
Covenant Companion—R
Decision
Disciple's Journal—R
Discovery—R
Dovetail—R
Emphasis/Faith & Living—R
E Street—R
Evangel—R
Evangelical Baptist—R
Evangelical Visitor—R
Expression Christian
Family Digest
Family Network—R
Fellowship Link—R
Fellowship Today—R
Focus on the Family
Foursquare World—R
Gem, The—R
God's Revivalist
Good News (AL)—R
Good News, Etc—R
Good News Journal—R
Gospel Tidings—R
Gospel Today
Guideposts
Healing Inn—R
Hearing Hearts
Heartlight Internet—R
Heavenly Thoughts—R
Home Times—R
Ideals—R
Indian Life—R
Inside Journal—R
Insights—R
Inspirer, The—R
Island Christian—R
John Milton—R
Jour/Christian Nursing—R
Keys to Living
Life Gate—R
Lifeglow—R
Light and Life
Liguorian
Live—R
Living—R
Living Church, The
Living with Teenagers—R
Lutheran Digest—R
Lutheran Journal—R
Lutheran Parent
Lutheran Witness—R
Marriage Partnership

Mature Years—R
Mennonite, The—R
Mennonite Brethren—R
MESSAGE
Messenger
Messenger/St. Anthony
Michigan Christian
Minnesota Christian—R
Montana Catholic—R
North American Voice
NW Christian Journal—R
Oblates
Our Sunday Visitor
ParentLife—R
Pegasus Review—R
Plain Truth—R
Pentecostal Testimony—R
Plenty Good Room
Plus—R
Power for Living—R
PrayerWorks—R
Presbyterian Outlook
Presbyterian Record—R
Presbyterians Today—R
Preserving Christian
    Homes—R
Progress—R
Purpose—R
Religious Broadcasting—R
St. Anthony Messenger
St. Joseph's Messenger—R
Seek—R
Sharing—R
Single Connection—R
Smile—R
Sojourners
Something Better—R
Standard—R
Standard, The—R
Stand Firm—R
Table Talk—R
TEAK Roundup—R
Time of Singing—R
Today's Christian Senior—R
Together—R
United Church Observer
U.S. Catholic
Vibrant Life—R
Voice, The—R
War Cry—R
Way of St. Francis—R
Wesleyan Advocate—R

CHILDREN
Club Connection—R
CLUBHOUSE—R
Counselor—R
Courage

Discovery (NY)—R
Focus/Clubhouse
Focus/Clubhouse Jr
Guideposts for Kids
Junior Trails—R
Live Wire—R
On the Line—R
Partners—R
Pockets—R
Primary Pal (IL)
R-A-D-A-R—R
Skipping Stones
Together Time
Touch—R
Wonder Time
Young Christian—R

*CHRISTIAN
EDUCATION/LIBRARY*
Baptist Leader—R
CE Connection—R
CE Counselor—R
CE Leadership—R
Children's Ministry
Church Educator—R
Evangelizing Today's
    Child—R
GROUP
Leader/Church School
    Today—R
Parish Teacher—R
Shining Star
Teacher's Interaction
Vision—R

MISSIONS
Catholic Near East
World Vision—R
Worldwide Challenge

MUSIC
Church Pianist
Creator—R
Plans & Pluses
Quest—R

PASTORS/LEADERS
Art+Plus
Catholic Servant
Celebration
Christian Camp—R
Christian Management—R
Church Bytes—R
Clergy Journal—R
Five Stones, The—R
GROUP's Jr. High
Let's Worship

Liturgy—R
Lutheran Forum—R
Modern Liturgy—R
Pastor's Family
Preacher's Magazine—R
Proclaim
Pulpit Helps—R
Vital Issues

TEEN/YOUNG ADULT
Alive!
Breakaway—R
Certainty
Challenge (GA)
Challenge (IL)
Christteen—R
Conqueror—R
Cornerstone—R
Devo'Zine—R
Listen—R
Straight—R
Teenage Christian—R
Teen Life (AG)—R
Teen Power—R
With—R
YOU!—R
Young & Alive—R
Young Christian—R
Young Salvationist—R
Youth 98

WOMEN
Anna's Journal—R
Aspire
DOMESTIQUE—R
Esprit—R
Handmaiden, The—R
Helping Hand—R
Horizons—R
Ishshah—R
Journey—R
Joyful Woman—R
Lutheran Woman's Quar.
Proverbs 31 Homemaker—R
Tea and Sunshine
Today's Christian Woman
Virtue—R
Woman's Touch—R

WRITERS
Inklings
Tickled by Thunder

HOME SCHOOLING

ADULT/GENERAL
Anglican Journal—R

Arlington Catholic
AXIOS—R
Banner, The
Bible Advocate—R
Bible Advocate Online—R
Catholic Digest—R
Catholic Insight
CBA Marketplace
Charisma/Christian Life
Christian Chronicle—R
Christian C.L. RECORD—R
Christian Computing
    (MO)—R
Christian Edge—R
Christian Motorsports
Christian Parenting—R
Christian Ranchman
Christian Single—R
Church Advocate—R
Disciple's Journal—R
Discovery—R
Evangelical Baptist—R
Expression Christian
Family Journal—R
Family Network—R
Focus on the Family
Good News (AL)—R
Good News, Etc—R
Good News Journal—R
Green Cross—R
Heavenly Thoughts—R
Homeschooling Today
Home Times—R
Insights—R
Inspirer, The—R
Island Christian—R
Life Gate—R
Liguorian
Live—R
Lutheran Life—R
Lutheran Parent
MESSAGE/Open Bible—R
Metro Voice—R
Michigan Christian
Minnesota Christian—R
NW Christian Journal—R
ParentLife—R
Preserving Christian
    Homes—R
Religious Education
Single Connection—R
Social Justice
Something Better—R
Sursum Corda!—R
Table Talk—R
Watchman, The
Wesleyan Advocate—R

CHILDREN
BREAD/God's Children—R
Focus/Clubhouse
Skipping Stones
Writers' Intl. Forum/Young
Young Christian—R

CHRISTIAN
EDUCATION/LIBRARY
CE Connection—R
Christian Educators Jour—R
Christian School

PASTORS/LEADERS
Church Bytes—R
Pastoral Life
Pastor's Family
Pulpit Helps—R
Today's Christian
     Preacher—R

TEEN/YOUNG ADULT
Christteen—R
Conqueror—R
YOU!—R
Young Christian—R

WOMEN
Esprit—R
Handmaiden, The—R
Helping Hand—R
Ishshah—R
Joyful Woman—R
Proverbs 31 Homemaker—R
Tea and Sunshine
Writers' Intl. Forum

HOW-TO ACTIVITIES
(JUV.)

ADULT/GENERAL
Christian Edge—R
Christian Ranchman
Church Herald/Holiness—R
Disciple's Journal—R
E Street—R
Family Network—R
Good News (AL)—R
Green Cross—R
Living—R
Living with Teenagers—R
Lutheran Life—R
Michigan Christian
ParentLife—R
Preserving Christian
     Homes—R
Table Talk—R

CHILDREN
BREAD/God's Children—R
Club Connection—R
Counselor—R
Courage
Crusader—R
Discovery (NY)—R
Focus/Clubhouse
Focus/Clubhouse Jr.
God's World Today
High Adventure—R
Junior Trails—R
Kids' Ministry Ideas—R
Listen
Live Wire—R
My Friend
Nature Friend—R
On the Line—R
Partners—R
Pockets—R
Primary Pal (IL)
R-A-D-A-R—R
Together Time
Touch—R
Wonder Time
Young Christian—R

CHRISTIAN
EDUCATION/LIBRARY
Church Educator—R
Evangelizing Today's
     Child—R
Junior Teacher—R
Leader/Church School
     Today—R
Perspective—R
Shining Star
Today's Catholic Teacher—R

PASTORS/LEADERS
Enrichment—R
GROUP's Jr. High
Networks—R

TEEN/YOUNG ADULT
Breakaway—R
Challenge (GA)
Listen—R
Teen Life (AG)—R
Teen Power—R
Young Christian—R
Young Salvationist—R
Youth 98

WOMEN
Esprit—R
Proverbs 31 Homemaker—R

Wesleyan Woman—R

HOW-TO

ADULT/GENERAL
At Ease—R
Baptist Informer
Believer, The—R
Biblical Reflections—R
Canada Lutheran—R
Catholic Digest—R
Catholic Twin Circle—R
CBA Frontline
CBA Marketplace
Charisma/Christian Life
Christian Arts Review
Christian Chronicle—R
Christian Edge—R
Christian Home & School
Christian Living—R
Christian Motorsports
Christian Parenting—R
Christian Ranchman
Christian Reader—R
Christian Single—R
Christian Standard—R
Christian Traveler—R
Church of God
     EVANGEL—R
Companion
Connecting Point—R
Conquest
Discipleship Journal
Discovery—R
Dovetail—R
Emphasis/Faith & Living—R
Expression Christian
Family Digest
Family Network—R
Fellowship Link—R
Good News (AL)—R
Good News, Etc.—R
Gospel Today
Green Cross—R
Hallelujah! (CAN)—R
Head to Head—R
Healing Inn—R
Hearing Hearts
Heavenly Thoughts—R
Home Times—R
Inland NW Christian
Island Christian—R
John Milton—R
Jour/Christian Nursing—R
Light and Life
Liguorian
Live—R
Living with Teenagers—R

Lutheran Digest—R
Lutheran Parent
Marriage Partnership
Mature Living
Mature Years—R
Mennonite, The—R
MESSAGE
MESSAGE/Open Bible—R
Michigan Christian
New Writing—R
Northwestern Lutheran—R
Our Sunday Visitor
ParentLife—R
Physician
Plain Truth—R
Plus—R
PrayerWorks—R
Pursuit—R
Quiet Revolution—R
Religious Broadcasting—R
Smart Dads
Smart Families
Standard—R
Standard, The—R
TEAK Roundup—R
Total Health
2-Soar—R
Vibrant Life—R
Visitation

CHILDREN
Discovery (NY)—R
High Adventure—R
Kids' Ministry Ideas—R

CHRISTIAN
EDUCATION/LIBRARY
Brigade Leader—R
Catechist
CE Connection—R
CE Connection
   Communique—R
CE Counselor—R
CE Leadership—R
Children's Ministry
Christian School
Church & Synagogue Lib.—R
Church Educator—R
Church Libraries—R
GROUP
Leader/Church School
   Today—R
Lollipops
Shining Star
Teacher's Interaction
Vision—R

MISSIONS
PFI World Report—R
Quiet Hour Echoes

MUSIC
Church Music Report
Gospel Industry Today
Plans & Pluses

PASTORS/LEADERS
Art+Plus
Christian Camp—R
Church Administration
Church Bytes—R
GROUP's Jr. High
Ivy Jungle Report—R
Journal/Christian Healing—R
Modern Liturgy—R
Newsletter Newsletter
Networks—R
Pastor's Family
Priest, The
Resource—R
Vital Issues
Youthworker—R

TEEN/YOUNG ADULT
Breakaway—R
Certainty
Challenge (GA)
Challenge (IL)
Christteen—R
Straight—R
Student Leadership—R
Teen Power—R
Teens on Target—R
With—R
YOU!—R
Young Christian—R
Youth Challenge—R

WOMEN
DOMESTIQUE—R
Esprit—R
Helping Hand—R
Horizons—R
Ishshah—R
Just Between Us—R
Kansas City Woman
Lutheran Woman Today
Today's Christian Woman
Wesleyan Woman—R

WRITERS
Byline
Canadian Writer's Jour—R
Christian Communicator—R

Cross & Quill—R
Housewife-Writer—R
NW Christian Author
Once Upon a Time
VA Christian Writer—R
W.I.N. Informer
Writers Connection—R
Writer's Digest—R
Writer's Exchange—R
Writer's Forum (OH)—R
Writer's Ink—R

HUMOR

ADULT/GENERAL
Alive!—R
alive now!
Angels on Earth
At Ease—R
AXIOS—R
Biblical Reflections—R
Canada Lutheran—R
Canadian Baptist
Catholic Digest—R
Catholic Forester—R
Catholic Parent
Catholic Twin Circle—R
CBA Frontline
Charisma/Christian Life
Christian Chronicle—R
Christian C.L. RECORD—R
Christian Computing
   (MO)—R
Christian Edge—R
Christian Home & School
Christian Living—R
Christian Motorsports
Christian Parenting—R
Christian Ranchman
Christian Reader—R
Christian Single—R
Church Herald/Holiness—R
Church of God
   EVANGEL—R
Companion
Connecting Point—R
Covenant Companion—R
Disciple's Journal—R
Door, The—R(satire)
Emphasis/Faith & Living—R
E Street—R
Evangelical Visitor—R
Faith Today
Family Digest
Family Journal—R
Family Network—R
Fellowship Link—R
Gem, The—R

Good News (AL)—R
Good News, Etc.—R
Good News Journal—R
Gospel Today
Head to Head—R
Healing Inn—R
Hearing Hearts
Home Times—R
Impact Magazine—R
Indian Life—R
Inland NW Christian
Insights—R
Island Christian—R
John Milton—R
Jour/Christian Nursing—R
Keys to Living
Life Gate—R
Light and Life
Liguorian
Live—R
Living—R
Living with Teenagers—R
Lookout—R
Lutheran, The—R
Lutheran Digest—R
Lutheran Journal—R
Lutheran Parent
Lutheran Witness—R
Marriage Partnership
Mature Living
Mature Years—R
Mennonite Brethren—R
MESSAGE/Open Bible—R
Messenger, The (MI)—R
Messenger/St. Anthony
Michigan Christian
Minnesota Christian—R
New Trumpet—R
Our Family—R
ParentLife—R
Pegasus Review—R
Pentecostal Testimony—R
PrayerWorks—R
Presbyterian Record—R
Presbyterians Today—R
Preserving Christian
    Homes—R
Pursuit—R
Religious Broadcasting—R
Single Connection—R
Single-Parent Family
Smile—R
Sojourners
Something Better—R
Standard—R
Standard, The—R
Stand Firm—R
Table Talk—R

Today's Christian Senior—R
Upsouth—R
Visitation
Voice, The—R
War Cry—R

CHILDREN
Club Connection—R
Courage
Discovery (NY)—R
Focus/Clubhouse
Focus/Clubhouse Jr
Guideposts for Kids
High Adventure—R
Live Wire—R
My Friend
On the Line—R
R-A-D-A-R—R
Touch—R
Wonder Time
Writers' Intl. Forum/Young

CHRISTIAN EDUCATION/LIBRARY
CE Leadership—R
Children's Ministry
Christian School
GROUP
Teachers in Focus—R
Teacher's Interaction
Team—R
Vision—R

MISSIONS
Areopagus—R
World Christian—R
Worldwide Challenge

MUSIC
Church Pianist, etc.
Creator—R
Quest—R

PASTORS/LEADERS
Art+Plus
Catholic Servant
Cell Life FORUM—R
Christian Camp—R
Clergy Journal—R
Five Stones, The—R
GROUP's Jr. High
Journal/Christian Healing—R
Minister's Family
Ministries Today
Modern Liturgy—R
Networks—R
Pastor's Family

Preacher's Illus. Service—R
Priest, The
Resource—R
Sermon Notes
Today's Parish
Vital Issues
WCA Monthly—R

TEEN/YOUNG ADULT
Breakaway—R
Brio
Certainty
Challenge (IL)
Christteen—R
Conqueror—R
Devo'Zine—R
Insight—R
Straight—R
Teen Life (AG)—R
Teen Power—R
With—R
YOU!—R
Young Adult Today

WOMEN
Aspire
DOMESTIQUE—R
Esprit—R
Handmaiden, The—R
Helping Hand—R
Horizons—R
Ishshah—R
Just Between Us—R
Lutheran Woman's Quar.
Lutheran Woman Today
Proverbs 31 Homemaker—R
Today's Christian Woman
Virtue—R
Virtuous Woman
Wesleyan Woman—R
Woman's Touch—R

WRITERS
Byline
Canadian Writer's Jour—R
Exchange—R
Housewife-Writer—R
Once Upon a Time—R
W.I.N. Informer
Writers' Intl. Forum

INSPIRATIONAL

ADULT/GENERAL
Angels on Earth
Annals of St. Anne
Arlington Catholic

At Ease—R
Banner, The
Bible Advocate—R
Bible Advocate Online—R
Bread of Life—R
Broken Streets
Canada Lutheran—R
Catholic Answer
Catholic Digest—R
Catholic Forester—R
Catholic Parent
Catholic Twin Circle—R
CBA Frontline
Celebrate Life—R
Charisma/Christian Life
Christian Arts Review
Christian Chronicle—R
Christian Edge—R
Christian Living—R
Christian Motorsports
Christian Parenting—R
Christian Reader—R
Christian Single—R
Church Advocate—R
Church Herald/Holiness—R
Church of God
   EVANGEL—R
Companion
Companions—R
Connecting Point—R
Covenant Companion—R
Disciple's Journal—R
Emphasis/Faith & Living—R
E Street—R
Evangel—R
Evangelical Baptist—R
Evangelical Visitor—R
Family Digest
Fellowship Link—R
Fellowship Today—R
Family Network—R
Foursquare World—R
Gem, The—R
God's Revivalist
Good News (AL)—R
Good News(KY)—R
Gospel Tidings—R
Gospel Today
Guideposts
Head to Head—R
Healing Inn—R
Hearing Hearts
Heartlight Internet—R
Heavenly Thoughts—R
Highway News—R
Home Times—R
Ideals—R
Indian Life—R

Inland NW Christian
Insights—R
Inspirer, The—R
Island Christian—R
Jewel Among Jewels—R
John Milton—R
Jour/Christian Nursing—R
Keys to Living
Life Gate—R
Lifeglow—R
Light and Life
Liguorian
Live—R
Living—R
Living Light News—R
Living with Teenagers—R
Lutheran, The—R
Lutheran Digest—R
Lutheran Journal—R
Lutheran Parent
Lutheran Witness—R
Marian Helpers—R
Marriage Partnership
Mature Living
Mature Years—R
Mennonite Brethren—R
MESSAGE
MESSAGE/Open Bible—R
Messenger, The (MI)—R
Messenger/Sacred Heart
Messenger/St. Anthony
Michigan Christian
New Covenant
New Heart, A—R
New Trumpet—R
New Writing—R
Northwestern Lutheran—R
Oblates
Our Sunday Visitor
ParentLife—R
Pegasus Review—R
Pentecostal Evangel—R
Plain Truth—R
Plenty Good Room
Plowman, The—R
Plus—R
Pourastan—R
Power for Living—R
PrayerWorks—R
Presbyterian Record—R
Presbyterians Today—R
Preserving Christian
   Homes—R
Purpose—R
Queen of All Hearts
Remembrance—R
Sacred Journey—R
St. Anthony Messenger

St. Joseph's Messenger—R
Second Stone
Seek—R
Shantyman, The—R
Smile—R
Sojourners
Something Better—R
Standard—R
Standard, The—R
Stand Firm—R
Sursum Corda!—R
TEAK Roundup—R
Time of Singing—R
Today's Christian Senior—R
Together—R
Total Health
2-Soar—R
Upscale Magazine
Upsouth—R
U.S. Catholic
Vision, The—R
Visitation
Voice, The—R
War Cry—R
Watchman, The
Way of St. Francis—R
Weavings—R
Wesleyan Advocate—R
Worldwide Challenge

CHILDREN
BREAD/God's Children—R
Club Connection—R
CLUBHOUSE—R
Discovery (NY)—R
Focus/Clubhouse
High Adventure—R
Partners—R
Touch—R
Wonder Time
Writers' Intl. Forum/Young

*CHRISTIAN
EDUCATION/LIBRARY*
Brigade Leader—R
CE Connection—R
CE Counselor—R
Children's Ministry
Christian School
Church & Synagogue Lib.
GROUP
Journal/Adventist Educ.—R
Junior Teacher—R
Leader/Church School
   Today—R
Shining Star
Teacher's Interaction
Vision—R

MISSIONS
American Horizon—R
Areopagus—R
Message of the Cross—R
Quiet Hour Echoes
World Vision—R

MUSIC
Creator—R
Quest—R
Senior Musician—R

PASTORS/LEADERS
Art+Plus
Catholic Servant
Cell Church—R
Cell Life FORUM—R
Christian Camp—R
Christian Management—R
Clergy Journal—R
Eucharistic Minister—R
Evangelism USA
Five Stones, The—R
GROUP's Jr. High
Journal/Christian Healing—R
Journal/Pastoral Care
Minister's Family
Ministry
Networks—R
Preacher's Magazine—R
Priest, The
PROCLAIM—R
Today's Christian
    Preacher—R
Vital Issues
Voice of the Vineyard —R

TEEN/YOUNG ADULT
Alive!
Breakaway—R
Challenge (GA)
Christteen—R
Conqueror—R
Devo'Zine—R
Insight—R
Teenage Christian—R
Teen Power—R
Teens on Target—R
Today's Christian Teen—R
With—R
YOU!—R
Young Adult Today
Young & Alive—R
Young Christian—R
Youth Challenge—R
Youth 98

WOMEN
Adam's Rib—R
Anna's Journal—R
Aspire
DOMESTIQUE—R
Esprit—R
Handmaiden, The—R
Helping Hand—R
Horizons—R
Ishshah—R
Journey—R
Just Between Us
Kansas City Woman
Lutheran Woman's Quar.
Lutheran Woman Today
Proverbs 31 Homemaker—R
Sisters Today
Tea and Sunshine
Today's Christian Woman
Virtue—R
Virtuous Woman
Wesleyan Woman—R
Woman's Touch—R
Women Alive!—R

WRITERS
Byline
Canadian Writer's Jour—R
Fellowscript—R
Once Upon a Time—R
VA Christian Writer—R
Writer's Digest—R
Writer's Forum (OH)—R
Writers' Intl. Forum

INTERVIEWS/PROFILES

ADULT/GENERAL
AGAIN—R
Alive!—R
Anglican Journal—R
Arkansas Catholic
Arlington Catholic
At Ease—R
AXIOS—R
Biblical Reflections—R
Canadian Baptist
Canadian Catholic
Canadian Mennonite
Catholic Digest—R
Catholic New York
Catholic Parent
Catholic Sentinel—R
Catholic Twin Circle—R
Charisma/Christian Life
Christian Advocate—R
Christian Arts Review

Christian Chronicle—R
Christian C.L. RECORD—R
Christian Courier (WI)—R
Christian Courier (CAN)—R
Christian Edge—R
Christian Motorsports
Christian News NW—R
Christian Parenting—R
Christian Ranchman
Christian Reader—R
Christian Renewal—R
Christian Single—R
Christianity Today—R
Church Advocate—R
Church & State—R
Columbia
Companion
Cornerstone—R (music)
Covenant Companion—R
Culture Wars—R
Disciple's Journal—R
Door, The
Dovetail—R
Emphasis/Faith & Living—R
Episcopal Life—R
Evangelical Baptist—R
Expression Christian
Faith Today
Family Digest
Family Journal—R
Focus on the Family
Gadfly—R
Good News (AL)—R
Good News(KY)—R
Good News, Etc—R
Gospel Today
Grail
Green Cross—R
Guideposts
Head to Head—R
Healing Inn—R
Hearing Hearts
Heartlight Internet—R
Heavenly Thoughts—R
Home Times—R
Impact Magazine—R
Indian Life—R
Inside Journal—R
Insights—R
Interim—R
Island Christian—R
Jewel Among Jewels—R
John Milton—R
Jour/Christian Nursing—R
Joyful Noise
Lifeglow—R
Liguorian
Living—R

Living Church
Living Light News—R
Living with Teenagers—R
Lutheran, The—R
Lutheran Journal
Lutheran Parent
Lutheran Witness—R
Marriage Partnership
Mature Living
Mature Years—R
Mennonite, The—R
Mennonite Historian—R
MESSAGE
Messenger
Messenger/St. Anthony
Metro Voice—R
Michigan Christian
Minnesota Christian—R
New Covenant
New Creation
New Heart, A—R
New Trumpet—R
New Writing—R
NW Christian Journal—R
Our Sunday Visitor
Pentecostal Evangel—R
Pentecostal Testimony—R
Physician
Plain Truth—R
Plenty Good Room
Poetry Forum—R
Power for Living—R
Presbyterian Layman
Presbyterian Outlook
Presbyterian Record—R
Presbyterians Today—R
Prism—R
ProLife News—R
Pursuit—R
Quiet Revolution—R
Religious Broadcasting—R
Sacred Journey—R
St. Anthony Messenger
SCP Journal—R
Second Stone
Signs of the Times—R
Single Connection—R
Single-Parent Family
Sojourners
Something Better—R
Standard—R
Standard, The—R
Stand Firm—R
Stewardship
Sursum Corda!—R
Table Talk—R
TEAK Roundup—R
Today's Christian Senior—R

Together—R
United Church Observer
Upscale Magazine
Upsouth—R
U.S. Catholic
Vibrant Life—R
Visitation
War Cry—R
Way of St. Francis—R

CHILDREN
Focus/Clubhouse
Guideposts for Kids
Live Wire—R
Pockets—R
Skipping Stones
Touch—R

CHRISTIAN EDUCATION/LIBRARY
Brigade Leader—R
Children's Ministry
CE Counselor—R
Christian Educators Jour—R
Christian Library Jour—R
Christian School
Church Libraries—R
GROUP
Perspective—R
Teachers in Focus—R
Vision—R

MISSIONS
American Horizon—R
East-West Church
Evangelical Missions—R
Leaders for Today
PFI World Report—R
Save Our World—R
Urban Mission—R
World Christian—R
World Pulse—R
World Mission People—R
Worldwide Challenge

MUSIC
Church Music World
Gospel Industry Today
Quest—R

PASTORS/LEADERS
Catholic Servant
Cell Church—R
Christian Camp—R
Christian Management—R
Church Bytes—R
Cross Currents—R

Evangelism USA
GROUP's Jr. High
Ivy Jungle Report—R
Journal/Christian Healing—R
Ministries Today
Modern Liturgy—R
Networks—R
Pastor's Family
Preacher, The—R
Preacher's Magazine—R
PROCLAIM—R
Sabbath School Leadership
Sermon Notes
Single Ad. Ministries Jour.
Technologies/Worship—R
Vital Issues
Voice of the Vineyard—R
WCA Monthly—R
Youthworker—R

TEEN/YOUNG ADULT
Breakaway—R
Challenge (GA)
Christteen—R
Devo'Zine—R
Insight—R
Sharing the VICTORY—R
Spirit
Straight—R
Teenage Christian—R
Teen Life (AG)—R
Teen Power—R
YOU!—R
Young Adult Today
Young & Alive—R
Young Salvationist—R
Youth 98

WOMEN
Aspire
Church Woman
Esprit—R
Handmaiden, The—R
Ishshah—R
Jour/Women's Ministries
Journey—R
Kansas City Woman
Lutheran Woman Today
Proverbs 31 Homemaker—R
Today's Christian Woman
Virtue—R

WRITERS
Canadian Writer's Jour—R
Christian Communicator, The—R
Cross & Quill—R

Fellowscript—R
Housewife-Writer—R
Inklings
NW Christian Author—R
Once Upon a Time—R
Tickled by Thunder
Writers Connection—R
Writer's Info
Writer's Ink—R

LEADERSHIP

ADULT/GENERAL
Angels on Earth
At Ease—R
Atlantic Baptist
Banner, The
Biblical Reflections—R
Canada Lutheran—R
Canadian Baptist
Catholic Digest—R
Catholic Forester—R
Christian Advocate—R
Christian Century
Christian Chronicle—R
Christian Edge—R
Christian Living—R
Christian Motorsports
Christian Ranchman
Christian Single—R
Christians in Business
Church Advocate—R
Companion
Covenant Companion—R
Culture Wars—R
Discipleship Journal
Disciple's Journal—R
Emphasis/Faith & Living—R
Evangelical Baptist—R
Expression Christian
Faith Today
Family Network—R
Foursquare World—R
Good News(KY)—R
Good News, Etc—R
Gospel Today
Hearing Hearts
Heartlight Internet—R
Heavenly Thoughts—R
Inland NW Christian
Insights—R
Island Christian—R
John Milton—R
Jour/Christian Nursing—R
Living Church
Lutheran Digest—R
Lutheran Journal—R
Lutheran Parent

MESSAGE/Open Bible—R
Messenger, The (MI)—R
Michigan Christian
NW Christian Journal—R
Our Family—R
Our Sunday Visitor
Perspectives
Pourastan—R
Presbyterian Layman
Presbyterian Outlook
Prism—R
Purpose—R
Religious Broadcasting—R
Religious Education
Sacred Journey—R
Single Connection—R
Something Better—R
Standard, The—R
Stand Firm—R
Trumpeter, The
United Church Observer
Watchman, The

CHILDREN
BREAD/God's Children—R
Club Connection—R

CHRISTIAN EDUCATION/LIBRARY
Baptist Leader—R
Brigade Leader—R
CE Connection—R
CE Connection
  Communique—R
CE Counselor—R
CE Leadership—R
Children's Ministry
Church Educator—R
Church Worship
GROUP
Leader/Church School
  Today—R
Perspective—R
Resource—R
Teacher's Interaction
Team—R
Vision—R

MISSIONS
American Horizon—R
East-West Church
Evangelical Missions—R
Leaders for Today
Missiology
Urban Mission—R
Worldwide Challenge

PASTORS/LEADERS
Catholic Servant
Cell Church—R
Cell Life FORUM—R
Christian Camp—R
Christian Century
Christian Management—R
Christian Ministry
Church Bytes—R
Church Growth Network—R
Church Management—R
Clergy Journal—R
Emmanuel
Enrichment—R
Evangelism USA
Five Stones, The—R
GROUP's Jr. High
Ivy Jungle Report—R
Journal/Christian Healing—R
Jour/Amer Soc/Chur
  Growth—R
Leadership Journal—R
Let's Worship
Lutheran Partners—R
Minister's Family
Ministries Today
Ministry
Pastoral Life
Pastor's Family
Preacher, The—R
Preacher's Magazine—R
Priest, The
Resource—R
Sabbath School Leadership
Sermon Notes
Today's Christian
  Preacher—R
Vital Issues
Voice of the Vineyard —R
WCA Monthly—R
Word & World
Worship Leader
Your Church—R
Youthworker—R

TEEN/YOUNG ADULT
Challenge (GA)
Student Leadership—R
Teenage Christian—R
YOU!—R

WOMEN
Aspire
Esprit—R
Helping Hand—R
Joyful Woman—R
Just Between Us—R

Sisters Today
Virtuous Woman
Woman's Touch—R

LITURGICAL

ADULT/GENERAL
AGAIN—R
alive now!
Annals of St. Anne
Arkansas Catholic
Arlington Catholic
Banner, The
Canada Lutheran—R
Canadian Catholic
Catholic Digest—R
Catholic Insight
Catholic Parent
Christian Century
Christian Motorsports
Commonweal
Companion
Cresset
Culture Wars—R
Episcopal Life—R
Family Digest
John Milton—R
Liguorian
Living Church
Lutheran Journal
Messenger (KY)
Messenger/ Sacred Heart
Messenger/St. Anthony
New Writing—R
North American Voice
Our Family—R
Our Sunday Visitor
Perspectives
Prairie Messenger—R
Presbyterian Record—R
St. Anthony Messenger
Silver Wings—R
Standard—R
Touchstone—R
United Church Observer
U.S. Catholic
Way of St. Francis—R

CHRISTIAN EDUCATION/LIBRARY
Catechist
Church Educator—R
Church Worship
Parish Teacher—R
Religion Teacher's Journal

MISSIONS
Areopagus—R
Catholic Near East

MUSIC
Church Pianist, etc.
Gospel Industry Today
Hymn, The

PASTORS/LEADERS
Catholic Servant
Catechumenate
Celebration
Christian Century
Christian Ministry
Church Administration
Church Bytes—R
Clergy Journal—R
Diocesan Dialogue—R
Emmanuel
Eucharistic Minister—R
Journal/Christian Healing—R
Liturgy
Lutheran Forum—R
Lutheran Partners—R
Ministries Today
Modern Liturgy—R
Parish Liturgy
Pastoral Life
Preacher's Illus. Service—R
Preacher's Magazine—R
Priest, The
PROCLAIM—R
Reformed Worship
Theology Today
Today's Parish
Word & World
Worship Leader

TEENS/YOUNG ADULT
YOU!—R
Youth Update

WOMEN
Handmaiden, The—R
Lutheran Woman Today
Sisters Today

MARRIAGE

ADULT/GENERAL
Alive!—R
America
American Tract Soc.—R
Angels on Earth
Annals of St. Anne
Arkansas Catholic

Arlington Catholic
At Ease—R
Atlantic Baptist
AXIOS—R
Banner, The
Bible Advocate—R
Biblical Reflections—R
Bread of Life—R
Canada Lutheran—R
Canadian Baptist
Canadian Catholic
Catholic Digest—R
Catholic Forester—R
Catholic Parent
Catholic Twin Circle—R
Celebrate Life—R
Charisma/Christian Life
Christian C.L. RECORD—R
Christian Courier (CAN)—R
Christian Edge—R
Christian Home & School
Christian Living—R
Christian Motorsports
Christian Parenting—R
Christian Ranchman
Christian Reader—R
Church Advocate—R
Church Herald/Holiness—R
Church of God
   EVANGEL—R
Columbia
Companion
Covenant Companion—R
Culture Wars—R
Decision
Disciple's Journal—R
Dovetail—R
Emphasis/Faith & Living—R
Evangel—R
Evangelical Baptist—R
Evangelical Visitor—R
Expression Christian
Faith Today
Family Digest
Family Network—R
Fellowship Today—R
Focus on the Family
Foursquare World—R
Gem, The—R
Good News (AL)—R
Good News, Etc—R
Good News Journal—R
Gospel Today
Guideposts
Head to Head—R
Hearing Hearts
Heartlight Internet—R
Heavenly Thoughts—R

Highway News—R
Home Times—R
Impact Magazine—R
Indian Life—R
Inside Journal—R
Insights—R
Island Christian—R
John Milton—R
Joyful Noise
Life Gate—R
Lifeglow—R
Light and Life
Liguorian
Live—R
Living—R
Lookout—R
Lutheran, The—R
Lutheran Digest—R
Lutheran Journal—R
Lutheran Parent
Lutheran Witness—R
Marriage Partnership
Mennonite, The—R
Mennonite Brethren—R
MESSAGE
Messenger, The (MI)—R
Messenger/St. Anthony
Metro Voice—R
Michigan Christian
Minnesota Christian—R
Montana Catholic—R
Moody—R
New Covenant
New Oxford Review
New Trumpet—R
North American Voice
NW Christian Journal—R
Our Family—R
Our Sunday Visitor
Pegasus Review—R
Pentecostal Testimony—R
Physician
Plain Truth—R
Plus—R
Pourastan—R
Prairie Messenger—R
PrayerWorks—R
Presbyterian Layman
Presbyterian Record—R
Presbyterians Today—R
Preserving Christian
    Homes—R
Prism—R
Progress—R
Purpose—R
Seek—R
Signs of the Times—R
Smart Dads

Smart Families
Social Justice
Something Better—R
Standard—R
Standard, The—R
Stand Firm—R
Star of Zion
Table Talk—R
Together—R
2-Soar—R
United Church Observer
Upsouth—R
U.S. Catholic
Vibrant Life—R
Vision, The—R
Voice, The—R
War Cry—R
Wesleyan Advocate—R

*CHRISTIAN
EDUCATION/LIBRARY*
CE Connection—R
Children's Ministry
GROUP

MISSIONS
Quiet Hour Echoes
Worldwide Challenge

PASTORS/LEADERS
Art+Plus
Catholic Servant
Cell Church—R
Five Stones, The—R
GROUP's Jr. High
Journal/Christian Healing—R
Journal/Pastoral Care
Lutheran Forum—R
Lutheran Partners—R
Minister's Family
Ministries Today
Networks—R
Pastoral Life
Pastor's Family
Preacher, The—R
Preacher's Illus. Service—R
PROCLAIM—R
Pulpit Helps—R
Today's Christian
    Preacher—R
Today's Parish
Vital Issues
Voice of the Vineyard —R
Word & World

TEEN/YOUNG ADULT
Straight—R

Today's Christian Teen—R
YOU!—R
Young Adult Today
Young & Alive—R
Young Christian—R
Youth Update

WOMEN
Adam's Rib—R
Aspire
Anna's Journal—R
DOMESTIQUE—R
Esprit—R
Handmaiden, The—R
Helping Hand—R
Horizons—R
Ishshah—R
Journey—R
Joyful Woman—R
Just Between Us—R
Lutheran Woman's Quar.
Lutheran Woman Today
Proverbs 31 Homemaker—R
Tea and Sunshine
Today's Christian Woman
Virtue—R
Virtuous Woman
Welcome Home
Woman's Touch—R
Women Alive!—R

MEN'S ISSUES

ADULT/GENERAL
Advent Christian Witness—R
Annals of St. Anne
Arlington Catholic
At Ease—R
Atlantic Baptist
AXIOS—R
Banner, The
Bible Advocate—R
Biblical Reflections—R
Bread of Life—R
Canada Lutheran—R
Canadian Baptist
Catholic Digest—R
Catholic Forester—R
Catholic Parent
CBA Marketplace
Celebrate Life—R
Charisma/Christian Life
Christian Edge—R
Christian Living—R
Christian Motorsports
Christian News NW—R
Christian Ranchman
Christian Reader—R

Christian Single—R
Christian Social Action—R
Chrysalis Reader
Church Herald/Holiness—R
Church of God
   EVANGEL—R
Columbia
Companion
Cornerstone—R
Covenant Companion—R
Decision
Disciple's Journal—R
Discovery—R
Emphasis/Faith & Living—R
Evangel—R
Evangelical Baptist—R
Expression Christian
Family Journal—R
Family Network—R
Fatted Calf Forum—R
Focus on the Family
Foursquare World—R
Gem, The—R
Good News (AL)—R
Good News, Etc—R
Good News Journal—R
Gospel Today
Healing Inn—R
Hearing Hearts
Heartlight Internet—R
Heavenly Thoughts—R
Highway News—R
Home Times—R
Indian Life—R
Inland NW Christian
Inside Journal—R
Insights—R
Island Christian—R
Jour/Christian Nursing—R
Joyful Noise
Life Gate—R
Liguorian
Light and Life
Live—R
Living—R
Lookout—R
Lutheran Parent
Marriage Partnership
Mennonite, The—R
MESSAGE/Open Bible—R
Messenger, The (MI)—R
Messenger/St. Anthony
Metro Voice—R
Michigan Christian
Moody—R
Newsline—R
New Trumpet—R
Our Family—R

Pentecostal Testimony—R
Physician
Plain Truth—R
Plus—R
PrayerWorks—R
Presbyterian Outlook
Preserving Christian
   Homes—R
Prism—R
Purpose—R
Single Connection—R
Smart Dads
Smart Families
Something Better—R
Standard, The—R
Stand Firm—R
Star of Zion
Table Talk—R
Together—R
Touchstone—R
Trumpeter, The
2-Soar—R
United Church Observer
Upsouth—R
Vibrant Life—R (health)
Voice, The—R

*CHRISTIAN
EDUCATION/LIBRARY*
Brigade Leader—R

MISSIONS
American Horizon—R
Brigade Leader—R
Worldwide Challenge

MUSIC
Quest—R

PASTORS/LEADERS
Art+Plus
Christian Ministry
Clergy Journal—R
Journal/Pastoral Care
Leadership Journal—R
Lutheran Partners—R
Ministries Today
Pastor's Family
Preacher, The—R
Preacher's Magazine—R
Pulpit Helps—R
Today's Christian
   Preacher—R
Voice of the Vineyard —R
Word & World

TEEN/YOUNG ADULT
Challenge (GA)
YOU!—R

WOMEN
Anna's Journal—R
Aspire
Horizons—R
Virtue—R

MIRACLES

ADULT/GENERAL
America
Angels on Earth
At Ease—R
Bible Advocate—R
Biblical Reflections—R
Bread of Life—R
Canadian Baptist
Canadian Catholic
Catholic Digest—R
Catholic Twin Circle—R
Charisma/Christian Life
Christian Chronicle—R
Christian Edge—R
Christian Motorsports
Christian Ranchman
Christian Single—R
Church Advocate—R
Church Herald/Holiness—R
Church of God
   EVANGEL—R
Companion
Connecting Point—R
Disciple's Journal—R
Culture Wars—R
Family Network—R
God's Revivalist
Good News (AL)—R
Good News, Etc—R
Good News Journal—R
Gospel Today
Guideposts
Hallelujah! (CAN)—R
Healing Inn—R
Heavenly Thoughts—R
Home Times—R
Impact Magazine—R
Insights—R
Island Christian—R
John Milton—R
Live—R
Lutheran Digest—R
Lutheran Parent
MESSAGE/Open Bible—R
Messenger/St. Anthony

Michigan Christian
New Oxford Review
North American Voice
Pegasus Review—R
Plain Truth—R
PrayerWorks—R
Queen of All Hearts
Single Connection—R
Something Better—R
Standard—R
Total Health
2-Soar—R
Upsouth—R
Vision, The—R
Watchman, The
Way of St. Francis—R

CHILDREN
BREAD/God's Children—R
Discovery (NY)—R

MISSIONS
American Horizon—R
Areopagus—R
Save Our World—R

PASTORS/LEADERS
Art+Plus
Journal/Christian Healing—R
Ministries Today
Networks—R
Voice of the Vineyard —R
Word & World

TEEN/YOUNG ADULT
Conqueror—R
Insight—R
Teen Life (AG)—R
YOU!—R
Young Adult Today
Young Christian—R

WOMEN
Handmaiden, The—R
Helping Hand—R
Lutheran Woman Today
Woman's Touch—R

MISSIONS

ADULT/GENERAL
Alive!—R
Anglican Journal—R
At Ease—R
Banner, The
Baptist Informer
B.C. Catholic—R

Bible Advocate—R
Biblical Reflections—R
Canada Lutheran—R
Canadian Baptist
Canadian Catholic
Canadian Mennonite
Catholic Digest—R
Catholic Twin Circle—R
Charisma/Christian Life
Christian Chronicle—R
Christian Edge—R
Christian Motorsports
Christian News NW—R
Christian Ranchman
Christian Reader—R
Christian Renewal—R
Christian Single—R
Christianity Today—R
Church Advocate—R
Church Herald/Holiness—R
Church of God
  EVANGEL—R
Companion
Companions—R
Connecting Point—R
Conquest
Cornerstone—R
Covenant Companion—R
Culture Wars—R
Disciple's Journal—R
Discipleship Journal
Decision
Episcopal Life—R
Evangel—R
Evangelical Baptist—R
Faith Today
Family Network—R
Gem, The—R
Good News (AL)—R
Good News (KY)—R
Good News, Etc—R
Gospel Today
Hallelujah! (CAN)—R
Healing Inn—R
Heavenly Thoughts—R
Indian Life—R
Insights—R
Island Christian—R
John Milton—R
Jour/Christian Nursing—R
Life Gate—R
Live—R
Living Church
Lutheran, The—R
Lutheran Journal—R
Lutheran Parent
Lutheran Witness—R
MESSAGE/Open Bible—R

Messenger, The (MI)—R
Messenger/St. Anthony
Michigan Christian
New Heart, A—R (medical)
New Oxford Review
New Trumpet—R
North American Voice
Our Family—R
Our Sunday Visitor
Power for Living—R
PrayerWorks—R
Presbyterian Layman
Presbyterian Outlook
Presbyterian Record—R
Presbyterians Today—R
Prism—R
Purpose—R
Queen of All Hearts
Seek—R
Single Connection—R
Something Better—R
Standard—R
Standard, The—R
Stand Firm—R
TEAK Roundup—R
2-Soar—R
Upsouth—R
Vision, The—R
Way of St. Francis—R

CHILDREN
BREAD/God's Children—R
Crusader (TN)
Lad
Partners—R
R-A-D-A-R—R

**CHRISTIAN
EDUCATION/LIBRARY**
Brigade Leader—R
Children's Ministry
Church Educator—R
Courage
Evangelizing Today's
  Child—R
GROUP
Shining Star

MISSIONS
(See alphabetical listings)

MUSIC
Quest—R

PASTORS/LEADERS
Art+Plus
Christian Management—R

Church Administration
Emmanuel
Enrichment—R
GROUP's Jr. High
Jour/Amer Soc/Chur
    Growth—R
Journal/Christian Healing—R
Lutheran Partners—R
Ministries Today
Networks—R
Preacher's Magazine—R
Priest, The
PROCLAIM—R
Pulpit Helps—R
Today's Christian
    Preacher—R
Vital Issues
Voice of the Vineyard —R
Word & World
Youthworker—R

TEEN/YOUNG ADULT
Alive!
Certainty
Challenge (GA)
Challenge (IL)
Christteen—R
Conqueror—R
Devo'Zine—R
Student Leadership—R
Teen Life (AG)—R
Teen Power—R
YOU!—R
Young Adult Today

WOMEN
Aspire
CoLaborer—R
Esprit—R
Handmaiden, The—R
Joyful Woman—R
Just Between Us—R
Lutheran Woman Today

MONEY MANAGEMENT

ADULT/GENERAL
Anglican Journal—R
At Ease—R
AXIOS—R
Banner, The
Biblical Reflections—R
Brethren Evangelist
Catholic Digest—R
Catholic Forester—R
Catholic Parent
Catholic Twin Circle—R

CBA Marketplace
Christian C.L. RECORD—R
Christian Edge—R
Christian Living—R
Christian Motorsports
Christian Parenting—R
Christian Ranchman
Christian Single—R
Christians in Business
Church Advocate—R
Connecting Point—R
Conquest
Covenant Companion—R
Disciple's Journal—R
Discovery—R
Emphasis/Faith & Living—R
Evangelical Baptist—R
Evangelical Visitor—R
Expression Christian
Family Network—R
Good News (AL)—R
Gospel Today
Head to Head—R
Healing Inn—R
Heartlight Internet—R
Heavenly Thoughts—R
Home Times—R
Indian Life—R
Inland NW Christian
Insights—R
Island Christian—R
Life Gate—R
Live—R
Living—R
Lutheran Digest—R
Lutheran Journal
Lutheran Parent
Marriage Partnership
Mennonite, The—R
MESSAGE
MESSAGE/Open Bible—R
Messenger, The (MI)—R
Michigan Christian
No-Debt Living—R
Parent Paper, The
Pentecostal Testimony—R
Physician
Presbyterian Layman
Preserving Christian
    Homes—R
Religious Broadcasting—R
Signs of the Times—R
Single Connection—R
Smart Dads
Smart Families
Something Better—R
Standard, The—R
Stand Firm—R

Star of Zion
Stewardship
Table Talk—R
Today's Christian Senior—R
2-Soar—R
Visitation
War Cry—R

CHILDREN
Courage
Young Christian—R

*CHRISTIAN
EDUCATION/LIBRARY*
Children's Ministry
CE Connection—R
Christian School
Church Educator—R
GROUP

MISSIONS
Quiet Hour Echoes
World Christian—R

PASTORS/LEADERS
Cell Church—R
Christian Ministry
Church Bytes—R
Clergy Journal—R
GROUP's Jr. High
Journal/Christian Healing—R
Leadership Journal—R
Ministries Today
Networks—R
Pastor's Family
Pastor's Tax & Money
Today's Christian
    Preacher—R
Today's Parish
Vital Issues
Your Church—R
Youthworker—R

TEEN/YOUNG ADULT
Certainty
Challenge (GA)
Challenge (IL)
Christteen—R
Today's Christian Teen—R
Young Adult Today
Young Christian—R

WOMEN
Adam's Rib—R
Aspire
DOMESTIQUE—R
Esprit—R

Ishshah—R
Journey—R
Just Between Us—R
Lutheran Woman Today
Proverbs 31 Homemaker—R
Today's Christian Woman
Virtuous Woman
Woman's Touch—R

MUSIC REVIEWS

ADULT/GENERAL
Arlington Catholic
Atlantic Baptist
Banner, The
Canadian Catholic
CBA Marketplace
Charisma/Christian Life
Christian Arts Review
Christian Edge—R
Christian Media—R
Christian Parenting—R
Christian Single—R
Christianity/Arts
Commonweal
Cornerstone—R
Disciple's Journal—R
Expression Christian
Fatted Calf Forum—R
Gadfly—R
Good News (AL)—R
Good News Journal—R
Good News - Salem
Head to Head—R
Heartlight Internet—R
Heavenly Thoughts—R
Home Times—R
Impact Magazine—R
Island Christian—R
Life Gate—R
Live—R
Living Light News—R
Living with Teenagers—R
Michigan Christian
MovieGuide
ParentLife—R
Pentecostal Testimony—R
Plowman, The—R
Presbyterian Record—R
Prism—R
Single Connection—R
Sojourners
Something Better—R
Stand Firm—R
Star of Zion
TEAK Roundup—R
United Church Observer
Upsouth—R

CHILDREN
Club Connection—R

CHRISTIAN EDUCATION/LIBRARY
CE Counselor—R
Church Libraries—R

MUSIC
CCM Magazine
Christian Country—R
Creator—R
Gospel Industry Today
Hymn, The
Quest—R

PASTORS/LEADERS
Ivy Jungle Report—R
Ministries Today
Technologies/Worship—R
WCA Monthly—R
Reformed Worship

TEEN/YOUNG ADULT
Challenge (GA)
Christteen—R
Devo'Zine—R
Teenage Christian—R
Teen Power—R
With—R
YOU!—R
Young Christian—R
Young Salvationist—R
Youth 98

WOMEN
Horizons—R
Kansas City Woman

WRITERS
Inklings

NATURE

ADULT/GENERAL
Alive!—R
AXIOS—R
Canadian Catholic
Catholic Digest—R
Catholic Forester—R
Christian Traveler—R
Chrysalis Reader
Companion
Covenant Companion—R
E Street—R
Fellowship Link—R

Good News (AL)—R
Good News - Salem
Green Cross—R
Heavenly Thoughts—R
Ideals—R
John Milton—R
Keys to Living
Lifeglow—R
Lutheran Digest—R
Lutheran Parent
Messenger/St. Anthony
Pegasus Review—R
Pourastan—R
PrayerWorks—R
Rosebud
Seek—R
Smile—R
Standard, The—R
TEAK Roundup—R
Time of Singing—R
Today's Christian Senior—R
2-Soar—R
Upsouth—R

CHILDREN
Club Connection—R
Counselor—R
Courage
Crusader—R
Focus/Clubhouse
Junior Trails—R
Live Wire—R
My Friend
Nature Friend—R
On the Line
Partners—R
R-A-D-A-R—R
Skipping Stones
Story Friends—R
Touch—R
Young Christian—R

CHRISTIAN EDUCATION/LIBRARY
Shining Star

PASTORS/LEADERS
Art+Plus
Christian Camp—R
Journal/Christian Healing—R
Word & World

TEEN/YOUNG ADULT
Challenge (GA)
Insight—R
Teenage Christian—R
YOU!—R

Young & Alive—R
Young Christian—R

WOMEN
Aspire
Esprit—R
Proverbs 31 Homemaker—R

NEWSPAPERS

Alabama Baptist
Alive
Anglican Journal
Arkansas Catholic
Arlington Catholic
Awareness TN Christian
Baptist Informer
B.C. Catholic
Catholic Courier
Catholic New York
Catholic Peace Voice
Catholic Sentinel
Catholic Servant
Catholic Telegraph
Catholic Twin Circle
Christian Advocate
Christian American
Christian Courier (WI)
Christian Courier (CAN)
Christian Crusade
Christian Edge
Christian Media
Christian News NW
Christian Observer
Christian Ranchman
Christian Renewal
Church Advocate
Dallas/Ft.Worth Heritage
Diocesan Dialogue
Disciple's Journal
Discovery
Episcopal Life
Expression Christian
Family Journal, The
Fatted Calf Forum
Good News (AL)
Good News, Etc.
Good News Journal
Good News - Salem
Harvest Press
Harvest Times
Home Times
Indian Life
Inland NW Christian
Inside Journal
Interchange
Interim
Island Christian Info

John Milton
Kentucky Christian News
Life Gate
Live Wire
Living
Living Light News
Mennonite Weekly
Messenger
Metro Voice
Michigan Christian
Minnesota Christian Chronicle
Montana Catholic
National Catholic Reporter
Network
Northstate Christian Times
NW Christian Journal
Oblate World
Our Sunday Visitor
Parent Paper
Plowman, The
Prayerworks
Presbyterian Layman
Pulpit Helps
Revelation Post
Save Our World
Second Stone
Shantyman, The
Single Connection
Something Better News
Star of Zion
Together
United Voice
YOU! (teen)

ONLINE MAGAZINES*

ADULT/GENERAL
Bible Advocate Online
Christian Arts Review
Head to Head
Heartlight
New Writing
Poet's Park
Religious Broadcasting
Seeds Magazine
Uplook Magazine
Village Life

PASTORS/LEADERS
Sermon Notes

OPINION PIECES

ADULT/GENERAL
Arlington Catholic
At Ease—R
AXIOS—R

Banner, The
B.C. Catholic—R
Bible Advocate—R
Biblical Reflections—R
Canadian Catholic
Canadian Mennonite
Catholic New York
Celebrate Life—R
Charisma/Christian Life
Christian Arts Review
Christian Chronicle—R
Christian Edge—R
Christian Living—R
Christian Motorsports
Christian News NW—R
Christian Renewal—R
Christian Social Action—R
Christianity Today—R
Commonweal
Compass
Cornerstone—R
Covenant Companion—R
Culture Wars—R
Door, The
Dovetail—R
Episcopal Life—R
Evangel—R
Evangelical Baptist—R
Faith Today
Family Journal—R
Family Network—R
Fellowship Today—R
First Things
Good News, Etc—R
Gospel Today
Grail
Head to Head—R
Healing Inn—R
Heavenly Thoughts—R
Home Times—R
Indian Life—R
Inland NW Christian
Insights—R
Interim—R
Jour/Christian Nursing—R
Light and Life
Lutheran, The—R
Lutheran Parent
Mennonite Brethren—R
Mennonite Weekly
MESSAGE/Open Bible—R
Messenger
Messenger/St. Anthony
Metro Voice—R
Michigan Christian
Minnesota Christian—R
New Creation
New Oxford Review

Perspectives
Plain Truth—R
PrayerWorks—R
Presbyterian Outlook
Presbyterian Record—R
Presbyterians Today—R
ProLife News—R
Quiet Revolution—R
Sacred Journey—R
St. Anthony Messenger
Second Stone
Single Connection—R
Social Justice
Sojourners
Standard, The—R
United Church Observer
Upsouth—R
U.S. Catholic
Visitation
Way of St. Francis—R

CHILDREN
Writers' Intl. Forum/Young

CHRISTIAN
EDUCATION/LIBRARY
CE Connection—R
Today's Catholic Teacher—R

MISSIONS
American Horizon—R
Areopagus—R
East-West Church
Save Our World—R

PASTORS/LEADERS
Cell Life FORUM—R
Christian Century
Journal/Christian Healing—R
Journal/Pastoral Care
Lutheran Forum—R
Priest, The
Pulpit Helps—R
Single Ad. Ministries Jour.
Word & World
Worship Leader

TEEN/YOUNG ADULT
Christteen—R
Insight—R
YOU!—R
Young Adult Today
Young Christian—R
Young Salvationist—R

WOMEN
Anna's Journal—R

Conscience—R
DOMESTIQUE—R
Handmaiden, The—R
Horizons—R
Lutheran Woman Today

WRITERS
Canadian Writer's Jour—R
Exchange—R
Once Upon a Time—R
W.I.N. Informer
Writer's Exchange—R
Writer's Ink—R
Writers' Intl. Forum

PARENTING

ADULT/GENERAL
American Tract Soc.—R
Angels on Earth
Annals of St. Anne
Arkansas Catholic
Arlington Catholic
Atlantic Baptist
AXIOS—R
Banner, The
Bible Advocate—R
Biblical Reflections—R
Bread of Life—R
Canada Lutheran—R
Canadian Baptist
Catholic Digest—R
Catholic Forester—R
Catholic Parent
Catholic Sentinel—R
Charisma/Christian Life
Christian Courier (CAN)—R
Christian Home & School
Christian Living—R
Christian Motorsports
Christian Parenting—R
Christian Ranchman
Christian Reader—R
Christian Single—R
Church Advocate—R
Church Herald/Holiness—R
Columbia
Companion
Covenant Companion—R
Culture Wars—R
Decision
Disciple's Journal—R
Dovetail—R
Emphasis/Faith & Living—R
E Street—R
Evangel—R
Evangelical Baptist—R
Evangelical Visitor—R

Expression Christian
Family Digest
Family Network—R
Fellowship Today—R
Focus on the Family
Foursquare World—R
Gem, The—R
God's Revivalist
Good News (AL)—R
Good News, Etc—R
Good News Journal—R
Good News - Salem
Good Shepherd
Gospel Tidings—R
Gospel Today
Green Cross—R
Hearing Hearts
Heartlight Internet—R
Highway News—R
Home Times—R
Impact Magazine—R
Indian Life—R
Inside Journal—R
Insights—R
Island Christian—R
Life Gate—R
Light and Life
Liguorian
Live—R
Living—R
Living with Teenagers—R
Lookout—R
Lutheran, The—R
Lutheran Digest—R
Lutheran Journal—R
Lutheran Parent
Marriage Partnership
Mennonite, The—R
Mennonite Brethren—R
MESSAGE
MESSAGE/Open Bible—R
Messenger/St. Anthony
Metro Voice—R
Michigan Christian
Moody—R
MovieGuide
New Covenant
New Oxford Review
Our Family—R
Our Sunday Visitor
ParentLife—R
Parent Paper, The
Pegasus Review—R
Pentecostal Evangel—R
Pentecostal Testimony—R
Plain Truth—R
Plus—R
Pourastan—R

Power for Living—R
PrayerWorks—R
Presbyterians Today—R
Preserving Christian
    Homes—R
Progress—R
Purpose—R
Religious Education
Sacred Journey—R
St. Joseph's Messenger—R
Seek—R
Single-Parent Family
Smart Dads
Smart Families
Social Justice
Sojourners
Standard—R
Standard, The—R
Stand Firm—R
Table Talk—R
Together—R
2-Soar—R
Upsouth—R
U.S. Catholic
Vibrant Life—R
Vision, The—R
War Cry—R
Wesleyan Advocate—R

*CHRISTIAN
EDUCATION/LIBRARY*
CE Connection—R
CE Counselor—R
Children's Ministry
Christian School
GROUP

MISSIONS
Quiet Hour Echoes
Worldwide Challenge

PASTORS/LEADERS
Art+Plus
Catholic Servant
Church Bytes—R
GROUP's Jr. High
Journal/Christian Healing—R
Minister's Family
Networks—R
Pastor's Family
Preacher's Illus. Service—R
Pulpit Helps—R
Single Ad. Ministries Jour.
Today's Christian
    Preacher—R
Vital Issues
Youthworker—R

WOMEN
Adam's Rib—R
Aspire
DOMESTIQUE—R
Esprit—R
Handmaiden, The—R
Helping Hand—R
Horizons—R
Ishshah—R
Joyful Woman—R
Just Between Us—R
Link & Visitor—R
Lutheran Woman's Quar.
Lutheran Woman Today
Proverbs 31 Homemaker—R
Tea and Sunshine
Today's Christian Woman
Virtue—R
Virtuous Woman
Welcome Home
Wesleyan Woman—R
Woman's Touch—R
Women Alive!—R

PERSONAL EXPERIENCE

ADULT/GENERAL
AGAIN—R
alive now!
Angels on Earth
Annals of St. Anne
At Ease—R
Banner, The
B.C. Catholic—R
Bible Advocate—R
Bible Advocate Online—R
Biblical Reflections—R
Canada Lutheran—R
Canadian Baptist
Canadian Mennonite
Catholic Digest—R
Catholic New York
Catholic Sentinel—R
Catholic Twin Circle—R
Celebrate Life—R
Christian Chronicle—R
Christian Courier (CAN)—R
Christian Edge—R
Christian Home & School
Christian Motorsports
Christian Ranchman
Christian Reader—R
Christian Renewal—R
Christian Single—R
Christian Traveler—R
Chrysalis Reader
Church Advocate—R
Church Herald/Holiness—R

Church of God
    EVANGEL—R
Comments/Friends—R
Commonweal
Companion
Companions—R
Compass
Conquest
Covenant Companion—R
Crossway/Newsline—R
Decision
Disciple's Journal—R
Door, The
Dovetail—R
Evangel—R
Evangelical Baptist—R
Evangelical Visitor—R
Family Journal—R
Family Network—R
Fellowship Today—R
Gem, The—R
God's Revivalist
Good News (AL)—R
Good News, Etc—R
Good News Journal
Good News - Salem
Gospel Today
Grail
Guideposts
Hallelujah! (CAN)—R
Head to Head—R
Healing Inn—R
Hearing Heart—R
Heavenly Thoughts—R
Highway News—R
Home Times—R
Ideals
Impact Magazine—R
Indian Life—R
Inland NW Christian
Insights—R
Inspirer, The—R
Inside Journal—R
Interim—R
Island Christian—R
John Milton—R
Jour/Christian Nursing—R
Keys to Living
Light and Life
Liguorian
Live—R
Living—R
Living with Teenagers—R
Lutheran, The—R
Lutheran Digest—R
Lutheran Journal—R
Lutheran Parent
Marian Helpers—R

Marriage Partnership
Mennonite, The—R
Mennonite Brethren—R
MESSAGE
MESSAGE/Open Bible—R
Messenger, The (MI)—R
Messenger/St. Anthony
Michigan Christian
Minnesota Christian—R
Moody—R
MovieGuide
New Covenant
New Heart, A—R
Newsline—R
New Trumpet—R
New Writing—R
North American Voice
Northwestern Lutheran—R
Oblates
Our Family—R
Pentecostal Evangel—R
Plain Truth—R
Plenty Good Room
Plus—R
PrayerWorks—R
Presbyterian Record—R
Presbyterians Today—R
Preserving Christian
    Homes—R
Progress—R
ProLife News—R
Purpose—R
Pursuit—R
Religious Broadcasting—R
Remembrance—R
Sacred Journey—R
St. Anthony Messenger
SCP Journal—R
Seek—R
Shantyman, The—R
Sharing—R
Single Connection—R
Single-Parent Family
Smile—R
Sojourners
Spiritual Life
Standard—R
Standard, The—R
Stand Firm—R
Stewardship
Sursum Corda!—R
Table Talk—R
Time of Singing—R
Together—R
United Church Observer
Upscale Magazine
Upsouth—R
VISION—R

Vision, The—R
Visitation
Voice, The—R
War Cry—R
Way of St. Francis—R
Weavings—R
Wesleyan Advocate—R

CHILDREN
Club Connection—R
Counselor—R
Courage
Discovery (NY)—R
GUIDE—R
Live Wire—R
Partners—R
Skipping Stones
Touch—R
Venture
Writers' Intl. Forum/Young

*CHRISTIAN
EDUCATION/LIBRARY*
Brigade Leader—R
CE Connection—R
CE Counselor—R
Children's Ministry
GROUP
Journal/Adventist Educ.—R
Perspective—R
Religion Teacher's Journal
Today's Catholic Teacher—R

MISSIONS
American Horizon—R
Areopagus—R
Heartbeat—R
P.I.M.E. World
Quiet Hour Echoes
Save Our World—R
World Christian—R
Worldwide Challenge

MUSIC
Plans & Pluses

PASTORS/LEADERS
Art+Plus
Catholic Servant
Cell Church—R
Cell Life FORUM—R
Christian Camp—R
Christian Century
Christian Ministry
Christian Recreation
Church Bytes—R
Eucharistic Minister—R

Five Stones, The—R
GROUP's Jr. High
Journal/Christian Healing—R
Journal/Pastoral Care
Leadership Journal—R
Minister's Family
Networks—R
Pastor's Family
Preacher's Illus. Service—R
Preacher's Magazine—R
Sabbath School Leadership
Theology Today (rarely)
Today's Parish
Vital Issues
Youthworker—R

TEEN/YOUNG ADULT
Alive!
Breakaway—R
Campus Life—R
Certainty
Challenge (GA)
Challenge (IL)
Christteen—R
Conqueror—R
Devo'Zine—R
Insight—R
Listen—R
Sharing the VICTORY—R
Spirit
Straight—R
Teen Life (AG)—R
Teen Power—R
Teens on Target—R
Today's Christian Teen—R
With—R (1st person teen)
YOU!—R
Young Adult Today
Young Christian—R
Young Salvationist—R
Youth Challenge—R
Youth 98
Youth World—R

WOMEN
Anna's Journal—R
Aspire
DOMESTIQUE—R
Esprit—R
Handmaiden, The—R
Helping Hand—R
Horizons—R
Ishshah—R
Journey—R
Jour/Women's Ministries
Joyful Woman—R
Just Between Us—R
Kansas City Woman

Lutheran Woman Today
Proverbs 31 Homemaker—R
Tea and Sunshine
Today's Christian Woman
Virtue—R
Welcome Home
Wesleyan Woman—R
Woman's Touch—R
Women Alive!—R

WRITERS
Byline
Fellowscript—R
Housewife-Writer—R
Inklings
Once Upon a Time—R
Tickled by Thunder
Writer's Ink—R
Writers' Intl. Forum
Writer's Nook News

PHOTOGRAPHS

Note: "Reprint" indicators (R) have been deleted from this section, and "B" for black & white glossy prints or "C" for color transparencies inserted. An asterisk (*) before a listing indicates they buy photos with articles only.

ADULT/GENERAL
ABS RECORD
Alive!—B
alive now!—B
American Tract Soc.
Anglican Journal—B/C
*Annals of St. Anne—B/C
Arlington Catholic—B
At Ease—B/C
Banner, The
Bible Advocate—B/C
Bible Today—B
Calvinist Contact—B/C
Canada Lutheran—B
*Canadian Baptist
Canadian Mennonite —B/C
*Cathedral Age—B
Catholic Courier—B
*Catholic Digest—B/C
Catholic Forester—B/C
Catholic Heritage
Catholic New York—B
Catholic Parent
Catholic Rural Life—B
*Catholic Sentinel—B/C
Catholic Telegraph—B

Catholic Twin Circle
CBA Frontline—C
CBA Marketplace—C
Celebrate Life—B/C
Charisma/Christian Life—C
Christian Advocate—B/C
Christian Century—B
Christian Courier—B
Christian Crusade—B
*Christian Edge—B
*Christian History—B/C
Christian Home & School—C
Christian Living—B
*Christian Motorsports—B
Christian Parenting
    Today—B/C
*Christian Reader—B/C
*Christian Single—C
Christian Social Action—B
Christian Standard—B/C
Christian Traveler—C
*Christianity Today—C
*Christmas—C
Church Advocate
Church & State
Church of God
    EVANGEL—C
Columbia—C
Comments/Friends—B
*Commonweal—B/C
Companion—B
Connecting Point—B
*Conquest—B/C
Cornerstone—B/C
Covenant Companion—B/C
Culture Wars—B/C
Episcopal Life—B
*E Street—C
*Evangel—B
Evangelical Baptist—B/C
Evangelical Beacon—B/C
Evangelical Visitor—B
Faith Today—B
Fellowship Today—B
Focus on the Family—B/C
Foursquare World—C
Gadfly—B/C
Good News (AL)—B
Good News, Etc—C
Good News Journal—B
Gospel Tidings—B
Grail—B/C
*Guideposts—B/C
Hallelujah—B
Head to Head—B/C
*Heavenly Thoughts
Highway News—B
*Home Times—B

Impact Magazine—C
Inland NW Christian—B
*Inside Journal—B
Insights
Inspirer, The—B
Interchange—B
Interim
*Journal/Christian
    Nursing—B/C
Joyful Noise
Liberty—B/C
*Lifeglow—B/C
Light and Life—B/C
*Liguorian—B/C
Live—C
Living—B/C
Living Church—B/C
Living Light News—B/C
Lookout—B/C
Lutheran, The—B
*Lutheran Journal—B/C
Lutheran Parent
Lutheran Witness—B/C
Marian Helpers—B/C
Mature Living
*Mature Years—C
Mennonite, The—B/C
Mennonite Brethren—B
Mennonite Weekly—B
MESSAGE—B/C
Messenger—B
*Messenger/St.
    Anthony—B/C
Michigan Christian—B
*Montana Catholic—B
Nat. Christian
    Reporter—B/C/prints
*New Heart, A—B
Northwestern Lutheran
Our Family—B/C
Our Sunday Visitor—B/C
Pentecostal Evangel—B/C
*Pentecostal Testimony—B/C
*Plain Truth—B/C (few)
Plenty Good Room—B
Poetry Forum—B
Poets' Paper
*Power for Living—B
*Prairie Messenger—C
*Presbyterian Layman—B
Presbyterian Outlook—B/C
Presbyterian Record—B/C
Presbyterians Today—B/C
Prism—B/C
Progress—C
*Purpose—B
Pursuit—B
Quiet Revolution—B

Revelation Post—B/C
Sacred Journey—B
*St. Anthony
    Messenger—B/C
SCP Journal—B/C
Second Stone—B
Seek—B
Signs of the Times—C
Sojourners—B/C
*Something Better
Spiritual Life—B
Sports Spectrum—C
Standard—B
Standard, The
Stand Firm—C
*Star of Zion
*Sursum Corda!—R
Together—B/C
Total Health—B/C
Twin Cities Christian—B
*United Church
    Observer—B/C
Upscale Magazine
*Vibrant Life—C
VISION—B/C
*Visitation
War Cry—B/C
Way of St. Francis—B
Wesleyan Advocate—C

CHILDREN
*Counselor—B/C
*Courage
Crusader
*Focus/Clubhouse Jr.—C
God's World Today—C
Guideposts for Kids—C
Junior Trails—C
Listen—C
Live Wire—C
Nature Friend—B/C
My Friend
On the Line—B/C
*Pockets—B/C
Power & Light—B
*Primary Pal (IL)
R-A-D-A-R—C (rarely)
*Skipping Stones—B
Story Friends—B
Together Time—C
Touch—C
Venture—C
Wonder Time—B/C

CHRISTIAN
EDUCATION/LIBRARY
Baptist Leader—B/C
Brigade Leader—B

CE Counselor—B/C
CE Leadership—B/C
Children's Ministry—C
Christian Librarian—B
Christian School—C
*Church Educator—B
*Church Libraries—B/C
Evangelizing Today's
    Child—B/C
GROUP—C
Journal/Adventist
    Education—B
Junior Teacher—B/C
*Leader/Church School
    Today—B
Lollipops
Parish Teacher—B
Religion Teacher's
    Journal—B/C
Teachers in Focus—C
*Teachers Interaction—B
Team—B/C
*Today's Catholic Teacher—C

DAILY DEVOTIONALS
Daily Dev for Deaf—C
Light from the Word—C
Secret Place—B/C
Words of Life—B/C

MISSIONS
American Horizon
Areopagus—B/C
Catholic Near East—C
Evangelical Missions
PFI World Report
*P.I.M.E. World—C
Intl Jour/Frontier—R
Message of the Cross—B/C
New World Outlook—C
*Wherever—B
World Christian—B/C
*World Pulse
*World Vision—C

MUSIC
Christian Country—B
Church Musician—B
*Creator—B/C
Plans & Pluses—B/C

PASTORS/LEADERS
Catholic Servant
*Cell Life FORUM—B/C
Christian Camp—B/C
Christian Century—B/C
Christian Ministry—B

Clergy Journal—B
Environment & Art—B/C
GROUP's Jr. High—C
Leadership Journal—B
Liturgy—B
Lutheran Forum—B
*Lutheran Partners—B
    (rarely)
Ministry—B
Networks—B
Pray!
*Preacher, The—B
Preacher's Magazine—B/C
Resource—B/C
Today's Parish—B/C
Vital Issues - C
WCA Monthly—C
*Worship Leader—C
*Your Church—B/C

TEEN/YOUNG ADULT
Breakaway—C
Brio—C
Campus Life—C
*Certainty—B
*Challenge (GA)—B/C
*Challenge (IL)
*Christteen—B/C
The Conqueror—B/C
Lighted Pathway—B/C
*Listen—B/C
*Sharing the VICTORY—C
Spirit—B/C
Straight—C
Student Leadership—B/C
Take Five—B/C
Teen Life (AG)—C
*Teen Power—B
Venture—B
With—B
Young Adult Today—B
Young & Alive—B(prefer)/C
Young Christian—B/C
Youth 98—B/C

WOMEN
Anna's Journal—B
Conscience—B
*Esprit—B
Helping Hand—B
*Horizons—B/C
*Ishshah—R
Jour/Women's Ministries—B
*Journey
Joyful Woman—C
Kansas City Woman—B
*Link & Visitor—B
Lutheran Woman Today—B

*Sisters Today—B
Today's Christian Woman—C
Virtue—B/C
Wesleyan Woman
Women Alive!—B

WRITERS
*Byline
Gotta Write—B
*Housewife-Writer—B
Tickled by Thunder
*Writer's Digest—R

POETRY

ADULT/GENERAL
alive now!
America
AXIOS—R
Banner, The
Bible Advocate—R
Bread of Life—R
Broken Streets—R
Burning Light—R
Christian Century
Christian Courier (CAN)—R
Christian Living—R
Christian Motorsports
Christian Ranchman
Christian Reader—R
Christianity/Arts
Christmas—R
Church Herald/Holiness—R
Commonweal
Companion
Connecting Point—R
Cornerstone—R
Covenant Companion—R
Creatively Yours
Cresset
Culture Wars—R
Decision
Disciple's Journal—R
Door, The
Dovetail—R
Evangel—R
Family Journal—R
Family Network—R
Fatted Calf Forum—R
First Things
Foursquare World—R
Gems of Truth—R
Good News (AL)—R
Good News - Salem
Gospel Today
Grail
Green Cross—R
Guideposts

Hallelujah! (CAN)—R
Head to Head—R
Healing Inn—R
Hearing Hearts
Heartlight Internet—R
Heavenly Thoughts—R
Home Times—R
Ideals—R
Impact Magazine—R
Insights—R
Inspirer, The—R
Island Christian—R
Jewel Among Jewels—R
John Milton—R
Jour/Christian Nursing—R
Joyful Noise (KY)
Keys to Living
Liberty (little)—R
Life Gate—R
Light and Life
Lighthouse Fiction
Live—R
Living Church
Lutheran Digest—R
Lutheran Journal
Mature Living
Mature Years—R
Mennonite, The—R
Mennonite Brethren—R
Messenger, The (MI)—R
Miraculous Medal
Moonletters—R
New Heart, A—R
New Trumpet—R
New Writing—R
North American Voice
Oblates
Our Family—R
Parent Paper, The
Pegasus Review—R
Pentecostal Testimony—R
Perspectives
Plowman, The—R
Poetry Forum—R
Poets' Paper—R
Poet's Park—R
Pourastan—R
Prairie Messenger—R
PrayerWorks—R
Presbyterian Layman
Presbyterian Record—R
Presbyterians Today—R
Purpose—R
Queen of All Hearts
Ratio
Remembrance—R
Revelation Post—R
Rosebud

Sacred Journey—R
St. Anthony Messenger
St. Joseph's Messenger—R
San Diego Co. Christian
Second Stone
Sharing—R
Silver Wings—R
Smile—R
Sojourners
Standard—R
Star of Zion
Table Talk—R
TEAK Roundup—R
Time for Rhyme
Time of Singing—R
Today's Christian Senior—R
2-Soar—R
Upsouth—R
U.S. Catholic
Vision, The—R
Voice, The—R
War Cry—R
Weavings—R
Wesleyan Advocate—R

CHILDREN
Club Connection—R
CLUBHOUSE—R
Creatively Yours
Discovery (NY)—R
Focus/Clubhouse Jr
Guideposts for Kids
Junior Trails—R
Listen
Mission
Nature Friend—R
On the Line—R
Our Little Friend—R
Partners—R
Pockets—R
Primary Treasure—R
R-A-D-A-R—R
Skipping Stones
Story Friends—R
Story Mates—R
Together Time
Touch—R
Young Christian—R

*CHRISTIAN
EDUCATION/LIBRARY*
Baptist Leader—R
Christian Educators Jour—R
Christian School
Church Educator—R
Lollipops
Resource—R
Shining Star

Teacher Interaction
Today's Catholic Teacher—R
Vision—R

DAILY DEVOTIONALS
Living Words—R
Secret Place

MISSIONS
Quiet Hour Echoes

MUSIC
Choir Herald, etc.
Church Pianist, etc.
Glory Songs—R
Hymn, The (hymns only)
Plans & Pluses
Quest—R
Senior Musician—R
Tradition

PASTORS/LEADERS
Art+Plus
Catechumenate
Cell Life FORUM—R
Christian Century
Cross Currents—R
Emmanuel
Journal/Christian Healing—R
Journal/Pastoral Care
Let's Worship
Liturgy
Lutheran Forum—R
Lutheran Partners—R
Minister's Family
Networks—R
Preacher, The—R
Preacher's Illus. Service—R
Pulpit Helps—R
Review for Religious
Theology Today

TEEN/YOUNG ADULT
Alive!
Campus Life
Christteen—R
Devo'Zine—R
Insight—R
Sharing the VICTORY—R
Straight—R
Student Leadership—R
Take Five—R
Teenage Christian—R
Teen Life (AG)—R
Teen Power—R (by teens)
YOU!—R
Young Christian—R

Young Salvationist—R
Youth 98 (by teens)
Youth World—R

WOMEN
Adam's Rib—R
Anna's Journal—R
Conscience—R
DOMESTIQUE—R
Esprit—R
Handmaiden, The—R
Horizons—R
Ishshah—R
Jour/Women's Ministries
Joyful Woman—R
Link & Visitor—R
Lutheran Woman Today
Proverbs 31 Homemaker—R
Sisters Today
Tea and Sunshine
Virtue—R
Virtuous Woman
Welcome Home
Wesleyan Woman—R
Women Alive!—R

WRITERS
Byline
Canadian Writer's Jour—R
Christian Communicator—R
Cross & Quill—R
Gotta Write
Heaven—R
Housewife-Writer—R
Inklings
My Legacy—R
Omnific—R
Once Upon a Time—R
Poetry Connection
Southwestern Writers—R
Tickled by Thunder
Today's $85,000 Freelance
W.I.N. Informer
Writer's Digest—R
Writer's Exchange—R
Writer's Ink—R
Write Touch—R

POLITICAL

ADULT/GENERAL
Anglican Journal—R
Arkansas Catholic
Arlington Catholic
AXIOS—R
Banner, The
Bible Advocate—R

Biblical Reflections—R
Canadian Catholic
Catholic Courier
Catholic Insight
Celebrate Life—R
Christian American
Christian Chronicle—R
Christian C.L. RECORD—R
Christian Courier (WI)—R
Christian Courier (CAN)—R
Christian Crusade
Christian Edge—R
Christian Motorsports
Christian Renewal—R
Christian Single—R
Christian Social Action—R
Christianity Today—R
Commonweal
Compass
Cornerstone—R
Cresset
Disciple's Journal—R
Evangelical Baptist—R
Faith Today
Fatted Calf Forum—R
First Things
Good News, Etc—R
Good News - Salem
Gospel Today
Green Cross—R
Head to Head—R
Heavenly Thoughts—R
Home Times—R
Indian Life—R
Inland NW Christian
Interim—R
Journal of Church & State
Metro Voice—R
Michigan Christian
Minnesota Christian—R
Perspectives
Presbyterian Outlook
Presbyterians Today—R
Prism—R
Religious Broadcasting—R
Religious Education
SCP Journal—R
Social Justice
Sojourners
Standard, The—R
Stand Firm—R
Trumpeter, The
Upsouth—R

CHRISTIAN
EDUCATION/LIBRARY
Today's Catholic Teacher—R

MISSIONS
Areopagus—R
East-West Church

PASTORS/LEADERS
Christian Century
Networks—R
Preacher's Illus. Service—R
Word & World

TEEN/YOUNG ADULT
Challenge (GA)
With—R
Young Adult Today
Young Christian—R

WOMEN
Conscience—R

PRAYER

ADULT/GENERAL
alive now!
Angels on Earth
Annals of St. Anne
At Ease—R
Atlantic Baptist
Banner, The
Baptist Informer
Bible Advocate—R
Bible Advocate Online—R
Bread of Life—R
Brethren Evangelist
Broken Streets
Canadian Baptist
Canadian Catholic
Catholic Digest—R
Celebrate Life—R
Charisma/Christian Life
Christian Chronicle—R
Christian Edge—R
Christianity Today—R
Christian Living—R
Christian Motorsports
Christian Parenting—R
Christian Ranchman
Christian Reader—R
Christian Single—R
Church Advocate—R
Church Herald/Holiness—R
Church of God
    EVANGEL—R
Columbia
Companion
Companions—R
Compass
Connecting Point—R

Conquest
Cornerstone—R
Covenant Companion—R
Culture Wars—R
Decision
Disciple's Journal—R
Discipleship Journal
Emphasis/Faith & Living—R
Episcopal life—R
Evangelical Baptist—R
Evangelical Visitor—R
Family Digest
Family Journal—R
Family Network—R
Fellowship Link—R
Fellowship Today—R
Focus on the Family
Foursquare World—R
God's Revivalist
Good News (KY)—R
Good News, Etc—R
Good News Journal—R
Good News - Salem
Gospel Today
Green Cross—R
Head to Head—R
Healing Inn—R
Hearing Hearts
Heartlight Internet—R
Heavenly Thoughts—R
Highway News—R
Home Times—R
Indian Life—R
Inland NW Christian
Insights—R
Inspirer, The—R
Island Christian—R
John Milton—R
Jour/Christian Nursing—R
Life Gate—R
Light and Life
Liguorian
Live—R
Living Church
Lookout—R
Lutheran, The—R
Lutheran Digest—R
Lutheran Journal—R
Lutheran Parent
Lutheran Witness—R
Marian Helpers—R
Marriage Partnership
Mennonite, The—R
Mennonite Brethren—R
MESSAGE
MESSAGE/Open Bible—R
Messenger/St. Anthony
Metro Voice—R

Michigan Christian
Moody—R
New Covenant
New Oxford Review
North American Voice
Northwestern Lutheran—R
Our Family—R
Our Sunday Visitor
ParentLife—R
Pegasus Review—R
Pentecostal Testimony—R
Plain Truth—R
Plowman, The—R
Plus—R
Poet's Park—R
Pourastan—R
Prairie Messenger—R
PrayerWorks—R
Presbyterian Outlook
Presbyterian Record—R
Presbyterians Today—R
Purpose—R
Queen of All Hearts
Sacred Journey—R
St. Anthony Messenger
Seek—R
Silver Wings—R
Social Justice
Sojourners
Something Better—R
Spiritual Life
Standard—R
Standard, The—R
Stand Firm—R
Table Talk—R
Time of Singing—R
Today's Christian Senior—R
Together—R
Upsouth—R
U.S. Catholic
Vision, The—R
War Cry—R
Watchman, The
Way of St. Francis—R
Weavings—R
Wesleyan Advocate—R

CHILDREN
BREAD/God's Children—R
Club Connection—R
Counselor—R
Courage
Discovery (NY)—R
Focus/Clubhouse
GUIDE—R
High Adventure—R
R-A-D-A-R—R
Touch—R

Wonder Time
Young Christian—R

*CHRISTIAN
EDUCATION/LIBRARY*
CE Connection—R
CE Counselor—R
Children's Ministry
Church Educator—R
Church Worship
Evangelizing Today's
   Child—R
GROUP
Leader/Church School
   Today—R
Religion Teacher's Journal
Shining Star
Teacher's Interaction
Vision—R

MISSIONS
American Horizon—R
Areopagus—R
Intl Jour/Frontier—R
Message of the Cross—R
PFI World Report—R
Save Our World—R
Worldwide Challenge

MUSIC
Creator—R
Quest—R
Quiet Hour Echoes

PASTORS/LEADERS
Art+Plus
Catholic Servant
Celebration
Cell Life FORUM—R
Clergy Journal—R
Emmanuel
Enrichment—R
Evangelism USA
Five Stones, The—R
GROUP's Jr. High
Journal/Christian Healing—R
Jour/Amer Soc/Chur
   Growth—R
Leadership Journal—R
Liturgy—R
Lutheran Partners—R
Minister's Family
Ministries Today
Ministry
Modern Liturgy—R
Networks—R
Pastoral Life

Pray!—R
Preacher, The—R
Preacher's Illus. Service—R
Preacher's Magazine—R
Priest, The
PROCLAIM—R
Reformed Worship
Resource—R
Theology Today
Today's Christian
   Preacher—R
Today's Parish
Vital Issues
Word & World
Worship Leader

TEEN/YOUNG ADULT
Certainty
Challenge (GA)
Challenge (IL)
Conqueror—R
Devo'Zine—R
Insight—R
Straight—R
Student Leadership—R
Teenage Christian—R
Teen Life (AG)—R
Teen Power—R
Teens on Target—R
Today's Christian Teen—R
Vision—R
With—R
YOU!—R
Young Adult Today
Young Christian—R
Young Salvationist—R
Youth Challenge—R
Youth 98
Youth Update

WOMEN
Adam's Rib—R
Aspire
CoLaborer—R
Esprit—R
Handmaiden, The—R
Helping Hand—R
Horizons—R
Journey—R
Just Between Us—R
Lutheran Woman's Quar.
Lutheran Woman Today
Proverbs 31 Homemaker—R
Sisters Today
Today's Christian Woman
Virtue—R
Virtuous Woman
Women Alive!—R

PROPHECY

ADULT/GENERAL
Apocalypse Chronicles—R
Banner, The
Bible Advocate—R
Bread of Life—R
Charisma/Christian Life
Christian Edge—R
Christian Motorsports
Church of God
   EVANGEL—R
Conquest
Disciple's Journal—R
Evangelical Baptist—R
Fellowship Link—R
Foursquare World—R
God's Revivalist
Good News, Etc—R
Good News - Salem
Hallelujah! (CAN)—R
Home Times—R
Insights—R
MESSAGE
MESSAGE/Open Bible—R
Metro Voice—R
Michigan Christian
New Writing—R
Our Family—R
Pentecostal Testimony—R
Plain Truth—R
Queen of All Hearts
Revelation Post—R
SCP Journal—R
Signs of the Times—R
Silver Wings—R
Single Connection—R
Today's Christian Senior—R
2-Soar—R
Upsouth—R
Watchman, The

MISSIONS
Quiet Hour Echoes

PASTORS/LEADERS
Journal/Christian Healing—R
Ministries Today
PROCLAIM—R
Today's Christian
   Preacher—R
Voice of the Vineyard —R
Word & World

TEEN/YOUNG ADULT
Certainty
Young Adult Today

WOMEN
Horizons—R
Woman's Touch—R

PSYCHOLOGY

ADULT/GENERAL
AXIOS—R
Banner, The
Biblical Reflections—R
Catholic Digest—R
Catholic Twin Circle—R
Christian Chronicle—R
Christian Motorsports
Christian Single—R
Chrysalis Reader
Church Advocate—R
Common Boundary
Companion
Disciple's Journal—R
Faith Today
Good News (AL)—R
Good News, Etc—R
Good News - Salem
Home Times—R
Insights—R
Island Christian—R (maybe)
Jewel Among Jewels—R
John Milton—R
Jour/Christian Nursing—R
MESSAGE/Open Bible—R
Michigan Christian
New Covenant
Our Family—R
ParentLife—R
Ratio
Religious Education
SCP Journal—R
Single Connection—R
Social Justice
Spiritual Life
Standard, The—R
Total Health
Upsouth—R

*CHRISTIAN
EDUCATION/LIBRARY*
Catechist
Church Educator—R

PASTORAL/LEADERS
Cell Church—R
Christian Counseling Today
Christian Ministry
Eucharistic Minister—R
Five Stones, The—R
Journal/Christian Healing—R

Journal/Pastoral Care
Lutheran Partners—R
Ministries Today
Priest, The
Single Ad. Ministries Jour.
Word & World

PUPPET PLAYS

Children's Ministry
Christian Parenting—R
Christian Recreation
Christianity/Arts
Church Street Press
Club Connection—R
Creatively Yours
Evangelizing Today's
    Child—R
Focus/Clubhouse
Focus/Clubhouse Jr
Kids' Ministry Ideas—R
Leader/Church School
    Today—R
Lillenas
Sheer Joy! Press
Shining Star
Touch—R

RELATIONSHIPS

ADULT/GENERAL
Angels on Earth
Annals of St. Anne
At Ease—R
AXIOS—R
Banner, The
Bible Advocate—R
Biblical Reflections—R
Canada Lutheran—R
Catholic Digest—R
Catholic Forester—R
Charisma/Christian Life
Christian Edge—R
Christian Living—R
Christian Motorsports
Christian Parenting—R
Christian Ranchman
Christian Reader—R
Christian Single—R
Chrysalis Reader
Church Advocate—R
Church of God
    EVANGEL—R
Columbia
Companion
Conquest
Covenant Companion—R
Discipleship Journal

Dovetail—R
Evangel—R
Evangelical Baptist—R
Family Digest
Family Network—R
Fellowship Link—R
Foursquare World—R
Gem, The—R
Good News (AL)—R
Good News, Etc—R
Good News Journal—R
Good News - Salem
Gospel Tidings—R
Gospel Today
Guideposts
Head to Head—R
Healing Inn—R
Hearing Hearts
Heartlight Internet—R
Heavenly Thoughts—R
Highway News—R
Home Times—R
Island Christian—R
Inside Journal—R
Insights—R
Jewel Among Jewels—R
John Milton—R
Jour/Christian Nursing—R
Life Gate—R
Lifeglow—R
Liguorian
Live—R
Living—R
Living with Teenagers—R
Lookout—R
Lutheran Digest—R
Lutheran Journal—R
Lutheran Parent
Marriage Partnership
MESSAGE
Messenger, The (MI)—R
Messenger/St. Anthony
Metro Voice—R
Michigan Christian
Moody—R
New Writing—R
ParentLife—R
Pegasus Review—R
Pentecostal Testimony—R
Plain Truth—R
Plus—R
Pourastan—R
PrayerWorks—R
Preserving Christian
    Homes—R
Progress—R
Purpose—R
Pursuit—R

Remembrance—R
Silver Wings—R
Single-Parent Family
Standard, The—R
Stand Firm—R
Table Talk—R
TEAK Roundup—R
Time of Singing—R
Together—R
Upscale Magazine
Upsouth—R
U.S. Catholic
Vibrant Life—R
Voice, The—R
War Cry—R

CHILDREN
BREAD for God's Children
Club Connection—R
Discovery (NY)—R
Focus/Clubhouse
Focus/Clubhouse Jr
GUIDE—R
High Adventure—R
R-A-D-A-R—R
Touch—R
Young Christian—R

CHRISTIAN
EDUCATION/LIBRARY
Children's Ministry
GROUP
Perspective—R

MISSIONS
American Horizon—R
Evangelical Missions—R
Message of the Cross—R
Quiet Hour Echoes
Worldwide Challenge

PASTORS/LEADERS
Art+Plus
Cell Church—R
Cell Life FORUM—R
Christian Camp—R
Five Stones, The—R
GROUP's Jr. High
Leadership Journal—R
Lutheran Partners—R
Minister's Family
Ministries Today
Ministry
Pastor's Family
Preacher's Magazine—R
Pulpit Helps—R
Today's Christian Preacher—R

Youthworker—R
Vital Issues
Voice of the Vineyard —R
Word & World

TEEN/YOUNG ADULT
Alive!
Certainty
Challenge (GA)
Challenge (IL)
Christteen—R
Devo'Zine—R
Insight—R
Listen—R
Straight—R
Student Leadership—R
Teenage Christian—R
Teen Life (AG)—R
Teen Power—R
Teens on Target—R
Today's Christian Teen—R
With—R
YOU!—R
Young Christian—R
Young Salvationist—R
Youth Challenge—R
Youth 98
Youth Update

WOMEN
Adam's Rib—R
Anna's Journal—R
Aspire
Esprit—R
Handmaiden, The—R
Helping Hand—R
Horizons—R
Ishshah—R
Journey—R
Just Between Us—R
Link & Visitor—R
Lutheran Woman's Quar.
Proverbs 31 Homemaker—R
Tea and Sunshine
Today's Christian Woman
Virtue—R
Virtuous Woman
Welcome Home
Wesleyan Woman—R
Woman's Touch—R

RELIGIOUS FREEDOM

ADULT/GENERAL
AGAIN—R
America
Annals of St. Anne

Arlington Catholic
AXIOS—R
Banner, The
Bible Advocate—R
Biblical Reflections—R
Bread of Life—R
Catholic Twin Circle—R
Charisma/Christian Life
Christian Advocate—R
Christian Arts Review
Christian Chronicle—R
Christian C.L. RECORD—R
Christian Courier (WI)—R
Christian Courier (CAN)—R
Christian Edge—R
Christian Motorsports
Christian Ranchman
Christian Single—R
Christianity Today—R
Church & State—R
Church Herald/Holiness—R
Church of God
   EVANGEL—R
Columbia
Comments/Friends—R
Connecting Point—R
Cornerstone—R
Covenant Companion—R
Cresset
Disciple's Journal—R
Episcopal Life—R
E Street—R
Family Journal—R
Faith Today
Fatted Calf Forum—R
First Things
God's Revivalist
Good News, Etc—R
Good News Journal—R
Good News - Salem
Grail
Hallelujah! (CAN)—R
Heavenly Thoughts—R
Home Times—R
John Milton—R
Journal of Church & State
Liberty—R
Life Gate—R
Live—R
MESSAGE
MESSAGE/Open Bible—R
Messenger, The (MI)—R
Messenger/St. Anthony
Metro Voice—R
Michigan Christian
Minnesota Christian—R
Moody—R
Our Family—R

Our Sunday Visitor
Pegasus Review—R
Pentecostal Testimony—R
Pourastan—R
Presbyterian Layman
Presbyterian Outlook
Presbyterians Today—R
Prism—R
Religious Broadcasting—R
Religious Education
SCP Journal—R
Single Connection—R
Social Justice
Something Better—R
Spiritual Life
Stand Firm—R
United Church Observer
U.S. Catholic
Upsouth—R

CHILDREN
Focus/Clubhouse
High Adventure—R

*CHRISTIAN
EDUCATION/LIBRARY*
CE Connection—R
Church Worship
Vision—R

MISSIONS
Areopagus—R
East-West Church
Evangelical Missions—R
Quiet Hour Echoes
World Pulse—R
Worldwide Challenge

MUSIC
Quest—R

PASTORS/LEADERS
Art+Plus
Catholic Servant
Cell Church—R
Christian Century
Christian Ministry
Five Stones, The—R
Journal/Christian Healing—R
Ministry
Networks—R
Theology Today
Today's Christian
    Preacher—R
Word & World

TEEN/YOUNG ADULT
Challenge (GA)
Conqueror—R
Young Adult Today
Young Christian—R

WOMEN
Esprit—R
Horizons—R

WRITERS
Christian Response—R

SALVATION TESTIMONIES

ADULT/GENERAL
AGAIN—R
American Tract Soc.—R
At Ease—R
Banner, The
Bible Advocate—R
Bible Advocate Online—R
Broken Streets
Christian Chronicle—R
Christian Motorsports
Christian Ranchman
Christian Single—R
Church of God
    EVANGEL—R
Connecting Point—R
Conquest
Covenant Companion—R
Crossway/Newsline—R
Decision
Emphasis/Faith & Living—R
Evangel—R
Evangelical Baptist—R
Family Network—R
Fellowship Link—R
Gem, The—R
God's Revivalist
Good News, Etc—R
Good News Journal
Good News - Salem
Guideposts
Hallelujah! (CAN)—R
Head to Head—R
Healing Inn—R
Hearing Hearts
Heavenly Thoughts—R
Home Times—R
Indian Life—R
Inside Journal—R
Insights—R
Inspirer, The—R
Island Christian—R
John Milton—R

Light and Life
Live—R
Living Light News—R
Lutheran Journal—R
Mennonite Brethren—R
MESSAGE/Open Bible—R
Michigan Christian
Moody—R
New Covenant
New Heart, A—R
New Oxford Review
New Trumpet—R
Pentecostal Testimony—R
Plain Truth—R
Power for Living—R
PrayerWorks—R
Pursuit—R
Revelation Post—R
SCP Journal—R
Shantyman, The—R
Silver Wings—R
Single Connection—R
Something Better—R
Standard—R
Stand Firm—R
Together—R
Upsouth—R
Voice, The—R
Watchman, The
Wesleyan Advocate—R

CHILDREN
BREAD/God's Children—R
Club Connection—R
Counselor—R
Courage

*CHRISTIAN
EDUCATION/LIBRARY*
Evangelizing Today's
    Child—R

MISSIONS
American Horizon—R
Save Our World—R
World Mission People—R
Worldwide Challenge

PASTORS/LEADERS
Art+Plus
Cell Church—R
Christian Camp—R
Journal/Christian Healing—R
Ministry
Networks—R
Preacher's Magazine—R

TEEN/YOUNG ADULT
Challenge (GA)
Challenge (IL)
Christteen—R
Conqueror—R
Insight—R
Teen Life (AG)—R
Teen Power—R
Today's Christian Teen—R
Young Adult Today
Young Salvationist—R

WOMEN
Esprit—R
Helping Hand—R
Horizons—R
Journey—R
Joyful Woman—R
Wesleyan Woman—R
Woman's Touch—R

SCIENCE

ADULT/GENERAL
AXIOS—R
Banner, The
Biblical Reflections—R
Canadian Catholic
Catholic Digest—R
Catholic Dossier
Catholic Twin Circle—R
Christian C.L. RECORD—R
Christian Courier (CAN)—R
Christian Motorsports
Christian Reader—R
Christian Single—R
Christianity Today—R
Compass
Cornerstone—R
Disciple's Journal—R
Family Journal—R
First Things
Good News (AL)—R
Good News - Salem
Home Times—R
John Milton—R
Lutheran Parent
Messenger/St. Anthony
Metro Voice—R
Michigan Christian
PrayerWorks—R
Religious Education
SCP Journal—R
Something Better—R
Standard, The—R
Upsouth—R

CHILDREN
Counselor—R
Discovery (AL)
Focus/Clubhouse
Live Wire—R
My Friend
Nature Friend—R
R-A-D-A-R—R

*CHRISTIAN
EDUCATION/LIBRARY*
Vision—R

PASTORS/LEADERS
Journal/Christian Healing—R
Lutheran Partners—R
Pulpit Helps—R
Technologies/Worship—R
Word & World

TEEN/YOUNG ADULT
Challenge (GA)
Young Adult Today

WOMEN
Aspire
Esprit—R

SELF-HELP

ADULT/GENERAL
Believer, The—R
Catholic Forester—R
Christian Edge—R
Christian Living—R
Christian Motorsports
Christian Ranchman
Christian Single—R
Companion
Discovery—R
Dovetail—R
Expression Christian
Family Digest
Fellowship Link—R
Good News (AL)—R
Good News - Salem
Insights—R
Island Christian—R
John Milton—R
Live—R
Living—R
Living with Teenagers—R
Lutheran Parent
Marriage Partnership
Mennonite, The—R
MESSAGE
Messenger/St. Anthony

Michigan Christian
New Writing—R
Our Family—R
St. Anthony Messenger
Single Connection—R
Social Justice
Stand Firm—R
TEAK Roundup—R
2-Soar—R

CHILDREN
Discovery (NY)—R

PASTORS/LEADERS
Art+Plus
Cell Church—R
Pastor's Family

TEEN/YOUNG ADULT
Challenge (GA)
Straight—R
Teenage Christian—B/C
With—R

WOMEN
DOMESTIQUE—R
Esprit—R
Horizons—R
Ishshah—R
Journey—R
Today's Christian Woman
Wesleyan Woman—R

SENIOR ADULT ISSUES

ADULT/GENERAL
Alive!—R
Angels on Earth
Anglican Journal—R
Annals of St. Anne
Atlantic Baptist
AXIOS—R
Banner, The
B.C. Catholic—R
Biblical Reflections—R
Canada Lutheran—R
Canadian Baptist
Catholic Digest—R
Catholic Forester—R
Christian Courier (CAN)—R
Christian Edge—R
Christian Home & School
Christian Living—R
Christian Motorsports
Church Advocate—R
Church Herald/Holiness—R
Church of God EVANGEL—R

Companion
Conquest
Covenant Companion—R
Disciple's Journal—R
Discovery—R
Emphasis/Faith & Living—R
Evangel—R
Evangelical Baptist—R
Family Network—R
Fellowship Link—R
Gem, The—R
Good News (AL)—R
Good News, Etc—R
Good News Journal—R
Good News - Salem
Hearing Hearts
Home Times—R
Inspirer, The—R
Island Christian—R
John Milton—R
Jour/Christian Nursing—R
Life Gate—R
Light and Life
Liguorian
Live—R
Living—R
Lutheran, The—R
Lutheran Digest—R
Mature Years—R
MESSAGE/Open Bible—R
Metro Voice—R
Michigan Christian
Minnesota Christian—R
Montana Catholic—R
Moody—R
NW Christian Journal—R
Our Family—R
Our Sunday Visitor
Pentecostal Evangel—R
Plain Truth—R
Plus—R
Power for Living—R
PrayerWorks—R
Presbyterian Record—R
Presbyterians Today—R
Purpose—R
Resource—R
Smile—R
Sojourners
Something Better—R
Standard—R
Standard, The—R
Star of Zion
Today's Christian Senior—R
U.S. Catholic
Voice, The—R
War Cry—R
Wesleyan Advocate—R

**CHRISTIAN
EDUCATION/LIBRARY**
CE Connection—R
CE Counselor—R
CE Leadership—R
Church Educator—R
Leader/Church School
   Today—R

MISSIONS
Worldwide Challenge

MUSIC
Senior Musician—R

PASTORS/LEADERS
Art+Plus
Clergy Journal—R
Diocesan Dialogue—R
Five Stones, The—R
Journal/Christian
   Healing—R
Lutheran Partners—R
Pastoral Life
Single Ad. Ministries Jour.
Word & World

WOMEN
Adam's Rib—R
Aspire
Esprit—R
Horizons—R
Today's Christian Woman
Wesleyan Woman—R
Woman's Touch—R
Canadian Writer's Jour—R

SERMONS

ADULT/GENERAL
Arlington Catholic
Banner, The
Cathedral Age
Christian Chronicle—R
Christian Motorsports
Church Herald/Holiness—R
Church of God
   EVANGEL—R
Cresset
Evangelical Baptist—R
God's Revivalist
Good News, Etc—R
Good News - Salem
Green Cross—R
Hallelujah! (CAN)—R
Healing Inn—R
Inspirer, The—R

Joyful Noise
Presbyterians Today—R
Sojourners
Standard, The—R
Star of Zion
Upsouth—R
Way of St. Francis—R
Weavings—R

**CHRISTIAN
EDUCATION/LIBRARY**
Church Worship

MISSIONS
Quiet Hour Echoes

PASTORS/LEADERS
Celebration
Clergy Journal—R
Enrichment—R
In Season
Journal/Christian Healing—R
Leadership Journal—R
Let's Worship
Preacher's Illus. Service—R
Preacher's Magazine—R
Preaching
PROCLAIM—R
Pulpit Helps—R
Sermon Notes
Today's Parish

**SHORT STORY:
ADULT/RELIGIOUS**

Adam's Rib—R
Alive!—R
alive now!
Annals of St. Anne
Anna's Journal—R
Baptist Informer
Burning Light—R
Canadian Writer's Jour—R
Catholic Forester—R
Chip Off Writer's Block—R
Christian Advocate—R
Christian Century
Christian Chronicle—R
Christian Courier (CAN)—R
Christian Educators Journal
Christian Living—R
Christian Motorsports
Christian Reader—R
Christian Renewal—R
Christian School
Christian Single—R
Christianity/Arts

Christmas—R
Church & Synagogue Lib.
Church Musician
Companion
Companions—R
Connecting Point—R
Conquest
Cornerstone—R
Covenant Companion—R
Discovery—R
DOMESTIQUE—R
Dreams & Visions—R
Emphasis/Faith & Living—R
Esprit—R
E Street—R
Evangel—R
Evangelical Baptist
Evangelical Visitor—R
Family Network—R
Fatted Calf Forum—R
Fellowship Link—R
Five Stones, The—R
Gem, The—R
Gems of Truth—R
God's Revivalist
Good News (AL)—R
Good News - Salem
Grail
Handmaiden, The—R
Head to Head—R
Healing Inn—R
Hearing Hearts
Heartlight Internet—R
Heaven
Heavenly Thoughts—R
Helping Hand—R
Highway News—R
Home Times—R
Horizons—R
Housewife-Writer—R
Impact Magazine—R
Inklings
Insights—R
Inspirer, The—R
John Milton—R
Journal/Christian Healing—R
Journal/Pastoral Care
Joyful Woman—R
Lighthouse Fiction
Liguorian
Live—R
Living—R
Living Light News—R
Lookout—R
Lutheran Digest
Lutheran Partners—R
Lutheran Witness—R
Lutheran Woman's Quar.

Lutheran Woman Today
Mature Living
Mature Years—R
Mennonite Brethren—R
Messenger/Sacred Heart
Messenger/St. Anthony
Miraculous Medal
Moody—R
My Legacy—R
New Trumpet—R
New Writing—R
North American Voice
Pegasus Review—R
Pentecostal Testimony—R
Perspectives
Plowman, The—R
Poetry Forum—R
PrayerWorks—R
Presbyterian Record—R
Preserving Christian
   Homes—R
Queen of All Hearts
Quest—R
Ratio
Rosebud
St. Anthony Messenger
St. Joseph's Messenger—R
San Diego Co. Christian
Seek—R
Single Connection—R
Sojourners
Standard—R
Star of Zion
Sursum Corda!—R
TEAK Roundup—R
Tickled by Thunder
Today's Christian Senior—R
Today's Christian Woman
Upsouth—R
U.S. Catholic
Virtue—R
Vision—R
War Cry—R
Weavings—R
Wherever
Women Alive!—R
Writers' Intl. Forum
Write Touch—R
YOU!—R

SHORT STORY:
ADVENTURE

ADULT
Alive!—R
Annals of St. Anne
Byline
Chip Off Writer's Block—R

Christian Courier (CAN)—R
Christian Single—R
Christianity/Arts
Dreams & Visions—R
Emphasis/Faith & Living—R
Good News (AL)—R
Healing Inn—R
Heartlight Internet—R
Heavenly Thoughts—R
Lighthouse Fiction
Liguorian
Live—R
Miraculous Medal
My Legacy—R
New Trumpet—R
New Writing—R
Standard—R
TEAK Roundup—R
Today's Christian Senior—R
Upsouth—R
Vision, The—R
Writers' Intl. Forum

CHILDREN
Annals of St. Anne
BREAD/God's Children—R
CLUBHOUSE—R
Connecting Point—R
Counselor—R
Courage
Crusader—R
Discoveries—R
Discovery (NY)—R
Focus/Clubhouse
Focus/Clubhouse Jr
Guideposts for Kids
Junior Trails—R
Lighthouse Fiction
Listen
Lollipops (young)
My Friend
Primary Pal (IL)
R-A-D-A-R—R
Story Friends—R
Writers' Intl. Forum
Writers' Intl. Forum/Young
Young Christian—R

TEEN/YOUNG ADULT
Annals of St. Anne
Breakaway—R
Challenge (GA)
Challenge (IL)
Christteen—R
Discovery—R
Lighthouse Fiction
Straight—R
Teenage Christian—R

Teen Life (AG)—R
Teens on Target—R
Teens Today—R
Writers' Intl. Forum
Writers' Intl. Forum/Young
Young Adult Today
Young Christian—R
Youth Challenge—R
Youth World—R

SHORT STORY: ALLEGORY

ADULT
Byline
Burning Light—R
Chip Off Writer's Block—R
Christianity/Arts
Christian Single—R
Cornerstone—R
Covenant Companion—R
Discovery—R
Dreams & Visions—R
Family Network—R
Fatted Calf Forum—R
Good News (AL)—R
Good News - Salem
Grail
Head to Head—R
Healing Inn—R
Hearing Hearts
Heartlight Internet—R
Heavenly Thoughts—R
Highway News—R
Home Times—R
Horizons—R
Inklings
Insights—R
Inspirer, The—R
Mennonite Brethren—R
Messenger/St. Anthony
My Legacy—R
New Trumpet—R
New Writing—R
Pentecostal Testimony—R
Prism—R
Ratio
Tea and Sunshine
Vision, The—R
Weavings—R

CHILDREN
Discovery (NY)—R
Head to Head—R
Pockets—R
Touch—R

TEENS/YOUNG ADULT
Conqueror—R
Discovery—R
Head to Head—R
John Milton—R
Student Leadership—R
Teen Life (AG)—R
With—R
YOU!—R
Youth World—R

SHORT STORY: BIBLICAL

ADULT
Annals of St. Anne
Christian Advocate—R
Christian Courier (CAN)—R
Christianity/Arts
Church & Synagogue Lib.
Church Herald/Holiness—R
Church Worship
Connecting Point—R
Cornerstone—R
Discovery—R
Dreams & Visions—R
Esprit—R
Emphasis/Faith & Living—R
Evangel—R
Family Network—R
Fatted Calf Forum—R
Fellowship Link—R
Five Stones, The—R
Good News (AL)—R
Grail
Handmaiden, The—R
Head to Head—R
Healing Inn—R
Hearing Hearts
Heartlight Internet—R
Highway News—R
Helping Hand—R
Impact Magazine—R
Insights—R
Inspirer, The—R
Joyful Woman—R
Lutheran Woman's Quar.
Lutheran Woman Today
Mature Years—R
Mennonite Brethren—R
Miraculous Medal
My Legacy—R
New Writing—R
Pentecostal Testimony—R
Perspectives
Plowman, The—R
Preacher's Illus. Service—R

Presbyterian Record—R
Preserving Christian
   Homes—R
Ratio
Sojourners
TEAK Roundup—R
Today's Christian Senior—R
Upsouth—R
U.S. Catholic
Virtue—R
War Cry—R
Weavings—R

CHILDREN
Annals of St. Anne
BREAD/God's Children—R
Discoveries—R
Discovery (NY)—R
Focus/Clubhouse
Focus/Clubhouse Jr
Head to Head—R
MESSAGE
John Milton—R
North American Voice
Pockets—R
Preacher's Illus. Service—R
R-A-D-A-R—R
Young Christian—R

TEEN/YOUNG ADULT
Annals of St. Anne
Challenge (GA)
Christteen—R
Conqueror—R
Discovery—R
Head to Head—R
John Milton—R
Preacher's Illus. Service—R
Student Leadership—R
Teenage Christian—R
Teen Life (AG)—R
Teen Power—R
Teens on Target—R
YOU!—R
Young Adult Today
Young Christian—R
Youth Challenge—R

SHORT STORY: CONTEMPORARY

ADULT
Annals of St. Anne
Burning Light
Byline
Canadian Lutheran—R
Chip Off Writer's Block—R

Christian Century
Christian Living—R
Christianity/Arts
Companion
Connecting Point—R
Conquest
Cornerstone—R
Covenant Companion—R
Dreams & Visions—R
Esprit—R
Evangel—R
Good News (AL)—R
Head to Head—R
Healing Inn—R
Hearing Hearts
Heartlight Internet—R
Heavenly Thoughts—R
Horizons—R
Housewife-Writer—R
Inklings
Inspirer, The—R
Lighthouse Fiction
Liguorian
Living Light News—R
Lookout—R
Messenger/St. Anthony
Miraculous Medal
Moody—R
My Legacy—R
New Trumpet—R
New Writing—R
Pentecostal Testimony—R
Perspectives
Poetry Forum—R
Rosebud
St. Anthony Messenger
St. Joseph's Messenger—R
Standard—R
TEAK Roundup—R
Tickled by Thunder
Tradition—R
Upsouth—R
U.S. Catholic
Virtue—R
War Cry—R
Writers' Intl. Forum

CHILDREN
Annals of St. Anne
BREAD/God's Children—R
Canada Lutheran—R
Discoveries—R
Discovery (NY)—R
Focus/Clubhouse
Focus/Clubhouse Jr
Guideposts for Kids
Head to Head—R
Junior Trails—R

Lighthouse Fiction
Listen
On the Line—R
Partners—R
Pockets—R
R-A-D-A-R—R
Story Friends—R
Together Time
Touch—R
Writers' Intl. Forum
Writers' Intl. Forum/Young
Young Christian—R

TEEN/YOUNG ADULT
Annals of St. Anne
BREAD/God's Children—R
Certainty
Challenge (IL)
Christteen—R
Discovery—R
Head to Head—R
Lighthouse Fiction
Listen—R
Spirit
Straight—R
Teenage Christian—R
Teen Life (AG)—R
Teen Power—R
Tradition—R
Writers' Intl. Forum
Writers' Intl. Forum/Young
Young Christian—R

SHORT STORY: ETHNIC

ADULT
Byline
Christian Living—R
Cornerstone—R
Dreams & Visions—R
Fellowship Link—R
Good News (AL)—R
Inklings
Live—R
Upsouth—R

CHILDREN
Counselor—R
Discovery (NY)—R
Skipping Stones

TEEN/YOUNG ADULT
Discovery—R
Straight—R
Teen Life (AG)—R
Young Salvationist—R

SHORT STORY: FANTASY

ADULT
Burning Light
Byline
Chip Off Writer's Block—R
Christian Courier (CAN)—R
Christianity/Arts
Connecting Point—R
Cornerstone—R
Dreams & Visions—R
Esprit—R
Inklings
Messenger/St. Anthony
Moonletters—R
My Legacy—R
New Creation
Presbyterian Record—R
Ratio
Tickled by Thunder
Writers' Intl. Forum

CHILDREN
Discovery (NY)—R
Guideposts for Kids
Lollipops (young)
Touch—R
Venture
Writers' Intl. Forum
Writers' Intl. Forum/Young
Young Christian—R

TEEN/YOUNG ADULT
Discovery—R
New Creation
Spirit
With—R
Writers' Intl. Forum
Writers' Intl. Forum/Young
Young Adult Today
Young Christian—R
Young Salvationist—R

SHORT STORY: FRONTIER

ADULT
Byline
Chip Off Writer's Block—R
Christianity/Arts
Connecting Point—R
Dreams & Visions—R
Good News (AL)—R
Inspirer, The—R
Lighthouse Fiction
Miraculous Medal
My Legacy—R

Upsouth—R
Writers' Intl. Forum

CHILDREN
Focus/Clubhouse
Focus/Clubhouse Jr
Guideposts for Kids
High Adventure—R
Lighthouse Fiction
Touch—R
Writers' Intl. Forum
Writers' Intl. Forum/Young
Young Christian—R

TEEN/YOUNG ADULT
Lighthouse Fiction
Writers' Intl. Forum
Writers' Intl. Forum/Young
Young Christian—R

SHORT STORY: FRONTIER/ROMANCE

Byline
Chip Off Writer's Block—R
Christianity/Arts
Connecting Point—R
Dreams & Visions—R
Healing Inn—R
Helping Hand—R
Lighthouse Fiction
Miraculous Medal
My Legacy—R
Writers' Intl. Forum
Young Christian—R

SHORT STORY: HISTORICAL

ADULT
Alive!—R
Byline
Chip Off Writer's Block—R
Christian Courier (CAN)—R
Christian Living—R
Christianity/Arts
Companions—R
Connecting Point—R
Conquest
Dreams & Visions—R
Esprit—R
Family Network—R
Fellowship Link—R
Good News (AL)—R
Handmaiden, The—R
Healing Inn—R
Heartlight Internet—R

Heavenly Thoughts—R
Home Times—R
Inklings
Lighthouse Fiction
Live—R
Lutheran Woman's Quar.
Messenger/St. Anthony
Miraculous Medal
My Legacy—R
New Writing—R
North American Voice
Pentecostal Testimony—R
Perspectives
Poetry Forum—R
Presbyterian Record—R
Ratio
Seek—R
TEAK Roundup—R
Today's Christian Senior—R
Tradition—R
Upsouth—R

CHILDREN
CLUBHOUSE—R
Counselor—R
Courage
Discovery (NY)—R
Focus/Clubhouse
Focus/Clubhouse Jr
Guideposts for Kids
High Adventure—R
Lighthouse Fiction
Friend
On the Line—R
R-A-D-A-R—R
Touch—R
Young Christian—R

TEEN/YOUNG ADULT
BREAD/God's Children—R
Challenge (GA)
Challenge (IL)
Discovery—R
John Milton—R
Lighthouse Fiction
Tradition—R
Young Adult Today
Young Christian—R
Youth—R

SHORT STORY: HISTORICAL/ROMANCE

Byline
Christianity/Arts
Connecting Point—R
Dreams & Visions—R
Healing Inn—R

Lighthouse Fiction
Messenger/St. Anthony
Miraculous Medal
My Legacy—R
Young Christian—R

SHORT STORY: HUMOROUS

ADULT
Alive!—R
Byline
Canada Lutheran—R
Catholic Forester—R
Chip Off Writer's Block—R
Christian Chronicle—R
Christian Courier (CAN)—R
Christian Single—R
Christianity/Arts
Church & Synagogue Lib.
Clergy Journal—R
Companion
Connecting Point—R
Conquest
Cornerstone—R
Covenant Companion—R
Dreams & Visions—R
Esprit—R
E Street—R
Fatted Calf Forum—R
Five Stones, The—R
Gem, The—R
Good News (AL)—R
Good News - Salem
Healing Inn—R
Helping Hand—R
Heartlight Internet—R
Highway News—R
Home Times—R
Horizons—R
Housewife-Writer—R
Impact—R
Insights—R
Inspirer, The—R
John Milton—R
Lighthouse Fiction
Liguorian
Live—R
Living—R
Living Light News—R
Mature Years—R
Messenger/St. Anthony
Miraculous Medal
My Legacy—R
New Trumpet—R
New Writing—R
ParentLife—R
Pentecostal Testimony—R

Preacher's Illus. Service—R
Presbyterian Record—R
Preserving Christian
  Homes—R
Rosebud
St. Joseph's Messenger—R
Seek—R
Single Connection—R
Sojourners
Table Talk—R
TEAK Roundup—R
Tickled by Thunder
Today's Christian Senior—R
Tradition—R
Upsouth—R
Virtue—R
Writers' Intl. Forum

CHILDREN
Crusader—R
Discovery (NY)—R
Focus/Clubhouse
Focus/Clubhouse Jr
Guideposts for Kids
High Adventure—R
Junior Trails—R
Lighthouse Fiction
Living—R
My Friend
Preacher's Illus. Service—R
R-A-D-A-R—R
Story Friends—R
Touch—R
Wonder Time
Writers' Intl. Forum
Writers' Intl. Forum/Young

TEEN/YOUNG ADULT
Breakaway—R
Brio—R
Campus Life—R
Challenge (GA)
Challenge (IL)
Discovery—R
Lighthouse Fiction
Preacher's Illus. Service—R
Straight—R
Student Leadership—R
Teenage Christian—R
Teen Life (AG)—R
Teen Power—R
Teens Today—R
Tradition—R
With—R
Writers' Intl. Forum
Writers' Intl. Forum/Young
YOU!—R
Young Adult Today

SHORT STORY: JUVENILE

Annals of St. Anne
Beginner's Friend—R
BREAD/God's Children—R
Catholic Forester—R
Challenge (GA)
Children's Church—R (6-8)
Christian Home & School
  (few)
Christmas—R
Church Educator—R
Church & Synagogue Lib.
Counselor—R
Courage
Crusader—R
Discoveries—R
Discovery (NY)—R
Evangelizing Today's
  Child—R
Focus/Clubhouse
Focus/Clubhouse Jr
Good News (AL)—R
Good News Journal—R
Guideposts for Kids
Head to Head—R
High Adventure—R
Insights—R
Junior Companion—R
MESSAGE
Messenger/St. Anthony
Junior Trails—R
Lighthouse Fiction
Listen (3-4's)
Living—R
Lollipops
Lutheran Woman Today
My Friend
My Legacy—R
On the Line—R
Partners—R
Pockets—R
Presbyterian Record—R
Primary Pal (IL)
Primary Pal (KS)—R
R-A-D-A-R—R
Skipping Stones
Story Friends—R
Today's Catholic Teacher—R
Together Time (3-4)
Touch—R
United Church Observer
Venture
Visitation
Wonder Time
Write Touch
Writers' Intl. Forum
Writers' Intl. Forum/Young

Young Christian—R

SHORT STORY: LITERARY

ADULT
Burning Light—R
Byline
Chip Off Writer's Block—R
Christian Century
Christian Courier (CAN)—R
Christian Living—R
Christianity/Arts
Compass
Conquest
Cornerstone—R
Covenant Companion—R
Chrysalis Reader
Dreams & Visions—R
Esprit—R
Fatted Calf Forum—R
Good News (AL)—R
Healing Inn—R
Heavenly Thoughts—R
Horizons—R
Housewife-Writer—R
Inklings
Mennonite Brethren
  Herald—R
Messenger/St. Anthony
Miraculous Medal
My Legacy—R
New Writing—R
Perspectives
Ratio
Rosebud
Sojourners
Standard—R
Tea and Sunshine
TEAK Roundup—R
Tickled by Thunder
Upsouth—R
Virtue—R
Weavings—R

CHILDREN
Discovery (NY)—R
Story Friends—R

SHORT STORY: MYSTERY

ADULT
Byline
Chip Off Writer's Block—R
Christian Courier (CAN)—R
Christianity/Arts
Connecting Point—R
Dreams & Visions—R

Healing Inn—R
Heartlight Internet—R
Housewife-Writer—R
Inklings
Lighthouse Fiction
Messenger/St. Anthony
Miraculous Medal
My Legacy—R
New Writing—R
Quest
TEAK Roundup—R
Writers' Intl. Forum

CHILDREN
Courage
Discovery (NY)—R
Focus/Clubhouse
Focus/Clubhouse Jr
Guideposts for Kids
Junior Trails—R
Lighthouse Fiction
On the Line—R
R-A-D-A-R—R
Touch—R
Writers' Intl. Forum
Writers' Intl. Forum/Young
Young Christian—R

TEEN/YOUNG ADULT
Challenge (IL)
Discovery—R
Lighthouse Fiction
Straight—R
Writers' Intl. Forum
Writers' Intl. Forum/Young
Young Adult Today
Young Christian—R

SHORT STORY: MYSTERY/ROMANCE

Byline
Chip Off Writer's Block—R
Christianity/Arts
Connecting Point—R
Dreams & Visions—R
Healing Inn—R
Lighthouse Fiction
Messenger/St. Anthony
Miraculous Medal
Standard—R
Writers' Intl. Forum
Young Christian—R

SHORT STORY: PARABLES

ADULT
alive now!
America
Annals of St. Anne
Catholic Twin Circle—R
Christian Advocate—R
Christian Chronicle—R
Christian Courier (CAN)—R
Christian Living—R
Christian Single—R
Christianity/Arts
Church Worship
Companion
Cornerstone—R
Covenant Companion—R
Discovery—R
Dreams & Visions—R
Emphasis/Faith & Living—R
Esprit—R
Family Network—R
Fellowship Link—R
Five Stones, The—R
God's Revivalist
Good News (AL)—R
Good News - Salem
Grail
Healing Inn—R
Hearing Hearts
Heartlight Internet—R
Heavenly Thoughts—R
Helping Hand—R
Highway News—R
Home Times—R
Horizons—R
Impact Magazine—R
Inklings
Insights—R
Inspirer, The—R
LA Catholic
Lutheran
Mennonite Brethren—R
MESSAGE
Messenger/St. Anthony
New Writing—R
Perspectives
Preacher's Illus. Service—R
Presbyterian Record—R
Ratio
Sojourners
Star of Zion
Upsouth—R
U.S. Catholic
Weavings—R

CHILDREN
Annals of St. Anne

Church Educator—R
Courage
Discovery (NY)—R
High Adventure—R
MESSAGE
John Milton—R
Pockets—R
Preacher's Illus. Service—R
R-A-D-A-R—R
Touch—R
Young Christian—R

TEEN/YOUNG ADULT
Annals of St. Anne
Church Educator—R
Discovery—R
John Milton—R
Preacher's Illus. Service—R
Student Leadership—R
Teen Life (AG)—R
With—R
YOU!—R
Young Adult Today
Young Christian—R

SHORT STORY: PLAYS

Baptist Leader—R
Burning Light—R
Challenge (IL)
Christian Recreation
Church Worship
Courage (short short)
Creatively Yours
Discovery (NY)—R
Esprit—R
Fellowship Link—R
Five Stones, The—R
Focus/Clubhouse Jr
Guideposts for Kids
Head to Head—R
Horizons—R
Inklings
Lutheran Digest
Messenger/St. Anthony
National Drama Service
New Writing—R
Plans & Pluses
Ratio
Shining Star
Touch—R
YOU!—R
Young Christian—R

SHORT STORY: ROMANCE

ADULT
Alive!—R

Byline
Chip Off Writer's Block—R
Christianity/Arts
Connecting Point—R
Dreams & Visions—R
Helping Hand—R
Housewife-Writer—R
Inklings
Kansas City Woman
Lighthouse Fiction
Messenger/St. Anthony
Miraculous Medal
Preserving Christian
    Homes—R
Ratio
St. Joseph's Messenger—R
Virtue—R
War Cry—R

TEEN/YOUNG ADULT
Brio
Discovery—R
Healing Inn—R
Lighthouse Fiction
Straight—R
Teen Life (AG)—R
Teens Today—R
With—R
Young Christian—R
Young Salvationist—R

SHORT STORY: SCIENCE FICTION

ADULT
Byline
Chip Off Writer's Block—R
Christian Courier (CAN)—R
Christianity/Arts
Connecting Point—R
Cornerstone—R
Dreams & Visions—R
Fatted Calf Forum—R
Impact Magazine—R
Inklings
Moonletters—R
Ratio
Tickled by Thunder
Writers' Intl. Forum

CHILDREN
Focus/Clubhouse Jr
Writers' Intl. Forum
Writers' Intl. Forum/Young

TEEN/YOUNG ADULT
Breakaway—R

Teen Life (AG)—R
With—R
Writers' Intl. Forum
Writers' Intl. Forum/Young
Young Adult Today
Young Salvationist—R

SHORT STORY: SKITS

ADULT
Baptist Leader—R
Christian Recreation
Church Worship
Esprit—R
Five Stones, The—R
Head to Head—R
Helping Hand—R
Horizons—R
New Writing—R
Wesleyan Woman—R

CHILDREN
Christian Recreation
Discovery (NY)—R
Head to Head—R
Shining Star
Touch—R

TEEN/YOUNG ADULT
Christian Recreation
Discovery—R
Head to Head—R
Student Leadership—R
YOU!—R

SHORT STORY: TEEN/YOUNG ADULT

Annals of St. Anne
Beautiful Christian Teen
BREAD/God's Children—R
Breakaway—R
Brio
Campus Life—R
Canada Lutheran—R
Catholic Forester—R
Certainty
Challenge (GA)
Challenge (IL)
Church & Synagogue Lib.
Church Educator—R
Christteen—R
CLUBHOUSE—R
CoLaborer—R
Companions—R
Conqueror—R
Discovery—R

Evangel—R
Five Stones, The—R
Gospel Tidings—R
Head to Head—R
High Adventure—R
Insights—R
Lighthouse Fiction
Liguorian
Listen—R
Parent Paper, The
Partners—R
Pentecostal Testimony—R
Presbyterian Record—R
Quest—R
Skipping Stones
Sojourners
Spirit
Star of Zion
Straight—R
Student Leadership
Teenage Christian—R
Teen Life (AG)—R
Teen Power—R
Teens on Target—R
Touch—R
With—R
Write Touch—R
Writers' Intl. Forum
Writers' Intl. Forum/Young
YOU!—R
Young Adult Today
Young Christian—R
Young Salvationist—R
Youth Challenge—R
Youth Compass—R
Youth World—R

SINGLES ISSUES

ADULT/GENERAL
American Tract Soc.—R
Annals of St. Anne
At Ease—R
Banner, The
Bible Advocate—R
Bible Advocate Online—R
Biblical Reflections—R
Canadian Baptist
Catholic Digest—R
Christian Advocate—R
Christian Courier (CAN)—R
Christian Living—R
Christian Motorsports
Christian Reader—R
Christian Single—R
Church Advocate—R
Church of God
    EVANGEL—R

Companion
Conquest
Cornerstone—R
Covenant Companion—R
Decision
Disciple's Journal—R
Emphasis/Faith & Living—R
Evangel—R
Evangelical Baptist—R
Faith Today
Family Journal—R
Family Network—R
Fatted Calf Forum—R
Foursquare World—R
Gem, The—R
Good News (AL)—R
Good News, Etc.—R
Good News Journal—R
Good News - Salem
Gospel Today
Hearing Hearts
Heartlight Internet—R
Heavenly Thoughts—R
Home Times—R
Indian Life—R
Insights—R
Island Christian—R
Light and Life
Liguorian
Live—R
Living—R
Lookout—R
Lutheran, The—R
Lutheran Digest—R
Lutheran Parent
Mennonite, The—R
MESSAGE
MESSAGE/Open Bible—R
Metro Voice—R
Michigan Christian
Minnesota Christian—R
Moody—R
Newsline—R
NW Christian Journal—R
Plain Truth—R
Power for Living—R
Presbyterian Layman
Presbyterian Record—R
Presbyterians Today—R
Purpose—R
Signs of the Times—R
Single Connection—R
Single-Parent Family
Sojourners
Something Better—R
Standard—R
Trumpeter, The
2-Soar—R

U.S. Catholic
War Cry—R
Wesleyan Advocate—R

*CHRISTIAN
EDUCATION/LIBRARY*
CE Connection—R
CE Leadership—R

MISSIONS
Worldwide Challenge

MUSIC
Quest—R

PASTORS/LEADERS
Art+Plus
Church Administration
Five Stones, The—R
Journal/Christian Healing—R
Lutheran Partners—R
Ministries Today
Pastoral Life
Resource—R
Single Ad. Ministries Jour.
Word & World

TEEN/YOUNG ADULT
Christteen—R
Conqueror—R
YOU!—R
Young Adult Today
Young Christian—R

WOMEN
Adam's Rib—R
Aspire
Esprit—R
Horizons—R
Ishshah—R
Today's Christian Woman
Virtue—R
Virtuous Woman
Wesleyan Woman—R

SOCIAL JUSTICE

ADULT/GENERAL
Arkansas Catholic
Arlington Catholic
Banner, The
Bible Advocate Online—R
Biblical Reflections—R
Brethren Evangelist
Canadian Baptist
Canadian Catholic

Catholic Digest—R
Catholic Insight
Catholic Rural Life
Catholic Sentinel—R
Charisma/Christian Life
Christian Advocate—R
Christian Century
Christian Chronicle—R
Christian Edge—R
Christian Living—R
Christian Motorsports
Christian Reader—R
Christian Social Action—R
Christianity Today—R
Church Advocate—R
Church of God
    EVANGEL—R
Commonweal
Covenant Companion—R
Cresset
Culture Wars—R
Disciple's Journal—R
Faith Today
Family Network—R
Foursquare World—R
Good News, Etc—R
Good News - Salem
Grail
Hallelujah! (CAN)—R
Head to Head—R
Heavenly Thoughts—R
Home Times—R
Indian Life—R
Inland NW Christian
Insights—R
Jour/Christian Nursing—R
Liguorian
Live—R
Living—R
Lookout—R
Lutheran Parent
Mennonite, The—R
Mennonite Brethren—R
MESSAGE/Open Bible—R
Messenger/St. Anthony
Michigan Christian
Moody—R
North American Voice
Our Family—R
Perspectives
Pourastan—R
Prairie Messenger—R
Presbyterian Layman
Prism—R
ProLife News—R
Purpose—R
Religious Broadcasting—R
St. Anthony Messenger

Second Stone
Single Connection—R
Social Justice
Sojourners
Something Better—R
Spiritual Life
United Church Observer
Upsouth—R
Voice, The—R
Way of St. Francis—R

CHILDREN
Skipping Stones

*CHRISTIAN
EDUCATION/LIBRARY*—R
Church Educator—R
Journal/Adventist Educ.—R
Religion Teacher's Journal

PASTORS/LEADERS
Art+Plus
Celebration
Emmanuel
Liturgy—R
Lutheran Partners—R
Ministries Today
Voice of the Vineyard —R

TEEN/YOUNG ADULT
Christteen—R
Devo'Zine—R
Teenage Christian—B/C
YOU!—R
Young Christian—R

WOMEN
Aspire
Horizons—R
Woman's Touch—R

SOCIOLOGY

ADULT/GENERAL
Anglican Journal—R
Biblical Reflections—R
Catholic Digest—R
Catholic Rural Life
Christian Advocate—R
Christian Courier (CAN)—R
Christian Edge—R
Commonweal
Compass
Covenant Companion—R
Culture Wars—R
Disciple's Journal—R
Faith Today

Family Network—R
Fellowship Link—R
Good News, Etc—R
Good News - Salem
Grail
Home Times—R
Journal of Church & State
Lutheran Parent
Michigan Christian
New Oxford Review
Quiet Revolution—R
SCP Journal—R
Seek—R
Social Justice
Standard, The—R
Upsouth—R

*CHRISTIAN
EDUCATION/LIBRARY*
Catechist
CE Connection—R
Church Educator—R

MISSIONS
Areopagus—R
Missiology
Urban Mission—R

PASTORS/LEADERS
Eucharistic Minister—R
Five Stones, The—R
Jour/Amer Soc/Chur
   Growth—R
Journal/Christian Healing—R
Single Ad. Ministries Jour.
Word & World

TEEN/YOUNG ADULT
Christteen—R
Young Adult Today

WOMEN
Aspire

SPIRITUALITY

ADULT/GENERAL
Acts 2
Advent Christian Witness—R
alive now!
American Tract Soc.—R
Angels on Earth
Annals of St. Anne
Arlington Catholic
At Ease—R
Banner, The
Bible Advocate—R

Bible Advocate Online—R
Bible Today
Biblical Reflections—R
Bread of Life—R
Brethren Evangelist
Canada Lutheran—R
Canadian Catholic
Cathedral Age
Catholic Digest—R
Catholic Insight
Catholic Parent
Catholic Rural Life
Charisma/Christian Life
Christian Advocate—R
Christian Century
Christian Chronicle—R
Christian Home & School
Christian Living—R
Christian Motorsports
Christian Parenting—R
Christian Reader—R
Christian Single—R
Christianity Today—R
Chrysalis Reader
Church Advocate—R
Columbia
Common Boundary
Commonweal
Companion
Companions—R
Compass
Conquest
Covenant Companion—R
Cresset
Chrysalis Reader
Culture Wars—R
Disciple's Journal—R
Door, The
Emphasis/Faith & Living—R
Episcopal Life—R
Evangelical Baptist—R
Faith Today
Family Digest
Family Network—R
Fellowship Link—R
Fellowship Today—R
Gem, The—R
God's Revivalist
Good News (KY)—R
Good News, Etc—R
Good News Journal—R
Good News - Salem
Gospel Today
Grail
Guideposts
Healing Inn—R
Hearing Hearts
Heartlight Internet—R

Heavenly Thoughts—R
Highway News—R
Inland NW Christian
Insights—R
Island Christian—R
Jewel Among Jewels—R
John Milton—R
Jour/Christian Nursing—R
Life Gate—R
Liguorian
Live—R
Living Church
Living with Teenagers—R
Lutheran, The—R
Lutheran Digest—R
Lutheran Journal
Lutheran Parent
Marriage Partnership
Mennonite, The—R
Mennonite Brethren—R
MESSAGE/Open Bible—R
Messenger/St. Anthony
Messenger of the Sacred
   Heart
Michigan Christian
Montana Catholic—R
New Covenant
New Oxford Review
Newsline—R
New Writing—R
North American Voice
Oblates
Our Family—R
Our Sunday Visitor
Pegasus Review—R
Perspectives
Plowman, The—R
Poet's Park—R
Prairie Messenger—R
Presbyterian Outlook
Presbyterian Record—R
Presbyterians Today—R
Preserving Christian
   Homes—R
Prism—R
Purpose—R
Queen of All Hearts
Religious Education
Sacred Journey—R
St. Anthony Messenger
St. Willibrord Journal
SCP Journal—R
Signs of the Times—R
Single Connection—R
Smile—R
Social Justice
Sojourners
Spiritual Life

Standard—R
Standard, The—R
Stand Firm—R
TEAK Roundup—R
2-Soar—R
United Church Observer
Upsouth—R
U.S. Catholic
Vision, The—R
Voice, The—R
War Cry—R
Way of St. Francis—R
Weavings—R
Wesleyan Advocate—R

CHILDREN
BREAD/God's Children—R
Discovery (NY)—R
Skipping Stones
Wonder Time

*CHRISTIAN
EDUCATION/LIBRARY*
CE Connection—R
Christian School
Church Educator—R
Church Worship
Religion Teacher's Journal
Teacher's Interaction
Vision—R

MISSIONS
Areopagus—R
Message of the Cross—R
Missiology
Quiet Hour Echoes
World Vision—R
Worldwide Challenge

MUSIC
Quest—R

PASTORS/LEADERS
Art+Plus
Celebration
Christian Century
Cross Currents—R
Emmanuel
Eucharistic Minister—R
Five Stones, The—R
Jour/Amer Soc/Chur
   Growth—R
Journal/Christian Healing—R
Journal/Pastoral Care
Lutheran Partners—R
Ministries Today
Ministry

Pastoral Life
Preacher's Illus. Service—R
Priest, The
PROCLAIM—R
Pulpit Helps—R
Reformed Worship
Review for Religious
Theology Today
Today's Christian
   Preacher—R
Today's Parish
Word & World
Youthworker—R

TEEN/YOUNG ADULT
Challenge (GA)
Christteen—R
Conqueror—R
Devo'Zine—R
Student Leadership—R
Teenage Christian—R
Teen Life (AG)—R
With—R
YOU!—R
Young Adult Today
Young Christian—R
Youth Update

WOMEN
Adam's Rib—R
Aspire
Esprit—R
Handmaiden, The—R
Horizons—R
Joyful Woman—R
Just Between Us—R
Lutheran Woman's Quar.
Lutheran Woman Today
Sisters Today
Today's Christian Woman
Virtue—R
Virtuous Woman
Wesleyan Woman—R

SPIRITUAL WARFARE

ADULT/GENERAL
Angels on Earth
Banner, The
Bible Advocate—R
Bible Advocate Online—R
Bread of Life—R
Charisma/Christian Life
Christian Advocate—R
Christian Chronicle—R
Christian Edge—R
Christian Motorsports

Christian Ranchman
Christian Single—R
Church Herald/Holiness—R
Church of God
    EVANGEL—R
Common Boundary
Companions—R
Disciple's Journal—R
Family Network—R
Fellowship Link—R
Good News (KY)—R
Good News, Etc—R
Good News - Salem
Hallelujah! (CAN)—R
Healing Inn—R
Hearing Hearts
Heartlight Internet—R
Heavenly Thoughts—R
Indian Life—R
Insights—R
Island Christian—R
John Milton—R
Life Gate—R
Lutheran Journal
Lutheran Parent
MESSAGE
MESSAGE/Open Bible—R
Pentecostal Evangel—R
PrayerWorks—R
Single Connection—R
Something Better—R
Standard, The—R
Stand Firm—R
Table Talk—R
2-Soar—R
Upsouth—R
Voice, The—R
Watchman, The

CHILDREN
BREAD/God's Children—R
Discovery (NY)—R
High Adventure—R

MISSIONS
Evangelical Missions—R
Quiet Hour Echoes

PASTORS/LEADERS
Art+Plus
Cell Church—R
Cell Life FORUM—R
Christian Camp—R
Enrichment—R
Jour/Amer Soc/Chur
    Growth—R
Ministries Today

Today's Christian Preacher—R

TEEN/YOUNG ADULT
Challenge (GA)
Christteen—R
Teen Life (AG)—R
Teen Power—R

WOMEN
Adam's Rib—R
Handmaiden, The—R
Ishshah—R
Just Between Us—R
Tea and Sunshine
Virtuous Woman

SPORTS/RECREATION

ADULT/GENERAL
American Tract Soc.—R
Angels on Earth
Arlington Catholic
AXIOS—R
Banner, The
Catholic Digest—R
Christian Courier (WI)—R
Christian Courier (CAN)—R
Christian Living—R
Christian Motorsports
Christian Ranchman
Christian Single—R
Columbia
Connecting Point—R
    (Special Olympics)
Covenant Companion—R
Disciple's Journal—R
Discovery—R
E Street—R
Expression Christian
Gem, The—R
Good News (AL)—R
Good News, Etc—R
Good News - Salem
Guideposts
Home Times—R
Indian Life—R
Lifeglow—R
Living Light News—R
Living with Teenagers—R
Lutheran Parent
Lutheran Witness—R
Messenger/St. Anthony
Metro Voice—R
Minnesota Christian—R
New Writing—R
NW Christian Journal—R
ParentLife—R

Single Connection—R
Something Better—R
Sports Spectrum
Standard, The—R
Stand Firm—R
Table Talk—R
TEAK Roundup—R
Trumpeter, The
Vibrant Life—R

CHILDREN
BREAD/God's Children—R
Club Connection—R
Counselor—R
Courage
Crusader—R
Focus/Clubhouse
Guideposts for Kids
High Adventure—R
Live Wire—R
On the Line—R
Touch—R
Young Christian—R

CHRISTIAN
EDUCATION/LIBRARY
Christian School

MISSIONS
Worldwide Challenge

MUSIC
Quest—R

PASTORS/LEADERS
Christian Recreation
Pastor's Family
Preacher's Illus. Service—R

TEEN/YOUNG ADULT
Breakaway—R
Certainty
Challenge (GA)
Challenge (IL)
Christteen—R
Devo'Zine—R
Sharing the VICTORY—R
Straight—R
Teen Life (AG)—R
Teen Power—R
Today's Christian Teen—R
YOU!—R
Young Adult Today
Young & Alive—R
Young Christian—R
Young Salvationist—R
Youth 98

WOMEN
Aspire
Esprit—R

STEWARDSHIP

ADULT/GENERAL
Angels on Earth
Banner, The
Bible Advocate—R
Biblical Reflections—R
Canadian Baptist
Canadian Catholic
Catholic Digest—R
Catholic Rural Life
Christian Edge—R
Christian Living—R
Christian Motorsports
Christian Ranchman
Christian Single—R
Church Advocate—R
Church Herald/Holiness—R
Church of God
    EVANGEL—R
Companions—R
Covenant Companion—R
Disciple's Journal—R
Discipleship Journal
Evangel—R
Family Network—R
Gem, The—R
Good News, Etc—R
Good News - Salem
Gospel Today
Green Cross—R
Healing Inn—R
Heavenly Thoughts—R
Insights—R
Island Christian—R
John Milton—R
Life Gate—R
Liguorian
Lutheran Journal—R
Lutheran Parent
Mennonite, The—R
Mennonite Brethren—R
MESSAGE
MESSAGE/Open Bible—R
Michigan Christian
Moody—R
Pentecostal Testimony—R
Plain Truth—R
Power for Living—R
Presbyterian Layman
Presbyterian Outlook
Preserving Christian
    Homes—R
Prism—R

Religious Broadcasting—R
Standard, The—R
Stand Firm—R
Stewardship
Today's Christian Senior—R
United Church Observer
U.S. Catholic
Watchman, The

CHILDREN
BREAD/God's Children—R
Crusader (TN)
Lad
R-A-D-A-R—R

CHRISTIAN
EDUCATION/LIBRARY
Children's Ministry
CE Leadership—R
Church Educator—R
GROUP
Leader/Church School
    Today—R

MISSIONS
Quiet Hour Echoes
Save Our World—R
World Mission People—R

PASTORS/LEADERS
Art+Plus
Cell Church—R
Enrichment—R
Five Stones, The—R
GROUP's Jr. High
Lutheran Partners—R
Ministries Today
Ministry
Preacher's Magazine—R
Pulpit Helps—R
Resource—R
Theology Today
Today's Christian
    Preacher—R
Your Church—R

TEEN/YOUNG ADULT
Challenge (GA)
Christteen—R
Straight—R
Teen Life (AG)—R
Teens on Target—R
Today's Christian Teen—R
With—R
YOU!—R
Youth Challenge—R

WOMEN
Aspire
Esprit—R
Handmaiden, The—R
Today's Christian Woman
Virtuous Woman
Wesleyan Woman—R

TAKE-HOME PAPERS

ADULT/GENERAL
Companions—R
Conquest
Evangel—R
Gems of Truth
Gem, The—R
Live—R
Lookout—R
Power for Living—R
Purpose
Seek—R
Standard—R
Vision—R

CHILDREN
Beginner's Friend
Counselor—R
Courage
Discoveries—R
Discovery (AL)
Good News for Children
Guide
Junior Companion
Junior Trails—R
On the Line—R
Our Little Friend—R
Partners
Power & Light
Primary Pal (IL)
Primary Pal (KS)
Primary Treasure
Promise
R-A-D-A-R—R
Seeds
Story Friends—R
Story Mates—R
Together Time
Venture
Wonder Time

TEEN/YOUNG ADULT
Certainty
Challenge
Cross Walk
Essential Connections
Insight
Rock, The

Straight—R
Teen Life (AG)—R
Teen Life (UPC)—R
Teen Power—R
Teens on Target
Visions
Youth Challenge
Youth Compass (KS)
Youth World—R

THEOLOGICAL

ADULT/GENERAL
AGAIN—R
America
Anglican Journal—R
Annals of St. Anne
Arlington Catholic
At Ease—R
Banner, The
Baptist Informer
B.C. Catholic—R
Bible Advocate—R
Biblical Reflections—R
Canadian Baptist
Canadian Catholic
Catholic Digest—R
Catholic Insight
Catholic Rural Life
Catholic Twin Circle—R
Charisma/Christian Life
Christian Century
Christian Motorsports
Christian Renewal—R
Christian Research
Christian Social Action—R
Christianity Today—R
Church Herald/Holiness—R
Church of God
        EVANGEL—R
Commonweal
Companion
Companions—R
Compass
Conquest
Cornerstone—R
Covenant Companion—R
Cresset
Culture Wars—R
Discipleship Journal
Emphasis/Faith & Living—R
Episcopal Life—R
Evangelical Baptist—R
Evangelical Visitor—R
Fellowship Link—R
First Things
Good News (KY)—R
Good News - Salem

Grail
Green Cross—R
Heavenly Thoughts—R
Insights—R
Interim—R
John Milton—R
Journal of Church & State
Liguorian
Living Church
Lutheran, The—R
Lutheran Digest—R
Lutheran Parent
Mennonite Brethren—R
Messenger/St. Anthony
Messenger of the Sacred
        Heart
Michigan Christian
New Oxford Review
North American Voice
Our Family—R
Our Sunday Visitor
Perspectives
Prairie Messenger—R
Presbyterian Layman
Presbyterian Outlook
Presbyterian Record—R
Presbyterians Today—R
Queen of All Hearts
Ratio
Religious Education
St. Anthony Messenger
St.Willibrord Journal
SCP Journal—R
Silver Wings—R
Social Justice
Sojourners
Spiritual Life
Standard, The—R
Touchstone—R
United Church Observer
U.S. Catholic
Watchman, The
Way of St. Francis—R
Weavings—R

CHRISTIAN
EDUCATION/LIBRARY
CE Connection—R
Church Educator—R
Church Worship
Teacher's Interaction

MISSIONS
Areopagus—R
East-West Church
Missiology
Quiet Hour Echoes
Urban Mission—R

Worldwide Challenge

PASTORS/LEADERS
Bibliotheca Sacra
Catechumenate
Celebration
Christian Camp—R
Christian Century
Christian Ministry
Cross Currents—R
Diocesan Dialogue—R
Emmanuel
Enrichment—R
Eucharistic Minister—R
Five Stones, The—R
Journal/Christian Healing—R
Journal/Pastoral Care
Jour/Amer Soc/Chur
        Growth—R
Lutheran Forum—R
Lutheran Partners—R
Ministries Today
Ministry
Modern Liturgy—R
Networks—R
Preacher's Illus. Service—R
Preacher's Magazine—R
Priest, The
PROCLAIM—R
Pulpit Helps—R
Quarterly Review
Review for Religious
Theology Today
Today's Christian
        Preacher—R
Today's Parish
Word & World
Youthworker—R

TEEN/YOUNG ADULT
Challenge (GA)
YOU!—R
Young Adult Today
Youth Update

WOMEN
Aspire
Conscience—R
Esprit—R
Handmaiden, The—R
Jour/Women's Ministries
Lutheran Woman Today
Sisters Today

THINK PIECES

ADULT/GENERAL
Alive!—R
American Tract Soc.—R
Annals of St. Anne
AXIOS—R
Banner, The
Bible Advocate—R
Bible Advocate Online—R
Biblical Reflections—R
Canada Lutheran—R
Canadian Catholic
Catholic Digest—R
Catholic Forester—R
Catholic Rural Life
Catholic Twin Circle—R
Christian Chronicle—R
Christian C.L. RECORD—R
Christian Courier (CAN)—R
Christian Edge—R
Christian Living—R
Christian Single—R
Christian Social Action—R
Church of God
       EVANGEL—R
Commonweal
Companion
Compass
Conquest
Cornerstone—R
Covenant Companion—R
Disciple's Journal—R
Discipleship Journal
Door, The
Episcopal Life—R
Evangel—R
Evangelical Baptist—R
Evangelical Visitor—R
Expression Christian
Family Journal—R
First Things
Good News (AL)—R
Good News, Etc—R
Good News - Salem
Green Cross—R
Head to Head—R
Healing Inn—R
Hearing Hearts
Heartlight Internet—R
Heavenly Thoughts—R
Home Times—R
Insights—R
Inspirer, The—R
Island Christian—R
John Milton—R
Lutheran, The—R
Lutheran Digest—R

Lutheran Journal—R
Mennonite Brethren—R
MESSAGE
MESSAGE/Open Bible—R
Metro Voice—R
Michigan Christian
Minnesota Christian—R
New Oxford Review
New Writing—R
Pegasus Review—R
Poet's Park—R
PrayerWorks—R
Presbyterian Layman
Presbyterian Outlook
Presbyterian Record—R
Presbyterians Today—R
Preserving Christian
       Homes—R
Purpose—R
Ratio
Religious Broadcasting—R
Religious Education
San Diego Co. Christian
Seek—R
Single Connection—R
Sojourners
Standard, The—R
Stand Firm—R
Star of Zion
Table Talk—R
TEAK Roundup—R
Upsouth—R
Wesleyan Advocate—R

CHILDREN
Discovery (NY)—R
Touch—R
Writers' Intl. Forum/Young

CHRISTIAN EDUCATION/LIBRARY
CE Connection—R
Resource—R
Vision—R

MISSIONS
Areopagus—R
Catholic Near East
World Vision—R

MUSIC
Quest—R
Tradition—R

PASTORS/LEADERS
Art+Plus
Catholic Servant

Celebration
Church Bytes—R
Eucharistic Minister—R
Journal/Christian Healing—R
Journal/Pastoral Care
Lutheran Partners—R
Ministries Today
Networks—R
Priest, The
Pulpit Helps—R
Technologies/Worship—R
Word & World

TEEN/YOUNG ADULT
Alive!
Certainty
Challenge (GA)
Christteen—R
Conqueror—R
Vision—R
YOU!—R
Young Adult Today
Young Christian—R

WOMEN
Anna's Journal—R
Aspire
DOMESTIQUE—R
Handmaiden, The—R
Horizons—R
Ishshah—R
Lutheran Woman Today
Tea and Sunshine
Virtue—R
Wesleyan Woman—R

WRITERS
Writer's Exchange—R
Writers' Intl. Forum

TRAVEL

ADULT/GENERAL
Alive!—R
Angels on Earth
Arlington Catholic
Catholic Digest—R
Catholic Twin Circle—R
Charisma/Christian Life
Christian Courier (CAN)—R
Christian Ranchman
Christian Traveler—R
Companion
Disciple's Journal—R
E Street—R
Family Digest
Fellowship Link—R

Good News (AL)—R
Good News - Salem
Home Times—R
Joyful Noise
Living with Teenagers—R
Lutheran Journal—R
Mature Living
Mennonite Historian—R
Messenger/St. Anthony
Michigan Christian
MovieGuide
ParentLife—R
Seek—R
Single Connection—R
Smart Dads
Smart Families
Standard, The—R
TEAK Roundup—R
Time of Singing—R
Today's Christian Senior—R
Upscale Magazine
Upsouth—R
Vibrant Life—R
Visitation

CHILDREN
High Adventure—R
R-A-D-A-R—R
Skipping Stones
Touch—R

MISSIONS
Areopagus—R
East-West Church
World Mission People—R

PASTORS/LEADERS
Preacher's Illus. Service—R

TEEN/YOUNG ADULT
Conqueror—R
Teenage Christian—R
Young Adult Today
Young & Alive—R
Young Christian—R

WOMEN
Aspire

TRUE STORIES

ADULT/GENERAL
AGAIN—R
Alive!—R
Angels on Earth
At Ease—R
Bible Advocate—R

Bible Advocate Online—R
Canada Lutheran—R
Canadian Baptist
Catholic Digest—R
Catholic Twin Circle—R
CBA Frontline
Christian Chronicle—R
Christian Edge—R
Christian Living—R
Christian Motorsports
Christian Ranchman
Christian Reader—R
Christian Single—R
Church Advocate—R
Church of God
   EVANGEL—R
Companion
Conquest
Cornerstone—R
Covenant Companion—R
Crossway/Newsline—R
Culture Wars—R
Decision
Disciple's Journal—R
Emphasis/Faith & Living—R
Evangel—R
Evangelical Visitor—R
Family Network—R
Fellowship Link—R
Foursquare World—R
Gem, The—R
God's Revivalist
Good News (AL)—R
Good News, Etc—R
Good News Journal
Good News - Salem
Gospel Today
Green Cross—R
Guideposts
Head to Head—R
Healing Inn—R
Hearing Hearts
Heartlight Internet—R
Heavenly Thoughts—R
Home Times—R
Impact Magazine—R
Indian Life—R
Insights—R
Inspirer, The—R
Island Christian—R
Jewel Among Jewels—R
John Milton—R
Jour/Christian Nursing—R
Lifeglow—R
Light and Life
Liguorian
Living—R
Living Light News—R

Lutheran, The—R
Lutheran Digest—R
Lutheran Journal—R
Lutheran Parent
Lutheran Witness—R
Mennonite, The—R
Mennonite Brethren—R
MESSAGE/Open Bible—R
Messenger, The (MI)—R
Messenger/St. Anthony
Metro Voice—R
Michigan Christian
Minnesota Christian—R
Moody—R
New Heart, A—R
New Trumpet—R
New Writing—R
Our Family—R
Pentecostal Evangel—R
Physician
Plain Truth—R
Plus—R
Power for Living—R
PrayerWorks—R
Presbyterian Record—R
Preserving Christian
   Homes—R
ProLife News—R
Pursuit—R
Quiet Revolution—R
Religious Broadcasting—R
Rosebud
SCP Journal—R
Seek—R
Signs of the Times—R
Single Connection—R
Something Better—R
Standard—R
Standard, The—R
Stand Firm—R
Table Talk—R
TEAK Roundup—R
Today's Christian Senior—R
2-Soar—R
Vision, The—R
War Cry—R
Wesleyan Advocate—R

CHILDREN
Club Connection—R
CLUBHOUSE—R
Counselor—R
Courage
Discovery (NY)—R
Focus/Clubhouse
Focus/Clubhouse Jr
GUIDE—R
Guideposts for Kids

High Adventure—R
Junior Trails—R
Listen
Live Wire—R
Mission
Nature Friend—R
Our Little Friend—R
Partners—R
Pockets—R
Primary Treasure—R
Skipping Stones
Story Friends—R
Touch—R

*CHRISTIAN
EDUCATION/LIBRARY*
CE Connection—R
Church Media Library—R
Leader/Church School
   Today—R
Perspective—R
Shining Star

MISSIONS
American Horizon—R
Areopagus—R
Heartbeat—R
Leaders for Today
Quiet Hour Echoes
Save Our World—R
Urban Mission—R
World Christian—R
World Mission People—R
World Vision—R
Worldwide Challenge

MUSIC
Quest—R

PASTORS/LEADERS
Cell Church—R
Cell Life FORUM—R
Eucharistic Minister—R
Five Stones, The—R
Leadership Journal—R
Minister's Family
Networks—R
Pastor's Family
Preacher's Illus. Service—R

TEEN/YOUNG ADULT
Alive!
Certainty
Challenge (GA)
Challenge (IL)
Christteen—R
Conqueror—R

Insight—R
Straight—R
Teen Life (AG)—R
Teen Power—R
Teens on Target—R
Today's Christian Teen—R
With—R
YOU!—R
Young Adult Today
Young & Alive—R
Young Christian—R
Young Salvationist—R
Youth Challenge—R
Youth World—R

WOMEN
Anna's Journal—R
Aspire
DOMESTIQUE—R
Esprit—R
Handmaiden, The—R
Helping Hand—R
Horizons—R
Ishshah—R
Journey—R
Just Between Us—R
Lutheran Woman Today
Proverbs 31 Homemaker—R
Today's Christian Woman
Virtue—R
Wesleyan Woman—R
Woman's Touch—R

WRITERS
Writer's Nook News

VIDEO REVIEWS

ADULT/GENERAL
Arlington Catholic
Believer, The—R
CBA Marketplace
Christian Arts Review
Christian Edge—R
Christian Single—R
Christianity/Arts
Companion
Disciple's Journal—R
Discovery—R
Expression Christian
Fatted Calf Forum—R
Gadfly—R
Good News (AL)—R
Good News - Salem
Home Times—R
Island Christian—R
Living Light News—R

Michigan Christian
MovieGuide
New Trumpet—R
ProLife News—R
Something Better—R
Stand Firm—R
Upsouth—R

CHILDREN
Club Connection—R

*CHRISTIAN
EDUCATION/LIBRARY*
Church Libraries—R

PASTORS/LEADERS
Five Stones, The—R
Lutheran Partners—R
Ministries Today

TEEN/YOUNG ADULT
Challenge (GA)
Devo'Zine—R

WOMEN
Esprit—R
Horizons—R

WOMEN'S ISSUES

ADULT/GENERAL
Advent Christian Witness—R
Anglican Journal—R
Annals of St. Anne
Arlington Catholic
At Ease—R
Atlantic Baptist
Banner, The
Bread of Life—R
Canada Lutheran—R
Canadian Baptist
Canadian Catholic
Catholic Digest—R
Catholic Forester—R
Catholic Insight
Catholic Parent
Catholic Rural Life
Catholic Twin Circle—R
CBA Marketplace
Celebrate Life—R
Charisma/Christian Life
Christian C.L. RECORD—R
Christian Courier (CAN)—R
Christian Edge—R
Christian Living—R
Christian News NW—R
Christian Ranchman

Christian Single—R
Christian Social Action—R
Christians in Business
Chrysalis Reader
Church Advocate—R
Church Herald/Holiness—R
Church of God
     EVANGEL—R
Columbia
Companion
Compass
Cornerstone—R
Covenant Companion—R
Decision
Disciple's Journal—R
Discovery—R
Emphasis/Faith & Living—R
Episcopal Life—R
Evangel—R
Evangelical Baptist—R
Expression Christian
Faith Today
Family Network—R
Fatted Calf Forum—R
Focus on the Family
Foursquare World—R
Gem, The—R
Good News (AL)—R
Good News, Etc—R
Good News Journal—R
Good News - Salem
Hallelujah! (CAN)—R
Healing Inn—R
Heartlight Internet—R
Heavenly Thoughts—R
Home Times—R
Indian Life—R
Interim—R
Island Christian—R
John Milton—R
Jour/Christian Nursing—R
Joyful Noise
Life Gate—R
Light and Life
Liguorian
Living—R
Living with Teenagers—R
Lookout—R
Lutheran, The—R
Marriage Partnership
MESSAGE
MESSAGE/Open Bible—R
Messenger, The (MI)—R
Messenger/St. Anthony
Metro Voice—R
Michigan Christian
Minnesota Christian—R
Moody—R

Newsline—R
New Writing—R
Our Sunday Visitor
ParentLife—R
Pentecostal Evangel—R
Pentecostal Testimony—R
Perspectives
Plain Truth—R
Plus—R
Presbyterian Layman
Presbyterian Outlook
Presbyterians Today—R
ProLife News—R
Purpose—R
St. Joseph's Messenger—R
Signs of the Times—R
Single Connection—R
Sojourners
Something Better—R
Standard—R
Standard, The—R
Table Talk—R
Together—R
Total Health
Trumpeter, The
2-Soar—R
United Church Observer
Vibrant Life—R
Voice, The—R
War Cry—R

*CHRISTIAN
EDUCATION/LIBRARY*
Leader/Church School
     Today—R
Resource—R

MISSIONS
American Horizon—R
East-West Church
Urban Mission—R
Worldwide Challenge

PASTORS/LEADERS
Art+Plus
Cell Church—R
Christian Century
Christian Ministry (feminist)
Clergy Journal—R
Journal/Christian Healing—R
Leadership Journal—R
Lutheran Partners—R
Ministries Today (little)
Ministry
Pastor's Family
Preacher's Magazine—R
Pulpit Helps—R

Single Ad. Ministries Jour.
Youthworker—R
Word & World

TEEN/YOUNG ADULT
Brio
Christteen—R
Vision—R
YOU!—R
Young Adult Today
Young Christian—R

WOMEN
(See alphabetical listing)

WORLD ISSUES

ADULT/GENERAL
Alive!
America
Annals of St. Anne
Arlington Catholic
At Ease—R
Atlantic Baptist
AXIOS—R
Banner, The
Baptist Informer
Bible Advocate—R
Bible Advocate Online—R
Biblical Reflections—R
Canada Lutheran—R
Canadian Baptist
Canadian Catholic
Catholic Digest—R
Catholic Twin Circle—R
Charisma/Christian Life
Christian Century
Christian Courier (CAN)—R
Christian Crusade
Christian Edge—R
Christian Living—R
Christian Motorsports
Christian Ranchman
Christian Single—R
Christian Social Action—R
Church of God
     EVANGEL—R
Commonweal
Companion
Compass
Covenant Companion—R
Culture Wars—R
Disciple's Journal—R
Emphasis/Faith & Living—R
Evangel—R
Evangelical Baptist—R
Evangelical Visitor—R

Expression Christian
Family Network—R
Fatted Calf Forum—R
First Things
God's Revivalist
Good News (AL)—R
Good News, Etc.—R
Good News - Salem
Gotta Write
Grail
Green Cross—R
Hallelujah! (CAN)—R
Healing Inn—R
Heartlight Internet—R
Heavenly Thoughts—R
Home Times—R
Inland NW Christian
Insights—R
Interchange
Island Christian—R
John Milton—R
Journal of Church & State
Liberty—R
Lutheran, The—R
Lutheran Journal
MESSAGE
MESSAGE/Open Bible—R
Messenger
Messenger/St. Anthony
Metro Voice—R
Michigan Christian
Minnesota Christian—R
Moody—R
Our Sunday Visitor
Pentecostal Testimony—R
Presbyterian Layman
Presbyterian Outlook
Presbyterian Record—R
Presbyterians Today—R
ProLife News—R
Quiet Revolution—R
Religious Broadcasting—R
Sacred Journey—R
SCP Journal—R
Single Connection—R
Sojourners
Something Better—R
Standard, The—R
Stand Firm—R
Table Talk—R
TEAK Roundup—R
2-Soar—R
United Church Observer
Vision, The—R
War Cry—R
Watchman, The

CHILDREN
Counselor—R
God's World Today
Skipping Stones

MISSIONS
Areopagus—R
Catholic Near East
East-West Church
Missiology
New World Outlook
P.I.M.E. World
Save Our World—R
Urban Mission—R
World Christian—R
World Vision—R
Worldwide Challenge

PASTORS/LEADERS
Cell Church—R
Christian Century
Lutheran Partners—R
Ministries Today
Networks—R
Preacher's Illus. Service—R
Preacher's Magazine—R
Word & World
Youthworker—R

TEEN/YOUNG ADULT
Challenge (GA)
Christteen—R
Conqueror—R
Student Leadership—R
Teenage Christian—R
YOU!—R
Young Adult Today
Young Christian—R

WOMEN
Aspire
Esprit—R
Helping Hand—R
Horizons—R
Lutheran Woman Today
Wesleyan Woman—R

WORSHIP

ADULT/GENERAL
Advent Christian Witness—R
alive now!
Angels on Earth
Annals of St. Anne
Arlington Catholic
At Ease—R
Atlantic Baptist

Baptist Informer
Bible Advocate—R
Bread of Life—R
Brethren Evangelist
Canada Lutheran—R
Canadian Baptist
Canadian Catholic
Canadian Mennonite
Cathedral Age
Catholic Digest—R
Charisma/Christian Life
Christian Century
Christian Edge—R
Christian Motorsports
Christian Single—R
Christianity Today—R
Church Herald/Holiness—R
Church of God EVANGEL—R
Commonweal
Companion
Companions—R
Conquest
Cornerstone—R
Covenant Companion—R
Cresset
Culture Wars—R
Decision
Disciple's Journal—R
Emphasis/Faith & Living—R
Evangel—R
Evangelical Baptist—R
Evangelical Visitor—R
Faith Today
Family Digest
Family Network—R
Fellowship Link—R
Fellowship Today—R
Foursquare World—R
Good News, Etc—R
Good News Journal—R
Good News - Salem
Green Cross—R
Healing Inn—R
Heavenly Thoughts—R
Insights—R
Inspirer, The—R
Island Christian—R
John Milton—R
Joyful Noise
Keys to Living
Life Gate—R
Liguorian
Living Church
Living with Teenagers—R
Lookout—R
Lutheran, The—R
Lutheran Journal—R
Lutheran Parent

Mennonite, The—R
Mennonite Brethren—R
MESSAGE/Open Bible—R
Messenger/St. Anthony
Michigan Christian
Moody—R
North American Voice
NW Christian Journal—R
Our Family—R
Our Sunday Visitor
Perspectives
Plain Truth—R
Plenty Good Room
Power for Living—R
Prairie Messenger—R
PrayerWorks—R
Presbyterian Outlook
Presbyterian Record—R
Presbyterians Today—R
St. Willibrord Journal
Seek—R
Silver Wings—R
Spiritual Life
Standard—R
Standard, The—R
Time of Singing—R
United Church Observer
U.S. Catholic
Voice, The—R
War Cry—R
Watchman, The
Weavings—R
Wesleyan Advocate—R

CHILDREN
BREAD/God's Children—R
R-A-D-A-R—R
Wonder Time

*CHRISTIAN
EDUCATION/LIBRARY*
Children's Ministry
CE Connection—R
Christian Ed Journal—R
CE Leadership—R
Church Educator—R
Church Media Library—R
Church Worship
Evangelizing Today's
    Child—R
GROUP
Leader/Church School
    Today—R
Shining Star

MISSIONS
American Horizon—R

Areopagus—R
Catholic Near East
Quiet Hour Echoes
Worldwide Challenge

MUSIC
Church Pianist, etc.
Creator—R
Glory Songs—R
Gospel Industry Today
Hymn, The

PASTORS/LEADERS
Celebration
Cell Church—R
Cell Life FORUM—R
Christian Century
Christian Management—R
Church Bytes—R
Clergy Journal—R
Emmanuel
Enrichment—R
Environment & Art
Five Stones, The—R
GROUP's Jr. High
Journal/Christian Healing—R
Jour/Amer Soc/Chur
    Growth—R
Leadership Journal—R
Let's Worship
Liturgy
Lutheran Forum—R
Lutheran Partners—R
Ministries Today
Ministry
Modern Liturgy—R
Networks—R
Preacher's Illus. Service—R
Preacher's Magazine—R
Preaching
Priest, The
PROCLAIM—R
Reformed Worship
Today's Christian
    Preacher—R
Today's Parish
Vital Issues
WCA Monthly—R
Word & World
Worship Leader
Youthworker—R

TEEN/YOUNG ADULT
Alive!
Challenge (GA)
Conqueror—R
Straight—R

Student Leadership—R
Teenage Christian—R
Teen Life (AG)—R
Teen Power—R
Teens on Target—R
Today's Christian Teen—R
YOU!—R
Young Adult Today
Young Salvationist—R
Youth Challenge—R
Youth Update

WOMEN
Adam's Rib—R
Aspire
Esprit—R
Handmaiden, The—R
Horizons—R
Ishshah—R
Lutheran Woman Today
Proverbs 31 Homemaker—R
Sisters Today
Virtue—R
Virtuous Woman
Wesleyan Woman—R

WRITING HOW-TO

ADULT/GENERAL
Believer, The—R
CBA Marketplace
Christian Edge—R
Good News - Salem
Home Times—R
Michigan Christian
New Writing—R
Poets' Paper—R
TEAK Roundup—R
2-Soar—R

CHILDREN
Challenge (GA)
Discovery (NY)—R

*CHRISTIAN
EDUCATION/LIBRARY*
Children's Ministry
GROUP
Leader/Church School
    Today—R

PASTORS/LEADERS
GROUP's Jr. High
Newsletter Newsletter
Technologies/Worship—R
Vital Issues

TEEN/YOUNG ADULT
Challenge (GA)

WOMEN
Esprit—R
Joyful Woman—R

WRITERS
Advanced Chris. Writer—R
Byline
Canadian Writer's Jour—R
Cross & Quill—R
Exchange—R
Fellowscript—R
NW Christian Author—R
Once Upon a Time—R
Teachers & Writers
Tickled by Thunder
Today's $85,000 Freelance
W.I.N. Informer
Writer, The
Writer's Digest—R
Writer's Exchange—R
Writer's Forum—R
Writing World

YOUTH ISSUES

ADULT/GENERAL
American Tract Soc.—R
Annals of St. Anne
Arlington Catholic
AXIOS—R
Banner, The
Canada Lutheran—R
Canadian Baptist
Canadian Catholic
Catholic Digest—R
Catholic Rural Life
Charisma/Christian Life
Christian Courier (CAN)—R
Christian Edge—R
Christian Living—R
Christian Motorsports
Christian Ranchman
Christian Social Action—R
Church Herald/Holiness—R
Church of God EVANGEL—R
Columbia
Companion
Covenant Companion—R
Culture Wars—R
Disciple's Journal—R
Decision
Emphasis/Faith & Living—R
Evangel—R
Evangelical Baptist—R

Expression Christian
Foursquare World—R
Good News (AL)—R
Good News, Etc—R
Good News Journal—R
Good News - Salem
Gospel Tidings—R
Gospel Today
Hallelujah! (CAN)—R
Home Times—R
Indian Life—R
Insights—R
Island Christian—R
Keys to Living
Life Gate—R
Light and Life
Liguorian
Living with Teenagers—R
Lutheran, The—R
Lutheran Digest—R
Lutheran Parent
Mennonite Brethren—R
MESSAGE
Messenger/St. Anthony
Metro Voice—R
Michigan Christian
New Oxford Review
Our Family—R
ParentLife—R
Prairie Messenger—R
Presbyterian Outlook
Presbyterian Record—R
Presbyterians Today—R
Prism—R
ProLife News—R
Religious Education
Smart Dads
Smart Families
Sojourners
Something Better—R
Standard, The—R
Table Talk—R
Trumpeter, The
2-Soar—R
U.S. Catholic
Voice, The—R

CHILDREN
BREAD/God's Children—R
Children's Ministry
Club Connection—R
CLUBHOUSE—R
Courage
Discovery (NY)—R
Focus/Clubhouse Jr
GUIDE—R
My Friend
On the Line—R

Power & Light—R
R-A-D-A-R—R
Skipping Stones
Touch—R

*CHRISTIAN
EDUCATION/LIBRARY*
CE Connection—R
CE Counselor—R
CE Leadership—R
Church Educator—R
Enrichment—R
GROUP
Journal/Adventist Educ.—R
Leader/Church School
   Today—R
Parish Teacher—R
Perspective—R
Resource—R
Team—R
Vision—R

MISSIONS
American Horizon—R
Quiet Hour Echoes
Worldwide Challenge

MUSIC
Quest—R

PASTORS/LEADERS
Art+Plus
Catholic Servant
Cell Church—R
Cell Life FORUM—R
Christian Camp—R
Five Stones, The—R
GROUP's Jr. High
Ivy Jungle Report—R
Journal/Christian Healing
Lutheran Partners—R
Minister's Family
Ministries Today
Pastoral Life
Vital Issues
Word & World
Youthworker—R

TEEN/YOUNG ADULT
(See alphabetical listing)

WOMEN
Esprit—R
Handmaiden, The—R
Horizons—R
Proverbs 31 Homemaker—R
Wesleyan Woman—R

ALPHABETICAL LISTINGS OF PERIODICALS

Following are the listings of periodicals. They are arranged alphabetically by type of periodical (see Table of Contents for a list of types). Nonpaying markets are indicated in bold letters within those listings, e.g., **NO PAYMENT**.

If a listing is preceded by an asterisk (*), it indicates that publisher did not send updated information. If it is preceded by a number symbol (#) it was updated from available sources or by phone. If it is preceded by a (+) it is a new listing. It is important that freelance writers request writer's guidelines and a recent sample copy before submitting to any of these publications, but especially to those with the * and # symbols.

If you do not find the publication you are looking for, look in the General Index. See the introduction of that index for the codes used to identify the current status of each unlisted publication.

For a detailed explanation of how to understand and get the most out of these listings, as well as solid marketing tips, see the "How to Use This Book" section at the front of the book. Unfamiliar terms are explained in the Glossary at the back of the book.

(*) An asterisk before a listing indicates no or unconfirmed information update.
(#) A number symbol before a listing means it was updated from the current writer's guidelines or other sources.
(+) A plus sign means it is a new listing.

ADULT/GENERAL MARKETS

+**ACCENT ON LIVING**, PO Box 700, Bloomington IL 61702. (309)378-2961. Fax (309)378-4420. Betty Garee, ed. Provides information on new devices and easier ways to do things, so people with physical disabilities can enjoy a better and more satisfying lifestyle. Quarterly mag; circ 20,000. Query. Pays .10/wd & up on publication for one-time rts. Articles 250-1,000 wds. Responds in 2 wks. Guidelines; copy $3.

Fillers: Cartoons; $20.

Tips: "We prefer an informal, rather than academic approach. We want to show individuals with disabilities getting involved in all aspects of life."

#**ADVENT CHRISTIAN WITNESS**, PO Box 23152, Charlotte NC 28227. (704)545-6161. Fax (704)573-0712. E-mail: Mayerpub@aol.com. Advent Christian General Conference. Robert J. Mayer, ed. Denominational. Monthly (10X) mag; 20 pgs; circ 3,200. Subscription $11. 10-15% freelance. Query or complete ms/cover letter; no phone/fax/e-mail query. Pays $15-25 on publication for one-time rts. Articles 1,500-2,000 wds (3-4/yr). Responds in 6-10 wks. Seasonal 7 mos ahead. Accepts simultaneous submissions & reprints. Accepts disk. Sidebars OK. Prefers NIV. Guidelines; copy for 9x12 SAE/4 stamps.

AGAIN MAGAZINE, PO Box 76, Ben Lomond CA 95005. (408)338-3644. Fax

(408)336-8882. E-mail: shouston@conciliarpress.com. Website: http://www. conciliarpress.com. Orthodox/Conciliar Press. Raymond Zell, mng ed. A call to the people of God to return to their roots of historical orthodoxy once AGAIN. Quarterly mag; 32 pgs; circ 5,000. Subscription $14.50. 1% freelance. Query. **PAYS IN COPIES.** Accepts simultaneous submissions & reprints. Articles 1,500-2,500 wds; fiction 1,500-2,500 wds; book reviews 500-700 wds. Responds in 16 wks. Seasonal 2 mos ahead. Serials 2 parts. Prefers disk. Copy $2.50/9x12 SAE/5 stamps.

#THE ALABAMA BAPTIST, 3310 Independence Dr., Birmingham AL 35209-5602. (205)870-4720. Fax (205)870-8957. E-mail: 70420.127@compuserve.com. Dr. Bob Terry, ed. Shares news and information relevant to members of Baptist churches in Alabama. Weekly newspaper; circ 117,000. Subscription $9.65. Open to freelance. Query. Not in topical listings. (Ads)

ALIVE! A MAGAZINE FOR CHRISTIAN SENIOR ADULTS, PO Box 46464, Cincinnati OH 45246-0464. (513)825-3681. Christian Seniors Fellowship. June Lang, office ed. Focuses on activities and opportunities for active, Christian senior adults, 55 and older; upbeat rather than nostalgic. Bimonthly mag; 28 pgs; circ 3,000. Subscription/membership $15. 70% freelance. Complete ms/cover letter. Pays .04-.06/wd on publication for one-time or reprint rts. Articles 600-1,200 wds (35-40/yr); fiction 600-1,200 wds (6-8/yr). Responds in 6-8 wks. Seasonal 4 mos ahead. Accepts reprints (tell when/where appeared). No disk. Few sidebars. Guidelines; copy for 9x12 SAE/3 stamps. (Ads)

> **Poetry:** Rarely use. Free verse, light verse, traditional; $3-10. Submit max. 3 poems.
>
> **Fillers:** Buys 20/yr. Anecdotes, cartoons, quizzes, short humor, and word puzzles, 50-500 wds; $5-25.
>
> **Columns/Departments:** Buys 35/yr. Heart Medicine (humor, grandparent/grandchild anecdotes), to 100 wds, $5-10.
>
> **Tips:** "Most open to fresh material of special appeal to Christian senior adults. Avoid nostalgia. Our market is seniors interested in living in the present, not dwelling on the past. We pay little attention to credits/bios. Articles stand on their own merit."

*ALIVE NOW! 1908 Grand Ave., Box 189, Nashville TN 37202-0189. (615)340-7218. Fax (615)340-7006. E-mail: 102615.3122@compuserve.com. United Methodist/The Upper Room. George R. Graham, ed. Short theme-based writings in attractive graphic setting for reflection and meditation. Bimonthly mag; 64 pgs; circ 65,000. 30% freelance. Complete ms/cover letter. Pays $25 or more on acceptance for newspaper, periodical & electronic rts. Articles 250-500 wds; fiction 250-750 wds. Responds 13 wks before issue date. Seasonal 6-8 mos ahead. Accepts disk. Guidelines/theme list; free copy.

> **Poetry:** Free verse, traditional; to 25 lines.
>
> **Fillers:** Cartoons, prayers.

#AMERICA, 106 W. 56th St., New York NY 10019-3893. (212)581-4640. Fax (212)399-3596. Catholic. Rev. George W. Hunt, S.J., ed. A national journal of opinion. Weekly mag; 24-32 pgs; circ 36,000. 100% freelance. Query or complete ms/cover letter; fax query OK. Pays $50-200 on acceptance for all rts. Articles 1,500-2,000 wds. Responds in 3 wks. Seasonal 3 mos ahead. Guidelines; copy $1.50.

Poetry: Patrick Samway, S.J. Light verse, serious poetry, unrhymed; 15-30 lines; $7.50-25 or $1.40/line (on publication). Submit max. 3 poems.

AMERICAN TRACT SOCIETY, Box 462008, Garland TX 75046. (972)276-9408. E-mail: amtract@aol.com or pcbr@earthlink.net. Website: http://www.gospelcom. net/ATS. Peter Batzing, tract ed. Majority of tracts written to win unbelievers. Bimonthly tracts; 25 million produced annually. 5% freelance. Query or complete ms/cover letter. **PAYS IN COPIES** for simultaneous rts. Tracts 800-1,200 wds. Responds in 6-8 wks. Seasonal 8-9 mos ahead. Accepts reprints. Guidelines/free samples for #10 SASE.

Special Needs: Current issues, working professionals, women, youth.

Tips: "Choose a subject that is very relevant to potential readers."

+ANGEL TIMES, 22 Perimiter Park, Atlanta GA 30341. Angelic Realms Unlimited, Inc. Linda Whitman Vephula, pub. Stories of true, angelic experiences. Quarterly mag. **NO PAYMENT.** Articles 1,500 wds. Not in topical listings.

ANGELS ON EARTH, 16 E. 34th St., New York NY 10016. (212)251-8100. Fax (212)684-0679. Website: http://www.guideposts.org. Guideposts. Colleen Hughes, mng. ed.; Celeste McCauley, ed. for features & fillers. Presents true stories about God's angels and humans who have played angelic roles on earth. Bimonthly mag.; circ 500,000. Subscription $15.95. Est. 1995. 90% freelance. Complete ms/cover letter. Pays to $400 on publication for all rts. Articles to 1,500 wds (all stories must be true). Responds in 12 wks. Seasonal 6 mos ahead. Sidebars OK. No disk. Guidelines; copy for 7x10 SAE/4 stamps.

Fillers: Buys many. Anecdotal shorts of similar nature; to 250 wds; $25-100.

Columns/Departments: Accepts many. Earning Their Wings (good deeds), 150 wds; Only Human? (human or angel?/mystery), 250 wds; $50-100.

#ANGLICAN JOURNAL, 600 Jarvis St., Toronto ON M4Y 2J6 Canada. (416)924-9192. Anglican Church of Canada. Carolyn Purden, ed; submit to Vianney Carriere, news ed. Informs Canadian Anglicans about the church at home and overseas. Newspaper (10x/yr); 24 pgs; circ 272,000. 25% freelance. Query only; phone query OK. Pays $50-300 CAN, on acceptance for 1st rts. Articles to 1,000 wds. Responds in 2 wks. Seasonal 2 mos ahead. Accepts reprints. Guidelines.

THE ANNALS OF SAINT ANNE DE BEAUPRE, PO Box 1000, St. Anne de Beaupre QC G0A 3C0 Canada. (418)827-4538. Fax (418)827-4530. Catholic/Redemptorist Fathers. Father Roch Achard, C.Ss.R., ed. Promotes Catholic family values. Monthly mag; 32 pgs; circ 45,000. Subscription $8.75 US, $9.25 CAN. 35% freelance. Complete ms/cover letter. Pays .03-.04/wd on acceptance for 1st rts. Articles & fiction (250/yr); 500-1,500 wds. Responds in 4 wks. Seasonal 4-5 mos ahead. No disk or sidebars. Guidelines; copy for 9x12 SAE/IRC.

Tips: "Writing must be uplifting and inspirational; clearly written, not filled with long quotations. We tend to stay away from extreme controversy and focus on the family, good family values, devotion and Christianity."

THE APOCALYPSE CHRONICLES, Box 448, Jacksonville OR 97530. (541)899-8888. Christian Media. James Lloyd, ed/pub. Deals with the apocalypse exclusively. Quarterly newsletter; circ 2,000-3,000. Query; prefers phone query. Payment negotiable for reprint rts. Articles. Responds in 3 wks. KJV only. Copy for #10 SAE/2 stamps.

Tips: "It's helpful if you understand your own prophetic position and are aware of its name, i.e., Futurist, Historicist, etc."

ARKANSAS CATHOLIC, PO Box 7417, Little Rock AR 72217. (501)664-0125. Fax (501)664-9075. E-mail: malea@alltel.net. Catholic Diocese of Little Rock. Malea Walters, ed. Regional newspaper for the local Diocese. Weekly tabloid; 12 pgs; circ 7,000. Subscription $15. 10% freelance. Query/clips; fax query OK. Pays on acceptance or publication for 1st rts. Articles (2/yr) 400-800 wds. Accepts simultaneous submissions. Accepts disk. Sidebars OK. Prefers Catholic Bible. Guidelines; copy for 7x10 SAE/2 stamps. (Ads)

> **Columns/Departments:** Leslie O'Malley. Accepts 2/yr. Seeds of Faith (education).

> **Tips:** "Make stories as localized as possible."

#ARLINGTON CATHOLIC HERALD, 200 N. Glebe Rd., Ste. 607, Arlington VA 22203. (703)841-2590. Fax (703)524-2782. E-mail: achflach@aol.com. Catholic Diocese of Arlington. Michael Flach, ed. Regional newspaper for the local Diocese. Weekly newspaper; 28 pgs; circ 53,000. Subscription $14. 10% freelance. Query; phone/fax/e-mail query OK. Pays $50-150 on publication for one-time rts. Articles 500-1,500 wds. Responds in 2 wks. Seasonal 3 mos ahead. Accepts simultaneous submissions. Prefers disk. Sidebars OK. Guidelines; copy for 11x17 SAE. (Ads)

> **Columns/Departments:** Sports; School News; Local Entertainment; 500 wds.

> **Tips:** "All submissions must be Catholic-related. Avoid controversial issues within the Church."

#AT EASE, 1445 Boonville Ave., Springfield MO 65802-1894. (417)862-2781. Fax (417)863-7276. Assemblies of God. Lemuel D. McElyea, ed. Devotional articles for military personnel. Bimonthly mag; 4 pgs; circ 28,000. Free to military. 90% freelance. Complete ms/cover letter; phone/fax query OK. Pays .03/wd on publication for 1st rts. Articles 400-700 wds (20/yr). Responds in 6 wks. Seasonal 6 mos ahead. Accepts simultaneous submissions & reprints. Accepts disk. Guidelines/copy for #10 SAE/1 stamp.

> **Fillers:** Buys 5/yr. Cartoons; $20-40.

> **Tips:** "Strong human interest; talk about real life. Make subject inspiring and uplifting. We want to win souls."

*ATLANTIC BAPTIST, PO Box 756, Kentville NS B4N 3X9 Canada. (902)681-6868. Fax (902)681-0315. Atlantic Baptist Convention. Michael A. Lipe, ed. Denominational. Monthly; 32-48 pgs; circ 7,500. Subscription $27.50. 25% freelance. Query or complete ms; fax query OK. Pays $15-30 on publication for one-time rts. Articles 750-1,500 wds. Responds in 2-5 wks. Guidelines.

*AWARENESS TENNESSEE CHRISTIAN COMMUNICATOR, PO Box 100415, Nashville TN 37224. Phone/fax (615)889-1791. Nondenominational. Karynthia Phillips, pub/ed. Provides national, international and local news. Monthly newspaper; 8 pgs; circ 10,000. Free subscription. 100% freelance. Query/clips. **PAYS IN COPIES.**

*AXIOS, 1501 E. Chapman Ave. #345, Fullerton CA 92631-4000. Orthodox Christian. Fr. Daniel John Gorham, ed. Review of public affairs, religion, literature and the arts, and is especially interested in the Orthodox Catholic Church and its world view. Bimonthly newsletter; 32 pgs; circ 15,672. Subscription $25. 90%

freelance. Complete ms/cover letter. Pays .04/wd & up ($25-500) on publication for 1st rts. Articles, any length (29/yr); book reviews 2,000 wds. Responds in 4-8 wks. Seasonal 4 mos ahead. Accepts simultaneous submissions & reprints. Kill fee 25%. Copy $4.20/9x12 SAE/$1.20 currency.

Poetry: Buys 6/yr. Traditional; any length; $5-25. Submit max. 3 poems.

Fillers: Buys 25/yr. Anecdotes, cartoons, facts.

Columns/Departments: Buys 80 religious book and film reviews/yr. Query.

Tips: "Most open to articles. Be sure you have an idea of who and what an orthodox Christian is."

** Axios was #58 on the 1994 Top 50 Christian Publishers list.

#THE BANNER, 2850 Kalamazoo Ave. SE, Grand Rapids MI 49560. (616)224-0732. Fax (616)224-0834. E-mail: banner@crcna.org. Christian Reformed Church. Malcolm McBryde, assoc. ed. Denominational. Weekly mag; 31 pgs; circ. 32,000. Subscription $41.95. 10% freelance. Query or complete ms/cover letter; phone/fax/e-mail query OK. Pays $100-125 on acceptance for all rts. Articles 850 or 1,200 wds (5/yr); book/music/video reviews, 850 wds, $50. Responds in 4 wks. Seasonal 6-8 mos ahead. Requires disk. Kill fee 50%. Sidebars OK. Prefers NIV. Guidelines/theme list; copy for 9x12 SAE/4 stamps. (Ads)

Poetry: Buys 10/yr. Any type; 5-10 lines; $32. Submit max. 5 poems.

Fillers: Buys 48/yr. Church related cartoons; $40.

Columns/Departments: Tuned In (critical critiques of movies, music, TV, etc), 800 wds; $50.

Tips: "One must really get to know the Christian Reformed Church. All of our articles are geared to this expression of faith."

** 1997 EPA Award of Merit—Denominational.

BANNER NEWS SERVICE, 7127 Little River Turnpike, Ste. 205, Annandale VA 22003. (703)750-3078. Fax (703)916-7773. E-mail: TWMgroup@ipo.net. Worldwide, nondenominational news organization. Fidelis Iyebote, ed. Provides companies, church organizations and individuals with news, information, ideas, innovations, and facts to promote business and individual growth. Subscription $150. Buys 20 articles/day; 2 typed, double-spaced pages. Query/clips or complete ms; fax query OK (prefers mail). Payment is attractive, but depends on quality. Responds in 4 wks. House style book available to accredited contributors and correspondents.

Tips: "Most open to exclusive, authentic, well-researched stories on topical current issues."

BAPTIST HISTORY AND HERITAGE, 901 Commerce St., Ste. 400, Nashville TN 37203-3630. (800)966-2278 or (615)244-0344. E-mail: jtaulman@juno.com. Southern Baptist. Jim Taulman, mng. ed., 517 Adamwood Dr., Nashville TN 37211, (615)834-8886. A scholarly journal focusing on Baptist history. Quarterly journal; 64 pgs; circ 2,000. 15-20% freelance. Query. Pays $192 (for assigned only) for all rts. Articles to 4,000 wds. Responds in 9 wks. Prefers disk. Guidelines.

Tips: "Most open to lesser known aspects of Baptist history based on primary sources."

*THE BAPTIST INFORMER, 603 S. Wilmington St., Raleigh NC 27601. (919)821-7466. Fax (919)836-0061. General Baptist. Archie D. Logan, ed. Regional African-American publication. Monthly tabloid; 16 pgs; circ 10,000. 10% freelance. Query or complete ms/cover letter; fax query OK. **PAYS IN COPIES** for one-time rts. Articles & fiction. Responds in 13 wks. Accepts simultaneous submissions. Prefers disk. Free copy.

*THE B.C. CATHOLIC, 150 Robson St., Vancouver BC V6B 2A7 Canada. (604)683-0281. Fax (604)683-8117. Catholic. Rev. Vincent Hawkswell, ed. News, education and inspiration for Canadian Catholics. Weekly (47X) newspaper; 16 pgs; circ 20,000. 70% freelance. Query; phone query OK. Pays variable rate on publication for 1st rts. Articles 400-500 wds. Responds in 6 wks. Seasonal 4 wks ahead. Accepts simultaneous submissions & reprints.

> **Tips:** "We prefer to use Catholic writers."

THE BELIEVER, 5375 Alderley Rd., Victoria BC V8Y 1X9 Canada. (250)658-2644. Fax (250)658-8481. E-mail: msbowes@islandnet.com or believer@islandnet.com. Website: http://www.islandnet.com/~believer. Tidewater Publishing Co. Madge S. Bowes, ed. Easy-to-read local news and inspiration for churches and businesses on Vancouver Island. Query; fax/e-mail query OK. Not copyrighted. **NO PAYMENT**. Articles 300-750 wds; little fiction; a few book/music reviews, 400 wds. Seasonal 2 mos ahead. Accepts simultaneous submissions & reprints. Accepts disk (Mac only). Copy for 9x12 SAE/IRCs or $1.

> **Poetry:** Accepts 24-36/yr.
>
> **Fillers:** Anecdotes; accepts few.
>
> **Tips:** "I want a 'diet' for our readers of Christian growth, how-tos for church, individual and family needs with a Christian perspective." Prefers not to have to return mss.

BIBLE ADVOCATE, Box 33677, Denver CO 80233. (303)452-7973. Fax (303)452-0657. E-mail: cofgsd@denver.net. Website: http://www.denver.net/~baonline. Church of God (Seventh Day). Calvin Burrell, ed; Sherri Langton, asst ed. Mostly older adult readers; 50% not members of the denomination. Mag published every 6 wks; 24 pgs; circ 12,500. Free subscription. 25% freelance. Complete ms/cover letter; e-mail query OK. Query for electronic submissions. Pays $15-35 on publication for 1st, one-time, reprint & simultaneous rts. Articles 1,000-2,000 wds (20-25/yr). Responds in 4-6 wks. Seasonal 9 mos ahead. Accepts simultaneous submissions & reprints (tell when/where appeared). Accepts disk. Kill fee up to 50%. Sidebars OK. Prefers NIV, KJV, NKJV, NAS. Guidelines; copy for 9x12 SAE/3 stamps.

> **Poetry:** Buys 10-20/yr. Free verse, light verse, traditional; 5-25 lines; $10. Submit max. 5 poems. Will be used mainly as fillers in '98.
>
> **Fillers:** Buys 5-10/yr. Facts, prose, quotes; 50-150 wds; $5-10.
>
> **Columns/Departments**: Accepts 6-10/yr. Viewpoint (social or religious issues), 600-700 wds, pays copies.
>
> **Special Needs:** Knowing Your Christian Life; Knowing About the Devil; Knowing the Church; Knowing Your Calling to Serve.
>
> **Tips:** "Viewpoint column and poetry most open. Keep your writing fresh. Have something different to say that is biblically sound and insightful, and stick to your focus. Going through a major face-lift to appeal to younger audience."

BIBLE ADVOCATE ONLINE, Box 33677, Denver CO 80233. (303)452-7973. Fax

(303)452-0657. E-mail: cofgsd@denver.net. Website: http://www.denver.net/ ~baonline. Church of God (Seventh Day). Calvin Burrell, ed; Sherri Langton, asst ed. Articles on salvation, Jesus, social issues, life problems that are inclusive of non-Christians. Monthly mag; distributed online. Est. 1996. 25-75% freelance. Complete ms/cover letter; phone/e-mail query OK. Pays $15-35 on publication for first, one-time rts, simultaneous & reprint rts. Articles 1,200-1,500 wds (20/yr). Responds in 4-6 wks. Seasonal 6 mos ahead. Accepts simultaneous submissions & reprints (tell when/where appeared). Accepts disk. Sidebars OK. Prefers NIV. Guidelines; copy of online article for 9x12 SAE/2 stamps.

Fillers: Buys 5-10/yr. Anecdotes, facts, prose, quotes; 50-100 wds. Pays $5-10.

Special Needs: Always need personal experience pieces showing a person's struggle that either brought him/her to Christ or deepened faith in God. Also need more articles on social issues.

Tips: "Be aware of world around you and how a non-Christian views it. Present truths of Christ in fresh ways that will grab the attention of skeptics and the unchurched. Be in tune with felt needs."

THE BIBLE TODAY, The Liturgical Press, Collegeville MN 56321-7500. (320)363-2213 or (800)858-5450. Fax (800)445-5899. Catholic/Benedictine Monks of St. John's Abbey. Mss to: Rev. Donald Senior, C.P., ed., 5401 S. Cornell Ave., Chicago IL 60615. Explains the meaning and context of particular biblical passages and books and encourages a regular, prayerful reading of the Bible. Bimonthly mag; 64 pgs; circ 7,000. Subscription $24. 20% freelance. Complete ms/cover letter; no phone/fax query. **PAYS 5 COPIES & 1 YR SUBSCRIPTION.** Articles to 2,000 wds (10/yr). Responds in 9 wks. Seasonal 6 mos ahead. Prefers disk. Some sidebars. Prefers NAB. Free guidelines/copy. (Ads)

Tips: "Most open to general articles on the Bible or biblical themes, biblical archaeology, biblical spirituality."

#BIBLICAL REFLECTIONS ON MODERN MEDICINE, PO Box 14488, Augusta GA 30919. (706)736-0161. Dr. Ed Payne, ed. For all Christians interested in medical-ethical issues. Bimonthly newsletter; circ 1,100. Subscription $19. 20% freelance. Complete ms/cover letter. **PAYS IN COPIES & SUBSCRIPTION**, for 1st rts. Articles to 1,500 wds (5/yr). Responds in 1-4 wks. Accepts simultaneous submissions & reprints. No sidebars. Guidelines/copy for #10 SAE/1 stamp.

+BOOKS & CULTURE, 465 Gundersen Dr., Carol Stream IL 60188. (630)260-6200. Fax (630)260-0114. E-mail: WilsonBKS@aol.com. Website: http://www. christianity.net/bc. Christianity Today, Inc. John Wilson, ed. To edify, sharpen, and nurture the evangelical intellectual community by engaging the world from all its complexity from a distinctly Christian perspective. Bimonthly mag; circ 12,000. Subscription $24.95. Open to freelance. Query. Not in topical listings. (Ads)

*THE BREAD OF LIFE, 209 Macnab St. N., Box 395, Hamilton ON L8N 3H8 Canada. (905)529-4496. Fax (905)529-5373. Catholic. Fr. Peter Coughlin, ed. Catholic Charismatic; to encourage spiritual growth in areas of renewal in the catholic church today. Bimonthly mag; 32 pgs; circ 5,200. Subscription $30. 10% freelance. Complete ms/cover letter; fax query OK. **PAYS IN COPIES.** Articles

1,200-1,400 wds; book reviews 250 wds. Responds in 2-3 wks. Seasonal 6 mos ahead. Accepts reprints (tell when/where appeared). No disk. No sidebars. Prefers NAB or NJB. Guidelines; copy for 9x12 SAE/6 stamps. (Ads)

Poetry: Accepts 12-15/yr. Traditional; 10-25 lines. Submit max. 2 poems.

Fillers: Accepts 10-12/yr. Facts, prose, quotes; to 250 wds.

THE BRETHREN EVANGELIST, 524 College Ave., Ashland OH 44805. (419)289-1708. Fax (419)281-0450. E-mail: Brethrench@aol.com. The Brethren Church. Richard C. Winfield, ed. Denominational. Monthly newsletter; 12 pgs; circ 7,950. Free to members/$14.50. 5% freelance. Complete ms/cover letter; no phone/fax/e-mail query. Pays to $50 on publication for one-time rts. Articles 750 wds (6/yr). Responds in 6 wks. Seasonal 3 mos ahead. Accepts simultaneous submissions. No disk. Some sidebars. Prefers NIV. Copy for 9x12 SAE/3 stamps.

BROKEN STREETS, 57 Morningside Dr. E., Bristol CT 06010. (203)582-2943. Ron Grossman, ed. For Christian writers of poetry, especially new writers. Semi-annual journal; 40-50 pgs; circ 500-1,000. Subscription $10. 99% freelance. Complete ms/cover letter. **PAYS IN COPIES**, for one-time rts. Articles 100-500 wds (5-10/yr). Responds in 1 wk. Accepts reprints. Guidelines; copy $2.50.

Poetry: Accepts 200/yr. All types; no length limit (prefers 5-15 lines). Submit max. 5 poems.

Fillers: Accepts 50/yr. Prose, devotionals, prayers, journal entries; to 500 wds.

Tips: "Buy a sample, write a good cover letter, and pray for guidance."

#BURNING LIGHT: A Journal of Christian Literature, 4 Robin Ln., West Milford NJ 07480-4037. Burning Light Press. Carl Simmons, ed/pub. A literary journal devoted to today's writer who is Christian. Quarterly jour; 32-48 pgs; circ 400. Subscription $14. Est. 1993. 100% freelance. Complete ms/cover letter; phone query OK. **PAYS IN COPIES/SUBSCRIPTION** for negotiable rts. Essays 1,000-3,000 wds (3-4/yr); fiction 1,000-10,000 wds (10/yr); book reviews, 200-400 wds. Responds in 3-4 wks. Seasonal 3-4 mos ahead. Accepts simultaneous submissions & reprints (rarely—tell when/where appeared). Accepts disk. No sidebars. Guidelines; copy $4.

Poetry: Buys 50-80/yr. Avant-garde, free verse, haiku, traditional; to 600 lines. Submit any number.

Tips: "Be real—don't say what you think God wants to hear; say what he's moved you to say. Prophetic voices are never pretty, but they're a lot more useful."

*CANADA LUTHERAN, 1512 St. James St., Winnipeg MB R3H 0L2 Canada. (204)786-6707. Fax (204)783-7548. Evangelical Lutheran Church in Canada. Kenn Ward, ed. Denominational. Monthly (11X) mag; 40 pgs; circ 23,000. Subscription $17 US. Up to 50% freelance. Query or complete ms/cover letter; fax query OK. Pays $40-110 CAN, on acceptance for one-time rts. Articles 800-1,500 wds (15/yr); fiction 850-1,200 wds (4/yr). Responds in 5 wks. Seasonal 10 mos ahead. Accepts simultaneous submissions & reprints. Prefers disk. Guidelines.

Tips: "Canadians/Lutherans receive priority, but not the only consideration. Want material that is clear, concise and fresh. Articles that talk about real life experiences of faith receive our best reader response."

THE CANADIAN BAPTIST, 414-195 The West Mall, Etobicoke ON M9C 5K1

Canada. (416)622-8600. Fax (416)622-0780. E-mail: Thecb@baptist.ca. Baptist Convention of Ontario and Quebec/Western Canada. Dr. Larry Matthews, ed. Covers issues relevant to and events/stories about people in the Baptist community. Monthly (10X) mag; 32 pgs; circ 9,000. Subscription $19.50. 95% freelance. Query; fax/e-mail query OK. Pays .10/wd, 4 wks after acceptance, for 1st rts. Not copyrighted. Articles. Responds in 4-8 wks. Seasonal 6 mos ahead. Accepts reprints only in exceptional cases (tell when/where appeared). Kill fee varies. Prefers disk. Some sidebars. Prefers NRSV. Guidelines; copy for 9x13 SAE/$1.56 US or $1.35 CAN postage. (Ads)

> **Columns/Departments:** Buys 9/yr. Points of Departure (inspirational meditations), 500 wds. Pays $50-100.
>
> **Tips:** "We use a wide variety of issues connected with life of the church, daily Christian living, current issues, and missions. Virtually all material draws from or is written by Canadian Baptists. Most is assigned."

THE CANADIAN CATHOLIC REVIEW, St. Thomas More College, 1437 College Dr., Saskatoon SK S7N 0W6 Canada. (306)966-8959. Fax (306)966-8904. E-mail: editor@ccr.nethosting.com. Website: http://ccr.nethosting.com/rev/. Catholic. Rev. T. Allan Smith, CSB, ed. For intelligent (but not scholarly) Catholics who take their faith seriously. Frequency & format under review; circ 1,000. Subscription $25 US. Query; phone/fax/e-mail query OK. Pays to $300 on publication for 1st NASR. Articles 500-6,000 wds (10/yr); book reviews 300-700 wds/$25. Responds in 4 wks. Seasonal 6 mos ahead. Prefers disk. No sidebars. Prefers RSV. Copy $3/9x12 SAE/IRCs. (Ads)

> **Tips:** "Most open to columns and general articles. Be lucid, articulate, faithful and brief."

CANADIAN MENNONITE (formerly **MENNONITE REPORTER**), 3-312 Marsland Dr., Waterloo ON N2J 3Z1 Canada. (519)884-3810. Fax (519)884-3331. Mennonite. Ron Rempel, ed. Denominational. Biweekly mag; 40 pgs; circ 20,000. 20% freelance. Query; fax query OK. Pays .10/wd on publication for 1st rts. Articles 750-1,250 wds; news 400-600 wds. Responds in 4 wks. Accepts simultaneous submissions. Guidelines; free copy.

> **Tips:** "Most of our readers are Canadians; give us a Canadian perspective."

*CATHEDRAL AGE, Mount St. Alban, Massachusetts & Wisconsin Aves NW, Washington DC 20016-5098. (202)537-6249. Fax (202)364-6600. Washington National Cathedral (Episcopal). Sherwood Harris, ed. About what's happening in and to cathedrals and their programs. Quarterly mag; 36 pgs; circ 32,000. Subscription $15. 20% freelance. Query/clips; phone/fax query OK. Pays to $500 on acceptance for all rts. Articles 1,000-1,500 wds (10/yr); book reviews 600 wds, $100. Responds in 4 wks. Seasonal 6 mos ahead. Requires disk. Kill fee 50%. Sidebars OK. Prefers RSV. Copy $5/9x12 SAE/5 stamps.

> **Special Needs:** Art, architecture, and music.
>
> **Tips:** "We assign all articles, so query/clips first. Always write from the viewpoint of an individual first, then move into a more general discussion of the topic. Human interest angle important."

*THE CATHOLIC ANSWER, 207 Adams St., Newark NJ 07105. (219)356-8400. Our Sunday Visitor/Catholic. Father Peter Stravinskas, mng. ed. Answers to questions of belief for orthodox Catholics. Bimonthly mag; 64 pgs; circ 60,000. 50%

freelance. Query/clips. Pays $100 on publication for 1st rts. Articles 1,200-2,200 wds (80/yr). Seasonal 6 mos ahead. Guidelines; free copy (from 200 Noll Plaza, Huntington IN 46750).

CATHOLIC COURIER, 1150 Buffalo Rd., Rochester NY 14624. (716)328-4340. Fax (716)328-8640. Website: http://www.catholiccourier.com. Catholic. Submit to The Editor. Newspaper for the Diocese of Rochester NY. Weekly newspaper; 20 pgs; circ 48,000. Subscription $20. Less than 1% freelance. Query/clips or complete ms/cover letter. Pays $30-100 on publication for one-time rts. Articles 1,200 wds. Responds in 4-9 wks. Accepts simultaneous submissions. Prefers disk. (Ads)

> **Columns/Departments:** News; Leisure; Opinion; Youth; 750 wds.
>
> **Tips:** "We publish very little freelance and virtually none from non-local writers."

CATHOLIC DIGEST, Box 64090, St. Paul MN 55164-0090. (612)962-6739. Fax (612)962-6758. E-mail: cdigest@stthomas.edu. Catholic/University of St. Thomas. Submit to Articles Editor. Readers have a stake in being Catholic and a wide range of interests: religion, family, health, human relationships, good works, nostalgia, and more. Monthly mag; 128 pgs; circ 503,500. Subscription $19.95. 25% freelance. Complete ms (for original material)/cover letter, tear sheets for reprints. Pays $200-400 ($100 for reprints) on acceptance for one-time rts. On-line only articles receive $100, plus half of any traceable revenue. Articles 1,000-3,500 wds (90-100/yr). Responds in 6-8 wks. Seasonal 4 mos ahead. Accepts reprints (tell when/where appeared). Accepts disk. Sidebars OK. Prefers NAB. Guidelines; copy for 7x10 SAE/2 stamps. (Ads)

> **Fillers:** Buys 200-300/yr. Anecdotes, cartoons, facts, games, jokes, quizzes, quotes, short humor; to 500 wds; $2/published line.
>
> **Columns/Departments:** Buys 100-150/yr. Open Door (personal stories of conversion to Catholicism); 200-500 wds; pays $2/published line. See guidelines for full list.
>
> **Special Needs:** Family and career concerns of Baby Boomers who have a stake in being Catholic.
>
> **Tips:** "We favor the anecdotal approach. Stories must be strongly focused on a definitive topic that is illustrated for the reader with a well-developed series of true-life, interconnected vignettes."
>
> ** This periodical was #27 on the 1997 Top 50 Christian Publishers list (#29 in 1996, #30 in 1995, #25 in 1994).

+CATHOLIC DOSSIER, PO Box 591120, San Francisco CA 94159-1120. (800)651-1531. Website: http://www.ignatius.com/mags/cd.htm. Examines Catholic beliefs from many perspectives, including philosophy, history, science, art and even fiction. New bimonthly magazine. Subscription $24.95. Incomplete topical listings.

CATHOLIC FORESTER, Box 3012, Naperville IL 60566-7012. (630)983-3381. Fax (630)983-3384. Catholic Order of Foresters. Mary Anne File, assoc. ed. For mixed audience, primarily parents and grandparents between the ages of 30 and 80. Bimonthly mag; 36 pgs; circ 100,000+. Free/membership. 10% freelance. Complete ms/cover letter. Pays .10/wd (.25/wd for fiction), on acceptance for all, 1st, one-time rts. Articles 1,200-1,500 wds (5/yr); fiction for all ages 500-1,200 wds (5/yr). Responds in 8-12 wks. Seasonal 4-6 mos ahead. Accepts simultaneous submissions & reprints (tell when/where appeared). Prefers disk. Kill fee 20-25%. Sidebars OK. Prefers Catholic version. Guidelines; copy for 9x12 SAE/4 stamps.

Poetry: Free verse, light verse, traditional. Pay varies. Submit max. 5 poems.

Fillers: Keith Halla. Cartoons, games. Pays $25.

Tips: "Looking for informational, inspirational articles. Writing should be energetic with good style and rhythm."

** This periodical was #28 on the 1997 Top 50 Christian Publishers list (#50 in 1996).

#**CATHOLIC HERITAGE**, 200 Noll Plaza, Huntington IN 46750. (219)356-8400. Fax (219)356-9117. E-mail: 76440.3571@compuserve.com. Catholic. Bill Dodds, ed. For those interested in Catholic history. Bimonthly mag; circ 25,000. 75% freelance. Query; e-mail query OK. Pays $200 on acceptance for 1st rts. Articles 1,000-1,200 wds (30/yr). Responds in 3-5 wks. Seasonal 6 mos ahead. Accepts reprints (payment negotiable). Kill fee 33% or $50-75. Prefers disk or e-mail. Guidelines; free copy.

Tips: "Most open to general features."

+**CATHOLIC INSIGHT**, PO Box 625, Adelaide Sta., 36 Adelaide St. E., Toronto ON M5C 2J8 Canada. (416)368-4558. Fax (416)368-8575. E-mail: interim@ direct.com. Life Ethics Information Center. Alphonse de Valk, ed/pub. News, analysis and commentary on social, ethical, political, and moral issues from a Catholic perspective. Monthly (10X) mag; 20-24 pgs; circ 3,100. Subscription $25 CAN, $28 US. 30-40% freelance. Query/clips; phone/fax query OK. Pays variable rates on publication for all rts. Articles 750-1,500 wds (20-30/yr); book/music/video reviews 750 wds. Responds in 6-8 wks. Seasonal 2 mos ahead. Accepts disk. Sidebars OK. Prefers RSV (Catholic). Copy $2.50 CAN/9x12 SAE/.90 postage or IRC. (Ads)

Tips: "We are interested in political/social/current affairs—Canadian—from viewpoint of informed readership and encouraging involvement in the political process as essential to social change."

***CATHOLIC NEW YORK**, 1011 1st Ave, 17th Fl., New York NY 10126. (212)688-2399. Fax (212)688-2642. Catholic. Anne Buckley, ed-in-chief. To inform New York Catholics. Weekly newspaper; 44 pgs; circ 130,000. Subscription $20. 10% freelance. Query or complete ms/cover letter. Pays $15-100 on publication for one-time rts. Articles 500-800 wds. Responds in 5 wks. Copy $1.

Columns/Departments: Comment; Catholic New Yorkers (profiles of unique individuals); 325 wds.

Tips: "Most open to articles that show how to integrate Catholic faith into work, hobbies or special interests."

CATHOLIC PARENT, 200 Noll Plaza, Huntington IN 46750. (800)348-2440. Catholic. Woodeene Koenig-Bricker, ed. Practical advice for Catholic parents, with a specifically Catholic slant. Bimonthly mag; 52 pgs; circ 40,000. Subscription $18. Est. 1993. 90% freelance. Query/clips or complete ms/cover letter; fax query OK. Pays $100-200 on acceptance for 1st rts. Articles 250-1,000 wds (30-40/yr). Responds in 6-8 wks. Seasonal 6 mos ahead. Kill fee. Accepts disk. Sidebars OK. Guidelines; copy $3/10x13 SAE/5 stamps.

Fillers: Mary Bazzett. Accepts 40/yr. Parenting tips, 100-200 wds, $25.

Columns/Departments: This Works! (short parenting tips).

Tips: "We need true-life, heart-warming stories dealing with family life and parenting."

** This periodical was #20 on the 1997 Top 50 Christian Publishers list (#51 in 1996, #25 in 1995, #26 in 1994).

CATHOLIC PEACE VOICE, 532 W. 8th, Erie PA 16502-1343. (814)453-4955. Fax (814)452-4784. E-mail: peacevoice@paxchristiusa.org. Website: http://www. nonviolence.org/~nvweb/pcusa. Dave Robinson, ed. For members of US Catholic Peace Movement. Quarterly newspaper; 16 pgs; circ 20,000. Distributed free. 5% freelance. Query; phone/fax/e-mail query OK. Pays on publication for one-time rts. Accepts simultaneous submissions & reprints. Prefers disk. Guidelines; copy for 9x12 SAE/2 stamps. Not in topical listings. (Ads)

Tips: "Emphasis is on nonviolence. No sexist language."

#CATHOLIC RURAL LIFE, 4625 Beaver Ave., Des Moines IA 50310-2199. (515)270-2634. Fax (515)270-9447. E-mail: ncrlc@aol.com. Website: http://www. netins.net/showcase/ncrlcnet. Catholic. Sandra A. LaBlanc, commun. dir. Semi-annual mag; 40 pgs; circ 3,000. Membership $25. 50% freelance. Query/clips; phone/fax/e-mail query OK. Pays for 1st rts. Articles 1,000-1,500 wds. Responds in 6 wks. Seasonal 6 mos ahead. Prefers disk. Sidebars OK. Guidelines/theme list; copy for 9x12 SAE/3 stamps.

Columns/Departments: Building Community, 350 wds; Closer Look (think piece), 750-1,000 wds; no payment.

*CATHOLIC SENTINEL, PO Box 18030, Portland OR 97218-0030. (503)281-1191. Fax (503)282-3486. Catholic. Robert Pfohman, ed. For Catholics in the Archdiocese of western and eastern Oregon. Weekly tabloid; 16-24 pgs; circ 15,000. Subscription $22. 25% freelance. Query; phone/fax query OK (if timely). Pays $25-150 on publication for one-time rts. Not copyrighted. Articles 800-1,800 wds (15/yr). Responds in 6 wks. Seasonal 1 month ahead. Accepts reprints (on columns, not news or features; tell them). Prefers disk or modem. Kill fee 100%. Sidebars OK. Copy 50 cents/9x12 SAE/2 stamps.

Columns/Departments: Buys about 30/yr. Opinion Page, 600 wds, $10. Send complete ms.

Tips: "Find active Catholics living their faith in specific, interesting, upbeat, positive ways."

*CATHOLIC TELEGRAPH, 100 E. 8th St., Cincinnati OH 45202. (513)421-3131. Fax (513)381-2242. Catholic. Tricia Hempel, gen. mng. Diocese newspaper for Cincinnati area. Weekly newspaper; 20 pgs; circ 27,000. 10% freelance. Send resume and writing samples for assignment. Pays varying rates on publication for all rts. Articles. Responds in 2-3 wks. Kill fee. Guidelines sent on acceptance; free copy.

Fillers: Newsbreaks (local).

CATHOLIC TWIN CIRCLE, 33 Rossotto Dr., Hamden CT 06514. (203)288-5600. Fax (203)288-5157. Catholic/Circle Media. Loretta G. Seyer, ed. Features writing for Catholics and/or Christian families of all ages. Weekly newspaper; 20 pgs; circ 30,000. 45% freelance. Complete ms/cover letter; fax/e-mail submissions OK. Pays $75 for opinion pcs; $74, $150, or $300 for features, on publication for all rts. Opinion pieces, 600 or 825 wds; features 600, 1,100, or 2,000 wds. Responds in 13 wks. Seasonal 2 mos ahead. Serials 3 parts. Kill fee. No sidebars. Prefers Catholic Bible. Guidelines/theme list; copy for 9x12 SAE/2 stamps or $2.

Columns/Departments: Point of View (opinion on various Catholic issues), 600-800 wds, $50.

+CATHOLIC WORLD REPORT, PO Box 591300, San Francisco CA 94159-1300. (800)651-1531. Website: http://ignatius.com/mags/cwr.htm. Catholic. A news magazine that not only reports on important events in the Church, but helps to shape them. Monthly mag. Subscription $39.95. Not in topical listings.

#CBA FRONTLINE, PO Box 200, Colorado Springs CO 80901-0200. (719)576-7880. Fax (719)576-0795. E-mail: publications@cba-intl.org. Website: http://www.cbaonline.org. Christian Booksellers Assn. Steve Parolini, ed. To give product knowledge and inspiration to the frontline staff in Christian retail bookstores. Monthly trade journal; 38 pgs; circ 11,000. Est. January 1997. 10-20% freelance. Query/clips; phone/fax/e-mail query OK. Pays .16-.25/wd. on acceptance for all rts. Articles. Responds in 4 wks. Seasonal 4-5 mos ahead. Accepts simultaneous submissions. Accepts disk. Kill fee. Sidebars OK. Prefers NIV. Guidelines/theme list.

Fillers: Buys many/yr. Anecdotes, cartoons, facts, ideas, newsbreaks, short humor; 25-100 wds. Pays $20.

Columns/Departments: Buys many/yr. Quick "did-you-know" product pieces in these columns: Music, Video, Software, Apparel, Books, Bibles, 25-100 wds. Inspiration (short devotionals), 250 wds; Humor (true retail-oriented anecdotes & cartoons), 25-100 wds. Pays $20.

Tips: "We rarely accept unsolicited mss, but assign 2-5 articles per month to freelancers based on our agenda. Send cover letter, including experience and areas of interest, plus clips. Also looking for retail and product anecdotes."

#CBA MARKETPLACE, PO Box 200, Colorado Springs CO 80901-0200. (800)252-1950. (719)576-7880. Fax (719)576-0795. E-mail: publications@cba-intl.org. Website: http://www.cbaonline.org. Christian Booksellers Assn. Sue Grise, ed. To provide Christian bookstore owners with professional retail skills, product information, and industry news. Monthly trade journal; 100-110 pgs; circ 8,000. Subscription $47. 10-20% freelance. Query/clips; phone/fax query OK. Pays .16-.25/wd on acceptance for all rts. Articles 1,500-2,500 wds (30/yr assigned); book reviews 150-200 wds, $30; music/video reviews 100-200 wds, $25. Responds in 4 wks. Seasonal 4-5 mos ahead. Accepts simultaneous submissions. Accepts disk. Kill fee 90%. Sidebars OK. Prefers NIV. Guidelines; copy $5/9x12 SAE/6 stamps. (Ads)

Fillers: Buys 12/yr. Anecdotes, cartoons ($100), facts, ideas, newsbreaks, short humor; $20.

Columns/Departments: Buys 10-20/yr. Industry Watch; Music News; Gift News; Video & software News; Book News; all 100-800 wds. Pays $25 or .25/wd. Query.

Tips: "All our articles focus on producing and selling Christian products. We rarely accept unsolicited mss, but assign 2-5 articles per month to freelancers. Send cover letter, including experience and areas of interest, plus clips. We also assign 25-30 book reviews, 8-12 music reviews, and 2-5 video reviews per month."

#CELEBRATE LIFE, Box 1350, Stafford VA 22555. (540)659-4171. Fax (540)659-2586. American Life League. Steve Dunham, mng ed. A pro-life, pro-family magazine for Christian audience. Bimonthly mag; 48 pgs; circ 145,000. Subscription $12.95. 60% freelance. Query; phone/fax/e-mail query OK. Pays $25-150 on publication for one-time rts. Articles 500-2,000 wds (70/yr); book reviews 250 wds, $25. Responds in 2-8 wks. Seasonal 6 mos ahead. Accepts reprints. Prefers disk. Kill fee. Sidebars OK. Guidelines/theme list; copy for 9x12 SAE/5 stamps.

> **Fillers:** Buys 6/yr. Newsbreaks (local or special pro-life news); 50-100 wds; $10.
>
> **Columns/Departments:** Buys 3/yr. Prayer and Fasting (personal spirituality), 500 wds, $25-50. Query.
>
> **Special Needs:** Abortion, adoption, euthanasia, post-abortion healing, natural family planning and teen chastity. Looking for articles by high school or college students.
>
> **Tips:** "We need good color photos to accompany human-interest stories. Most open to human-interest stories to fit themes."
>
> ** #66 on the 1994 Top 50.

+CGA WORLD, 430 Penn Ave., Scranton PA 18503. (717)342-3294. Fax (717)963-0149. Catholic Golden Age. Barbara Pegula, ed. For Catholics 50+. Quarterly mag; 32 pgs; circ 100,000. Subscription/membership $8. Query. Pays .10/wd on publication for 1st, one-time, or reprint rts. Articles & fiction (biblical & religious). Responds in 6 wks. Seasonal 6 mos ahead. Accepts reprints (tell when/where appeared). Accepts disk. Guidelines; copy for 9x12 SAE/3 stamps. Not in topical listings (uses topics of interest to senior adults). (Ads)

> **Fillers:** Games, ideas, prayers, word puzzles.

CHARISMA & CHRISTIAN LIFE, 600 Rinehart Rd., Lake Mary FL 32746. (407)333-0600. Fax (407)333-7133. E-mail: grady@strang.com. Website: http://charismamag.com/index.htm. Strang Communications. Lee Grady, exec. ed.; Marcia Ford, assoc. ed. (e-mail: mford@strng.com); Jimmy Stewart, book & music review ed. Primarily for the Pentecostal and Charismatic Christian community. Monthly mag; 100+ pgs; circ 220,000. Subscription $21.97. 75% freelance. Query; no phone/fax/e-mail query. Pays $100-800 on publication for 1st rts. Articles 2,000 wds (120/yr); book/music reviews, 200 wds, $20. Responds in 8-12 wks. Seasonal 4 mos ahead. Kill fee $50. Prefers disk. Sidebars OK. Guidelines; copy $3. (Ads)

> **Tips:** "Most open to news section, reviews or features. Query (published clips help a lot)."

CHESAPEAKE CITIZEN, 408 Cranes Roost, Annapolis MD 21401. (410)757-7599. Fax (410)757-6245. E-mail: CurtisEdit@aol.com. Maryland Family Forum. Carolyn Curtis, ed. To inform constituents of news events and public policy trends impacting pro-family Marylanders. Monthly newsletter; circ 4,500. Subscription $20. Open to freelance.

CHRISTIAN ADVOCATE, PO Box 30, Beech Grove IN 46107. (317)787-3291. Fax (317)787-3325. Reporter-Times, Inc. Joe Skuarenina, ed. Indianapolis-area regional paper for the evangelical Christian community (conservative). Monthly newspaper; circ. 16,000. Subscription $18. 99% freelance. Query or complete ms/cover letter; phone query OK. **NO PAYMENT.** Articles 500-700 wds (up to

100/yr); book reviews, 500-700 wds. Responds in 2 wks. Seasonal 2 mos ahead. Accepts simultaneous submissions & reprints. Kill fee 30%. Accepts disk. Sidebars OK. Any version. Copy $1. (Ads)

Columns/Departments: Accepts up to 40/yr. Query.

#CHRISTIAN AMERICAN NEWSPAPER, 1801-L Sara Dr., Chesapeake VA 23320. (757)424-2630. Fax (757)424-4326. E-mail: letters@cc.org. Christian Coalition, Inc. Michael Ebert, ed. To provide a Christian perspective on the news, enabling readers to be more effective citizens by being better informed. Bimonthly newspaper; circ 400,000. Subscription $14.95. Open to freelance. Query. (Ads)

#THE CHRISTIAN ARTS REVIEW, 803 Hwy. 90E., Chipley FL 32428. (908)638-0643. E-mail: BRIGHT@aol.com. Website: http://www.christianlink.com/home/arts. Brightwater Communications Group. William Curtis Bridenback, ed. For evangelical Christians, 25-55, who enjoy Christian books and music. Quarterly newsletter; on-line edition updated monthly, and 2 special editions/yr; 6-8 pgs; circ 1,500. Subscription $12. 50% freelance. Query/clips; e-mail query OK. Pays $5-25 on publication for 1st & electronic rts. Articles 175-350 wds (10-15/yr); book/music/video reviews 75-150 wds, $5/product. Responds in 2 wks. Seasonal 4-5 mos ahead. Prefers disk. Kill fee. Sidebars OK. Guidelines/theme list; copy for #10 SAE/1 stamp. (Ads)

Fillers: Buys 50/yr. Anecdotes, facts, newsbreaks, quotes; 75-150 wds; $5-25.

Columns/Departments: Buys 10-15/yr. Feature Artist (celebrity interview/profile), 350 wds; Spotlight (new product), 275 wds; Etcetera (news & information soundbites), 75-150 wds. Pays $5-25.

Special Needs: Bible reviews, essays on Christian media. Always looking for good reviewers who have the time and enjoy the work.

Contest: At end of year, gives $25 certificates to best writers in each area.

Tips: "Short items are a good way to go. We'd like to do more issues-oriented stories and op/ed pieces on Christian media. Our summer special issue is also a good place to start; write for topic information."

*THE CHRISTIAN CHRONICLE, PO Box 12623, Reading PA 19612-2623. (610)378-1245. Fax (610)378-1378. Nondenominational. Alice Swoyer-Smolkowicz, pub. For non-Charismatic Christians. Bimonthly newsletter; 8 pgs; circ. 2,000. Subscription $12. Est. 1994. 90% freelance. Complete ms/cover letter; phone/fax/e-mail query OK. **NO PAYMENT** for one-time rts. Articles 100-500 wds (18/yr); fiction (2/yr). Seasonal 3 mos ahead. Accepts reprints. Prefers disk. Prefers NIV. Copy for #10 SAE/1 stamp.

Fillers: Accepts 24/yr. Anecdotes, cartoons, facts, ideas, quotes, short humor; 50-200 wds.

THE CHRISTIAN CIVIC LEAGUE OF MAINE RECORD, Box 5459, Augusta ME 04332. (207)622-7634. Fax (207)621-0035. E-mail: email@cclmaine.org. Michael Heathe, ed. Focuses on church, public service and political action. Monthly newsletter; 12 pgs; circ 4,600. 10% freelance. Query. **NO PAYMENT** for one-time rts. Articles (10-12/yr). Responds in 4-8 wks. Seasonal 2 mos ahead. Accepts simultaneous query & reprints. Free copy. Not in topical listings.

#CHRISTIAN COMPUTING MAGAZINE, PO Box 198, 309 S. Washington, Raymore MO 64083. (816)331-3881. Fax (816)331-5510. E-mail: steve@ccmag.com or bob@ccmag.com. Website: http://www.ccmag.com. Steve Hewitt, ed-in-chief; Bob Dasal, mng. ed. For Christian/church computer users. Monthly (11X) mag; 2 pgs; circ. 90,000. Subscription $14.95. 40% freelance. Query/clips; fax/e-mail query OK. **NO PAYMENT** for all rts. Articles 1,000-1,800 wds (12/yr). Responds in 4 wks. Seasonal 2 mos ahead. Accepts reprints. Requires disk. Sidebars OK. Guidelines; copy for 9x12 SAE.

Fillers: Accepts 6 cartoons/yr.

Columns/Departments: Accepts 12/yr. Telecommunications (computer), 1,500-1,800 wds.

Special Needs: Articles on Internet, DTP, and computing.

*THE CHRISTIAN COURIER, 1933 W. Wisconsin Ave., Milwaukee WI 53233. (414)344-7300. Fax (414)344-7375. ProBuColls Assn. John M. Fisco, Jr., pub. To propagate the Gospel of Jesus Christ in the Midwest. Monthly newspaper; circ 10,000. 10% freelance. Query. **PAYS IN COPIES**, for one-time rts. Not copyrighted. Articles 300-1,500 wds (6/yr). Responds in 2-4 wks. Seasonal 2 mos ahead. Accepts reprints. Guidelines; free copy.

Fillers: Anecdotes, facts, newsbreaks; 10-100 wds.

CHRISTIAN COURIER, 4-261 Martindale Rd., St. Catherines ON L2W 1A1 Canada. (US address: Box 110, Lewiston NY 14092-0110.) (416)682-8311. Fax (416)682-8313. E-mail: cceditor@aol.com. Independent (Protestant Reformed). Bert Witvoet, ed; Bob Vander Vennen, book review ed. To present Canadian and international news, both religious and secular, from a Reformed Christian perspective. Weekly (44X) newspaper; 20 pgs; circ 5,000. 25% freelance. Complete ms/cover letter; phone query OK. Pays .05-.10/wd on publication for one-time rts. Articles 700-1,000 wds (20/yr); fiction 1,000-2,000 wds (10/yr); book reviews 100-500 wds. Responds in 3 wks. Seasonal 1 yr ahead. Accepts reprints. Guidelines; copy for 9x12 SAE/IRC.

Poetry: Buys 20/yr. Avant-garde, free verse, traditional; 10-30 lines; $15-30. Submit max. 5 poems.

CHRISTIAN CRUSADE NEWSPAPER, PO Box 279, Neosho MO 64850. (918)438-4234. Fax (417)451-4319. Interdenominational. Billy James Hargis, pub. A Christian, pro-American approach to current social and political issues. Monthly newspaper; 24 pgs; circ 25,000. 50% freelance. Query. Pays varying rates on publication for all rts. Articles (any length). Responds in 9 wks. Free copy.

CHRISTIAN DRAMA MAGAZINE, 1824 Celestia Blvd., Walla Walla WA 99362-3619. (509)522-5242. Suspending publication until March 1999.

*THE CHRISTIAN EDGE, 6501 Bronson Ln., Bakersfield CA 93309. Phone/fax (805)837-1378. E-mail: thechredge@aol.com. Chase Productions/evangelical. Don Chase, pub. Activity and resources guide; not an issues-driven publication. Monthly newspaper; 8-12 pgs; circ 15,000. Subscription $18. 10% freelance. Query/clips; e-mail query OK. **NO PAYMENT** for one-time rts. Articles 350-1,000 wds (10/yr); book/music/video reviews 150 wds. Responds in 3 wks. Seasonal 2 mos ahead. Accepts simultaneous submissions & reprints (tell when/where appeared). Prefers disk. Sidebars OK. Copy for 9x12 SAE/4 stamps. (Ads)

+CHRISTIAN ENTERTAINMENT, PO Box 314, Anniston AL 36202. (205)238-

8336. Fax (205)238-8336. Consolidated Publishing Co. Darryal W. Ray, ed. To highlight options for the Christian family in various forms of entertainment. Monthly mag; circ 100,000. Subscription $30. Query. Not in topical listings. (Ads)

#CHRISTIAN HISTORY, 465 Gundersen Dr., Carol Stream IL 60188. (630)260-6200. Fax (630)260-0114. E-mail: CHedit@aol.com. Website: http://www. christianity.net/christianhistory. Christianity Today, Inc. Mark Galli, ed. To teach Christian history to educated readers in an engaging manner. Quarterly mag; 52 pgs; circ 70,000. Subscription $19.95. 75% freelance. Query; fax/e-mail query OK. Pays .10/wd on acceptance for 1st, electronic & some ancillary rts. Articles 1,000-3,000 wds (1/yr). Responds in 2 wks. Accepts reprints (tell when/where appeared). Requires disk. Kill fee 50%. Sidebars OK. Guidelines/theme list; copy $5.50. (Ads)

> **Tips:** "Let us know your particular areas of specialization and any books or papers you have written in the area of Christian history."
> ** 1997 & 1995 EPA Award of Merit—General.

CHRISTIAN HOME & SCHOOL, 3350 East Paris Ave. SE, Box 8709, Grand Rapids MI 49512. (616)957-1070x234. Fax (616)957-5022. E-mail: chsschlnt@ aol.com. Website: http://www.gospelcom.net/csi/chs. Christian Schools Intl. Roger Schmurr, sr. ed. Focuses on parenting and Christian education; for parents who send their children to Christian schools. Bimonthly mag; 32 pgs; circ 62,000. Subscription $11.95. 60% freelance. Complete ms. Pays $125-200 on publication for 1st rts. Articles 750-2,000 wds (30/yr); fiction 1,200-2,000 wds (5/yr); book reviews $25 (assigned). Responds in 1 wk. Seasonal 5 mos ahead. Accepts simultaneous query. Accepts disk (prefers clean copy they can scan). Sidebars OK. Prefers NIV. Guidelines/theme list; copy for 9x12 SAE/4 stamps. (Ads)

> **Fillers:** Ideas; 75-100 wds. Pays $25-40.
> **Tips:** Most open to features. Needs Christmas fiction.
> ** 1997 & 1995 EPA Award of Merit—Organizational.

#THE CHRISTIAN LEADER, PO Box V, Hillsboro KS 67063. (316)947-5543. Fax (316)947-3266. Mennonite Brethren. Don Ratzlaff, ed. Denominational. Monthly mag; circ. 9,800. Subscription $16. Query. Open to freelance. Not in topical listings.

CHRISTIAN LIVING, 616 Walnut Ave., Scottdale PA 15683-1999. (412)887-8500. Fax (412)887-3111. E-mail: SKRISS%MPH@mcimail.com. Mennonite. Steve Kriss, ed. Denominational with focus on contemporary stories of faith in action in a variety of contexts. Monthly (8X) mag; 28-36 pgs; circ 4,500. Subscription $21.95. 95% freelance. Complete ms/cover letter; no electronic submissions. Pays .04-.06/wd on publication for 1st, one-time, reprint or simultaneous rts. Articles 700-1,500 wds (25/yr); fiction 800-1,500 wds (1-2/yr). Responds in 6-8 wks. Seasonal 4-6 mos ahead. Accepts simultaneous submissions & reprints (tell when/where appeared). Accepts disk. Sidebars OK. Prefers NRSV. Guidelines/theme list; copy for 9x12 SAE/3 stamps. (Ads)

> **Poetry:** Buys 15-20/yr. Free verse, haiku; 3-25 lines; pays $1/line. Submit max. 5 poems.
> **Fillers:** Buys 2-3/yr. Newsbreaks, prayers; 50-30 wds; $5-20.
> **Ethnic:** Targets all ethnic groups involved in the Mennonite religion. Needs articles on issues of race.

Tips: "Looking for good articles on peace issues. A good understanding of issues related to our emphasis and community, family and peace and justice will help the writer."

** This periodical was #51 on the 1995 Top 50 Christian Publishers list (#56 in 1994).

CHRISTIAN MEDIA, Box 448, Jacksonville OR 97530. (541)899-8888. James Lloyd, ed./pub. For emerging Christian songwriters, artists, and other professionals involved in music, video, film, print, and broadcasting. Bimonthly tabloid; 16 pgs; circ 2,000-6,000. Query; prefers phone query. **NO PAYMENT** for negotiable rts. Articles; book & music reviews, 3 paragraphs. Accepts simultaneous submissions & reprints. Prefers disk. KJV only. Copy for 9x12 SAE/2 stamps.

Special Needs: Particularly interested in stories that expose dirty practices in the industry—royalty rip-offs, misleading ads, financial misconduct, etc. No flowery pieces on celebrities; wants well-documented articles on abuse in the media.

+CHRISTIAN MOTORSPORTS ILLUSTRATED, PO Box 129, Mansfield PA 16933. (717)549-2282. Fax (717)549-3366. E-mail: cpo@epix.net. CPO Publishing. Roland Osborne, pub. Covers Christian involved in motorsports. Bimonthly mag; 64 pgs; circ 40,000. Subscription $19.96. 50% freelance. Complete ms; no phone/fax/e-mail query. Pays .20/wd on publication for 1st rts. Articles 500-2,000 wds (30/yr); fiction 500-2,000 wds (30/yr). Seasonal 4 mos ahead. Requires disk. Sidebars OK. Free copy. (Ads)

Poetry: Buys 10/yr. Any type. Pays .20/wd. Submit max. 10 poems.

Fillers: Buys 100/yr. Anecdotes, cartoons, facts, games, ideas, jokes, newsbreaks, prayers, prose, quizzes, quotes, short humor. Pays .20/wd.

Columns/Departments: Buys 10/yr.

Tips: "Send a story on a Christian involved in motorsports."

+CHRISTIAN NEWS NORTHWEST, PO Box 974, Newberg OR 97132. Phone/fax (503)537-9220. E-mail: cnnw@juno.com. John Fortmeyer, ed. News of ministry in the evangelical Christian community in western and central Oregon and southwest Washington; distributed primarily through evangelical churches. Monthly newspaper; 20-28 pgs; circ 20,000. Subscription $15. 10-15% freelance. Query; phone/fax/e-mail query OK. **NO PAYMENT.** Not copyrighted. Articles 300-400 wds (100/yr). Responds in 4 wks. Seasonal 3 mos ahead. Accepts reprints (tell when/where appeared). Sidebars OK. Guidelines; copy $1.50. (Ads)

Tips: "Emphasis is on news in our local area."

#THE CHRISTIAN OBSERVER, 9400 Fairview Ave., Ste. 200, Manassas VA 22110. (703)335-2844. Fax (703)368-4817. E-mail: Christiano@aol.com. Christian Observer Foundation; Presbyterian Reformed. Edwin P. Elliott, ed. To encourage and edify God's people and families. Monthly newspaper; circ 2,000. Subscription $27. Query. Not in topical listings. (Ads)

CHRISTIAN PARENTING TODAY, 4050 Lee Vance View, Colorado Springs CO 80918-7100. (719)531-7776. Fax (719)535-0172. E-mail: CPTmag@aol.com. Cook Communications. Erin Healy, ed; submit to Kathy Davis, assoc. ed.. Practical advice for parents (of kids birth-12), from a Christian perspective, that runs the whole gamut of needs: social, educational, spiritual, medical, etc. Bimonthly mag; 72-92 pgs; circ 118,000. Subscription $16.95. 80-90% freelance. Query or complete ms/cover letter; fax/e-mail query OK. Pays $30-650 on acceptance for assigned (on publication for unsolicited) for 1st and reprint rts. Articles 600-1,800 wds (180-200/yr); product reviews (games, toys, etc), 150 wds, $25-35. Responds in 8-10 wks. Seasonal 8-12 mos ahead. Accepts reprints (tell when/where appeared). Accepts disk. Kill fee 25%. Sidebars OK. Prefers NIV. Guidelines; copy for 9x12 SAE/$3 postage. (Ads)

Columns/Departments: Buys 75-80/yr. Train Them Up, 700 wds, $125; Healthy & Safe, 400-450 wds, $50-75; The Lighter Side, 600-700 wds, $125; Parent Exchange (parenting tips), 25-100 wds, $30; Life in Our House (humorous anecdotes), 25-100 wds, $30.

Tips: "Study past issues. Cultivate journalism skills. Start by writing for columns. Be selective in sending clips that demonstrate the kind of writing we publish. Demonstrate that you can identify with our readers."

** This periodical was #1 on the 1997 Top 50 Christian Publishers list (#20 in 1996, #2 in 1995, #27 in 1994). 1996 EPA Award for Most Improved Publication.

*THE CHRISTIAN RANCHMAN, 7022-A Lake County Dr., Fort Worth TX 76179. (817)236-0023. Fax (817)236-0024. Interdenominational. Monthly tabloid; 12 pgs; circ 28,000. No subscription. Open to freelance. Complete ms/cover letter. **NO PAYMENT** for all rts. Articles; book/video reviews (length open). No sidebars.

Poetry: Accepts 40/yr. Free verse. Submit max. 3 poems.

Fillers: Accepts all types.

#CHRISTIAN READER, 465 Gundersen Dr., Carol Stream IL 60188-2498. (630)260-6200. Fax (630)260-0114. E-mail: creditoria@aol.com. Website: http://www. christianity.net/cr/cr.html. Christianity Today, Inc. Bonne Steffen, ed. A Christian "Reader's Digest" that uses both reprints and original material. Bimonthly mag; 112 pgs; circ 225,000. Subscription $17.50. 35% freelance. Complete ms/cover letter; phone/fax/e-mail query OK. Pays $100-250 (.10/wd) on acceptance for 1st rts. Articles 500-1,500 wds (50/yr). Responds in 3 wks. Seasonal 9 mos ahead. Accepts reprints ($50-100, tell when/where appeared). Kill fee. No sidebars. Guidelines/theme list; copy for 6x9 SAE/4 stamps. (Ads)

Poetry: Buys 2/yr. Free verse, light verse, traditional; 5-35 lines; $10-50. Submit max. 3 poems.

Fillers: Buys 25-35/yr. Anecdotes, facts, short humor (see Lite Fare); 25-400 wds; pays $15-25.

Columns/Departments: Cynthia Thomas. Buys 150/yr. Lite Fare (adult church humor); Kids of the Kingdom (kids say and do funny things); Rolling Down the Aisle (true humor from weddings/rehearsals); all to 250 wds; $25-35.

Tips: "Keep articles short; we edit everything. First-person nonfiction stories are a top priority editorially for final selection."

Contest: Annual contest, March 1 deadline. Prizes $1,000, $500, $250. Send SASE for contest fact sheet.

** This periodical was #29 on the 1997 Top 50 Christian Publishers list (#7 in 1996, #63 in 1995).

CHRISTIAN RENEWAL, Box 770, Lewiston NY 14092-0770. (905)562-5719. Fax (905)562-7828. E-mail: JVANDYK@aol.com. Reformed (Conservative). John Van Dyk, mng. ed. Church-related and world news for members of the Reformed community of churches in North America. Biweekly newspaper; 20 pgs; circ 4,000. Subscription $29. 5% freelance. Query/clips; e-mail query OK. Pays $25-100 for one-time rts. Articles 500-3,000 wds; fiction 2,000 wds (6/yr); book reviews 50-200 wds. Responds in 9 wks. Seasonal 3 mos ahead. Accepts simultaneous submissions & reprints. Prefers disk. Copy $1. (Ads)

CHRISTIAN RESEARCH JOURNAL, 30162 Tomas, Rancho Santa Margarita, CA 92688. (714)858-6100. Fax (714)858-6111. Christian Research Institute. Elliot Miller, ed-in-chief. For those who have been affected by cults and the occult. Quarterly journal; 56 pgs; circ 35,000. Subscription $20. 1% freelance. Query or complete ms/cover letter; fax query OK. Pays .15/wd on publication for 1st rts. Articles to 5,000 wds (1/yr); book reviews 1,800-2,500 wds. Responds in 16-20 wks. Accepts simultaneous submissions. Kill fee to 50%. Requires disk. Sidebars assigned. Guidelines; copy $6. (Ads)

> **Columns/Departments:** Witnessing Tips (evangelism), 1,000 wds; Viewpoint (opinion on cults, ethics, etc.), 875 wds.
>
> **Tips:** "Be patient; we sometimes review mss only twice a year, but we will get back to you. Most open to features (on cults), book reviews, opinion pieces and witnessing tips."
>
> ** 1997 & 1996 EPA Award of Merit—Organizational.

CHRISTIAN RETAILING, 600 Rinehart Rd., Lake Mary FL 32746. (407)333-0600. Fax (407)333-7133. E-mail: retailing@strang.com or stertzer@strang.com. Website: http://www.strang.com/cr/cr.html. Strang Communications Co. Marcia Ford, mng ed. This publisher is now using only assignment writers and has more writers than they can use.

CHRISTIAN SINGLE, 127 9th Ave. N, Nashville TN 37234-0140. (615)251-2230. Fax (615)251-5008. E-mail: christiansingle@bssb.com or wgibson@bssb.com. Website: http://www.bssb.com. Southern Baptist. Stephen Felts, ed-in-chief; Wendi Gibson, copy ed. To encourage singles, primarily in their 20s and 30s, to integrate the biblical principles of their faith into their everyday lifestyle. Monthly mag; 50 pgs; circ 63,000. Subscription $19.95. 20% freelance. Query/clips. Pays .10-20/wd on acceptance for all, 1st, one-time, reprint, and electronic rts. Articles 600-2,400 wds (24/yr) & fiction 600-2,400 wds (24/yr); book/music/video reviews 200 wds, $75. Responds in 13 wks. Seasonal 6 mos ahead. Accepts reprints (tell when/where appeared). Accepts disk. Likes sidebars. Prefers NIV & THE MESSAGE. Guidelines/theme list; copy for 9x12 SAE/4 stamps. (Ads)

> **Fillers:** Facts, quotes, short humor; 50-100 wds. Pay negotiable.
>
> **Columns/Departments:** Single Parenting (self-help), 1,200 wds; Body Shop (physical, mental, emotional, spiritual fitness), 1,200 wds; Closing Moment (devotional), 150 wds; Micro Info (filler bits), 800 wds; Profiles (singles putting faith to work), 2,000 wds. Query.
>
> **Tips:** "Most open to general features. Send writing samples, study publication before you query, and know your market. Need more humor."
>
> ** This periodical was #43 on the 1997 Top 50 Christian Publishers list (#30 in 1996, #47 in 1995 & 1994). Also 1997 EPA Award of Excellence—Denominational.

CHRISTIAN SOCIAL ACTION, 100 Maryland Ave. NE, Washington DC 20002. (202)488-5621. Fax (202)488-1617. E-mail: LRANCK@igc.org. United Methodist. Lee Ranck, ed. Information and analysis of critical social issues from the perspective of Christian faith. Monthly (11X) mag; 40 pgs; circ 2,000. Subscription $15. 20% freelance. Query/clips or complete ms/cover letter. Pays $75-150 on publication for all rts (negotiable). Articles 2,000 wds (12/yr); book reviews 500 wds, $25. Responds in 4 wks. Consider simultaneous submissions & reprints (tell when/where appeared). Prefers disk. Sidebars OK. Prefers RSV. Guidelines; copy for 9x12 SAE/2 stamps. (Ads)

> **Columns/Departments:** Buys 10/yr. Talking (reader's write), 1,000 wds; Media Watch (reviews), 500 wds. Pays $25-50.
>
> **Special Needs:** Urban issues, children's issues, and environment.
>
> **Tips:** "Most open to regular articles on issues."

#CHRISTIAN STANDARD, 8121 Hamilton Ave., Cincinnati OH 45231. (513)931-4050. Fax (513)931-0950. Standard Publishing/Christian Churches/Churches of Christ. Sam E. Stone, ed. Devoted to the restoration of New Testament Christianity, its doctrines, its ordinances, and its fruits. Weekly mag; 24 pgs; circ 59,000. Subscription $20. 50% freelance. Complete ms/cover letter. Pays $10-80 on publication for 1st or one-time rts. Articles 400-1,600 wds (200/yr). Responds in 9 wks. Seasonal 8-12 mos ahead. Accepts reprints. Guidelines; copy for 9x12 SAE/3 stamps or $1. (Ads)

+THE CHRISTIAN TRAVELER, PO Box 1736, Holland MI 49422. (616)494-0907. Fax (616)494-0912. E-mail: tct@iserv.net. Amy Eckert, ed. Features travel destinations of significance to Christians. Bimonthly mag. 85% freelance. Query; fax/e-mail query OK. Query for electronic submissions. Pays .30/wd on publication for 1st, one-time, reprint & electronic rts. Articles 1,000-2,500 wds. Responds in 4-6 wks. Seasonal 6 mos ahead. Accepts reprints (tell when/where appeared). Prefers disk. Sidebars OK. Prefers NIV. Guidelines; copy for 9x12 SAE/2 stamps. (Ads)

> **Fillers:** Anecdotes, facts, ideas, newsbreaks, quizzes, quotes, short humor, tips on healthy travel or travel budgeting. No payment.
>
> **Columns/Departments:** Buys 12/yr. Emmaus Road (personal experience essay) 800 wds; Working Vacations (missions/outreach projects) 1,000 wds; Wilderness Wanderings (outdoor nature traveling) 1,000 wds; Family (destinations of interest to all ages) 1,000 wds; and Retreats (great retreat/getaways) 1,000 wds.
>
> **Tips:** "Looking for destinations outside the US and Europe. Take time to learn the art of travel writing, which is different from other types of non-fiction. We look for writers who are talented and willing to grow with us as we become a better established publication."

CHRISTIANITY AND THE ARTS, 1100 N. Lake Shore #33-A, Chicago IL 60611. (312)642-8606. Fax (312)266-7719. E-mail: chrnarts@aol.com. Website: http://members.aol.com/chrarts/chrnarts.html. Nondenominational. Marci Whitney-Schenck, ed/pub. Celebrates the revelation of God through the arts and encourages Christian artistic expression. Quarterly mag; 56 pgs; circ 3,000. Subscription $21. Est. 1994. 75% freelance. Complete ms/cover letter; phone/fax/e-mail query OK. Sometimes pays $100 on acceptance or publication for 1st rts. Articles 2,000 wds (20/yr); fiction 2,000 wds (uses little); book, music, video reviews 500 wds. Responds in 3 wks. Seasonal 6 mos ahead. Accepts simultaneous submissions. Accepts disk. Sidebars OK. Theme list; copy $6.

Poetry: Robert Engler, c/o Richard J. Daley College, 7500 S. Pulaski, Chicago IL 60652. Buys 12/yr. Avant-garde, free verse, haiku, traditional.

Special Needs: Visual arts, dance, music, literature, drama.

Tips: "Interested in features and interviews that focus on ethnic celebration of Christian arts, social problems and the arts, and Jewish-Christian links. I need three contributors to write on drama, dance, and film (four articles a year—No payment). Be knowledgeable, but readable to mass market."

CHRISTIANITY TODAY, 465 Gundersen Dr., Carol Stream IL 60188-2498. (630)260-6200. Fax (630)260-0114. E-mail: ctedit@aol.com. Website: http://www.christianity.net. Carol Thiessen, ed. For evangelical Christian thought leaders who seek to integrate their faith commitment with responsible action. Magazine published 14X/yr; 80-120 pgs; circ 172,500. Subscription $24.95. 80% (little unassigned) freelance. Query; phone/fax/e-mail query OK. Pays $100-1,000 (.10/wd) on acceptance for one-time rts. Articles 2,000-4,000 wds (60/yr); book reviews 800-1,000 wds, pays per-page rate. Responds in 12 wks. Seasonal 8 mos ahead. Accepts reprints (tell when/where appeared—payment 25% of regular rate). Kill fee 25%. No sidebars. Prefers NIV. Guidelines; copy for 9x12 SAE/3 stamps. (Ads)

Columns/Departments: Buys 7-10/yr. Church in Action (profile of unusual person/ministry), 900-1,000 wds (query); Arts, 850 wds; $75.

Tips: "We are developing more of our own manuscripts and requiring a much more professional quality from others. An SASE a must."

** This periodical was #61 on the 1997 Top 50 Christian Publisher's list. 1996 EPA Award of Merit—General.

+CHRISTIANS IN BUSINESS, 3595 Webb Bridge Rd., Alphretta GA 30203. (770)442-1500. Fax (770)442-1844. E-mail: Hillman.cib@mindspring.com. Website: http://www.cibmagazine.com. Aslan Group Publishing, Inc. Os Hillman, ed. To reflect Christ in the marketplace. Est. 1997. Bimonthly mag; 32 pgs. Subscription $16.95. Complete ms; phone/fax/e-mail query/submissions OK. (Ads)

Tips: "If you have a story in which Christ was reflected in your marketplace, we want to hear about it."

*CHRISTMAS, An Annual Treasury, Box 1209, Minneapolis MN 55440. (612)330-3442. Fax (612)330-3215. Augsburg Fortress. Bob Klausmeier, ed. Birth of Christ central to celebration of Christmas. Annual book; 64 pgs; circ 40,000. 75% freelance. Complete ms/cover letter. Pays $150-300 on acceptance for one-time rts. Articles 1,500-2,500 wds (2-3/yr); fiction 1,500-2,000 wds (3-4/yr). Responds in 12 wks. Works 14-18 mos ahead. Accepts reprints. Guidelines/themes; copy $12.95 + postage (call 800-328-4648).

Poetry: Buys 3-4/yr. Free verse, light verse, traditional; to 30 lines; $75-125. Submit max. 3 poems. Nothing on Santa Claus.

Tips: "Short stories related to Christmas only. Nonfiction related to yearly theme, check first."

CHRYSALIS READER, Rte. 1 Box 184, Dillwyn VA 23936. (804)983-3021. Fax (804)983-1074. E-mail: lawson@aba.org. Swedenborg Foundation. Carol S. Lawson, ed. Focuses on spiritual life and literature. A semiannual collection of stories, articles and poetry in book form; 192 pgs; circ. 3,000. $13.95/issue. 60% freelance. Query. Pays $50-150 (plus 5 copies) on publication for one-time rts. Articles and short stories (15-20/yr) 2,000-3,500 wds. Responds in 8 wks. Prefers disk. No sidebars. Guidelines/theme list; copy $10/9x12 SAE/5 stamps.

Poetry: Robert Lawson. Buys 15/yr. Avant-garde, free verse, haiku; $25 plus 2 copies. Submit max. 6 poems.

Tips: "Each issue is on a theme, so we always need essays on those themes; also literary fiction."

THE CHURCH ADVOCATE, Box 926, 700 E. Melrose Ave., Findlay OH 45839. (419)424-1961. Fax (419)424-3433. E-mail: ejs@brt.bright.net. Churches of God General Conference. Evelyn J. Sloat, ed. Denominational. Quarterly tabloid; 16 pgs; circ 13,000. Subscription free to denomination. Little freelance. Complete ms. Pays $10/printed pg. on publication for one-time rts. Articles 750 wds & up (6/yr). Seasonal 6 mos ahead. Accepts simultaneous submissions & reprints. Sidebars OK. Prefers NIV. Guidelines; copy for 9x12 SAE.

Tips: Most open to personal experience.

#CHURCH & STATE, 1816 Jefferson Pl. NW, Washington DC 20036. (202)466-3234. Fax (202)466-2587. Americans United for Separation of Church and State. Joseph L. Conn, mng. ed. Emphasizes religious liberty and church/state relations matters. Monthly mag; 24-32 pgs; circ 33,000. 10% freelance. Query. Pays negotiable fee on acceptance for all rts. Articles 600-2,600 wds (11/yr), prefers 800-1,600. Responds in 9 wks. Accepts simultaneous query & reprints. Guidelines; copy for 9x12 SAE/3 stamps.

Tips: "We are not a religious magazine. You need to see our magazine before you try to write for it."

CHURCH HERALD AND HOLINESS BANNER, 7415 Metcalf, Box 4060, Overland Park KS 66204. (913)432-0331. Fax (913)722-0351. E-mail: mavery@juno.com. Website: http://www.sunflower.org/~kccbslib. Church of God (Holiness)/Herald and Banner Press. Mark D. Avery, ed. Denominational; conservative/Wesleyan/evangelical people. Biweekly mag; 20 pgs; circ 1,700. Subscription $12.50. 50% freelance. Complete ms/cover letter. **NO PAYMENT** for one-time, reprint or simultaneous rts. Not copyrighted. Articles 200-800 wds (40/yr); fiction 500-1,000 wds. Responds in 8 wks. Seasonal 6 mos ahead. Accepts simultaneous submissions & reprints (tell when/where appeared). Accepts disk. Prefers KJV. Guidelines.

Poetry: Buys few. Traditional; 8-24 lines.

Fillers: Anecdotes, facts, prose, quotes; 150-400 wds.

Tips: "Most open to devotional articles. Must be concise, well-written, and get one main point across; 200-400 wds."

CHURCH OF GOD EVANGEL, PO Box 2250, Cleveland TN 37320-2250. (423)478-7589. Fax (423)478-7521. Church of God (Cleveland, TN). Wilma Amison, mng ed. Denominational. Monthly mag; 36 pgs; circ 51,000. Subscription $12. 25% freelance. Complete ms/cover letter. Pays $10-50 on acceptance for 1st, one-time, simultaneous or reprint rts. Articles 300-1,200 wds (150/yr). Responds in 2-3 wks. Seasonal 4 mos ahead. Accepts simultaneous submissions & reprints. Accepts disk. Some sidebars. Prefers KJV, NKVJ, NIV. Free guidelines/copy.

Fillers: Anecdotes & ideas.

Tips: "Need human interest articles. Always willing to buy thoughtful, well-written pieces that speak to people where they live. Always need humor with a point."

COLUMBIA, PO Box 1670, 1 Columbus Plaza, New Haven CT 06510. (203)772-2130. Fax (203)777-0114. Knights of Columbus (Catholic). Richard McMunn, ed. Geared to a general Catholic family audience. Monthly mag; 32 pgs; circ 1.5 million. Subscription $6; foreign add $2. 25% freelance. Query. Pays to $250-500 on acceptance for 1st rts. Articles 1,000-1,500 wds (20/yr). Responds in 3-4 wks. Seasonal 6 mos ahead. Prefers disk. Kill fee $100. Some sidebars. Free guidelines/copy.

Tips: "Keep eye out for K of C activity in local area and send a query letter about it. Also articles on Catholic family life. Articles must be accompanied by photos or transparencies."

** This periodical was #38 on the 1997 Top 50 Christian Publishers list (#25 in 1996, #32 in 1995, #19 in 1994).

COMMENTS FROM THE FRIENDS, Box 819, Assonet MA 02702. Website: http://www.webshowplace.com/CommentsfromtheFriends. David A. Reed, ed. For ex-Jehovah's Witnesses, their relatives, Christians reaching out to them, and dissident Witnesses. Quarterly newsletter; 16 pgs; circ 1,200. Subscription $11. 5% freelance. Complete ms/cover letter. Pays $20 (sometimes copies or subscription) on publication for all rts. Articles 100-1,000 wds (4/yr); book reviews 50-1,000 wds. Responds in 4-8 wks. Seasonal 3 mos ahead. Accepts simultaneous submissions & reprints. Macintosh disks only. No sidebars. Any version. Guidelines; copy $1/8x10 SAE/2 stamps.

Columns/Departments: Witnessing Tips, 500-1,000 wds.

Tips: "Acquaint us with why you are qualified to write about J.W.'s. Write well-documented, concise articles relevant to J.W.'s today. We automatically reject all material not specifically about Jehovah's Witnesses."

COMMON BOUNDARY, 5272 River Rd., Ste. 650 Bethesda MD 20816-1405. (301)652-9495. E-mail: connect@commonboundary.org. Ecumenical. Ann Simpkinson, ed. Explores relationship between psychotherapy and spirituality. Bimonthly mag; 64 pgs; circ 26,000. 50% freelance. Query. Pays varying rates on publication for 1st rts. Articles 3,000-4,000 wds. Responds in 13-26 wks. Accepts simultaneous submissions. Kill fee 1/3. Guidelines; copy $5.

Fillers: Newsbreaks, 200-600 wds.

Contest: Annual $1,000 Dissertation/Thesis award for best psycho-spiritual topic.

COMMONWEAL, 475 Riverside Dr., Room 405, New York NY 10115-0499. (212)662-4200. Fax (212)662-4183. E-mail: commonweal@msn.com. Commonweal Foundation/Catholic. Patrick Jordan, mng ed. A review of public affairs, religion, literature and the arts, for an intellectually engaged readership. Biweekly mag; 32 pgs; circ 19,000. Subscription $44. 20% freelance. Query/clips. Pays $50-100 (.03/wd) on acceptance or publication for all rts. Articles 1,000 or 3,000 wds (20/yr). Responds 4 wks. Seasonal 2 mos ahead. Prefers disk. Kill fee 2%. Occasional sidebars. Guidelines; copy for 9x12 SAE/4 stamps. (Ads)

Poetry: Rosemary Deen. Buys 20/yr. Free verse, traditional; to 75 lines;

.75/line. Submit max. 5 poems. Submit October-May.

Columns/Departments: Upfronts (brief, newsy facts and info behind the headlines), 750-1,000 wds; The Last Word (commentary based on insight from personal experience or reflection), 700 wds.

Tips: "Most open to meaningful articles on social, political, religious and cultural topics; or columns."

#COMPANION MAGAZINE, Box 535, Station F., Toronto ON M4Y 2L8 Canada. (800)461-1619. Fax (416)690-3320. E-mail: 102532.1737@compuserve.com. Website: http://www.cmpa.ca. Catholic/Franciscan. Fr. R. Riccioli, ed; submit to Betty McCrimmon, mng. ed. An adult, Catholic, inspirational, devotional family magazine. Monthly (11X) mag; 32 pgs; circ 5,000. Subscription $16 CAN or $18 US & foreign. 50% freelance. Complete ms/cover letter; phone/fax/e-mail query OK. Pays .06/wd CAN on publication for 1st rts. Articles 500-1,000 wds (35/yr); fiction 500-1,000 wds (7/yr). Responds in 6 wks. Seasonal 5 mos ahead. Accepts disk (Mac). Guidelines; copy for 7x10 SAE with IRCs. (Ads)

Poetry: Free verse, light verse, traditional. Pays .60/line CAN.

Fillers: Anecdotes, cartoons, prayers, quotes, short humor, word puzzles.

Special Needs: Articles on St. Francis, Franciscan spirituality, and social justice.

Tips: Most open to human interest.

COMPANIONS, Rt. 4 Box 3926, Seymour MO 65746-9009. Mennonite/Christian Light Publications. Roger L. Berry, ed. Consistent with conservative Mennonite doctrine: believer baptism, nonresistance, and nonconformity. Monthly take-home paper; 4 pgs; circ 8,000. Subscription $8.40. 75% freelance. Complete ms. Pays .02-.05/wd on acceptance for all, 1st, one-time or reprint rts. Articles 100-800 wds (100/yr); fiction 800-2,000 wds (50/yr), or serials 1,800 wds and up. Responds in 6-8 wks. Seasonal 6 mos ahead. Accepts reprints (tell when/where appeared). No disk or sidebars. KJV only. Guidelines/theme list; copy for 9x12 SAE/2 stamps.

Fillers: Buys 20/yr. Anecdotes, prose, quotes; 30-100 wds.

Columns/Departments: Buys 12/yr. Science and Scripture (creationist/Biblicist), 400-700; Archaeology and Scripture (archaeology that supports biblical truths); 400-700 wds.

Tips: "Looking for Anabaptist history/theology/ethics. Don't submit to us without studying the do's & don'ts in our guidelines. Stories (fiction or true) are the most difficult to write for us because of the conservative and spiritual lifestyle we promote."

** This periodical was #51 on the 1997 Top 50 Christian Publishers list (#45 in 1996, #14 in 1995, #28 in 1994).

#COMPASS: A Jesuit Journal, Box 400, Sta. F, 50 St. Charles St. E., Toronto ON M4Y 2L8 Canada. (416)921-0653. Fax (416)921-1864. E-mail: leischod@ hookup.net. Website: http://home.ican.net/~gvanv/compass/comphome.html. Catholic; Jesuits of English Canada. Robert Chodos, ed. Ethical and ecumenical discussion of social and religious topics; for educated, but non-specialized readership. Bimonthly mag; 52 pgs; circ 3,700. Subscription $20.33 CAN, $19 US & foreign. 10% freelance. Query/clips. Pays $100-500 CAN, on publication for 1st rts. Articles 1,500-2,500 wds (60/yr); fiction 1,000-2,500 wds/pays $100-250);

book reviews 2,000 wds/$300. Responds in 8 wks. No seasonal. Accepts simultaneous submissions. Prefers disk. Kill fee 50%. Guidelines/theme list; copy $2/9x12 SAE/$1.35 postage CAN.

Fillers: Accepts 60/yr. Short, pithy quotes from other writers; 10-150 wds. Pays 1-yr subscription.

Columns/Departments: Buys 24/yr. Testament (contemporary application of scripture); Colloquy (theology & daily life); Saint (fresh perspective on a Saint); all 750 wds; $100-150. Query.

Special Needs: Every January/February issue examines the state of peace on earth.

Tips: "We are interested primarily in analytical and reflective articles. Write for themes."

+COMPUTING TODAY, 465 Gundersen Dr., Carol Stream IL 60189-2498. (630)260-6200. Fax (630)260-0114. E-mail: computingt@aol.com. Christianity Today, Inc. Mark Galli, ed. To provide Christian computer users with practical information to help them in their ministries and personal use. Quarterly mag; 50 pgs; circ 100,000. Subscription $9.95. 75% freelance. Query; fax/e-mail query OK. Pays variable rates on acceptance publication for 1st rts. Articles 1,000-1,500 wds (15/yr). Responds in 4 wks. Seasonal 9 mos ahead. Accepts reprints (tell when/where appeared). Requires disk or e-mail. Kill fee 50%. Sidebars OK. Prefers NIV. Guidelines; copy for 9x12 SAE. Limited reference in topical listings (accepts all types of articles).

Fillers: Buys10/yr. Cartoons, short humor; $125 for cartoons.

#CONNECTING POINT, Box 685, Cocoa FL 32923. (407)632-0130. Linda G. Howard, ed. For and by the mentally challenged (retarded) community; primarily deals with spiritual and self-advocacy issues. Monthly mag; circ 1,000. 75% freelance. Complete ms. **NO PAYMENT** for 1st rts. Articles (24/yr) & fiction (12/yr), 250-750 wds; book reviews 150 wds. Responds in 3-6 wks. Seasonal 3 mos ahead. Accepts simultaneous submissions & reprints. Guidelines; copy for 9x12 SAE/6 stamps.

Poetry: Accepts 4/yr. Any type; 4-66 lines. Submit max. 10 poems.

Fillers: Accepts 12/yr. Cartoons, games, word puzzles; 50-250 wds.

Columns/Departments: Accepts 24/yr. Devotion Page, 1,000 wds; Bible Study, 500 wds. Query.

Special Needs: Record reviews, self-advocacy, integration/normalization, justice system.

Tips: "All mss need to be in primary vocabulary."

CONQUEST, 1300 N Meacham Rd., Schaumburg IL 60173-4888. (847)843-1600. Fax (847)843-3757. Regular Baptist. Joan E. Alexander, ed. For adults associated with fundamental Baptist Churches. Weekly take-home paper. Note: This periodical is being redesigned as we go to press. Send for new guidelines before submitting.

CORNERSTONE, 939 W. Wilson Ave., Chicago IL 60640-5718. (773)561-2450. Fax (773)989-2076. Cornerstone Communications, Inc. Joyce Paskewich, submissions ed. For young adults, 18-35; to communicate doctrinal truth based on Scripture and to break the "normal Christian" mold with a stance that has cultural relevancy. Quarterly (3-4 issues) mag; 70 pgs; circ 38,000. Subscription $15/8 issues. 10% freelance. Complete ms/cover letter; fax query OK. Pays .08-.10/wd on publication for 1st, one-time, reprint & simultaneous rts. Articles to 4,000 wds (20/yr); fiction 250-4,000 wds (1-4/yr); book/music reviews 500-1,000 wds. Responds in 13-26 wks to accepted mss only (discards others, don't send SASE). Seasonal 6 mos ahead. Accepts simultaneous submissions & reprints (tell when/where appeared). Prefers disk. Sidebars OK. Guidelines; copy for 9x12 SAE/5 stamps. (Ads)

> **Poetry:** Tammy Perlmutter. Buys 15-24/yr. Avant-garde, free verse, haiku, light verse; $10-25. Submit any number.
>
> **Fillers:** Buys 1-4/yr. Cartoons, prayers; 500-1,000 wds. Pays .08-.10/wd
>
> **Columns/Departments:** Buys 3-4/yr. News items, 500-1,000 wds; Music Interviews (Christian & secular artists) to 2,700 wds; Music & Book Reviews (Christian & secular).
>
> **Tips:** "Most open to stream-of-consciousness fiction and book reviews."

#THE COVENANT COMPANION, 5101 N. Francisco Ave., Chicago IL 60625. (773)784-3000x328. Fax (773)784-1540. E-mail: 73430.3316@compuserve. com. Website: http://www.npcts.edu/cov/. Evangelical Covenant Church. Jane K. Swanson-Nystrom, mng ed. Denominational. Monthly mag; 40 pgs; circ 20,000. Subscription $26. 10-15% freelance. Complete ms/cover letter; fax/e-mail query OK. Pays $25-75 on publication for one-time or simultaneous rts. Articles 500-1,200 wds (15/yr), fiction 750-1,200 (3/yr). Responds in 4 wks. Seasonal 4 mos ahead. Accepts simultaneous submissions & reprints (tell when/where appeared). Some kill fees. Sidebars OK. Prefers NRSV. Guidelines/theme list; copy for 9x12 SAE/4 stamps; or $2.50. (Ads)

> **Poetry:** Buys 5-10/yr. Avant-garde, free verse, traditional; $15-25. Submit max. 10 poems.
>
> **Fillers:** Cartoons, short humor, word puzzles.
>
> **Tips:** "We are placing more emphasis on the coverage of current events from an evangelical perspective."

*CREATION ILLUSTRATED, PO Box 7955, Auburn CA 95604. (800)360-2732. 68 pgs. New. Not in topical listings.

+CREATION SPIRITUALITY NETWORK, 2141 Broadway, Oakland CA 94612-2309. Rebecca Bier, ed. Focuses on life and the creation spirituality movement. Pays .02-.05/wd on publication. Essays 1,500-2,500 wds. Not in topical listings.

> **Poetry:** Buys poetry.

THE CRESSET, A Review of Arts, Literature & Public Affairs, Huegli Hall #29, Valparaiso IN 46383. (219)464-5274. Fax (219)464-5496. E-mail: geifrig@exodus. valpo.edu. Valparaiso University/Lutheran. Gail McGrew Eifrig, ed. For college educated, professors, pastors, lay people; serious review essays on religious-cultural affairs. Bimonthly (7X) mag; 36 pgs; circ 4,700. Subscription $8.50. 50% freelance. Complete ms/cover letter. Pays $35 on publication for 1st rts. Articles 2,500-5,000 wds (20-30/yr). Responds in 12 wks. Seasonal 3 mos ahead. Prefers disk. No sidebars. Copy for 9x12 SAE/5 stamps.

> **Poetry:** John Ruff. Buys 15-20/yr. Avant-garde, free verse, traditional; to 40 lines; $15. Submit max. 5 poems.

*CROSSWAY/NEWSLINE, 103 Ambleside Rd., Lightwater, Surrey GU185UJ England. Tel. 02764 72724. Airline Aviation & Aerospace Christian Fellowship.

J. Brown, gen. sec. For non-Christians working in aviation. Crossway is an annual magazine; Newsline a quarterly newsletter; 16 pgs. Free subscription. 100% freelance. Complete ms/cover letter. **NO PAYMENT.** Sometimes copyrighted. Articles on aviation to 2,000 wds. Accepts simultaneous submissions & reprints. Guidelines.

CULTURE WARS (formerly **FIDELITY MAGAZINE**), 206 Marquette Ave., South Bend IN 46617. (219)289-9786. Fax (219)289-1461. E-mail: 71554.445@ compuserve.com. Ultramontagne Associates, Inc. Dr. E. Michael Jones, ed. Issues relating to Catholic families and issues affecting America that impact all people. Monthly (11X) mag; 35 pgs; circ. 3,500. Subscription $25. 20% freelance. Complete ms/cover letter; fax/e-mail query OK. Pays $100 & up on publication for all rts. Articles (25/yr); book reviews $50. Responds in 12-24 wks. Query about reprints. Prefers disk. Some sidebars. Developing guidelines; copy for 9x12 SAE/5 stamps.

> **Poetry:** Buys 15/yr. Free verse, light verse, traditional; 10-50 lines; $25. Submit max. 2 poems.
>
> **Fillers:** Buys 15/yr. Cartoons, quotes; 25 wds & up; variable payment.
>
> **Columns/Departments:** Buys 25/yr. Commentary, 2,500 wds; Feature, 5,000 wds; $100-250.
>
> **Tips:** "All fairly open except cartoons. Single-spaced preferred; avoid dot matrix; photocopies must be clear."

#THE DALLAS/FORT WORTH HERITAGE, PO Box 1424, Ennis TX 75120. (972)846-2900. Fax (972)846-2800. E-mail: DFWHER@fni.com. John J. Dwyer, ed. To help preserve and sustain America's Christian heritage and pass it on to the nation's children. Monthly newspaper; 40-44 pgs; circ 45,000. Subscription $25. Open to freelance. Query. (Ads)

DECISION, PO Box 779, Minneapolis MN 55440-0779. (612)338-0500. Fax (612)335-1299. E-mail: Decision@graham-assn.org. Website: http://www. graham-assn.org/decision. Billy Graham Evangelistic Assn. Submit to The Editor. Evangelism/Christian nurture. Monthly mag; 44 pgs; circ 1,800,000. Subscription $9. 25% freelance. Complete ms/cover letter; no phone/fax/e-mail query. Pays $55-230 on publication for all or 1st rts. Articles 1,000-1,400 wds (40/yr). Responds 10-12 wks. Seasonal 10-12 mos ahead. Accepts disk. Kill fee. Sidebars OK. Guidelines/theme list; copy for 10x13 SAE/3 stamps.

> **Poetry:** Buys 6/yr. Free verse, light verse, traditional; 4-16 lines; .60/wd. Submit max. 7 poems.
>
> **Fillers:** Buys 50/yr. Anecdotes, prose; 300-600 wds; $25-75.
>
> **Columns/Departments:** Buys 12/yr. Where Are They Now? (people who have become Christian through Billy Graham ministries); 600-800 wds; $85.
>
> **Tips:** "We want personal experience articles that show how you learned and grew in a specific situation. What have you experienced that has caused you to grow closer to Christ? How have you applied biblical principles in a difficult situation? Let us see what you did—let us learn with you."
>
> ** #59 on the 1994 Top 50.

DISCIPLESHIP JOURNAL, Box 35004, Colorado Springs CO 80935. (719)531-3529. Fax (719)598-7128. E-mail: susan_maycinik@navigators.org. Website: http://www.gospelcom.net/navs/NP/djhome.html. The Navigators. Susan Maycinik, ed. For motivated, maturing Christians desiring to grow spiritually and to help others grow; biblical and practical. Bimonthly mag; 96+ pgs; circ 110,000. Subscription $21.97. 95% freelance. Query; fax/e-mail query OK; query for electronic submissions. Pays .20/wd (.05/wd for reprints) on acceptance for 1st & electronic rts. Articles 1,500-2,500 wds (60/yr); fiction 1,500-2,500 wds (1-2/yr). Responds in 4-6 wks. Accepts simultaneous submissions. Prefers disk. Kill fee 50%. Sidebars OK. Prefers NIV. Guidelines/theme list. (Ads)

> **Columns/Departments:** Buys 15+/yr. On the Home Front (Q & A regarding family issues); 1,000 wds; Bible Study Methods (how-to), to 1,000 wds; DJ Plus (ministry how-to on missions, evangelism, serving, discipling, teaching & small groups), to 500 wds. Pays .20/wd.

> **Tips:** "Most open to non-theme articles, departments, DJ Plus and sidebars. Our articles focus on biblical passages or topics. Articles should derive main principles from a thorough study of Scripture; should illustrate each principle; should show how to put each principle into practice; and should demonstrate with personal illustrations and vulnerability that the author has wrestled with the subject in his or her life."

> ** This periodical was #10 on the 1997 Top 50 Christian Publishers list. (#2 in 1996 , #15 in 1995, #8 in 1994). Also 1997 EPA Award of Excellence— General (1996 EPA Award of Merit—General.)

DISCIPLE'S JOURNAL, PO Box 100, Wilmington MA 01887. (508)657-7373. Fax (508)657-5411. E-mail: dddj@disciplesdirectory.com. Kenneth A. Dorothy, ed. To strengthen, edify, inform and unite the body of Christ. Monthly newspaper; 16-32 pgs; circ 10,000. Subscription $9.95. Est. 1995. 25% freelance. Query; fax/e-mail query OK. **NO PAYMENT** for one-time rts. Articles 400 wds (24/yr); book/music/video reviews 200 wds. Responds in 2 wks. Seasonal 2 mos ahead. Accepts simultaneous submissions & reprints (tell when/where appeared). Prefers disk. Some sidebars. Prefers NIV. Guidelines/theme list; copy for 9x12 SAE/$1.70 postage. (Ads)

> **Poetry:** Accepts 12/yr. All types; 12-24 lines. Submit max. 6 poems.

> **Fillers:** Accepts 12/yr. All types; 100-400 wds.

> **Columns/Departments:** Financial; Singles; Men; Women; Business; Parenting. 400 wds.

> **Contest:** Poetry contest.

> **Tips:** "Most open to men's, women's or singles' issues; missions; or home schooling. Send sample of articles for review."

DISCOVERY, 400 W. Lake Brantley Rd., Altamonte Springs FL 32714-2715. (407)682-9494. Fax (407)682-7005. E-mail: joyful953@aol.com. Website: http://www.wtln.com. Radio Station WTLN FM/AM. Chris Shenk, features ed. For Christian community in Central Florida. Monthly newspaper; circ 25,000. Subscription free/$9 for home delivery. 20% freelance. Complete ms; phone/fax query OK. **NO PAYMENT**. Not copyrighted. News driven & informative articles under 500 wds. Seasonal 1+ mos ahead. Accepts reprints. Sidebars OK. No disk. Theme list. (Ads)

> **Columns/Departments:** Local/National News, Local Ministries, Broadcaster's Information, Sports, Christian Living, Seasonal themed features.

> **Tips:** "We may submit articles to our other publications in Knoxville and Philadelphia."

THE DOOR, PO Box 1444, Waco TX 76703-1444. (817)752-1468. Fax (817)752-4915. E-mail: 103361.23@compuserve.com. Trinity Foundation. Robert Darden, ed. Satire of evangelical church plus issue-oriented interviews. Bimonthly mag; 44 pgs; circ 16,000. Subscription $24. 90% freelance. Complete ms. Pays $40-200 after publication for 1st rts. Not copyrighted. Articles 750-1,500 wds (25/yr). Responds in 6 wks. Accepts simultaneous submissions & reprints (if from non-competing markets). Kill fee $40-50. Sidebars OK. Guidelines; copy $4.50.

> **Tips:** "We look for biting satire/humor—National Lampoon not Reader's Digest. You must understand our satirical slant. Read more than one issue to understand our 'wavelength.' We desperately need genuinely funny articles with a smart, satiric bent."

DOVETAIL: A Journal by and for Jewish/Christian Families, PO Box 19945, Kalamazoo MI 49019. (616)342-2900. Fax (616)342-1012. E-mail: dovetail@mich.com. Joan C. Hawxhurst, ed. Offers balanced, non-judgmental articles for interfaith families and the professionals who serve them. Bimonthly journal; 16-20 pgs; circ 1,500. Subscription $24.99. 50% freelance. Complete ms/cover letter; fax/e-mail query OK. Pays $10-20 on publication for 1st or reprint rts. Articles 800-1,000 wds (15/yr); book reviews 500 wds, $10. Responds in 6-8 wks. Seasonal 4 mos ahead. Accepts simultaneous submissions & reprints (tell when/where appeared). Prefers disk. Sidebars OK. Guidelines/theme list; copy for 9x12 SAE/3 stamps. (Ads)

> **Poetry:** Buys 1-2/yr. Traditional; $10-20.

> **Tips:** "Please do not send articles that deal with Christian theology or beliefs. Our audience is families with two faiths, and articles should address this specific situation."

DREAMS & VISIONS, 35 Peter St. S., Orillia ON L3V 5A8 Canada. Fax (705)329-1770. E-mail: skysong@bconnex.net. Website: http://www.bconnex.net/~skysong. Skysong Press. Steve Stanton, ed. An international showcase for short literary fiction written from a Christian perspective. Irregular journal; 56 pgs; circ 200. Subscription $12. 100% freelance. Complete ms/cover letter; fax/e-mail query OK. Pays .005/wd on publication for 1st rts & one non-exclusive reprint. Fiction 2,000-6,000 wds (10/yr). Responds in 4-6 wks. Seasonal 6 mos ahead. Accepts simultaneous submissions & reprints (tell when/where appeared). Accepts disk. Guidelines; copy $4.95 (4 back issues to writers $10).

#EMPHASIS ON FAITH AND LIVING, Box 9127, Fort Wayne IN 46899-9127. (219)747-2027. Fax (219)747-5331. E-mail: missionary.church@internetmci.com. Missionary Church. Robert Ransom, mng ed. Denominational; for adults 40 and older. Bimonthly mag; 16 pgs; circ 13,000. Subscription free. 10% freelance. Query or complete ms/cover letter. Pays .03-.04/wd on publication for 1st, one-time, reprint or simultaneous rts. Not copyrighted. Articles 200-800 wds (3/yr); fiction 200-1,600 wds (1-2/yr). Responds in 4-8 wks. Seasonal 4 mos ahead. Accepts simultaneous submissions & reprints. Guidelines; copy for 9x12 SAE/2 stamps. (Ads)

> **Tips:** "Our publication provides church news, missions information, and spiritual reading for members and friends of the Missionary Church denomination. We seek material that is compatible with our Wesleyan-Armenian church doctrine."

Columns/Departments: Buys 5/yr. Pays $5.

*EPISCOPAL LIFE, 815 2nd Ave., New York NY 10017. (212)922-5398. Episcopal Church. Jerrold F. Hames, ed; Edward P. Stannard, mng. ed. Denominational. Monthly newspaper; 32 pgs; circ 180,000. 35% freelance. Query/clips or complete ms/cover letter; phone query on breaking news only. Pays $50-300 on publication for 1st, one-time or simultaneous rts. Articles 250-1,200 wds (12/yr); assigned book reviews 400 wds ($35). Responds in 5 wks. Seasonal 4 mos ahead. Accepts simultaneous submissions & reprints. Kill fee 50%. Free copy.

Columns/Departments: Nan Cobbey. Buys 36/yr. Commentary on political/religious topics; 300-600 wds; $35-75. Query.

Tips: "All articles must have Episcopal Church slant or specifics. We need topical/issues, not devotional stuff. Most open to feature stories about Episcopalians—clergy, lay, churches, involvement in local efforts, movements, ministries."

+E STREET, 2930 Flowers Rd., Ste. 107, Atlanta GA 30341. (770)936-5312. Fax (770)936-5260. E-mail: 70420.301@compuserve.com. The Christian Index/ Georgia Baptist Convention. John D. Pierce, mng. ed. Positive, faith-affirming feature magazine, but not a church "insider" piece. Quarterly mag; 56 pgs; circ 11,000. Subscription $8. 50% freelance. Query/clips; fax query OK. Pays $75-250 on publication for 1st rts. Articles 700-1,200 wds (6/yr); fiction 1,200-1,600 wds (25/yr). Responds in 2 wks. Seasonal 6 mos ahead. Accepts reprints (tell when/where appeared). Prefers disk. Sidebars OK. Guidelines; copy for 9x12 SAE. (Ads)

Fillers: Buys 6/yr. Cartoons, prose, short humor. Pays $25-50.

Tips: "Most open to fiction or profiles of famous or unknowns who have good personal stories with faith foundation. Avoid 'church language.'"

EVANGEL, Box 535002, Indianapolis IN 46253-5002. (317)244-3660. Free Methodist/Light and Life Communications. Julie Innes, ed. For young to middle-aged adults; encourages spiritual growth. Weekly take-home paper; 8 pgs; circ 19,000-20,000. Subscription $7.40. 100% freelance. Query. Pays .04/wd (.03/wd for reprints) on publication for one-time rts. Articles to 1,200 wds (100/yr); fiction to 1,200 wds (100/yr). Responds in 6-8 wks. Seasonal 9-12 mos ahead. Accepts simultaneous submissions & reprints (tell when/where appeared). Accepts disk. Some sidebars. Prefers NIV. Guidelines; copy for #10 SAE/1 stamp.

Poetry: Buys 30/yr. Free verse, light verse; 3-16 lines; $10. Submit max. 5 poems. Rhyming poetry not usually taken too seriously.

Fillers: Buys 20/yr. Cartoons, short humor; to 100 wds; humor $10, cartoons $20.

Tips: "Write about a topic that is new and fresh. Avoid redundancy and focus on thesis for clarity of submission."

#THE EVANGEL, PO Box 348, Marlow OK 73055. (405)658-5631. Fax (405)658-2867. E-mail: UMI.MHR@juno.com. Home Mission Board, Southern Baptist Church. Michael H. Reynolds, ed. To expose Mormonism and explain its views of doctrine, history and current events. Bimonthly; circ 20,000. Subscription free. Open to freelance. Complete ms. Not in topical listings. (Ads)

#THE EVANGELICAL ADVOCATE, 1426 Lancaster Pike, Circleville OH 43113. (614)474-8856. Fax (614)477-7766. Churches of Christ in Christian Union. Wes

Humble, ed. Denominational; emphasizing fundamental evangelical holiness. Monthly mag; circ 5,000. Subscription $10. Open to freelance. Query. Not in topical listings. (Ads)

#THE EVANGELICAL BAPTIST, 679 Southgate Dr., Guelph ON N1G 4S2 Canada. (519)821-4830. Fax (519)821-9829. E-mail: LoisPeck@compuserve.com. The Fellowship of Evangelical Baptist Churches in Canada. Lois Peck, mng ed. Denominational; conservative evangelical. Monthly (11X) mag; 36 pgs; circ 4,000. Subscription $14.95 CAN, $16.95 US. 20-30% freelance. Query or complete ms/cover letter; phone/fax query OK. Pays $25-50 on publication for one-time rts. Articles 750-1,500 wds; fiction 750-1,500 wds; book reviews 200-375 wds. Responds in 5 wks. Seasonal 2 mos ahead. Accepts simultaneous submissions & reprints. Accepts disk. Rarely uses sidebars. Guidelines; copy for 9x12 SAE/Canadian postage. (Ads)

> **Tips:** "If you expect payment for your submission, you must say so when submitting."

#THE EVANGELICAL BEACON, 901 E. 78th St., Minneapolis MN 55420-1360. (612)854-1300. Fax (612)853-8488. Evangelical Free Church of America. Timothy Addington, ed. Denominational; informational, inspirational, and evangelistic. Monthly (7x) mag; 32 pgs; circ 30,000. Subscription $12. Very little freelance. Query or complete ms. Feature articles assigned. Looking for short news items, 150-200 words about exciting ministries, prayer movements, or evangelistic efforts of Evangelical Free Churches. B&W or color prints that illustrate the story a plus. Responds in 6 wks. Accepts simultaneous submissions & reprints. Guidelines; copy $1/ 9x12 SAE/4 stamps. (Ads)

#EVANGELICAL VISITOR, PO Box 166, Nappanee IN 46550-0166. (219)773-3164. Fax (219)773-5934. Brethren in Christ. Glen Pierce, ed. Denominational. Monthly mag; circ 4,500. Subscription $12. 10% freelance. Complete ms. Pays $15-39 on publication for reprint rts. Articles 750-1,200 wds (3-5 pgs); fiction or true stories 900 wds. Responds in 10 wks. Seasonal 3-4 mos ahead. Accepts simultaneous submissions. Guidelines; copy $1. (Ads)

EXPRESSION CHRISTIAN NEWSPAPER, 200 Dinsmore Ave., Pittsburgh PA 15205. (412)921-1300. Fax (412)921-1537. E-mail: express@nauticom.net. Website: http://www.nauticom.net/www/express. The Sonshine Foundation. Barbara Wilson, dir. Geared toward bringing unity among the churches in the Pittsburgh and west PA area. Monthly newspaper; 24-32 pgs; circ 15,000. Subscription $20 (first year free). 75% freelance. Query; fax/e-mail query OK. Pays $25-100 on publication for one-time rts. Not copyrighted. Articles 300-500 or 750-1,000 wds; book/music/video reviews 300 wds (no pay). Responds in 3-4 wks. Seasonal 2 mos ahead. Accepts simultaneous submissions. Kill fee. Sidebars OK. Accepts disk. Guidelines/theme list; copy for 9x12 SAE/3 stamps. (Ads)

> **Fillers:** Buys 4-6/yr. Cartoons; $10-25.
>
> **Tips:** "Send local/state stories, for example: Interview with local guy, Mel Blount (ex-Steeler), who has a half-way house for boys. Most open to editorials; PA stories of interest."

FAITH TODAY, M.I.P. Box 3745, Markham ON L3R 0Y4 Canada. (905)479-5885. Fax (905)479-4742. E-mail: ft@efc-canada.com. Evangelical Fellowship of Canada. Marianne Meed Ward, mng ed. Informing Canadian evangelicals on thoughts, trends, issues and events. Bimonthly mag; 62-80 pgs; circ 18,000. Subscription $17.65 CAN. 80% freelance. Query/clips; fax/e-mail query OK. Query for electronic submissions. Pays $50-800 on publication for 1st rts. Articles (90/yr) 400-3,000 wds; news stories 400 wds; profiles 900 wds. Responds in 2 wks. Prefers disk or e-mail. Kill fee 30-50%. Sidebars OK. Guidelines/theme list; copy for 9x12 SAE/$1.35 Canadian postage. (Ads)

Fillers: Buys 6/yr. Cartoons. Pays $25.

Columns/Departments: Buys 6/yr. Other Voices (current social/political/religious issues of concern to Canadian church); 600 wds; .15/wd.

Special Needs: "Canadian news. All topics to be approached in a journalistic—not personal viewpoint—style (except for 'Other Voices')."

Contest: The God Uses Ink Awards Contest, held in conjunction with annual writer's conference. See listing under Canadian conferences. Open to Canadian Christian writers. Categories: Nonfiction book or article and fiction book or short story.

Tips: "Most open to Other Voices. Suggest a short news piece; if I'm happy with the idea and delivery, I'll assign a larger feature article."

** This periodical was #4 on the 1997 Top 50 Christian Publishers List. (#65 in 1996, #43 in 1994).

THE FAMILY DIGEST, PO Box 40137, Fort Wayne IN 46804. Catholic. Corine B. Erlandson, ed. Dedicated to the joy and fulfillment of Catholic family life and its relationship to the Catholic parish. Bimonthly journal/booklet; 48 pgs; circ 150,000. Distributed through parishes. 90% freelance. Complete ms/cover letter. Pays $40-60, 4-6 wks after acceptance, for 1st rts. Articles 700-1,200 wds (60/yr). Responds in 4-8 wks. Seasonal 7 mos ahead. Occasionally buys reprints. No disk or sidebars. Prefers NAB. Guidelines; copy for 6x9 SAE/2 stamps. (Ads—Call 612-929-6765)

Fillers: Buys 24/yr. Anecdotes drawn from experience, 20-100 wds, $20.

Tips: "Prospective freelance writers should be familiar with the types of articles we accept and publish. Need upbeat articles which affirm simple ways in which the Catholic faith is expressed in daily life. Articles on family life, parish life, seasonal articles, how-to pieces, inspirational, prayer, spiritual life and Church traditions will be gladly reviewed for possible acceptance and publication."

** This periodical was #52 on the 1995 Top 50 Christian Publishers list (#57 in 1994).

*****THE FAMILY JOURNAL**, PO Box 506, Bath NY 14810-0506. (607)776-4151. Fax (607)776-6929. E-mail: famlife@aol.com Interdenominational. Jack Hager, ed. A ministry center and 8 radio stations in northern PA and southern NY. Bimonthly newspaper; circ 22,000. Free to donors. 10% freelance. Complete ms/cover letter; phone/fax query OK. **NO PAYMENT.** Not copyrighted. Articles 250-500 wds (6/yr). Responds in 1 wk. Seasonal 3 mos ahead. Accepts simultaneous submissions & reprints. Requires disk. No sidebars. Copy for 10x13 SAE/2 stamps. (Ads)

Poetry: Accepts 4/yr. Free verse, light verse, traditional; 32-40 lines. Submit max. 3 poems.

Tips: "We lean, but not exclusively, on stories/writers from NY and PA."

*THE FAMILY NETWORK, RR1 Box 354, Claude TX 79019. Phone/fax (806)944-5414. Stacy Lewis, ed. To encourage Christian living, purity, modesty, home education, trusting God in family planning, homebirth, and prayer. Bimonthly newsletter; 12 pgs; circ 150. Subscription $15. 100% freelance. Complete ms; phone query OK. **NO PAYMENT.** Not copyrighted. Articles 50-800 wds (50/yr); fiction to 800 wds (15/yr). Responds in 3 wks. Seasonal 4 mos ahead. Accepts simultaneous submissions & reprints. Accepts disk. Sidebars OK. Guidelines; copy $3. (Ads)

> **Poetry:** Accepts 12-20/yr. Any type; any length. Submit max. 5 poems.
> **Fillers:** Accepts 30/yr. All types.
> **Columns/Departments:** Accepts 6/yr. Herbs (how to grow, dry, prepare own medicinals) 50-200; Child Training 50-1,000 wds; Marriage 50-1,000 wds.
> **Special Needs:** Organizational helps and large family concerns.
> **Tips:** "Any family/marriage/serving-God type articles. We love testimonies, articles that glorify God and encourage the believer."

*FATTED CALF FORUM, Fatted Calf Enterprises, Box 4031, San Marcos CA 92069. Department Editor. Regional Christian newspaper. Quarterly mag; 32+ pgs; circ 100. Subscription $20. 100% freelance. Complete ms. **PAYS IN COPIES/SUBSCRIPTION** for one-time rts. Articles to 2,000 wds (6/yr); fiction up to 2,000 wds (20/yr); music/video reviews, 250 wds. Responds in 6 wks. Seasonal 3 mos ahead. Accepts simultaneous submissions & reprints (tell when/where appeared). Prefers disk. Some sidebars. Guidelines; copy $2/9x12 SAE/4 stamps. (Ads)

> **Poetry:** Accepts 20/yr. All types; any reasonable length. Submit max. 3 poems.
> **Columns/Departments:** Accepts 4/yr. Pastor's Corner (church issues), 500 wds.
> **Contest:** Sponsors a contest.
> **Tips:** "We specialize in the unusual. Make me think. No self-help or counseling. Fiction! Poetry! Commentary, satire; preferably with an attitude. If everyone else is afraid of it, send it along."

*THE FELLOWSHIP LINK, 679 Southgate Dr., Guelph ON N1G 4S2 Canada. (519)821-4830. Fax (519)821-9829. Fellowship of Evangelical Baptist Churches in Canada. Dr. T. Starr, ed. To edify and strengthen people 55+ through the various stages of aging. Quarterly mag; 24 pgs; circ. 2,000. Subscription $12. 90% freelance. Query w/wo clips. **NO PAYMENT** for all rts. Not copyrighted. Articles 300-350 wds (12/yr); fiction 300-350 wds (12/yr); book reviews 100 wds. Responds in 2 weeks. Seasonal 3 mos ahead. Accepts simultaneous submissions & reprints (tell when/where appeared). Guidelines; copy for 9x12 SAE/.90 postage or IRCs. (Ads)

> **Poetry:** Accepts 3/yr. Traditional; short. Submit max. 2 poems.
> **Fillers:** Accepts 6/yr. Anecdotes, cartoons, games, ideas, jokes, quizzes, short humor; to 250 wds.
> **Tips:** "Most open to devotional articles or short stories, true or fictional."

*FELLOWSHIP TODAY, Box 237, Barrie ON L4M 4T2, Canada. (705)737-0114. United Church Renewal Fellowship. Gail Reid, mng. ed. Not in topical listings.

#FELLOWSHIP TODAY, Fellowship Press, 4909 E. Buckeye Rd., Madison WI

53716. (608)221-1528. Fax (608)221-4934. E-mail: LAKECITY@MSN. FULLFEED.COM. Fellowship of Christian Assemblies. Kim Cortez, ed. Inspirational and teaching, informational. Monthly mag; circ 3,900. Subscription $10.60. 15% freelance. Query. Pays $7-20 on publication for 1st or reprint rts. Articles 500-1,800 wds (12/yr). Responds in 8 wks. Seasonal 3-4 mos ahead. Accepts simultaneous submissions. Guidelines; copy for 9x12 SAE/3 stamps. (Ads)

FIRST THINGS: A Monthly Journal of Religion and Public Life, 156 Fifth Ave., Ste. 400, New York NY 10010. (212)627-1985. Fax (212)627-2184. Website: http://www.firstthings.com. Institute on Religion & Public Life. James Nuechterlein, ed. Shows relation of religion and religious insights to contemporary issues of public life. Monthly (10X) mag; 64-84 pgs; circ 31,500. Subscription $29. 70% freelance. Complete ms/cover letter. Pays $250-700 on publication for all rts. Articles 4,000-6,000 wds, opinion 1,500 wds; (50-60/yr); book reviews, 1,500 wds, $125. Responds in 2 wks. Seasonal 4-5 mos ahead. Prefers disk. Kill fee. No sidebars. Guidelines; copy for 9x12 SAE/9 stamps. (Ads)

> **Poetry:** Poetry Editor. Buys 30/yr. Traditional; to 40 lines; $50.
>
> **Columns/Departments:** Opinion, 1,000-2,000 wds.
>
> **Tips:** "Most open to opinion and articles."

FOCUS ON THE FAMILY MAGAZINE, 8605 Explorer Dr., Colorado Springs CO 80920. (719)548-5881. Fax (719)531-3499. Focus on the Family. Tom Neven, ed. To help families utilize Christian principles in the problems and situations of everyday living. Monthly mag; 16 pgs; circ 2,500,000. Free to donors. 1% freelance. Query/clip; no phone/fax query. Pays $100-800 on acceptance for 1st rts. Articles 700-1,000 wds (8/yr). Responds in 2-3 wks. Seasonal 6 mos ahead. Accepts disk. Kill fee 25%. Sidebars OK. Prefers NIV. Guidelines; copy for 9x12 SAE/2 stamps.

> **Tips:** "This magazine is 99% generated from within our ministry. It's very hard to break in. Must be a unique look at a subject or very interesting topic not usually seen in our magazine, but still fitting the audience."
>
> **This periodical was #11 on the 1997 Top 50 Christian Publishers list (#54 in 1994).

#FOURSQUARE WORLD ADVANCE, 1910 W. Sunset Blvd., Ste. 200, Los Angeles CA 90026-0176. (213)484-2400. Fax (213)413-3824. E-mail: comm@ foursquare.org. Website: http://www.foursquare.org/advmag. International Church of the Foursquare Gospel. Dr. Ronald Williams, ed. Denominational. Bimonthly magazine; 23 pgs; circ 98,000. Subscription free. 5% freelance. Complete ms/cover letter. Pays $75 on publication for 1st, one-time, simultaneous, or reprint rts. Not copyrighted. Articles 1,000-1,200 wds (2-3/yr); fiction. Responds in 2 wks. Seasonal 6 mos ahead. Accepts simultaneous submissions & reprints. Sidebars OK. Free guidelines/theme list/copy. (Ads)

> **Poetry:** Buys 1-2/yr. Pays $50.
>
> **Fillers:** Buys 1-2/yr. Anecdotes, cartoons; 250-300 wds; $50.

+GADFLY MAGAZINE (formerly **RUTHERFORD MAGAZINE**), PO Box 7482, Charlottesville VA 22901. (804)975-1652. Fax (804)978-1789. E-mail: editor@ gadfly.org. Website: http://www.gadfly.org. Gadfly Productions. Amy Nickell, ed. Devoted to cultural advancement in education, literature, television, music, film and the arts; don't gear toward religious audience. Monthly mag; 28 pgs; circ.

18,000. Subscription $21. Est. 1996. 30% freelance. Query/clips; phone/fax/e-mail query OK. Pays $50-500 on acceptance for all rts. Articles 400-4,000 wds (10/yr); book/music/video reviews, 500 wds, pays $75-100. Responds in 4-12 wks. Seasonal 4 mos ahead. Accepts reprints (tell when/where appeared). Accepts disk. Kill fee. Sidebars OK. Guidelines; copy for 2 stamps. (Ads)

> **Tips:** "We almost never accept unsolicited mss. Instead we assign articles to freelancers. Best to send writing samples and ask to be added to our list of freelancers. Especially open to reviews written for general (including secular) audience. Also, articles on the arts and/or popular culture."

THE GEM, 700 E. Melrose Ave., Box 926, Findlay OH 45839-0926. (419)424-1961. Fax (419)424-3433. E-mail: ejs@brt.bright.net. Churches of God, General Conference. Evelyn J. Sloat, ed. Weekly take-home paper for adults; 8 pgs; circ 7,000. Subscription $9. 90% freelance. Complete ms/cover letter; e-mail query OK. Pays $7.50-15 on publication for one-time rts. Not copyrighted. Articles 100-1,500 wds (125/yr); fiction 100-1,500 wds. Responds in 8 wks. Seasonal 6 mos ahead. Accepts simultaneous submissions & reprints (tell when/where appeared). Accepts disk. No sidebars. Prefers NIV. Guidelines/copy for #10 SAE/1 stamp.

> **Poetry:** Buys 5/yr. Free verse, traditional. Pays $7.50. Submit max. 5 poems.
>
> **Fillers:** Buys 15/yr. Anecdotes, cartoons, prose, short humor; 100-200 wds. Pays $5.
>
> **Tips:** "We are accepting more material that is 400 wds or less as fillers (pays $5-10). Holiday material always welcome, although often we don't use it the first year we have it."

+GEMS OF TRUTH, PO Box 4060, Overland Park KS 66204. (913)432-0331. Fax (913)722-0351. Church of God (holiness)/Herald & Banner Press. Arlene McGehee, Sunday school ed. Denominational. Weekly adult take-home paper; 8 pgs; circ 14,000. Subscription $1.90. Complete ms/cover letter; phone/fax query OK. Pays .005/wd on publication for 1st rts. Fiction 1,000-2,000 wds. Seasonal 6-8 mos ahead. Accepts simultaneous submissions & reprints (tell when/where appeared). Prefers KJV. Guidelines/theme list; copy. Not in topical listings.

> **Poetry:** Traditional; pays .25/line.

+GENERAL BAPTIST MESSENGER, 400 Stinson Dr., Poplar Bluff MO 63901. (573)686-9051. Fax (573)686-5198. E-mail: Sam_Ramdial.PART1@F.CUNET. ORG. General Baptist Education and Publications, Inc. Sam Ramdial, ed. Denominational. Monthly mag; circ 5,600. Subscription $8. Open to freelance. Query. Not in topical listings. (Ads)

GOD'S REVIVALIST, 1810 Young St., Cincinnati OH 45210. (513)721-7944x296. Fax (513)721-3971. Larry Smith, ed. Salvation theme; Wesleyan persuasion. Monthly mag; 24 pgs; circ 20,000. Subscription $8. 75% freelance (currently overstocked). Complete ms/cover letter. **NO PAYMENT** for one-time rts. Articles 600-1,400 wds (3/yr). Responds in 9 wks. Seasonal 2 mos ahead. Accepts simultaneous submissions. Guidelines; copy $1/9x12 SAE.

> **Poetry:** Accepts 5/yr. Free verse, light verse, traditional; 8-20 lines. Submit max. 10 poems.
>
> **Fillers:** Accepts 5/yr. Facts, ideas, prose, short humor; 50-90 wds.
>
> **Tips:** "We need some information about the author."

+GOOD NEWS (AL), PO Box 26617, Hoover AL 35260-6617. (205)978-6008. Fax

(205)823-5263. E-mail: FJBritton@aol.com. Shades Mountain Independent Church. Jackie Britton, ed. Community newspaper with a Christian slant; not preachy. Bimonthly tabloid; 24 pgs; circ 20,000. Subscription free. 100% freelance. Complete ms/cover letter; phone/fax/e-mail query OK. **PAYS 3 COPIES** for one-time rts. Articles 300-600 wds (30/yr); fiction 500 wds (6/yr); book/music/video reviews, 300 wds (no pay). Responds in 3-4 wks. Seasonal 3 mos ahead. Accepts simultaneous submissions & reprints (tell when/where appeared). Accepts disk. Sidebars OK. Guidelines; copy for 9x12 SAE/2 stamps. (Ads)

Poetry: Accepts 3-4/yr. Light verse, traditional; 8-12 lines.

Fillers: Anecdotes, cartoons, facts, ideas, jokes, quizzes, quotes, short humor, word puzzles; 100-200 wds.

Tips: "We especially like articles dealing with Alabamians and/or life-changing situations."

GOOD NEWS (KY), 308 E. Main St., Wilmore KY 40390. (606)858-4661. Fax (606)858-4972. E-mail: gnmag@aol.com. Website: http://www.goshen.net/gnm, United Methodist/Forum for Scriptural Christianity, Inc. Steve Beard, ed. Focus is evangelical renewal within the denomination. Bimonthly mag; 44 pgs; circ 65,000. Subscription $20. 20% freelance. Query only; no phone/fax/e-mail query. Pays .05-.07/wd on publication for one-time rts. Articles 1,500 wds (25/yr). Responds in 24 wks. Seasonal 6 mos ahead. Accepts simultaneous submissions & reprints (tell when/where appeared). Accepts disk. Kill fee. Sidebars OK. Prefers NIV. Guidelines; copy $2.75/9x12 SAE. (Ads)

Tips: "Most open to features."

GOOD NEWS, ETC., PO Box 2660, Vista CA 92085. (760)724-3075. Fax (760)724-8311. E-mail: rmonroe@goodnewsetc.com. Good News Publishers, Inc. of California. Rick Monroe, ed. Feature stories and local news of interest to Christians in San Diego County. Monthly tabloid; 24-32 pgs; circ 40,000. Subscription $15. 2% freelance. Query; e-mail query OK. Pays $20 on publication for all, 1st, one-time or reprint rts. Articles 500-700 wds (15/yr). Responds in 2 wks. Seasonal 2 mos ahead. Accepts simultaneous submissions & reprints (tell when/where appeared). Prefers disk. Sidebars OK. Prefers NIV. Guidelines/theme list; copy for 9x12 SAE/4 stamps. (Ads)

Tips: "Most open to local, personality-type articles."

** 1994 EPA Award of Merit—Newspaper.

#GOOD NEWS JOURNAL, Box 1882, 10900 E Hwy WW, Columbia MO 65205. (573)875-8755. Fax (573)874-4964. E-mail: goodnews@digmo.org. Good News Publishers. Lenna Truman, ed. Christian newspaper for mid-Missouri area. Monthly (10X) tabloid; 16 pgs; circ 35,000. Subscription $20. 25% freelance. Query/clips; phone/fax query OK. **NO PAYMENT**, for one-time rts. Not copyrighted. Articles 250-1,000 wds (12-24/yr); kid's fiction 500-1,000 wds (6-12/yr); book/music reviews, 50-100 wds. Responds in 9 wks. Seasonal 2 mos ahead. Accepts simultaneous submissions & reprints. Prefers disk. Sidebars OK. Copy $1/ 9x12 SAE. (Ads)

Fillers: Accepts 12/yr. Cartoons, games, quizzes, quotes, word puzzles.

Columns/Departments: Accepts 12/yr. Good News Kids (fiction for kids up to 12 yrs), 500-750 wds; Golden Digest (testimonies or devotionals for those over 55), 1,000 wds.

Special Needs: Testimonies of healing with verification of physician.

Tips: "Interested in testimonies and personal experience stories that illustrate Christian growth or Christian principles."

+GOOD NEWS—SALEM, 1164 Madison St. NE, Salem OR 97303. (503)315-2094. E-mail: GNAmerica@juno.com. Ed Mongo, pub. The first in a series of local Christian newspapers that will reach both Christians & non-Christians. Monthly newspaper; 16-24 pgs. Subscription $15. Est. 1997. Query; phone/e-mail query OK. Pays $10-25 (wants donated articles through 1998) on publication. Articles & little fiction. (Ads)

Poetry: Buys 12-24/yr. Any type. Pays $5-10. Submit max. 3 poems.

Fillers: Anecdotes, cartoons, facts, games, ideas, jokes, newsbreaks, prayers, prose, quizzes, quotes, short humor, word puzzles; 50-500 wds. Pays $5-25.

Columns/Departments: Uses many.

Tips: "Most areas open. Looking for a wide variety of Christian and good human-interest articles; items that encourage, uplift, and bring out the positive."

+THE GOOD SHEPHERD, 171 White Plains Rd., Bronxville NY 10708. (914)337-5172. Fax (914)779-5274. E-mail: shepherd@concordia-ny.edu. Website: http://www.shepherdcenter.org. A publication for Christian families. Viji George, mng. ed. Quarterly mag. Incomplete topical listings.

GOSPEL TIDINGS, 5800 S. 14th St., Omaha NE 68104-3584. (402)731-4780. Fax (402)731-1173. E-mail: febcoma@aol.com. Fellowship of Evangelical Bible Churches. Robert L. Frey, ed. To inform, educate and edify members of affiliate churches. Bimonthly mag; 20 pgs; circ 2,300. Subscription $8. 5% freelance. Complete ms/cover letter; fax/e-mail query OK. Pays to $15-35 on publication for all rts. Articles (2/yr) & fiction (1/yr); 1,500/2,500 wds. Responds ASAP. Seasonal 3 mos ahead. Accepts simultaneous submissions & reprints (tell when/where appeared). Accepts disk. Some sidebars. Prefers NIV. Guidelines; copy for 9x12 SAE/3 stamps.

Poetry: Light verse, traditional.

GOSPEL TODAY MAGAZINE, 761 Old Hickory Blvd. Ste. 205, Brentwood TN 37027. (615)376-5656. Fax (615)376-0882. E-mail: gospel@usit.net. Website: http://www.gospeltoday.com. Horizon Concepts. Iris Raeshaun, assoc. ed. Ministry and Christian/gospel music; Christian lifestyles directed toward African Americans. Bimonthly (8X) mag; 60 pgs; circ 50,000. Subscription $20. 50% freelance. Query; fax query OK. Pays $150-250 on publication for all, one-time or simultaneous rts. Articles 1,000-3,500 wds (4/yr); book reviews 1,00-1,500 wds. Responds in 4 wks. Seasonal 4 mos ahead. Requires disk. Kill fee 15%. Sidebars OK. Prefers KJV. Guidelines/theme list; copy for 10x13 SAE/8 stamps. (Ads)

Poetry: Accepts.

Columns/Departments: Precious Memories (historic overview of renowned personality), 1,500-2,000 wds; From the Pulpit (issue-oriented observation from clergy), 2,500-3,000 wds; Life & Style (travel, health, beauty, fashion tip, etc.), 1,500-2,500 wds. **NO PAYMENT.**

Tips: "Looking for more human-interest pieces—ordinary people doing extraordinary things."

+GRAIL: An Ecumenical Journal, 223 Main St., Ottawa ON K1S 1C4 Canada.

(613)782-3036. Fax (613)751-4020. E-mail: cgreen@spu.stpaul.uottawa.ca. Novalis–St. Paul University. Caryl Green, mng. ed. A contemporary and ecumenical journal. Quarterly journal; 100 pgs; circ 1,300. Subscription $22 CAN & $25 US. 80% freelance. Complete ms/cover letter; phone/fax/e-mail query OK. Pays an honorarium on publication for all rts. Articles 1,000-2,000 wds (12/yr); fiction 1,000-1,500 wds (4/yr); book reviews, 1,000 wds, $50. Responds in 3-4 wks. Prefers disk. Sidebars OK. Prefers NRSV or Jerusalem. Copy for 7x10 SASE.

Poetry: Buys 16-20/yr. Free verse, traditional; $25.

GREEN CROSS MAGAZINE, 10 E. Lancaster Ave., Wynnewood PA 19096. (610)645-9390. Fax (610)649-8090. E-mail: gcross@esa.mhs.compuserve.com. Evangelicals for Social Action. Michael Crook, ed. For Christians who care about earth stewardship. Quarterly mag; 20 pgs; circ 5,000. Subscription $25. 90% freelance. Query; fax/e-mail query OK. Query for electronic submissions (crook@esa.online.org). Pays to $150 on publication for one-time & electronic rts. Articles 500-1,200 wds (20/yr); book reviews 200 wds (no payment). Responds in 6-8 wks. Seasonal 4 mos ahead. Accepts reprints (tell when/where appeared). Prefers disk. Sidebars OK. Prefers NRSV or NIV. Guidelines; copy for 10x13 SAE/4 stamps. (Ads)

Poetry: All types; 5-30 lines. No payment. Submit max. 3 poems.

Fillers: Buys 10-12/yr. Cartoons, newsbreaks, prayers, short humor; 50-250 wds; $10-25.

Tips: "Looking for well-written personal testimony on writer's discovery of Christian/biblical basis for conservation. Other than that, we don't need articles that say "What a surprise! The Bible says to care for God's creation."

GUIDEPOSTS, 16 E 34th St., New York NY 10016. (212)251-8100. Website: http://www.guideposts.org. Interfaith. Submit to The Editor. Personal faith stories showing how faith in God helps each person cope with life in some particular way. Monthly mag; 48 pgs; circ 3.8 million. Subscription $13.94. 60% freelance. Complete ms/cover letter. Pays $250-500 on acceptance for all rts. Articles 750-1,500 wds (75/yr). Responds in 4-8 wks. Seasonal 6 mos ahead. Accepts simultaneous submissions. Kill fee 25%. Some sidebars. Free guidelines/copy.

Poetry: Celeste McCauley. Buys 6/yr. Free verse, light verse, traditional; 2-12 lines; $15-25. Submit max. 2 poems.

Fillers: Celeste McCauley. Buys 15-20/yr. Anecdotes; quotes, short humor; 10-200 wds; $25-100.

Columns/Departments: Celeste McCauley. Buys 24/yr. His Mysterious Ways (divine intervention), 250 wds; What Prayer Can Do, 250 wds; Angels Among Us, 400 wds; Divine Touch (tangible evidence of God's help), 400 wds. ("This is our most open area. Write in 3rd person."); $100.

Contest: Writers Workshop Contest held on even years with June 30 deadline. Also Young Writers Contest; $25,000 college scholarship; best stories to 1,200 wds; deadline November 30.

Tips: "Be able to tell a good story, with drama, suspense, description and dialogue. The point of the story should be some practical spiritual help the reader receives from what the author learned through his experience." First person only.

** This periodical was #47 on the 1996 Top 50 Christian Publishers list. (#54 in 1995, #44 in 1994)

*HALLELUJAH!, PO Box 223, Postal Stn. A, Vancouver BC V6C 2M3 Canada. (604)498-3895. Cable: Hallelujah. Bible Holiness Movement. Wesley H. Wakefield, ed. For evangelism and promotion of holiness revivals; readership mostly ethnic, non-white minorities. Bimonthly mag; 32-40 pgs; circ 5,000. Subscription $5. 3-5% freelance. Query or complete ms; no phone query. Pays $10-50 on acceptance for one-time or simultaneous rts. Articles 300-2,500 wds (4/yr). Responds in 5 wks. Accepts simultaneous submissions & reprints (tell when/where appeared). No disk. No sidebars. Prefers KJV. Guidelines; copy for 6x9 SAE/$1 postage.

> **Poetry:** Buys 4/yr. Traditional, hymn length (5 stanzas). Pays $5 or royalties. Submit max. 5 poems. Prefers poetry of hymn or song quality with identifiable meter.
>
> **Fillers:** Buys few. Prefers striking quotes from early Methodism or salvationers; 10-50 wds; $5.
>
> **Special Needs:** Spiritual warfare; religious conditions in southern Sudan; child labor/slavery; and Christian revival movements.
>
> **Ethnic:** Distributes to Nigeria, Canada and US
>
> **Tips:** "Avoid Americanisms. No Calvinistic articles or premillenialism. Be very familiar with evangelistic emphasis, doctrines, life standards, social stands of holiness churches."

+HARVEST PRESS, PO Box 2876, Newport News VA 23609. (757)886-0713. Fax (757)886-1295. E-mail: EPublish@Juno.com. Tyrone Campbell, ed. To proclaim the gospel of Jesus Christ, to reach the unreached and promote unity within the body of Christ. Monthly newspaper; circ 20,000. Subscription $25. Open to freelance. Query. Not in topical listings. (Ads)

*HARVEST TIMES, PO Box 868, Cleveland TX 77328. (713)592-4224. George Brohawn, ed. To spread the gospel, unite the church body, strengthen families and the community, encourage the body, and bring good community news. Biweekly newspaper; circ 3,000. Subscription $20. Open to freelance. Not in topical listings. (Ads)

HEAD TO HEAD, PO Box 711, St. Johnsbury VT 05819-0711. Phone/fax (802)748-8000. E-mail: hthtbi@aol.com. Website: http://www.bypass.com/~pwebb/hth.htm. Nondenominational. Paul A. Webb, ed-in-chief. Shows Christ as the greatest hope for brain-injury survivors and caretakers. Irregularly published mag; 24+ pgs; circ world-wide on the Internet. Subscription free on the Internet. 50% freelance. Complete ms/cover letter; fax query OK. **PAYS IN COPIES** for 1st rts. Articles 250-1,200 wds (to 36/yr); fiction for all ages 500-1,000 wds; book/music/video reviews, 500 wds. Responds in 8 wks. Seasonal 6 mos ahead. Accepts reprints. Prefers disk. Guidelines/theme list for #10 SAE/2 stamps.

> **Poetry:** Accepts 12/yr. All types, 4-60 lines. Submit max. 5 poems.
>
> **Fillers:** Most types; 50-250 wds.
>
> **Columns/Departments:** Tips & Hints; Caregiver Concerns & Family Matters, 250 wds.
>
> **Special Needs:** All topics should relate to brain injury, traumatic or congenital brain injury, cerebral palsy, encephalitis, multiple sclerosis, strokes, or alcohol/drug-induced brain injury.

New Features: Articles and stories about (1) Christian Evangelism, (2) Prophetic exhortation and admonition to the Christian church, its leadership and parishioners, (3) Current issues and the biblical view.

Tips: "Need how-tos on survival, coping skills, cognitive strategies, social skills, job skills, and communication."

THE HEALING INN, 18524 Linden N. #306, Shoreline WA 98133. Phone/fax (206)542-0210. Christian Airline Personnel Missionary Outreach. June Shafhid, ed. Offers healing for Christians wounded by a church or religious cult. Semiannual mag; 20 pgs; circ. 5,000. No subscriptions. 100% freelance. Complete ms; phone/fax query OK. **PAYS IN COPIES** for 1st or reprint rts. Articles 500-2,500 wds; fiction 500-3,000 wds. Responds in 3-4 wks. Seasonal 6 mos ahead. Accepts simultaneous submissions & reprints (tell when/where appeared). No disk. Some sidebars. Prefers KJV, NIV or NAS. Theme list; free copy. (Ads)

Poetry: All types; 5-20 lines. Accepts 10-20/yr. Submit max. 10 poems.

Fillers: Accepts 20/yr. Anecdotes, facts, games, ideas, jokes, newsbreaks, prose, quizzes, prayers, quotes, short humor, word puzzles.

Tips: "All areas open. Looking for stories that will woo the lost back to Christ."

*HEARING HEARTS, 4 Silo Mill Ct., Sterling VA 20164. Phone/fax (703)430-7387. American Ministries to the Deaf. Beverly Cox, ed. For deaf adults and those with whom they live, work and worship. Quarterly mag; 24 pgs; circ 500. Subscription $12. 75% freelance. Query/clips; phone/fax query OK. **PAYS IN COPIES.** Articles 100-600 wds (50-100/yr). Responds in 2 wks. Seasonal 3 mos ahead. Sidebars OK. Theme list; copy for 9x12 SAE/4 stamps.

Poetry: Accepts 100/yr. Free verse, haiku, light verse, traditional; 5-30 lines. Submit max. 5 poems.

Fillers: Cartoons, games, ideas, party ideas, quizzes, word puzzles.

Special Needs: Wants interviews with interesting deaf Christians.

Tips: "Needs Bible-application articles—lively & brief. Best if it can have a deaf twist—not using standard verses that refer to deaf. Show creativity to touch people within the 'don't fix me; I ain't broke' deaf culture."

+HEARTLIGHT INTERNET MAGAZINE, 8332 Mesa Dr., Austin TX 78759. (514)345-6386. Fax (512)345-6634. E-mail: phil@heartlight.org. Website: http://www.hearlight.org. Phil Ware, pres. Offers positive Christian resources for living in today's world. Weekly e-zine (see Website above); 20+ pgs; circ 6,000. Subscription free. Est. 1996. 20% freelance. E-mail query. **NO PAYMENT** for electronic rts. Articles 300-450 wds (25-35/yr); fiction 500-700 wds (12-15/yr). Responds in 3 wks. Seasonal 2 mos ahead. Accepts simultaneous submissions & reprints (tell when/where appeared). Prefers disk or e-mail. Sidebars OK. Prefers NIV. Copy available on the Internet.

Poetry: Accepts 10/yr. Free verse, light verse, traditional. Submit max. 10 poems.

Fillers: Accepts 12/yr. Anecdotes, cartoons, games, ideas, jokes, newsbreaks, prayers, prose, quotes, short humor, word puzzles; to 350 wds.

Tips: "Most open to feature articles, Just for Men or Just for Women, or Heartlight for Children."

+HEAVENLY THOUGHTS NEWSLETTER, PO Box 700, Bellevue NE 68005-

0700. E-mail: LeeWJr@aol.com. Website: http://www.trader.com/users/5011/ 3495/Heaven.htm. Lee Warren, ed. For the Christian who wants to mature in faith and the searching nonbeliever. Quarterly newsletter; 12 pgs; circ 430. Subscription free (donations). 100% freelance. Complete ms. **PAYS 5 COPIES** one-time, reprint, simultaneous, and electronic rts. Articles to 1,500 wds (35/yr); fiction to 1,500 wds (4/yr); book reviews 1,500 wds. Responds in 8 wks. Seasonal 3 mos ahead. Accepts simultaneous submissions & reprints (tell when/where appeared). Accepts disk. Few sidebars. Guidelines; copy for 2 stamps. (Ads)

Poetry: Accepts 12-15/yr. Any type or length.

Fillers: Accepts 4-6/yr. Anecdotes, prayers, prose.

Tips: "Written in a free format—no departments or themes. No divisive issues. Write clearly and concisely, with a specific point."

HERALD OF HOLINESS, 6401 The Paseo, Kansas City MO 64131. (816)333-7000 x2302. Fax (816)333-1748. Church of the Nazarene. Wes Eby, ed. Not accepting freelance material this year.

** This periodical was #16 on the 1997 Top 50 Christian Publishers list.

HIGHWAY NEWS AND GOOD NEWS, PO. Box 303, Denver PA 17517-0303. (717)721-9800. Fax (717)721-9351. E-mail: GoTFC@aol.com. Lisa Graham, ed. For truck drivers and their families; evangelistic; with articles for Christian growth. Monthly mag; 16 pgs; circ 35,000. Subscription $25. 75% freelance. Complete ms/cover letter; phone, fax, e-mail query OK. **PAYS IN COPIES** for rights offered. Articles 600 or 1,200 wds & fiction 1,200-1,400 wds. Seasonal 4 mos ahead. Accepts simultaneous submissions & reprints (tell when/where appeared). Accepts disk. Some sidebars. Prefers NIV. Guidelines/theme list; free copy for 9x12 SAE.

Fillers: Short humor, 100 wds.

Tips: "All articles/stories must relate to truckers; need pieces on marriage, parenting, and fatherhood. Most open to features."

#HOMESCHOOLING TODAY, PO Box 1425, Melrose FL 32666. Phone/fax (352)475-3088. E-mail: 74672.2004@compuserve.com. S. Squared Productions. Debbie Ward, ed. To equip and minister to homeschool parents/teachers with ready-to-use products and resources for the purpose of educating their children. Bimonthly; circ 21,000. Subscription $17.95. Open to freelance. Query. (Ads)

HOME TIMES, 3676 Collins Dr. #12, West Palm Beach FL 33406. (561)439-3509. E-mail: hometimes@aol.com. Neighbor News, Inc. Dennis Lombard, ed/pub. Conservative, pro-Christian community newspaper. Monthly tabloid; 24 pgs; circ 4,000. Subscription $12. 50% freelance. Complete ms only/cover letter; no phone/e-mail query. Pays $5-25 on publication for one-time rts. Articles 200-800 wds (20/yr); fiction 200-800 wds (5/yr); book/video reviews 400 wds ($5); video reviews 400 wds; $5-15. Responds in 3-4 wks. Seasonal 6 wks ahead. Accepts simultaneous submissions & reprints (tell when/where appeared). No disk. Sidebars OK. Prefers NIV. Guidelines; 1 copy for $1/3 for $3. (Ads)

Poetry: Buys 6/yr. Light verse, traditional; 2-32 lines; $5. Submit max. 3 poems.

Fillers: Accepts 15-20/yr. Anecdotes, cartoons, jokes, newsbreaks, quotes, short humor; 25-100 wds; pays 6 issues.

Columns/Departments: Buys 20/yr. See guidelines for columns, to 600 wds; $5-15.

Special Needs: Articles on heroes and angels.

Contest: May do one in 1998.

Tips: "Very open to new writers, but study guidelines and sample first; we are different. We need timely movie reviews, not too moralistic. Published by Christians, but not religious."

#IDEALS MAGAZINE, Ideals Publishing, Inc., PO Box 305300, Nashville TN 37230-5300. (615)333-0478. Lisa Ragan, ed. Seasonal, inspirational, nostalgic magazine for mature men and women of traditional values. Mag published 6 times/yr; 88 pgs; circ 180,000. Subscription $19.95. 95% freelance. Complete ms/cover letter; no phone query. Pays .10/wd on publication for one-time rts. Articles 800-1,000 wds (20/yr). Responds in 13 wks. Seasonal 8 mos ahead. Accepts simultaneous submissions & reprints (tell when/where appeared). No disk. No sidebars. Prefers KJV. Guidelines; copy $4.

> **Poetry:** Buys 100+/yr. Free verse, light verse, traditional; 8-40 lines; $10. Submit max. 5 poems.

> **Tips:** "Most open to optimistic poetry oriented around a season or theme."

*IMMACULATE HEART MESSENGER, 240 - 5th St. W., Alexandria SD 57311-0158. Catholic/Fatima Family Apostate. Fr. Robert J. Fox, ed. Bimonthly mag; circ. 10,000. Subscription $13. 50% freelance. **NO PAYMENT** for one-time rts. Articles 5 double-spaced pgs. Seasonal 6 mos ahead. Not in topical listings.

#IMPACT MAGAZINE, 12 B East Coast Rd., 1542 Singapore XX 428723. 65-345-0444. Fax 65-345-3045. Evangelical Fellowship of Singapore. Andrew Goh, ed. To help young working adults apply Christian principles to contemporary issues. Bimonthly mag; circ 6,000. Subscription $12. 10-15% freelance. Query or complete ms/cover letter; phone query OK. **NO PAYMENT** up to $20/pg, for all rts. Articles (12/yr) & fiction (6/yr); 1,000-2,000 wds. Seasonal 2 mos ahead. Accepts reprints. Copy for $3 & $1.70 postage (surface mail). (Ads)

> **Poetry:** Accepts 2-3 poems/yr. Free verse, 20-40 lines. Submit max. 3 poems.

> **Fillers:** Accepts 6/yr. Anecdotes, cartoons, jokes, quizzes, short humor, and word puzzles.

> **Columns/Departments:** Closing Thoughts (current social issues), 600-800 wds; Testimony (personal experience), 1,500-2,000 wds; Parenting (Asian context), 1,000-1,500 wds.

> **Tips:** "We're most open to fillers."

#INDIAN LIFE, PO Box 3765, RPO Redwood Center, Winnipeg MB R2W 3R6 Canada. US address: Box 32, Pembina ND 58271. (204)661-9333. Fax (204)661-3982. E-mail: indianlife@compuserve.com. Website: http://www.indianlife.org. Indian Life Ministries. Jim Uttley, ed; Viola Fehr, asst. ed. An evangelistic publication for English-speaking aboriginal people in North America. Bimonthly newspaper; 16 pgs; circ 38,000. Subscription $7. 20% freelance. Query; fax/e-mail query OK. **NO PAYMENT** for 1st rts. Articles 1,000-1,200 wds (6/yr). Responds in 4 wks. Seasonal 6 mos ahead. Accepts reprints. Sidebars OK. Accepts disk. Guidelines; copy $1. (Ads)

> **Columns/Departments:** Jim Uttley. Accepts 12/yr. Family Life (native families); Native Business (natives in business); Crossword Puzzles; native pastor's column; all 500 wds.

> **Tips:** "Most open to historical pieces, news items and personal experience.

Native authors preferred, but some others are published. Aim at an 8th grade reading level; short paragraphs; avoid multi-syllable words and long sentences."

#INLAND NORTHWEST CHRISTIAN NEWS, 222 W. Mission #132, Spokane WA 99201. (509)328-0820. Fax (509)326-4921. Zeda Leonard, ed. To inform, motivate and encourage evangelical Christians in Spokane and the inland Northwest. Newspaper published 18X/yr; 12 pgs; circ 2,500. Subscription $17.95. 30% freelance. Query; phone query OK. Pays $1/column inch on publication for 1st rts. Articles 500 wds. Responds in 9 wks. Copy $1.50. (Ads)

#INSIDE JOURNAL, PO Box 17429, Washington DC 20041-0429. (703)478-0100x560. Fax (703)318-0235. E-mail: 74171.511@compuserve.com. Prison Fellowship Ministries. Terry White, ed. To proclaim the gospel to non-Christian prisoners within the context of a prison newspaper. Bimonthly (8X) tabloid; circ 375,000. Subscription $10. 60% freelance. Query; phone/fax/e-mail query OK. Modest payment, depending on situation, on acceptance for one-time rts. Articles to 1,200 wds (25/yr). Responds in 4 wks. Seasonal 4 mos ahead. Accepts disk. Sidebars OK. Guidelines; free copy. (Ads)

> **Columns/Departments:** Buys 15-20/yr. Shortimer (those preparing for release within 6 wks), 500 wds; Especially for Women (issues for incarcerated women), 600-800 wds. Variable payment.

> **Tips:** "Always need seasonal material for Christmas, Easter and Thanksgiving. Also celebrity stories that demonstrate triumph over adversity."

> ** 1995 EPA Award of Merit—Newspaper.

+INSIGHTS, 15 - 1725 - 30th Ave. NE, Calgary AB T2E 7P6 Canada. (403)291-3179. Fax (403)291-9674. E-mail: yfccal@cadvision.com. Youth for Christ/Calgary. Doug Willems, ed. Encouragement for Christian living, especially for families. Quarterly mag; 24 pgs; circ 13,500. Subscription free. 30% freelance. Complete ms/cover letter; phone/fax/e-mail query OK. Query for electronic submissions. Pays $25 on publication for one-time rts. Not copyrighted. Articles 500-1,200 wds (8/yr); fiction 500-1,200 wds (4/yr). Responds in 4 wks. Seasonal 3 mos ahead. Accepts simultaneous submissions & reprints (tell when/where appeared). Prefers disk. Sidebars OK. Prefers NIV. No guidelines; theme list/copy for 9x12 SAE/4 stamps. (Ads)

> **Poetry:** Buys 4/yr. Light verse, traditional; 5-30 lines. Pays to $25. Submit max. 5 poems.

> **Fillers:** Buys 8yr. Anecdotes, cartoons, facts, jokes, newsbreaks, prayers, prose, quizzes, quotes, short humor; 10-500 wds. Pays $25.

> **Tips:** "Call editor and talk to us directly about your ideas. We're pretty open (and flexible) to new ideas. We value personal experience stories quite highly (especially if they are local). Particularly interested in stories from Alberta writers, but we accept all others too."

#INSPIRATIONAL NEWS NETWORK, 20 Main St., Shenandoah PA 17976-2016. (717)628-2166. Fax (717)628-2167. Shirley C. Cicioni, pres/ed. A syndication that distributes articles dealing with news from an inspirational point of view. Not in topical listings.

THE INSPIRER, 737 Kimsey Ln. #620, Henderson KY 42420-4917. (502)826-5720. Billy Edwards, ed. To encourage believers in their Christian life. (Especially open to writers who are physically disabled.) Quarterly newsletter; 8 pgs; circ 2,500. Subscription for donation. 50% freelance. Query. Articles 250-700 wds (15/yr); fiction 250-500 wds (5/yr); book reviews, 500 wds. **PAYS IN COPIES/SUBSCRIPTION.** Not copyrighted. Responds in 2 wks. Seasonal 2 mos ahead. Accepts simultaneous submissions & reprints. No sidebars. Prefers KJV. Guidelines; copy for #10 SASE/2 stamps.

> **Poetry:** Accepts 5-10/yr. Traditional, 10-50 lines. Submit max. 3 poems.
>
> **Fillers:** Accepts 10-15/yr. Anecdotes, cartoons, facts, games, ideas, jokes, newsbreaks, prose, quizzes, prayers, quotes, short humor, word puzzles; 50-250 wds.
>
> **Columns/Departments:** Accepts 10/yr. Let the Redeemed Say So (testimonies), 250-500 wds; The Lighter Side (humor), to 300 wds.
>
> **Special Needs:** Issues of interest to (and from) the physically disabled; biblically based and Christ-centered.

*INTERCHANGE, 412 Sycamore St., Cincinnati OH 45202. (513)421-0311. Fax (513)421-0315. Episcopal. Michael R. Barwell, ed. Regional paper for the Episcopal and Anglican Church in southern Ohio. Bimonthly tabloid; 28 pgs; circ 12,600. Free. 5% freelance. Query or complete ms/cover letter. Pays $35-50 on publication for all rts. Articles 500-2,000 wds (1-2/yr). Responds in 9 wks. Accepts simultaneous submissions. Prefers disk (Mac compatible). Sidebars OK. Copy for 9x12 SASE.

> **Tips:** "Most open to features, especially with a local angle."

*THE INTERIM, 53 Dundas St. E. #306, Toronto ON M5B 1C6 Canada. (416)368-0250. Fax (416)368-8575. Catholic. Peter Muggeridge, ed. Abortion, euthanasia, pornography, feminism and religion from a pro-life perspective. Monthly newspaper; circ 25,000. 50% freelance. Query; phone query OK. Pays $100-150 CAN, on publication. Articles 700-1,000 wds. Responds in 2 wks. Seasonal 2 mos ahead. Accepts simultaneous submissions & reprints.

ISLAND CHRISTIAN INFO, PO Box 5062, Sta. B, Victoria BC V8R 6N3 Canada. (250)592-6071. Fax (250)592-8217. E-mail: cine@ampsc.com. Vancouver Island Christian Communication Society. Adele Wickett, ed. Easy-to-read local news and inspiration for churches and businesses on Vancouver Island. Monthly tabloid; 20 pgs; circ. 13,000. Subscription $20, $25 US 98% freelance. Query; fax/e-mail query OK. Not copyrighted. **NO PAYMENT.** Articles 200-400 wds; a few book/music reviews, 400 wds. Seasonal 2 mos ahead. Accepts simultaneous submissions & reprints (tell when/where appeared). Prefers disk. Prefers NIV. Copy for 9x12 SAE/IRCs or $1. (Ads)

> **Fillers:** Anecdotes; accepts few.

*JEWEL AMONG JEWELS ADOPTION NEWS, 9302 Seascape Dr., Indianapolis IN 46256. Phone/fax (317)849-5651. Independent Christian. Sherrie Eldridge, ed. Targets the interests and needs of adoptees and those touched by adoption. Quarterly newsletter; circ. 1,500. Free subscription in US. Est. 1994. Complete ms/cover letter; fax/e-mail query OK. **NO PAYMENT.** Articles 250-500 wds. Responds in 2 wks. Seasonal 3 mos ahead. Accepts simultaneous submissions & reprints. Prefers disk. Prefers NIV. Guidelines/theme list; copy for 1 stamp.

> **Poetry:** Free verse, traditional. Submit any number.
>
> **Fillers:** Accepts 10/yr. Anecdotes, cartoons, facts, ideas, newsbreaks, prose,

quizzes, prayers, quotes, short humor, word puzzles; 25-300 wds.

Columns/Departments: Common Threads, Passages of Adoption, The Great Awakening, Trigger Points, Reframing the Loss, The Blessings of Adoption; all 250 wds. See guidelines for descriptions.

Special Needs: Adoptive parenting, adoption, grief & loss, identity in Christ, bonding & attachment perspectives, 12-step writing about adoption, how to find therapist who understands adoption issues.

Tips: "Most open to columns and transparent testimonials from adoptees willing to share their stories."

JOHN MILTON MAGAZINE, 475 Riverside Dr., Rm. 455, New York NY 10115. (212)870-3335. Fax (212)870-3229. John Milton Society for the Blind/nonsectarian. Darcy Quigley, mng dir. Reprints material from over 60 religious periodicals in a large-type digest for the visually impaired. Quarterly tabloid; 24 pgs; circ 5,285. Free to visually impaired. 1% freelance. Complete ms/cover letter; fax query OK. **NO PAYMENT,** for reprint rts. Not copyrighted. Articles 750-1,500 (1/yr); fiction 750-1,500 (1/yr). Responds in 6 wks. Seasonal 9-12 mos ahead. Accepts simultaneous submissions & reprints (tell when/where appeared). Accepts disk. Few sidebars. Guidelines; copy for 9x12 SAE/3 stamps.

Poetry: Accepts 4/yr. Any type; 5-30 lines. Submit max. 3 poems. Seasonal/holiday.

Fillers: Accepts 1/yr. Anecdotes, cartoons, facts, games, prayers, prose, quotes, short humor; 10-150 wds.

Tips: "Most open to poetry/prayers pertaining to Christian holidays/seasonal themes and visual impairments. If writing about blindness, don't be patronizing. Send complete manuscripts requiring little or no editing. Look at the magazines we typically reprint from (see guidelines)."

JOURNAL OF CHRISTIAN NURSING, PO Box 1650, Downers Grove IL 60515-0780. (630)887-2500. Fax (630)887-2520. E-mail: jcn@ivpress.com. Nurses Christian Fellowship of InterVarsity Christian Fellowship. Melodee Yohe, mng. ed. Personal, professional, practical articles that help nurses integrate Christian faith with nursing profession. Quarterly mag.; 48 pgs; circ 9,000. Subscription $19.95. 35% freelance. Complete ms/cover letter; phone/fax query OK. Pays $25-80 on publication for all (rarely), one-time or reprint rts (few). Not copyrighted. Articles 6-12 pgs (20/yr). Responds in 4-6 wks. Seasonal 1 yr ahead. Accepts some reprints (tell when/where appeared). Accepts disk. Kill fee 50%. Sidebars OK. Prefers NRSV. Guidelines/theme list; copy $4.50/9x12 SAE/6 stamps. (Ads)

Columns/Departments: Pulse Beats (this and that).

Special Needs: Congregational health, nursing history, environmental issues, professional issues, conflict management, and dealing with disabilities.

Contests: Sponsors an occasional contest. None planned for now.

Tips: "All topics must relate to nursing, or contain illustrations using nurses. freelancers can interview and write about Christian nurses involved in creative ministry (include pictures). Interview/profile a Christian nurse involved in a creative ministry."

** 1996 EPA Award of Merit—Christian Ministry.

JOURNAL OF CHURCH AND STATE, Baylor University, PO Box 97308, Waco

TX 76798-7308. (254)710-1510. Fax (254)710-1571. E-mail: Derek_Davis@ Baylor.edu. Baylor University/Interdenominational. Dr. Derek H. Davis, dir. Provides a forum for the critical examination of the interaction of religion and government worldwide. Quarterly jour; 225 pgs; circ 1,700. Subscription $20. 50% freelance. Complete ms (3 copies)/cover letter. **NO PAYMENT** for all rights. Articles 25-30 pgs/footnotes (24/yr). Responds in 6-8 wks. Prefers disk. No sidebars. Guidelines; copy $8 + $1.50 postage. (Ads)

Special Needs: Church-state issues.

*JOYFUL NOISE, 4259 Elkcam Blvd. SE, St. Petersburg FL 33705-4216. Nondenominational. William W. Maxwell, ed. Deals with African-American life and religious culture. Bimonthly mag. Est. 1993. Complete ms/cover letter or query/clips. Pays $50-250 on acceptance for 1st rts. Articles 700-3,000 wds. Guidelines.

#JOYFUL NOISE: A Journal of Christian Poetry, PO Box 401, Bowling Green KY 42102. (502)781-3831. Jim Erskine, ed. Christian-oriented poetry. Quarterly. Est. 1996. Accepts simultaneous submissions. Complete ms. **PAYS IN COPIES-** for one-time rts. Responds in 5 wks. Guidelines/copy.

Poetry: Christian; any style; to 25 lines.

Tips: "We prefer personal, small subjects, over large themes such as love, brotherhood, etc. No political, new age, or social issues."

#THE KANSAS CHRISTIAN, PO Box 47003, Topeka KS 66647. (913)273-4424. Fax (913)272-5595. E-mail: ChrstnNews@aol.com. Eagle Christians, Inc. Everett R. Daves, ed. To promote the gospel of Jesus Christ. Weekly; circ 4,000. Subscription $18 donation. Open to freelance. Query or complete ms. Not in topical listings. (Ads)

*KENTUCKY CHRISTIAN NEWS, 3191 Nicholasville Rd., Ste. 600, Lexington KY 40503. Beverly Byrd, ed. Christian Newspaper. Not in topical listings.

+KEYS TO LIVING, PO Box 154, Washingtonville PA 17884. (717)437-2891. E-mail: owcam@sunlink.net. Connie Mertz, ed/pub. Educates and encourages readers through inspirational writings while presenting an appreciation for God's natural world. Bimonthly newsletter; 10 pgs; circ 125. Subscription $9. 20% freelance. Complete ms/cover letter. **PAYS 3 COPIES** for one-time or reprint rts. Articles 350-500 wds. Responds in 4 wks. Seasonal 2-4 mos ahead. Accepts reprints. No disk. Prefers NIV. Guidelines/theme list; copy for 8x10 SAE/2 stamps.

Poetry: Any type; to 20 lines. Religious or nature.

Fillers: Cartoons, games, jokes, quizzes, quotes, short humor; to 100 wds.

Tips: "Always looking for personal experiences or devotions on themes (get theme list). Seasonal poetry on nature is open for all issues."

LIBERTY, Religious Liberty Dept., 12501 Old Columbia Pike, Silver Springs MD 20904. (301)680-6448. Fax (301)680-6695. E-mail: 74617.263@compuserve. com. Seventh-day Adventist. Clifford R. Goldstein, ed. Deals with religious liberty issues for government officials, civic leaders, and laymen. Bimonthly mag; 32 pgs; circ 250,000. 90% freelance. Query; phone/fax/e-mail query OK. Pays $500-750 on acceptance for 1st rts. Articles & essays to 2,500 wds. Responds in 4 wks. Requires disk. Guidelines.

#LIFE GATE, 2026 Boulder Run Dr., Richmond VA 23233. Phone/fax (804)750-1504. By His Design, Inc. Randy Moore, ed. Positive news for Protestant Christians. Monthly tabloid; circ. 23,000. 40% freelance. Query; fax/e-mail query OK. **NO PAYMENT.** Articles 250-500 wds (12/yr); book/music reviews 350 wds. Seasonal 4 mos ahead. Accepts simultaneous submissions & reprints. Prefers disk. Prefers NIV. Copy $1.50.

Poetry: Accepts 8-10/yr. Avant-garde, free verse, light verse, traditional; 100-500 wds. Submit max. 5 poems.

Fillers: Anecdotes, facts.

*LIFEGLOW, Box 6097, Lincoln NE 68506. (402)489-5922. Christian Record Services. Richard J. Kaiser, ed-in-chief. For sight-impaired adults over 25; interdenominational Christian audience. Quarterly mag; 65-70 pgs (lg. print); circ 30,000. Free to sight-impaired. 95% freelance. Query; phone query OK. Pays .04-.05/wd on acceptance for one-time rts. Articles & true stories 750-1,400 wds. Responds in 1-4 wks. Seasonal 18 mos ahead. Accepts simultaneous query & reprints. Guidelines; copy for 9x12 SAE/5 stamps.

Special Needs: Nostalgia. Overstocked on historical.

Tips: "Remember the readers are sight impaired or physically handicapped. Would the topics be relevant to them?"

#LIGHT AND LIFE, Box 535002, Indianapolis IN 46253. (317)244-3660. Fax (317)244-1247. Free Methodist Church of North America. Doug Newton, ed. Christian growth, ministry to saved and unsaved, denominational news. Monthly mag; 32 pgs; circ 23,000. Subscription $16. 40% freelance. Query; phone query OK. Pays .04-.05/wd on publication for 1st, one-time, or simultaneous rts. Articles 500-600 or 1,000-1,200 wds (60/yr). Responds in 4-6 wks. Seasonal 8 mos ahead. Accepts simultaneous submissions. Prefers disk (WordPerfect); pays $2 extra. Kill fee 50%. Sidebars OK. Guidelines; copy $1.50. (Ads)

Poetry: Buys 6-10/yr. Free verse, traditional; 4-16 lines; $10. Send max. 5 poems. Uses as sidebars to articles.

Columns/Departments: Buys 6-10/yr. Personal Opinion; Young Voice (ages 16-22); 500-600 wds.

Tips: "Most open to feature articles. Write to the readers' interest. Our age groupings are approximately: 25% baby boomers, 25% over 65, 30% between boomers and retired; 20% younger than boomers."

** 1994 EPA Award of Excellence—Denominational.

*LIGHTHOUSE FICTION COLLECTION, PO Box 1377, Auburn WA 98071-1377. Tim Clinton, ed/pub. Timeless fiction for the whole family. Quarterly mag; 56 pgs; circ 300. Subscription $7.95 for 6/$14.95 for 12. 100% freelance. Complete ms/cover letter. Pays to $5-50 on publication for 1st or one-time rts. Fiction for all ages 250-5,000 wds (40-50/yr). Responds in 6-18 wks. Seasonal any time. Guidelines; copy $3.

Poetry: Buys 12-20/yr. Free-verse, light verse, traditional; 6-80 lines; $1-5. Submit max. 5 poems.

Tips: "Read and follow guidelines. Basic need is for good stories and poems—well-written, interesting, new plot."

#LIGUORIAN, One Liguori Dr., Liguori MO 63057-9999. (314)464-2500. Fax (800)325-9526. E-mail: 104626.1547@compuserve.com. Website: http://www.liguori.org. Catholic. Allan Weinert, CSSR, ed-in-chief. To help readers lead a fuller Christian life through the sharing of experiences, scriptural knowledge, and a better understanding of the church. Monthly mag; 72 pgs; circ 300,000. Subscription $18. 25% freelance. Query or complete ms/cover letter; phone/fax/e-mail query OK. Pays .10-.12/wd (to $200) on acceptance for all rts. Articles 400-2,000 wds (60/yr); fiction 2,000 wds (12/yr). Responds in up to 26 wks. Seasonal 6 mos ahead. Prefers disk. Some sidebars. Guidelines; copy for 6x9 SAE/3 stamps.

Fillers: Anecdotes, jokes, prose, prayers, short humor; .10/wd.

Columns/Departments: Buys 12/yr. Five-Minute Meditation (reflective essay), 750 wds. Complete ms.

Tips: "Polish your own ms. Need marriage and parenting articles, articles that touch a reader's life in a personal way. If writing a personal experience piece, beware of limited subjectivity. Most open to Five-Minute Meditation, fiction and fillers."

LIVE, 1445 Boonville Ave., Springfield MO 65802-1894. (417)862-2781x4356. Fax (417)862-6059. Assemblies of God. Paul W. Smith, adult ed. Inspiration and encouragement for adults. Weekly take-home paper; 8 pgs; circ 130,000. Subscription $9.20. 100% freelance. Complete ms; no phone/fax query. Pays .05/wd (.03/wd for reprints) on acceptance for 1st, one-time simultaneous or reprint rts. Articles 700-1,600 wds (75/yr); fiction 700-1,600 wds (30/yr). Responds in 6-8 wks. Seasonal 1 yr ahead. Accepts simultaneous submissions & reprints (tell when/where appeared). No disk. Few sidebars. Prefers NIV. Guidelines/copy for 6x9 SAE/2 stamps.

Poetry: Buys 15-25/yr. Free verse, traditional; 12-24 lines; $15 when scheduled. Submit max. 3 poems.

Fillers: Buys 50/yr. Anecdotes, facts, prose, short humor, word puzzles; to 200-700 wds; $15.

Tips: "Encourage our readers to live more productive Christian lives. We want them to be uplifted, not preached at or merely informed. Our purpose is mainly Christian inspiration and encouragement. Send no more than two articles in the same envelope and send an SASE. We always need seasonal articles, other than Christmas."

** This periodical was #31 on the 1997 Top 50 Christian Publishers list. (#26 in 1996, #16 in 1995, #20 in 1994)

LIVING, Rt. 2 Box 656, Grottoes VA 24441. Phone/fax (540)249-3177. E-mail: Tgether@aol.com. Shalom Foundation, Inc. Melodie Davis, ed. A positive, practical and uplifting publication for the whole family; mass distribution. Quarterly tabloid; 32 pgs; circ 250,000. Free. 80% freelance. Query or complete ms/cover letter; e-mail query OK. Pays $25-50 on publication for one-time rts. Articles 500-1,000 wds (36/yr); fiction (4/yr). Responds in 12-16 wks. Seasonal 4 mos ahead. Accepts simultaneous submissions & reprints (tell when/where appeared). Accepts disk. Some sidebars. Prefers NIV. Guidelines/theme list; copy for 9x12 SAE/4 stamps. (Ads)

Fillers: Buys 4-8/yr. Anecdotes, short humor; 100-200 wds; $20-25.

Tips: "We are directed toward the general public, many of whom have no Christian interests, and we're trying to publish high-quality writing on family issues/concerns from a Christian perspective. That means religious language must be low key. Too much of what we receive is directed toward a Christian reader. We use fiction for adults or children, 6-14 (has to be emotionally moving/involving)."

#THE LIVING CHURCH, PO Box 92936, Milwaukee WI 53202-0936. (414)276-5420. Fax (414)276-7483. E-mail: livngchrch@aol.com. Episcopal/The Living Church Foundation, Inc. John Schuessler, mng ed. Independent news coverage of the Episcopal Church for clergy and lay leaders. Weekly mag; 16+ pgs; circ 9,000. Subscription $39.50. 50% freelance. Complete ms/cover letter; phone/fax/e-mail query OK. Pays $25-100 (for solicited articles) for one-time rts. Articles 1,000 wds (10/yr); fiction (1/yr). Responds in 2-4 wks. Seasonal 1 mo ahead. Accepts disk. Sidebars OK. Free copy. (Ads)

> **Poetry:** Accepts 5-10/yr. Light verse, traditional; 4-15 lines. Submit max. 3 poems.
>
> **Columns/Departments:** Accepts 10/yr. Benediction (devotional/inspirational), 200 wds.
>
> **Tips:** "Most open to features, as long as they have something to do with the Episcopal Church."

LIVING LIGHT NEWS, #200, 5304-89 St., Edmonton AB T6E 5P9 Canada. (403)468-6397. Fax (403)468-6872. E-mail: livinglight@enable.ab.ca. Living Light Ministries. Jeff Caporale, ed. To motivate and encourage Christians; witnessing tool to the lost. Bimonthly tabloid; 28 pgs; circ 10,000. Subscription $19.95 US. Est. 1995. 75% freelance. Query; phone/fax/e-mail query OK. Pays $20-125 (.05-.10/wd), $20-50 for fiction, on publication for 1st, one-time, simultaneous or reprint rts. Not copyrighted. Articles 300-750 wds (20/yr); fiction to 1,500 wds (3/yr for Christmas only); book reviews 350 wds, music reviews 250 wds, & video reviews 300 wds; .10/wd. Responds in 4 wks. Seasonal 3-4 mos ahead. Accepts simultaneous submissions & reprints (tell when/where appeared). Accepts disk. Sidebars OK. Prefers NIV. Guidelines/theme list; copy for 10x13 SAE/$2.25 postage. (Ads)

> **Special Needs:** Celebrity interviews/testimonials of well-known sports figures; interesting fiction and nonfiction stories related to Christmas; unique ministries.
>
> ** 1997 EPA Award of Excellence—Newspaper.

LIVING WITH TEENAGERS, 127 Ninth Ave. N, Nashville TN 37234-0140. (615)251-2229. (615)251-5008. E-mail: lwt@bssb.com. Website: http://www.bssb.com. LifeWay Press. Jeff Large, mng ed. Christian parenting for parents of teenagers. Monthly mag; 36 pgs; circ. 42,000. Subscription $18.95. 30% freelance. Query/clips; fax/e-mail query OK. Pays $100-500 on acceptance for all, 1st, one-time, or electronic rts. Articles 400-1,000 wds (35/yr). Responds in 6-8 wks. Seasonal 8 mos ahead. Accepts simultaneous submissions & reprints rarely (tell when/where appeared). Accepts disk. Sidebars OK. Prefers NIV. Guidelines; copy for 9x12 SAE/3 stamps.

> **Fillers:** Buys 25/yr. Party ideas, short humor, parent/teen devotional ideas; 100-500 wds; $25-150.
>
> **Tips:** "Most open to articles."
>
> ** This periodical was #15 on the 1997 Top 50 Christian Publishers list.

#THE LOOKOUT, 8121 Hamilton Ave., Cincinnati OH 45231-9981. (513)931-4050. Fax (513)931-0950. Standard Publishing. Andrea Ritze, mng ed. For adults in Sunday school who are interested in learning more about applying the gospel to their lives. Weekly take-home paper; 16 pgs; circ 105,000. Subscription $23.50. 40-50% freelance. Complete ms; no phone/fax/e-mail query. Pays .05-.15/wd on acceptance for 1st, one-time, simultaneous or reprint rts. Articles 400-1,800 wds or 400-700 wds(50/yr). Responds in 18 wks. Seasonal 6 mos ahead. Accepts simultaneous submissions & reprints (tell when/where appeared). Accepts disk. Kill fee 33%. Sidebars OK. Prefers NIV. Guidelines/theme list; copy for .75.

    Fillers: Cartoons, $50.

    Columns/Departments: Buys 24/yr. Outlook (personal opinion), 500-900 wds; Salt & Light (innovative ways to reach out into the community), 500-900 wds. Pays .05-.07/wd.

    Tips: "We now focus our articles in three main areas: personal Christian growth, home and family, and social issues from a Christian perspective."

    ** This periodical was #40 on the 1997 Top 50 Christian Publishers list (#1 in 1996, #3 in 1993 & 1995). Also EPA 1996 Award of Excellence—Sunday School Take-Home.

THE LUTHERAN, 8765 W. Higgins Rd., Chicago IL 60631-4183. (773)380-2540. Fax (773)380-2751. E-mail: lutheran@elca.org. Website: http://www. thelutheran.org. Evangelical Lutheran Church in America. Edgar R. Trexler, ed.; Roger R. Kahle, mng ed.; submit to David L. Miller, sr. ed. Addresses broad constituency of the church. Monthly mag; 68 pgs; circ 150,000. 10% freelance. Query only; fax/e-mail query OK. Pays $300-700 (assigned), $100-500 (unsolicited) on acceptance for 1st rts. Articles 1,000-1,500 wds (40/yr). Responds in 4-6 wks. Seasonal 4 mos ahead. Accepts reprints. Disk/modem OK. Kill fee 50%. Guidelines/theme list; free copy.

    Fillers: Roger Kahle. Buys 50/yr. Cartoons, jokes, short humor. Uses only true anecdotes from ELCA congregations.

    Columns/Departments: Roger Kahle. Lite Side (church and religious humor), 25-100 wds; $10.

    Tips: "Most open to feature articles."

    ** This periodical was #12 on the 1997 Top 50 Christian Publishers list. (#31 in 1996, #7 in 1995, #9 in 1994)

#THE LUTHERAN AMBASSADOR, 86286 Pine Grove Rd., Eugene OR 97402. (541)687-8643. Fax (541)683-8496. E-mail: cjohnson@efn.org. Assn. of Free Lutheran Congregations. Craig Johnson, ed. Denominational. Magazine published 16X/yr; circ 4,800. Subscription $16. Open to freelance. Query or complete ms. Not in topical listings.

THE LUTHERAN DIGEST, Box 4250, Hopkins MN 55343. (612)933-2820. Fax (612)933-5708. Lutheran. David L. Tank, ed. Blend of secular and light theological material used to win non-believers to the Lutheran faith. Quarterly mag; 72 pgs; circ 155,000. Subscription $20/2 yrs. 100% freelance. Query/clips or complete ms/cover letter. Pays $25 on acceptance for one-time rts. Articles to 1,000 wds (25-30/yr). Responds in 4-9 wks. Seasonal 6-9 mos ahead. Accepts reprints (70% is reprints). No disk. Some sidebars. Guidelines; copy $2/6x9 SAE/3 stamps.

    Poetry: Accepts 45-50/yr. Light verse, traditional; any length; no payment. Submit max. 3 poems.

Fillers: Anecdotes, cartoons, facts, jokes, short humor; to 100 wds; no payment.

Tips: "We would like more short articles, 1 page or less. We also look for good-quality nature articles."

** #50 on the 1994 Top 50.

THE LUTHERAN JOURNAL, 7317 Cahill Rd., Ste. 201, Minneapolis MN 55439-2081. (612)941-6830. Fax (612)941-3010. Macalester Park Publishing. Rev. Armin Deye, ed. Family magazine for church members, middle age and older. Quarterly (3X) mag; 32 pgs; circ 127,000. Subscription $6. 60% freelance. Complete ms/cover letter; fax query OK. Pays .03/wd on publication for one-time rts. Articles 400-1,700 wds (30/yr); book reviews, 150 wds, $5. Responds in 8-10 wks. Seasonal 4-5 mos ahead. Accepts simultaneous submissions. Sidebars OK. Prefers NIV, ASV or KJV. Accepts disk. Guidelines; copy for 9x12 SAE/3 stamps. (Ads)

Poetry: Buys 10/yr. Free verse, haiku, light verse, traditional; to 2 pgs. Pays $5-30. Submit max. 5 poems.

Fillers: Buys 5/yr. Anecdotes, cartoons, facts, games, prose, quizzes, quotes, short humor; to 100 wds; $5-30.

Columns/Departments: Buys 40/yr. Apron Strings (short recipes); About Books (reviews), 50-150 wds. Pays $5-25.

Tips: "Most open to Lutheran lifestyles or Lutherans in action."

+LUTHERAN PARENT, 1250 N. 113th St. Milwaukee WI 53226-3284. (414)454-2104. Fax (414)454-2170. Northwestern Publishing House. Kenneth J. Kremer, ed. Scriptural guidance, encouragement, and resources for Christian parents. Bimonthly mag; 16 pgs; circ 7,300. Subscription $13.99. Est. 1995. Pays .05/wd on acceptance for 1st, one-time, or reprint rts. Articles 500-1,600 wds. Prefers disk. Sidebars OK. Prefers NIV. Guidelines/theme list; copy for $3.50/9x12 SAE.

Columns/Departments: Buys 24/yr. Child Development, Home/School, Question & Answer, and Carpenter's Square; all 400 wds. Pays $50.

Special Needs: Special edition written exclusively by children.

+LUTHERAN PARENT'S WELLSPRING, 1250 N. 113th St. Milwaukee WI 53226-3284. (414)454-2104. Fax (414)454-2170. Northwestern Publishing House. Kenneth J. Kremer, ed. A devotional magazine for the whole family. Bimonthly mag. Subscription $10.99.

#LUTHERAN WITNESS, 1333 S. Kirkwood Rd., St. Louis MO 63122-7295. (314)965-9000. Fax (314)965-3396. E-mail: ic_mahsmadl@lcms.org. Lutheran Church-Missouri Synod. Rev. David Mahsman, ed; submit to David L. Strand, mng ed. Denominational. Monthly mag; 26 pgs; circ 325,000. 50% freelance. Complete ms/cover letter. Pays $100-300 on acceptance for 1st rts. Articles 250-1,600 wds (40-50/yr); fiction 500-1,500 wds. Responds in 9 wks. Seasonal 6 mos ahead. Considers simultaneous submissions & reprints. Kill fee 50%. Free guidelines/copy.

Fillers: Accepts 60+/yr. Cartoons ($50), short humor; no payment.

Columns/Departments: Buys 60/yr. Bible Studies, Humor, Opinion; $50-100.

*MARIAN HELPERS BULLETIN, PO Box 951, Stockbridge MA 01263. (413)298-3691. Catholic. Vincent Flynn, ed. Quarterly mag; circ 500,000. 20%

freelance. Query/clips or complete ms/cover letter. Pays .10/wd on acceptance for all, 1st, or reprint rts. Articles 500-900 wds; book reviews. Responds in 3 wks. Seasonal 6 mos ahead. Accepts reprints. Kill fee 30%. Free guidelines/copy.

Tips: "Also needs articles on mercy in action or devotion to Blessed Virgin Mary."

#MARRIAGE PARTNERSHIP, 465 Gundersen Dr., Carol Stream IL 60188. (630)260-6200. Fax (630)260-0114. E-mail: MPedit@aol.com. Website: http://www. christianity.net/mp/current. Christianity Today, Inc. Louise Ferrebee, assoc. ed. To promote and strengthen Christian marriages. Quarterly mag; 80 pgs; circ 55,000. Subscription $19.95. 5% freelance. Query only; fax/e-mail query OK. Pays $50-300 (.15/wd) on acceptance for 1st rts. Articles 500-2,000 wds. Responds in 8-10 wks. Seasonal 6 mos ahead. Some sidebars. Guidelines; copy $5.

Fillers: Cartoons; pays $75.

Columns/Departments: For Women Only (women's issues) & For Men Only (men's issues), 400-500 wds; Work it Out (working out a marriage problem).

#MATURE LIVING, 127 9th Ave. N., Nashville TN 37234. (615)251-2274. Fax (615)251-5008. Southern Baptist. Al Shackleford, ed.; submit to Judy Pregel, mng. ed. Christian leisure-reading for senior adults (50+) characterized by human interest and Christian warmth. Monthly mag; circ 350,000. 70% freelance. Complete ms. Pays .055/wd ($75 min.) on acceptance for all (preferred) or one-time rts. Articles 600-1,200 (100/yr); fiction 900-1,200 wds (12/yr). Responds in 13 wks. Seasonal 1 yr ahead. Serials. Guidelines; copy for 9x12 SAE/4 stamps.

Poetry: Buys 30/yr. Light verse, traditional; senior adult themes; any length; $13-20. Submit max. 5 poems.

Fillers: Buys 120/yr. Anecdotes, facts, games, short humor; to 50 wds; $10.

Columns/Departments: Cracker Barrel (brief humor), $10; Grandparent's Brag Board, $10.

Tips: "Most open to human-interest stories. All articles and fiction must relate to senior adults."

** This periodical was #53 on the 1997 Top 50 Christian Publishers list.

MATURE YEARS, Box 801, Nashville TN 37202. (615)749-6292. Fax (615)749-6512. United Methodist. Marvin W. Cropsey, ed. Inspiration, information, and leisure reading for persons of retirement age. Quarterly mag; 112 pgs; circ 70,000. Subscription $12. 50% freelance. Complete ms/cover letter. Pays .05/wd on acceptance for one-time rts. Articles 900-2,000 wds (60/yr); fiction 1,200-2,000 wds (4/yr). Responds in 3-8 wks. Seasonal 14 mos ahead. Accepts reprints. Sidebars OK. Guidelines; copy $3.75.

Poetry: Buys 24/yr. Free verse, haiku, light verse, traditional; 4-16 lines; pays .50-$1/line. Submit max. 6 poems.

Fillers: Buys 20/yr. Cartoons, jokes, prayers, word puzzles (religious only); to 30 wds; $5-25.

Columns/Departments: Buys 20/yr. Health Hints, 900-1,200 wds; Modern Revelations (inspirational), 900-1,100 wds; Fragments of Life (true life inspirational), 250-600 wds; Going Places (travel), 1,000-1,500 wds; Money Matters, 1,200-1,800 wds.

Special Needs: Articles on crafts and pets. Fiction on older adult situation.

** This periodical was #63 on the 1997 Top 50 Christian Publishers list. (#56 in 1996, #65 in 1995, #51 in 1994)

THE MENNONITE, Box 347, Newton KS 67114. (316)283-5100. Fax (316)283-0454. E-mail: TheMennonite@gcmc.org. General conference Mennonite Church. J. Lorne Peachey, ed. Practical articles on aspects of Christian living. Semimonthly mag; 24 pgs; circ 8,000. Subscription $28. 10% freelance. Complete ms/cover letter; fax/e-mail query OK. Pays .05/wd on publication for one-time rts. Articles 700-1,200 wds (10/yr); book/music/video reviews, 300 wds, $10. Responds in 1-2 wks. Seasonal 6 mos ahead. Accepts simultaneous submissions & reprints (tell when/where appeared). Accepts disk. Kill fee 50%. Sidebars OK. Prefers NRSV. Guidelines/theme list; copy for 9x12 SAE/6 stamps.

Poetry: Buys 5-10/yr. Avant-garde, free verse; $20-50. Submit max. 3 poems.

Fillers: Buys 3-5/yr. Anecdotes, cartoons, facts; 25-100 wds; $10-30.

Columns/Departments: Buys 5/yr. Speaking Out (opinion); Bible (Bible study with application); Profile (example of discipleship); all 700 wds. Pays .05/wd.

Tips: "Most open to feature articles (1,000-1,500 wds): should be anecdotal, with practical ideas for living the Christian life; stories of people who have changed for the better are especially considered; needs to fit Mennonite theology." Note: This publication just merged with Gospel Herald.

MENNONITE BRETHREN HERALD, 3-169 Riverton Ave., Winnipeg MB R2L 2E5 Canada. (204)669-6575. Fax (204)654-1865. E-mail: mbherald@cdnmbconf.ca. Website: http://www.cdnmbconf.ca/mb/mbherald/htm. Canadian Conference of Mennonite Brethren Churches. Susan Brandt, mng. ed. Denominational; for information, communication and spiritual enrichment. Biweekly mag; 32 pgs; circ 15,000. Subscription $30. 40% freelance. Complete ms/cover letter. Pays .07/wd on publication for 1st rts. Articles 1,200 wds (40/yr); fiction 1,000-2,000 wds (10/yr). Responds in 20 wks. Seasonal 5 mos ahead. Accepts reprints (tell when/where appeared). Prefers disk. Sidebars OK. Prefers NIV. Guidelines/theme list; copy for 9x12 SAE/$1 Canadian postage. (Ads)

Poetry: Buys 15/yr. Avant-garde, free verse, traditional; any length; pays to $10.

*****MENNONITE HISTORIAN**, 600 Shaftesbury Blvd., Winnipeg MB R3P 0M4 Canada. (204)888-6781. Fax (204)831-5675. Conference of Mennonites in Canada. Lawrence Klippenstein, ed. Gathers and shares historical material related to Mennonites; focus on North America, but also beyond. Quarterly newsletter; 8 pgs; circ. 2,600. Subscription $9. 60% freelance. Complete ms/cover letter; phone/fax query OK. **NO PAYMENT EXCEPT BY SPECIAL ARRANGEMENT** for 1st rts. Articles 250-1,000 wds (6/yr). Responds in 3 wks. Seasonal 3 mos ahead. Accepts simultaneous submissions & reprints (depending on where published). Copy $1/9x12 SAE.

Tips: "Most open to lead articles. Write with your ideas. Also genealogical articles."

MENNONITE WEEKLY REVIEW, Box 568, Newton KS 67114-0568. (316)283-3670. Fax (316)283-6502. E-mail: menwkrv@southwind.net. Mennonite. Paul Schrag, ed. Features religious and Mennonite news. Weekly newspaper; 12-16 pgs; circ 11,000. 5% freelance. Complete ms/cover letter. Pays .05/wd on publication for one-time rts. Articles 400-500 wds. Responds in 5 wks. Accepts simultaneous submissions. Copy $1/SAE/2 stamps.

Tips: "Topic must be Mennonite; we are exclusively a Mennonite publication."

MESSAGE, Review and Herald Pub. Assn., 55 W. Oak Ridge Dr., Hagerstown MD 21740. (301)791-7000. Fax (301)714-1753. E-mail: 74617.3047@compuserve. com. Seventh-day Adventist. Stephen P. Ruff, ed. Blacks and other minorities who have an interest in current issues and are seeking a better lifestyle. Bimonthly mag; 32 pgs; circ 70,000. Subscription $12.97. 25% freelance. Complete ms/cover letter; fax query OK. Pays $50-300 ($50-75 for fiction) on acceptance for 1st rts. Articles 700-1,200 wds (50/yr); parables; fiction (6/yr) for children (ages 5-8), 500 wds. Responds in 6-10 wks. Seasonal 6 mos ahead. Prefers disk. Sidebars OK. Prefers NIV. Guidelines/theme list; free copy for 9x12 SAE. (Ads)

Fillers: Facts, games, quizzes, word puzzles; to 500 wds; $50-75.

Columns/Departments: Buys 12/yr. Healthspan (health issues), 700 wds; MESSAGE Jr. (biblical stories or stories with clear-cut moral for ages 5-8), 500 wds. Pays $75-150.

Contests: Sometimes has a black history contest and/or Bible-related contest.

Tips: "As with any publication, writers should have a working knowledge of MESSAGE. They should have some knowledge of our style and our readers."
** This periodical was #18 on the 1997 Top 50 Christian Publishers list. (#28 in 1995). Also 1996 EPA Award of Merit—Missionary.

MESSAGE OF THE OPEN BIBLE, 2020 Bell Ave., Des Moines IA 50315-1096. (515)288-6761. Fax (515)288-2510. Open Bible Churches. Andrea Johnson, ed. To inspire, inform and educate the Open Bible family. Bimonthly mag; 16 pgs; circ 4,300. Subscription $9.75. 5% freelance. Complete ms/cover letter. **PAYS 5 COPIES**. Not copyrighted. Articles 750 wds (2/yr). Responds in 4 wks. Seasonal 4 mos ahead. Accepts simultaneous submissions & reprints (tell when/where appeared). Accepts disk. Sidebars OK. Prefers NIV. Guidelines/theme list; copy for 9x12 SAE/2 stamps.

Fillers: Accepts 6/yr. Cartoons, facts, quotes, short humor; 50 wds.

Tips: "Most open to inspiration or evangelistic pieces. A writer can best break in by giving us something valuable for an upcoming theme or something that would inspire or uplift the average church member, specifically as they relate to Open Bible."
** 1996 EPA Award of Merit—Denominational.

*MESSENGER, Box 18068, Covington KY 41018-0068. (606)283-6270. Catholic. Jean Bach, news ed. Diocese paper of Covington KY. Weekly (45X) newspaper; 24 pgs; circ 16,000. Subscription $18. 40% freelance. Query/clips. Pays $1.25/column inch on publication for 1st rts. Articles 500-800 wds. Responds in 1 wk. Seasonal 1 mo ahead. Accepts simultaneous submissions. Guidelines; free copy.

+THE MESSENGER, 1001 E. Beltline Ave. NE, Grand Rapids MI 49525. (616)949-5300x1343. Fax (616)222-1434. E-mail: jelmore@cornerstone.edu. Cornerstone College/Grand Rapids Baptist Seminary. John Elmore, public relations. General Assn. of Regular Baptists. Quarterly mag; 16 pgs; circ 27,000. Free. Query; query for electronic submissions. **NO PAYMENT** for one-time & electronic rts. Articles 2,000-2,200 or 3,000 wds. Responds in 2-3 wks. Seasonal 6 mos ahead. Accepts simultaneous submissions & reprints (tell when/where appeared). Prefers disk. Sidebars OK. Prefers NIV & NAS.

Poetry: Free verse, light verse. Inspirational, theologically Bible-based, encouraging.

Fillers: Cartoons, quotes.

MESSENGER OF THE SACRED HEART, 661 Greenwood Ave., Toronto ON M4J 4B3 Canada. (416)466-1195. Catholic/Apostleship of Prayer. Rev. F.J. Power, S.J., ed. Help for daily living on a spiritual level. Monthly mag; 32 pgs; circ 14,000. Subscription $12. 40% freelance. Complete ms; no phone query. Pays .04/wd on acceptance for 1st rts. Articles 800-1,500 wds (30/yr); fiction 800-1,500 wds (12/yr). Responds in 3 wks. Seasonal 6 mos ahead. No disk or sidebars. Guidelines; copy $1/9x12 SAE.

Tips: "Most open to inspirational stories and articles."

THE MESSENGER OF ST. ANTHONY, Via Orto Botanico, 11, 35123 Padova, Italy (no longer has a US editor or address). (011)3949 822 5000. Fax (010)3949 822 5651. E-mail: m.conte@mess-s-antonio.it. Catholic. Martin De Sa'Pinto, ed. asst. For middle-age and older Catholics in English-speaking world; articles that address current issues. Monthly mag; 40 pgs; circ 20,000. Subscription $27 US. 80% freelance. Query; phone/fax/e-mail query OK. Pays .10-.15/wd on publication for all rts. Articles 600-2,000 wds (150/yr); fiction 600-1,400 wds (11/yr). Responds in 6-8 wks. Seasonal 4 mos ahead. Prefers disk. Sidebars OK. Prefers Liguori Faithware. Guidelines; free copy.

Fillers: Buys 11/yr. Anecdotes, cartoons, facts, ideas, quotes; 600-800 wds. Pays $55.

Columns/Departments: Buys 40-50/yr. Documentary (issues), 600-2,000 wds; Spirituality, 600-2,000 wds; Church Life, 600-2,000 wds; Saint Anthony (devotional), 600-1,400 wds; Living Today (family life), 600-1,400 wds. Pays $55-165.

Tips: "We prefer articles with accompanying photos. Articles on parishes dedicated to St. Anthony; topical articles, e.g., we are opening a series of 2-page articles on Rwanda, Sudan, and Kenya. Also family life articles, especially observations and advice."

METHODIST HISTORY, 36 Madison Ave., Madison NJ 07940. (973)408-3189. Fax (973)408-3909. United Methodist. Charles Yrigoyen Jr., ed. History of the United Methodism and Methodist/Wesleyan churches. Quarterly journal; 64 pgs; circ 1,000. 100% freelance. Query; phone query OK. **PAYS IN COPIES** for all rts. Historical articles to 5,000 wds (15/yr); book reviews 500 wds. Responds in 8 wks. Requires disk. No sidebars. Guidelines; copy $5. (Ads)

METRO VOICE (formerly **KANSAS CITY CHRISTIAN NEWSPAPER**), 108 SE 3rd St., Lee's Summit MO 64063. (816)524-4522. Fax (816)525-4423. Nondenominational. Dwight & Anita Widaman, pubs; Melanie Miles, ed. To promote Christian business, ministries and organizations; provide thought-provoking commentary for edification of the body of Christ. Monthly newspaper; circ 35,000. Subscription $14. 50% freelance. Complete ms/cover letter; short phone query OK. **PAYS IN COPIES** or limited amount for well-researched pieces, for one-time or reprint rts. Not copyrighted. Articles to 1,200 wds (100/yr). Responds in 6 wks. Seasonal 6 mos ahead. Accepts reprints. Guidelines; copy for 9x12 SAE/$1 postage.

Fillers: Accepts 12/yr. Anecdotes, cartoons, ideas, newsbreaks, quotes, short humor; to 500 wds.

Tips: "We look for up-to-date information. Willing to work with new writers who want to learn."

+MICHIGAN CHRISTIAN ADVOCATE, 316 Springbrook Ave., Adrian MI 49221. (517)265-2075. Fax (517)263-7422. United Methodist. Erik Alsgaard, ed. For Michigan United Methodists. Biweekly tabloid; 16 pgs; circ 12,000. Subscription $12. 75% freelance. Complete ms/cover letter; fax query OK. Pays $30-50 on publication for one-time rts. Articles 400-550 wds; book/music/video reviews, 200 wds, $15. Responds in 4 wks. Seasonal 3 mos ahead. Accepts simultaneous submissions. Accepts disk. Sidebars OK. Prefers NRSV. Copy available. (Ads)

Fillers: Buys 30-35/yr. Cartoons, word puzzles. Pay varies.

Columns/Departments: Buys 20-26/yr. My Experience (true), 450-550 wds; In My Opinion (church topics), 400-500 wds. Pays $30.

Special Needs: Easter My Experience columns, 350-450 wds.

Tips: "Always looking for touching true experience columns—be brief, not sappy. Always looking for good cartoonists—pay $25-50 depending on artist. Young cartoonists please apply."

#MINNESOTA CHRISTIAN CHRONICLE, 7317 Cahill Rd., Minneapolis MN 55439. (612)941-1605. Fax (612)941-3010. E-mail: trouten@compuserve.com. Beard Communications. Doug Trouten, ed. Local news and features of interest to the Christian community. Biweekly newspaper; 36 pgs; circ 7,000. Subscription $19.95. 10% freelance. Query; phone query OK. Pays .05/wd after publication for one-time rts. Articles 500-1,000 wds (50/yr); book reviews 500 wds. Responds in 13 wks. Seasonal 2 mos ahead. Accepts simultaneous query & reprints. Guidelines; copy $2. (Ads)

Tips: "Not interested in anything without a Minnesota 'hook.' Inspiration section has room for two general personality features each issue; tell us about people and ministries we're not aware of."

** 1997 Award of Merit—Newspaper. (1996 EPA Award of Excellence—Newspaper.)

THE MIRACULOUS MEDAL, 475 E. Chelten Ave., Philadelphia PA 19144-5785. (215)848-1010. Catholic. Rev. William J. O'Brien, ed. Fiction & poetry for Catholic adults, mostly women. Quarterly mag; 36 pgs; circ 340,000. 100% freelance. Complete ms/cover letter. Pays .02/wd on acceptance for 1st rts. Religious fiction 1,600-2,400 wds (6/yr). Responds in 26 wks. Seasonal anytime. Accepts simultaneous submissions. Guidelines; copy for 2 stamps.

Poetry: Buys 6/yr. Free verse, traditional; to 20 lines; .50 & up/line. Send any number. "Must have religious theme, preferably about the Blessed Virgin Mary."

THE MONTANA CATHOLIC, PO Box 1729, Helena MT 59624-1729. (406)442-5820. Fax (406)442-5191. E-mail: GMKorson@aol.com. Catholic. Gerald M. Korson, ed. News and features for the Catholic community of western Montana.

Tabloid published 16X/yr; 20-24 pgs; circ 9,300. Subscription $18. 5% freelance. Complete ms/cover letter or query; e-mail query OK. Pays .05-.10/wd on acceptance for 1st, one-time, simultaneous or reprint rts. Articles 200-950 wds (12/yr); book reviews, 200-600 wds. Responds in 3 wks. Seasonal 2 mos ahead. Accepts simultaneous submissions & reprints (tell when/where appeared). Accepts disk. Kill fee 35%. Sidebars OK. Prefers NAS or RSV. Guidelines; copy $2/9x12 SAE. (Ads)

> **Tips:** "Our greatest need is for freelance writers who reside in western Montana, have an understanding of the Catholic Church, and are willing to take on news and feature writing assignments of local interest. Photographic ability helpful. On rare occasions we use feature articles by other freelancers, particularly when geared toward seasons and days of the liturgical year or our semi-annual special sections on religious vocations."

MOODY MAGAZINE, 820 N. LaSalle Blvd., Chicago IL 60610. (312)329-2164. Fax (312)329-2149. E-mail: MoodyLtrs@moody.edu. Website: http://www. moody.edu/MOODYMAG. Moody Bible Institute. Andrew Scheer, mng. ed. To encourage and equip evangelical Christians to think and live biblically. Bimonthly mag; 84-96 pgs; circ 115,000. Subscription $18.95. 60% freelance. Query only; no phone/fax/e-mail query. Query for electronic submissions. Pays $210-500 (.15-.20/wd) on acceptance for 1st & non-exclusive electronic rts. Articles 1,200-2,500 wds (60/yr); fiction 1,200-2,500 wds (1-3/yr). Responds in 6-8 wks. Seasonal 9 mos ahead. Accepts reprints (tell when/where appeared). Kill fee 50%. Requires disk. Sidebars OK. Prefers NIV. Guidelines; copy for 9x12 SASE/8 stamps. (Ads)

> **Columns/Departments:** Buys 12/yr. Just For Parents (application of scriptural principle to parenting), 1,500-1,600 wds; First Person (salvation testimonies—may be as-told-to), 800-900 wds; $150-225.

> **Tips:** "We want feature articles from freelancers for the second (non-cover) section of each issue. In generating article ideas, consider these questions: What has God been working on in my life the last few years? How am I applying a new realization of what the Bible is directing me to do? What difference has this obedience made? Answers should lead you to appropriate content for a Moody article."

> ****** This periodical was #13 on the 1997 Top 50 Christian Publishers list. (#9 in 1996, #4 in 1995 & 1994)

+MOONLETTERS, 7210 W. 5th Pl., Summit IL 60501. (708)496-8802. E-mail: shaunaskye@aol.com. Shauna Skye, ed/pub. Secular (with Christian editor). Publishes science fiction, fantasy, poetry, and speculative fiction. Mag. Published 3-4x/yr.; variable length; circ under 1,000. Est. 1995. 100% freelance. Complete ms/cover letter; e-mail query OK. Query for electronic submissions. **PAYS IN COPIES** for one-time rts. Articles (3-4/yr); fiction to 2,000 wds (16-20/yr). Responds in 4 wks. Seasonal 4 mos ahead. Accepts some reprints (query). Prefers disk. Guidelines; copy $3. (Ads)

> **Poetry:** Accepts many/yr. Up to one page. Pays one copy. Submit reasonable number.

> **Fillers:** Ideas, jokes, prose. "Fillers should relate to and fit with the fiction/poetry of our publication."

> **Columns/Departments:** Query.

> **Contest:** See Moonmaid Press (books).

Tips: "Science fiction and fantasy fiction must be set in another world. Cover letters a must."

MOVIEGUIDE, 2510-G Los Posas Rd. #502, Camarillo CA 93010. (805)383-2000. Fax (805)383-4089. E-mail: tbaehr@jetlink.net. Good News Communications/Christian Film & TV Commission. Dr. Theodore Baehr, pub. Family guide to media entertainment from a biblical perspective. Biweekly mag; 30+ pgs.; circ 7,000. Subscription $40. 40% freelance. Query/clips. **NO PAYMENT** for all rts. Articles 1,200 wds (100/yr); book/music/video/movie reviews, 1,200 wds. Responds in 6 wks. Seasonal 6 mos ahead. Accepts disk. Sidebars OK. Guidelines/theme list; copy for SAE/4 stamps. (Ads)

Fillers: Accepts 1,000/yr; all types; 20-50 wds.

Columns/Departments: MovieGuide; TravelGuide; VideoGuide; CDGuide, etc.; 1,200 wds.

NATIONAL CATHOLIC REPORTER, 115 E. Armour Blvd., Kansas City MO 64111. (816)531-0538. Fax (816)968-2280. E-mail: natcath@aol.com. Website: http://www.natcath.com. Catholic. Thomas Fox, pub; Michael Farrell, ed. Independent. Weekly (44X) newspaper; 44-48 pgs; circ 48,000. Query/clips. Pays varying rates on publication. Articles any length. Responds in 9 wks. Accepts simultaneous submissions.

Columns/Departments: Query with ideas for columns.

#NETWORK, PO Box 131165, Birmingham AL 35213-6165. (205)328-7112. Interdenominational. Dolores Milazzo Hicks, ed/pub. To encourage and nurture dialog, understanding and unity in Jewish and Christian communities. Monthly tabloid; 12-16 pgs; circ 15,000. 50% freelance. Negotiable payment. Not copyrighted. Accepts simultaneous submissions. Articles and news.

*NEW COVENANT, 200 Noll Plaza, Huntington IN 46750. (219)356-8400. Fax (219)356-8472. E-mail: NewCov@aol.com. Catholic/Our Sunday Visitor. Mike Aquilina, ed. Serves readers interested in orthodox Catholic spirituality. Monthly mag; 36 pgs; circ 20,000. Subscription $18. 85% freelance. Query/clips or complete ms/cover letter; fax/e-mail query OK. Pays $100-200 on acceptance for 1st or one-time rts. Articles 1,000-1,200 wds (40/yr). Responds in 5 wks. Seasonal 5 mos ahead. Prefers disk. Guidelines; copy for 9x12 SAE/5 stamps. (Ads)

Tips: "Most open to practical, useful approaches to deepening one's spiritual life and relationship with Christ. Be familiar with New Covenant's style so you can speak to our audience."

** This periodical was #67 on the 1997 Top 50 Christian Publishers list. (#33 in 1996, #48 in 1995, #46 in 1994)

+NEW CREATION, PO Box 254, Temple City CA 91780. (562)948-2008. E-mail: DEnsign888@aol.com. Christian Comics Arts Society. Ralph E. Miley, exec. ed. Reports on the Christian comics movement. Bimonthly newsletter; 8-10 pgs; circ 64. Subscription $12. Est. 1996. 20-30% freelance. Query; phone/e-mail query OK. **NO PAYMENT** for all rts. Articles 700 wds (6/yr); book reviews 200 wds. Responds in 3 wks. Accepts reprints (tell when/where appeared). No sidebars. Prefers KJV. Guidelines/theme list; copy for SAE/ stamps. (Ads)

Fillers: Accepts 6 cartoons/yr.

Columns/Departments: Accepts 6/yr. Editorials, 700 wds; Forerunner reviews, 200 wds.

Special Needs: Comic book, cartoon strip and animation news, Christian oriented. Fantasy fiction.

A NEW HEART, Box 4004, San Clemente CA 92674-4004. (714)496-7655. Fax (714)496-8465. Aubrey Beauchamp, ed. For Christian healthcare-givers; info regarding medical/Christian issues. Quarterly mag; 16 pgs; circ 5,000. Subscription $20. 20% freelance. Complete ms/cover letter; phone/fax query OK. **PAYS 2 COPIES** for one-time rts. Not copyrighted. Articles 600-1,800 wds (20-25/yr). Responds in 2-3 wks. Accepts simultaneous submissions & reprints. No sidebars. Guidelines; copy for 9x12 SAE/ 3 stamps.

Poetry: Accepts 1-2/yr. Submit max. 1-3 poems.

Fillers: Accepts 3-4/yr. Anecdotes, cartoons, facts, jokes, short humor; 100-120 wds.

Columns/Departments: Accepts 20-25/yr. Chaplain's Corner, 200-250 wds; Physician's Corner, 200-250 wds.

Tips: "Most open to true stories, short, medically related, including caregivers."

#NEW HORIZONS, 607 N. Easton Rd., Bldg. E, PO Box P, Willow Grove PA 19090-0920. (215)830-0900. Fax (215)830-0350. E-mail: tomtyson@aol.com. Committee on Christian Education, Orthodox Presbyterian Church. Thomas E. Tyson, ed. Denominational. Monthly (11X) newsletter; circ 12,000. Subscription $15. Open to freelance. Query or complete ms. Not in topical listings. (Ads)

NEW OXFORD REVIEW, 1069 Kains Ave., Berkeley CA 94706. (510)526-5374. Catholic. Dale Vree, ed. Orthodox Catholic, but open to compatible evangelical views; highly educated audience. Monthly (11X) mag; 40 pgs; circ 15,250. Subscription $19. 50% freelance. Query or complete ms; phone query OK. **PAYS IN COPIES**, for all rts. Articles 750-3,750 wds (20/yr). Responds in 3-6 wks. Seasonal 4 mos ahead. Copy for $3.50.

Tips: "Manuscripts must have intellectual depth."

NEW TRUMPET, TH130 590 Lower Landing Rd., Blackwood NJ 08012. (609)228-4243. Mae Hart Lovett, ed. To help Christians in their walk and to prepare them for the return of Christ. Irregular newsletter; 16 pgs; circ 1,200. 100% freelance. Complete ms/cover letter; phone query OK. **PAYS IN COPIES** for one-time rts. Articles 350-800 wds (33/yr); fiction 1,500-2,000 wds (3/yr); book/video reviews, 300 wds. Responds in 4 wks. Accepts simultaneous submissions & reprints (tell when/where appeared). Prefers disk. Sidebars OK. Prefers NIV or NAS. Guidelines; copy for 2 stamps.

Poetry: Accepts 3-5/yr. Free verse, light verse, traditional; 4-24 lines. Submit max. 3-6 poems.

Fillers: Accepts 3-4/yr. Anecdotes, cartoons, facts, ideas, jokes, prayers, prose, quizzes, quotes, short humor; 15-30 wds.

Tips: "Call to discuss your idea. Looking for male writers. Your idea should excite you and the reader, be biblically based, and comfort or build the reader's faith. I like stories, fact or fiction."

NEW WRITING MAGAZINE, Box 1812, Amherst NY 14226-7812. (716)834-1067. E-mail: newwriting@aol.com. Website: http://1812.simplemet.com. New Writing Agency. Richard Lynch, co-ed. The best of new writing by beginning and established writers. Annual electronic mag. Free on the Internet. 95% freelance.

Complete ms/cover letter; e-mail query OK. **NO PAYMENT** for 1st rts. Not copyrighted. Articles (5/yr); fiction (20/yr). Responds in 6-8 wks. Seasonal 6 mos ahead. Accepts simultaneous submissions & reprints (tell when/where appeared). Guidelines. (Ads)

Poetry: Buys 20/yr. Avant-garde, free verse, traditional; any length. Submit max. 5 poems.

Contest: "We run a writing contest and agency. Visit http://members. aol.com/newwriting.contest.html."

NO-DEBT LIVING, PO Box 282, Veradale WA 99037-0282. Phone/fax (509)927-1322 (call for fax). E-mail: nodebt@gntech.net. Website: http://www.nodebtnews. com. Robert E. Frank, ed. Financial and home-management information from a Christian perspective. Monthly newsletter; 12 pgs; circ. 1,000. Subscription $25.95. 50% freelance. Query/clips or resume; fax/e-mail query OK. Pays $30-60 on publication for one-time & reprint rts. Articles 300-1,200 wds (40/yr); 400-600 wds (vignettes); book reviews 300 wds. Responds in 4 wks. Seasonal 2-3 mos ahead. Accepts simultaneous submissions & reprints (tell when/where appeared). Prefers disk or e-mail in ASCII format. Sidebars OK. Prefers NAS. Guidelines/theme list; copy for 7x10 SAE/2 stamps.

Special Needs: Consumer-related news, investment, and taxes.

Tips: "Follow AP style. Use original quotes from two well-known professionals (preferably Christians). Link story to a current news trend or issue. Most open to money-management (if writer has experience and/or professional expertise)."

THE NORTH AMERICAN VOICE OF FATIMA, 1023 Swan Rd., Youngstown NY 14174. (716)754-7489. Fax (716)754-9130. E-mail: OurLadFati@aol.com. Barnabite Fathers, Inc./Catholic. Father Paul Keeling, ed. A Marian publication with emphasis on apparitions of Our Lady of Fatima. Bimonthly mag; 20 pgs; circ 3,000. Subscription $4.50. 50% freelance. Complete ms/cover letter. Pays .04/wd on publication for 1st rts. Not copyrighted. Articles & fiction 1,000 wds. Responds in 6 wks. Seasonal 4 mos ahead. Accepts simultaneous submissions & reprints. No disk. Sidebars OK. Guidelines/copy for #10 SAE.

Poetry: Buys 20/yr. Free verse, traditional. Pays $10.

*NORTHSTATE CHRISTIAN TIMES,, PO Box 493954, Redding CA 96049. (916)221-0326. Rick Flynn, ed. Christian Newspaper. Not in topical listings.

NORTHWEST CHRISTIAN JOURNAL, Box 59014, Renton WA 98058. (425)255-3552. Fax (425)228-8749. E-mail: storysearc@aol.com. Tami Tedrow, ed. Local, national, and international news with an evangelical perspective. Monthly tabloid newspaper; 16-40 pgs; circ 26,000. Subscription $15. Little freelance. Query/clips; no phone queries. Pays $40 on publication for one-time or simultaneous rts. Articles 500-750 wds. Accepts simultaneous submissions & reprints. Accepts disk or e-mail. Some sidebars. Prefers NIV. Guidelines (2 stamps); copy $1.50. (Ads)

Fillers: Limited interest in cartoons.

Special Needs: Advertising themes: January—Marriage; March & October—Christian Education Guide.

Tips: "This is a news publication, which limits our interest to stories that are timely and localized for the Northwest. No devotional material, columns, poetry, personal testimonies (unless localized with a news angle) or promotions of business (contact our advertising dept). Local writers preferred."

NORTHWESTERN LUTHERAN, 2929 N Mayfair Rd., Milwaukee WI 53222-4398. (414)256-3888. Fax (414)256-3899. E-mail: garyb@host3.sab.wels.net. Wisconsin Evangelical Lutheran Synod. Gary P. Baumler, ed. Denominational. Monthly mag; 36 pgs; circ 55,000. Subscription $9. 25% freelance. Complete ms/cover letter; no phone/fax/e-mail query. Pays $50/pg on publication for one-time rts. Articles 500-1,000 wds (50/yr). Responds in 4-6 wks. Seasonal 4 mos ahead. Accepts reprints (tell when/where appeared). Accepts disk. Sidebars OK. Prefers NIV. Guidelines; copy for 9x12 SAE/2 stamps.

Tips: "Most of our writers belong to the denomination and write about our members, organizations or institutions. Most open to strong personal witness; strong inspirational example of Christian living."

#OBLATES, 9480 N. De Mazenod Dr., Belleville IL 62223-1160. (618)398-4848. Fax (618)398-8788. Catholic/Missionary Assn. of Missionary Oblates of Mary Immaculate. Mary Mohrman, mss ed. To inspire, comfort, uplift, and motivate an older Catholic/Christian audience. Bimonthly mag; 20 pgs; circ 500,000. Free to members. 30-50% freelance. Complete ms only/cover letter; no phone/fax query. Pays $80 on acceptance for 1st rts. Articles 500-600 wds (40/yr). Responds in 9 wks. Seasonal 6 mos ahead. Considers simultaneous submissions. No disk. No sidebars. Prefers NAB. Guidelines; copy for 6x9 SAE/2 stamps.

Poetry: Buys 20-25/yr. Free verse, traditional; 8-16 lines; $30. Submit max. 2 poems.

Tips: "Need personal, inspirational articles with a strong spiritual theme firmly grounded to a particular incident and poetry."

OUR FAMILY, Box 249, Battleford SK S0M 0E0 Canada. (306)937-7771. Fax (306)937-7644. Catholic/Missionary Oblates of St. Mary's Province. Fr. Nestor Gregoire, ed. All aspects of family life in the light of Christian faith. Monthly (11X) mag; 40 pgs; circ 14,300. Subscription $15.98. 60% freelance. Query or complete ms; phone query OK. Pays .07-.10/wd on acceptance for all, 1st, one-time, simultaneous, or reprint rts. Articles 500-2,500 wds (72-88/yr). Responds in 5 wks. Seasonal 4 mos ahead. Accepts simultaneous submissions & reprints. Kill fee 100%. Sidebars OK. Guidelines/theme list; copy $2.50/9x12 SAE./Canadian postage or IRCs. (Ads)

Poetry: Buys 48-110/yr. Free verse, haiku, light verse, traditional; 2-25 lines; $.75-$1/line.

Fillers: Buys 24-110/yr. Anecdotes, cartoons, jokes, short humor; to 150 wds.

Tips: "Your SASE must have Canadian postage. We aim at the average reader. Looking for articles which deal with specific Catholic issues; articles that are rooted in social justice, service to others, and the Sunday liturgy. Articles need an experiential point of view with practical guidelines."

** This periodical was #47 on the 1997 Top 50 Christian Publishers list. (#39 in 1996 & 1995, #29 in 1994)

*OUR SUNDAY VISITOR, 200 Noll Plaza, Huntington IN 46750. (219)356-8400. Fax (219)356-8472. Catholic. David Scott, ed. Vital news, spirituality for today's Catholic. Weekly newspaper; 24 pgs; circ 120,000. Subscription $36. 5% freelance. Query. Pays $150-250 on acceptance for 1st rts. Articles to 1,000 wds

(25/yr). Responds in 5 wks. Seasonal 2 mos ahead. Kill fee. Guidelines; Copy for #10 SASE.

Columns/Departments: Buys 50/yr. Viewpoint (editorial/op-ed), 750 wds, $100.

Tips: "Need familiarity with Catholic Church issues and with Catholic Press—newspapers and magazines."

** #1 on the 1994 Top 50.

PARENTLIFE, 127 Ninth Ave. N., Nashville TN 37234-0140. (615)251-2229. Fax (615)251-5008. E-mail: parentlife@bssb.com. Southern Baptist/LifeWay Press. Jeff Large, mng ed. For parents of children—birth to 12 years. Monthly mag; 50 pgs; circ 115,000. Subscription $19.95. Est. 1994. 30% freelance. Query/clips; fax/e-mail query OK. Pays $100-500 on acceptance for all, first, one-time & electronic rts. Articles 800-1,200 wds (75/yr). Responds in 6-8 wks. Seasonal 8 mos ahead. Considers simultaneous submissions. Accepts disk. Sidebars OK. Prefers NIV. Guidelines; copy for 9x12 SAE/3 stamps.

Fillers: Buys 50/yr. Anecdotes, games, ideas, party ideas; 75-100 wds; $25-100.

Tips: "Looking for articles on specific aspects of parenting. Good topics are developmental articles, school, home school, family life. You must send an SASE, or no response."

** This periodical was #3 on the 1997 Top 50 Christian Publishers list. (#27 in 1996, #40 in 1995)

THE PARENT PAPER, PO Box 1313, Manchester TN 37349. (931)728-8309. Fax (931)723-1902. E-mail: rhurst@edge.net. Rebekah Hurst, pub. A Christian perspective on topics that benefit the family. Monthly newspaper; circ. 5,000; subscription $15. Complete ms. **PAYS 3 COPIES FOR NOW** for 1st or reprint rts. Articles; fiction from youth writers (400-600 words). Seasonal 6 mos ahead. Accepts simultaneous submissions & reprints. Guidelines; copy for 9x12 SAE/4 stamps.

Poetry: Accepts 6/yr.

THE PEGASUS REVIEW, PO Box 88, Henderson MD 21640-0088. (410)482-6736. Art Bounds, ed. Theme-oriented poetry, short fiction & essays; not necessarily religious; in calligraphy. Bimonthly mag; 10-12 pgs; circ 130. Subscription $10. 100% freelance. Query or complete ms/cover letter. **PAYS 2 COPIES** for one-time rts. Fiction 2 1/2 pgs, single-spaced (6-10/yr); also one-page essays. Responds in 4 wks. Seasonal 2 mos ahead. Accepts simultaneous submissions & reprints (tell when/where appeared). No disk or sidebars. Prefers KJV. Guidelines/theme list; copy $2.50.

Poetry: Accepts 60-100/yr. Any type; to 24 lines (shorter the better). Theme oriented. Submit max. 5 poems.

Fillers: Accepts 10-20/yr. Cartoons, prose, quotes; short.

Special Needs: 1998 themes are Beginnings, Dreams, Creativity, Country (USA), Nature, and Parents.

Tips: "Zero in on a theme, submit 3-5 poems or one story, and heed editor's suggestions."

PENTECOSTAL EVANGEL, 1445 Boonville, Springfield MO 65802-1894. (417)862-2781. Fax (417)862-0416. E-mail: pevangel@ag.org. Assemblies of

God. Hal Donaldson, ed. Denominational; Pentecostal. Weekly mag; 32 pgs; circ 250,000. Subscription $21.95. 20% freelance. Complete ms/cover letter. Pays .06-.08/wd (.03/wd for reprints) on acceptance for 1st and electronic rts. Articles 800-1,000 wds (70/yr). Responds in 6-8 wks. Seasonal 6-8 mos ahead. Accepts reprints (tell when/where appeared). Kill fee 100%. Prefers disk. Sidebars OK. Prefers NIV or KJV. Guidelines; copy $1/9x12 SAE/4 stamps. (Ads)

> **Fillers:** Practical, how-to pieces on family life, devotions, evangelism, seasonal, current issues, Christian living; 50-200 wds. Pays $20.

> **Tips:** "General inspirational articles with a strong focus; salvation-type articles for the unsaved; feature articles targeted to the unsaved (we will have 12 evangelism issues a year)." Note: This publication is undergoing a redesign in both layout and editorial content. Send for new guidelines.

> ** This periodical was #28 on the 1996 Top 50 Christian Publishers list. (#11 in 1995, #23 in 1994)

THE PENTECOSTAL TESTIMONY, 6745 Century Ave., Mississauga ON L5N 6P7 Canada. (905)542-7400. Fax (905)542-7313. E-mail: testimony@paoc.org. The Pentecostal Assemblies of Canada. Rick Hiebert, ed. Focus is inspirational and Christian living; Pentecostal holiness slant. Monthly mag; 28 pgs; circ 21,650. Subscription $24 US/$17 CAN. 20% freelance. Query; fax query OK. Pays $20-75 ($100 for fiction) on publication for 1st or reprint rts. Articles 800-1,200 wds (12/yr); fiction 1,000-1,500 wds (5/yr); book/music reviews, 400 wds ($20 or copy of book). Responds in 6-8 wks. Seasonal 4 mos ahead. Accepts reprints (tell when/where appeared). Prefers disk. Sidebars OK. Prefers NIV. Guidelines; copy $2/9x12 SAE. (Ads)

> **Special Needs:** Youth-related articles; native issues. Looking for young writers able to write for young readers (teens through 20-something).

> **Tips:** "Our readership is 98% Canadian. We prefer Canadian writers or at least writers who understand that Canadians are not Americans in long underwear."

PERSPECTIVES, A Journal of Reformed Thought, PO Box 470, Ada MI 49301-0470. (616)285-8074. Fax (616)285-9828. E-mail: 70134.222@compuserve.com. Reformed Church Press. Craig W. Stapert, mng ed. To express the Reformed faith theologically; to engage issues that Reformed Christians meet in personal, ecclesiastical, and societal life. Monthly (10X) mag; 24 pgs; circ. 3,000. Subscription $24.95. Complete ms/cover letter; fax/e-mail query OK. **PAYS IN COPIES** for all rts (usually). Articles (10/yr) and fiction (3/yr), 2,000-2,500 wds; book reviews 500-1,500 wds. Responds in 4-6 wks. Seasonal 4 mos ahead. Prefers disk. Sidebars rare. Prefers NRSV. Copy for 9x12 SAE/$1.50 postage. (Ads)

> **Poetry:** Francis Fike. Free verse, traditional. Accepts 5-7/yr. Submit max. 2 poems.

> **Columns/Departments:** Accepts 20-24/yr. As We See It (editorial/opinion) 750-1,500 wds; Inside Out (biblical exegesis) 750 wds. Complete ms.

PHYSICIAN, 8605 Explorer Dr., Colorado Springs CO 80920. (719)531-3400. Fax (719)531-3499. E-mail: coxmr@fotf.org. Focus on the Family. Melissa Cox, ed. To encourage physicians and their families. Bimonthly mag; 24 pgs; circ 68,820. Free to medical profession. 10% freelance. Complete ms/cover letter; fax/e-mail query OK. Pays $100-500 on publication for 1st rts. Articles 800-2,400 wds.

Responds in 6 wks. Prefers disk. Kill fee. Sidebars OK. Prefers NIV. Copy available.

Fillers: Cartoons; $50-75.

Tips: "Call ahead. Be a physician. Understand the medical industry."

** 1997 EPA Award of Excellence—Christian Ministry.

THE PLAIN TRUTH, 300 W. Green St., Pasadena CA 91129. Fax (818)795-0107. E-mail: Susan_Stewart@ptm.org. Website: http://www.ptm.org/index.htm. Plain Truth Ministries. Susan Stewart, mng ed. Proclaims the Gospel of Jesus Christ, emphasizing the central teachings of Christianity and making those teachings plain and truthful. Bimonthly mag; 68 pgs; circ 135,000. Subscription $12.95. 60-70% freelance. Query/clips or complete ms/cover letter; fax/e-mail query OK. Pays .25/wd (.15/wd for reprints) on publication for 1st, one-time, reprint, and world (all languages) rts. Articles 750-2,000 wds (25/yr); book/music/video reviews 100 wds, $25. Responds in 4-6 wks. Seasonal 6-8 mos ahead. Accepts simultaneous submissions & reprints (tell when/where appeared). Requires disk. Kill fee 75%. Sidebars OK. Prefers NIV. Guidelines; copy for 9x12 SAE/4 stamps. (Ads)

> **Columns/Departments:** Buys 18/yr. Family (family issues), 1,500 wds; Commentary (hot topic editorials), 550-650 wds; Christian People (testimonial/interviews), 1,500 wds. Query or complete ms.
>
> **Tips:** "Best to send tear sheets of previously published articles and submit detailed query for standard articles."

*****PLENTY GOOD ROOM,** 1800 N. Hermitage Ave., Chicago IL 60622-1101. (773)486-8970. Catholic. J. Glen Murray, ed. Focuses on African-American worship within the church. Bimonthly mag; 12 pgs. Est. 1993. Query. Pays $25/pg, for all rts. Articles. Responds in 13 wks. Guidelines; free copy.

#PLOUGH, Spring Valley, RD 2 Box 446, Farmington PA 15437. (800)521-8011 or (412)329-1100. Fax (412)329-0914. E-mail: PlghSec@bruderhof.com. Website: http://www.bruderhof.org/ploughs/index.htm. Bruderhof Communities. Christoph Arnold, ed. Dedicated to all who work for a personal transformation in Christ and for a radical turn away from the materialism, militarism, racism, and impurity of this world towards the coming of God's kingdom. Quarterly mag; circ 7,500. Subscription $10. Some freelance. Query. Not in topical listings. (Ads)

THE PLOWMAN, Box 414, Whitby ON L1N 5S4 Canada. (905)668-7803. The Plowman Ministries/Christian. Tony Scavetta, pub. Poetry and prose of social commentary; any topics. Quarterly journal; 20 pgs; circ 5,000. Subscription $10 US. 90% freelance. Query; phone query OK. **NO PAYMENT.** Articles (10/yr) & fiction (50/yr), 1,000 wds. Responds in 1-2 wks. Accepts simultaneous submissions & reprints. No disk or sidebars. Free guidelines/copy for 9x12 SAE. (Ads)

> **Poetry:** Accepts 100/yr. Free verse, haiku, light verse, traditional; to 38 lines (55 characters across max.). Submit max. 4 poems.
>
> **Fillers:** Accepts 25/yr. Prose, prayers; 25-30 wds.
>
> **Special Needs:** Also publishes chapbooks; 20% royalties. Open to all topics.
>
> **Contest:** Sponsors a poetry contest; $2/poem entry fee.

PLUS, 66 E. Main St., Pawling NY 12564. (914)855-5000. Fax (914)855-1462. Peale Center for Christian Living. Pat Planeta, ed. Spiritually oriented, based on positive thinking and faith. Monthly (10X) mag; 36 pgs; circ 600,000. Subscription

$10. 30% freelance. Complete ms/cover letter; phone/fax query OK. Pays $25/pg on publication for 1st or one-time rts. Articles 500-2,500 wds (8/yr). Responds in 3-4 wks. Seasonal 6 mos ahead. Accepts reprints. Some sidebars. Guidelines; copy for #10 SAE/1 stamp.

Tips: "Have a deep, living knowledge of Christianity. Our audience is 65-70% female, average age is 55."

** This periodical was #31 on the 1995 Top 50 Christian Publishers list.

POETRY FORUM SHORT STORIES, 5713 Larchmont Dr., Erie PA 16509. Phone/fax (814)866-2543. E-mail: 75562.670@compuserve.com. Interdenominational. Gunvor Skogsholm, ed. Poetry and prose that takes an honest look at the human condition. Bimonthly mag; 20 pgs; circ 400. Subscription $22. 90% freelance. Complete ms by fax or e-mail. **NO PAYMENT** for one-time rts (buys only from subscribers). Articles 300 wds; fiction 3,000 wds (150/yr); book reviews 200 wds. Responds in 8 wks. Seasonal 2 mos ahead. Accepts simultaneous submissions & reprints (tell when/where appeared). Prefers disk. Guidelines; copy $3. (Ads)

Poetry: Accepts 300/yr. Inspirational; any type; to 50 lines.

Contest: Poetry & short stories. Send SASE for information.

POETS' PAPER (formerly **FEELINGS QUARTERLY**), PO Box 85, Easton PA 18044-0085. (610)559-9287. E-mail: irregular@silo.com. Anderie Poetry Press. Carole J. Heffley, exec. ed; submit to Michael Steffen, acq. ed. For the publication of fine poetry. Quarterly journal; 56-60 pgs; circ 3,000. Subscription $24. Est. 12/96. 90% freelance. Complete ms/cover letter; phone/e-mail query OK. Query for electronic submissions. **NO PAYMENT** for one-time rts. Responds in 4-6 wks. Seasonal 6 mos ahead. Reprints if it's been more than a year (tell when/where appeared). Guidelines; copies $6.50. (Ads)

Poetry: Accepts 1,000+/yr; to 38 lines. Submit max. 3 poems.

Fillers: Quotes: must pertain to poetry, poets or writing. Pays one copy.

Columns/Departments: Buys 20/yr. Pays $25. "Would accept a column on writing inspirational poetry; markets for inspirational poetry."

Contest: Sponsors several contests. Send for guidelines. Also collects poetry for an annual edition of praise poetry; 100 poems/edition.

Tips: "We do not accept overly religious poems. Use subtle images of our Creator—mostly in nature."

#POET'S PARK, 2745 Monterey Hwy #76, San Jose CA 95111-3129. E-mail: poet@soos.com. Website: http://www.soos.com/poetpark. Redwood Family Chapel. Submit to The Editor at e-mail. Known as "the resting spot on the information super highway;" on-line to provide spiritual refreshing for those who are browsing the Web. Quarterly mag. Free. 100% freelance. Query on-line only/one poem. **NO PAYMENT** for one-time rts. Articles 350-2,500 wds (12/yr). Responds in 4 wks. Accepts simultaneous submissions & reprints. Requires disk or e-mail. Sidebars OK. Guidelines; view online only at above Website. (Ads)

Poetry: Accepts 600-800/yr. Any type; 1-60 lines; submit via e-mail; one only.

*POURASTAN, 615 Stuart Ave., Outremont QB H2V 3H2 Canada. (514)279-3066. Fax (514)276-9960. Canadian Diocese of the Armenian Holy Apostolic Church. Mr. N. Ouzounian, ed. Denominational; religious, social and community oriented.

Bimonthly mag; 24-28 pgs; circ 1,000. Free for donations. 100% freelance. Complete ms/cover letter; phone/fax query OK. **NO PAYMENT.** Not copyrighted. Articles 250-1,500 wds (10/yr); book reviews, 300 wds. Seasonal 1 mo ahead. Accepts simultaneous submissions & reprints. No sidebars. Accepts disk. Copy for 9x12 SAE/90 cents.

Poetry: Accepts 10/yr. Traditional, 4-40 lines. Submit max. 2 poems.

Fillers: Anecdotes, ideas, prayers, quotes, short humor, 10-50 wds.

Note: This publication is published in Armenian with occasional English and French.

POWER FOR LIVING, Box 36640, Colorado Springs CO 80936. (719)536-0100. Cook Communications/Scripture Press Publications. Don Alban Jr., ed. To communicate biblical principles for godly living through articles focused on evangelism, exposition, or edification. Weekly take-home paper; 8 pgs; circ 250,000. Subscription $10. 25% freelance. Complete ms; no phone/fax/e-mail query. Pays up to .15/wd (reprints up to .10/wd) on acceptance for 1st or one-time rts. Articles 700-1,500 wds (20/yr). Responds in 4 wks. Seasonal 1 yr ahead. Accepts simultaneous submissions & reprints (tell when/where appeared). Prefers disk. Kill fee. Few sidebars. Paraphrase Bible verses (avoids direct quotes). Guidelines/copy for #10 SAE/1 stamp.

Special Needs: Third-person profiles of truly out-of-the-ordinary Christians who express their faith uniquely.

Tips: "Most open to vignettes, 450-1,000 wds, of prominent Christians with solid testimonies or profiles from church history. Focus on the unusual. Signed releases required."

** This periodical was #11 on the 1996 Top 50 Christian Publishers list. (#9 in 1995, #21 in 1994)

PRAIRIE MESSENGER, PO Box 190, Muenster SK S0K 2Y0 Canada. (306)682-1772. Fax (306)682-5285. E-mail: pmessenger@sk.sympatico.ca. Catholic. Marion Noll, OSU, assoc. ed. For Catholics in Saskatchewan & Manitoba, and Christians in other faith communities. Weekly journal; circ 7,800. Subscription $25 CAN. 10% freelance. Complete ms/cover letter; phone/fax/e-mail query OK. Pays to $40-60 ($2/column inch for news items) on publication for 1st, one-time, simultaneous & reprint rts. Not copyrighted. Articles to 250-600 wds (15/yr). Responds in 9 wks. Seasonal 3 mos ahead. Accepts simultaneous submissions & reprints. Sidebars OK. Guidelines; copy for 9x12 SAE/$1 CAN/$1.24 US.

Poetry: Accepts 46/yr. Free verse; 6-25 lines.

Special Needs: Ecumenism; social justice; native concerns.

Tips: "Comment/feature section is most open. Send topic of concern or interest to Prairie readership. It's difficult to break into our publication."

** This periodical was selected #1 for general excellence by the Canadian Church Press (10 times during the last 16 years).

PRAYERWORKS, PO Box 301363, Portland OR 97294. (503)761-2072. Fax (503)760-1184. E-mail: 7653.3202@compuserve.com. V. Ann Mandeville, ed. For prayer warriors in retirement centers; focuses on prayer. Weekly newspaper; 4 pgs; circ 600. Free subscription. 100% freelance. Complete ms; phone/fax query OK. **PAYS IN COPIES,** for one-time rts. Not copyrighted. Articles (30-40/yr) & fiction (30/yr); 300-500 wds. Responds in 3 wks. Seasonal 2 mos ahead. Accepts simultaneous submissions & reprints. No sidebars. Guidelines; copy for #10 SAE/1 stamp.

Poetry: Accepts 20-30/yr. Free verse, haiku, light verse, traditional. Submit max. 10 poems.

Fillers: Accepts up to 50/yr. Facts, jokes, prayers, quotes, short humor; to 50 wds.

Tips: "Write tight. Half our audience is over 70, but 30% is young families. Subject matter isn't important as long as it is scriptural and designed to help people pray."

#THE PRESBYTERIAN LAYMAN, 136 Tremont Park, PO Box 2210, Lenoir NC 28645. (704)758-8716. Fax (704)758-0920. Presbyterian Lay Committee. Parker T. Williamson, exec. ed. For the conservative/evangelical members of the Presbyterian Church (USA). Bimonthly newspaper; 24 pgs; circ. 520,000. No subscriptions. 10% freelance. Query. Pays negotiable rates on publication for 1st rts. Articles 800-1,200 wds (12/yr). Responds in 2 wks. Seasonal 2 mos ahead. Prefers disk. Sidebars OK. Copy for 9x12 SAE/3 stamps.

Poetry: Traditional; pay negotiable. Submit max. 1 poem.

THE PRESBYTERIAN OUTLOOK, Box 85623, Richmond VA 23285-5623. (804)359-8442. Fax (804)353-6369. E-mail: outlook.parti@pcusa.org. Presbyterian Church (USA)/Independent. Robert H. Bullock Jr., ed. For ministers, members and staff of the denomination. Weekly (43X) mag; 16-40 pgs; circ 11,900. Subscription $28. 5% freelance. Query; phone/fax/e-mail query OK. **NO PAYMENT** for all rts. Not copyrighted. Articles to 1,000 wds; book reviews 1 1/2 pgs. Responds in 1-2 wks. Seasonal 2 mos ahead. Requires disk. Some sidebar. Prefers NRSV. Guidelines; free copy. (Ads)

Tips: "Correspond with editor regarding current needs. Most material is commissioned; anything submitted should be of interest to Presbyterians."

PRESBYTERIAN RECORD, 50 Wynford Dr., North York ON M3C 1J7 Canada. (416)444-1111. Fax (416)441-2825. E-mail: pcrecord@presbyterian.ca. Website: http://www.presbycan.ca/. The Presbyterian Church in Canada. Rev. John Congram, ed. Denominational. Monthly (11X) mag; 52 pgs; circ 55,000. 50% freelance. Query (preferred) or complete ms/cover letter; fax query OK. Pays $50 CAN on publication for 1st, one-time, reprint or simultaneous rts. Articles 1,000-1,500 wds (15-20/yr); book/music reviews, to 400 wds/no pay. Responds in 9-13 wks. Seasonal 3 mos ahead. Accepts simultaneous submissions & reprints. Sidebars OK. Guidelines; copy for 9x12 SAE/$1 Canadian postage or IRCs from US writers.

Poetry: Thomas Dickey. Buys 8-15/yr. Free verse, haiku, light verse, traditional; 10-30 lines preferred; $35. Send any number.

Fillers: Buys 6/yr. Anecdotes, cartoons, facts, ideas, prose, prayers, short humor; to 200 wds; $15-25.

Columns/Departments: Buys 12/yr. Vox Populi (controversial issues), 750 wds; $35-50.

Tips: "It helps if submissions have some connection to Canada and/or the Presbyterian Church."

PRESBYTERIANS TODAY, 100 Witherspoon St., Louisville KY 40202-1396. (502)569-5637. Fax (502)569-8632. E-mail: today@pcusa.org. Website: http://www.pcusa.org/pcusa/today. Presbyterian Church (USA). Catherine Cottingham, mng. ed.; submit to Eva Stimson, ed. Denominational; not as conservative or evangelical as some. Monthly (10X) mag; 44 pgs; circ 90,000. Subscription $12.95. 65% freelance. Complete ms/cover letter; fax/e-mail query OK. Pays $200 before publication for 1st rts. Articles 1,000-1,500 wds (20/yr). Responds in 4-5 wks. Seasonal 4 mos ahead. Some reprints. Kill fee. Guidelines; free copy. (Ads)

Fillers: Cartoons, $25, short humor to 100 wds, no payment.

Tips: "Most open to feature articles or news articles about Presbyterian people and programs (600-800 wds, $75). Do not often use inspirational or testimony-type articles."

** This periodical was #48 on the 1997 Top 50 Christian Publishers list. (#64 in 1996, #41 in 1995)

PRESERVING CHRISTIAN HOMES (formerly **PENTECOSTAL HOMELIFE**), 8855 Dunn Rd., Hazelwood MO 63042-2299. (314)837-7300. Fax (314)837-4503. E-mail: Gyouth8855@aol.com. United Pentecostal Church. Scott Graham, ed. Addresses relevant topics for the Christian family. Bimonthly mag; 16 pgs; circ 4,000. 40% freelance. Complete ms/cover letter; phone/fax/e-mail query OK. Pays $30 on publication for one-time or simultaneous rts. Articles 500-1,500 wds (12/yr); fiction 500-1,500 wds (12/yr). Responds in 3-4 wks. Seasonal 6 mos ahead. Accepts simultaneous submissions & reprints (tell when/where appeared). No disk. Some sidebars. Prefers KJV. Guidelines; copy for 10x13 SAE.

Poetry: Buys 3-4/yr. Light verse, traditional; 4-50 lines. Pays $15-30. Submit max. 2 poems.

Fillers: Buys 2/yr. Cartoons, games, quizzes, word puzzles. Pays $15-30.

Tips: "Most open to fiction and relationships."

#PRISM, 10 Lancaster Ave., Wynnewood PA 19096-3495. (610)645-9390. Fax (610)649-8090. E-mail: prism@esa.mhs.compuserve.com. Website: http://www.libertynet.org/~esa/prism. Evangelicals for Social Action. Dwight Ozard, ed. For Christians who are interested in the social and political dimensions of the gospel. Bimonthly mag; 44 pgs; circ 6,000. Subscription $25. 15% freelance. Query/clips; fax/e-mail query OK. Pays $200 ($100 for fiction) 6 wks after publication for 1st or reprint rts. Articles 500-2,800 wds (5/yr); fiction, 700-1,600 wds (1/yr); book/video reviews, 500 wds, $0-100. Responds in 8-12 wks. Seasonal 6 mos ahead. Accepts reprints (tell when/where appeared). Prefers disk. Sidebars OK. Prefers NRSV. Guidelines; copy $3. (Ads)

Tips: "Looking for analysis on religious right; social justice fiction. Understand progressive evangelicals and E.S.A. Read Tony Campolo, Ron Sider and Richard Foster. Most open to features."

PROGRESS, Box 9609, Kansas City MO 64134-0609. (816)763-7800. Fax (816)765-2522. Stonecroft Ministries. Susan Collard, mng. ed. For women and their families who are involved in some aspect of Stonecroft Ministries. Bimonthly mag; 64 pgs; circ 30,000. Subscription $8.50. 15% freelance. Complete ms/cover letter; phone/fax query OK. **PAYS IN COPIES**, for 1st rts. Not copyrighted. Articles 300-600 wds (15/yr). Responds in 2 wks. Seasonal 6 mos ahead. Accepts reprints (tell when/where appeared). Accepts disk. Some sidebars. Prefers NIV. Guidelines; copy for 6x9 SAE/4 stamps.

Columns/Departments: Buys 12/yr. Coping Series (how God helped through crisis or stress—prefers other than illness); Family Builders (help for families); 1,000-1,200 wds. These columns most open to freelance.

Tips: "We do not include controversial or doctrinal issues about which Christians disagree. Material should be Christ-centered and biblically based."

+PROLIFE NEWS CANADA, B1 - 90 Garry St., Winnipeg MB R3C 4H1 Canada. (204)943-5273. Fax (204)943-9283. Barbara LeBow, mng. ed. For those who respect and protect life, from conception to natural death. Monthly (10X) mag;16 pgs; circ 30,000. Subscription $21.40 (GST incl.). Variable freelance. Complete ms/cover letter; phone/fax/e-mail query OK. Pays $50 CAN on publication for all rts. Articles 1,000-1,200 wds (10-20/yr); book or some video reviews, under 1,000 wds. Responds in 4 wks. Seasonal 2 mos ahead. Accepts simultaneous submissions & reprints (tell when/where appeared). No disk. Some sidebars. Guidelines; copy for 10x13 SAE/.90 CAN postage. (Ads)

Special Needs: Human rights, rights of the child in the womb, euthanasia.

PURPOSE, 616 Walnut Ave., Scottdale PA 15683. (412)887-8500. Fax (412)887-3111. E-mail: horsch%mph@mcimail.com. Mennonite Church. James E. Horsch, ed. Denominational, for older youth and adults. Weekly take-home paper; 8 pgs; circ 13,000. Subscription $16.10. 95% freelance. Complete ms (only)/cover letter; phone query OK. Pays .05/wd on acceptance for one-time rts. Articles & fiction, to 750 wds (130/yr). Responds in 9 wks. Seasonal 6 mos ahead. Accepts simultaneous submissions & reprints (tell when/where appeared). Sidebars OK. Guidelines; copy for 6x9 SAE/2 stamps.

Poetry: Buys 130/yr. Free verse, light verse, traditional; 3-12 lines; up to $2/line. Submit max. 10 poems.

Fillers: Buys 15/yr. Anecdotes, cartoons, short humor; 200-500 wds; .04/wd.

Tips: "Articles must carry a strong story line. First person is preferred. Don't exceed maximum word length."

** This periodical was #49 on the 1997 Top 50 Christian Publishers list. (#48 in 1996, #20 in 1995, #22 in 1994)

#PURSUIT, 901 E. 78th St., Minneapolis MN 55420. (800)995-5360 or (612)854-1300. Fax (612)853-8488. Evangelical Free Church. Timothy Addington, ed. An evangelistic magazine written for the unchurched. Quarterly mag; 32 pgs; circ 50,000. Subscription $10. 100% freelance. Query. Pays .10/wd on publication for one-time rts. Articles 800-2,000 wds (20/yr). Responds in 4-6 wks. Seasonal 6 months ahead. Accepts simultaneous submissions & reprints, if advised. Kill fee 25%. Guidelines; copy $1/9x12 SAE/4 stamps. (Ads)

Tips: "Study the magazine. Write about what the unchurched are interested in, touching especially on felt needs. Along with complete article, please submit suggested theme for issue and two or three companion article ideas."

QUEEN OF ALL HEARTS, 26 S. Saxon Ave., Bay Shore NY 11706-8993. (516)665-0726. Fax (516)665-4349. E-mail: Q.O.A.H.@aol.com. Catholic/Montfort Missionaries. Rev. Roger M. Charest, SMM, mng. ed. Focus is Mary, the Mother of Jesus. Bimonthly journal; 48 pgs; circ 2,800. Subscription $17. 80% freelance. Complete ms/cover letter. Pays $25-75 ($40-60 for fiction) on publication for 1st rts. Not copyrighted. Articles (40/yr) and fiction (6/yr) 1,500-2,000 wds; book reviews 100 wds. Responds in 3 wks. Seasonal 4 mos ahead. No disk. Some sidebars. Prefers NRSV. Guidelines; copy for 9x12 SAE/4 stamps.

Poetry: Buys 12/yr. Free verse; to 25 lines; Marian themes only. Pays 2 year subscription and 6 copies. Submit max. 2 poems.

*THE QUIET REVOLUTION, 1655 St. Charles St., Jackson MS 39209. (601)353-1635. Voice of Calvary Ministries. Cornelius J. Jones, ed. Interracial ministry to the poor; conservative/evangelical. Quarterly mag; 7 pgs; circ 3,000. 10% freelance. Query or complete ms/cover letter. **NO PAYMENT** for one-time rts. Articles 3-4 pgs. Responds in 5 wks. Accepts reprints. Free copy.

Tips: "Most open to articles about ministering to the poor."

#RATIO: Essays in Christian Thought, 323 E. Matilija St. #110-208, Ojai CA 93023-2740. Jeff Bearce, ed. For an academic/intellectual audience anchored in the humanities; deals with theology, biblical studies, psychology, science, etc. Semiannual journal; circ 100. 15-20% freelance. Query. **NO PAYMENT.** Not copyrighted. Articles, fiction and book reviews.

+REAL FAMILYLIFE, 3900 N. Rodney Parham, Little Rock AR 72212. (501)223-8663. Fax (501)228-2394. E-mail: RealFLmag@aol.com. FamilyLife/Campus Crusade for Christ. David Boehi, ed. Provides practical, biblical help for families. Bimonthly (7X) mag; circ 100,000. Subscription free. Accepts freelance. Query. Not in topical listings. (Ads)

+REASON AND REVELATION, 230 Landmark Dr., Montgomery AL 36117. (800)234-8558 or (334)272-8558. Fax (800)234-2882 or (334)270-2002. Website: http://www.ApologeticsPress.org. Bert Thompson & Wayne Jackson, eds. Monthly journal. Not in topical listings.

#RELIGIOUS BROADCASTING, National Religious Broadcasters, 7839 Ashton Ave., Manassas VA 22109. (703)330-7000. Fax (703)330-6996. E-mail: ssmith@nrb.com. Website: http://www.nrb.com. Christine L. Pryor, assoc. ed. Topics relate to Christian radio, television and satellite; promoting access excellence in religious broadcasting. Monthly (10X) mag, with online version; 84 pgs; circ 9,000. Subscription $24. 70% freelance. Complete ms/cover letter; fax/e-mail query OK. **PAYS 6 COPIES** ($75-150 for assigned) on publication for 1st or reprint rts. Articles 2,000-3,000 wds (30/yr). Responds in 2-5 wks. Seasonal 6 mos ahead. Accepts simultaneous submissions & reprints (tell when/where appeared). Prefers disk. Sidebars OK. Prefers NIV & KVJ. Free guidelines/theme list/copy. (Ads)

Columns/Departments: Sarah E. Smith. Accepts 10/yr. Trade Talk or Media Focus (news items/events in religious broadcasting), 300 wds; Socially Speaking (social issues), 1,000 wds.

Special Needs: Electronic media; education. All articles must relate in some way to broadcasting; radio, TV, programs on radio/TV.

Tips: "Most open to feature articles relevant to religious broadcasters. Become acquainted with religious broadcasters in your area and note their struggles, concerns, and victories. Find out what they would like to know, research the topic, then write about it."

RELIGIOUS EDUCATION, 15600 Mulholland Dr., Los Angeles CA 90077. (310)476-9777. Fax (310)471-1278. University of Judaism. Dr. Hanan Alexander, ed-in-chief. Scholarly journal for professors of religious education of all faiths. Quarterly journal; 130-160 pgs; circ 2,000. Call for subscription/membership rate. 100% freelance. Complete ms/cover letter; phone/fax/e-mail query OK.

PAYS 3 COPIES for all rts. Articles to 6,500 wds; book reviews, 250 wds. Responds in 8-12 wks. Requires disk. No sidebars. Guidelines; copy $3/9x12 SAE. (Ads)

> **Columns/Departments:** Insights from Scholarship; Insights from Practice; Forum (diverse points of view on topics of interest); and Critique (reviews of books, media and curricula).

> **Special Needs:** Spiritual, cultural & social issues; policy & practice; models & methods; traditions & trends; sacred texts, moral values, & character education, religious education, and educational theory.

#REMEMBRANCE, Box 394, Society Hill SC 29593. E-mail: EBOONE@aol.com. RSVP Press. Gene Boone, ed. A tribute to loved ones who have passed away. Biannual mag (semi-book form); 60 pgs; circ 250. Subscription $8.95. Est. 1996. 100% freelance. Complete ms/cover letter; e-mail query OK. **PAYS ONE COPY** for one-time rts. Articles to 200-3,000 wds (50/yr). Responds in 5 wks. Accepts reprints (tell when/where appeared). Accepts disk. No sidebars. Guidelines/theme list; copy $4.95.

> **Poetry:** Accepts 100-200/yr. Free verse, traditional; 3-50 lines.

THE REVELATION POST, 187 Cooper St., Cambridge ON N3C 2N9 Canada. (519)651-2896. Fax (519)651-2521. E-mail: forerunner@compuserve.com. Shining Light Ministries. Brent Hackett, ed. Gospel outreach newspaper sent to all homes in area; focus is evangelical. Irregular (as funds provide) newspaper; 8-12 pgs; circ. 15,000-45,000. Freewill gifts. Query. **NO PAYMENT** for one-time rts. Articles 300-1,000 wds (flexible). Responds in 2 wks upon request. Accepts simultaneous submissions & reprints. Prefers disk. KJV only. Guidelines/theme list; copy for 6x9 SAE.

> **Poetry:** Accepts 1-2/yr. Traditional. Submit max. 2 poems.

> **Fillers:** Accepts 4-5/yr. Facts, quotes. Must be Bible-based with strong supporting Scripture reference.

> **Special Needs:** Current events in relation to Bible prophecy.

+THE RIVER, 5375 Alderley Rd., Victoria BC V8Y 1X9 Canada. (250)658-2644. Fax (250)658-8481. E-mail: msbowes@islandnet.com or believer@islandnet.com. Website: http://www.islandnet.com/~believer. Tidewater Publishing Co. Madge S. Bowes, ed. Focuses on renewal and revival. Quarterly mag; circ. 1,000. Subscription $8. Receives most submissions by e-mail. Not copyrighted. **NO PAYMENT**. Articles 300-750 wds. Seasonal 2 mos ahead. Accepts simultaneous submissions & reprints. Accepts disk (Mac only). Copy for 9x12 SAE/IRCs or $1.

+ROSEBUD, Rosebud, Inc., PO Box 459, Cambridge WI 53523. (608)423-9609. Fax (608)423-9690. Roderick Clark, ed. For people who enjoy good writing. Quarterly mag; 136 pgs; circ 10,000. Subscription $22. 95% freelance. Complete ms/cover letter. Pays $45-185 shortly after publication for one-time rts. Articles/essays (10/yr) & fiction (60/yr) 1,200 wds. Responds in 16 wks. Accepts simultaneous submissions. No disk. Sidebars OK. Guidelines; copy $5.50/9x12SAE/5 stamps. (Ads)

> **Poetry:** John Smelcer. Buys 20/yr. Free verse; any length. Pays $45-185. Submit max. 5 poems.

> **Columns/Departments:** Includes 21 departments; see guidelines.

Tips: "We like good storytelling, real emotion, and authentic voice."

SACRED JOURNEY: FELLOWSHIP IN PRAYER (formerly **FELLOWSHIP IN PRAYER**), 291 Witherspoon St., Princeton NJ 08542. (609)924-6863. Fax (609)924-6910. Fellowship In Prayer, Inc. Rebecca Laird, ed. An interfaith spirituality journal. Bimonthly journal; 48 pgs; circ 10,000. Subscription $16. 100% freelance. Complete ms/cover letter; fax query OK. **PAYS IN COPIES & SUBSCRIPTION** for one-time & electronic rts. Articles to 1,500 wds (40/yr); book reviews 400 wds. Responds in 8 wks. Seasonal 4 mos ahead. Accepts simultaneous submissions & reprints (tell when/where appeared). Requires disk. No sidebars. Guidelines; copy for 6x9 SAE/3 stamps.

> **Poetry:** Accepts 6-8/yr. Free-verse, haiku, light verse, traditional; 10-35 lines. Submit max. 3 poems.
>
> **Columns/Departments:** Buys 30/yr. A Transforming Experience (personal experience of spiritual significance); Pilgrimage (journey taken for spiritual growth of service); Spirituality and the Family; Spirituality and Aging; to 750 wds.
>
> **Tips:** "Write well about your own spiritual experience and we'll consider it."

ST. ANTHONY MESSENGER, 1615 Republic St., Cincinnati OH 45210-1298. (513)241-5615. Fax (513)241-0399. E-mail: StAnthony@AmericanCatholic.org. Website: http://www.AmericanCatholic.org. Catholic. Norman Perry, O.F.M., ed. Catholic. Monthly mag; 56 pgs; circ 359,000. Subscription $19. 40% freelance. Query or complete ms/cover letter; fax/e-mail query OK. Pays .15/wd on acceptance for 1st, reprint (right to reprint), & electronic rts. Articles 2,000-2,500 wds (45-50/yr); fiction 2,000 wds (12/yr); book reviews 500 wds/$25. Responds in 8 wks. Seasonal 6 mos ahead. Kill fee. Some sidebars. Prefers NAB. Guidelines; copy for 9x12 SAE. (Ads)

> **Poetry:** Susan Hines-Brigger. Buys 30-35/yr. Free verse, haiku, traditional; 3-25 lines; $2/line ($10 min.) Submit max. 2 poems.
>
> **Tips:** "Most open to articles, profiles, interviews of Catholic personalities. Writing must be professional, use Catholic terminology and vocabulary. Writing must be faithful to Catholic belief and teaching, life and experience."
>
> ** This periodical was #55 on the 1997 Top 50 Christian Publishers list (#40 in 1994).

#ST. JOSEPH'S MESSENGER AND ADVOCATE OF THE BLIND, PO Box 288, Jersey City NJ 07303-0288. (201)798-4141. Catholic/Sisters of St. Joseph of Peace. Sister Ursula Maphet, CSJP, ed. For older Catholics interested in supporting ministry to the aged, young, blind, and needy. Semiannual mag; 16 pgs; circ 15,500. Subscription $5. 30% freelance. Complete ms. Pays $3-15 ($6-25 for fiction) on publication for 1st rts. Articles 500-1,000 wds (24/yr); fiction 1,000-1,500 wds (30/yr). Responds in 5 wks. Seasonal 3 mos ahead. Accepts simultaneous submissions & reprints. No sidebars. Guidelines; copy for 9x12 SAE/2 stamps.

> **Poetry:** Buys 25/yr. Light verse, traditional; 4-40 lines; $5-20 on publication. Submit max. 10 poems.
>
> **Fillers:** Buys 20/yr. Ideas, 50-100 wds; $5-10.
>
> **Tips:** "Most open to contemporary fiction."

*ST. WILLIBRORD JOURNAL, Box 271751, Houston TX 77277-1751. Christ

Catholic Church. Charles E. Harrison, ed. Strictly Catholic; concentrating on the unchurched. Quarterly journal; 40 pgs; circ 500. 5% freelance. Complete ms/cover letter. **NO PAYMENT** for one-time rts. Not copyrighted. Articles to 1,000 wds. Responds in 9 wks. Seasonal 6 mos ahead. Copy $2.

Columns/Departments: Question Box; Q & A column on doctrinal and biblical questions.

Tips: "We will read anything if it is sincere and orthodox. Most open to what's happening in the Christian church: doctrinal changes, attitude adjustments, moral attitudes."

#SCP JOURNAL, (Spiritual Counterfeits Project), PO Box 4308, Berkeley CA 94704-4308. (510)540-0300. Fax (510)540-1107. E-mail: scp@dnai.com. Website: http://www.scp-inc.org/. Tal Brooke, ed. Christian apologetics for the college educated. Quarterly newsletter; 55 pgs; circ 18,000. Subscription $25. 5-10% freelance. Query/clips; phone query encouraged. Pays $20-35/typeset pg on publication for negotiable rts. Articles 2,500-3,500 wds (5/yr); book reviews 1,500 wds. Responds in 13 wks. Accepts simultaneous query & reprints. Guidelines; copy $8.75

Tips: "Talk to us first."

+SECOND STONE, PO Box 8340, New Orleans LA 70182. Fax (504)899-4014. E-mail: secstone@aol.com. Submit to The Editor. National news journal for gay and lesbian Christians, and others who care about justice and equality for Gays and Lesbians in church and society. Bimonthly tabloid; 20-24 pgs. Query or complete ms sent by fax or e-mail (preferred, but will accept by mail). Pays. Articles 1,200-1,500 wds; book reviews 800-1,200 wds. Accepts reprints (no payment). Prefers disk.

Poetry: Accepts poetry; to 40 lines. No payment.

Fillers: Newsbreaks. No payment.

+SEEDS MAGAZINE, PO Box 6170, Waco TX 76706-0170. (817)755-7745. E-mail: SeedsHope@aol.com. Website: http://www.helwys.com/chliving.html. Seeds of Hope, Inc. L. Katherine Cook, ed. Committed to the healing of hunger and poverty in our world. Quarterly online mag. Sprouts edition published 8X/yr. Subscription $20. Not in topical listings.

SEEK, 8121 Hamilton Ave., Cincinnati OH 45231. (513)931-4050x365. Standard Publishing. Eileen H. Wilmoth, ed. For young and middle-age adults. Weekly take-home paper; 8 pgs; circ 45,000. 98% freelance. Complete ms/cover letter. Pays .05-.07/wd on acceptance for 1st rts, .025/wd for reprint rts. Articles 400-1,200 wds (150-200/yr); fiction 400-1,200 wds. Responds in 13 wks. Seasonal 1 yr ahead. Accepts reprints. Guidelines; copy for 6x9 SAE/2 stamps.

Fillers: Buys 50/yr. Ideas, jokes, short humor; $15.

** This periodical was #56 on the 1997 Top 50 Christian Publishers list. (#49 in 1996, #57 in 1995, #36 in 1994)

*THE SHANTYMAN, 2476 Argentia Rd., Ste. 213, Mississauga ON L5N 6M1 Canada. (905)821-6310. Fax (905)821-6311. Shantymen's Christian Assn. Margaret Sharpe, mng ed. Distributed by their missionaries in remote areas of Canada and northern US as an evangelism tool. Bimonthly mini-tabloid; 16 pgs; circ 17,000. Subscription $6. 90% freelance. Complete ms/cover letter; no phone/fax query. Pays $20-50 CAN, on publication for one-time or reprint rts. Articles

800-1,600 wds (30/yr). Responds in 4-6 wks. Seasonal 6 mos ahead. Accepts reprints (tell when/where appeared). No disk. Some sidebars. Prefers NASB. Guidelines; copy for #10 SAE/2 stamps or IRC's.

Columns/Departments: Accepts 6/yr. Way of Salvation (fresh look at gospel message), 300-400 wds.

Tips: "We always have a need for salvation testimonies, first person (preferred) or as-told-to. We always have too many inspirational stories. No reprints, please, until 1998."

SHARING, A Journal of Christian Healing, 6807 Forest Haven St., San Antonio TX 78240-3343. (210)681-5146. Fax (210)681-5146. Order of St. Luke the Physician. Marjorie George, ed. For Christians interested in spiritual and physical healing. Monthly journal; 32 pgs; circ 9,000. Subscription $12. 100% freelance. Complete ms/cover letter. **NO PAYMENT** for one-time or reprint rts. Articles 750-900 wds (50/yr). Responds in 3 wks. Seasonal 2 mos ahead. Accepts simultaneous submissions & reprints (tell when/where appeared). Prefers disk. Some kill fees. Some sidebars. Prefers RSV. Guidelines; copy for 8x10 SAE/2 stamps.

Poetry: Accepts 10-12/yr. Free verse, traditional; 6-14 lines.

Tips: "The entire magazine is open. We're looking for crisp, clear, well-written articles on the theology of healing and personal witness of healing. We do not return mss or poems, nor do we reply to inquiries regarding mss status."

#SIGNS OF THE TIMES, Box 5353, Nampa ID 83653-5353. (208)465-2577. Fax (208)465-2531. E-mail: signs@pacificpress.com. Website: http://www.pacificpress. com. Seventh-day Adventist. Marvin Moore, ed. Biblical principles relevant to all of life; for general public. Monthly mag; 32 pgs; circ 245,000. 40% freelance. Query/clips or complete ms. Pays $100-400 (to .20/wd) on acceptance for 1st rts. Articles 500-2,000 wds (75/yr). Responds in 4-9 wks. Seasonal 8 mos ahead. Accepts reprints (tell when/where appeared). Kill fee 50%. Guidelines; copy for 9x12 SAE/3 stamps.

** This periodical was #33 on the 1997 Top 50 Christian Publishers list. (#34 in 1996, #42 in 1995, #33 in 1994)

SILVER WINGS, PO Box 1000, Pearblossom CA 93553. (805)264-3726. E-mail: poetwing@aol.com. Jackson Wilcox, ed. Christian understanding and uplift through poetry. Quarterly mag; 24 pgs; circ 300. Subscription $7. 100% freelance. Complete ms. **PAYS 1 COPY** for 1st rts. Not copyrighted. Responds in 4 wks. Seasonal before October. Accepts simultaneous submissions. No disk. Prefers KJV. Guidelines; copy $2/6x9 SAE/2 stamps.

Poetry: Accepts 200/yr. Any type; 2-20 lines. Submit max. 4 poems.

Contest: Annual poetry contest; send SAE for details.

+SINGLE CONNECTION, PO Box 17519, Pittsburgh PA 15235. Phone/fax (412)856-1039. JoAnne McBriar, pub/ed. A resource and forum for single adults. Bimonthly newspaper; 12 pgs; circ 30,000. Subscription $12. Est. 1997. Complete ms. **NO PAYMENT.** Articles/fiction 600-800 wds (25/yr). Responds in 4-6 wks. Seasonal 4 mos ahead. Accepts simultaneous submissions & reprints (tell when/where appeared). Sidebars OK. Copy $3. (Ads)

Fillers: Cartoons, facts, jokes, party ideas, quizzes, short humor, word puzzles.

Tips: "Material used as space permits."

SINGLE-PARENT FAMILY, 8605 Explorer Dr., Colorado Springs CO 80920. (719)548-4588. Fax (719)531-3499. Focus on the Family. Dr. Lynda Hunter, ed. To encourage and equip single parents to do the best job they can at creating stable, godly homes for themselves and their children. Monthly mag; 24 pgs; circ. 50,000. Membership $15. 13% freelance. Query or complete ms. Pays .10-.15/wd. Articles 600-1,200 wds. (Ads)

SMART DADS, Box 270616, San Diego CA 92198-2616. (619)487-7099. Fax (619)487-7356. E-mail: familyu@aol.com. Website: http://www.familyuniversity. com. Mike Yorkey, ed. Christian fathering/parenting, with strong crossover to secular dads. Bimonthly newsletter; 8 pgs; circ 10,000. Subscription $24 (includes 2 tapes). Little freelance. Complete ms preferred; fax query OK. Pays $50-250 on publication for 1st rts. Articles 250-900 wds (5/yr). Responds in 2-4 wks. Seasonal 4 mos ahead. Accepts simultaneous submissions. Prefers disk. Some sidebars. Copy for 10x13 SAE/3 stamps.

> **Fillers:** Buys a lot. Games, ideas, quotes.
>
> **Tips:** "We are not a magazine and have tight length requirements. Because of crossover audience, we do not regularly print Scripture references or use traditional God-word language."

+SMART FAMILIES, Box 270616, San Diego CA 92198-2616. (619)487-7099. Fax (619)487-7356. E-mail: familyu@aol.com. Website: http://www.familyuniversity. com. Mike Yorkey, ed. Christian parenting, with strong crossover to secular families. Quarterly newsletter; 16 pgs; circ 140,000. Subscription $24 (includes 2 tapes). Little freelance. Complete ms preferred; fax query OK. Pays $50-250 on publication for 1st rts. Articles 250-900 wds. Responds in 2-4 wks. Seasonal 4 mos ahead. Accepts simultaneous submissions. Prefers disk. Some sidebars. Copy for 10x13 SAE/3 stamps.

> **Fillers:** Buys a lot. Games, ideas, quotes.
>
> **Tips:** "We are not a magazine and have tight length requirements. Because of crossover audience, we do not regularly print Scripture references or use traditional God-word language."

SMILE, PO Box 5090, Brookfield CT 06804-5090. Joyce M. Johnson, ed. Poetry devoted to cheering up people. Quarterly mag; 22 pgs; circ 230. Subscription $10. 90% freelance. Complete ms/cover letter. **PAYS ONE COPY** for 1st or reprint rts. Not copyrighted. Articles 200 wds (essay or first-person reminiscences—8/yr.). Responds in 2 wks. Seasonal 2 mos ahead. Accepts reprints (tell when/where appeared). No disk. Prefers NIV or New Jerusalem. Guidelines; copy $3.

> **Poetry:** Free verse, haiku, light verse, traditional (on Christian values); 3-24 lines; 40 characters wide maximum.
>
> **Fillers:** Accepts 18-20/yr. Anecdotes, cartoons, jokes, quotes (state source), short humor and word puzzles; 25-50 wds.
>
> **Contest:** You must be a subscriber to be eligible for poetry prizes awarded four times per year. Prizes of $15, $10 and $5. Send 3-32 cent stamps with submission. Deadline is October 31.
>
> **Tips:** "We encourage new poets. We like light, humorous verse about facing the daily problems in life. Especially welcome older-aged poets and shut-ins, with their spiritual wisdom."

SOCIAL JUSTICE REVIEW, 3835 Westminster Pl., St. Louis MO 63108-3472. (314)371-1653. Catholic Central Union of America. Rev. John H. Miller, C.S.C., ed. For those interested in the social teaching of the Catholic Church. Bimonthly journal; 32 pgs; circ 4,750. Subscription $20. 90% freelance. Query or complete ms. Pays .02/wd on publication for one-time rts. Not copyrighted. Articles to 3,000 wds (80/yr); book reviews 500 wds **(no pay)**. Responds in 1 wk. Seasonal 3 mos ahead. Accepts reprints (tell when/where appeared). No disk or sidebars. Guidelines; copy for 9x12 SAE/3 stamps.

> **Columns/Departments:** Virtue; Economic Justice; variable length. Query.

> **Tips:** "Fidelity to papal teaching and clarity and simplicity of style; thoughtful and thought-provoking writing."

#SOJOURNERS, 2401 - 15th St. NW, Washington DC 20009. (202)328-8842. Fax (202)328-8757. E-mail: sojourners@ari.net. Website: http://www.sojourners.com/sojourners/home.html. Karen Lattea, mng ed. For those who seek to turn their lives toward the biblical vision of justice and peace. Bimonthly mag; 68 pgs; circ. 24,000. Subscription $30. 30% freelance. Query. Pays $75-200 on publication for variable rts (no reprints). Articles 600-3,600 wds (10/yr); fiction 600-3,600 wds; book/music reviews, 650-1,300 wds, $50-100. Responds in 6 wks. Seasonal 6 mos ahead. Kill fee. Prefers NRSV. Sidebars OK. Guidelines; copy for 9x12 SAE. (Ads)

> **Poetry:** Rose Marie Berger. Accepts 6-10/yr. Free verse, haiku; $50.

> **Fillers:** Accepts 6 cartoons/yr.

> **Columns/Departments:** Buys 15/yr. Culture Watch (reviews), 650-1,300 wds; Commentary (editorials), 650 wds; New Wineskins (faith issues), 650 wds; and Close to Home (parenting, family, singles), 650 wds; $50-75.

> **Tips:** "Most open to features, Culture Watch, New Wineskins, or Close to Home."

> ** 1997 EPA Award of Merit—General.

THE SOMETHING BETTER NEWS,, 3300 - 28th St. SW #1, Grandville MI 49418-1423. (616)530-3957. Fax (616)530-0728. Something Better Publications, Inc. Jerry Fennell, ed. Christian Newspaper. Monthly newspaper; 16 pgs; circ 75,000. Subscription $20. 10% freelance. Query/clips; phone query OK. . **NO PAYMENT** for 1st rts. Articles 500 wds (10-20/yr); book/music reviews 300 wds, music/video reviews 750-1,000 wds, $10. Responds in 4 wks. Seasonal 2 mos ahead. Accepts reprints (tell when/where appeared). Prefers disk. Sidebars OK. Prefers KJV. Guidelines/theme list; copy for 10x13 SAE/$1.50 postage. (Ads)

> **Columns/Departments:** Accepts 10-20/yr. God & Money; Revival; Advice; all 1,000 wds. Query or complete ms.

> **Special Needs:** Wants to expand their Christian entertainment section. Always looking for sports/recreation pieces.

> **Tips:** "Most open to concert reviews and news stories."

***SPIRIT OF REVIVAL**, 2000 Morris Dr., Niles MI 49102. (616)684-5905. Fax (616)684-0923. Life Action Ministries. Nancy Leigh DeMoss, ed. Proclaiming and preserving the message of revival. Biannual mag; circ 74,000. Subscription free. Open to freelance. Query. Not in topical listings.

#SPIRITUAL LIFE, 2131 Lincoln Rd. NE, Washington DC 20002-1199. (202)832-

8489. Fax (202)832-8967. E-mail: edodonnell@aol.com. Website: http://www. ocd.or.at/. Catholic. Edward O'Donnell, O.C.D., ed. For college-educated Christians interested in spirituality. Quarterly mag; 64 pgs; circ 12,000. Subscription $15. 80% freelance. Complete ms/cover letter; phone/fax query OK. Pays $50-250 ($10/ms pg) on acceptance for 1st rts. Articles/essays 3,000-5,000 wds (20/yr); book reviews 1,500 wds, $15. Responds in 9 wks. Seasonal 9 mos ahead. Accepts simultaneous submissions. Requires disk. No sidebars. Prefers NAB. Guidelines; copy for 7x10 SAE/5 stamps.

Tips: "No stories of personal healing, conversion, miracles, etc."

SPORTS SPECTRUM, 3000 Kraft SE, Grand Rapids MI 49512. (616)954-1276. Fax (616)957-5741. E-mail: ssmag@sport.org. Discovery House Publishers. Dave Branon, mng. ed. An evangelistic tool that sports fans can use to witness to non-Christian friends. Monthly (10X) mag; 32 pgs; circ 50,000. Subscription $15.97. 65% freelance. Query/clips; fax/e-mail query OK. Pays .18/wd on acceptance for 1st & electronic rts. Not copyrighted. Articles 725-2,000 wds (70/yr). Responds in 3-4 wks. Accepts disk. Kill fee 30-50%. Sidebars OK. Prefers NIV. Guidelines; copy for 9x12 SAE/4 stamps.

Columns/Departments: Buys 30/yr. Leaderboard (Christian athletes serving others), 725 wds; Front Row (on the scene sports scenarios), 800-1,200 wds; Champions (lesser-known athletes), 250 wds. Pays .18/wd.

Tips: "Show an ability to interview professional athletes and create a well-written article from that interview. Don't interview an athlete on our behalf without our approval. We do welcome ideas/leads from freelancers."

** #69 on the 1994 Top 50. 1996 EPA Award of Merit—General.

STANDARD, 6401 The Paseo, Kansas City MO 64131. (816)333-7000. Fax (816)333-4439. Website: http://www.nazarene.org. Nazarene. Rev. Everett Leadingham, ed. Examples of Christianity in everyday life for adults college-age through retirement. Weekly take-home paper; 8 pgs; circ 150,000. Subscription $8.95. 80% freelance. Complete ms. Pays .035/wd (.02/wd for reprints) on acceptance for 1st or reprint rts. Articles (20/yr) or fiction (200/yr) 800-1,200 wds. Responds in 8-12 wks. Seasonal 6 mos ahead. Accepts simultaneous submissions & reprints (tell when/where appeared). No disk. Kill fee. No sidebars. Prefers NIV. Guidelines/theme list/copy for #10 SAE/2 stamps.

Poetry: Buys 100/yr. Free verse, haiku, traditional; to 25 lines; $5-12.50. Submit max. 5 poems.

Fillers: Buys 50/yr. Word puzzles; $20.

Tips: "Fiction or true-experience stories must demonstrate Christianity in action. Show us, don't tell us. Action in stories must conform to Wesleyan-Armenian theology and practices."

** This periodical was #68 on the 1997 Top 50 Christian Publishers list. (#41 in 1996, #12 in 1995, #2 in 1994)

THE STANDARD, 2002 S. Arlington Hts. Rd., Arlington Hts. IL 60005. (847)228-0200. Fax (847)228-5376. E-mail: gmbgcstd@aol.com. Baptist General Conference. Jodi Hanning, mng. ed. Denominational. Monthly (10X) mag; 32 pgs; circ. 11,000. Subscription $15.75. 40-50% freelance. Query or complete ms; fax/e-mail query OK. Pays $20-200 on publication for 1st rts. Articles 400-1,200 wds (20-30/yr). Responds in 4-6 wks. Seasonal 6 mos ahead. Accepts reprints. Kill fee

50%. Prefers disk (or e-mail). Kill fee. Sidebars OK ($20). Prefers NIV. Guidelines/theme list; copy for 9x12 SAE/4 stamps. (Ads)

Tips: "When we use a general article, it has to be tailor-made to fit our themes."
** 1996 EPA Award of Excellence—Denominational.

STAND FIRM, God's Challenge for Today's Man, 127 Ninth Ave. N., Nashville TN 37234-0140. (615)251-5955. Fax (615)251-5008. E-mail: vhancoc@bssb.com. Lifeway Press/Baptist Sunday School board. Valerie Hancock, copy ed. Addresses the unique and distinctive needs of men of the 90s. Monthly digest-size mag; 36 pgs; circ 40,000. Subscription $18.95. 25-30% freelance. Complete ms/cover letter; fax/e-mail query OK. Pays negotiable rates on acceptance for all (preferred), 1st, or electronic rts. Articles 50-400 wds; book/music/video reviews, 20-50 wds. Responds in 4-6 wks. Seasonal 6-8 mos ahead. Accepts simultaneous submissions & reprints (tell when/where appeared). Prefers disk. Sidebars OK. Prefers NIV. Guidelines/theme list; copy for 6x9 SAE/3 stamps.

Tips: "Looking for feature articles for weekends; interviews with recognized Christian leaders, reviews of men's products/books/events, news/ideas/projects/activities for men, ministry news, and insights into sports, finances, and other topics of interest to men."

THE STAR OF ZION, 401 E. 2nd St., Charlotte NC 28231. (704)377-4329. Fax (704)377-2809. E-mail: starozion@juno.com. African Methodist Episcopal Zion Church. Dr. Marie P. Tann, assoc. ed. Ethnic publication; moderate; conservative. Biweekly tabloid; 16-20 pgs; circ 8,000. Subscription $33. 90% freelance. Query; phone query OK. PAYS 5 COPIES. Articles & fiction to 600 wds. Responds in 9 wks. Seasonal 2 mos ahead. Accepts simultaneous submissions. No sidebars. Copy $1/10x14 SAE/2 stamps.

Poetry: African-American themes.

Fillers: Short humor.

*STEWARDSHIP, 32401 Industrial Dr., Madison Heights MI 48071. (248)585-7800. Fax (248)585-2193. Parish Publications, Inc. Richard Meurer, ed. To help church members understand stewardship. Monthly newsletter; 4 pgs. 50% freelance. Query or complete ms/cover letter; fax query OK. Pays $25-100 on publication for all rts. Articles 200-300 wds. Free copy.

SUNDAY DIGEST, 4050 Lee Vance View, Colorado Springs CO 80918-7100. (719)536-0100. Fax (719)536-3296. Cook Communications. This publication will cease publishing as of the June 1998 quarter. They are accepting no further submissions.

+SURSUM CORDA! The Catholic Revival, PO Box 993, Ridgefield CT 06877. Fax (203)438-1305. E-mail: roger.mccaffrey@internetmci.com. Foundation for Catholic Reform. Roger McCaffrey, ed; submit to Tom Woods, mng. ed. Covers the good things that happen in the Catholic Church; includes a 16-page homeschooling section. Quarterly mag; circ 16,000. Complete ms; fax query OK. Pays $150-500 on publication for one-time or reprint rts. Articles 2,000-5,000 wds (2/yr); religious fiction. Responds in 5-9 wks. Accepts simultaneous submissions & reprints. Free copy.

Tips: "Keep in mind that the theme of our magazine is the orthodox Catholic Revival. We are conservative."

*TABLE TALK, 6401 The Paseo, Kansas City MO 64131. (816)333-7000x2359. Fax

(816)333-4439. E-mail: childmin@nazarene.org. Website: http://www.nazarene. org. Nazarene. Submit to Kathleen Johnson, asst. ed. A family magazine for parents of elementary age children; offers helps, hints, ideas and encouragement. Quarterly mag; 80 pgs; circ 12,000. Subscription $6.75. 40% freelance. Complete ms/cover letter; phone/fax/e-mail query OK. Pays $25 or .05/wd (.03 for reprints) on publication for multi-use rts. Articles 1,200 wds (20/yr). Responds in 16 wks. Seasonal 15 mos ahead. Accepts simultaneous submissions & reprints (tell when/where appeared). Accepts disk. Some sidebars. Prefers NIV. Guidelines; copy for 6x9 SAE/4 stamps.

Poetry: Free verse, light verse, traditional; $10 or .05/wd.

Fillers: Buys 12/yr. Anecdotes, cartoons, games, ideas, short humor; 75-1500 wds; $10 or .05/wd.

Tips: "Offer encouragement and advice on how to deal with family and parenting issues." Margins should be 1.5" all around.

TEAK ROUNDUP, #5 - 9060 Tronson Rd., Vernon BC V1H 1E7 Canada. (250)545-4186. Fax (250)545-4194. West Coast Paradise Publishing. Robert G. Anstey, ed. General, family-oriented poetry and prose. Quarterly mag; 52 pgs; circ. 200. Subscription $13 US, $17 CAN. Query; phone/fax query OK. **NO PAYMENT** for one-time rts. Articles (100/yr) & fiction to 1,000 wds; book reviews to 1,000 wds. Responds in 1 wk. Seasonal 2 mos ahead. Accepts reprints. Accepts disks. Sidebars OK. Prefers KJV. Guidelines; copy $3 US/$5 CAN/6x9 SAE/.90 CAN postage or $1.17 US. (Ads)

Poetry: Accepts 100/yr. Any type; to 40 lines. Submit max. 5 poems.

Fillers: Anecdotes, cartoons, ideas, newsbreaks, party idea, prose, short humor. Also accepts line-art drawings.

Contest: For subscribers only.

Tips: Subscribers only are eligible for publication.

THIS ROCK, 7290 Engineer Rd. Ste. H, PO Box 17490, San Diego CA 92111. (619)541-1131. Fax (619)541-1154. E-mail: editor@catholic.com. Website: http://www.catholic.com. Catholic. Karl Keating, ed. Deals with doctrine, evangelization and apologetics. Monthly (11X) mag; 48 pgs; circ 12,000. Subscription $29.95. 70% freelance. Query. Pays $300 on publication for 1st rts. Articles 1,500-3,500 wds. Responds in 5-13 wks. Guidelines; copy $4.

TIME FOR RHYME, PO Box 1055, Battleford SK S0M 0E0 Canada. (306)445-5172. Richard W. Unger, ed. Poetry only; not strictly Christian (but editor is). Quarterly mag; 32 pgs. Subscription $12, US or CAN. 80% freelance. Complete ms/cover letter. **PAYS IN COPIES** for 1st rts. Seasonal 1 yr ahead. Guidelines; copy $3.25 US or CAN. (Ads)

Poetry: Buys 60/yr; 2-32 lines. Rhyming only; light or serious. Submit max. 5 poems. Not keen on holiday poems.

*TIME OF SINGING, A Magazine of Christian Poetry, PO Box 149, Conneaut Lake PA 16316. (814)382-5911. High Street Community Church. Charles A. Waugaman, ed. We try to appeal to all poets and lovers of poetry. Quarterly mag; 44 pgs; circ 300. Subscription $15. 95% freelance. Complete ms/cover letter; phone query OK. Pays $1-4/poem or .25/line on publication for 1st or reprint rts. Poetry only. Responds in 4-6 wks. Seasonal 4-6 mos ahead. Accepts some reprints. Guidelines/theme list; copy $4/6x9 SAE.

Poetry: Buys 150-200/yr. Free verse, haiku, light verse (rarely), traditional; any length (prefers short). Submit max. 5 poems.

Contest: Sponsors an annual poetry contest (send SASE for rules).

Tips: "We only review books by our poets. Send SASE and put name and address on every poem."

TODAY'S CHRISTIAN DOCTOR, PO Box 5, Bristol TN 37621-0005. (423)844-1000. Fax (423)844-1005. E-mail: davebiebel@aol.com. Christian Medical & Dental Society. David B. Biebel, ed. To change the face of health care by changing the hearts of doctors/dentists. Bimonthly mag; circ 12,000. Subscription $25. Open to freelance (mostly from medical professionals). Query. Articles 8-10 pgs. Guidelines. Not in topical listings. (Ads)

TODAY'S CHRISTIAN SENIOR, 10 Webster Rd., Shelburne VT 05482. (802)985-5744. Fax (802)985-2811. E-mail: BryanBice@aol.com. Scepter Publication. Bryan Bice, ed. Geared to senior citizens in the areas of health, finances, ministry and travel. Quarterly mag; 16 pgs; circ 50,000. Free subscription. Est. 1996. 15% freelance. Complete ms/cover letter; e-mail query OK. Pays $150 on publication for 1st, one-time or simultaneous rts. Articles & fiction 900-1,000 wds. Responds in 4 wks. Seasonal 9 mos ahead. Accepts reprints (tell when/where appeared). Prefers disk. Sidebars OK. Prefers KJV. Guidelines/theme list; copy for 9x12 SAE/3stamps. (Ads)

Poetry: Light verse, traditional. Pays $25. Submit max. 3 poems.

Fillers: Cartoons, jokes, quizzes, word puzzles; $10.

+TOGETHER, Rt. 2 Box 656, Grottoes VA 24441. (540)249-3900. Fax (540)249-3177. E-mail: Tgether@aol.com. Shalom Foundation, Inc. Melodie Davis, ed. An outreach magazine distributed by churches to attract the general public to Christian faith & life. Quarterly tabloid; 8 pgs; circ 150,000. Free. 90% freelance. Complete ms/cover letter; e-mail query OK. Pays $30-50 on publication for one-time rts. Articles 500-1,200 wds (16/yr). Responds in 12-16 wks. Seasonal 4 mos ahead. Accepts simultaneous submissions & reprints. Accepts disk. Some sidebars. Prefers NIV. Guidelines/theme list; copy for 9x12 SAE/4 stamps. (Ads)

*TOTAL HEALTH, 165 N. 100 E. Ste 2, St. George UT 84770-2505. Submit to Arpi Coliglow, asst. ed. A family health magazine. Bimonthly mag; 70 pgs; circ 90,000. Subscription $16. 75% freelance. Query or complete ms. Pays $50-75 on publication for all and reprint rts. Articles 1,400-1,800 wds (48/yr). Responds in 4 wks. Seasonal 4 mos ahead. Accepts simultaneous submissions. Query or complete ms/cover letter. Sidebars OK. Requires disk (Mac). Guidelines; copy $1/9x12 SAE/5 stamps.

Columns/Departments: Contemporary Herbal, 1,000 wds, $50.

Tips: "Most open to self-help and prevention articles."

TOUCHSTONE, A Journal of Ecumenical Orthodoxy, PO Box 18237, Chicago IL 60618. (773)267-1440. Fax (773)267-6754. E-mail: fstjames@aol.com. Fellowship of St. James. James Kushiner, ed. News and opinion devoted to a thoughtful appreciation of orthodox Christian faith. Bimonthly jour; 48 pgs; circ 1,800. 15% freelance. Query; e-mail query OK. **PAYS IN COPIES** for one-time rts. Articles 8,000-15,000 wds; book reviews 700-3,000 wds. Responds in 4 wks. Seasonal 4 mos ahead. Accepts simultaneous submissions & reprints (tell when/where appeared). Prefers disk. Sidebars OK. Prefers RSV or NIV. Guidelines; copy for 10x13 SAE/7 stamps. (Ads)

Fillers: Cartoons.

+THE TRUMPETER, First Union Bank Bldg., 7100 N. Kendall Dr., Ste. 100, Miami FL 33156. Fax (305)670-7771. E-mail: Trumpeter@supernet.win.net or info@thetrumpeter.com. Website: http://www.thetrumpeter.com. Martiele Swanko, ed-in-chief. Unites all South Florida Christian denominations, ethnic groups, and cultures. Bimonthly mag; circ 50,000. Complete ms/cover letter; fax/e-mail query OK. Features & sports, 900-1,000 wds; articles 400-700 wds. **PAYS IN COPIES.** Sidebars OK. Guidelines (on Website). Not in topical listings.

Columns/Departments: Around town (local talk), 100-125 wds; Arts & Entertainment, 400 wds; Legal, 450 wds; Political/Viewpoint, 100-125 wds.

+2-SOAR, PO Box 574, South Bend IN 46624. (219)289-8760. Church of God in Christ (Pentecost). Izola Bird, ed. Denominational. Quarterly mag; 12 pgs; circ 7,000. Subscription $15. 95% freelance. Query or complete ms/cover letter. **PAYS IN COPIES** for one-time rts. Articles 4 pgs. Responds in 2 wks. Accepts reprints (tell when/where appeared). Guidelines/copy. (Ads)

Poetry: Accepts 50/yr. Light verse, traditional, love; 20 lines. Submit max. 4 poems.

Contest: Spring & Fall poetry contests. Prizes of $25-100. Send for details.

Tips: "We want to hear from African-American writers."

THE UNITED CHURCH OBSERVER, 478 Huron St., Toronto ON M5R 2R3 Canada. (416)960-8500. Fax (416)960-8477. E-mail: general@ucobserver.org. United Church of Canada. Muriel Duncan, ed. Denominational news. Monthly (11X) newsmag; 52-60 pgs; circ 120,000. Subscription $20. 20% freelance. Query (preferred) or complete ms/cover letter; fax/e-mail query OK. Pays negotiable rates on publication for 1st or sometimes all rts. Articles to 1,200 wds (8/yr); juvenile fiction (6-12 yrs), query; book reviews (all assigned), $50. Responds in 12 wks. Seasonal 3-4 mos ahead. Kill fee. Some sidebars. Guidelines; copy $2. (Ads)

Fillers: Buys 24 cartoons/yr; $20.

Columns/Departments: Buys 40-50/yr. Faith; Living; World; Ministry; Front Page (church-related opinion pc.), 800 wds. Pays $200.

#UNITED VOICE, 8032 Cottonwood, Lenexa KS 66215-4120. (913)438-2607. Fax (913)438-2608. E-mail: DLLeBLANC@aol.com. Episcopalians United for Revelation Renewal and Reformation. Douglas LeBlanc, ed. To provide reporting and commentary on the Episcopal church for supporters and friends. Bimonthly newspaper; circ 25,000. Free subscription. Open to freelance. Query or complete ms. (Ads)

** 1997 EPA Award of Merit—Newspaper.

+UPLOOK MAGAZINE, PO Box 2041, Grand Rapids MI 49501-2041. E-mail: editor@uplook.org. Website: http://www.gospelcom.net/uplook/home.html. Uplook Ministries. Print and online magazine. Submit to e-mail address. Not in topical listings.

Columns/Departments: Accepts material for Frontlines or What's Going On columns.

+UPSCALE MAGAZINE, The Successful Black Magazine, 600 Bronner Brothers

Way SW, Atlanta GA 30310. (404)758-7467. Fax (404)755-9892. Upscale Communications, Inc. Sheila Bronner, ed-in-chief; submit to Paula M. White, assoc. ed. To inspire, inform, and entertain African-Americans. Monthly mag; circ 242,000. 75-80% freelance. Query. Pays $150 & up for all rts. Articles (135/yr); novel excerpts. Seasonal 4 mos ahead. Accepts simultaneous submissions. Kill fee 25%. Guidelines; copy $2.

Columns/Departments: Lee Bliss. Buys 50/yr. Positively You, Viewpoint, Perspective (personal inspiration/perspective). Query. Pays $75. These columns most open to freelance.

Tips: "We are open to queries for exciting and informative nonfiction." Uses inspirational and religious articles.

UPSOUTH, 3627 Hammett Hill Rd., Bowling Green KY 42101. (502)843-8018. E-mail: galen.smith@BGAmug.org. Christian. Galen Smith, ed. By freelance poets and writers interested in spiritual and Southern life and issues. Quarterly newsletter; 12-16 pgs; circ 75. Subscription $8. 98% freelance. Query; e-mail query OK. **PAYS FREE COPY** for one-time rts. Articles & fiction to 500 wds; book/music/video reviews to 500 wds. Responds in 2 wks. Accepts simultaneous submissions & reprints. No disk or sidebars. Guidelines; copy $2/#10 SAE/1 stamp.

Poetry: Buys large number. Any type, to 25 lines. Submit max. 3 poems.

Tips: "Prefer short, concise pieces that are crisp, interesting and uplifting. Writing about the South should be culture-centered. Most open to good poetry—spiritual, inspirational and uplifting poems that can move a reader."

U.S. CATHOLIC, 205 W. Monroe St., Chicago IL 60606. (312)236-7782. Fax (312)236-7230. E-mail: uscath@aol.com. Website: http://www.claret.org/~uscath. Catholic/Claretian. Tom McGrath, exec. ed.; Patrice Tuohy, mng ed. Devoted to starting and continuing a dialogue with Catholics of diverse lifestyles and opinions about the way they live their faith. Monthly mag; 52 pgs; circ 35,000. Subscription $18. 95% freelance. Complete ms/cover letter; phone/fax/e-mail query OK. Pays $250-600 (fiction $300-400) on acceptance for all rts. Articles 2,500-4,000 wds; fiction 2,500-3,500 wds. Responds in 2 wks. Seasonal 2 mos ahead. Accepts disk. Sidebars OK. Guidelines; free copy. (Ads)

Poetry: Buys poetry. Pays $100.

Columns/Departments: (See guidelines first.) Sounding Board, 1,100-1,300 wds, $250; Gray Matter and A Modest Proposal, 1,100-1,800 wds, $250; Practicing Catholic, 750 wds, $150.

Tips: "All articles (except for fiction or poetry) should have an explicit religious dimension that enables readers to see the interaction between their faith and the issue at hand. Fiction should be well-written, creative, with solid character development."

VIBRANT LIFE, 55 W. Oak Ridge Dr., Hagerstown MD 21740-7390. (301)791-7000. Fax (301)790-9734. E-mail: vleditor@rhpa.org. Seventh-day Adventist/Review & Herald. Larry Becker, ed. Total health publication (physical, mental and spiritual); plus articles on family and marriage improvement; ages 30-50. Bimonthly mag; 32 pgs; circ 40,000. Subscription $9.97. 80% freelance. Query/clips. Pays $75-250 on acceptance for 1st rts. Not copyrighted. Articles 500-1,500 wds (20-25/yr). Responds in 2-4 wks. Seasonal 7 mos ahead. Accepts simultaneous submissions & reprints (tell when/where appeared). Accepts disk. Kill fee. Sidebars OK. Prefers NIV. Guidelines; copy $1/9x12 SAE. (Ads)

Columns/Departments: Buys 6/yr. Fit People (people whose lives are changed for the better when applying timeless health principles/before & after photos), 500 wds; $100-150.

Tips: "Freelancers can sell us a well-written feature. Make sure it has practical application to a person's daily life. Sidebars help."

** This periodical was #57 on the 1997 Top 50 Christian Publishers List (#22 in 1996).

+VILLAGE LIFE, PO Box 816, Ellicott City MD 21041-0816. Fax (410)203-9063. Website: http://www.villagelife.org. Kaleidoscope Ministries, Ltd. Submit to The Editor. An interactive weekly news site on the World Wide Web. Query; phone/fax/e-mail (preferred) query OK. Pays $75-100 after publication for 1st & electronic rts. Articles; book reviews, $30-40. Accepts few reprints (tell when/where appeared). Prefers e-mail submissions. Guidelines on the Website. Not in topical listings.

Poetry: Buys Accepts /yr. ; lines. Pays . Submit max. poems.

Tips: "Authors are expected to have an e-mail address, which will be included in the credits of published articles."

THE VISION, 8855 Dunn Rd., Hazelwood MO 63042-2299. (314)837-7300. Fax (314)837-4503. E-mail: WAPDavis@aol.com. Website: http://www.upci.org. United Pentecostal Church. Richard M. Davis, ed. Denominational. Weekly take-home paper; 4 pgs; circ 10,000. Subscription $4.40. 95% freelance. Complete ms/cover letter. Pays $18-25 on publication for 1st rts. Articles 1,200-1,600 wds (to 120/yr); fiction 1,200-1,600 wds (to 120/yr). Seasonal 9 months ahead. Accepts simultaneous submissions & reprints. Guidelines; free copy.

Poetry: Buys 30/yr. Pays $3-12.

Tips: "Most open to good stories and articles for a traditional, fundamental, conservative church." Accepts material primarily from members of the denomination.

+VISITATION, A Source for Non-Traditional Families, PO Box 91345, Austin TX 78709-1345. (512)338-1125. Fax (512)338-0564. E-mail: takechg@worldnet. att.net. Take Charge Productions. Mary Roland, ed; Stephanie Mosher, mng. ed. Deals with parenting issues for single parents, step-parents, adoptive, non-custodial, grandparents, and blended families. Bimonthly mag; circ 20,000. 30% freelance. Query; e-mail query/submission OK. Pays $25-45 on publication for one-time rts. Articles 600-850 wds (8-15/yr); fiction 400-600 wds (children's short stories—6/yr). Responds in 5 wks. Seasonal 3 mos ahead. Guidelines; copy $5/SAE.

Fillers: Buys 6-12/yr. Anecdotes, facts, short humor, gags to be illustrated by cartoonist; 50-250 wds. Pays $10-20.

Columns/Departments: Buys 6/yr. Travel Tips, 650-850 wds; Money Matters, 650-850 wds. Pays $45.

Tips: "Our focus is on positive resolutions to parenting issues. We want an inspirational, not religious focus."

*VOICE, PO Box 19714, Irvine CA 92713-9714. (714)754-1400. Fax (714)557-9916. Full Gospel Business Men's Fellowship Intl. Jerry Jensen, ed. An evangelistic outreach to the business men in the marketplace. Monthly mag; 40 pgs; circ

200,000. Subscription $7.95. 20% freelance. Query; fax query OK. **NO PAY-MENT**. First-Person Male Testimonies (spirit-filled) 600-2,500 wds (200/yr). Responds in 2 wks. Seasonal 2 mos ahead. Accepts simultaneous submissions & reprints. Guidelines; copy for 6x9 SAE/2 stamps. (Ads)

*THE VOICE, 7537 Holly Park Dr. S. #665, Seattle WA 98118. (206)721-1983. A & A Enterprises/Pentecostal. Rev. Daniel Ashcraft, ed. Christ-honoring poetry and devotionals for street people and everyday folks. Monthly newsletter; 1 pg; circ 500. Subscription $10. 100% freelance. Complete ms. **PAYS IN COPIES** for all rts. Articles 25-75 wds. Responds in 4 wks. Seasonal 6 mos ahead. Accepts simultaneous submissions & reprints. No sidebars. Guidelines/theme list; copy for $2/#10 SAE/1 stamp.

> **Poetry:** Accepts 50/yr. Free verse, light verse, traditional; 5-20 lines. Submit max. 5 poems.
>
> **Tips:** "Most open to poetry. Avoid preaching. Keep it simple, to the point and neat."

WAR CRY, 615 Slaters Ln., Alexandria VA 22314. (703)684-5500. Fax (703)684-5539. E-mail: USWarCry@aol.com. Website: http://www.salvationarmy.org. The Salvation Army. Lt. Col. Marlene Chase, ed. Pluralistic readership reaching all socioeconomic strata and including distribution in institutions. Biweekly mag; 24 pgs; circ 300,000. Subscription $7.50. 5% freelance. Complete ms/brief cover letter; no phone/fax/e-mail query. Pays .20/wd (.15/wd for reprints) on acceptance for one-time or reprint rts. Articles & fiction 1,000-1,500 wds (60/yr). Responds in 4 wks. Seasonal 6 mos ahead. Accepts simultaneous submissions & reprints (tell when/where appeared). Requires disk. Sidebars OK. Prefers NIV. Guidelines/theme list; copy for 9x12 SAE/3 stamps.

> **Poetry:** Buys 3-6/yr. Free verse, traditional; to 16 lines. Pays by the word.
>
> **Tips:** "Much of what we receive consists of personal experience pieces, which don't fit our format. We prefer essays about 800 wds."
>
> ** This periodical was #25 on the 1997 Top 50 Christian Publishers List. (#6 in 1996, #70 in 1994)

*THE WATCHMAN, PO Box 614, Madison FL 32341. (904)973-6101. Nondenominational. Lu Castillo, ed. End-time Bible prophecy subjects; general Christian growth; articles of interest to home churches. Quarterly newsletter; 8 pgs. 20% freelance. Complete ms/cover letter. **NO PAYMENT.** Not copyrighted. Articles.

THE WAY OF ST. FRANCIS, 1500 - 34th Ave., Oakland CA 94601-3092. (916)443-5717. Fax (916)443-2019. E-mail: ofmcaway@woldnet.att.net. Franciscan Friars of California/Catholic. Camille Franicevich, mng. ed. For those interested in the message of St. Francis of Assisi as lived out by contemporary people. Bimonthly mag; 48 pgs; circ 5,000. Subscription $12. 15% freelance. Complete ms/cover letter; no phone/fax/e-mail query. Pays $25-100 on publication for 1st rts. Articles 500-1,500 wds (4-6/yr). Responds in 6 wks. Seasonal 6 mos ahead. Accepts simultaneous submissions & reprints (tell when/where appeared). Prefers disk. Sidebars OK. Guidelines/theme list; copy for 6x9 SAE/6 stamps.

> **Fillers:** Anecdotes, cartoons, facts, prayers, prose; to 100 wds. Pays $25-50.
>
> **Columns/Departments:** Buys 12/yr. First Person (opinion/issue), to 900 wds; Portrait (interview or personality), to 1,200 wds; Inspirations (spiritual), to 1,200 wds. Pays $25-50.

Tips: "Most open to columns. Make direct connection to Francis or the Franciscan way of life."

WEAVINGS, 1908 Grand Ave., PO Box 189, Nashville TN 37202-0189. (615)340-7254. Fax (615)340-7006. E-mail: weavings@upperroom.org. Website: http://www. upperroom.org. The Upper Room. John S. Mogabgab, ed.; submit to Kathleen Stephens, assoc. ed. A thoughtful, thematic focus on the Christian spiritual life. Bimonthly journal; 48 pgs; circ. 40,000. Subscription $24. 75% freelance. Complete ms/cover letter; e-mail query OK. Pays .12 & up/wd on publication for all, one-time or reprint rts. Articles 1,250-2,500 wds (2/yr); fiction (6/yr) 2,000 wds (vignettes 500 wds); book reviews 750 wds. Responds in 8 wks. Seasonal 9 mos ahead. Accepts reprints (tell when/where appeared). Accept disk. Kill fee. No sidebars. Prefers NRSV. Guidelines/theme list; copy for 7x10 SAE/5stamps.

> **Poetry:** Buys 1/yr. Free verse, light verse, traditional. Must have a spiritual focus; $75 & up.

#WESLEYAN ADVOCATE, Box 50434, Indianapolis IN 46250-0434. (317)576-8156. Fax (317)842-1649. E-mail: weslyndoc@aol.com. The Wesleyan Church. Jerry Brecheisen, mng ed. A full salvation family mag; denominational. Monthly mag; 36 pgs; circ 20,000. Subscription $15. 50% freelance. Complete ms/cover letter; phone query OK. Pays $10-40 for assigned, $5-25 for unsolicited, .01-.02/wd for reprints on publication for 1st or simultaneous rts. Not copyrighted. Articles 250-650 wds (50/yr). Responds in 2 wks. Seasonal 6 mos ahead. Accepts simultaneous submissions & reprints. Guidelines; copy $2. (Ads)

> **Poetry:** Buys 30/yr. Free verse or traditional; $5-10. Send max. 6 poems.
> **Fillers:** Prose, 100-300 wds. Pays $2-6.
> **Columns/Departments:** Personal Experiences, 700 wds; Ministry Tips, 600 wds; $10.

+WHO CARES, 1511 K St. NW #412, Washington DC 20005. (202)628-1691. Fax (202)628-2063. Who Cares, Inc. Samantha Stainburn, mng. ed. A business magazine for people who do good works (secular). Bimonthly mag; 48 pgs; circ 50,000. Subscription free. 80-100% freelance. Query/clips; fax query OK. Pays .10/wd on publication for first, reprint & electronic rts. Articles 700-3,000 wds (many/yr). Responds in 8 wks. Seasonal 3-4 mos ahead. Accepts reprints (tell when/where appeared). Prefers disk. Kill fee 25%. Sidebars OK. Guidelines; copy for 9x12 SAE/5 stamps.

> **Columns/Departments:** Tool box, 700-1,200 wds; Civil Society, 700-1,200 wds. Pays $70-120. See guidelines for details.
> **Special Needs:** May/June Legacy issue: The history of service.
> **Tips:** "We have an ongoing need for writers who can discuss religion as an impetus for community service with a secular audience. We also seek case studies of churches and church leaders who take innovative approaches to service."

*THE WICHITA CHRONICLE, PO Box 781079, Wichita KS 67278. Karen McBride, ed.

CHILDREN'S MARKETS

+BEGINNER'S FRIEND, PO Box 4060, Overland Park KS 66204. (913)432-0331. Fax (913)722-0351. Church of God (holiness)/Herald and Banner Press. Arlene

McGehee, Sunday school ed. Denominational; for young children. Weekly take-home paper; 4 pgs; circ 2,700. Subscription $1.30. Complete ms/cover letter; phone/fax query OK. Pays .005/wd on publication for 1st rts. Fiction 500-800 wds. Seasonal 6-8 mos ahead. Accepts simultaneous submissions & reprints (tell when/where appeared). Prefers KJV. Guidelines/theme list; copy. Not in topical listings.

BREAD FOR GOD'S CHILDREN, Box 1017, Arcadia FL 34265-1017. (941)494-6214. Fax (941)993-0154. E-mail: bread@desoto.net. Bread Ministries, Inc. Judith M. Gibbs, ed. A family magazine for serious Christians who are concerned about their children or grandchildren (ages 6-18). Monthly (8X) mag; 32 pgs; circ 10,000. Free subscription. 20-25% freelance. Complete ms. Pays $20-30 ($30-50 for fiction) on publication for 1st or one-time rts. Not copyrighted. Articles 600-800 wds (6/yr); fiction & true stories 600-900 wds for 4-10 yrs, 900-1,500 wds for teens (15/yr). Responds in 8-12 wks (may hold longer). Some simultaneous submissions & reprints (tell when/where appeared). Some sidebars. Prefers KJV. Guidelines; 3 copies for 9x12 SAE/5 stamps; 1 copy 3 stamps.

> **Columns/Departments:** Buys 5-8/yr. Let's chat (discussion issues facing children), 500-800 wds; Teen Page (teen issues), 600-900 wds; and Idea Page (object lessons or crafts for kids), 300-800 wds.. Pays $10-30.
>
> **Tips:** "Most open to fiction. Stories should teach Christian values and life-style without preaching. No tag endings or adult solutions coming from children. Create realistic characters and situations. No 'sudden inspiration' solutions."

CLUB CONNECTION, 1445 Boonville Ave., Springfield MO 65802-1894. (417)862-2781. Fax (417)862-0503. E-mail: mettes@ag.org. Kerry Clarensau, ed. For girls ages 3 through high school (with leader edition for Missionettes leaders). Est. 1997. Quarterly mag; 32 pgs; circ 18,000-20,000. Subscription $6.50 (leader's $7.50). 10% freelance. Complete ms/cover letter. Pays $10-50 on publication for 1st or one-time rts. Articles 500 wds (4-6/yr). Responds in 10 wks. Seasonal 10-12 mos ahead. Accepts simultaneous submissions & reprints (tell when/where appeared). Accepts disk. Kill fee. Sidebars OK. Prefers NIV. Guidelines/theme list; copy for 9x12 SAE/3 stamps.

> **Poetry:** Buys 1-2 /yr. Light verse; 4-20 lines; $5-10. Submit max. 2 poems.
>
> **Fillers:** Buys 6-8/yr. Anecdotes, cartoons, facts, games, ideas, jokes, news-breaks, party ideas, quizzes, short humor, word puzzles; 20-50 or 100 wds; $5-20.
>
> **Columns/Departments:** Buys 4-6/yr. Pays $10-50.
>
> **Tips:** "Articles with a Christian slant of interest to girls."

*CLUBHOUSE, c/o Your Story Hour, Box 15, Berrien Springs MI 49103. (616)471-3701. Fax (616)471-4661. Non-denominational. Krista Phillips, ed. To help young people (9-14) feel good about themselves. Monthly newsletter; 4 pgs; circ 8,000. Subscription $5. 75% freelance. Complete ms. Pays $12-35 on acceptance for one-time rts. Articles 25-1,200 wds (150/yr); fiction 100-1,200 wds (30/yr). Responds in 4-5 wks. Seasonal 6 mos ahead. Accepts simultaneous submissions & reprints. No disk. Guidelines; copy for 5x7 SAE/2 stamps.

> **Poetry:** Buys 60/yr. Free verse, light verse, traditional; to 12 lines; $12. Submit max. 3 poems.

Fillers: Buys 60/yr. Anecdotes, cartoons, games, jokes, word puzzles; 50-100 wds; $12.

Tips: "Send all material once a year in March."

** This periodical was #50 on the 1996 Top 50 Christian Publishers List.

COUNSELOR, 4050 Lee Vance View, Colorado Springs CO 80918. (719)536-0100. Fax (719)536-3243. Cook Communications Ministries. Janice K. Burton, ed. Presents the way spiritual truths in the weekly lesson can be worked out in everyday life—a correlated teaching tool for 8-12 yr olds. Weekly take-home paper; 4 pgs. Subscription $11.50. 50% freelance. Complete ms/cover letter; no phone/fax query. Pays .07-.10/wd on acceptance for all, 1st, one-time, or reprint rts. Articles 300 wds (12/yr); fiction/true stories 800-1,000 wds (12/yr). Responds in 6-8 wks. Seasonal 1 yr ahead. Accepts simultaneous submissions & reprints (tell when/where appeared—pays .05-.07/wd). Prefers hard copy. Some kill fees. No sidebars. Prefers KJV or NIV. Guidelines/theme list; copy for #10 SAE/1 stamp.

Fillers: Buys 10-12/yr. Cartoons, puzzles, quizzes, fun activities; 100-150 wds. Pays $7-25.

Columns/Departments: Buys 12/yr. God's Wonders (science themes); World Series (missions story from child's perspective); 300-400 wds.

Tips: "Should have a feel for the age level. Know your readers and what is appropriate in terms of concepts and vocabulary. Submit only best quality manuscripts. All must have a Christian emphasis." Uses ethnic short stories. Include Social Security number.

** This periodical was #61 on the 1996 Top 50 Christian Publishers List. (#67 in 1994). 1996 EPA Award of Merit—Sunday School Take-Home.

COURAGE, 1300 N. Meacham Rd., Schaumburg IL 60173-4888. (847)843-1600. Fax (847)843-3757. Regular Baptist Press. Joan Alexander, ed. For children, 9-12, in Sunday school. Weekly take-home paper. Note: This periodical is being redesigned as we go to press. Send for new guidelines before submitting.

CRUSADER, 1333 Alger SE, Grand Rapids MI 49507. (616)241-5616. Fax (616)241-5558. E-mail: cadets@aol.com. Calvinist Cadet Corp. G. Richard Broene, ed. To show cadets and their friends, boys 9-14, how God is at work in their lives and in the world around them. Mag published 7X/yr; 24 pgs; circ 14,000. Subscription $9.50. 35% freelance. Complete ms/cover letter. Pays .02-.05/wd on acceptance for 1st, one-time, or reprint rts. Articles 500-1,000 wds (7/yr); fiction 900-1,500 wds (14/yr). Responds in 4 wks. Seasonal 5 mos ahead. Accepts simultaneous submissions & reprints (tell when/where appeared). Accepts disk. Sidebars OK. Prefers NIV. Guidelines/theme list; copy for 9x12 SAE/4 stamps. (Ads)

Fillers: Buys 12-18/yr. Cartoons, quizzes, word puzzles; 20-200 wds; $5 & up.

Tips: "Fiction tied to themes or fillers; request new theme list in February of each year."

** 1995 EPA Award of Merit—Youth.

#CRUSADER, 4200 N. Point Pkwy, Alpharetta GA 30022-4174. Southern Baptist. James Warren, ed. For children, primarily boys, grades 4-6; missions education. Monthly mag; 20 pgs; circ. 60,000. Subscription $12.36. Complete ms/cover letter; fax query OK. Pays variable rate on acceptance for all rts. Responds in 4 wks. Seasonal 1 yr ahead. Prefers NAS. Guidelines/theme list; copy $1.25/9x12 SAE/4 stamps.

Tips: "Be Southern Baptist—involved in Royal Ambassadors or children's missions education group."

DISCOVERIES, 6401 The Paseo, Kansas City MO 64131. (816)333-7000. Fax (816)333-4439. Website: http://www.nazarene.org. Nazarene/Word Action Publishing. Kathleen Johnson, asst. ed. For 8-9 yr olds, emphasizing Christian values and holy living. Weekly take-home paper; 4 pgs; circ 30,000. 75% freelance. Complete ms/cover letter; fax query OK. Pays .05/wd on publication for multi-use rts. Articles (10/yr) & fiction (30/yr), to 500 wds. Responds in 6 wks. Seasonal 6 mos ahead. Accepts reprints (tell when/where appeared). No disk. Kill fee. Sidebars OK. Prefers NIV. Guidelines/theme list/copy for #10 SAE/2 stamps.

Tips: "Follow guidelines and theme list. Most open to nonfiction and fiction."

+DISCOVERY (AL), 230 Landmark Dr., Montgomery AL 36117. (800)234-8558 or (334)272-8558. Fax (800)234-2882 or (334)270-2002. Website: http://www. ApologeticsPress.org. Bert Thompson & Wayne Jackson, eds. Focus is Scripture and science; for 4th-6th graders. Monthly take-home paper; 8 pgs. Incomplete topical listings.

DISCOVERY (NY), 475 Riverside Dr., Rm. 455, New York NY 10115. (212)870-3335. Fax (212)870-3229. The John Milton Society for the Blind. Ingrid Peck, asst. ed. For blind children ages 8-18, in Braille; reprints articles from Christian and other magazines for youth. Quarterly mag; 44 pgs; circ 2,060. Free subscription. 5% freelance. Complete ms/cover letter; phone query OK. **NO PAYMENT** for reprint rts. Not copyrighted. Articles 500-1,500 wds (1/yr); fiction 500-1,500 wds (1/yr). Responds in 6 wks. Seasonal 9-12 mos ahead. Accepts simultaneous submissions & reprints (tell when/where appeared). Accepts disk. No sidebars. Guidelines; free copy.

Poetry: Accepts 1/yr. Any type; 5-30 lines.

Fillers: Anecdotes, games, ideas, jokes, quizzes, prayers, quotes, short humor, word puzzles; 10-150 wds.

Tips: "Look at magazines we typically reprint from (see guidelines). Send complete manuscript with little or no editing required. We are most in need of poetry/prayers pertaining to Christian themes/holidays & seasons."

FOCUS ON THE FAMILY CLUBHOUSE, 8605 Explorer Dr., Colorado Springs CO 80920. (719)531-3400. Fax (719)531-3499. Focus on the Family. Jesse Florea, ed. For children 8-12 yrs in Christian homes. Monthly mag; 24 pgs; circ 100,000. Subscription $15. 40% freelance. Complete ms/cover letter; fax query OK. Pays $25-250 for articles, $50-250 for fiction on acceptance for 1st rts. Articles 400-600 wds (5/yr); fiction 400-600 wds (30/yr). Responds in 4-6 wks. Seasonal 5 mos ahead. No disk. Kill fee. Sidebars OK. Prefers NIV. Guidelines; copy for 9x12 SAE/5 stamps.

Fillers: Buys 10/yr. Games, party ideas, quizzes, word puzzles; 150-500 wds; $25-100.

Contest: Contests only for children 8-12 years.

Tips: "Biggest need is for fiction. Send mss with list of credentials. Read past issues."

** This periodical was #2 on the 1997 Top 50 Christian Publishers list. (#62 in 1996, #38 in 1995, #15 in 1994) Also 1997 & 1995 EPA Award of Merit—Youth.

#FOCUS ON THE FAMILY CLUBHOUSE JR., 8605 Explorer Dr., Colorado Springs CO 80920. (719)548-4595. Fax (719)531-3499. Focus on the Family. Jesse Florea, ed. For ages 4-8 yrs. Monthly mag; 16 pgs; circ 80,000. Subscription $12. 25% freelance. Complete ms/cover letter; fax query OK. Pays $100 ($100-200 for fiction) on acceptance for 1st rts. Articles 300-750 wds (1-2/yr); fiction 300-1,000 wds (10/yr). Responds in 4 wks. Seasonal 5-6 mos ahead. Kill fee. No sidebars. Guidelines; copy for 9x12 SAE/2 stamps.

> **Poetry:** Buys 3/yr. Free verse, light verse, traditional; 10-25 lines; $25-100.
>
> **Fillers:** Buys 1-2/yr. Cartoons, games, word puzzles; $15-30.
>
> **Special Needs:** Bible stories.
>
> **Tips:** "Most open to short, non-preachy fiction, beginning reader stories, and read-to-me."
>
> ****** This periodical was #52 on the 1997 Top 50 Christian Publishers list. (#53 in 1996 & 1995, #15 in 1994) 1996 EPA Award of Excellence—Youth.

#GOD'S WORLD TODAY/IT'S GOD'S WORLD, PO Box 2330, Asheville NC 28802. (704)253-8063. Fax (704)253-1556. God's World Publications. Norman W. Bomer, ed. Current events, published in 5 editions, for kindergarten through jr. high students, mostly in Christian and home schools. Weekly newsletter (during school yr); 8 pgs; circ 301,000. Subscription $19.95. 16% freelance. Complete ms/cover letter. Pays $75 on acceptance for one-time rts. Articles 700-900 wds. Responds in 9 wks. Guidelines; free copy. (Ads)

> **Tips:** "Keep vocabulary simple. Must present a distinctly Christian world view without being moralistic."

GOOD NEWS FOR CHILDREN, 330 Progress Rd., Dayton OH 45449. (937)847-5900. Fax (937)847-5910. E-mail: pliservice@aol.com. Website: http://www. pflaum.com.Catholic. Joan Mitchell CSJ, ed. For 2nd & 3rd graders. Weekly (32X) take-home paper; 4 pgs. Not in topical listings.

GUIDE, 55 W. Oak Ridge Dr., Hagerstown MD 21740. (301)791-7000. Fax (301)790-9734. E-mail: GUIDE@chpa.org. Seventh-day Adventist. Tim Lale, ed.; Randy Fishell, assoc. ed. A Christian journal for 10-14 yr olds, presenting true stories relevant to their needs. Weekly take-home paper; 32 pgs; circ 33,000. Subscription $39.97/yr. 100% freelance. Complete ms/cover letter; fax/e-mail query OK. Pays .03-.12/wd on acceptance for one-time, reprint, simultaneous or electronic rts. Articles 1,200 wds or true stories (150/yr). Responds in 3-4 wks. Seasonal 6 mos ahead. Accepts simultaneous submissions & reprints (tell when/where appeared—pays 1/2). Prefers disk. Sidebars usually assigned. Guidelines/theme list; copy for #10 SAE/2 stamps.

> **Fillers:** Buys 50-75/yr. Games, quizzes & word puzzles on a spiritual themes; 20-50 wds; $25-50.
>
> **Special Needs:** "Most open to true action/adventure and Christian humor. Kids want that—put it together with dialogue and a spiritual slant, and you're on the 'write' track for our readers. School life."
>
> ****** This periodical was #22 on the 1995 Top 50 Christian Publishers list. (#38 in 1994)

GUIDEPOSTS FOR KIDS, PO Box 638, Chesterton IN 46304. Fax (219)926-3839. E-mail: WALLYT5232@aol.com. Website: http://www.guideposts.org. Guideposts, Inc. Mary Lou Carney, ed; Betsy Berlin, articles & fiction editor. For kids 7-12 yrs (emphasis at upper level). Bimonthly mag; 32 pgs; circ 200,000. Subscription $15.95. 75% freelance. Query/clips (complete ms for fiction); no electronic submissions. Pays $150-450 ($250-400 for fiction) on acceptance for all & electronic rts. Articles 300-1,200 wds (30/yr); fiction 500-1,200 wds (10/yr). Responds in 4-6 wks. Seasonal 6 mos ahead. No disk. Kill fee. Likes sidebars. Prefers NIV. Guidelines; copy $3.25/10x13 SAE.

> **Poetry:** Mary Lou Carney. Buys 4-6/yr. Free verse, haiku, light verse, traditional; 3-20 lines; $15-50. Submit max. 5 poems.
>
> **Fillers:** Buys 15-20/yr. Facts, games, jokes, quizzes, short humor, word puzzles; to 300 wds; $20-75.
>
> **Columns/Departments:** Buys 20/yr. Featuring Kids (true, interesting kid profiles), 300-600 wds; Tips from the Top (Christian celebrities/sport figures), 500-700 wds; $150-350.
>
> **Tips:** "Looking for historical fiction; mini-series/brain teasers; true action stories suitable comic book format."
>
> ** This periodical was #30 on the 1997 Top 50 Christian Publishers list. (#54 in 1996, #55 in 1995)

*HIGH ADVENTURE, 1445 Boonville Ave., Springfield MO 65802-1894. (417)862-2781x4178. Fax (417)831-8230. Assemblies of God. Marshall Bruner, ed-in-chief. For the Royal Rangers (boys), 5-17 yrs; slanted toward teens. Quarterly mag; 16 pgs; circ 86,000. 90% freelance. Complete ms/cover letter. Pays .03-.04/wd on acceptance for 1st, one-time, simultaneous or reprint rts. Articles 500-900 wds (30/yr); fiction 500-900 wds (15/yr). Responds in 4-5 wks. Seasonal 7 mos ahead. Accepts simultaneous submissions & reprints (tell when/where appeared). Sidebars OK. Prefers NIV. Guidelines/theme list; copy for 9x12 SAE/3 stamps.

> **Fillers:** Buys 30/yr. Cartoons, jokes, short humor; 50 wds; $2-20.
>
> ** This periodical was #14 on the 1997 Top 50 Christian Publishers list.

+JUNIOR COMPANION, PO Box 4060, Overland Park KS 66204. (913)432-0331. Fax (913)722-0351. Church of God (holiness)/Herald and Banner Press. Arlene McGehee, Sunday school ed. Denominational; for 4th-6th graders. Weekly take-home paper; 4 pgs; circ 3,500. Subscription $1.30. Complete ms/cover letter; phone/fax query OK. Pays .005/wd on publication for 1st rts. Fiction 500-1,200 wds. Seasonal 6-8 mos ahead. Accepts simultaneous submissions & reprints (tell when/where appeared). Prefers KJV. Guidelines/theme list; copy. Not in topical listings.

JUNIOR TRAILS, 1445 Boonville Ave., Springfield MO 65802-1894. (417)862-2781. E-mail: UElemCurr@ag.org. Assemblies of God. Sinda S. Zinn, ed. Teaching of Christian principles through fiction stories about children (10-12 yrs). Weekly take-home paper; 8 pgs; circ 50,000. Subscription $6.20. 98% freelance. Complete ms. Pays .03-.05/wd on acceptance for one-time rts. Articles 300-500 wds (50/yr); fiction 1,000-1,200 wds (50/yr). Responds in 2-4 wks. Seasonal 15-18 mos ahead. Accepts simultaneous submissions & reprints. No disk. No sidebars. Prefers NIV. Guidelines/theme list; copy for #10 SAE/1 stamp.

Poetry: Buys 6-8/yr. Free verse, haiku, light verse, traditional; $5 & up. Submit max. 3 poems.

Fillers: Buys 8-10/yr. Facts, short humor; 300-500 wds; .03-.05/wd.

Tips: "Most open to fiction based on relevant problems for today's kids. Submit well-written, believable stories in which character overcomes real problem based on biblical principles. Use third person; move story through action and dialogue, rather than narration."

** This periodical was #36 on the 1997 Top 50 Christian Publishers list. (#17 in 1996, #23 in 1995)

KEYS FOR KIDS, Box 1, Grand Rapids MI 49501. (616)451-2009. Fax (616)451-0032. E-mail: cbh@cbhonline.com. Website: http://www.cbhonline.com. Hazel Marett, ed. A daily devotional booklet for children (8-14) or for family devotions. Bimonthly booklet; 96 pgs; circ 40,000. No subscriptions. 100% freelance. Complete ms. Pays $12-16 on acceptance for 1st or simultaneous rts. Not copyrighted. Devotionals (includes short fiction story) 375-425 wds (60-70/yr). Responds in 2-4 wks. Seasonal 4-5 mos ahead. Accepts simultaneous submissions & reprints. Prefers KJV or NIV. Guidelines; copy for 6x9 SAE/$1.24 postage.

Tips: "If you are rejected, go back to the sample and study it some more."

#LAD, 4200 n. Point Pkwy, Alpharetta GA 30022-4174. Southern Baptist. Charlotte Teas, ed. For boys, grades 1-3; missions education. Monthly mag; 20 pgs; circ. 60,000. Subscription $12.36. Complete ms/cover letter; fax query OK. Pays variable rate on acceptance for all rts. Responds in 4 wks. Seasonal 1 yr ahead. Prefers NAS. Guidelines/theme list; copy $1.25/9x12 SAE/4 stamps.

Tips: "Be Southern Baptist—involved in Royal Ambassadors or children's missions education group."

LISTEN, 6401 The Paseo, Kansas City MO 64131. (816)333-7000 x2358. Fax (816)333-4439. E-mail: gpryor@nazarene.org. Website: http://www.nazarene. org. Nazarene/Wesleyan/WordAction. Lynda Boardman, ed. Weekly activity/story paper for 3-4 yr olds; 4 pgs; circ 7,500. Subscription $9.20. 30% freelance. Query. Pays .05/wd on publication for one-time & reprint rts. Not copyrighted. Articles 100-200 wds (0/yr); contemporary fiction & true stories 300-400 wds (45/yr). Responds in 4 wks. Seasonal 12 mos ahead. No disk. No sidebars. Prefers NIV. Guidelines/theme list/copy for #10 SAE/1 stamp.

Poetry: Buys 35/yr. Light verse, traditional; 4-10 lines; $2 or .25/line. Submit max. 10 poems.

Fillers: Buys 15/yr. Games, ideas/activities (age-appropriate), prayers; $5-15.

Special Needs: Exciting, age-appropriate activities for back page; adventure stories and children's life situation stories; poetry.

+LIVE WIRE, 8121 Hamilton Ave., Cincinnati OH 45231. (513)931-4050. Fax (513)931-0950. E-mail: standardpub@attmail.com. Carla J. Crane, ed. Geared to 10-12 year olds who want to connect to Christ. Weekly newspaper; 4 pgs; circ 40,000. Subscription $11.99. 100% freelance. Complete ms. Pays .05-.07/wd on acceptance for all, 1st, & reprint rts. Articles 250-350 wds. Responds in 9-13 wks. Seasonal 1 yr ahead. Accepts simultaneous submissions & reprints (tell when/where appeared). Accepts disk. Sidebars OK. Prefers NIV. Guidelines/theme list; copy for #10 SAE/2 stamps.

Fillers: Facts, games, ideas, jokes, party ideas, quotes, word puzzles.

#MY FRIEND, The Catholic Magazine for Kids, 50 St. Paul's Ave., Boston MA 02130-3491. (617)522-8911. Fax (617)541-9805. E-mail: chaire@interramp. com. Website: http://www.pauline.org (click on Kidstuff). Pauline Books & Media. Sr. Kathryn James, mng. ed. Christian values and basic Catholic doctrines for children, ages 6-12. Monthly (10X) mag; 32 pgs; circ 12,000. Subscription $18. 20-60+% freelance. Complete ms/cover letter; fax/e-mail query OK. Pays $35-100 after acceptance for all or 1st rts. Articles 150-800 wds (20/yr) & fiction 500-900 wds (8/yr). Responds in 9 wks. Seasonal 6 mos ahead. No disk. Kill fee. Sidebars OK. Guidelines; copy $2.95.

> **Fillers:** New area. Cartoons, jokes; $7-15.
>
> **Tips:** "In fiction, include physically challenged, and universality or ethnic inclusion."
>
> ** This periodical was #66 on the 1997 Top 50 Christian Publishers list. (#32 in 1996, #34 in 1995, #39 in 1994)

NATURE FRIEND MAGAZINE, 22777 State Rd. 119, Goshen IN 46526. (219)534-2245. Fax (219)534-2333. Pilgrim Publishers/Fundamental Creationist. Mrs. Stanley Brubaker, ed. For children (ages 4-14); about God's wonderful world of nature and wildlife. Monthly mag; 36 pgs; circ 7,600. Subscription $22. 50% freelance. Complete ms/cover letter. Pays .05/wd on publication for one-time rts. Articles 500-1,200 wds; or true stories 500-1200 wds (40/yr). Responds in 4-12 wks. Seasonal 3-6 mos ahead. Accepts simultaneous submissions & reprints (tell when/where appeared). No disk. Some sidebars. Prefers KJV. Guidelines; copy $2.50/9x12 SAE/3 stamps.

> **Poetry:** Buys 10-20/yr. Traditional; $8-20. Submit max. 5 poems.
>
> **Fillers:** Buys 12/yr. Quizzes, word puzzles; 100-500 wds. Pays $10-25.
>
> **Tips:** "Don't bother submitting to us unless you have seen our guidelines and a sample copy. We are very conservative in our approach."

+NEW CHILDREN'S MAGAZINE (This magazine did not have a name at press time), 119 S. Lakewood Dr., Ridgeley WV 26753. (304)738-2136. Fountain Publishing. Patricia Timbrook, pub/ed-in-chief; Susan Titus Osborn, ed. For children 6-12 yrs. First issue October 1998. Bimonthly mag; 32 pgs. Guidelines. Not in topical listings.

> **Tips:** "We are seeking fiction and nonfiction stories, poems, rebuses, and art samples."

ON THE LINE, 616 Walnut Ave., Scottdale PA 15683-1999. (412)887-8500. Fax (412)887-3111. E-mail: otl%mph@mcimail.com. Mennonite/Herald Press. Mary Clemens Meyer, ed. Reinforces Christian values in 10-14 yr olds. Monthly mag; 28 pgs; circ 6,000. Subscription $19.85. 90% freelance. Complete ms; fax/e-mail query OK. Pays .03-.05/wd on acceptance for one-time or reprint rts. Articles 300-500 wds (25-30/yr); fiction 1,000-1,800 wds (45-50/yr). Responds in 4 wks. Seasonal 6 mos ahead. Accepts simultaneous submissions & reprints (tell when/where appeared). Sidebars OK. Prefers NIV or NRSV. Guidelines; copy for 7x10 SAE/2 stamps.

> **Poetry:** Buys 10-15/yr. Free verse, haiku, light verse, traditional; 3-24 lines; $10-25.
>
> **Fillers:** Buys 25-30/yr. Cartoons, facts, games, jokes, party ideas, quizzes, word puzzles; to 350 wds; $10-25.

Ethnic: Targets all ethnic groups involved in the Mennonite religion.

Tips: "Watch kids 10-14. Listen to them talk. Write stories that sound natural—not moralizing, preachy, with adults quoting Scripture. Our readers like puzzles, especially theme crosswords."

** This periodical was #59 on the 1997 Top 50 Christian Publishers list. (#38 in 1996, #44 in 1995, #52 in 1994)

#OUR LITTLE FRIEND, Box 5353, Nampa ID 83653-5353. (208)465-2580. Fax (208)465-2531. E-mail: ailsox@pacificpress.com. Website: http://www.pacificpress. com. Seventh-day Adventist. Aileen Andres Sox, ed. For theme and comments, see **Primary Treasure**. Weekly take-home paper for 1-6 yr olds (through 1st grade); 8 pgs; circ 45,000-50,000. 40% freelance (assigned), 10% unsolicited. Complete ms; fax/e-mail query OK (not preferred). Pays $25-50 on acceptance for one-time or reprint rts. True stories to 650 wds. Responds in 13 wks. Seasonal 7 mos ahead. Accepts simultaneous submissions & reprints. No disk. Guidelines (also on Website)/theme list; copy for 9x12 SAE/2 stamps.

Poetry: 12 lines; $1/line.

Tips: "Stories need to be crafted for this age reader in plot and vocabulary."

PARTNERS, Christian Light Publications, Inc., Box 1212, Harrisonburg VA 22801-1212. (540)434-0768. Fax (540)433-8896. Mennonite. Crystal Shank, ed. For 9-14 yr olds. Weekly take-home paper; 4 pgs; circ 5,800. Subscription $9.20. Almost 100% freelance. Complete ms. Pays up to .03/wd on acceptance for all, 1st, or reprint rts. Articles 200-1,000 wds (50/yr); fiction & true stories 1,000-1,600 wds (50-75/yr); serial stories up to 1,600/installment; short-short stories to 400 wds. Responds in 6 wks. Seasonal 6 mos ahead. Accepts simultaneous submissions (treated as reprints) & reprints (tell when/where appeared); serials 2-13 parts (2-4 parts preferred). Requires KJV. Guidelines/theme list/copy for 9x12 SAE/3 stamps.

Poetry: Buys 25/yr. Traditional, story poems; 4-24 lines; .50/line. Submit max. 6 poems.

Fillers: Buys 50-75/yr. Quizzes, word puzzles (Bible related). Payment varies, about $5.

Columns/Departments: Character Corner; Cultures & Customs; Historical Highlights; Maker's Masterpiece; Missionary Mail; Torches of Truth; or Nature Nooks; all 200-800 or 1,000 wds.

Tips: "Personal familiarity with conservative Mennonite applications of biblical truth is very helpful. Follow themes. We do not require that you be Mennonite, but we do send a questionnaire for you to fill out."

** This periodical was #44 on the 1997 Top 50 Christian Publishers list. (#63 in 1996, #66 in 1995)

POCKETS, PO Box 189, Nashville TN 37202-0189. (615)340-7333. Fax (615)340-7006. E-mail: pockets@upperroom.org. United Methodist. Janet Knight, ed; submit to Lynn W. Gilliam, assoc. ed. Devotional magazine for children (6-11 yrs). Monthly (11X) mag; 48 pgs; circ 93,000. Subscription $16.95. 75% freelance. Complete ms. Pays .14/wd on acceptance for 1st rts. (Will start buying software application rts if commissioned.) Articles 400-800 wds (20/yr) & fiction 500-1,600 wds (55/yr). Responds in 4 wks. Seasonal 1 yr ahead. Accepts reprints (tell when/where appeared). Kill fee 33%. Some sidebars. Prefers NRSV. Guidelines/theme list (new each Dec.); copy for 7x9 SAE/4 stamps.

Poetry: Buys 30/yr. Free verse, haiku, light verse, traditional; 4-20 lines; $25-50 or $2/line. Submit max. 7 poems.

Fillers: Buys 44 games/puzzles/yr. Games, ideas, jokes, prayers, riddles, word puzzles; $25.

Columns/Departments: Buys 40/yr. Kids Cook; Pocketsful of Love (ways to show love), 200-300 wds; Peacemakers at Work, 500-800 wds; Pocketsful of Prayer, 400-600 wds.

Special Needs: "New feature is a 2-pg story for ages 5-8, 650 words max. Need role model stories and retold Bible stories. Stories about someone you'd like to know. Interesting articles about children doing unusual things, 250-600 wds."

Contest: Fiction-writing contest; submit between 4/1 & 8/15 every yr. Prize $1,000. Length 1,000-1,600 wds. Must be unpublished and not historical fiction. Previous winners not eligible. Send to Pockets Fiction Contest at above address.

Tips: "Get our theme list first. Nonfiction probably easiest to sell and Peacemakers at Work."

** This periodical was #22 on the 1997 Top 50 Christian Publishers list. (#10 in 1996, #8 in 1995, #18 in 1994)

POWER AND LIGHT, 6401 The Paseo, Kansas City MO 64131. (816)333-7000x2243. Fax (816)333-4439. E-mail: bpostlewait@nazarene.org. Website: http://www.nazarene.org. Nazarene/WordAction Publishing Co. Beula Postlewait, ed. For pre-teens, 11-12 year olds. Weekly take-home paper; 8 pgs; circ 40,000. Subscription $28. 25% freelance. Query or complete ms/cover letter; fax/e-mail query OK. Pays .05/wd on publication for multiple use rts (writer retains right to reuse). Articles 600 wds (10/yr); fiction 700 wds (10/yr). Responds in 2 wks. Accepts simultaneous submissions & reprints (.035/wd—tell when/where appeared). Kill fee $15. Accepts disk. No sidebars. NIV only. Guidelines/theme list; copy for #10 SAE/2 stamps.

Fillers: Buys 104/yr. Cartoons, games, jokes, short humor, word puzzles; $15.

Tips: "Most open to fiction, puzzles and cartoons. Request a theme list. Write about preteens from a preteen perspective."

PRIMARY PAL (IL), 1300 N. Meacham Rd., Schaumburg IL 60173-4888. (847)843-1600. Fax (847)843-3757. Regular Baptist Press. Joan Alexander, ed. For ages 6-8; fundamental, conservative. Weekly take-home paper. Note: This periodical is being redesigned as we go to press. Send for new guidelines before submitting.

+PRIMARY PAL (KS), PO Box 4060, Overland Park KS 66204. (913)432-0331. Fax (913)722-0351. Church of God (holiness)/Herald and Banner Press. Arlene McGehee, Sunday school ed. Denominational; for 1st-3rd graders. Weekly take-home paper; 4 pgs; circ 2,900. Subscription $1.30. Complete ms/cover letter; phone/fax query OK. Pays .005/wd on publication for 1st rts. Fiction 500-1,000 wds. Seasonal 6-8 mos ahead. Accepts simultaneous submissions & reprints (tell when/where appeared). Prefers KJV. Guidelines/theme list; copy. Not in topical listings.

#PRIMARY TREASURE, Box 5353, Nampa ID 83653-5353. (208)465-2500. Fax (208)465-2531. E-mail: ailsox@pacificpress.com. Website: http://www.pacificpress. com. Seventh-day Adventist. Aileen Andres Sox, ed. To teach children Christian belief, values, and practice. God's loving us and our loving Him makes a difference in every facet of life, from how we think and act to how we feel. Weekly take-home paper for 7-9 yr olds (2nd-4th grades); 16 pgs; circ 35,000. 25% freelance (assigned), 75% reprints or unsolicited. Complete ms; fax/e-mail query OK (not preferred). Pays $25-50 on acceptance for one-time or reprint rts. True stories 900-1,000 wds; articles used rarely (query). Responds in 13 wks. Seasonal 7 mos ahead. Accepts simultaneous submissions; serials to 10 parts (query). No disk. Guidelines (also on Website); copy for 9x12 SAE/2 stamps.

> **Poetry:** 12 lines; $1/line.
>
> **Tips:** "We need positive, lively stories about children facing modern problems and making good choices. We always need strong stories about boys. We need a spiritual element that frequently is missing from submissions. We're changing; refer to guidelines."

PROMISE, 330 Progress Rd., Dayton OH 45449. (937)847-5900. Fax (937)847-5910. E-mail: pliservice@aol.com. Website: http://www.pflaum.com. Catholic. Joan Mitchell CSJ, ed. For Kindergarten & Grade 1; encourages them to participate in parish worship. Weekly (32X) take-home paper. Not in topical listings.

R-A-D-A-R, 8121 Hamilton Ave., Cincinnati OH 45231. (513)931-4050. Fax (513)931-0904. Standard Publishing. Gary Thacker, ed. For 8-11 yr olds; correlates with Sunday-school lesson themes. Weekly take-home paper; 12 pgs; circ 56,000. Subscription $12. 80-90% freelance. Complete ms/cover letter; no phone/fax query. Pays .03-.07/wd on acceptance for 1st, one-time, simultaneous or reprint rts. Articles 300-500 wds (50/yr) & fiction 700-1,000 wds (50/yr). Responds in 2-4 wks. Seasonal 1 yr ahead. Accepts simultaneous submissions & reprints (tell when/where appeared). No disk. Few sidebars. Prefers NIV. Guidelines/theme list/copy for #10 SAE/2 stamps.

> **Poetry:** Buys 20-25/yr. Traditional, any length; pays .50/line. Submit any number.
>
> **Fillers:** Buys 75/yr. Cartoons, facts, games, jokes, quizzes, prayers, word puzzles; .03-.07/wd.
>
> **Tips:** "We mail theme list automatically if you request to be put on list. Follow our theme list (published quarterly). Articles should deal with issues relevant to third and fourth graders and use age-appropriate language."
>
> ** This periodical was #41 on the 1997 Top 50 Christian Publishers list. (#24 in 1996 & 1995, #13 in 1994)

+SEEDS, 330 Progress Rd., Dayton OH 45449. (937)847-5900. Fax (937)847-5910. E-mail: pliservice@aol.com. Website: http://www.pflaum.com. Catholic. Joan Mitchell CSJ, ed. For preschoolers. Weekly (32X) take-home paper; 4 pgs. Not in topical listings.

SKIPPING STONES, A Multicultural Children's Quarterly, PO Box 3939, Eugene OR 97403. (541)342-4956. Not specifically Christian. Arun N. Toke, ed. A multi-cultural awareness and nature appreciation magazine for young people 7-17, world-wide. Bimonthly mag; 36 pgs; circ 2,500. Subscription $25. 80% freelance. Query or complete ms/cover letter; no phone query. **PAYS IN COPIES**

for 1st, electronic or reprint rts. Articles (15-25/yr) 500-750 wds; fiction for teens, 750-1,000 wds; book reviews 100 wds; video reviews 50 wds. Responds in 3-6 wks. Seasonal 2-4 months ahead. Accepts simultaneous submissions. Accepts disk. Sidebars OK. Guidelines/theme list; copy $5/9x12 SAE/5 stamps.

Poetry: Only from kids under 18. Accepts 100/yr. Any type; 3-30 lines. Submit max. 4-5 poems.

Fillers: Accepts 10-20/yr. Anecdotes, cartoons, quizzes, quotes, word puzzles; to 200 wds.

Columns/Departments: Accepts 10/yr. Noteworthy News (multicultural/nature/international/social, appropriate for youth), 200 wds.

Special Needs: Challenging disability; living in other cultures/countries; cross-cultural communications; rewards and punishments.

Contest: Annual Youth Honor Awards. June 20, 1998 deadline for students 7-17. Send SASE for guidelines.

Tips: "We're seeking submissions by minority, multicultural, international, and/or youth writers. Do not be judgmental or preachy; be open or receptive to diverse opinions."

STORY FRIENDS, 616 Walnut St., Scottdale PA 15683. (412)887-8500. Fax (412)887-3111. E-mail: Rose%MPH@mcimail.com. Mennonite. Rose Mary Stutzman, ed. For children 4-9 yrs; reinforces Christian values in a non-moralistic manner. Monthly mag; 20 pgs; circ 7,000. Subscription $10. 75% freelance. Complete ms. Pays .03-.05/wd on acceptance for one-time rts. Articles (5-10/yr) & fiction (30/yr), 300-800 wds. Responds in 8 wks. Seasonal 6 mos ahead. Accepts simultaneous submissions & reprints (tell when/where appeared). Prefers NIV. Guidelines; copy for 9x12 SAE/2 stamps.

Poetry: Buys 12/yr. Traditional; 4-12 lines; $10. Submit max. 3 poems.

Fillers: Buys 2-3/yr. Cartoons, word puzzles.

Ethnic: Targets all ethnic groups involved in the Mennonite religion.

Tips: "Send stories that show rather than tell. Realistic fiction (no fantasy). Send good literary quality with a touch of humor that will appeal to children. Cover letter should give your experience with children."

STORY MATES, Christian Light Publications, Inc., Box 1212, Harrisonburg VA 22801-1212. (703)434-0768. Mennonite. Chrystal Shank, ed. For 4-8 yr olds. Weekly take-home paper; 4 pgs; circ 5,500. 90% freelance. Complete ms/cover letter. Pays up to .03/wd on acceptance for all, 1st, & reprint rts. Realistic or true stories to 800-900 wds (50-75/yr); picture stories 120-150 wds. Responds in 6 wks. Seasonal 6 mos ahead. Accepts simultaneous submissions & reprints (tell when/where appeared). No disk. Requires KJV. Guidelines/theme list; copy for 9x12 SAE/3 stamps. Will send questionnaire to fill out.

Poetry: Buys 25/yr. Traditional, any length. Likes story poems. Pays up to .50/line.

Fillers: Quizzes, word puzzles, craft ideas. "Need fillers that correlate with theme list; Bible related." Pays about $5.

Tips: "We would welcome more puzzles for this age group. Carefully read our guidelines and understand our conservative Mennonite applications of Bible principles." Very conservative.

TOGETHER TIME, 6401 The Paseo, Kansas City MO 64131. (816)333-

7000x2347. Fax (816)333-4439. E-mail: lboardman@nazarene.org. Website: http://www.nazarene.org. WordAction Publishing Co./Church of the Nazarene. Lynda Boardman, ed. For 3-4 yr olds and parents. Weekly take-home paper; 4 pgs; circ 19,000. Subscription $9.95. 75% freelance. Query; fax/e-mail query OK. Pays .05/wd on publication for all rts. Articles 150-200 wds, fiction 150-200 wds (30/yr). Responds in 8-10 wks. Seasonal 12 mos ahead. Accepts simultaneous submissions. Kill fee 5%. Prefers disk. Prefers NIV. Guidelines/theme list; copy for #10 SAE/1 stamp.

> **Poetry:** Buys 52/yr. Free verse, traditional; 4-8 lines; .25/line. Submit max. 5 poems.

> **Fillers:** Games, ideas, activities; 150-200 wds. Pays $15 for crafts & ideas, finger plays.

> **Tips:** "Know the age level of 3-4 year olds. Integrate Christian education throughout; don't tack it on the end."

TOUCH, Box 7259, Grand Rapids MI 49510. (616)241-5616. Fax (616)241-5558. GEMS Girls Clubs (Christian Reformed, Reformed, and Presbyterian). Carol Smith, mng ed. To show girls, ages 9-14, that God is at work in their lives and the world around them. Monthly mag; 24 pgs; circ 14,000. Subscription $12.50. 70% freelance. Complete ms. Pays $5-20 ($15-50 for fiction) or .03/wd on publication for 1st, reprint or simultaneous rts. Articles 200-400 wds (10/yr); fiction 400-1,000 wds (30/yr). Responds in 3 wks. Seasonal 10 mos ahead. Accepts simultaneous submissions & reprints. Accepts disk. Sidebars OK. Prefers NIV. Guidelines/theme list; copy $1/9x12 SAE/3 stamps.

> **Poetry:** Buys 3/yr. Haiku, light verse, traditional; 4-12 lines; $5-10. Poetry fits themes.

> **Fillers:** Buys 10/yr. Games, party ideas, prayers, quizzes, short humor; 50-200 wds; $5-15.

> **Special Needs:** Annual theme is "Come, Celebrate the King!" so all articles and stories should be of a celebrative nature. See Update for ideas.

> **Tips:** "Fiction most open to freelancers. Know what girls face today and how they cope in their daily lives. We need angles from home life and friendships, peer pressure and the normal growing-up challenges girls deal with."

> ** This periodical was #42 on the 1996 Top 50 Christian Publishers list. (#45 in 1995)

VENTURE, 330 Progress Rd., Dayton OH 45449. (937)847-5900. Fax (937)847-5910. E-mail: pliservice@aol.com. Website: http://www.pflaum.com. Joan Mitchell, ed. Connects young people's real life experiences—successes and conflicts in family, neighborhoods, classrooms, playgrounds—with the Sunday gospels; for intermediate-age children. Weekly (32X) take-home paper; 8 pgs; circ 140,000. 40% freelance. Query. Pays $125 on publication for all rts. Articles (6-8/yr) & fiction (8-10/yr), 800-900 wds. Responds in 2-8 wks. Seasonal 4-6 mos ahead. Accepts simultaneous query. Guidelines; copy $1.85.

> **Tips:** "We want realistic fiction and nonfiction that raises current ethical religious questions and conflicts in multi-racial settings, believable and detailed, to which intermediate-age children can relate."

WONDER TIME, 6401 The Paseo, Kansas City MO 64131. (816)333-7000. Fax (816)333-4439. Website: http://www.nazarene.org. Church of the Nazarene. Shirley Smith, asst. ed. For 6-8 yr olds (1st & 2nd graders); emphasis on principles, character-building, and brotherhood. Weekly take-home paper; 4 pgs; circ 40,000. 75-85% freelance. Complete ms; no phone/fax query. Pays $25 on acceptance for all rts. Fiction 250-350 wds (52/yr). Responds in 4-6 wks. Accepts disk. Kill fee $15. Prefers NIV. Guidelines/theme list; copy for #10 SAE/2 stamps.

> **Tips:** "We accept freelance stories that follow our theme list. Stories should be contemporary, life-related, at a 1st-2nd grade readability, and directly correlate with our Sunday school curriculum. Avoid trite situations."

+WRITERS' INTERNATIONAL FORUM FOR YOUNG AUTHORS, PO Box 516, Tracyton WA 98393. Bristol Services Intl. Sandra E. Haven, ed. For writers aged 16 and under; used in some homeschooling groups. Monthly (10X) newsletter; 6-8 pgs. Subscription $24. Est. 1997. 25% freelance. Complete ms/cover letter; no phone/fax/e-mail query. Pays $10-30 (essays), $10-30 for fiction, on acceptance for 1st rts. Essays to 1,000 wds (4/yr); fiction to 1,000 wds (8/yr). Responds in 6 wks. Seasonal 4 mos ahead. No disk. Guidelines; copy for $3/#10 SAE/1 stamp.

> **Contest:** Sponsors two contests a year for young writers. Send SASE for details.
>
> **Tips:** "We use well-crafted essays or short stories only. Rarely use writing-related essays and no slices-of-life or vignettes."

CHRISTIAN EDUCATION/LIBRARY MARKETS

BAPTIST LEADER, Box 851, Valley Forge PA 19482-0851. (610)768-2143. Fax (610)768-2056. E-mail: Don_Ng@ecunet.org. American Baptist. Donald Ng, ed. Practical "how-to" or thought-provoking articles for local church Christian education lay leaders and teachers. Quarterly mag; 32 pgs; circ 5,000. Subscription $8. 5% freelance. Complete ms/cover letter; fax/e-mail query OK. Pays $10-75 ($25-75 for fiction) on acceptance for 1st, one-time or reprint rts. Articles 1,300-2,000 wds (10/yr); fiction (2-3/yr); book & video reviews 200 wds (assigned). Responds in 12 wks. Seasonal 1 yr ahead. Accepts simultaneous submissions & reprints (tell when/where appeared). Prefers disk. Sidebars OK. Prefers NRSV. Guidelines; copy $1.50. (Ads)

> **Poetry:** Accepts 2-3/yr. Haiku, light verse, traditional; $10-20.
>
> **Fillers:** Buys 4-8/yr. Cartoons, jokes, prayers; 25-100 wds; $10-20.
>
> **Special Needs:** Plays & skits related to holidays that churches celebrate: Christmas, Easter, Mother's Day, Children's Day, Reformation Sunday, Black History Month, etc; 1,300-2,000 wds; pays $25-50. Play & skits are the only fiction used.
>
> **Tips:** "Most open to feature articles, new program ideas for holidays, and holiday-related dramas or plays."

BRIGADE LEADER, Box 150, Wheaton IL 60187. (630)665-0630. Fax (630)665-0372. E-mail: BrigadeCSB@aol.com. Christian Service Brigade. Deborah Christensen, mng. ed. For men leading boy's clubs; emphasis on fathering issues. Quarterly mag; 16 pgs; circ 5,000. Subscription $10. 50% freelance. Query (most articles assigned); no e-mail query. Pays .05-.10/wd on publication for 1st or reprint rts. Articles 500-1,000 wds (4-8/yr). Responds in 2 wks. Accepts reprints (tell when/where appeared). Prefers disk. Kill fee $35. Sidebars OK. Prefers NIV.

Guidelines; copy $1.50/9x12 SAE/4 stamps.

Tips: "We're especially looking for men who are familiar with Christian Service Brigade and how to disciple boys."

*CARAVAN: A Resource for Adult Religious Educators, 90 Parent Ave., Ottawa ON K1N 7B1 Canada. (613)241-9461. Fax (613)241-8117. Canadian conference of Catholic Bishops. Joanne Chafe, ed. A resources for adult educators who work in church settings. Quarterly mag; 16 pgs; circ 1,500. Subscription $17.12. 100% freelance. Complete ms/cover letter. Pays variable rate on acceptance or publication. Copyrighted; rights released on request. Articles (30-40/yr). Responds in 4-6 wks. Seasonal 3 mos ahead. Accepts simultaneous submissions. Sidebars OK. Guidelines/copy.

> **Columns/Departments:** Adult religious education: New Initiatives, New Releases, Creative program ideas.
>
> **Special Needs:** Workshop models.

CATECHIST, 330 Progress Rd., Dayton OH 45449. (937)847-5900. Fax (937)847-5910. E-mail: raffio@aol.com. Website: http://www.pflaum.com. Catholic. Patricia Fischer, ed. For Catholic school teachers and parish volunteer catechists. Mag. published 7X/yr; 52 pgs; circ 50,000. Query (preferred) or complete ms. Pays $25-150 on publication for all rts. Articles 1,200-1,500 wds. Responds in 9-18 wks. Guidelines (also on Website); copy $2.50.

CE CONNECTION, Box 12609, Oklahoma City OK 73157. (405)787-7110. Fax (405)789-3957. E-mail: cathy@iphc.com. Website: http://www.iphc.org. General Christian Education Dept./IPHC. Cathy Harper, ed. Targets pastors and local Christian education workers/leaders for training/how-to. Quarterly mag/newsletter; circ 6,600. 100% freelance. Complete ms/cover letter. **NO PAYMENT.** Not copyrighted. Articles. Seasonal 4 mos ahead. Accepts reprints. Free copy.

CE CONNECTION COMMUNIQUE, PO Box 12624, Roanoke VA 24027. Phone/fax (540)342-7511. E-mail: ccmbbr@juno.com. Betty Robertson, ed. Virginia Christian Education Assn. Bimonthly newsletter; 8 pgs; circ 1,350. Subscription $19.95. 25% freelance. Query; no phone/fax/e-mail query. Pays $5-10 on acceptance for 1st, one-time, simultaneous rts. Not copyrighted. Articles 100-600 wds. Responds in 6 wks. Seasonal 6 mos ahead. Accepts simultaneous submissions & reprints. Guidelines; copy $3.

CHILDREN'S MINISTRY, PO Box 481, Loveland CO 80539. (970)669-3836. Fax (970)679-4372. E-mail: cfosmo@grouppublishing.com. Website: http://www.grouppublishing.com. Group Publishing. Corinna Fosmo, asst. ed. For Christians who work with kids from birth to 6th grade. Bimonthly mag; 85 pgs; circ 65,000. Subscription $24.95. 73% freelance. Query/clips or complete ms/cover letter; fax/e-mail query OK. Pays $35-175 on acceptance for all rts. Articles 500-1,700 wds (40/yr). Responds in 4-8 wks. Seasonal 5 mos ahead. Accepts disk. Sidebars OK. Prefers New Century. Guidelines; copy $2/9x12 SASE. (Ads)

> **Fillers:** Buys 5-10/yr. Cartoons, games, ideas; $15-35.
>
> **Columns/Departments:** Buys 50/yr. For Parents Only (practical parenting tips); Preschool Page (hints, songs, Bible activities); Nursery Notes; Group Games; Seasonal Specials (parties, service projects, worship celebrations—4-5 mos ahead); 5-Minute Messages; 50-125 wds; $15-35. Complete mss.

Special Needs: Crafts, hobbies, children's tends; tried and true ideas that work.

Tips: "Potential authors should be familiar with *Children's Ministry* and its style. Most successful authors are ones who have experience working with children in the church. We like new ideas with 'ah-has'."

CHRISTIAN EDUCATION COUNSELOR, 1445 Boonville Ave., Springfield MO 65802-1894. (417)862-2781. Fax (417)862-0503. E-mail: ceeditor@ag.org. Assemblies of God. Sylvia Lee, ed. Presents teaching and administrative helps to lay leaders in local churches. Bimonthly mag; 32 pgs; circ 20,000. Subscription $12. 5% freelance. Complete ms/cover letter. Pays .08-.12/wd on acceptance for 1st, simultaneous & reprint rts. Articles 300-800 wds (50/yr); book reviews, 400-500 wds, $35. Responds in 4 wks. Seasonal 6 mos ahead. Accepts simultaneous submissions & reprints. Accepts disk. Sidebars OK. Guidelines; copy for 9x12 SAE/2 stamps.

Fillers: Buys cartoons, games, ideas, quizzes; $35-85.

Tips: "Writers should have first-hand experience in Christian education in the local church. Articles strong on how-to. Offer practical material for classroom teachers who are short on time and resources."

** This periodical was #52 on the 1996 Top 50 Christian Publishers list. (#62 in 1995, #64 in 1994)

+CHRISTIAN EDUCATION JOURNAL, 2065 Half Day Rd., Deerfield IL 60015. Trinity Evangelical Divinity School. Dr. Perry G. Downs, ed. Articles 10-25 pgs, on Christian education topics. Guidelines. Not in topical listings.

#CHRISTIAN EDUCATION LEADERSHIP, 1080 Montgomery Ave., Cleveland TN 37311. (423)476-4512. Fax (423)478-7521. E-mail: lancewc@aol.com. Pentecostal Church of God/Pathway Press. Lance Colkmire, ed. For Christian education teachers and leaders. Quarterly mag; 32 pgs; circ 9,800. Subscription $7. 40% freelance. Complete ms/cover letter. Pays $25-55 on acceptance for one-time, simultaneous or reprint rts. Articles 500-1,200 wds (12/yr). Responds in 4 wks. Seasonal 4 mos ahead. Accepts simultaneous submissions & reprints (tell when/where appeared). Accepts disk. Sidebars OK. Guidelines; copy for 9x12 SAE/4 stamps. (Ads)

Columns/Departments: Sunday School; Singles Ministry; Outreach; Music Ministry; The Pastor and C.E.; Kid's Church; 400-800 wds; $25-50.

Special Needs: Articles on children's ministry and Sunday school.

#CHRISTIAN EDUCATORS JOURNAL, Dordt College, 498 - 4th Ave. NE, Sioux Center IA 51250-1697. (712)722-6252. Fax (712)722-1185. E-mail: lgilst@dordt.edu. Christian Educators Journal Assn. Lorna Van Gilst, mng. ed. For educators in Christian day schools at the elementary, secondary, and college levels. Quarterly journal; 36 pgs; circ 4,200. Subscription $7.50. 50% freelance. Query; phone query OK. Pays $30 on publication for one-time rts. Articles 600-1,200 wds (20/yr); fiction 600-1,200 wds. Responds in 5 wks. Seasonal 4 mos ahead. Accepts simultaneous submissions & reprints. Guidelines/theme list; copy $1 or 9x12 SAE/4 stamps. (Ads)

Poetry: Buys 6/yr. On teaching day school; 4-30 lines; $10. Submit max. 5 poems.

Tips: "No articles on Sunday school, only Christian day school. Most open to theme topics and features."

THE CHRISTIAN LIBRARIAN, Box 4000, Three Hills AB T0M 2N0 Canada. US address: Box 4, Cedarville OH 45314. (403)443-5511x3343. Fax (403)443-5540. E-mail: ron.jordahl@pbi.ab.ca. Assn. of Christian Librarians. Ron Jordahl, ed. Christian librarianship. Quarterly (3X) jour; 40 pgs; circ 500. Subscription $25. 25% freelance. Query; phone/fax query OK. **NO PAYMENT** for one-time rts. Not copyrighted. Articles 1,000-3,500 words; research articles to 5,000 wds (6/yr); reviews 150-300 wds. Responds in 5 wks. Accepts simultaneous query & reprints. Prefers disk. Sidebars OK. Guidelines; copy $5.

Fillers: Anecdotes, cartoons, newsbreaks, short humor; 25-300 wds.

Special Needs: Articles on libraries, books, and reading.

CHRISTIAN LIBRARY JOURNAL, 1101 SW Rogue River Ave., Grants Pass OR 97526-2736. (541)479-5277. Fax (541)479-5178. E-mail: nancyhclj@aol.com. Christian Library Services. Nancy Hesch, ed/pub. Submit to Andrew M. Seddon, ed., 4328 Trailmaster Dr., Billings MT 59101. Fax (406)238-2868. Primarily published for the Christian school (K-12) library and teachers of reading and English; also of interest to librarians, teachers, and home-schooling parents. Bimonthly (5X) mag; 88 pgs; circ. 1,000. Subscription $45. Est. 1995. 10% freelance. Query or complete ms/cover letter; fax/e-mail query OK; query for electronic submissions. Pays $50-100 on publication for 1st or reprint rts. Articles (15/yr) 500-1,200 wds; book reviews, 200-400 wds (ask Nancy Hesch to be a reviewer), no payment. Responds in 8-12 wks. Seasonal 4 mos ahead. Accepts reprints (tell when/where appeared). Prefers disk. Sidebars OK. Free guidelines/copy (order from OR address). (Ads)

Fillers: Quotes; 10-100 wds. No payment.

Columns/Departments: Accepts 4-6/yr. Book Nook (using books with students), 500-800 wds; No payment. Complete ms.

Tips: "Looking for discussions of various genres of Christian literature, especially as related to K-12 and staff."

CHRISTIAN SCHOOL, 1308 Santa Rosa, Wheaton IL 60187. (630)653-4588. Phil Landrum, pub. A publication for Christian-school educators and parents. Quarterly mag; 48 pgs; circ 3,000 schools. 2% freelance. Query; phone query OK. **NO PAYMENT.** Articles 500-1,500 wds (1/yr); fiction 1,000-1,500 (1/yr). Responds in 2-4 wks. Free guidelines/copy.

Poetry: Accepts 1/yr. Traditional. Submit max. 5 poems.

Fillers: Accepts 1/yr. Anecdotes.

Special Needs: Education how-to; youth trends; training techniques; children's books.

CHURCH & SYNAGOGUE LIBRARIES, PO Box 19357, Portland OR 97280-0357. (503)244-6919. Fax (503)977-3734. E-mail: csla@worldaccessnet.com. Website: http://www.worldaccessnet.com/~csla. Church and Synagogue Library Assn. Judith Janzen, exec. dir. To help librarians run congregational libraries. Bimonthly; 20 pgs.; circ. 3,000. Subscription $25, $35 CAN, $45 foreign. Query. **NO PAYMENT.** Requires disk. Articles. Book & video reviews 1-2 paragraphs. (Ads)

Fillers: Ideas.

CHURCH EDUCATOR, 165 Plaza Dr., Prescott AZ 86303. (520)771-8601. Fax (520)771-8621. E-mail: edmin2@aol.com. Linda Davidson, ed. For mainline Protestant Christian educators. Monthly journal; 36 pgs; circ 4,500. Subscription

$28. 90% freelance. Complete ms/cover letter; phone/fax/e-mail query OK. Pays .03/wd on publication for 1st rts. Articles 700-1,500 wds (100/yr). Responds in 4-6 wks. Seasonal 4 mos ahead. Accepts simultaneous submissions & reprints (tell when/where appeared). Sidebars OK. Guidelines/theme list; copy for 9x12 SAE/4 stamps.

Fillers: Bible games and Bible puzzles.

Columns/Departments: Buys 20/yr. Noah's Ark (crafts for children); Youth Notebook (tips for working with teens); 200-500 wds.

Tips: "Talk to the educator at your church. What would they find useful? Most open to seasonal articles dealing with the liturgical year. Write up church programs with specific how-tos of putting the program together."

CHURCH LIBRARIES, 9731 Fox Glen Dr. #6F, Niles IL 60714-5861. (847)296-3964. Fax (847)296-0754. E-mail: linjohnson@compuserve.com. Evangelical Church Library Assn. Lin Johnson, ed. To assist church librarians in setting up, maintaining, and promoting church libraries and media centers. Quarterly mag; 40-48 pgs; circ 600. Subscription $20. 99% freelance. Complete ms; fax/e-mail query OK. Pays .04/wd on acceptance for 1st, reprint or simultaneous rts. Articles 500-1,000 wds (20/yr); book/music/video/cassette reviews by assignment, 75-150 wds, free product. Responds in 4-6 wks. Seasonal 6 mos ahead. Accepts simultaneous submissions & reprints (tell when/where appeared). Requires disk or e-mail. Sidebars OK. Prefers NIV. Guidelines; copy for 9x12 SAE/6 stamps. (Ads)

Columns/Departments: Buys 16/yr. Idea Exchange (brief hints on any aspect of running a library), 100-200 wds; pays a free book.

Tips: "Talk to church librarians or get involved in library or reading programs. Most open to articles, Idea Exchange, and promotional ideas; profiles of church libraries; round-ups on best books in a category. Need for reviewers fluctuates; if interested send SASE for questionnaire."

#CHURCH MEDIA LIBRARY MAGAZINE, 127 9th Ave. N., Nashville TN 37234. (615)251-2752. Fax (615)251-5607. Southern Baptist. Floyd B. Simpson, ed. Supports the establishment and development of church media libraries; provides how-to articles and articles of inspiration and encouragement to media library workers. Quarterly mag; 52 pgs; circ 30,000. Query. Pays .055/wd on publication for all, 1st, or reprint rts. Articles 600-1,500 wds (10-15/yr). Responds in 5 wks. Seasonal 14 mos ahead. Free guidelines/copy.

CHURCH WORSHIP, 165 Plaza Dr., Prescott AZ 86303. (520)771-8601. Fax (520)771-8621. E-mail: edmin2@aol.com. Robert Davidson, ed. Supplementary resources for church worship leaders. Monthly journal; 24 pgs; circ 1,200. Subscription $24. 75% freelance. Complete ms/cover letter; phone/fax/e-mail query OK. Pays .03/wd on publication for 1st rts. Articles to 100-1,500 wds; fiction 100-1,500 wds. Responds in 2-6 wks. Seasonal 4 mos ahead. Guidelines/theme list; copy for 9x12 SAE/3 stamps.

Special Needs: Complete worship services; seasonal sermons.

Tips: "Most open to creative worship services using music, drama or art."

EVANGELIZING TODAY'S CHILD, Box 348, Warrenton MO 63383-0348. (314)456-4321. Fax (314)456-2078. E-mail: ETCLIP@aol.com. Child Evangelism Fellowship. Elsie C. Lippy, ed. To equip Christians to win the world's children (4-11) to Christ and disciple them. Bimonthly mag; 64 pgs; circ 15,000.

Subscription $20. 50% freelance. Complete ms; no phone/fax/e-mail query. Pays .10-.12/wd (.07/wd for fiction) within 60 days of acceptance for all, 1st, one-time or reprint rts. Articles 1,200-1,500 wds (24/yr); fiction 700-900 (12/yr). Responds in 4-6 wks. Seasonal 1 yr ahead. Accepts reprints (tell when/where appeared). Accepts disk. Kill fee 30%. Sidebars OK. Prefers NIV. Guidelines; copy $2/9x12 SAE/6 stamps. (Ads)

> **Resource Center:** Buys 40-60/yr. Complete ms, 200-250 wds. Pays $15-25 for teaching hints, bulletin board ideas, object lessons, missions incentives, etc.

> **Special Needs:** Salvation testimonies of adults saved before age 12, 700-900 wds; 6/yr. Creative ideas for involving children in ministry.

> **Tips:** "Most open to Resource Center. Study the publication. Know children and/or children's workers."

> ** This periodical was #62 on the 1997 Top 50 Christian Publishers list. (#64 in 1995, #49 in 1994)

GROUP MAGAZINE, Box 481, Loveland CO 80538. (970)669-3836. Fax (970)669-3269. E-mail: kdieterich@grouppublishing.com. Kathleen Dieterich, asst. ed. Aimed at leaders of high-school-age, Christian youth groups. Bimonthly mag; 85 pgs; circ 55,000. Subscription $25.95. 70% freelance. Query or complete ms/cover letter; fax/e-mail query OK. Pays $35-225 on acceptance for all rts. Articles 500-1,700 wds (30-40/yr). Responds in 4-8 wks. Seasonal 5 mos ahead. Accepts disk. Sidebars OK. Guidelines; copy $2/9x12 SASE. (Ads)

> **Fillers:** Buys 5-10/yr. Cartoons, games, ideas; $15-35.

> **Columns/Departments:** Buys 30-40/yr. Try This One (youth group activities), 300 wds; Strange But True (strange youth-ministry stories), 500 wds; Hands-on Help (tips for leaders), 300 wds; Good News About Kids (positive news about teens), 350 wds; $35. Complete ms.

> **Special Needs:** Articles geared toward working with teens; programming ideas; youth ministry issues.

> **Tips:** "Looking for articles that demonstrate cutting-edge activity in the area of youth ministry."

*INSIGHT INTO CHRISTIAN EDUCATION, Box 23152, Charlotte NC 28227-0272. (704)545-6161. Fax (704)573-0712. Advent Christian. Millie Griswold, ed. For local church Christian education volunteers. Quarterly mag; 8 pgs; circ 2,200. Subscription $6. 20% freelance. Query or complete ms. Pays $25 on publication. Articles 600-1,000 wds. Accepts reprints. Seasonal 6 mos ahead. Free copy.

THE JOURNAL OF ADVENTIST EDUCATION, 12501 Old Columbia Pike, Silver Springs MD 20904-6600. (301)680-5075. Fax (301)622-9627. E-mail: 74617,1231@compuserve.com. Seventh-day Adventist. Beverly J. Rumble, ed. For Seventh-day teachers teaching in the church's school system, K-University. Bimonthly journal; 48 pgs; circ 7,400. Subscription $17.25. 10% freelance. Query or complete ms; phone/fax/e-mail query OK. Pays $25-100 on publication for 1st & translation rts. Articles to 1,000-1,500 wds (2-20/yr); book reviews to $25. Responds in 6 wks. Seasonal 6 mos ahead. Accepts reprints (tell when/where appeared). Accepts disk. Kill fee to 25%. Sidebars OK. Guidelines; copy for 9x12 SAE/$2 postage.

> **Fillers:** Cartoons only, no pay.

Special Needs: "All articles in the context of parochial schools (*not* Sunday school tips); professional enrichment and teaching tips for Christian teachers. Need feature articles."

KIDS' MINISTRY IDEAS (formerly **KIDS' STUFF**), 55 W. Oak Ridge Dr., Hagerstown MD 21740. (301)791-7000. Fax (301)790-9734. Seventh-day Adventist. Patricia Fritz, ed; Dwain Esmond, asst. ed. For adults leading children (birth-eighth grade) to Christ. Quarterly mag; 32-40 pgs; circ. 7,500. Subscription $16.97. 10% freelance. Query; fax/e-mail query OK. Pays $25-125 on acceptance for one-time or reprint rts. Articles 500-1,300 wds (10/yr). Responds in 6-8 wks. Seasonal 9 mos ahead. Accepts simultaneous submissions & reprints (tell when/where appeared). Sidebars OK. Prefers NIV. Guidelines; copy for 9x12 SAE/4 stamps.

> **Columns/Departments:** Try This (short ideas that have worked in teaching kids), 2-3 paragraphs. Pays free book.
>
> **Tips:** "Looking for program ideas, outreach ideas, something that has worked to draw kids closer to Jesus. This is a how-to oriented magazine. I'd be interested in active teaching ideas on general themes, such as faith, trust, prayer and grace."

LEADER IN THE CHURCH SCHOOL TODAY, 201 Eighth Ave. N, Nashville TN 37202. (615)749-6488. Fax (615)749-6512. E-mail: 102521.1513@compuserve. com. United Methodist. Jill S. Reddig, ed. For pastors and Christian education leaders in the church. Quarterly mag; 64 pgs; circ 9,000. Subscription $16. 50% freelance. Complete ms/cover letter; phone/fax/e-mail query OK. Pays .05/wd on publication for all, 1st, one-time or reprint rts. Articles 400-2,500 wds (98/yr); book reviews 150 wds. Responds in 6-8 wks. Seasonal 6 mos ahead. Accepts reprints (tell when/where appeared). Prefers disk. Some sidebars. Prefers NRSV (never Living). Guidelines/search list; copy $4.50/9x12 SAE.

> **Columns/Departments:** Buys 30/yr. Idea Exchange (what worked for us; for children/youth/adult classes), 50-150 wds; Teacher/leader Development (teacher training), 700-2,500 wds; Days & Seasons (seasonal Christian ed.), 700-2,500 wds.
>
> ** This periodical was #45 on the 1997 Top 50 Christian Publishers List. (#66 in 1996)

*LOLLIPOPS, The Magazine for Early Childhood Educators, Good Apple, Inc., Box 2649, Columbus OH 43216-2649. Donna Borst, ed. Easy-to-use, hands-on, practical teaching ideas and suggestions for early childhood educators. Magazine published 5X/yr; circ 20,000. 20% freelance. Query or complete ms. Pays $10-100 on publication for all rts. Articles 200-1,000 wds; fiction (for young children) 500-1,200 wds. Seasonal 6 mos ahead. Guidelines (2 stamps); copy for 9x12 SAE/3 stamps.

> **Poetry:** Light verse.
>
> **Tips:** "Looking for something new and different for teachers of young children; seasonal material."

PARISH TEACHER, Box 1209, Minneapolis MN 55440-1209. (612)330-3423. E-mail: grinerr@augsburg-fortress.org. ELCA/Augsburg Fortress Publishers. Randi Sundet Griner, ed. Articles and ideas for Lutheran church school teachers. Monthly (9X) mag; 16 pgs; circ 50,000. Subscription $9.95. 12.5% freelance.

Complete ms/cover letter. Pays $50 on publication for 1st rts. Not copyrighted. Articles 550-650 wds (15/yr); plays 400-800 wds (1-2/yr). Responds in 12-16 wks. Seasonal 4-6 mos ahead. Accepts simultaneous submissions & reprints. Requires disk. No sidebars. Prefers NRSV. Guidelines; copy for 9x12 SAE/4 stamps.

Fillers: Buys 100 ideas/yr.; 100-200 wds; $20.

Tips: "Most open to ideas or feature articles that are practical and inspirational in Christian education settings."

#PERSPECTIVE, Box 788, Wheaton IL 60189-0788. (630)293-1600x340/342. Fax (630)293-3053. E-mail: pclubs@ix.netcom.com. Website: http://www.pioneerclubs. org. Pioneer Clubs. Rebecca Powell Parat, ed. To help and encourage Pioneer Club leaders (for children ages 2-18). Triennial mag; 32 pgs; circ 24,000. Subscription $6. 15% freelance. Query/clips (preferred); fax query OK. Pays .05-.10/wd ($40-90) on acceptance for 1st or reprint rts. Articles 1,000-1,500 wds (0-3/yr). Responds in 9 wks. Seasonal 9 mos ahead. Accepts simultaneous query & reprints (tell when/where appeared). Prefers disk. Sidebars OK. Prefers NIV. Guidelines; copy $1.75/9x12 SAE/6 stamps.

Fillers: Buys 1-2/yr. Games, party ideas.

Columns/Departments: Buys 2-3/yr. Storehouse (ideas for crafts, games, service projects, tips for leaders, etc.); 150-250 wds; $8-15. Complete ms.

Tips: "Most articles done on assignment. We'd like to hear from freelancers who have experience with, or access to, a Pioneer Clubs program or Camp Cherith. They should send samples of their work along with a letter introducing themselves."

REACHING CHILDREN AT RISK, PO Box 633, Oxford OX2 ONX, England UK. Phone + 44 1865 450 800. Fax + 44 1865 203 567. E-mail: rrobinson@viva.org. The Viva Network. B. Ripley Robinson, ed. To meet the needs of project leaders and workers ministering to children at high risk (street children of the world). Journal. Est. 1996. Query; phone/e-mail query OK. **PAYS IN COPIES.** Articles 1,500-3,000 wds. Guidelines. Not in topical listings.

Tips: "We are forming a pool of writers who would contribute material on an ongoing basis. A contributing writer may be asked to write one or two articles a year. Topics will be suggested by the writers."

RELIGION TEACHER'S JOURNAL, Box 180, Mystic CT 06355. (860)536-2611. Fax (860)572-0788. E-mail: ttpubsedit@aol.com. Twenty-Third Publications/ Catholic. Gwen Costello, ed. dir. For volunteer religion teachers who need practical, hands-on information as well as theological background for teaching religion to K through high school. 7X yearly mag; 40 pgs; circ 40,000. Subscription $18.95. 40% freelance. Query; fax/e-mail query OK. Pays to $100 on acceptance for 1st rts. Not copyrighted. Articles to 6 pgs (50/yr). Responds in 2-4 wks. Seasonal 2 mos ahead. Prefers disk. Sidebars OK. Guidelines/theme list; copy for 9x12 SAE/4 stamps. (Ads)

Fillers: Jennifer Johnson. Buys 20-30/yr. Anecdotes (about teaching), games, ideas, prayers, successful class activities; to 1 pg; $5-25.

Tips: "Know our audience and address their needs. Most open to feature articles about teaching skills, spirituality, successful class activities or projects."

#RESOURCE, 6401 The Paseo, Kansas City MO 64131. (816)333-7000x2224. Fax

(816)363-7092. E-mail: dfelter@nazarene.org. Website: http://www.nazarene.org. Church of the Nazarene. David Felter, ed. To provide information, training, and inspiration to those who are involved in ministering within the Christian Life and Sunday school departments of the local church. Quarterly journal; 34 pgs; circ 9,000. Subscription $6.25. 50-65% freelance. Complete ms/cover letter; fax/e-mail query OK. Query for electronic submissions. Pays .04/wd on acceptance for all, 1st, one-time, or reprint rts. Articles 1,000-4,000 wds (150/yr); book reviews 300 wds. Responds in 2 wks. Seasonal 6 mos ahead. Accepts reprints. Accepts disk. Sidebars OK. Prefers NIV or NRSV. Guidelines/theme list; copy for 9x12 SAE/2 stamps. (Ads)

Poetry: Buys 4/yr. Seasonal or on outreach/Sunday school; to 30 lines; .25/line, $5 minimum. Submit max. 1 poem.

Fillers: Buys 4 cartoons/yr; $10-25.

Tips: "Looking for succinct pieces that instruct, train, motivate, etc."

** This periodical was #50 on the 1997 Top 50 Christian Publishers list. (#18 in 1996, #10 in 1995)

SHINING STAR MAGAZINE, 1204 Buchanan, Carthage IL 62321. (217)357-6091. Fax (217)357-6095. Frank Schaeffer Publications. Mary Tucker, ed. Reproducible Bible activities for Sunday school, VBS & Christian schools; pre-K-6th grades. Quarterly mag; 80 pgs; circ 12,000. Subscription $16.95. 90% freelance. Query; phone/fax query OK. Pays $15-30 on publication for all rts. Articles 1 page (uses mostly activities). Responds in 6 wks. Seasonal 9 mos ahead. No sidebars. Prefers NIV. Guidelines/theme list; copy for 9x12 SAE/$1.93 postage.

Poetry: Buys 10/yr. Traditional; 8-36 lines; $10-30. Submit max. 4 poems.

Fillers: Buys 25/yr. Anecdotes, facts, games, ideas, quotes, word puzzles; 100-300 wds; $10-40.

Special Needs: Puzzles, games, crafts for kids.

Tips: "Try out material on children before you consider it ready to submit."

#TEACHERS IN FOCUS, 8605 Explorer Dr., Colorado Springs CO 80920. (719)548-4578. Fax (719)531-3499. Focus on the Family. Charles W. Johnson, ed. To encourage, inform and support Christian teachers in public and private education (K-12). Monthly (9X) mag; 32 pgs; circ 35,000. Subscription $20. 80% freelance. Query; fax query OK. Pays $200 & up on acceptance for 1st rts. Articles 1,500 wds (4/yr); book reviews (educational resources), $25-50. Responds in 4 wks. Accepts reprints (tell when/where appeared). Accepts disk. Kill fee 50%. Sidebars OK. Prefers NIV. Guidelines/theme list; copy for 9x12 SAE/4 stamps.

Fillers: Buys 50/yr. Humorous classroom anecdotes; 50-150 wds; $25.

Columns/Departments: Accepts 9/yr. Laughs From the Lounge (student humor), 100-150 wds; Teammates (profiles on support staff), 500 wds. Pays $75.

Tips: "Uses articles of interest to teachers trying to cope in the classroom situation. Education issues. Avoid educational and religious jargon."

** This periodical was #23 on the 1997 Top 50 Christian Publishers list (#12 in 1996, #29 in 1995, #55 in 1994). 1997 EPA Award of Merit—Christian Ministry (1995 EPA Award of Excellence—Christian Ministry).

TEACHERS INTERACTION, 3558 S. Jefferson Ave., St. Louis MO 63118-3968.

(314)268-1083. Fax (314)268-1329. E-mail: nummelata@cphnet.org. Concordia Publishing House/Lutheran Church-Missouri Synod. Tom Nummela, ed. A magazine church-school workers grow by. Quarterly mag; 32 pgs; circ. 20,400. Subscription $10.25. 25% freelance. Complete ms/cover letter; fax/e-mail query OK. Pays $20-100 on acceptance or publication for all rts. How-tos to 100 wds, articles 700 wds (10/yr). Responds in 4 wks. Seasonal 1 yr ahead. Prefers disk. Some sidebars. Prefers NIV. Guidelines/theme list; copy for 9x12 SAE/3 stamps.

> **Poetry:** Buys 4/yr. Any type; 6-10 or 20 lines; $20-30. Submit max. 2 poems. Also Christian songs.
>
> **Fillers:** Buys 48/yr. Teacher tips/ideas, 50 wds.
>
> **Special Needs:** Practical, how-to articles that will help the volunteer church worker.
>
> **Tips:** "We need feature articles in four areas—inspiration, theology, practical and informational—in the area of volunteer Christian education. Theology must be compatible with Lutheranism."

TEAM, Box 7259, Grand Rapids MI 49510. (616)241-5616. Fax (616)241-5558. Young Calvinist Federation. Submit to The Editor. Geared to leaders of youth programs, not Sunday school. Quarterly mag; circ 2,000. 10% freelance. Complete ms. Pays $30 on publication for 1st, simultaneous or reprint rts. Articles 700-2,000 wds (6/yr). Responds in 5 wks. Seasonal 6 mos ahead. Kill fee 50%. Accepts simultaneous submissions & reprints. Guidelines; copy $1/9x12 SAE/2 stamps.

> **Fillers:** Cartoons, ideas, party ideas, short humor.
>
> **Columns/Departments:** Street Beat (issues in urban youth ministry).

#TODAY'S CATHOLIC TEACHER, 330 Progress Rd., Dayton OH 45449-2386. (937)847-5900. Fax (937)847-5910. Catholic/Peter Li Education Group. Mary C. Noschang, ed. Directed to personal and professional concerns of teachers and administrators in K-12 Catholic schools. Monthly mag (6X during school yr); 60 pgs; circ 50,000. Subscription $14.95. 40% freelance. Complete ms/cover letter; phone/fax query OK. Pays $150-250 after publication for all rts. Articles 800-2,000 wds (40-50/yr). Responds in 18 wks. Seasonal 3 mos ahead. Accepts simultaneous submissions & reprints (tell when/where appeared). Kill fee. Prefers disk. Sidebars OK. Guidelines/theme list; copy $3. (Ads)

> **Special Needs:** Activity pages teachers can copy and pass out to students to work on. Try to provide classroom-ready material teachers can use to supplement curriculum.
>
> **Tips:** "Looking for material teachers in grades 3-9 can use to supplement curriculum material. Most open to articles or lesson plans."

#VISION MAGAZINE, Box 41300, Pasadena CA 91114. (818)798-1124. Fax (818)798-2346. E-mail: ceaieduca@aol.com. Christian Educators Assn., Intl. Judy Turpen, ed. To encourage and equip Christian educators and parents in public education; inserted in Teachers in Focus. Monthly (9X) insert; 8 pgs; circ 6,000. Subscription $35 (free to donors). 50% freelance. Query; fax query OK. Pays $30-40 on publication for 1st & reprint rts. Articles 50-1,200 wds (2/yr); book reviews, 40-50 wds, pays copies. Responds in 4-6 wks. Seasonal 4 mos ahead. Accepts simultaneous submissions & reprints. Sidebars OK. Guidelines/theme list; copy for 9x12 SAE/6 stamps. (Ads)

Poetry: Accepts 3-4/yr. Free verse, haiku, light verse, traditional; 4-16 lines; no payment. Submit max. 3 poems.

Fillers: Accepts 2-6/yr. Anecdotes, cartoons, facts, ideas, newsbreaks, prose, prayers, quotes; 100 wds; no payment. Educational only.

Special Needs: Legal and other issues in public education.

Tips: "Know public education, write from a positive perspective as our readers are involved in public education by calling and choice. Most open to tips for teachers for living out their faith in the classroom in legally appropriate ways."

DAILY DEVOTIONAL MARKETS

Due to the nature of the daily devotional market, the following market listings may include only the name, address, phone number (if available) and editor's name. Because most of these markets assign all material, they do not wish to be listed in the usual way, if at all.

If you are interested in writing daily devotionals, send to the following markets for guidelines and sample copies, write up sample devotionals to fit each one's particular format, and send to the editor with a request for an assignment. **DO NOT** submit any other type of material to these markets unless indicated.

*COME YE APART, Box 419527, Kansas City MO 64131. Paul Martin, ed.

DAILY DEVOTIONS FOR THE DEAF, 21199 Greenview Rd., Council Bluffs IA 51503-4190. (712)322-5493. Fax (712)322-7792. E-mail: DeafMissions@ deafmissions.com. Duane King, ed. Prefers to see completed devotionals; 225 wds. **NO PAYMENT.**

*DEVOTIONS, 8121 Hamilton Ave., Cincinnati OH 45231. (513)931-4050. Eileen Wilmoth, ed. No devotions or poetry. Buys photos only.

FORWARD DAY BY DAY, 412 Sycamore St., Cincinnati OH 45202-4195. (513)721-6659. Fax (513)721-0729. E-mail: forward.movement@ecunet.org. Website: http://www.dfms.org/forward-movement. E. S. Gleason, ed. Send a couple of sample devotions to fit our format and request an assignment. Devotionals each 1305 characters. Pays about $200 for a month's devotions. Uses almost no freelance.

THE HOME ALTAR, Box 1209, Minneapolis MN 55440-1209. (612)330-3211. E-mail: grinerr@augsburg-fortress.org. Randi Sundet Griner, ed. Devotional material for families with elementary-school-aged children. Devotional booklet; 64 pgs. Pays $20/pg.

*LIGHT FROM THE WORD, Box 50434, Indianapolis IN 46250-0434. (317)570-5204. Fax (317)570-5260. Carl W. Pierce, sr. ed.

PATHWAYS TO GOD, PO Box 2499, Anderson IN 46018-9988. (800)347-7721. (765)644-7721. Fax (765)622-9511. Kathleen Buehler, ed. Send an SASE for information on becoming a Pathways writer.

*THE QUIET HOUR, 4050 Lee Vance View, Colorado Springs CO 80919. Cook Communications Ministries. Gary Wilde, ed. Pays $15 on acceptance. Send resume and list of credits, rather than a sample.

*REJOICE!, 1218 Franklin St. NW, Salem OR 97304-3902. (503)585-4458. Mennonite. Philip Wiebe, ed. Quarterly. Pays $110 for 7-day assigned meditations,

300 wds. Doesn't send a samples or guidelines to unsolicited writers. Prefers that you send a couple of sample devotions and inquire about assignment procedures. Don't apply for assignment unless you are familiar with the publication and Anabaptist theology.

*THE SECRET PLACE, Box 851, Valley Forge PA 19482-0851. (610)768-2240. Kathleen Hayes, mng. ed. Prefers to see completed devotionals, 125-200 wds (use unfamiliar Scripture passages). Uses poetry and photos. 64 pgs. Pays $15 for 1st rts. Guidelines.

THE UPPER ROOM, PO Box 189, Nashville TN 37202-0189. (615)340-7252 (no "cold" calls; get guidelines first). Fax (615)340-7006. Website: http://www. upperroom.org. Mary Lou Redding, mng. ed. 95% freelance. Pays $20 per 250-word devotional. 72 pgs. Note: This publication does accept freelance submissions and does not make assignments. Phone/fax/e-mail query OK. Send devotionals up to 250 wds. Buys one-time use of art work (transparencies/slides requested). No disk. Guidelines; copy for 5x7 SAE/2 stamps.

> **Tips:** "We do not return submissions. Accepted submissions will be notified in 6-9 wks. Follow guidelines."

THE WORD IN SEASON, PO Box 1209, Minneapolis MN 55440-1209. (800)426-0115x216. Fax (612)330-3455. Andrea Lee Schieber, ed. 96 pgs. Devotions 250 wds. Pays $15/devotion. Guidelines for #10 SAE/2 stamps.

> **Tips:** "We prefer that you write for guidelines. We will send instructions for preparing sample devotions. We accept new writers based on the sample devotions we request and make assignments after acceptance."

+WORDS OF LIFE, Novalis, 223 Main St., Ottawa ON K1S 1C4 Canada. (613)782-3036. Fax (613)751-4020. E-mail: cgreen@spu.stpaul.uottawa.ca. Caryl Green, ed. Send samples and request an assignment. Prefers 125 wds. Pays $40.

MISSIONS MARKETS

+AMERICAN BAPTISTS IN MISSION, PO Box 851, Valley Forge PA 19482-0851. (610)768-2077. Fax (610)768-2320. E-mail: rich_schramm@ecunet.org. Richard W. Schramm, ed. Denominational. Bimonthly mag; 24-32 pgs; circ 39,000. Subscription free. 10% freelance. Query. Pays negotiable rates on publication. Articles 750-1,000 wds (few/yr).Guidelines; copy. Not in topical listings.

#AMERICAN HORIZON, 1445 Boonville Ave., Springfield MO 65802-1894. (417)862-2781x3264. Fax (417)863-7276. Assemblies of God. Dan Van Veen, ed. Denominational magazine of home missions, mostly on assignment. Bimonthly mag; 20 pgs; circ 39,200. Free to contributors. 75% freelance. Query or complete ms/cover letter; phone query OK. Pay .03/wd on publication for 1st rts. Articles 750-1,200 wds (17/yr). Responds in 6 wks. Seasonal 5 mos ahead. Accepts simultaneous submissions & reprints. Free guidelines/copy. (Ads)

#AREOPAGUS MAGAZINE, PO Box 33, Shatin, New Territories, Hong Kong. (852)691-1904. Fax (852)265-9885. E-mail: areopagus@imal.com. Website: http://www.areopagus.com. Tao Fong Shan Christian Centre. John G. LeMond, ed. Provides a forum for dialogue between the good news of Jesus Christ and people of faith both in major world religions and new religious movements. Quarterly mag; 50 pgs; circ 1,000. Subscription $24. 75% freelance. Complete ms; e-mail OK. Pays $100-300 on publication for 1st rts. Articles 1,000-5,000 wds (40/yr); book reviews, 500-750 wds, $100. Responds in 6-13 wks. Seasonal 6 mos ahead. Accepts simultaneous submissions & reprints. Prefers disk. Kill fee 50%. Guidelines; copy $4.

Columns/Departments: Buys 10/yr. Complete ms. Pays $50-100.

Special Needs: Interfaith dialogue.

Tips: "We look for compassionate, direct, and unself-conscious prose that reflects a writer who is firmly rooted in his/her own tradition but is unafraid to encounter other religions."

CATHOLIC NEAR EAST, 1011 First Ave., New York NY 10022-4195. (212)826-1480. Fax (212)826-8979. Catholic. Michael La Civita, ed. Interest in cultural, religious, human rights development in Middle East, NE Africa, India and Eastern Europe. Bimonthly mag; 32 pgs; circ 100,000. Subscription $12. 50% freelance. Query/clips; phone query OK. Pays .20/edited wd on publication for 1st rts. Articles 1,500-2,000 wds (15/yr). Responds in 9 wks. Seasonal 4 mos ahead. Kill fee. Sidebars OK. Guidelines; copy for 7x10 SAE/2 stamps.

Tips: "We strive to educate our readers about the culture, faith, history, issues and people who form the Eastern Christian churches. Material should not be academic."

EAST-WEST CHURCH AND MINISTRY REPORT, Dept. IEWCS, Wheaton College, Wheaton IL 60187-5593. (630)752-5917. Fax (630)752-5916. E-mail: melliott@wheaton.edu. Institute for East-West Christian Studies. Dr. Mark Elliot, ed. Encourages Western Christian ministry in East Central Europe and the former Soviet Union that is effective, culturally sensitive and cooperative. Quarterly newsletter; 16 pgs; circ. 430. Subscription $42.75. 75% freelance. Complete ms/cover letter; e-mail query OK. **NO PAYMENT** for all rts. Articles 1,500 wds (3/yr); book reviews, 100 wds. Responds in 4 wks. Accepts disk. Sidebars OK. Guidelines; copy $10.

Tips: "All submissions must relate to East-Central Europe, the former Soviet Union or evangelical missions."

+EVANGELICAL MISSIONS QUARTERLY, PO Box 794, Wheaton IL 60189. (630)653-2158. Fax (630)653-0520. E-mail: emqjournal@.aol.com. Evangelical Missions Information Service. Gary Corwin, ed. For missionaries and others interested in missions-trends, strategies, issues, problems, and resources. Quarterly journal; 128 pgs; circ 7,000. Subscription $21.95. 65% freelance. Query. Pays $100 on publication for all rts. Articles 2,500 wds (70/yr); book reviews 400 wds (query), $25. Responds in 4 wks. Accepts few reprints (tell when/where appeared). Prefers disk. Sidebars OK. Prefers NIV. Free guidelines/copy. (Ads)

Columns/Departments: Buys 4/yr. In the Workshop (tips to increase missionary effectiveness), 1,000-2,000 wds. Pays $100.

#HEARTBEAT, PO Box 5002, Antioch TN 37011-5002. (615)731-6812. Fax (615)731-5345. E-mail: heartbeat@naFwb.org. Free Will Baptist. Don Robirds, ed. To inform and challenge church members with mission needs. Bimonthly mag; 16 pgs; circ 20,000. Subscription free. 3% freelance. Query; fax/e-mail query OK. Pays .03/wd on publication for one-time rts. Articles 600-1,000 wds (2/yr). Responds in 6 wks. Seasonal 4 mos ahead. Accepts reprints. No sidebars. Guidelines; copy for 9x12 SAE. (Ads)

*INTERNATIONAL JOURNAL OF FRONTIER MISSIONS, 321 W. Rio

Grande, El Paso TX 79902. (915)533-4975. Fax (915)532-0990. E-mail: 103121,2610 @compuserve.com. Hans Weerstra, ed. Dedicated to frontier missions in people groups that have no viable Christian church. Quarterly journal; circ 600. Subscription $15. 100% freelance. Complete ms/cover letter; phone/fax/e-mail query OK. **NO PAYMENT**, for one-time rts. Articles 6-7 pgs. Seasonal 3 mos ahead. Accepts simultaneous submissions & reprints. Guidelines/theme list; copy $1/ 9x12 SAE/$1.05 postage. (Ads)

> **Special Needs:** Contextualization, church in missions, comparative religions, training for missions, trends for missions, biblical basis for missions.

> **Tips:** "Although the circulation is small, the print run is 3,000 and used for motivational purposes."

#LATIN AMERICA EVANGELIST, Box 52-7900, Miami FL 33152-7900. (305)884-8400. Fax (305)885-8649. E-mail: info@lam.org. Latin America Mission. John D. Maust, ed. To present God's work through the churches and missionaries in Latin America. Quarterly mag; 22 pgs; circ 17,000. Subscription $10. 10% freelance. Query only. Pays variable rates on publication for 1st rts. Articles 1,000 wds. Reporting time varies. Accepts simultaneous submissions. Not in topical listings. Free copy.

> **Tips:** "Looking for news and analysis of the religious climate and social conditions in Latin America."

LEADERS FOR TODAY, Box 13, Atlanta GA 30370. (770)449-8869. Fax (770)449-8457. E-mail: hiatlanta@haggai.institute.com. Haggai Institute. Scott Schreffler, sr ed. Primarily for donors to ministry; focus is alumni success stories. Quarterly mag; 24 pgs; circ 6,500. 75% freelance. Query; fax query OK. Pays .10-.25/wd on acceptance for all rts. Articles 1,000-2,000 wds. Responds in 2-3 wks. Requires disk. Kill fee 100%. Sidebars OK. Prefers NIV. Guidelines/theme list; copy for 9x12 SAE/4 stamps.

> **Tips:** "All articles are pre-assigned. Query first."

THE MAP INTERNATIONAL REPORT, MAP International, Box 215000, Brunswick GA 31521-5000. (912)265-6010. Fax (912)265-6170. E-mail: mnyenhuis@ map.org. Website: http://www.map.org. Michael Nyenhuis, ed. Deals with health care in developing countries. Bimonthly newsletter; 8-12 pgs; circ 13,500. 5% freelance. Prefers query. **NO MENTION OF PAYMENT.** Articles 500 wds. Seasonal 4 mos ahead. Free guidelines/theme list/copy. Not in topical listings.

#MESSAGE OF THE CROSS, 6820 Auto Club Rd., Ste D, Minneapolis MN 55438. (612)829-2492. Fax (612)829-2753. Bethany Fellowship, Inc. George Foster, ed. Deeper life and Christian missions for a general Christian public. Quarterly mag; 32 pgs; circ 10,000. Subscription free. 20% freelance. Query or complete ms/cover letter; fax query OK. Pays $20-35 on publication for 1st or reprint rts. Articles (8/yr). Responds in 4 wks. Seasonal 6 mos ahead. Accepts reprints. No sidebars. Copy for 6x9 SAE. (Ads)

MISSIOLOGY: An International Review, Asbury Theological Seminary, Wilmore KY 40390. (606)858-2215/2216. Fax (606)858-2375. American Society of Missiology. Darrell L. Whiteman, ed. A professional organization for mission studies. Quarterly journal; 128 pgs; circ 2,000. Subscription $18. 75% freelance. Complete ms (3 copies)/cover letter; phone/fax query OK. **PAYS 20 COPIES** for one-time & reprint rts. Articles to 20 typed pgs (20/yr); book reviews, 200 wds. Responds in 8 wks. Requires disk. Guidelines; copy for 7x10 SAE. (Ads)

> **Tips:** "Whole journal is open to freelancers as long as they write from a missiological perspective and have adequate documentation."

#NEW WORLD OUTLOOK, 475 Riverside Dr., Room 1333, New York NY 10115-0122. (212)870-3600. Fax (212)870-3940. E-mail: nwo@gbgm-umc.org. Website: http://www.gbgm-ums.org. United Methodist. Alma Graham, ed.; submit to Christie R. House. Denominational missions. Bimonthly mag; 48 pgs; circ 30,000. Subscription $12. 20% freelance. Query; phone/fax query OK. Pays $50-300 on publication for all rts. Articles 500-2,000 wds (24/yr); book reviews 200-500 wds (assigned). No guaranteed response time. Seasonal 4 mos ahead. Kill fee 50%. Prefers disk (WordPerfect preferred). Sidebars OK. Prefers NRSV. Guidelines; copy $2.50.

> **Tips:** "Ask for a list of United Methodist mission workers and projects in your area. Investigate them, propose a story, and consult with the editors before writing. Most open to articles and/or color photos of US or foreign mission sites visited as a stringer, after consultation with the editor."

*THE OBLATE WORLD AND VOICE OF HOPE, Box 680, 486 Chandler St., Tewksbury MA 01876. (508)851-7258. Missionary Society of the Oblate Fathers of Texas. Rev. Thomas J. Reddy, OMI, ed. Missions publication for Catholic clergy and laity. Bimonthly newspaper; circ 25,000. Pays .01-.02/wd on acceptance. Missions stories 1,000-1,600 wds. Responds in 3 wks. Not in topical listings. Copy.

#PFI WORLD REPORT, Box 17434, Washington DC 20041. (703)481-0000. Fax (703)481-0003. E-mail: chris@pfi.org. Prison Fellowship, Intl. Christopher P. Nicholson, mng. ed. Targets issues and needs of prisoners, ex-prisoners, justice officials, victims, families and PFI staff, and volunteers in 75 countries. Bimonthly newsletter; 4-8 pgs; circ 4,750. Free subscription. 15% freelance. Query; phone/fax/e-mail query OK. Pays to $250 on acceptance. Articles 500-700 wds (3/yr). Responds in 3 wks. Seasonal 4 mos ahead. Accepts simultaneous submissions & reprints (tell when/where appeared). Accepts disk. Kill fee. Sidebars OK. Copy for #10 SAE/ 1 stamp.

> **Special Needs:** Prison issues, justice issues, anything that relates to international prison ministry.

> **Tips:** "Looking for personal profiles of people active in prison ministry (preferably PFI officials); ex-prisoner success stories; how-to articles about various aspects of prison ministry. Avoid American slant."

P.I.M.E. WORLD, 17330 Quincy St., Detroit MI 48221-2765. (313)342-4066. Fax (313)342-6816. Pontifical Inst. for Foreign Missions/Catholic. Paul W. Witte, mng. ed. For those interested in and supportive of foreign missions. Monthly (10X) mag; 16 pgs; circ 26,000. Subscription $5. 15% freelance. Complete ms/cover letter; query for electronic submissions. Pays .06/wd on publication for all rts. Photos $10. Not copyrighted. Articles 800-1,200 wds. Responds in 4 wks. Seasonal 2 mos ahead. Accepts simultaneous submissions & reprints (tell when/where appeared). Prefers disk. Sidebars OK. Prefers NAB. Guidelines; copy for 2 stamps.

> **Tips:** "Issues like hunger, human rights, women's rights, peace and justice

as they are dealt with in developing countries by missionaries and locals alike; stories of missionary service."

*THE QUIET HOUR ECHOES, 630 Brookside Ave., Box 3000, Redlands CA 92373. (909)793-2588. Fax (909)793-4754. The Quiet Hour (radio broadcast). Sharon Bird, gen. mgr. Provides radio listeners with challenges from the mission field and heart-to-heart messages from God. Monthly mag; 32 pgs; circ. 80,000. Subscription $5. 50% freelance. Query only. **NO PAYMENT.** Not copyrighted. Few sidebars. Prefers KJV.

> **Poetry:** Accepts 12-36/yr. Traditional.

> **Tips:** Most open to articles on health and poetry.

*THE RAILROAD EVANGELIST, PO Box 3846, Vancouver WA 98662. (360)699-7208. Joe Spooner, ed. For railroad and transportation employees and their families. Quarterly mag; circ 2,500. Subscription $6. 100% freelance. Complete ms; phone query OK. **NO PAYMENT.** Articles 100-700 wds (10-15/yr). Seasonal 4 months ahead. Accepts simultaneous submissions & reprints. Guidelines; copy for 9x12 SAE/2 stamps.

> **Poetry:** Accepts 4-8/yr. Traditional, any length. Send any number.

> **Fillers:** Accepts many. Anecdotes, cartoons, quotes; to 100 wds.

> **Tips:** "We need 400-700 word salvation testimonies."

*SAVE OUR WORLD (S.O.W.), 2490 Keith St. NW, PO Box 8016, Cleveland TN 37320-8016. (423)478-7190. Fax (423)478-7155. E-mail: tlr@cogwm.org. Church of God (Cleveland TN). Robert D. McCall, ed. Denominational publication for missions awareness. Quarterly tabloid; 16 pgs; circ. 97,000. Free. 10% freelance. Query/clips; phone/fax/e-mail query OK. **NO PAYMENT** (pays $50 for some) for one-time rts. Articles 400-650 wds. Responds in 4 wks. Accepts reprints. Prefers disk. Sidebars OK. Prefers KJV. Copy $3/9x12 SAE.

> **Fillers:** Accepts 4/yr. Facts, newsbreaks; 50-100 wds.

> **Tips:** "Most open to missions trips made to foreign fields, missions experiences, material promoting missions giving and its rewards, missions-related stories, etc."

*URBAN MISSION, Box 27009, Philadelphia PA 19118. (215)887-5511. Fax (215)887-5404. Westminster Theological Seminary. H. M. Conn, ed. Dedicated to advancement of Christ in cities throughout the world. Quarterly journal; circ 1,300. Subscription $16. 100% freelance. Complete ms/cover letter. **PAYS 3 COPIES.** Articles 2,100-6,000 wds (40/yr). Responds in 1-2 wks. Accepts reprints.

WHEREVER, Box 969, Wheaton IL 60189-0969. (630)653-5300. Fax (630)653-1826. E-mail: dfelmly@teamworld.org. The Evangelical Alliance Mission/interdenominational. Dana Felmly, ed. coord. For yg. adults interested in overseas missions, short or long term. Triennial mag; 16 pgs; circ 30,000. Free subscription. 70% freelance. Query. Pays $75-125 on publication for all or one-time rts. Articles 500-1,000 wds (13/yr); fiction 500-1,000 wds (1/yr). Sidebars OK. Guidelines/theme list; copy for 9x12 SAE/3 stamps. (Ads)

> **Tips:** "We're looking for people who can write with a Generation-X flair and style."

*WORLD CHRISTIAN, Box 25, Colfax WA 99111. Independent. Submit to Gordon Aeschliman, ed.; June Mears, mng. ed. Missions slant. Monthly mag; circ 40,000. Query. **NO PAYMENT FOR NOW.** Responds in 6-8 wks. Accepts reprints.

Articles 1,500-4,500 wds. Accepts simultaneous query. Guidelines/theme list; copy for SASE.

WORLD MISSION PEOPLE, PO Box 535002, Indianapolis IN 46253-5002. (317)244-3660. Fax (317)244-1247. Free Methodist World Missions. Daniel V. Runyon, ed. People features and worldwide news for supporters of Free Methodist missions. Bimonthly mag; 32 pgs; circ. 7,000. Subscription $10. 90% freelance. Complete ms/cover letter; no phone/fax query OK. **NO PAYMENT** for one-time rts. Articles 100-2,000 wds. Responds in 4 wks. Considers simultaneous submissions & reprints (tell when/where appeared). Accepts disk. Sidebars OK. Prefers NIV. No guidelines/copy.

> **Tips:** "Visit a Free Methodist overseas ministry and tell us about your experience."

+WORLD PULSE, PO Box 794, Wheaton IL 60189. (630)653-2158. Fax (630)653-0520. E-mail: pulsenews@aol.com. Stan Guthrie, mng. ed. Articles and news items from around the world, related to missions and Christians. Bimonthly newsletter; 8 pgs; circ 5,000. Subscription $26.95. Query; fax/e-mail query OK. Pays $100 on publication for all rts. Articles 700-800 wds. Responds in 2 wks. Accepts reprints (tell when/where appeared). Prefers disk. Kill fee 60%. No sidebars. Free guidelines/copy.

> **Tips:** "Send specific ideas on what missions and national churches are actually doing."

#WORLD VISION MAGAZINE, PO Box 9716, Federal Way WA 98063-9716. (206)815-1000. Fax (206)815-3445. E-mail: worvismag@aol.com. World Vision Inc. Larry Wilson, sr ed.; Shelly Ngo, mng ed. Relevant issues pertaining to the US and the Third World, as well as poverty. Bimonthly mag; 24 pgs; circ 78,000. Subscription free. 50% freelance. Query/clips only; fax query OK. Pays to $1,500 for assigned, to $850 for unsolicited or .20-.25/wd on acceptance for 1st & electronic rts. Articles 1,200-2,000 wds (6/yr). Responds in 2-3 wks. Seasonal 6 mos ahead. Accepts simultaneous submissions & reprints (tell when/where appeared). Accepts disk. Kill fee. Sidebars OK. Prefers NRSV. Free guidelines/copy. (Ads)

> **Columns/Departments:** Buys 6/yr. Turning Points (personal experience relating to poor), 450-700 wds; .20/wd.

> **Tips:** "Send us copies of anything written previously. Have experience in nonfiction writing for publications. Be fairly knowledgeable about the Third World. To break in, call an editor—Terry Madison, Bruce Brander or Larry Wilson."

> ** This periodical was #19 on the 1997 Top 50 Christian Publishers list (#59 in 1996, #36 in 1995, #61 in 1994). Also 1997 & 1996 EPA Award of Merit—Missionary.

WORLDWIDE CHALLENGE, 100 Sunport Ln., Dept. 1600, Orlando FL 32809. (407)826-2390. Fax (407)826-2374. E-mail: WChallenge@aol.com. Website: http://www.ccci.org/WWC. Campus Crusade for Christ. Bill Sundstrom, ed. For financial supporters of Campus Crusade. Bimonthly mag; 48 pgs; circ 100,000. Subscription $12.95. 5% freelance. Query only/clips. Pays .10/wd + a flat fee of $100-200 (depending on research) on acceptance for 1st rts (all rts for assigned articles). Articles 800-1,600 wds (6/yr). Responds in 6-8 wks. Seasonal 6-8 mos

ahead. Accepts simultaneous submissions. Prefers disk. Kill fee 50%. Sidebars
OK. Prefers NAS. Guidelines; copy for 9x12 SAE/5 stamps. (Ads)

    Columns/Departments: Buys 6/yr. Upfront (personal experience/commentary); 400-800 wds; query or complete ms; Susie Hilsman, ed. History's
Heroes (positive examples), 1,250 wds, query, Lisa Master, ed.

    Tips: "Give the human face behind a topic or story. Show how the topic
relates to evangelism and/or discipleship."

    ** This periodical was #43 on the 1996 Top 50 Christian Publishers List.
(#35 in 1994) Also 1996 EPA Award of Merit—Organizational.

MUSIC MARKETS

#CCM MAGAZINE, 107 Kenner Ave., Nashville TN 37205. (615)386-3011. Fax
(615)385-4112 or (615)386-3380. E-mail: feedback@ccmcom.com. Website:
http://www.ccmcom.com. April Hefner, mng ed. Encourages spiritual growth
through contemporary music; provides news and information about the Christian
music market. Monthly mag; 80 pgs; circ. 85,000. Subscription $21.95. 75%
freelance. Query/clips; phone/fax query OK. Pays .20/wd for short pieces, or
$100/published page for features, on publication for all rts. Articles 500-2,500
wds; music reviews 250-350 wds. Responds slowly. Seasonal 3 mos ahead. Kill
fee 50%. Prefers disk or e-mail. Sidebars OK. Guidelines; copy for 9x12 SAE/$4.
(Ads)

    ** 1996 EPA Award of Merit—Youth.

CHRISTIAN COMPOSER, Box 448, Jacksonville OR 97530. (541)899-8888.
James Lloyd, ed/pub. The only songwriter and artists Top Sheet in the business;
includes a relevant essay on music-related subjects. Bimonthly newsletter, supplement to Christian Media; circ 2,000-6,000. Query; prefers phone query. **PAYS IN
COPIES OR PRODUCT** for all rts. Articles; book & music reviews, 3 paragraphs. Responds in 3 wks. Accepts simultaneous submissions & reprints. Prefers
disk. KJV only. Copy for 9x12 SAE/2 stamps. Not in topical listings.

    Special Needs: Material should focus on the craft of song writing, musical
performance, or marketing of the same.

    Tips: "We like 'street-smarts' when it comes to articles. Tell it like it is in the
music industry; we want our readers forewarned about the various pitfalls in
Christian music."

#CHRISTIAN COUNTRY RESEARCH BULLETIN (CCRB), 7057 Bluffwood
Ct., Brownsburg IN 46112. (317)892-5031. Fax (317)892-5034. E-mail:
ccrb@ai2a.net. Website: http://www.achiever.com/freehmpg/christiancountry.
Joyful Sounds. Les Roberts, ed. Trade journal for Christian country radio industry. Biweekly trade journal; 8-12 pgs; circ. 300-1,200. Subscription $36. 75%
freelance. Query or complete ms/cover letter; phone/fax/e-mail query OK. Negotiable payment & rights. Articles 600-2,000 wds; music reviews, 100-300 wds.
Responds in 2 wks. Seasonal 2 mos ahead. Accepts reprints. Requires disk (DOS-
ASCII). Copy for 9x12 SAE/2 stamps. (Ads)

    Fillers: Cartoons, short humor.

    Columns/Departments: Insider (artist interview); Programming 101 (radio
technique); retail, inspirational, especially for musicians and radio people;
600-2,000 wds.

Tips: "Most open to artist interviews. Must be familiar with Christian country music."

#CHURCH MUSICIAN TODAY (formerly THE CHURCH MUSICIAN), 127 9th Ave. N., Nashville TN 37234. (615)251-2961. Fax (615)251-2614 or 5951. Southern Baptist. Jere Adams, ed. For church music leaders. Monthly; 16 pages (music), 98 pgs total; circ 16,000. 20% freelance. Complete ms. Pays to .055/wd (.06 on disk) on acceptance for all rts. Articles & fiction (related to church music), to 1,300 wds. Responds in 9 wks. Accepts reprints (pays 50%—tell when/where appeared). Copy for 9x12 SAE/3 stamps.

Fillers: Short humor (with a musical slant); $5-15.

#THE CHURCH MUSIC REPORT, Box 1179, Grapevine TX 76099. (817)488-0141. Fax (817)481-4191. Bill Rayborn, ed. For church music leaders. Monthly newsletter; 8-12 pgs; circ 6,200. Ideas, tips, how-tos, and the like. Articles; interviews.

*CHURCH PIANIST/SAB CHOIR/THE CHOIR HERALD, Box 268, Alcoa TN 37701. Now a division of The Lorenz Corp. Hugh S. Livingston Jr., ed. Each of these music magazines has one page devoted to articles that deal with problems/solutions of choirs and accompanists. Bimonthly mag; 36-52 pgs; circ 25,000. 45% freelance. Complete ms/cover letter. Pay $15-150 on publication for all rts. Articles 250-1,250 wds (10-20/yr). Seasonal 1 yr ahead. Responds in 3-6 wks. Guidelines; copy for 9x12 SAE/3 stamps.

Poetry: Accepts 25/yr. Free verse, light verse, traditional, or poetry suitable for song lyrics; $10. Submit max. 5 poems.

Fillers: Accepts 5-10/yr. Anecdotes, cartoons.

Special Needs: Choir experiences; pianist/organist articles.

Tips: "Best approach is from direct experience in music with the small church."

#CREATOR MAGAZINE, PO Box 64775, Tucson AZ 85748. (520)888-0600. Fax (520)577-4967. E-mail: creatormag@aol.com. Marshall Sanders, pub. For interdenominational music ministry; promoting quality, diverse music programs in the church. Bimonthly mag; 48-56 pgs; circ 6,000. 35% freelance. Query or complete ms/cover letter; fax/e-mail query OK. Pays $35-75 on publication for 1st or one-time rts. Articles 1,000-10,000 wds (20/yr); book reviews $20. Responds in 4-12 wks. Seasonal 4 mos ahead. Accepts simultaneous submissions & reprints (tell when/where appeared). Prefers disk. Sidebars OK. Prefers NRSV. Guidelines/theme list; copy for 9x12 SAE/5 stamps. (Ads)

Fillers: Buys 20/yr. Anecdotes, cartoons, ideas, jokes, party ideas, short humor; 10-75 wds; $5-25.

Special Needs: Articles on worship; staff relationships.

#GLORY SONGS, 127 9th Ave. N. Nashville TN 37234. (615)251-2913. (615)251-2614. Southern Baptist. Jere V. Adams, ed. Easy choral music for church choirs; practical how-to articles for small church music programs. Quarterly mag; 26 pgs; circ 85,000. 100% freelance. Complete ms. Pays .055/wd on acceptance for 1st rts. Articles 550-1,000 wds (6-7/yr). Responds in 2-4 wks. Seasonal 1 yr ahead. Accepts simultaneous submissions & reprints. Guidelines; free copy.

Poetry: Buys 2-3/yr. Free verse, traditional.

Fillers: Cartoons, ideas, party ideas, musical quizzes, short humor.

Special Needs: Vocal techniques, choir etiquette, mission/outreach ideas, music training, etc.

GOSPEL INDUSTRY TODAY, 761 Old Hickory Blvd., Ste. 205, Brentwood TN 37027-4513. E-mail: gospel@usit.net. Website: http://www.gospeltoday.com/gospel_industry.htm. Horizon Concepts. Teresa Hairston, pub.; submit to Iris Raeshaun. About the Christian and Gospel music industry. Monthly (10X) mag; 16 pgs; circ 3,500. Subscription $24. 50% freelance. Query; fax/e-mail query OK. Pays $75-250 on publication for 1st rts. Articles 1,500-3,000 wds. Responds in 5-9 wks. Seasonal 3 mos ahead. Prefers disk. Kill fee 10%. Sidebars OK. Prefers KJV. Guidelines/theme list; copy for 10x13 SAE/8 stamps. (Ads)

*THE HYMN, School of Theology, Boston University, 745 Commonwealth Ave., Boston MA 02215-1401. (800)THEHYMN. Hymn Society in the US & Canada. Carl P. Daw, Jr., exec. dir. For church musicians, hymnologists, scholars; articles related to the congregational song. Quarterly journal; 60 pgs; circ 3,000. Subscription $45. 100% freelance. Query. **NO PAYMENT** for all rts. Articles any length (12/yr); book & music reviews any length. Responds in 4 wks. Seasonal 4 mos ahead. Prefers disk. Sidebars OK. Guidelines; free copy.

    Poetry: Hymn poetry.

    Special Needs: Hymns and articles on history of hymns.

#MUSIC MAKERS, 127 9th Ave. N., Nashville TN 37234. (615)251-2000. Southern Baptist. Darrell Billingsley, ed. For children ages 6-11. Quarterly mag; circ 105,000. Pays .06/wd on acceptance for all rts. Articles & fiction 250-500 wds. Responds in 4 wks. Guidelines/copy. Not in topical listings.

#MUSIC TIME, 127 9th Ave. N., Nashville TN 37234. (615)251-2000. Southern Baptist. Darrell Billingsley, literary design ed. For 4 & 5 yr olds; directly related to unit material found in **The Music Leader.** Quarterly mag; circ 60,000. Complete ms. Pays .05/wd for stories. Pays $9-12 on acceptance for all rts. Stories for 4 & 5 yr olds. Responds in 2-5 wks. Not in topical listings. Guidelines; free copy.

    Poetry: 1-7 lines; $5-9.

PLANS & PLUSES (formerly **THE MUSIC LEADER**), 127 9th Ave. N., Nashville TN 37234. (615)251-2513. Fax (615)251-2614. Southern Baptist. Anne Trudel & Rhonda Edge Buescher, eds. How-to material for leaders of preschool and children's choirs. Quarterly mag; 92 pgs; circ 35,000. 5% freelance. Complete ms/cover letter. Pays .055-.065/wd on acceptance for all or one-time rts. Articles 75-80 lines (to 800 wds), or 150-170 lines typed 40 characters/line; 250 lines max. Seasonal dramas, 7-8 pgs. Responds in 5 wks. Guidelines; copy $3.

    Poetry: For choir leaders.

*QUEST, PO Box 14804, Columbus OH 43214. Rick Welke, ed. Geared to 16-30 year olds and radio personnel. Monthly newsletter. Est. 1995. Query; fax query OK. **PAYS A SUBSCRIPTION.** Articles 100-500 wds (4/yr); fiction, 150-750 wds (4/yr); book/music reviews, 30-75 wds. Seasonal 3 mos ahead. Accepts simultaneous submissions & reprints. Theme list; copy for #10 SAE/2 stamps.

    Poetry: Accepts 12/yr. Any type, 4-24 lines. Submit max. 4 poems.

    Fillers: Accepts 36/yr. Cartoons, facts, jokes, quizzes, quotes, short humor, word puzzles.

    Columns/Departments: Artist Action (any specific artist information).

Special Needs: Organizational pieces; new music releases/photos; artist's concert schedules; radio station playlists.

Tips: "Submit between the 10th and 20th of each month for best review."

*RENAISSANCE, The Resource Publication for the Christian Musician, Box 2134, Lynnwood WA 98036. Renaissance Artists Group/Christian Artists International. Nathan L. Csakany, ed. Issues of interest to Christian musicians. Not in topical listings. Copy.

*RING! PO Box 1179, Grapevine TX 76099-1179. (817)488-0141. Fax (817)481-4191. TCMR Communications Inc. Lynann Rayborn, ed. For handbell choir members. Monthly (10X) newsletter.

#THE SENIOR MUSICIAN, 127 9th Ave. N, Nashville TN 37234. (615)251-2913. Fax (615)251-2614. Southern Baptist. Jere V. Adams, ed. For music directors and choir members of senior adult choirs. Quarterly mag; 26 pgs; circ 32,000. 100% freelance. Complete ms. Pays .055/wd on acceptance for 1st rts. Articles 500-900 wds (6-7/yr). Responds in 2-4 wks. Seasonal 1 yr ahead. Some simultaneous submissions; reprints. Guidelines; free copy.

   Poetry: Buys 2-3/yr. Traditional.

   Fillers: Buys 3-4/yr. Cartoons, ideas, party ideas, musical quizzes, short humor.

   Special Needs: Senior adults' testimonials, inspirational stories, personal growth and development, music training, and choir projects.

   Tips: "All topics must relate to senior adult musicians and senior choirs—anything else will be returned."

(SEVEN) 7 BALL, 2525-C Lebanon Pike, Box 6, Nashville TN 37214. (615)872-8080. Fax (615)872-9786. E-mail: bruce7ball@7ball.com. Website: http://www.7ball.com. Voxcorp, Inc. Bruce A. Brown, mng ed. Covers modern and alternative Christian rock. Bimonthly mag; circ 50,000. Open to freelance. Not in topical listings. (Ads)

*SING! PO Box 1179, Grapevine TX 76099-1179. (817)488-0141. Fax (817)481-4191. TCMR Communications Inc. Lynann Rayborn, ed. For adult choir members. Monthly newsletter.

*SING! JR., PO Box 1179, Grapevine TX 76099-1179. (817)488-0141. Fax (817)481-4191. TCMR Communications Inc. Lynann Rayborn, ed. For children's choir members & their parents. Monthly (9X) newsletter.

*TRADITION, Box 438, Walnut IA 51577. (712)366-1136. Prairie Press Ltd. Robert Everhart, ed. Devoted to acoustic traditional music with an over-35 audience. Bimonthly mag; circ 2,500. 20% freelance. Query. Pays $10-15 on publication for one-time rts. Not copyrighted. Articles 800-1,200 wds (2/yr). Responds in 5 wks. Seasonal 6 mos ahead. Accepts simultaneous query & reprints. Copy $1.

   Poetry: Buys 4/yr. Free verse, traditional; 5-20 lines; $2-5. Submit max. 2 poems.

   Fillers: Buys 5/yr. Anecdotes, clippings, jokes; 15-50 wds; $5-10.

   Special Needs: Articles on gospel music.

PASTOR/LEADERSHIP MARKETS

ART+PLUS, Reproducible Resources, Box 4710, Sarasota FL 34230-4710. (941)955-2950. Fax (941)955-5723. E-mail: Mail@MMI-art.com. Mission Media Inc. Wayne Hepburn, pub. Reproducible illustrations and verse for church bulletins and newsletters. Quarterly mag; 26 pgs; circ 3,000. Subscription $39.97. 100% freelance. Complete ms; phone/fax/e-mail query OK. Pays $5-25 on acceptance for all rts only. Anecdotes 100 wds max. Responds in 12 wks. Seasonal 6 mos ahead. Accepts simultaneous submissions. Accepts disk. Guidelines/theme list; copy $2/9x12 SAE.

Poetry: Buys 12-20/yr. Traditional only; 4-24 lines; $15. Submit max. 20 poems.

Fillers: Buys 40-100/yr. Anecdotes, cartoons; to 50 wds; $8.

Tips: "We are seasonally oriented; more open to art/images than writing. We need 3-5 poems per quarter and 3-10 anecdotes or fillers."

+BIBLIOTHECA SACRA, 3909 Swiss Ave., Dallas TX 75204. (214)841-3735. Fax (214)841-3532. Dallas Theological Seminary. Roy B. Zuck, ed. For pastors, church leaders, serious lay persons, students, scholars and teachers; covers biblical, theological, and ministerial issues from a conservative, evangelical perspective. Quarterly journal; 128 pgs; circ 8,500. Subscription $18. 50% freelance. Complete ms/cover letter. Pays $100 on publication for all rts. Articles 5,000-7,500 wds (20/yr). Responds in 4-6 wks. Requires disk. No sidebars. Prefers NAS. Copy $4.50/6x9 SAE/$2 postage.

Tips: "Ours is the oldest theological journal in the western hemisphere."

CATECHUMENATE: A JOURNAL OF CHRISTIAN INITIATION, 1800 N. Hermitage Ave., Chicago IL 60622-1101. (773)486-8970. Fax (800)933-7094. E-mail: editors@ltp.org. Catholic. Victoria M. Tufano, ed. For clergy and laity who work with those who are planning to become Catholic. Bimonthly jour; 48 pgs; circ 5,600. Subscription $20. Complete ms/cover letter; phone/fax/e-mail query OK. Pays $100-250 on publication for all rts (poetry, one-time rts). Articles 1,500-3,000 wds (10/yr). Responds in 2-6 wks. Accepts simultaneous submissions. Prefers disk. Kill fee. No sidebars. Guidelines; copy for 6x9 SAE/4 stamps.

Poetry: Buys 6/yr. Free verse, traditional; 5-20 lines; $75. Submit max. 5 poems.

Columns/Departments: Buys 12/yr. Sunday Word (Scripture reflection on Sunday readings, aimed at catechumers); 450 wds; $200-250. Query for assignment.

Special Needs: Christian initiation; reconciliation.

Tips: "It helps if the writer has experience working with Christian initiation. Approach is that this is something we are all learning together through experience and scholarship."

+THE CATHOLIC SERVANT, PO Box 24142, Minneapolis MN 55410. (612)929-8110. Fax (612)929-8146. Catholic. John Sondag, pub. For Catholic evangelization, catechesis, and apologetics. Monthly newspaper; 12 pgs; circ 24,000. Query/clips; fax query OK. Pays $50-60 on publication. Articles 1,000 wds (12/yr). Responds in 4 wks. Seasonal 3 mos ahead. Prefers disk. Some sidebars. (Ads)

Fillers: Cartoons & short humor.

Tips: "We buy features only."

*CELEBRATION, 207 Hillsboro Dr., Silver Spring MD 20902-3125. William J. Freburger, ed. National Catholic Reporter Publishing House. Monthly mag; 48

pgs; circ 9,000. Subscription $64.95. 15% freelance. Complete ms/cover letter. Pays $100-200 on acceptance for one-time rts. Articles 1,000-2,500 wds (15-20/yr). Responds in 2 wks. Seasonal 7 mos ahead. Prefers disk. No sidebars. Copy for 10x13 SAE/4 stamps. (Ads)

Contest: Monthly contest on different themes, usually worship ideas for specific occasions (New Year, Easter, etc.).

Tips: "I am always looking for descriptions of worship services (texts), ideas for worship occasions (seasonal., special), unsentimental and non-obvious stories as teaching/preaching aids, etc."

CELL CHURCH MAGAZINE, PO Box 19888, Houston TX 77224. (281)497-7901. Fax (281)497-0904. Website: http://www.touchusa.org. Touch Outreach Ministries. Les Brickman, ed. For Cell Church pastors, leaders and consultants working to impact the world for Christ through the church. Quarterly mag; 24 pgs; circ 12,000. Subscription $14. 70-80% freelance. Query/clips; fax/e-mail query OK. **PAYS 10 COPIES.** Articles 1,000-1,500 wds (20-30/yr). Responds in 2 wks. Seasonal 3 mos ahead. Accepts simultaneous submissions & reprints (tell when/where appeared). Prefers disk. Some sidebars. Prefers NIV. Guidelines/theme list; copy $3.50/9x12 SAE/3 stamps. (Ads)

Columns/Departments: Accepts 20-25/yr. Youth, Children's Ministry, Transitioning (to Cell Church), Global Input, Lone Service (lone pastor/supervisor), Pastor's Pilgrimage (pastor's testimonial about Cell Church), and Heart to Heart (heartfelt testimony about cell life); all 1,000-1,500 wds.

Special Needs: Global issues; practical tips and ideas relevant to Cell Church concept. Needs youth Cell Church writer.

CELL LIFE FORUM, 131 Tilman Cir., Markham ON L3P 6A4 Canada. (905)471-5015. Fax (905)471-6912. E-mail: 75273,3241@compuserve.com. World Team Canada. Nancy J. Lindquist, ed. A resource to connect cell-based churches across Canada. Quarterly mag; 16 pgs; circ. 300+. Subscription $12 CAN. Est. 1994. 75% freelance. Query; phone/e-mail query OK. Pays .05/wd on publication for 1st or one-time rts. Not copyrighted. Articles 500-2,000 wds (8-12/yr); book/music reviews, 100-500 wds, $5-25. Responds in 3-4 wks. Accepts simultaneous submissions & reprints. Accepts disk (prefers e-mail). Sidebars OK. Prefers NIV. Guidelines/theme list; copy for 9x12 SAE. (Ads)

Poetry: Buys 4/yr. Any type as long as on theme; 5-30 lines; $5-10. Submit max. 4 poems.

Fillers: Buys 8+/yr. Anecdotes, cartoons, tips; to 100 wds; $5-10.

Tips: "All material must relate to Canadian cell churches or Canadians involved in cell churches. Most open to profiles, My Story, or fillers."

CHRISTIAN CAMP & CONFERENCE JOURNAL (formerly **JOURNAL OF CHRISTIAN CAMPING**), 405 W. Rockrimmon Blvd. Colorado Springs CO 80919. (719)260-9400. Fax (719)260-6398. E-mail: editors@cciusa.org. Christian Camping Intl./USA. Dean Ridings, ed. To inform, inspire, and motivate all who serve in Christian camping. Bimonthly mag; 32-40 pgs; circ 7,500. Subscription $24.95. 80% freelance. Query; fax/e-mail query OK. Pays .12/wd on publication for 1st, reprint & electronic rts. Articles 1,000-2,500 wds (12/yr). Responds in 4-6 wks. Seasonal 4 mos ahead. Accepts simultaneous submissions & reprints (tell when/where appeared). Prefers disk. Kill fee. Sidebars OK. Prefers NIV.

Guidelines; copy $2.25/9x12 SAE/5 stamps. (Ads)

Special Needs: Outdoor setting; purpose and objectives; administration and organization; personnel development; camper/guest needs; programming; health and safety; food service; site/facilities maintenance; business/operations; marketing and PR; and fund raising.

Tips: "Get guidelines first. Don't send general camping-related articles. We print stories specifically related to Christian camp and conference facilities; changed lives or innovative programs; how a Christian camp or conference experience affected a present-day leader."

CHRISTIAN CENTURY, 407 S. Dearborn St., Ste. 1405, Chicago IL 60605-1150. (312)427-5380. Fax (312)427-1302. Christian Century Foundation. Submit to Manuscripts. For ministers, educators and church leaders interested in events and theological issues of concern to the ecumenical church. Weekly magazine; 32 pgs; circ 30,000. Subscription $40. 90% freelance. Query (complete ms for fiction); phone/fax query OK. Pays $75-150 ($100-200 for fiction) on publication for all rts. Articles 1,500-3,000 wds (140/yr); fiction 2,000-3,000 wds (3/yr); book reviews, 800-1,500 wds; music or video reviews 1,000 wds; pays $0-75. Responds in 3-4 wks. Seasonal 2-3 mos ahead. No disk. Kill fee. Sidebars OK. Prefers NRSV. Guidelines/theme list; copy $2/9x12 SAE/4 stamps or just $3. (Ads)

Poetry: Buys 50/yr. Any type (religious but not sentimental); to 20 lines; $50. Submit max. 10 poems.

Tips: "Looking for more fiction. Keep in mind our audience of sophisticated readers, eager for analysis and critical perspective that goes beyond the obvious."

#CHRISTIAN COUNSELING TODAY, 1821 Walden Office Sq., Ste. 111, Schaumburg IL 60173-4267. (847)303-6675. Fax (847)303-5957. E-mail: 1CCTatAACC@aol.com. Dr. Gary Collins, ed. Provides practical, relevant, up-to-date biblically and psychologically accurate information about Christian counseling for professional, pastoral, and lay counselors. Quarterly mag; circ. 20,000. Subscription $35. Open to freelance. Query. (Ads)

#CHRISTIAN MANAGEMENT REPORT, 1969 E. Broadway #3, Tempe AZ 85282. (602)967-9122. Fax (602)967-8298. E-mail: 103253.2444@compuserve. com. Church Management Association. DeWayne Herbrandson, ed. For Christian managers of nonprofit organizations and people from ministries in general. Bi-monthly journal; 40 pgs; circ 2,300. Subscription $29.95. 75% freelance. Query or complete ms/cover letter; fax query OK. **NO PAYMENT** for all rts. Articles 800 wds (20/yr); book reviews 200-500 wds. Responds in 5-13 wks. Seasonal 6 mos ahead. Accepts simultaneous submissions & reprints. Guidelines; free copy. (Ads)

Fillers: Anecdotes, cartoons, facts, newsbreaks, prose, prayers, quotes, short humor; 50-100 wds.

Columns/Departments: Management Q & A; Hiring Insights; both 500-700 wds. Query.

Special Needs: Non-profit management; fund-raising; marketing; and hiring issues.

CHRISTIAN MINISTRY, 407 S. Dearborn St., Ste. 1405, Chicago IL 60605-1150. (312)427-5380. Fax (312)427-1302. Website: http://www.christianmin.org. The

Press. Marshall N. Surratt, ed. Reviews of faith-based software, as well as stories about how churches, ministries, individuals and families are using computer technology. Bimonthly mag; 48 pgs; circ 10,000. Subscription $24. 40% freelance. Query; e-mail query OK. Pays $50 on publication for 1st & electronic rts. Articles 1,200-2,000 wds (20-30/yr); book reviews, 1,200-1,600 wds, $50. Responds in 2-3 wks. Seasonal 3-4 mos ahead. Accepts simultaneous submissions & reprints (tell when/where appeared). Requires disk. Sidebars OK. Guidelines; copy for 9x12 SAE/6 stamps. (Ads)

> **Special Needs:** Computing; computer technology, multimedia, Internet, and software.

> **Tips:** "We want articles that tell a story about people using computer technology to enhance ministry or to enhance their families' lives. We are also interested in how computer technology is being used and what difference that makes in our lives and for our faith."

CHURCH GROWTH NETWORK, PO Box 892589, Temecula CA 92589-2589. Phone/fax (909)506-3086. Dr. Gary L. McIntosh, ed. For pastors and church leaders interested in church growth. Monthly newsletter; 2 pgs; circ 8,000. Subscription $15. 10% freelance. Query; fax query OK. **PAYS IN COPIES** for one-time rts. Not copyrighted. Articles 1,000-2,000 wds (2/yr). Responds in 4 wks. Accepts simultaneous submissions & reprints. Prefers disk. No sidebars. Copy for #10 SAE/1 stamp.

> **Tips:** "All articles must have a church-growth slant. Should be very practical, how-to material; very tightly written with bullets, etc."

THE CLERGY JOURNAL, 6160 Carmen Ave. E., Inver Grove Heights MN 55076-4422. (612)451-9945. Fax (612)457-4617. Logos Productions, Inc. Sharilyn Figueroa, mng. ed. "How-to" articles on church administration, ministry/personal issues for Protestant ministers, Christian educators and church personnel. Monthly mag; 96 pgs; circ 10,000. Subscription $27. 60% freelance. Query/clips or complete ms/cover letter. Pays $50-150 on publication for 1st rts. Articles 1,000-3,000 wds (50/yr); fiction 1,000 wds (10/yr). Responds in 2 wks. Seasonal 1 yr ahead. Accepts reprints (tell when/where appeared). Prefers disk. Sidebars OK. Prefers NRSV. Guidelines/theme list; copy for 9x12 SAE/4 stamps. (Ads)

> **Fillers:** Cartoons, prayers; 50-150 wds; $10-25.

> **Special Needs:** Humorous fiction for pastors and children's sermons.

> **Tips:** "On the religious spectrum from very conservative to very liberal, our audience is in the middle to left. We are interested in meeting the personal and professional needs of clergy in areas like worship planning, church and personal finances, and self care-spiritual, physical and emotional. "

CROSS CURRENTS, College of New Rochelle, 29 Castle Pl., New Rochelle NY 10805-2339. (914)235-1439. Fax (914)235-1584. E-mail: aril@ecunet.org. Website: http://www.aril.org. Association for Religion and Intellectual Life. Shelley Schiff, mng ed. For thoughtful activists for social justice and church reform. Quarterly jour; 144 pgs; circ 5,000. Subscription $30. 99% freelance. Mostly written by academics. Complete ms/cover letter; phone/fax query OK. **PAYS IN COPIES** for all rts. Articles 3,000-5,000 wds; book reviews 1,000 wds (James Giles). Responds in 6-8 wks. Seasonal 6 mos ahead. Accepts simultaneous submissions & reprints. Requires disk. No sidebars. Guidelines; copy for 6x9 SAE/4 stamps. (Ads)

Poetry: Tom O'Brien. Accepts 12/yr. Any type or length; no payment. Submit max. 5 poems.

Tips: "Send 3 double-spaced copies; SASE; use Chicago Manual of Style; non-sexist language."

+CURRENT THOUGHTS & TRENDS, PO Box 35004, Colorado Springs CO 80935-3504. (719)531-3585. Fax (719)598-7128. E-mail: dsevcik@navigato. mhs.compuserve.com. The Navigators. Dennis Cone, ed. To enhance the ministry of Christian leaders by providing concise, timely summaries of contemporary trends in Christian and secular thought. Monthly newsletter; circ 17,000. Subscription $36. Open to freelance. Query. Not in topical listings. (Ads)

*DIOCESAN DIALOGUE, 16565 S. State St., South Holland IL 60473. (708)331-5485. Fax (708)331-5484. Catholic. Fr. Michael Gilligan, editorial dir. Targets Latin-Rite dioceses in the US that sponsor a mass broadcast on TV or radio. Semiannual tabloid; circ. 750. Free. 20% freelance. Complete ms/cover letter; no phone/fax query. Pays on publication for all rts. Responds in 10 wks. Accepts simultaneous submissions & reprints. Prefers NAB (Confraternity). Copy $3/9x12 SAE/2 stamps.

Fillers: Cartoons, 2/yr.

EMMANUEL, 5384 Wilson Mills Rd., Cleveland OH 44143-3092. (440)449-2103. Fax (440)449-3862. Catholic. Rev. Anthony Schueller, ed.; book reviews to Dr. Patrick Riley. Eucharistic spirituality for priests and others in church ministry. Monthly (10X) mag; 60 pgs; circ 4,000+. Subscription $19.95. 75% freelance. Query or complete ms/cover letter; fax query OK. Pays $75-150 for articles, $50 for meditations, on publication for all rts. Articles 2,000-2,750 wds; meditations 1,000-1,250 wds; book reviews 500-750 wds. Responds in 2 wks. Seasonal 4 mos ahead. Accepts disk. Prefers RNAB. Guidelines/theme list. (Ads)

Poetry: Buys 15/yr. Free verse; 25-100 lines. Pays $35-50. Submit max. 2-3 poems.

ENRICHMENT: A Journal for Pentecostal Ministry, 1445 Boonville Ave., Springfield MO 65802. (417)862-2781. Fax (417)862-0416. E-mail: enrichment@ ag.org. Assemblies of God. Rick Knoth, mng ed. Directed to part- or full-time denominational ministers and church leaders. Quarterly jour; 128-124 pgs; circ 32,000. Subscription $18. 5-10% freelance. Complete ms/cover letter. Pays .03-.10/wd ($75-175) on publication for 1st, one-time or reprint rts. Articles 1,200-2,500 wds (25/yr); book reviews, 250 wds, $25. Responds in 8-12 wks. Seasonal 6 mos ahead. Accepts simultaneous submissions & reprints (tell when/where appeared). Prefers disk. Kill fee 50%. Sidebars OK. Prefers NIV. Guidelines/theme list; copy for 10x13 SAE/4 stamps. (Ads)

Fillers: Cartoons, ideas, short humor, sermon illustrations, sermon outlines, ministry ideas; 200-500 wds. Pays $10-50.

Columns/Departments: Buys many/yr. For Women in Ministry (leadership ideas), Associate Ministers (related issues), Managing Your Ministry (how-to), Financial Concepts (church stewardship issues), Family Matters (ministers family), View from the Pew (layperson's perspective on ministry); all 1,200-1,500 wds. Pays $125-150.

Tips: "Most open to sermon outlines, how-to articles (fillers), sermon illustrations, practical ideas on ministry-related topics."
** 1997 EPA Award of Merit—Denominational & Most Improved Publication 1997.

*ENVIRONMENT & ART LETTER, 1800 N. Hermitage Ave., Chicago IL 60622-1101. (773)486-8970x64. Fax (773)486-7094. Catholic. David Philippart, ed. For artists, architects, building professionals, pastors, parish committees interested in church architecture, art and decoration. Monthly newsletter; 12 pgs; circ 2,500. Subscription $20. 80% freelance. Query/clips; phone/fax query OK. Pays $25/ms page on publication for all rts. Responds in 18 wks. Seasonal 2 mos ahead. Accepts simultaneous submissions. Theme list; copy for 9x12 SAE/3 stamps.

Tips: "Need a thorough knowledge of the liturgical documents pertaining to architecture and art, especially environment and art for Catholic worship."

EUCHARISTIC MINISTER, 115 E. Armour Blvd., Box 419493, Kansas City MO 64111. (816)531-0538. Fax (816)968-2280. E-mail: newsward@aol.com. Website: http://www.natcath.com. Catholic. Beatrice Fleo, ed. For eucharistic ministers. Monthly newsletter; 4-8 pgs; circ 50,000. 90% freelance. Complete ms. Pays $20-200 on acceptance for one-time rts. Articles 200-2,000 wds (30+/yr). Responds in 1-2 wks. Seasonal 4-6 mos ahead. Accepts simultaneous submissions & reprints. Guidelines; free copy.

Fillers: Buys 10-12/yr. Anecdotes, cartoons, short humor.

Tips: "We want articles to be practical, inspirational, or motivational. They need to be simple and direct enough for the average person to read easily—no heavy theology, pious inspiration, or excess verbiage."

*EVANGELISM USA, PO Box 12609, Oklahoma City OK 73157. (405)787-7110. Fax (405)789-3957. International Pentecostal Holiness Church. Talmadge Gardner, ed. For pastors/leaders interested in church growth/revitalization, church planting, and intercultural ministries. Monthly (10X) mag; 8 pgs. 100% freelance. Complete ms/cover letter. **NO PAYMENT** for all rts. Not copyrighted. Articles; book reviews 1 column long. Responds in 1 wk. Accepts disk. Sidebars OK. Free guidelines/copy.

THE FIVE STONES, 135 Pine St., Norton MA 02766-2812. Phone/fax (508)285-7145. E-mail: TONY_PAPPAS@ecunet.com. American Baptist. Anthony G. Pappas, ed. Primarily to small church pastors and laity, denominational staff, and seminaries; to equip for service. Quarterly journal; 24 pgs; circ 1,200. Subscription $8-12. 100% freelance. Complete ms/cover letter. Pays $5 on publication for one-time rights. Not copyrighted. Articles (20/yr) & fiction (4/yr), 500-2,000 wds; book reviews 500 wds, $5. Responds in 10-12 wks. Seasonal 10 mos ahead. Accepts simultaneous submissions & reprints. Accepts disk. Guidelines/theme list; copy for 9x12 SAE/4 stamps.

Fillers: Buys 12/yr. Anecdotes, cartoons, ideas, jokes, short humor; 20-200 wds; $5.

Tips: "Always looking for everything related to small church life (nature and dynamics of small churches); fresh programming. Good place for unpublished to break in. Best to call and talk."

GROUP'S JR. HIGH MINISTRY, Box 481, Loveland CO 80539. (970)669-3836.

Fax (970)679-4372. E-mail: nfriscia@grouppublishing.com. Website: http://www. grouppublishing.com. Group Publications, Inc. Nancy Friscia, ed. asst. For youth ministers who work with the junior-high age group. Mag published 5X/yr; 45 pgs; circ 25,000. Subscription $19.95. 60% freelance. Query/clips or complete ms/cover letter; fax/e-mail query OK. Pays $35-175 on acceptance for all rts. Articles 500-1,700 wds (60/yr). Responds in 4-8 wks. Seasonal 5 mos ahead. Sidebars OK. Guidelines; copy $2/9x12 SASE. (Ads)

> **Fillers:** Buys 5-10/yr. Cartoons, games, ideas; 150 wds. Pays $15-35.

> **Columns/Departments:** Buys 30/yr. Parents Page (tips for parents of junior-highers), 150 wds; Pick 'n Choose Games or Pick 'n Choose Ideas 200-300 wds; $25-35.

> **Special Needs:** Articles geared toward junior-highers; computers in ministry; and games for junior-highers.

> **Tips:** "Writers must be involved with junior high school or youth ministry. We are interested in articles about understanding junior high kids. Focus on faith in action and special life situations. Offer step-by-step instructions and objectives for retreats and group discussions."

+ISSACHARFILE, PO Box 12609, Oklahoma City OK 73157. (405)787-7110. Fax (405)789-3957. Intl. Pentecostal Holiness Church. Shirley G. Spencer, ed. Denominational; keeping church leaders in touch with the times. Monthly mag; circ 3,000. Subscription $9.75. Open to freelance. Query. Not in topical listings. (Ads)

#THE IVY JUNGLE REPORT, 1025 Austin St., Bellingham WA 98226-2643. (360)733-6212. Fax (360)738-8057. E-mail: ivyjungle@aol.com. Woodruff Resources. Mike Woodruff, pub. For people who minister to collegians. Quarterly mag; circ 800. Subscription $20. 75% freelance. Query; fax/e-mail query OK. **NO PAYMENT** for one-time rts. Not copyrighted. Articles 500-1,500 wds (16/yr); book/music reviews, 500 wds. Responds in 2 wks. Accepts simultaneous submissions & reprints. Prefers disk. Sidebars OK. Copy for 2 stamps. (Ads)

> **Fillers:** Accepts 10+/yr. Anecdotes, cartoons, facts, jokes, newsbreaks, quizzes, quotes, short humor; 15-100 wds.

> **Columns/Departments:** Out of the Classroom (student missions), 750-1,000 wds (4/yr). Query.

> **Tips:** "We are looking for writers who understand the unique demands and challenges of college ministry, both church and parachurch."

JOURNAL OF CHRISTIAN HEALING, 6728 Old McLean Village Dr., McLean VA 22101. (703)556-9222. Fax (703)556-8729. Assoc. of Christian Therapists. Father Louis Lussier, OSCAS, ed. Focuses on the healing power and presence of Jesus Christ, for health and mental health professionals and healing ministries. Quarterly journal; 40 pgs; circ 1,200. 100% freelance. Complete ms/cover letter; phone query OK. **PAYS IN COPIES** for all rts. Articles 10-20 pgs (12/yr); fiction 2-5 pgs; book reviews, 2-5 pgs. Accepts reprints. Responds in 8 wks. Guidelines; copy $8.

> **Poetry:** Charles Zeiders. Accepts 12/yr. Free verse, haiku, light verse or traditional; to 40 lines. Submit max. 10 poems.

> **Fillers:** Accepts 10/yr. Various; to 250 wds.

> **Columns/Departments:** Accepts 12/yr. Resources, Medical Practices, Nursing, Pastoral Ministry, Psychiatry, Prayer Ministry, Sexuality, Dreams; 2-5 pgs.

Tips: "All articles or short stories must relate to healing."

THE JOURNAL OF PASTORAL CARE, 1068 Harbor Dr. SW, Calabash NC 28467. Phone/fax (910)579-5084. E-mail: OrloS@aol.com. Orlo Strunk, Jr., mng ed. For chaplains/pastors/professionals involved with pastoral care and counseling in other than a church setting. Quarterly jour; 116 pgs; circ. 10,000. Subscription $22.50. 80% freelance. Query; phone/fax/e-mail query OK. **PAYS IN COPIES** for 1st rts. Articles 5,000 wds or 20 pgs (30/yr); book reviews 5 pgs. Responds in 8 wks. Requires disk. No sidebars. Guidelines; copy $2.50/6x9 SAE. (Ads)

>**Poetry:** Accepts 16/yr. Free verse; 5-16 lines. Submit max. 3 poems.

>**Tips:** "Readers are highly trained clinically, as well as holding professional degrees in religion/theology. Writers need to be professionals on topics covered."

JOURNAL OF THE AMERICAN SOCIETY FOR CHURCH GROWTH, 1230 US Hwy 6, Coronna IN 46730. (219)281-2452. Fax (219)436-0974. American Society of Church Growth. Dr. Gary L. McIntosh, ed. Targets professors, pastors, denominational executives and seminary students interested in church growth and evangelism. Quarterly journal (3X—fall, winter, spring); 100 pgs; circ. 300. Subscription $24. 100% freelance. Complete ms/cover letter; phone/fax query OK. **PAYS IN COPIES** for one-time rts. Not copyrighted. Articles 15 pgs or 4,000-5,000 wds (10/yr); book reviews 750-2,000 wds. Responds in 8-12 wks. Accepts simultaneous submissions & reprints (tell when/where appeared). Prefers disk. No sidebars. Guidelines/theme list; copy $10. (Ads)

>**Tips:** "All articles must have a church-growth slant. We're open to new writers at this time."

+THE JOYFUL NOISELETTER, PO Box 895, Portage MI 49081-0895. (616)324-0990. Fax (616)324-3984. E-mail: JoyfulNZ@aol.com. Cal Samra, ed. To provide pastors and local church bulletin editors of all denominations with clean jokes, uplifting anecdotes, and cartoons to use and reprint. Monthly newsletter; circ 10,000. Subscription $22. Open to freelance. Query. Partial topical listings. (Ads)

#LEADERSHIP JOURNAL, 465 Gundersen Dr., Carol Stream IL 60188. (630)260-6200. Fax (630)260-0114. E-mail: LeaderJ@aol.com. Website: http://www.christianity.net/leadership. Christianity Today, Inc. Kevin A. Miller, ed. Practical help for pastors/church leaders. Quarterly journal; 130 pgs; circ 70,000. Subscription $22. 75% freelance. Query or complete ms; fax/e-mail query OK. Pays $75-375 (.10/wd) on acceptance for 1st rts, rt. to reprint & electronic rts. Articles 500-3,000 wds (50/yr). Responds in 6-9 wks. Seasonal 6 mos ahead. Accepts reprints (tell when/where appeared). Accepts disk. Kill fee 50%. Sidebars OK. Guidelines/theme list; copy $3. (Ads)

>**Fillers:** Buys 80/yr. Anecdotes, cartoons, ideas, short humor; to 150 wds. Pays $25-50.

>**Columns/Departments:** Buys 80/yr. Ideas That Work, 150 wds; To Illustrate (sermon illustrations), 150 wds; To Quip (humorous sermon illustrations); Back Page (opinion), 1,200 wds. Complete ms. Pays $25-50.

>**Special Needs:** Material on pastoral care, church health, contemporary preaching, and the pastor's soul.

Tips: "Writers should be involved in the ministry/leadership of the church."
** This periodical was #14 on the 1996 Top 50 Christian Publishers list. (#27 in 1995, #16 in 1994)

+LET'S WORSHIP, MSN 157, 127 9th Ave. N., Nashville TN 37234. (615)251-3837. Fax (615)251-3609. Southern Baptist. Dean Richardson, ms. asst. To help pastors and other worship leaders in their preaching/worship ministry. Quarterly mag; 100 pgs. Subscription $62.25. Est. 1996. 75% freelance. Complete ms/cover letter; no phone/fax query. Pays $200 (.065/wd) on acceptance for all rts. Articles 1,600-2,000 wds. Responds in 6-8 wks. Seasonal 6-12 mos ahead. Accepts simultaneous submissions. Prefers disk. Kill fee. Sidebars OK. Prefers NIV. Guidelines; copy for 9x12 SAE/$2 postage.

Poetry: Buys 16/yr. Free verse, traditional; 4-48 lines. Pays $20-120.

Tips: "Most open to short dramas, dramatic readings, dramatic monologues/dialogues."

LITURGY, 8750 Georgia Ave., Ste. 123, Silver Spring MD 20910-3621. (301)495-0885. Fax (301)495-5945. E-mail: litconf@aol.com. The Liturgical Conference. Blair Gilmer Meeks, ed. For clergy, liturgy planners, musicians, and religious educators. Quarterly jour; 86 pgs; circ 2,300. Subscription $45. 5% freelance. Query; phone/fax/e-mail query OK. Pays $30-50 on publication for all rts. Articles 2,000-2,500 wds (3/yr). Responds in 8 wks. Seasonal 6 mos ahead. Accepts simultaneous submissions & reprints (tell when/where appeared). Requires disk. Some sidebars. Prefers NRSV. Guidelines/theme list; copy $10.95.

Tips: "An ecumenical perspective is required. Writers should be recommended by another of our writers or board members."

+THE LIVING LIGHT, U.S. Catholic Conference, Dept. E, Box 45, The Catholic University of America, Washington DC 20064. Berard L. Marthaler, ed. Theoretical and practical articles on religious education, catechesis, and pastoral ministry; 1,500-4,000 wds. Not in topical listings.

*LUTHERAN FORUM, PO Box 327, Delhi NY 13753-0327. (607)746-7511. Fax (607)829-2158. American Lutheran Publicity Bureau. Ronald Bagnall, ed. For church leadership—clerical and laity. Quarterly journal; 64 pgs; circ 3,200. 100% freelance. Complete ms/cover letter. **NO PAYMENT.** Articles 1,000-3,000 wds. Responds in 26-32 wks. Accepts simultaneous submissions & reprints. Requires disk. Guidelines; copy for 9x12 SAE/6 stamps. (Ads)

LUTHERAN PARTNERS, 8765 W. Higgins Rd., Chicago IL 60631-4195. (800)638-3522x2875 or 2884. (773)380-2875. Fax (773)380-2829. E-mail: 1partmag@elca.org or LUTHERAN_PARTNERS.parti@ecunet.org. Evangelical Lutheran Church in America. Carl E. Linder, ed. To encourage and challenge rostered leaders in the ELCA, including pastors and lay leaders. Bimonthly mag; 40-48 pgs; circ 20,000. Subscription $10 (free to leaders). 10-15% freelance. Query or complete ms/cover letter; phone/fax/e-mail query OK. Query for electronic submissions. Pays $100-150 on publication for one-time rts. Articles 500-2,500 wds (12-15/yr). Responds in 16 wks. Seasonal 9 mos ahead. Accepts simultaneous submissions & reprints (tell when/where appeared). Kill fee (rare). Prefers disk. Sidebars OK. Prefers NRSV. Guidelines/theme list; copy $2/9x12 SAE/5 stamps. (Ads)

Poetry: Buys 6-10/yr. Free verse, traditional: $50-75. Keep concise. Submit max. 6-10 poems.

Fillers: Buys 4-5/yr. Cartoons; ideas for parish ministry (called Jottings); to 500 wds; $25.

Special Needs: Book reviews. Query Thelma Megill-Cobbler, Trinity Lutheran Seminary, 2199 E. Main St., Columbus OH 43209, (614)235-4136. Uses books predominately from mainline denominational publishers. Payment is copy of book.

Tips: "Query us with solid idea. Understand Lutheran Christian theology and congregational life. Be able to see life from a pastor/lay leader's point of view. With limited freelance, most sections hard to get into, but you might try the Jottings section first (see Fillers)."

+THE MINISTER'S FAMILY, MSN 157, 127 9th Ave. N., Nashville TN 37234. (615)251-3837. Fax (615)251-3609. Southern Baptist. Dean Richardson, ms. asst. A leisure-reading magazine designed to encourage, inspire, inform, and enrich the lives of ministers and their families. Quarterly mag; 52 pgs. Subscription $17.95. 20% freelance. Complete ms/cover letter; no phone/fax query. Pays $200 (.065/wd) on acceptance for all rts. Articles 1,600-2,000 wds. Responds in 6-8 wks. Seasonal 6-12 mos ahead. Accepts simultaneous submissions. Prefers disk. Kill fee. Sidebars OK. Prefers NIV. Guidelines; copy for 9x12 SAE.

Poetry: Buys 5/yr. Light verse; 4-20 lines. Pays $20-100. Submit max. 4 poems.

Fillers: Games & ideas.

Tips: "Most open to experience-based humor."

MINISTRIES TODAY, 600 Rinehart Rd., Lake Mary FL 32746. (407)333-0600. Fax (407)333-7133. E-mail: grady@strang.com. Strang Communications. Lee Grady, exec. ed; Marcia Ford, assoc. ed (e-mail: mford@strng.com); Jimmy Stewart, book & music review ed. Helps for pastors and church leaders primarily in Pentecostal/charismatic churches. Bimonthly mag; 90 pgs; circ 30,000. Subscription $24.95. 60-80% freelance. Query; fax/e-mail query OK. Pays $50 or $500-800 on publication for all rts. Articles 2,000-2,500 wds (25/yr); book/music/video reviews, 300 wds, $25. Responds in 4 wks. Prefers disk. Kill fee. Sidebars OK. Prefers NIV. Guidelines; copy $4/9x12 SAE. (Ads)

Columns/Departments: Michele Buckingham. Buys 36/yr. Soap Box (opinion pcs); The Next Generation (youth/children's ministry); 800 or 1,050 wds; $100-150.

Tips: "Most open to columns. Write for guidelines and study the magazine."

MINISTRY MAGAZINE: International Journal for Pastors, 12501 Old Columbia Pike, Silver Spring MD 20904. (301)680-6510. Fax (301)680-6502. E-mail: 74532.2425@compuserve.com. Seventh-day Adventist. Julia W. Norcott, asst. ed.. For Pastors. Monthly journal; 32 pgs.; circ.20,000. Subscription $26.95. 90% freelance. Query; fax/e-mail query OK. Pays $50-150 on acceptance for all rts. Articles 1,000-1,500 wds; book reviews 100-150 wds ($25). Responds in 2-3 wks. Prefers disk. No sidebars. Guidelines/theme list; copy for 9x12 SAE/5 stamps. (Ads)

+MINISTRY NOW PROFILES, PO Box 2430, Cleveland TN 37320-2430. (423)478-7055. Fax (423)478-7966. E-mail: MNprofiles@aol.com. Church of God (Cleveland TN). Tom George, ed. To provide denominational ministers with church news and inspirational, informational, and practical how-to articles.

Monthly mag; circ 13,500. Subscription free. Open to freelance. Query. Not in topical listings. (Ads)

#MODERN LITURGY, 160 E. Virginia St. #290, San Jose CA 95112. (408)286-8505. Fax (408)287-8748. E-mail: mdrnlitrgy@aol.com. Resource Publications, Inc. Nick Wagner, ed. dir. To help liturgists and ministers make the imaginative connection between liturgy and life. Monthly (10X) mag; 50 pgs; circ 20,000. Subscription $45. Query only; fax/e-mail query OK. Query for electronic submissions. **PAYS IN COPIES & SUBSCRIPTION** on publication for 1st rts. Articles 1,000 wds (30/yr). Responds in 4 wks. Seasonal 6 mos ahead. Accepts reprints (tell when/where appeared). Requires disk. Sidebars OK. Guidelines/theme list; copy $4/11x14 SAE/2stamps. (Ads)

> **Contest:** Visual Arts Awards.

NATIONAL DRAMA SERVICE, MSN 170, 127 Ninth Ave. N, MSN 158, Nashville TN 37234. (615)251-5045. Fax (615)251-2614. Southern Baptist. Conservative, evangelical dramas for stage, street and sanctuary. Drama, puppets, clowns, mime, movement, comedy, seeker-oriented, dramatic worship service plans. Quarterly script collections; 5,000 subscription base. 100% freelance. Complete ms/cover letter. Pays about $25/published page. Scripts 5-7 minutes in length. No one-acts, full length or musicals. Responds in 10 wks. Seasonal 9 mos ahead. Accepts simultaneous submissions. Prefers NIV. Guidelines.

*NETWORKS, Box 685, Cocoa FL 32923. (407)632-0130. Fax (407)631-8207. Christian Council on Persons with Disabilities. Linda G. Howard, ed. For those with specialized ministry to the mentally retarded. Bimonthly newsletter; 8 pgs; circ 1,700. 80% freelance. Query or complete ms. **NO PAYMENT** for 1st rts. Articles 250-450 wds (12/yr); book reviews 350 wds. Responds in 6 wks. Seasonal 4 mos ahead. Accepts simultaneous submissions & reprints. Guidelines; copy for 9x12 SAE/6 stamps.

> **Poetry:** Accepts 4/yr. Any type; to 66 lines. Submit max. 10 poems.
>
> **Columns/Departments:** Accepts 8/yr. Program Highlights, 1,000 wds; Teachers' Tips, 750 wds.
>
> **Special Needs:** Advocacy, normalization/integration, church/state issues. June 15 deadline for annual issue on the Christian Council on Persons with Disabilities.

THE NEWSLETTER NEWSLETTER, 4150 Belden Village St. 4th Floor, Canton OH 44718. (330)493-7880. Fax (330)493-7897. E-mail: newsletter@comresources. com. Communication Resources. Timothy Merrill, ed. To help church secretaries and church newsletter editors prepare their newsletter. Monthly newsletter; 12 pgs. Subscription $39.95. 30% freelance. Complete ms. Pays $150 on acceptance for all rts. Articles 800-1,000 wds (8/yr). Responds in 4 wks. Seasonal 8 mos ahead. Accepts simultaneous submissions. Requires disk. Kill fee. Sidebars OK. Copy for 9x12 SAE/3 stamps.

*PARISH LITURGY, 16565 S. State St., South Holland IL 60473. (708)331-5485. Catholic. Father Gilligan, ed. dir. A planning tool for Sunday and Holyday liturgy. Quarterly mag; 32 pgs; circ 22,000. Subscription $18/2 yrs. 10% freelance. Query; no phone query. All rts. Articles 400 wds. Responds in 4 wks. Seasonal 4 mos ahead. Accepts simultaneous submissions & reprints (tell when/where appeared). Some sidebars. Prefers NAB.

PASTORAL LIFE, 9531 Akron-Canfield Rd., Canfield OH 44406-0595. (330)533-5503. Fax (330)533-1076. Catholic. Rev. Anthony Chenevey, ed. Focuses on the current problems, needs, issues and all important activities related to all phases of pastoral work and life. Monthly (11X) mag; 64 pgs; circ 1,800. Subscription $17. 50% freelance. Query. Pays .04/wd on publication for one-time rts. Not copyrighted. Articles (50/yr) to 3,000 wds; book reviews 300-500 wds (no pay). Responds in 3 wks. Seasonal 4 mos ahead. No disk. Some kill fees. Prefers NAB. Guidelines/theme list; copy for 6x9 SAE/4 stamps. (Ads)

> **Tips:** "We feature pastoral homilies for Sundays and Holydays. Articles should be eminently pastoral in approach and content."

PASTOR'S FAMILY, 8605 Explorer Dr., Colorado Springs CO 80920. (719)548-5884. Fax (719)531-3499. E-mail: dahlmasj@fotf.org. Focus on the Family. Simon J. Dahlman, ed. To support and strengthen ministers and other church workers, their spouses, and children in the area of family life. Bimonthly mag; 32 pgs; circ 28,500. Subscription $18. Est. 1996. 50% freelance. Query; phone/fax/e-mail query OK. Pays .10-.20/wd on acceptance for 1st & electronic rts. Articles 400-2,000 wds (60/yr); book reviews 100 wds, pays $20 + book. Responds in 8 wks. Seasonal 8-10 mos ahead. Accepts disk. Kill fee 25%. Sidebars OK. Prefers NIV. Guidelines; copy for 9x12 SAE.

> **Fillers:** Buys 40/yr. Anecdotes, cartoons, quotes; 25-100 wds. Pays $15.

> **Columns/Departments:** After Church (roundtable on specific topic), 1,500 wds, query; Better Homes and Parsons (humorous anecdotes related to ministry lifestyle), 30-100 wds, complete ms. Pays $15-250.

> **Tips:** "We are looking for solid, lively and candid profiles of people whose families are in ministry. We also look for creative how-to articles that offer fresh help for people in a unique situation. Familiarity with ministry life is a must."

> ** This periodical was #16 on the 1997 Top 50 Christian Publishers list.

*PASTOR'S TAX & MONEY, PO Box 50188, Indianapolis IN 46250. (800)877-3158. Daniel D. Busby, ed. Guidance for pastors in management of church and personal finances. Quarterly newsletter; 8 pgs; circ 6,000. Subscription $59.95. 50% freelance. Complete ms/cover letter. Pays $50 on publication for 1st rts. Articles 600-800 wds (8/yr). Responds in 13 wks. No sidebars. Copy $1/6x9 SAE/2 stamps.

> **Special Needs:** Minister's taxes; computers; personal finances and church finances.

+PLUGGED IN, 8605 Explorer Dr., Colorado Springs CO 80920. (719)531-3400. Fax (719)531-3347. Focus on the Family. Bob Smithouser, ed. Monthly newsletter; circ 50,000. Subscription $20. Freelance OK. Query. Not in topical listings. (Ads)

+PRAY!, PO Box 35008, Colorado Springs CO 80935-3508. (719)531-3507. Fax (719)598-7128. E-mail: pray-mag@navigators.org. Website: http://www.navigators. org. Jonathan L. Graf, ed. A magazine entirely about prayer, geared toward intercessors and prayer mobilizers (pastors and leaders who encourage prayer). Bimonthly mag; 32-40 pgs; circ 25,000. Subscription $14.97. 75% freelance. Complete ms/cover letter; fax/e-mail query OK. Pays .10/wd on acceptance for 1st, reprint & electronic rts. Articles 600-1,500 wds (30/yr). Responds in 6-8 wks.

Accepts simultaneous submissions & reprints (tell when/where appeared). Accepts disk. Kill fee 50%. Sidebars OK. Prefers NIV. Guidelines/theme list; copy for 9x12 SAE. (Ads)

Fillers: Ideas on prayer; 75-500 wds. Pays $20.

Special Needs: Non-theme feature articles on various aspects of prayer.

Tips: "Personal experience pieces are okay, but they need to teach something significant about prayer, not just be a look-what-I-did article. The ideas section is easiest place to break in. We are looking for short pieces that enhance, encourage, or promote individual or corporate prayer."

THE PREACHER, PO Box 757800, Memphis TN 38175-7800. (901)757-7977. Fax (901)757-1372. E-mail: olford@memphisonline.com. Encounter Ministries, Inc. Mark N. Boorman, assoc. ed. Triennial mag; 20-24 pgs; circ. 4,500. Subscription $10 (voluntary). 10% freelance. Query; phone query OK. **NO PAYMENT** for one-time rts. Articles (1-3/yr) 500 wds; book/video reviews 250 wds. Responds in 2-3 wks. Seasonal 3-4 mos ahead. Might accept reprints (tell when/where appeared). Prefers disk. Sidebars OK. Prefers NKJV. Copy for 9x12 SAE/4 stamps.

Poetry: Accepts 1-2 /yr. Traditional; 4-20 lines. Submit max. 2 poems.

Fillers: Accepts 4-6/yr. Prayers, 100-200 wds.

Tips: "Call and ask if we need article complementary to theme of upcoming issue."

*PREACHER'S ILLUSTRATION SERVICE, Box 3102, Margate NJ 08402. (609)822-9401. Fax (609)822-1638. James Colaianni, pub. Sermon illustration resource for professional clergy. Bimonthly loose-leaf booklet, 16 pgs. 15% freelance. Complete ms. Pays .15/wd on publication for any rts. Illustrations/anecdotes 50-250 wds. Responds in 6 wks. Seasonal 4 mos ahead. Accepts reprints. Prefers disk. Guidelines/topical index; copy for 9x12 SAE.

Poetry: Light verse, traditional; 50-250 lines; .15/wd. Submit max. 3 poems.

Fillers: Various; sermon illustrations; 50-250 wds; .15/wd.

THE PREACHER'S MAGAZINE, 10814 E. Broadway, Spokane WA 99206. (509)226-3464. Fax (509)926-8740. Nazarene. Rev. Randal E. Denny, ed. A professional journal for holiness pastors and other preachers. Quarterly mag; 80 pgs; circ 18,000. Subscription $7.50. 30% freelance. Complete ms/cover letter; phone query OK. Pays .035/wd on publication for one-time rts. Articles 700-2,500 wds (40/yr); book reviews 300-400 wds. Responds in 4-6 wks. Seasonal 6 mos ahead. Accepts simultaneous submissions & reprints (tell when/where appeared). No disk. Some sidebars. Prefers NIV. Guidelines.

Fillers: Buys 10/yr. Anecdotes, cartoons, ideas; 300-700 wds.

Tips: "Material must be relevant to pastor's ministry or personal life."

PREACHING, PO Box 369, Jackson TN 38302-0369. (901)668-9948. Fax (901)668-9633. E-mail: preaching@compuserve.com. Website: http://www.preaching. com/preaching/index.htm. Preaching Resources, Inc. Dr. Michael Duduit, ed; submit to Mark Johnson, mng ed. Professional magazine for evangelical preachers; focus is on preaching and worship leadership. Bimonthly mag; 64 pgs; circ 10,000-12,000. Subscription $24.95. 90-95% freelance. Query or complete ms/cover letter; phone/fax/e-mail query OK. Pays $35-50 on publication for 1st rts. Articles 1,200-1,500 wds (30-40/yr). Responds in 2 wks. Seasonal 6-8 mos ahead. Prefers disk. Sidebars OK. Prefers NIV. Some sidebars. Guidelines; copy $2/9x12 SAE. (Ads)

> **Fillers:** Buys 10-15/yr. Cartoons only; $25.
>
> **Tips:** "Need how-to articles about specific areas of preaching and worship leadership. We only accept articles from pastors or seminary/college faculty."

THE PRIEST, 200 Noll Plaza, Huntington IN 46750-4304. (219)356-8400. Fax (219)359-9117. Catholic/Our Sunday Visitor, Inc. Msgr. Owen F. Campion, ed. For Catholic priests, deacons and seminarians; to help in all aspects of ministry. Monthly mag; 48 pgs; circ 7,800. Subscription $35.97. 80% freelance. Complete ms/cover letter; phone query OK. Pays $175-250 on acceptance for 1st rts. Articles to 1,500-5,000 wds (96/yr); some 2-parts. Responds in 6-8 wks. Seasonal 6 mos ahead. Free guidelines/copy. (Ads)

> **Fillers:** George Foster. Cartoons; $35.
>
> **Columns/Departments:** Buys 36/yr. Viewpoint (about priests or the church), under 1,000 wds, $50. Complete ms.
>
> **Tips:** "Write to the point, with interest. Most open to features. Keep the audience in mind. Include Social Security number."
>
> ** #62 on the 1994 Top 50.

PROCLAIM, 127 Ninth Ave. N, Nashville TN 37234. (615)251-2874. Fax (615)251-3866. Southern Baptist. George Clark, ed. Sermons, illustrations and worship materials for pastors. Quarterly mag; 50 pgs; circ 15,000. Subscription $13.30. 75% freelance. Query; phone query OK. Pays .055/wd ($8 min) on acceptance for all or 1st rts. Articles 600-4,000 wds (50-60/yr). Responds in 2-16 wks. Seasonal 6 mos ahead. Accepts reprints. No sidebars. Guidelines; free copy for 9x12 SAE.

> **Columns/Departments:** Features, 2,400 wds; Sermon Workshop (sermon helps), 50-700 wds; Worship Workshop, 2,400 wds; Pulpit Performance, 3,000 wds.
>
> ** #68 on the 1994 Top 50.

PULPIT HELPS, 6815 Shallowford Rd., Chattanooga TN 37421. (800)251-7206. Fax (423)894-6863. E-mail: AMGpublish@aol.com. Ted Kyle, ed. To help preachers and serious students of the Bible. Monthly tabloid; 32 pgs; circ 106,000. Subscription $15. 20% freelance. Complete ms; fax/e-mail query OK. **NO PAYMENT**. Articles to 100-1,200 wds, prefers 1,000 (60-80/yr). Responds in 3 wks. Seasonal 4 mos ahead. Accepts simultaneous submissions & reprints (tell when/where appeared). Accepts disk. Few sidebars. Prefers KJV or NIV. Guidelines/theme list; copy for 9x12 SAE/2 stamps. (Ads)

> **Poetry:** Accepts 10-12/yr. Traditional; short. Submit max. 3 poems.
>
> **Fillers:** Anecdotes, prose; quotes; 50-250 wds.
>
> **Columns/Departments**: Family Helps, 100-1,000 wds; Illustrations (for sermons), 50-100 wds; Sermon Starters (brief).
>
> **Tips:** "Most open to Illustrations & Sermon Starters—short, pointed anecdotes/articles preachers can use as illustrations. "

*QUARTERLY REVIEW, A Journal of Theological Resources for Ministry, 1001 - 19th Ave. S., Nashville TN 37202-0871. (615)340-7334. Fax (615)340-7048. United Methodist. Dr. Sharon J. Hels, ed. A theological approach to subjects of interest to clergy—Scripture study, ethics, and practice of ministry in Wesleyan tradition. Quarterly journal; 112 pgs; circ 1,500. Subscription $24. 75% freelance.

Complete ms/cover letter; phone/fax query OK. **PAYS IN COPIES** for 1st rts. Articles to 5,000 wds (20/yr); book reviews to 1,000 wds. Responds in 6-8 wks. Seasonal 8 mos ahead. Prefers disk. No sidebars. Prefers NRSV. Guidelines/theme list; copy for 9x12 SAE/$2 postage.

Tips: "We look for writers who have strong academic/theological training and whose work addresses concerns and interests of those in ministry. Awareness of current scholarly literature, a well-developed argument, and clear expository prose are essential."

REFORMED WORSHIP, 2850 Kalamazoo SE, Grand Rapids MI 49560-0001. (616)224-0785. Fax (616)224-0834. E-mail: rw@crcpublications.org. Christian Reformed Church in North America. Dr. Emily R. Brink, ed. To provide liturgical and musical resources for pastors, church musicians, and other worship leaders. Quarterly mag; 48 pgs; circ 4,000. Subscription $23.95. 5% freelance. Complete ms/cover letter; e-mail query OK. Query for electronic submissions. Pays .05/wd on publication for all rts (negotiable). Articles 2,000 wds; book reviews 250 wds, $25. Responds in 4 wks. Seasonal 6 mos ahead. Rarely accepts reprints (tell when/where appeared). Kill fee 50%. Prefers disk. Sidebars OK. Prefers NIV or NRSV. Guidelines/theme list; copy for 9x12 SAE/$2 postage.

Fillers: Buys 4-5/yr. Cartoons, prayers; $20-50.

Columns/Departments: View From the Pew (humorous or reflective vignettes on worship experiences), 1,000-1,500 wds.

Tips: "You need to understand the Reformed tradition of worship."

RESOURCE: The National Leadership Magazine, 6745 Century Ave., Mississauga ON L5N 6P7 Canada. (905)542-7400. Fax (905)542-7313. Pentecostal Assemblies of Canada. Michael Horban, ed. For church leadership and practical how-tos on leadership issues. Bimonthly mag; 48 pgs; circ 10,000. Subscription $20. 20% freelance. Query. Pays $30-100 on publication for all rts. Articles 500-1,500 wds (8-10/yr); book reviews 250 wds, $20. Responds in 4-6 wks. Seasonal 3 mos ahead. Accepts reprints. Prefers disk. Sidebars OK. Guidelines/theme list; copy $2/9x12 SAE.

Fillers: Buys 4-8/yr. Anecdotes, cartoons, short humor; 200-300 wds; $20-30.

Special Needs: Good missions promotional features.

Tips: "Say something positive to leaders that stretches and enriches them."

REVIEW FOR RELIGIOUS, 3601 Lindell Blvd., Rm. 428, St. Louis MO 63108-3393. (314)977-7363. Fax (314)977-7362. E-mail: FOPPEMA@slu.edu. Catholic/Jesuits of Missouri Province. Rev. David L. Fleming, S.J., ed. For Catholic Women and Men Religious, clergy and laity involved in church ministry; to reflect on the church's rich heritage of spirituality. Bimonthly journal; 112 pgs; circ 9,000. Subscription $20. 85% freelance. Complete ms/cover letter; no phone/fax/e-mail query. Pays $18-72 on publication for 1st rts. Articles 2,000-5,000 wds (50/yr). Responds in 8 wks. Seasonal 8 mos ahead. Accepts disk. No sidebars. Prefers RSV or NAB. Guidelines; copy for 10x13 SAE/5 stamps.

Poetry: Buys 10/yr. Light verse, traditional; 3-12 lines; $6. Submit max. 4 poems.

Tips: "Be familiar with at least three past issues."

+SABBATH SCHOOL LEADERSHIP, 55 W. Oak Ridge Dr. (301)791-7000x2547. Fax (301)790-9734. E-mail: fcrumbly@rhpa.org. Faith Johnson Crumbly, ed.

Denominational; nurtures, educates and supports adult Sabbath school leaders by providing program helps, resources, instructional material, and networking opportunities. Open to freelance. Complete ms. Pays on publication (on acceptance for solicited material) 1st rts. Articles 70-800 wds. Responds in 6-8 wks. Seasonal 4-6 mos ahead. Requires disk. Guidelines/theme list; copy.

SERMON NOTES, 1420 Osborne St., Ste. 10, Humboldt TN 38343. (901)784-9239. Fax (901)784-8154. E-mail: stevemay@sermonnotes.com. Website: http://www. sermonnotes.com. Alderson Press. Stephen May, ed. Sermon helps for ministers. Bimonthly mag; 64 pgs; circ 5,000. Subscription $39. Est. 1994. 25% freelance. Complete ms/cover letter; fax/e-mail query OK. Pays $35-50 for articles & sermons ($5 for illustrations on publication for one-time rts. Sermons & articles (8/yr) 1,500 wds; illustrations 80-100 wds); book reviews 500 wds ($20). Responds in 5 wks. Seasonal 4 mos ahead. Accepts reprints (tell when/where appeared). Prefers disk. Sidebars OK. Prefers NIV. Guidelines/theme list; copy $2/6x9 SAE. (Ads)

> **Fillers:** Buys 12/yr. Cartoons, short humor or church newsletter ideas. Pays $15.

> **Columns/Departments:** Buys 6/yr. Q & A (interview with Christian leader), 1,000-1,500 wds; Pastor's Library (book or product review), 500 wds. Pays $35-50.

> **Tips:** "We are always interested in sermons. Right now we have an even greater interest in articles about church growth, preaching, or about a particular minister who is pastoring a growing church of any size." Also publishes on diskette and online.

#SINGLE ADULT MINISTRIES JOURNAL, Box 62056, Colorado Springs CO 80962. (800)487-4726. Fax (719)533-3041. E-mail: 70702.1001@compuserve. com. Cook Communications Ministries. Jene Jackson, ed. For pastors and lay leaders involved in ministry with single adults. Bimonthly journal; 16-24 pgs; circ 5,000. Subscription $24. 5% freelance. Query; fax/e-mail query OK. **USUALLY NO PAYMENT** for 1st rts. Articles 200-2,500 wds (0-4/yr); book reviews 50-300 wds/$15-75. Responds in 6-12 wks. Seasonal 4-6 mos ahead. Prefers disk. Theme list; copy for 9x12 SAE/4 stamps. (Ads)

> **Fillers:** Buys 0-5/yr. Facts, newsbreaks, quotes; 25-200 wds; $10-50.

> **Tips:** "Write to the pastor or leader, not to singles themselves. Interview singles or the leaders who work with them."

*SUNDAY SERMONS, PO Box 3102, Margate NJ 08402. (609)822-9401. Fax (609)822-1638. Ecumenical. J. Colaianni, ed-in-chief. Full-text sermon resource for clergy. Bimonthly bound workbook; 54-60 pgs. 5% freelance. Pays on publication for all rts. Responds in 6 wks. Seasonal 6 mos ahead. Accepts reprints. Prefers disk. Guidelines/theme list; copy for 9x12 SAE. Not in topical listings.

> **Tips:** "Sermons must include several relevant illustrations."

TECHNOLOGIES FOR WORSHIP, PO Box 35, Aurora ON L4G 3H1 Canada. (905)830-4300. Fax (905)853-5096. E-mail: amip@~inforamp.net. Website: http://www.TFWM.com. TWM Media. Neil Sutton, ed. Bimonthly mag; 32-40 pgs; circ. 10,000. Subscription $29.95. 90% freelance. Query; phone/fax/e-mail query OK. **NO PAYMENT** for one-time rts. Articles 700-1,200 wds. Responds in

2 wks. Seasonal 2 mos ahead. Accepts simultaneous submissions & reprints (tell when/where appeared). Accepts disk. Some sidebars. Free guidelines/theme list/copy. (Ads)

Special Needs: Technologies: audio, video, music, computers, broadcast, lighting, and drama; 750-2,500 wds.

Tips: Call the editor to discuss idea for article or column. Should know a lot about today's technologies.

THEOLOGY TODAY, PO Box 29, Princeton NJ 08542. (609)497-7714. Fax (609)497-7870. Submit to The Editor. Explores key issues, current thoughts and trends in the fields of religion and theology. Quarterly jour; 144-160 pgs; circ 13,000+. Subscription $24. Little unsolicited accepted. Complete ms/cover letter; phone query OK. Pays to $200 on publication for all rts. Articles 13-17 manuscript pgs; book reviews 500-750 pgs. Responds in several wks. Seasonal 1 yr ahead. No disk. Sidebars OK. Guidelines; free copy. (Display ads)

Poetry: Buys 12/yr. Free verse, traditional; $50. Submit max. 5 poems.

Tips: "We rarely accept unsolicited material, but do look for new talent. The best route to acceptance is strong familiarity with the journal and types of articles we publish. We expect exclusive language."

TODAY'S CHRISTIAN PREACHER, 40 Berkshire Ct., Wyomissing PA 19610-1224. (610)372-1111. Fax (610)372-1122. E-mail: Jerry@netmpi.clrs.com. Marketing Partners. Jerry Thacker, ed. To provide material on current topics to help preachers in their personal lives. Quarterly mag; 24 pgs; circ 25,000. Free subscription. Est. 1993. 20% freelance. Complete ms/cover letter; fax query OK. Pays $150 on publication for one-time or simultaneous rts. Not copyrighted. Articles 800-1,000 wds (10-15/yr). Responds in 3-4 wks. Seasonal 1 yr ahead. Accepts simultaneous submissions & reprints (tell when/where appeared). Prefers disk. Sidebars OK. Prefers KJV. Guidelines; copy for 9x12SAE/3stamps. (Ads)

TODAY'S PARISH, Box 180, Mystic CT 06355. (860)536-2611. Fax (860)572-0788. E-mail: ttpubsedit@aol.com.Catholic. Daniel Connors, ed. Practical ideas and issues relating to parish life, management and ministry. Mag published 7X/yr; 40 pgs; circ 14,800. Subscription $22.95. 25% freelance. Query or complete ms. Pays $75-100 on publication for 1st rts. Articles 800-1,800 wds (15/yr). Responds 13 wks. Seasonal 6 mos ahead. Guidelines; copy for 9x12 SASE.

+VITAL MINISTRY, PO Box 481, 1515 Cascade Ave., Loveland CO 80538. (970)669-3836. Fax (970)679-4372. E-mail: krector@grouppublishing.com. Website: http://www.grouppublishing.com. Group Publishing, Inc. Kristi Rector, asst. ed. For senior pastors and church leaders who provide vision and cultivate the spiritual life of the church; practical. Mag; 45 pgs; circ 25,000. 70% freelance. Query or complete ms/cover letter; fax/e-mail query OK. Pays $40-250 on acceptance for all rts. Articles 500-1,700 wds. Responds in 4-8 wks. Seasonal 5 mos ahead. Accepts disk. Sidebars OK. Guidelines; copy $2/9x12 SAE/ 5 stamps. (Ads)

Fillers: Buys 5-10/yr. Cartoons, games, ideas. Pays $15-35.

Columns/Departments: Family Ministry, Effective Outreach, Meaningful Worship, Preaching & Teaching, Staff & Volunteers, Practical Discipleship, all 200-400 wds. Pays $40-50.

Tips: "We want new and fresh, cutting-edge ideas and articles."

#VOICE OF THE VINEYARD, PO Box 18329, Anaheim CA 92817. (714)777-1433. Fax (714)777-8841. E-mail: vov@earthlink.net. Assn. of Vineyard Churches. Jon Bogart, ed. Quarterly mag; 24 pgs; circ. 40,000. Subscription $12. 5% freelance. Query; fax/e-mail query OK. Pays negotiable rates on publication for 1st rts. Articles 750-1,200 wds; book reviews 300 wds. Responds in 2 wks. Accepts simultaneous submissions & reprints (tell when/where appeared). Requires disk. Kill fee, Prefers NIV. Sidebars OK. Copy for 9x12 SAE/2 stamps. (Ads)

> **Fillers:** Anecdotes, cartoons, facts, games, ideas, jokes, newsbreaks, quizzes, quotes, short humor, word puzzles; 50 wds.

#WCA MONTHLY, PO Box 3188, Barrington IL 60011-5046. (847)765-0070. Fax (847)765-5046. E-mail: BraoudaP@willowcreek.org. Website: http://www.willowcreek.org. Willow Creek Assn. Paul Braoudakis, mng ed. For church leaders who are willing to take risks for the sake of the gospel. Bimonthly newsletter; 16-20 pgs; circ. 6,000. Subscription $29. 10% freelance. Query/clips; phone/fax/e-mail query OK. Pays $25 on publication for all rts. Articles 500-1,000 wds; book/music reviews 500 wds, video reviews 300 wds. Responds in 2 wks. Seasonal 2 mos ahead. Accepts simultaneous submissions & reprints (tell when/where appeared). Requires disk. Some sidebars. Prefers NIV. Free copy. (Ads)

> **Fillers:** Accepts many. Cartoons, ideas, short humor; 50-75 wds. Pays $10.
>
> **Columns/Departments:** On the Lighter Side (humor), 100 wds; News From the Frontlines (creative ministries within the church), 50-100 wds; Strategic Trends (trends from growing churches), 200-250 wds. Pays $10-25. Complete ms.
>
> **Tips:** "Any articles that pertain to doing a seeker-sensitive type of ministry will be considered."

*WORD & WORLD: Theology for Christian Ministry, 2481 Como Ave., St. Paul MN 55108. (612)641-3482. Fax (612)641-3354. E.L.C.A./Luther Northwestern Theological Seminary. Frederick J. Gaiser, ed. Addresses ecclesiastical and secular issues from a theological perspective and addresses pastors and church leaders with the best fruits of theological research. Quarterly journal; 104 pgs; circ 3,100. Subscription $18. 10% freelance. Complete ms/cover letter; phone query OK. Pays $50 on publication for all rts. Articles 5,000-6,000 wds. Responds in 2-8 wks. Guidelines/theme list; copy $5.

> **Tips:** "Most open to general articles. We look for serious theology addressed clearly and interestingly to people in the practice of ministry. Creativity and usefulness in ministry are highly valued."

#WORSHIP LEADER, 107 Kenner Ave., Nashville TN 37205-2207. (615)386-3011. Fax (615)385-4112 or (615)386-3380. E-mail: mriddle@ccmcom.com. CCM Communications. Melissa L. Riddle, mng ed. Intellectual tone with practical advice on leading worship. Bimonthly mag; 55 pgs; circ 41,000. Subscription $19.95. 20-40% freelance. Query/clips or complete ms. Pays .20/wd on publication for all rts. Articles 800-2,000 wds (15/yr). Responds in 6-8 wks. Seasonal 6-8 mos ahead. Kill fee 50%. Prefers disk. Sidebars OK. Prefers NIV. Guidelines. (Ads)

> **Fillers:** Buys 6-12/yr. Anecdotes, quotes; 150-300 wds.

Columns/Departments: Buys 6-12/yr. Viewpoint (op/ed), 600-800 wds; Putting it All Together (experience with church), 1,200 wds. Several others, see guidelines.

Tips: "We need writers from all parts of the country to do profiles of churches, worship leaders/ministers of music in their home cities. Also, suggest articles on worship applications outside the church."

YOUR CHURCH, 465 Gundersen Dr., Carol Stream IL 60188. (630)260-6200. Fax (630)260-0114. E-mail: YCEditor@aol.com. Christianity Today Inc. Phyllis Ten Elshof, mng ed. Focuses on church business/administration, purchasing and facilities management. Bimonthly mag; 80+ pgs; circ 150,000. Subscription free to qualified readers. 20% freelance. Query or complete ms/cover letter; fax/e-mail query OK. Query for electronic submissions. Pays $100 & up on acceptance for 1st rts. Articles 1,000-1,500 wds (60/yr). Responds in 2-4 wks. Seasonal 6 mos ahead. Accepts reprints (tell when/where appeared). Prefers disk. Kill fee 50%. Sidebars OK. Prefers NIV. Guidelines/theme list; copy for $1 postage. (Ads)

Fillers: Cartoons, $150.

Columns/Departments: Query. Pays $100.

Special Needs: Church management articles; audio/visual equipment; books/ curriculum resources; music equipment; church products; furnishings; office equipment; computers/software.

Tips: "Almost all articles are assigned to writers with expertise in a certain area. Write and ask for an assignment; tell your strengths, interests and background."

** This periodical was #42 on the 1997 Top 50 Christian Publishers list.

#YOUTHWORKER, 1224 Greenfield Dr., El Cajon CA 92021. (619)440-2333. Fax (619)440-4939. E-mail: urb@youthspecialties.com. Website: http://www.youth-specialties.com. Youth Specialties Inc. Dave Urbanski, ed. For youth workers/church and parachurch. Monthly journal; 72 pgs; circ 13,200. Subscription $39.95. 90% freelance. Query; phone query OK. Pays $100-150 on acceptance for 1st & reprint rts. Articles 2,000-3,500 wds (30/yr). Responds in 5 wks. Seasonal 10 mos ahead. Accepts reprints. Kill fee $50. Guidelines/theme list; copy $3/10x13 SAE.

Columns/Departments: Buys 10/yr. High School Minister; Middle School Minister; 2,000-3,000 wds; $100-150.

Special Needs: Upcoming themes include Music in Ministry, Growing Up: pitfalls, conflict, conflict, expectations.

Tips: "Read Youthworker; imbibe its tone (professional, though not academic; conversational, though not chatty). Query me with specific, focused ideas that conform to our needs. Writer needs to be a youth minister."

** This periodical was #60 on the 1997 Top 50 Christian Publishers list. (#46 in 1995, #53 in 1994) Also 1995 EPA Award of Merit—Christian Ministry.

TEEN/YOUNG ADULT MARKETS

+ALIVE!, PO Box 779, Minneapolis MN 55440-0779. (612)338-0500. Fax (612)335-1299. E-mail: alive@graham-assn.org. Website: http://www.graham-assn.org/bgea/alive/home.htm. Billy Graham Evangelistic Assn. Ann McCaffrey Elder, ed. Evangelistic publication for teens. Quarterly mag; 16 pgs; circ 50,000+.

Subscription $5. 10% freelance. Complete ms/cover letter; no electronic submissions. Pays on acceptance (solicited) or publication (unsolicited) for all, some first, and electronic rts. Articles 200-900 wds. Responds in 4-6 wks. Seasonal 10-12 mos ahead. Accepts disk. Sidebars OK. Prefers NIV. Guidelines; 2 copies for 9x12 SAE/3 stamps.

Poetry: By teens only. Submit max. 10. poems.

Special Needs: We are especially interested in teen-aged writers.

Tips: "All articles must have a take-away value. Keep in mind that our focus is evangelistic."

BEAUTIFUL CHRISTIAN TEEN, #7 Bergoo Rd., Webster Springs WV 26288. (304)847-7537. (304)847-7552. Baptist. Kimberly Short Wolfe, ed. Conservative publication for Christian teen girls. Bimonthly mag; 24-28 pgs; circ under 5,000. 75% freelance. Complete ms/cover letter. **NO PAYMENT.** Columns & fiction. Guidelines; copy $3. (Ads)

#BREAKAWAY, 8605 Explorer Dr., Colorado Springs CO 80920. (719)548-4576. Fax (719)531-3499. Focus on the Family. Michael Ross, ed. The 14-year-old, unchurched teen (boy) in the public school is our target; boys 11-18 yrs. Monthly mag; 24-32 pgs; circ 90,000. Subscription $15. 60-70% freelance. Complete ms/cover letter; phone query OK. Pays .12-.15/wd on acceptance for all, 1st, one-time & reprint rts. Articles 400-1,800 wds (40/yr); fiction 1,200-2,200 wds (15/yr); music reviews, 300 wds, $30-40. Responds in 5 wks. Seasonal 8 mos ahead. Accepts simultaneous submissions & reprints. Kill fee 33-50%. Guidelines/theme list; copy for 9x12 SAE/3 stamps. (Ads)

Fillers: Buys 50/yr. Cartoons ($75), facts, quizzes; 200-600 wds; .20-.25/wd.

Columns/Departments: Buys 12/yr. Plugged In (devotional); 700-900 wds.

Tips: "Need strong lead. Brevity and levity a must. Have a teen guy or two read it. Make sure the language is up-to-date, but not overly hip."

** This periodical was #9 on the 1997 Top 50 Christian Publishers list. (#3 in 1996, #6 in 1995, #5 in 1994)

#BRIO, 8605 Explorer Dr., Colorado Springs CO 80920. (719)548-4577. Fax (719)531-3499. Focus on the Family. Susie Shellenberger, ed; submit to Susan Stevens. For teen girls, 12-16 yrs. Monthly mag; 32 pgs; circ 170,000. Subscription $15. 60% freelance. Complete ms/cover letter; phone query OK. Pays .08-.15/wd on acceptance for 1st rts. Articles 800-1,000 wds (10/yr); fiction 1,200-2,000 wds (10/yr). Responds in 4-9 wks. Seasonal 5 mos ahead. Kill fee $100. Guidelines; copy $1.50. (Ads)

Fillers: Buys 15/yr. Cartoons, facts, ideas, quizzes, short humor; 50-200 wds. Pays $75-100.

Special Needs: All topics of interest to female teens are welcome: boys, make-up, dating, weight, ordinary girls who have the extraordinary, female adjustments to puberty, etc. Also teen-related female fiction.

Tips: "Study at least 3 issues of *Brio* before submitting. We're looking for a certain, fresh, hip-hop conversational style. Most open to fiction, articles and quizzes."

** This periodical was #58 on the 1997 Top 50 Christian Publishers list. (#60 in 1996, #61 in 1995, #37 in 1994) Also 1995 EPA Award of Merit—Youth.

#CAMPUS LIFE, 465 Gundersen Dr., Carol Stream IL 60188. (708)260-6200. Fax

(708)260-0114. E-mail: cledit@aol.com. Website: http://www.christianity.net/campuslife. Christianity Today, Inc. Christopher Lutes, mng. ed. Seeks to help high school students and early college students navigate adolescence with their faith intact; not overtly religious. Monthly (9X) mag; 62 pgs; circ 100,000. Subscription $19.95. 35% freelance. Query/clips; fax query OK. Pays .15-.20/wd on acceptance for 1st or one-time rts. Articles 750-1,500 (5-10/yr); fiction 1,000-2,000 wds (1-5/yr). Responds in 5-9 wks. Seasonal 5 mos ahead. Accepts simultaneous submissions & reprints (tell when/where appeared). Accepts disk. Kill fee 50%. Sidebars OK. Guidelines; copy $3/9x12 SAE/3 stamps. (Ads)

Poetry: Buys 1-5/yr. Free verse; 5-20 lines; $25-50. Submit max. 2 poems.

Fillers: Buys 30 cartoons/yr; $50; anecdotes, facts, short humor, 25-250 wds, $10-50.

Columns/Departments: Buys 20/yr. Making the Grade (study tips), 100-250 wds, $25-50.

Tips: "Most open to as-told-to stories. Interview students and get their stories."

** This periodical was #37 on the 1996 Top 50 Christian Publishers list. (#49 in 1995, #63 in 1994)

CERTAINTY, 1300 N. Meacham Rd., Schaumburg IL 60173-4888. (847)843-1600. Fax (847)843-3757. Regular Baptist Press. Joan E. Alexander, ed. For senior high youth (15-18); conservative/fundamental. Weekly take-home paper. Note: This periodical is being redesigned as we go to press. Send for new guidelines before submitting.

CHALLENGE (GA), 4200 N. Point Pkwy, Alpharetta GA 30202-4176. (770)410-6000. Fax (770)410-6018. Website: http://www.namb.net. North American Mission Board/Southern Baptist. Joe Conway, ed. Missions interest articles for young men, ages 12-18. Monthly mag; 24 pgs; circ 21,000. Subscription $13.08. 40% freelance. Query/clips. Pays $20-100 on publication for 1st rts. Articles 700-1,000 wds (36/yr); fiction 700-1,000 wds (12/yr); book/music/video reviews 250 wds, $20. Responds in 4-6 wks. Seasonal 8 mos ahead. Accepts simultaneous submissions. Accepts disk. Sidebars OK. Prefers NAS. Guidelines/theme list; copy for 9x12 SAE/3 stamps.

Special Needs: Internet computer innovation for youth.

Tips: "Looking for articles of male youth interest and articles with a Christian testimony, especially sports. Mission stories involving youth are also very good. Present relevant youth issues in an entertaining way."

CHALLENGE (IL), 1300 N. Meacham Rd., Schaumburg IL 60173-4888. (847)843-1600. Fax (847)843-3757. Regular Baptist Press. Joan E. Alexander, ed. For junior high youth (12-14); conservative/fundamental. Weekly take-home paper. Note: This periodical is being redesigned as we go to press. Send for new guidelines before submitting.

CHRISTTEEN MAGAZINE, PO Box 1519, Inglewood CA 90308. (213)750-7573. Franklin Publications. Sharon Jones, mng. ed. For African-American teens and their parents. Quarterly mag. Subscription $15. Est. 1994. Complete ms/cover letter. **PAYS IN COPIES** (for now) for 1st rts. Articles 500-1,100 wds (18/yr); open to fiction; book, music, movie reviews, 200 wds. Responds in 6-8 wks. Seasonal 6 mos ahead. Accepts simultaneous submissions & reprints. Wants sidebars. Prefers KJV or NIV. Guidelines; copy $3/9x12 SAE/5 stamps.

Poetry: From teens only. Free verse, traditional. Submit max. 2 poems.

Fillers: Various; 25-150 wds.

Columns/Departments: Teenview (by teens), 400-500 wds; Education (info on career planning, college, etc.), 500-850 wds.; The Way They Do It (youth programs), 400 wds; Parent Exchange (encouraging info/testimonies by parents), 500-850 wds; Let's Celebrate (holidays/special ways to celebrate), 400-500 wds.

Tips: "All departments & feature articles open (you don't have to be African-American to write for us). Write in a down-to-earth style, with lots of anecdotes, and don't use a lot of slang."

*THE CONQUEROR, 8855 Dunn Rd., Hazelwood MO 63042. (314)837-7300. United Pentecostal Church, Intl. Nathan C. Reever, ed. For teenagers in the denomination. Bimonthly mag; 16 pgs; circ 6,000. Subscription $7.50. 90% freelance. Complete ms. Pays $20-30 on publication for various rts. Articles & fiction (many/yr) 600-800. Responds in 10 wks. Seasonal 4 mos ahead. Accepts simultaneous submissions & reprints. Prefers KJV. Guidelines; copy for 11x14 SAE/2 stamps.

Fillers: Various.

Tips: "Articles should be written with the idea of strict morals, standards and ethics in mind."

CROSS WALK, 6401 The Paseo, Kansas City MO 64131. (816)333-7000x2211. Fax (816)333-4315. E-mail: crosswalk@nazarene.org. Website: http://www.nazarene. org. Holiness denominations. James K. Hampton, ed. Written by teens (and youth leaders) for teens. Weekly take-home paper; circ 35,000. Subscription $7.60. Est. 1995. By assignment only. Query only. Pays on acceptance for all rts. Responds in 2 wks. Kill fee 50%. No sidebars. Guidelines; copy for 9x12 SAE/2 stamps.

Tips: "Open only to a youth worker (professional or volunteer) and five teens from his/her youth group. The youth leader will write devotionals for Saturday and Sunday, and the five teens will write devotionals for Monday-Friday." Writers must be subscribers.

*DEVO'ZINE, 1908 Grand Ave., Nashville TN 37202-9890. (615)340-7247. Fax (615)340-7006. E-mail: 102615.3145@compuserve.com. The Upper Room. Robin Pippin, ed. Devotional; to help teens (12-18) maintain their maximum connection with God and other Christians. Bimonthly mag; 64 pgs; circ 58,000. Subscription $16.95. Est. 1996. 100% freelance. Query; phone/fax/e-mail query OK. Pays $20 for meditations, $75 for feature articles (assigned) on acceptance for one-time, electronic rts (newspaper, software-driven format). Meditations 150-250 wds (350/yr), articles 350-500 wds; book/music/video reviews, 350-500 wds, $75. Responds in 16 wks. Seasonal 6-8 mos ahead. Accepts reprints (tell when/where appeared). Accepts disk. Kill fee. Sidebars OK. Prefers NRSV, NIV, CEV. Guidelines/theme list; copy $1/7x10 SAE.

Poetry: Buys 25-30/yr. Free verse, light verse, haiku, traditional.; to 150 wds. Pays 20. Submit max. 1 poem/theme, 9 themes/issue.

Tips: " Call with ideas for week-end features related to specific themes."

** This periodical was #6 on the 1997 Top 50 Christian Publishers list.

ESSENTIAL CONNECTIONS, 127 Ninth Ave. N., Nashville TN 37234. (615)251-

5679. Fax (615)251-5091. E-mail: DwayneUlmer@bssb.com. Website: http://www.youthscape.com. Southern Baptist. Dwayne Ulmer, ed.

I.D., 4050 Lee Vance View, Colorado Springs CO 80918. (719)536-0100. Fax (719)536-3296. Cook Communications Ministries. No freelance until 1999.

** 1997 EPA Award of Excellence - Sunday School Take-home paper.

INSIGHT, 55 W. Oak Ridge Dr., Hagerstown MD 21740-7301. (301)791-7000. Fax (301)790-9734. E-mail: INSIGHT@rhpa.org. Review and Herald/Seventh-day Adventist. Lori Peckham, ed. For Adventist teenagers, 14-19 yrs; a forum for teen-authors to share their spiritual triumphs and struggles. Weekly mag; 16 pgs; circ 20,000. Subscription $37.97. 80-90% freelance. Complete ms/cover letter; phone/fax/e-mail query OK. Pays $30-85 on acceptance for one-time rts. Not copyrighted. Articles 500-1,200 wds (120/yr). Responds in 8-10 wks. Seasonal 6 mos ahead. Accepts simultaneous submissions & reprints (tell when/where appeared). Requires disk. Kill fee. Sidebars OK. Prefers NIV. Guidelines; copy for 9x12 SAE/4 stamps. (Ads)

> **Poetry:** Buys to 36/yr. All types; to 1 pg. By teens only.
>
> **Columns/Departments:** Buys 52/yr. Well-Versed (personal story that demonstrates truth of a Bible verse), 1,000-1,500 wds; On the Edge (drama in real life), 800-1,500 wds, $75-125. It Happened To Me (personal experience in first-person), 600-900 wds, $50-100. So I Said (true shorts or opinion pcs.), 200-400 wds, $40-60. How I Became Friends with God, 600-900 wds, $50-100; Service with a Smile, 600-1,500 wds, $50-125.
>
> **Contest:** Sponsors a fiction & poetry contest; includes a category for students under 21. Prizes to $250. May deadline (may vary). Send SASE for rules.
>
> **Tips:** "Send us stories from a teen's perspective that clearly illustrate a Christian point. We want material from teen authors; but we also encourage freelance authors to share with us teen-relevant articles and stories. "
>
> ** This periodical was #5 on the 1997 Top 50 Christian Publishers list. (#8 in 1996, #18 in 1995, #6 in 1994)

#LISTEN, 55 W. Oak Ridge Dr., Hagerstown MD 21740. (301)745-3888. Fax (301)790-9734. E-mail: 74617.3102@compuserve.com. The Health Connection. Lincoln Steed, ed. To educate teens against alcohol/drugs in a uniquely positive way; emphasizes moral values in a secular tone. Monthly mag; 32 pgs; circ. 65,000. Subscription $24.95. 75% freelance. Query; phone/fax query OK. Pays .05-.10/wd on acceptance for 1st or reprint rts. Articles 1,000-1,200 wds (30-50/yr); fiction 1,200 wds (20/yr). Responds in 9 wks. Seasonal 6 mos ahead. Accepts simultaneous submissions & reprints (tell when/where appeared). Accepts disk. Sidebars OK. Guidelines; copy $1/9x12 SAE/2 stamps. (Ads)

> ** This periodical was #21 on the 1997 Top 50 Christian Publishers List. (#15 in 1996)

+RIGHTSIDE UP MAGAZINE, PO Box 2041, Grand Rapids MI 49501-2041. Website: http://www.gospelcom.net/uplook/home.html. Uplook Ministries. Est. 1997. Quarterly; circ. 1,500. Not in topical listings.

THE ROCK, 4050 Lee Vance View, Colorado Springs CO 80918-7100. "We are not currently accepting freelance material; perhaps in a year or two."

#SHARING THE VICTORY, 8701 Leeds Rd., Kansas City MO 64129-1680.

Christian Century Foundation. Victoria Rebeck, mng. ed. For clergy seeking thoughtful, practical advice for parish ministry challenges. Bimonthly mag; 48 pgs; circ 6,600. Subscription $15. 60% freelance. Query/clips or complete ms/cover letter; fax query OK. Pays $50-100 on publication for all rts. Articles 1,200-1,800 wds (60/yr); book reviews, 500 wds (keep book). Responds in 6 wks. Seasonal 8 mos ahead. Kill fee 50%. Sidebars OK. Prefers disk. Sidebars OK. Prefers NRSV. Guidelines/theme list; copy for 9x12 SAE/4 stamps. (Ads)

> **Columns/Departments:** Buys 15/yr. Tricks of the Trade (brief practical tips), 400 wds.; Women of the Word (about women pastors), 2,000 wds; Congregational Computing (software for congregational ministry), 2,000 wds. Complete ms. Pays $20-60.
>
> **Special Needs:** Leadership, lay ministry, reaching men, maintaining and designing church buildings.
>
> **Contest:** Sponsors a sermon contest. Write for qualifications and requirements.
>
> **Tips:** "Most open to Reflections on Ministry; pastors offering personal thoughts on a real-life experience they have had. Writer should understand the life and intellectual abilities of the mainline pastor. Should have a sophisticated theology. Articles should not be preachy."

*CHRISTIAN RECREATION, 127 Ninth Ave. N, Nashville TN 37234. (615)251-3841. Southern Baptist. Submit to The Editor. Focus is on using recreation in all church programs. Quarterly mag; 60 pgs; circ 17,000. 70% freelance. Query or complete ms/cover letter; fax query OK. Pays .055/wd on acceptance for all or one-time rts. Articles 800 wds; fiction (scripts, skits, puppet plays and monologues) 800-1,200 wds. Responds in 5 wks. Accepts simultaneous submissions. Prefers disk. Guidelines; copy for 9x12 SASE.

*THE CHRISTIAN SENTINEL, Box 11322, Philadelphia PA 19137. (215)289-7885. Fax (215)289-8808. Calvary Chapel. Jackie Alnor, ed. Leaders-oriented publication exploring Christian apologetics issues; cults; issues affecting the church. Quarterly mag; 36 pgs; circ 10,000. 10% freelance. Query/clips. **NO PAYMENT** for 1st rts. Articles 100-700 wds; book reviews 500 wds. Responds in 2 wks. Sidebars OK. Copy for 9x12 SAE/2 stamps.

> **Fillers:** Accepts 10/yr. Cartoons.
>
> **Special Needs:** Heresy in the church; defense of the faith; signs of the times; eye-witness accounts of the introduction of lying signs and wonders in the church.
>
> **Tips:** "Be called to a discernment ministry; be provoked by evil and false teachings. Most open to news. Be big on fact, short on opinion."

#CHURCH ADMINISTRATION, MSN 157, 127 9th Ave. N., Nashville TN 37234. (615)251-2062. Fax (615)251-3866. Southern Baptist. Submit to The Editor. Practical pastoral ministry/church administration ideas for pastors and staff. Monthly mag; 50 pgs; circ 12,000. 15% freelance. Query. Pays .065/wd on acceptance for all rts. Articles 1,600-2,000 wds (60/yr). Responds in 8 wks. Guidelines/copy for #10 SAE/2 stamps.

> **Columns/Departments:** Buys 60/yr. Weekday Dialogue; Minister's Mate; Secretary's File; all 2,000 wds.

CHURCH BYTES, 8992 Preston Rd., Ste. 110-120, Frisco TX 75034-3964. (972)335-3201. Fax (972)377-9705. E-mail: mnsurratt@aol.com. Deerhaven

(816)921-0909. Fax (816)921-8755. E-mail: stv@fca.org. Website: http://www.
fca/org. Fellowship of Christian Athletes (Protestant and Catholic). John Dod-
deridge, ed. Equipping and encouraging athletes and coaches to take their faith
seriously, in and out of competition. Monthly (Sept-May, 9X) mag; 32 pgs; circ
60,000. Subscription $18. 50% freelance. Query only/clips. Pays $50-200 on
publication for 1st rts. Articles 500-1,500 wds (5-20/yr). Responds in 9 wks.
Seasonal 3 mos ahead. Accepts reprints (pays 50%). Kill fee. Sidebars OK.
Guidelines; copy $1/9x12 SAE/3 stamps. (Ads)

Poetry: Buys 9/yr. Free verse; 8-24 lines; $25. Submit max. 3 poems.

Special Needs: Articles on FCA camp experiences (40th anniversary of
camps). All articles must have an athletic angle.

Tips: "FCA angle important; pro & college athletes and coaches giving solid
Christian testimony; we run stories according to athletic season; need arti-
cles/poetry on female athletes."

** 1997 EPA Award of Merit—Organizational.

#SPIRIT, Lectionary-based Weekly for Catholic Teens, 1884 Randolph Ave., St. Paul
MN 55105-1700. (612)690-7005. Fax: (612)690-7039. Catholic. Therese Sher-
lock, CSJ, mng. ed. For the religious education of high schoolers (14-18 yrs).
Weekly newsletter; 4 pgs; circ 26,000. 50% freelance. Query. Pays $75-150 on
publication for all rts. Articles & fiction 1,100-1,200 wds (12 ea./yr). Responds in
6-13 wks. Seasonal 6 mos ahead. Accepts simultaneous submissions. Free guide-
lines/copy.

STRAIGHT, 8121 Hamilton Ave., Cincinnati OH 45231. (513)931-4050. Fax
(513)931-0950. Standard Publishing. Heather Wallace, ed. For Christian teens
(12-19 yrs). Weekly take-home paper; 12 pgs; circ 30,000. Subscription $11.99.
90% freelance. Complete ms/cover letter; no phone/fax query. Pays .05-.07/wd on
acceptance for 1st, one-time, or reprint rts. Articles to 900-1,100 wds (40/yr);
fiction 900-1,500 wds (100/yr). Responds in 6-8 wks. Seasonal 9-12 mos ahead.
Accepts simultaneous submissions & reprints. No disk. Some sidebars. Prefers
NIV. Guidelines/theme list; copy for #10 SAE/2 stamps.

Poetry: Buys 20/yr. Free verse, light verse, traditional; from teens only; $10.
Submit max. 5 poems.

Fillers: Buys 10-15/yr. Prayers, short humor, 300-700 wds.

Columns/Departments: Buys 12/yr. Straight Spotlight (teens making a difference), 900-1,000 wds.

Tips: "Request to be put on our theme list. Writers should have a good grasp
of what today's teens are like. How do they act? What do they like/dislike?
What are their concerns?"

** This periodical was #17 on the 1997 Top 50 Christian Publishers list. (#13
in 1996, #5 in 1995, #17 in 1994)

#STUDENT LEADERSHIP JOURNAL, Box 7895, Madison WI 53707-7895.
(608)274-9001x425. Fax (608)274-7882. E-mail: slj@ivcf.org. Website:
http://www.gospelcom.net/iv. InterVarsity Christian Fellowship. Jeff Yourison, ed.
Undergraduate college student Christian leaders, single, ages 18-36. Quarterly
journal; 32 pgs; circ 8,500. Subscription $20. 20-30% freelance. Query/clips.
Pays $35-125 on acceptance for 1st or one-time rts. Articles to 2,000 wds (1/yr);
fiction to 1,500 wds (0-1/yr), $25-100; book reviews 150-400 wds, $25-50. Re-

sponds in 16 wks. Seasonal 8 mos ahead. Accepts reprints. Guidelines/theme list; copy $3/9x12 SAE/4 stamps. (Ads)

Poetry: Buys 4-6/yr. Avant-garde, free verse; to 15 lines; $25-50. Submit max. 5 poems.

Fillers: Buys 0-5/yr. Facts, games, party ideas, quizzes; to 200 wds; $10-50.

Columns/Departments: Buys 6-10/yr. Collegiate Trends, 20-100 wds; Student Leadership Network, 500-800 wds; Chapter Strategy (how-to planning strategy for campus groups), 500-800; $10-75. Query.

Special Needs: Campus issues/trends/ministry/spiritual growth/leadership; Kingdom values.

Tips: "Most open to main features targeted to college-age students. Be upbeat, interesting and fresh. Use both Scripture and life illustrations."

** 1997 & 1996 EPA Award of Merit—Christian Ministry.

TAKE FIVE, 1445 Boonville Ave., Springfield MO 65802. (417)862-2781x4359. Fax (417)862-8558. E-mail: YouthCurr@ag.org. Assemblies of God. Tammy Bicket, youth ed. A daily devotional for teens, grades 7-12. Quarterly booklet; 112 pgs; circ 30,000. Subscription $8. 80% freelance. Write for assignment. Pays $15/devotion on acceptance for all rts (one-time rts for poetry). Responds in 13 wks. Seasonal 15 mos ahead. Accepts simultaneous submissions & reprints on poetry only. Prefers disk. Guidelines; copy for 6x9 SAE/3 stamps.

Poetry: Buys 36/yr. Any type; 8-20 lines; $15. Submit max. 5 poems. "Poetry is held on file unless writer requests its return."

Special Needs: Photos; photos of ethnic groups are a plus. Poetry from teens (SASE required for return).

Tips: "All devotional writing is done on assignment to Assemblies of God writers only. Sample devotional or similar writing can be submitted for editors evaluation and for future consideration when writing assignments are made."

*****TEENAGE CHRISTIAN,** PO Box 549, Murray KY 42071-0549. (800)637-2613. Church of Christ/Christian Publishing Inc. Jim Pounders, ed. Spiritual answers to tough questions for Christian teens (13-19 yrs). Bimonthly mag; 32 pgs; circ 10,500. Subscription $14.95. 50% freelance. Complete ms/cover letter. Pays $35 on publication for one-time & reprint rts. Articles 600-1,200 wds (20/yr); fiction 600-1,500 wds (9/yr). Responds in 3-4 wks. Accepts disk. Seasonal 6 mos ahead. Accepts simultaneous submissions & reprints (tell when/where appeared). Rarely uses sidebars. Prefers NIV. Copy for 9x12 SAE/$2.50. (Ads)

Poetry: Buys 3-4/yr. Free verse; 10-25 lines; $15-25. Submit max. 5 poems.

Fillers: Buys 5-10/yr. Cartoons, quizzes, prayers, word puzzles; 150-350 wds; $15-25.

Tips: "Most open to practical nonfiction. Fiction should be excellent, realistic, and up to date."

TEEN LIFE (AG), 1445 Boonville Ave., Springfield MO 65802-1894. (417)862-2781. Fax (417)862-6059. E-mail: YouthCurr@ag.org. Assemblies of God. Teen Life Editor. To emphasize Christian living through biblical principles for Spirit-filled young people ages 12-19. Quarterly mag; 64 pgs; circ 50,000. Subscription $10. 25% freelance. Complete ms/cover letter; no phone/fax query. Pays $50-100 ($25-50 for fiction) or .05/wd on acceptance for 1st, reprint or simultaneous rts. Articles 1,000-1,200 wds (10/yr); fiction 500-800 wds (15/yr). Responds in 6-8 wks. Seasonal 18 mos ahead. Accepts simultaneous submissions & reprints (tell when/where appeared). Prefers disk. Sidebars OK. Prefers NIV. Guidelines/theme list; copy for 9x12 SAE/2 stamps

Fillers: Buys 1-2/yr. Cartoons, facts, newsbreaks, Top 10 lists; 100-250 wds; no payment.

Special Needs: We like to highlight actual events/testimonies of teens: what they're doing in their church or community.

Tips: "The best opening is in the area of short story, true or fiction. It should be relevant to what teens are facing, but not provide pat, clichéd answers. Be willing to address the tough issues. Good humor pieces always needed."

** This periodical was #37 on the 1996 Top 50 Christian Publishers list. (#37 in 1995, #11 in 1994)

*TEEN LIFE (UPC), 8855 Dunn Rd., Hazelwood MO 63042. (314)837-7304. United Pentecostal Church. R. M. Davis, ed. For teens 13-15 yrs. Weekly take-home paper. 90% freelance. Complete ms. Pays $8-25 on publication for all rts. Articles 800-1,800 wds (up to 120/yr); fiction 1,200-1,800 wds (up to 120/yr). Seasonal 9 mos ahead. Accepts simultaneous submissions & reprints. Guidelines; free copy.

Poetry: Accepts 30/yr; $3-12.

Tips: "Most open to good stories and articles for a traditional, fundamental audience."

#TEEN POWER, PO Box 36640, Colorado Springs CO 80936. (719)533-3044. Fax (719)533-3045. Cook Communications/Scripture Press. Sarah M. Peterson, ed. To help young teens (11-15 yrs) explore ways Jesus relates to them in everyday life. Weekly take-home paper; 8 pgs. Subscription $11.50. 100% freelance. Complete ms/cover letter. Pays $25-120 on acceptance for one-time or simultaneous rts. Articles 300-1,000 wds (75/yr); fiction & true stories 600-1,200 wds (75/yr— $45-120). Responds in 13 wks. Seasonal 6 mos ahead. Accepts simultaneous submissions & reprints (pays .05-.07/wd). Guidelines/theme list/copy for #10 SAE/1 stamp.

Poetry: From teens only. Free verse, light verse, traditional.

Fillers: Buys 10/yr. Cartoons, jokes, prose, quizzes, word puzzles; $15.

Tips: "Looking for fresh, creative true stories, true-to-life fiction and articles. Show how God and the Bible are relevant in the lives of today's teens. Use slice-of-life vignettes. All manuscripts must have a clear, spiritual message." Send Social Security number.

** This periodical was #34 on the 1997 Top 50 Christian Publishers list. (#21 in 1996 & 1995, #41 in 1994)

TEENS ON TARGET, 8855 Dunn Rd., Hazelwood MO 63042. (314)837-7300. Fax (314)837-4503. E-mail: wapeditor@aol.com. Website: http://www.upci.org. Word Aflame Publications. P. Daniel Buford, assoc. ed. For teens 12-14 years. Weekly take-home paper; circ. 7,000. Subscription $4.40. 75% freelance. Complete ms/cover letter. Pays .01-.02/wd on publication for 1st or simultaneous rts. Articles 1,200-1,400 wds; fiction 1,200-1,400 wds (40/yr). Seasonal 1 yr ahead. Accepts simultaneous submissions & reprints. Few sidebars. Prefers KJV. Guidelines; copy for 6x9 SAE/2 stamps.

Fillers: Buys 2-3/yr. Quizzes, word puzzles; $5-12.

Tips: "Articles should be human interest with practical application of Christian principles for 12-14 year olds."

TODAY'S CHRISTIAN TEEN, 40 Berkshire Ct., Wyomissing PA 19610-1224. (610)372-1111. Fax (610)372-1122. E-mail: Jerry@netmpi.clrs.com. Marketing Partners. Jerry Thacker, ed. To help today's Christian teens by presenting material which applies the Bible to contemporary issues; conservative. Quarterly mag; 24 pgs; circ 39,800. Free subscription. 20% freelance. Complete ms/cover letter; fax/e-mail query OK. Pays $150 on publication for first, one-time or reprint rts. Not copyrighted. Articles 800-1,000 wds (4/yr). Responds in 6 wks. Seasonal 6 mos ahead. Accepts reprints (tell when/where appeared). Prefers disk. Sidebars OK. Prefers KJV. Guidelines; copy for 9x12 SAE/4 stamps.

   Contest: Essay contest. Prize is full scholarship to a youth conference for high school students. Send SASE for information.

VISIONS, Lectionary-based Weekly for Catholic Junior Highs, 330 Progress Rd., Dayton OH 45449. (937)847-5900. Fax (937)847-5910. E-mail: pliservice@ aol.com. Website: http://www.pflaum.com. Peter Li, Inc./Catholic. Joan Mitchell, CSJ, mng. ed. Connects young people's real-life experiences—successes and conflicts in family, neighborhood, classroom—with the Sunday gospels; for grades 7-9. Weekly (32X during school yr) take-home paper; circ 140,000. 40% freelance. Query; e-mail query OK. Pays $150 on publication for all rts. Articles (6-8/yr) & fiction (8-10/yr), 900-1,000 wds. Responds in 2-8 wks. Seasonal 4-6 mos ahead. Accepts simultaneous query. Guidelines; copy $1.85.

WITH, The Magazine for Radical Christian Youth, Box 347, Newton KS 67114-0347. (316)283-5100. Fax (316)283-0454. Faith & Life Press/Mennonite, Brethren & Mennonite Brethren. Carol Duerksen (fillers & poetry) & Eddy Hall (articles & fiction), co-eds. For high-school teens (15-18 yrs), Christian and non-Christian. 8 time/yr mag; 32 pgs; circ 6,000. Subscription $18.95. 80% freelance. Query (on first-person and how-to articles); complete ms on others/cover letter; no phone/fax query. Pays .05/wd (.03/wd for reprints) on acceptance for 1st, one-time, simultaneous or reprint rts. Articles 500-1,800 wds (15/yr); fiction 1,000-2,000 wds (15/yr); music reviews, 500 wds, .05/wd (query for assignment). Responds in 4 wks. Seasonal 6 mos ahead. Accepts simultaneous submissions & reprints (tell when/where appeared). No disk. Kill fee 25-50%. Sidebars OK. Prefers NRSV. Guidelines/theme list; copy for 9x12 SAE/4 stamps. Separate guidelines for 1st-person and how-to articles sent only when requested. (Ads)

   Fillers: Buys 20 cartoons/yr; $35-40.

   Contest: Sponsors contests for teen writers only.

   Tips: "Most open to fiction; match upcoming theme."

   ** This periodical was #35 on the 1997 Top 50 Christian Publishers list. (#23 in 1996, #17 in 1995, #12 in 1994) Also 1997 EPA Award of Merit—Youth.

YOU! MAGAZINE, Youth for the Next Millennium, 31194 La Baya Dr., Suite 200, Westlake Village CA 91362-4022. (818)991-1813. Fax (818)991-2024. E-mail: youmag@earthlink.net. Website: http://www/home.earthlink.net/~youmag/. Catholic. Submissions Editor. An alternative teen magazine (13-23 yrs) aimed at bridging the gap between religion and pop culture. Monthly (10X) mag; 35 pgs; circ 35,000. (Youthbeat, a newspaper insert, also available.) Subscription $19.95. 40% freelance. Query; fax/e-mail query OK. **PAYS IN COPIES** for all rts. Articles

900 wds (130/yr); fiction 900 wds (15/yr); book reviews 200 wds; music reviews 150 wds; video reviews 100 wds. Responds in 2 wks. Seasonal 3 mos ahead. Accepts simultaneous query & reprints (tell when/where appeared). Accepts disk. Sidebars OK. Prefers NAB. Guidelines/theme list; copy $2/9x12 SAE/4 stamps. (Ads)

Poetry: Accepts 24/yr. Free verse, light verse, traditional, 5-30 lines. Submit max. 3 poems.

Fillers: Cartoons, games, jokes, prayers, quizzes, quotes, and word puzzles; to 300 wds.

Columns/Departments: Patrick Lorenz. Watch It/Hear It (positive movie & music reviews), 50-150 wds.

Special Needs: Teen issues, sports, back to school, pro-life issues, religious vocations, and alternative Christian music.

Tips: "Write in the language of teens. Must be 'hip.' Most open to sports, school, friends & family, sexuality, and Your Stuff. Be brief, positive and powerful."

YOUNG ADULT TODAY, 1551 Regency Ct., Calumet City IL 60409. (708)868-7100. Fax (708)868-7105. Urban Ministries, Inc. Steven Beverly, ed., phone/fax (765)643-8518, e-mail: stvnbl@aol.com. Young adult curriculum for ages 18-24 (student and teacher manuals). Quarterly booklet; 72 pgs; circ 7,500. 60% freelance. Complete ms. Pays $35-50 on publication for all rts. Articles (24/yr) & fiction (12/yr); 2,900-3,500 characters. Responds in 1-2 wks. Seasonal 3 mos ahead. Free guidelines/theme list/copy.

Tips: "Send resumé and writing sample. Writer must be able to relate the writing to the outline given and the biblical material."

*YOUNG AND ALIVE, Box 6097, Lincoln NE 68506. (402)488-0981. Christian Record Services. Richard Kaiser, ed. For sight-impaired young adults, 16-20 yrs; for interdenominational Christian audience. Quarterly mag; 65-70 pgs; circ 26,000. 90% freelance. Query or complete ms/cover letter; phone query OK. Pays .03-.05/wd on acceptance for one-time rts. Articles & true stories 800-1,400 wds (30/yr). Responds in 9-13 wks. Seasonal 1 yr ahead. Accepts simultaneous query & reprints. Guidelines; copy for 9x12 SAE/6 stamps.

Special Needs: Adventure and relationships for the handicapped.

Tips: "Although many blind and visually impaired young adults have the same interests as their sighted counterparts, the material should meet their needs specifically."

Note: This publication has cut back to fewer issues and is overstocked.

*YOUNG CHRISTIAN, PO Box 1264, Huntington WV 25714. Tellstar Productions. Shannon Bridget Murphy, ed. For young Christians—children, teens and young adults. Bimonthly mag; circ. 1,500. Subscription $18. 95-100% freelance. Complete ms/cover letter. Pays on publication for 1st or one-time rts. Articles 500+ wds; fiction 500+ wds (24/yr). Responds in 4-8 wks. Seasonal 2-6 mos ahead. Accepts simultaneous submissions & reprints. Sidebars OK. Guidelines; copy $3 ($5 for 2).

Columns/Departments: Open to suggestions for columns.

Special Needs: How to write and make sales; articles for or by teens/young adults; food/recipes; party ideas for children and young adults.

Contest: Sponsors contests throughout the year. Send SASE for details.

Tips: "Submissions always welcome from children, teens or young adults. Writers, artists, or photographers should send a resume or letter with info on experiences and background."

YOUNG SALVATIONIST, PO Box 269, Alexandria VA 22313. (703)684-5500. Fax (703)684-5539. E-mail: ys@usn.salvationarmy.org. Website: http://www.salvation army.org. The Salvation Army. Lesa Davis, mng ed. For teens & young adults in the Salvation Army. Monthly (10X) mag; 16 pgs; circ 48,000. Subscription $4. 90% freelance. Complete ms; e-mail query OK. Pays .15/wd (.10 for reprints) on acceptance for 1st, one-time or reprint rts. Articles (40/yr) & fiction (10/yr); 1,000-1,500 wds. Responds in 4-6 wks. Seasonal 6 mos ahead. Accepts reprints (tell when/where appeared). Accepts disk. Some sidebars. Prefers NIV. Guidelines/theme list; copy for 9x12 SAE/3 stamps.

Contest: Sponsors a contest for fiction, nonfiction, poetry, original art and photography. Send SASE for details.

Tips: "We are always looking for articles/interviews about Christian entertainers or athletes; also current issues. Ask for theme list. Be contemporary— no stories about how it used to be."

** This periodical was #24 on the 1997 Top 50 Christian Publishers list. (#36 in 1996, #43 in 1995, 314 in 1994)

YOUTH CHALLENGE, 8855 Dunn Rd., Hazelwood MO 63042. (314)837-7300. Fax (314)837-4503. E-mail: wapeditor@aol.com. Website: http://www.upci.org. Word Aflame Publications. P. Daniel Buford, assoc. ed. For teens in 10th-12th grades. Weekly take-home paper; circ. 5,500. Subscription $4.40. 75% freelance. Complete ms/cover letter. Pays .01-.02/wd on publication for 1st or simultaneous rts. Articles 1,200-1,400 wds; fiction 1,200-1,400 wds (40/yr). Seasonal 1 yr ahead. Accepts simultaneous submissions & reprints. Few sidebars. Prefers KJV. Guidelines; copy for 6x9 SAE/2 stamps.

Fillers: Buys 2-3/yr. Quizzes, word puzzles; $5-12.

Tips: "Articles should be human interest with practical application of Christian principles for 15-17 year olds."

+YOUTH COMPASS (KS), PO Box 4060, Overland Park KS 66204. (913)432-0331. Fax (913)722-0351. Church of God (holiness)/Herald and Banner Press. Arlene McGehee, Sunday school ed. Denominational; for teens. Weekly take-home paper; 4 pgs; circ 4,800. Subscription $1.30. Complete ms/cover letter; phone/fax query OK. Pays .005/wd on publication for 1st rts. Fiction 800-1,500 wds. Seasonal 6-8 mos ahead. Accepts simultaneous submissions & reprints (tell when/where appeared). Prefers KJV. Guidelines/theme list; copy. Not in topical listings.

YOUTH 98, PO Box 4350, Evansville IN 47724. Phone/fax (812)867-8978. E-mail: YouthEdit@aol.com. House of White Birches/interdenominational. Rick Shallenberger, ed. Real answers to real questions based on Christian values; targets 15-19 year olds. Bimonthly mag; 40-70 pgs; circ. 40,000. Subscription $14.95. 75% freelance. Query or complete ms/cover letter; e-mail query OK. Pays $50-150/pg on acceptance for 1st rts. Articles 700 wds (30/yr) & fiction 1,400 wds (6/yr); book (200 wds)/music (175 wds) reviews, $50. Responds in 2-4 wks. Seasonal 6 mos ahead. Accepts simultaneous submissions & few reprints (tell when/where appeared). Prefers disk. Kill fee 50%. Sidebars OK. Prefers NIV. Guidelines; copy for 9x12 SAE/3 stamps. (Ads)

Poetry: By teens only. Accepts 30/yr. Any type; to 50 lines. Submit max. 3 poems. No payment.

Columns/Departments: Kerri Dowd/Michael Warren. Buys 12-20/yr. News, Trends & Hot Tips (short pieces to improve life, health), 50-200 wds; $20-50.

Tips: "Write to an older teenager in a style that relates to teens. Avoid slang. Most open to feature articles, nonfiction, first-person, personal experience or with interviews on social issues."

** This periodical was #8 on the 1997 Top 50 Christian Publishers list.

YOUTH UPDATE, 1615 Republic St., Cincinnati OH 45210-1298. (513)241-5615. St. Anthony Messenger Press/Catholic. Carol Ann Morrow, ed. For high-school teens, to support their growth in a life of faith. Monthly newsletter; 4 pgs; circ 18,000. 90% freelance. Query. Pays .15/wd on acceptance for 1st & electronic rts. Articles 2,200-2,300 wds (12/yr). Responds in 13 wks. Seasonal 6 mos ahead. Prefers disk. Sidebars OK. Prefers NAB. Guidelines; copy for #10 SAE/1 stamp.

*YOUTH WORLD, 8855 Dunn Rd., Hazelwood MO 63042. (314)837-7304. United Pentecostal Church. R. M. Davis, ed. For teens 13-15 yrs. Weekly take-home paper. 90% freelance. Complete ms. Pays $8-25 on publication for all rts. Articles 800-1,800 wds (up to 120/yr); fiction 1,200-1,800 wds (up to 120/yr). Seasonal 9 mos ahead. Accepts simultaneous submissions & reprints. Guidelines; free copy.

Poetry: Accepts 30/yr; $3-12.

Tips: "Most open to good stories and articles for a traditional, fundamental audience."

WOMEN'S MARKETS

+ADAM'S RIB, 5620 Hummer Lake Rd., Oxford MI 48371. Phone/fax (810)628-5953. E-mail: AdamRibU@aol.com. Website: http://crossplaza.com/wotp. Women of the Promise (wives of Promise Keepers). Gina Lawton, ed-in-chief. For women who desire to walk with God. Bimonthly newsletter. Subscription $9. Est. 1995. Open to freelance. Complete ms; fax/e-mail query/submission OK. **PAYS IN COPIES.** Articles to 1,000 wds; fiction to 1,000 wds. Seasonal 3 mos ahead. Accepts reprints (tell when/where appeared). Prefers disk. Prefers KJV or NIV. Guidelines/theme list; copy for 6x9 SAE/ 2 stamps. (Ads)

Poetry: Accepts.

Tips: "Follow themes and have mss in our hands no later than 8 weeks before an issue is printed (earlier is better)."

ANNA'S JOURNAL, PO Box 341, Ellijay GA 30540. Phone/fax (706)276-2309. E-mail: annas@ellijay.com. Catherine Ward-Long, ed. Spiritual support for childless couples who for the most part have decided to stay that way. Quarterly newsletter; 8 pgs; circ. 40. Subscription $14. Est. 1995. 90% freelance. Query or complete ms; e-mail query OK. **PAYS IN COPIES & SUBSCRIPTION** for 1st, simultaneous or reprint rts. Not copyrighted. Articles 500-2,000 wds (8-12/yr); fiction 1,000-2,000 wds (1-3/yr). Responds in 4-8 wks. Seasonal 3 months ahead. Accepts simultaneous submissions & reprints (tell when/where appeared). No disk. No sidebars. Prefers KJV. Guidelines/theme list; copy $3/9x12 SAE/3 stamps.

Poetry: Accepts 4-10/yr. Any type. Submit max. 3 poems.

Fillers: Accepts 3-4/yr. Anecdotes, facts, newsbreaks, prose, prayers, quizzes, quotes, letters; 50-250 wds.

Special Needs: Articles from married, childless men; articles discussing the meaning of childless, childfree and childless by choice.

Tips: "Looking for innovative ways to improve the child-free lifestyle and self-esteem. It helps if writer is childless or knows someone who is."

ASPIRE, 107 Kenner Ave., Nashville TN 37205. (615)386-3011. Fax (615)385-4112. CCM Communications. Wendy Lee Nentwig, mng ed. For women who feel they don't always fit the stereotype prescribed by the world, and sometimes the church, but who want to understand what it means to be fully of God and fully human. Bimonthly mag; circ. 50,000. Subscription $19.95. Est. 1994. 80% freelance. Query/clips; fax/e-mail query OK. Pays .20-.30/wd on acceptance (for assigned) and publication (for unsolicited) for 1st rts. Articles 900-1,500 wds (6/yr). Responds in 8-15 wks. Seasonal 6 mos. ahead. Accepts simultaneous submissions & some reprints (tell when/where appeared). Sidebars OK. Prefers NKJV. Guidelines; copy $2.50/9x12 SAE/$1.50 postage. (Ads)

Columns/Departments: Family Matters, Food for Thought, BodyWise, Your Image, Money Sense, The Great Outdoors, and On the Job; 1,000 wds; $200-300.

Special Needs: Stories about the latest news and trends on weddings for an annual wedding section.

Tips: "Read us and other women's magazines. Be in touch with latest journalism techniques. Have a savvy sense on what's news, and what's revealing, insightful, and unique for Christian women. Look for fresh twists to put on every story. Back up the relevance of a story with anecdotes, statistics, expert opinion,, and real women's candid thoughts and insights."

** This periodical was #26 on the 1997 Top 50 Christian Publishers list. (#19 in 1996, #59 in 1995)

*THE CHURCH WOMAN, 475 Riverside Dr., Room 812, New York NY 10115. (212)870-2347. Fax (212)870-2338. Church Women United. Margaret Schiffert, ed. Highlights women's, peace and justice issues. Quarterly mag; 24 pgs; circ 10,000. Little freelance. Query. **PAYS IN COPIES.** Articles to 3 pgs. Guidelines; copy $1.

COLABORER, Box 5002, Antioch TN 37011-5002. (615)731-6812. Fax (615)731-0071. E-mail: colaborer@nafwb.com. Free Will Baptist/Women Nationally Active for Christ. Suzanne Franks, ed. To help Free Will Baptist women fulfill the great commission. Bimonthly mag; 32 pgs; circ 11,000. Subscription $6.75. 5% freelance. Query; e-mail query OK. **PAYS IN COPIES** for one-time rts. Articles (1/yr) 1,500-2,000 wds; fiction (1/yr) 1,000-2,000. Responds in 4 wks. Seasonal 6 mos ahead. Accepts reprints (tell when/where appeared). Accepts disk. Some sidebars. Guidelines; copy $1.25.

Fillers: Accepts 1-2/yr. Anecdotes, party ideas; 200-500 wds.

Tips: "Most open to missions nonfiction stories."

Contest: Creative Arts Contest open to women in the Free Will Baptist Church. March 1 deadline each year. $25 first prize, plus others. Categories include art, feature articles, plays, poetry, and programs. Send SASE for details.

#CONSCIENCE, A Newsjournal of Prochoice Catholic Opinion, 1436 U St. NW, Ste. 301, Washington DC 20009-3997. (202)986-6093. E-mail: cffc@ige.apc.org. Catholic. Maggie Hume, ed. For laypeople, theologians, policymakers, and clergy. Quarterly newsjournal; 48 pgs; circ 12,000. Subscription $10. 80% freelance. Query/clips or complete ms/cover letter. Pays $25-150 on publication for 1st rts. Articles 1,000-3,500 wds (8-12/yr); book reviews 500-800 wds, $25-150. Responds in 18 wks. Seasonal 6 mos ahead. Accepts simultaneous submissions & reprints (tell when/where appeared). Kill fee. Guidelines; copy for 9x12 SAE/4 stamps.

> **Poetry:** Buys 16/yr. Any type, on subject, to 50 lines; $10 + copies. Submit max. 5 poems.
>
> **Fillers:** Buys 6/yr. Newsbreaks; 100-300 wds; $25-35.
>
> **Tips:** "Focus on issues of reproductive choice. Raise serious ethical questions within a generally prochoice framework. Most open to feature articles and book reviews."

DOMESTIQUE, Penworks, 917 S. Waugh St., Kokomo IN 46901-5563. E-mail: PenWorks@netusa1.net. Website: http://www.freeyellow.com/members/domestique/. PenWorks Publishing. Penny E. Stone, ed. For women who run a home. Bimonthly, spiral-bound journal; 20-24 pgs; circ 200 & growing. Subscription $22.50. Est. 1996. 95% freelance. Complete ms/cover letter; e-mail query OK (no attachments). Pays $5 (an extra $5 if put on the Website) after publication for 1st, one-time, simultaneous, electronic or reprint rts. Not copyrighted. Articles to 1,500 wds (100/yr); fiction to 2,500 wds. Responds in 4-8 wks. Seasonal 4 mos ahead. Accepts simultaneous submissions & reprints (tell when/where appeared). No disk. Prefers KJV or NKJV. Few sidebars. Guidelines (also on-line); copy $5. (Classified ads)

> **Poetry:** Buys 10-15/yr; 4-12 lines; $5.
>
> **Fillers:** Anecdotes, facts, jokes, prose, short humor, household tips, spiritual questions. Pays 2 copies.
>
> **Columns/Departments:** Behind the Scenes (pertinent news items), to 600 wds; Rejuvenate! (morale-building, self-help, positive thinking), to 1,200 wds; Domestic Engineering (household tips), to 1,200 wds; Tea Time (short humor—pays in copies); Ways to Date Your Mate, to 1,000 wds; Home Front (parenting), to 1,000 wds; Quiet Moments (devotional with scripture from KJV), to 800 wds; Homespun Goodness (recipes—pays in copies); A Penny for Your Thoughts (opinion), to 1,200 wds. See guidelines for additional columns.
>
> **Tips:** "We need articles which fit within our column guidelines. We try to touch on most aspects of domestic engineers. Preferred writers are subscribers."

ESPRIT, Evangelical Lutheran Women, 1512 St. James St., Winnipeg MB R2K 3B4 Canada. (204)775-8591. Fax (204)775-8628. E-mail: esprit@elcic.ca. Evangelical Lutheran Church in Canada. Gayle Johonnesson, ed. For denominational women. Quarterly mag; 56 pgs; circ 7,000. Subscription $15.50 CAN, $25 US. 50% freelance. Complete ms/cover letter; phone/fax/e-mail query OK. Pays $12.50-15/pg CAN on publication for 1st, one-time or reprint rts. Articles (34/yr) and fiction (4/yr) 325-1,400 wds; book reviews 150 wds ($6.25 CAN). Responds in 2-4 wks. Seasonal 4 mos ahead. Accepts simultaneous submissions & reprints (tell when/where appeared). Accepts disk (Macintosh). Sidebars OK. Prefers NRSV. Guidelines/theme list; copy for 6x9 SAE/.90 CAN postage or $1 US.

Poetry: Buys 8-12/yr. Free verse, light verse, traditional; 8-100 lines; $10-20. Submit max. 2 poems.

Fillers: Buys 20/yr. Anecdotes, cartoons, facts, prayers, short humor; 50-350 wds; $3.25-12.50.

Columns/Departments: Buys 4/yr. Over the Fence (conversational), 325 wds. Pays $12.50-15/pg.

Tips: "Be a Lutheran woman living in Canada. Use inclusive language (no male pronoun references to God), focus on women and spiritual/faith issues. Check our theme calendar; almost all articles and poems are theme related."

+THE HANDMAIDEN: A Journal for Women Serving God in the Orthodox Tradition, PO Box 76, Ben Lomond CA 95005. (408)336-5118. Fax (408)336-8882. E-mail: czell@conciliarpress.com. Website: http://www.conciliar-press.com. Conciliar Press. Katherine Hyde, ed. To provide support, encouragement, a sense of community, spiritual teaching, and appropriate role models for Orthodox Christian women. Quarterly journal; 64 pgs; circ 2,500. Subscription $15. 90% freelance. Query/clips; fax/e-mail query OK. **PAYS IN COPIES** for one-time rts. Not copyrighted. Articles 1,000-3,000 wds (40/yr); fiction 1,000-3,000 wds (1-2/yr); book reviews 500-1,000 wds. Responds in 2-6 wks. Seasonal 6 mos ahead. Accepts reprints (tell when/where appeared). Accepts disk. Sidebars OK. Prefers NKJV. Guidelines/theme list; copy for 7x10 SAE/5 stamps.

Poetry: Donna Farley, 9642 - 139 St., Surrey BC V3T 5H3 Canada. Accepts 4-12/yr. Any type; to 1 pg.

Fillers: Cartoons, newsbreaks, prayers, quotes; 20-150 wds.

Columns/Departments: Accepts 30-35/yr. Heroines of the Faith (saints), 1,000-3,000 wds; Orthodox Home; Women Making a Difference, 2,000-3,000 wds; The Clergy Wife's Voice, 800-1,200 wds; Daughters of the King (teens), 400-1,200 wds; Encounters with Grace (personal experiences), 400-1,200 wds; What's Happening (news items), up to 300 wds.

Special Needs: Articles on living the simple life.

Tips: "Be an excellent writer and an Orthodox Christian with something worthwhile to say."

THE HELPING HAND, Box 12609, Oklahoma City OK 73157-2609. (405)787-7110. Fax (405)789-3957. Pentecostal Holiness Church/Women's Ministries. Mary Belle Johnson, ed. Denominational; for women. Bimonthly mag; 16 pgs; circ 3,000. Subscription $9.95. 50% freelance. Complete ms/cover letter. Pays $20 on publication for one-time or simultaneous rts. Articles 500-1,300 wds (30/yr); fiction 500-1,300 wds (20/yr). Responds in 3 wks. Seasonal 3-4 mos ahead. Accepts simultaneous submissions & reprints (tell when/where appeared). Accepts disk. Prefers NIV. Guidelines; copy for 9x12 SAE/2 stamps.

Poetry: Buys 5/yr. Traditional; $10-20. Submit max. 4 poems.

HORIZONS, 100 Witherspoon St., Louisville KY 40202-1396. (502)569-5379. Fax (502)569-8085. Presbyterian Church (USA). Submit to The Editor. Justice issues and spiritual life for Presbyterian women. Bimonthly (7X) mag & annual Bible study; 40 pgs; circ 25,000. Subscription $14. 40% freelance. Complete ms/cover letter; fax query OK. Pays $50/printed page on publication for all rts. Articles 500-1,200 wds (10/yr) & fiction 500-1,200 wds (5/yr); book/music/video reviews 100-150 wds. Responds in 4 wks. Seasonal 5 mos ahead. Accepts reprints (tell when/where appeared). Prefers disk. Sidebars OK. Prefers NRSV. Guidelines/theme list; copy for 9x12 SAE/2 stamps.

Poetry: Buys 5/yr. All types; $50-100. Submit max. 5 poems.

Fillers: Cartoons, church-related graphics; $50.

Tips: "Poetry, features, fiction are open to freelancers. Should be relevant to Presbyterian women and church leadership. Devotionals for the inside front cover are also accepted. Seasonal fiction or nonfiction are most likely to be used. Be familiar with the 6 annual themes."

+ISHSHAH, PO Box 1519, Inglewood CA 90308. (310)419-0656. Fax (310)677-2434. E-mail: Ishshahmag@aol.com. Ishshah Publications. Sharon Jones, ed-in-chief; Lanette White, mng. ed. A multi-cultural magazine for and about women of color—all colors. Quarterly mag; 48 pgs. Subscription $10. 75% freelance. Query or complete ms/cover letter; e-mail query OK. Query for electronic submissions. **PAYS IN COPIES** for 1st, reprint or simultaneous rts. Articles 1,000-1,200 wds; little fiction. Responds in 8-10 wks. Seasonal 4 mos ahead. Accepts simultaneous submissions & reprints (tell when/where appeared). Prefers disk. Sidebars OK. Prefers KJV or NIV. Guidelines/theme list; copy for 9x12 SAE/4 stamps. (Ads)

Poetry: Accepts few (for fillers only); 4-12 lines.

Fillers: Accepts 15/yr. Cartoons, facts, jokes, quotes, short humor; 50-150 wds.

Columns/Departments: Accepts 24/yr. Treasures from Experience (mature insight), Manna (cooking & recipes/photo), Single Living, Quiver Management (parenting), A Time to Laugh (humor), and Speak Brother (male viewpoint), all to 500 wds.

Special Needs: 1998 themes are: racial issues, sexuality, relationships, holiness, and holidays.

Tips: "We love to know that our writers feel the heartbeat of our vision to minister to women of every ethnic background. Give us pieces that celebrate our differences yet point out our similarities as women in Christ."

JOURNAL OF WOMEN'S MINISTRIES, 216 Clinton St., Oak Park IL 60302. (800)334-7626. Fax (708)763-9454. Website: http://www.dfms.org/women or http://www.ecusa.anglican.org/woman. Episcopal/Council for Women's Ministries. Marcy Darin, ed. Deals with issues of interest to women from a liberal perspective. Biannual mag; 36 pgs; circ 10,000. Query. Pays $50 on publication for 1st rts. Articles 1,200-1,500 wds. Responds in 5 wks. Seasonal 3 mos ahead. Guidelines; copy for 9x12 SAE/3 stamps.

Poetry: Free verse, traditional. Submit max. 2 poems.

JOURNEY, 127 Ninth Ave. N., Nashville TN 37234. (615)251-5659. Fax (615)251-5008. Southern Baptist. Pamela Nixon, mng. ed. Devotional magazine for women of the 90s (30-45 years old). Monthly mag; 44 pgs; circ 150,000. 20% freelance. Subscription $18.95. Query/clips or complete ms/cover letter; no phone/fax/e-mail query. Pays $25-150 on acceptance for all, 1st, one-time or reprint rts. Articles 350-1,000 wds (10-12/yr). Responds in 8 wks. Seasonal 6-7 mos ahead.

Accepts simultaneous submissions & reprints (tell when/where appeared). Sidebars OK. Prefers NIV. Accepts disk. Guidelines; copy for 6x9 SAE/2 stamps.

Fillers: Prayers, short humor; 200-350 wds.

Special Needs: Strong feature articles 90-1,000 words; profiles of Christian women in leadership positions.

Tips: "Would like to see articles for our week-end pages and an occasional 3-page feature article on topics of interest to women 30-45 years old."

** This periodical was #54 on the 1997 Top 50 Christian Publishers List. (#55 in 1996)

THE JOYFUL WOMAN, PO Box 90028, Chattanooga TN 37412-6028. (706)866-5522. (706)866-2432. E-mail: JoyfulCMI@aol.com. Joyful Christian Ministries. Joy Rice Martin, exec. dir. For and about Bible-believing women who want God's best. Bimonthly mag; 24-28 pgs; circ 7,000. Subscription $16. 50% freelance. Query only, with first page of article. Pays $20-30 on publication for 1st rts. Articles & fiction 500-1,000 wds (15/yr); music reviews, 200-400 wds, $20. Responds in 6-8 wks. Seasonal 3 mos ahead. Accepts simultaneous submissions & reprints (tell when/where appeared). Accepts disk. Kill fee. Sidebars OK. KJV only. Guidelines/theme list; copy $3/9x12 SAE/4 stamps. (Ads)

Poetry: Buys 6/yr. Free verse, light verse, traditional; 15-40 lines; $15-40. Submit max. 2 poems.

Fillers: Buys 10/yr. Cartoons, jokes, newsbreaks, prayers, quotes, short humor; 25-300 wds; $15-25.

Columns/Departments: Query. Pays $20-30.

Tips: "Our biggest need is true-life stories. We prefer 1,000 word or less manuscripts, and would like color pictures of author and/or manuscript subject. Please allow 16 weeks before you call about your manuscript."

#JUST BETWEEN US, 777 S. Barker Rd., Brookfield WI 53045. (414)786-6478 or (800)260-3342. Fax (414)796-5752. Elmbrook Church, Inc. Shelly Esser, ed. Ideas, encouragement and resources for wives of evangelical ministers. Quarterly mag; 32 pgs; circ 5,000. Subscription $14.95. 90% freelance. Query; phone/fax query OK. **NO PAYMENT** for one-time rts. Articles 250-500 wds or 800-1,500 wds (50/yr). Responds in 6 wks. Accepts simultaneous submissions & reprints. Sidebars OK. Prefers NIV. Guidelines/theme list; copy $2/9x12 SAE. (Ads)

Fillers: Buys 15/yr. Anecdotes, cartoons, ideas, prayers, quotes, short humor; 50-250 wds.

Columns/Departments: Buys 12/yr. Money Savers; Keeping Your Kids Christian; Women's Ministry (program ideas); all 500-700 wds.

Tips: "Articles need to relate to unique ministry issues. Most open to columns or feature articles. Follow themes."

+KANSAS CITY WOMAN, One Heart, Many Faces, PO Box 1860, Blue Springs MO 64013-1860. Phone/fax (816)228-9838. E-mail: kcwoman@discoverynet. com. Secular. Debi Stack, ed. dir. Publishes the best profiles, business and family news, how-tos, features and spiritual encouragement to keep the woman's heartbeat going strong. Monthly mag. Launch date is May 1998. Query or query/clips (for cover stories & features). Pays .10/wd on publication for 1st (preferred), one-time, or reprint rts. Cover stories 1,500-2,500 wds, profiles 400-800 wds, features 750-1,000 wds, personal experience 750-850 wds, how-to 375-750 wds;

fiction 3,000-5,000 wds (to be serialized in 3 issues); book/music reviews 50-100 wds. Seasonal 9-12 mos ahead. Accepts reprints (tell when/where appeared). Guidelines.

Poetry: Assigned only.

Tips: "We want to see light, inspirational material."

THE LINK & VISITOR, 30 Arlington Ave., Toronto ON M6G 3K8 Canada. (416)651-7192. Fax (416)651-0438. Baptist Women's Missionary Society of Ontario and Quebec. Esther Barnes, ed. A positive, practical magazine for Canadian Baptist women who want to make a difference in our world. Monthly (9X) mag; 16 pgs; circ 4,500. Subscription $14 CAN, $12 US. 50% freelance. Complete ms/cover letter; phone query OK. Pays .05/wd CAN, on publication for one-time or simultaneous rts. Articles 700-2,000 wds (15/yr). Responds in 36 wks. Seasonal 3 mos ahead. Accepts simultaneous submissions & reprints (tell when/where appeared). Accepts disk. Prefers NIV (inclusive language), NRSV, or LB. Guidelines/theme list; copy for 9x12 SAE/$1 Canadian postage.

Poetry: Buys 6/yr. Free verse; 12-32 lines; $10-25. Submit max. 4 poems.

Tips: "Looking for articles on joy. Canadian writers preferred. If US writers send US postage for returns, they will be rejected. Too many writers seem too focused on themselves and their own experiences. Canadian perspective, please."

#LUTHERAN WOMAN TODAY, 8765 W. Higgins Ave., Chicago IL 60631-4189. (773)380-2743. Evangelical Lutheran Church in America. Nancy J. Stelling, ed. For women in the denomination. Monthly (11X) mag: 48 pgs; circ 230,000. 25% freelance. Complete ms/cover letter or query. Pays $60-280 on publication for 1st rts. Articles (24/yr) & fiction (5/yr), to 1,050 wds. Responds in 16 wks. Seasonal 7 mos ahead. Guidelines/theme list; copy $1.

Poetry: Buys 5/yr. Free verse, haiku, light verse, traditional; to 60 lines; $15-60. Submit max. 3 poems. Poetry must have a spiritual and women's focus.

Columns/Departments: Buys 5/yr. Devotion, 350 wds; Season's Best (reflection on the church year), 350-700 wds; About Women; Forum (essay); $50-250.

Tips: "Submit a short, well-written article using inclusive language and offering a women's and spiritual focus."

*LUTHERAN WOMAN'S QUARTERLY, 1860 Greenfield Dr., El Cajon CA 92021. Phone/fax (619)444-6089. Lutheran Women's Missionary League. Patricia Beach Schutte, ed-in-chief. For women of the Lutheran Church—Missouri Synod. Quarterly mag; 48 pgs; circ. 200,000. Subscription $2.50. 100% freelance. Complete ms/cover letter. **NO PAYMENT.** Not copyrighted. Articles 750-1,200 wds (4/yr); fiction 750-1,200 wds (4/yr). Responds in 2 wks. Seasonal 5 mos ahead. Sidebars OK. Prefers NIV. Guidelines/theme list.

Tips: "Most open to articles. Must reflect the Missouri Synod teachings. Most of our writers are from the denomination."

*THE PROVERBS 31 HOMEMAKER, PO Box 17155, Charlotte NC 28227. (704)849-2270. Fax (704)849-2270. E-mail: P31home@aol.com. Mary Ellen Bianco, ed. Encouragement and information for stay-at-home mothers. Monthly newsletter; 10 pgs; circ. 2,000. Subscription $15. 90% freelance. Query. **NO**

PAYMENT for one-time rts. Articles 200-400 wds (24/yr); book reviews 200-250 wds. Responds in 4 wks. Seasonal 4 mos ahead. Accepts simultaneous submissions & reprints (tell when/where appeared). No disk. Sidebars OK. Prefers NIV. Guidelines/theme list; copy for 9x12 SAE/2 stamps.

Poetry: Accepts up to 12/yr.

Fillers: Accepts 12/yr. Anecdotes, cartoons, ideas, party ideas, prose, prayers, quotes, short humor; to 100 wds.

Tips: "Looking for articles on relationship with God; how homemakers organize time; marital relationships; how to keep kids busy."

SISTERS TODAY, The Liturgical Press, St. John's Abbey, PO Box 7500, Collegeville MN 56321-7500. (320)363-2213. Fax (800)445-5899 or (320)363-7130. E-mail: mwagner@csbsju.edu. Website: http://www.csbsju/osb.sisters/public. html. Currently not accepting freelance submissions.

TEA AND SUNSHINE, S63 W 35530 Piper Rd., Eagle WI 53119. (414)392-9761. E-mail: MLJBeen@aol.com. Margaret Been, pub. For women whose hearts are at home. Quarterly mag; 24-40 pgs. Est. 1995. Subscription free (donations welcome). 60% freelance. Complete ms/cover letter; e-mail query OK. **PAYS IN COPIES.** for one-time rts (author retains rights). Not copyrighted. Articles/essays 600-1,200 wds (24-40/yr); fiction 700-1,500 wds (4-12/yr); Christian apologetics & current issues 600-1,200 wds (6-12/yr). Responds in 2-4 wks. Seasonal 12-16 mos ahead. Some reprints. No disk. Some sidebars. Prefers KJV or NIV. Guidelines; copy for 9x12 SAE/ 3 stamps.

Poetry: Accepts many/yr. Literary; around 3-76 lines.

Fillers: Prose, short essays, vignettes, testimonies, devotionals, book reviews, recipes.

Columns/Departments: Rivers of Living Water (spiritual growth essays), to 1,000 wds; Gleanings from the Garret (fine arts, literature, drama), to 1,000 wds.

Tips: "We focus on beauty, creativity, 'slow-lane' quality of life, and God's victory over circumstances. We are a home place for Christian writers who are 'keepers at home'; we welcome input from writers on various aspects of writing."

#TODAY'S CHRISTIAN WOMAN, 465 Gundersen Dr., Carol Stream IL 60188-2498. (630)260-6200. Fax (630)260-0114. E-mail: TCWedit@aol.com. Website: http://www.christianity.net/tcw. Submit to Camerin Courtney, asst. ed. To help Christian women grow in their relationship to God by providing practical, biblical perspectives on marriage, sex, parenting, work, health, friendship, and self. Bimonthly mag; 80-150 pgs; circ 351,000. Subscription $17.95. 25% freelance. Query only; fax/e-mail query OK. Query for electronic submissions. Pays .15/wd on publication (on acceptance for assignments) for 1st or reprint rts. Articles 1,500-1,800 wds (6-12/yr); no fiction. Responds in 4-6 wks. Seasonal 6 mos ahead. Accepts simultaneous submissions & reprints (tell when/where appeared). Some sidebars. Prefers NIV. Guidelines; copy $5. (Ads)

Columns/Departments: Buys 12/yr. One Woman's Story (dramatic story of overcoming a difficult situation), 1,000-1,500 wds, $150, query; Faith on Job (sharing faith at work), 100-200 wds, $25; Small Talk (humorous, inspirational anecdotes), 50-100 wds, $25. Send complete ms for last two/not acknowledged or returned.

Tips: "Most open to One Woman's Story: Should tell how you, through a personal experience, came to a spiritual turning point, solved a problem, or overcame a difficult situation."

** This periodical was #57 on the 1996 Top 50 Christian Publishers List. (#34 in 1994) Also 1997 EPA Award of Merit—General.

VIRTUE: Helping Women Build Christ-Like Character, 4050 Lee Vance View, Colorado Springs CO 80918-7102. (719)531-7776. Fax (719)535-0172. E-mail: VirtueMag@aol.com. Cook Communications Ministries. Debbie Colclough, assoc. ed. For Christian women who seek spiritual perspectives and personal enrichment in every aspect of their lives. Bimonthly mag; 80 pgs; circ 110,000. Subscription $18.95. 70% freelance. Query/clips; fax query OK. Pays .15-.25/wd on acceptance (for solicited) or on publication (for unsolicited) for 1st rts. Articles 800-1,500 wds (30/yr) & fiction 800-1,200 wds (4-6/yr). Responds in 6-8 wks. Seasonal 6 mos ahead. Accepts reprints only from non-competing markets (tell when/where appeared). Accepts disk. Kill fee 25%. Encourages sidebars. Prefers NIV. Guidelines; copy for 9x12 SAE/9 stamps or $3. (Ads)

> **Poetry:** Buys 3/yr. Free verse, light verse, traditional; $20-50. Submit max. 3 poems.
>
> **Departments:** Buys 40/yr. Family Matters (news and information for families), 50-300 wds; Virtue in Action (about virtue, values and character in our culture), 50-300 wds. Pays $20-50
>
> **Tips:** "Writers who clearly know our target audience, demonstrate an understanding of the issues our readers care about, and write a strong, specific query have the best chance of attracting our interest."
>
> ** #42 on the 1994 Top 50.

+VIRTUOUS WOMAN, 241 Old Mobile Rd., McCaysville GA 30555. (706)492-3332. E-mail: virtuouswoman@wingnet.net. Website: http://www.virtuouswoman. com. Sonja S. Key, ed. Interdenominational. Quarterly mag; 40-60 pgs; circ 350. And on-line mag (see Website above). Subscription $16. 60% freelance. Complete ms/cover letter; e-mail query OK. **PAYS 3 COPIES** for 1st & electronic rts. Articles 1,200 wds (25/yr); book reviews 200 wds, music reviews 100 wds. Responds in 8 wks. Accepts simultaneous submissions. No disk. Sidebars OK. Prefers Amplified Bible. Guidelines; copy for 9x12 SAE/$2 postage. (Ads)

> **Poetry:** Accepts 50/yr. Free verse, light verse, traditional; 8-25 lines. Submit max.5 poems.
>
> **Fillers:** Accepts 8/yr. Anecdotes, cartoons, prayers, prose, quizzes, quotes; 50-100 wds.
>
> **Columns/Departments:** Accepts 25/yr. Rivers of Living Waters (work of the Holy Spirit); Earthen Vessels (body, diet, grooming, etc); Broken & Poured Out (soul, mind, will, emotions); all 1,000 wds.
>
> **Tips:** "Most open to articles which offer advice to women already established in ministry, such as better or innovative ways to reach women with the gospel, how to train women for ministry, or how to build a thriving women's ministry."

*WELCOME HOME, 8310A Old Courthouse Rd., Vienna VA 22182. (703)827-5903 or (800)783-4MOM. Fax(703)790-8587. Mothers at Home, Inc. Submit to Manuscript Coordinator. For women who have chosen to stay at home with their children. Monthly jour; circ. 15,000. Subscription $18. 100% freelance. Complete ms/cover letter. **NO (OR LIMITED) PAYMENT** for one-time rts. Articles to 2,400 wds, most 500-1,500 wds (20/yr). Responds in 6-12 wks. Seasonal 1 yr ahead. Some sidebars. Guidelines (request specific guidelines for departments interested in); copy $2/7x10 SAE.

> **Poetry:** Winnie Peterson Cross. Accepts 48/yr. Free verse, haiku, light verse, traditional.

> **Columns/Departments:** Accepts 36/yr. From a Mother (surprising/sudden insights); Resource Roundup (books/resources); New Dimensions (personal growth/development); Heartwarming (cooking/recipes); Health & Safety (mother's/child's health, family safety); Time to Care (volunteer work; all 700-1,000 wds.

THE WESLEYAN WOMAN, PO Box 50434, Indianapolis IN 46250-0434. (317)570-5164. Fax (317)570-5254. E-mail: wwi@wesleyan.org. Wesleyan Church. Martha Blackburn, mng ed. Inspiration, education and sharing to meet the needs of Wesleyan women. Quarterly mag; 24 pgs; circ 3,500. Subscription $12.95. 75% freelance. Complete ms/cover letter; phone/fax query OK. Pays .04/wd (.02-.03/wd for reprints) on publication for one-time or reprint rts. Articles 500-700 wds (1-10/yr). Responds in 3 wks. Seasonal 6 mos ahead. Accepts simultaneous submissions & reprints (tell when/where appeared). Accepts disk. Sidebars OK. Guidelines/theme list; free copy.

> **Poetry:** Accepts 4/yr. Free verse, light verse, traditional. Pays .04/wd, up to $10. Submit max. 2 poems.

> **Fillers:** Accepts few. Anecdotes, cartoons, ideas, party ideas, quotes, short humor; 150-350 wds.

> **Tips:** "Most open to personal stories of 'guts' and grace to follow the Lord. Ways you see God at work in your life—personal, not preachy."

WOMAN'S TOUCH, 1445 Boonville Ave., Springfield MO 65802-1894. (417)862-2781. Fax (417)862-0503. E-mail: womanstouch@ag.org. Assemblies of God. Peggy Musgrove, ed. A general readership magazine committed to providing help and inspiration for Christian women, strengthening family life, and reaching out in witness to others; also leadership edition. Bimonthly mag; 36 pgs; circ 16,000+. Subscription $7/leader $8.50. 90% freelance. Complete ms/cover letter. Pays $10-40 (.03/wd) on publication for 1st, one-time, or reprint rts. Articles to 1,200 wds (50-60/yr). Responds in 10 wks. Seasonal 10-12 mos ahead. Accepts simultaneous submissions & reprints (tell when/where appeared). Accepts disk. Kill fee. Sidebars OK. Prefers KJV or NIV. Guidelines/theme list; copy for 9x12 SAE/3 stamps.

> **Fillers:** Buys 10/yr. Anecdotes, ideas; 50-200 wds; $5-15.

> **Columns/Departments:** Buys 30/yr. A Better You (health/fitness), 500 wds; A Final Touch (human interest on home/family/career), 350 wds; A Lighter Touch (true humorous anecdotes); 100 wds; History's Women (great women of faith), 500 wds. Pays $10-40.

> ** This periodical was #35 on the 1996 Top 50 Christian Publishers List.

WOMEN ALIVE!, Box 4683, Overland Park KS 66204. Phone/fax (913)649-8583. Aletha Hinthorn, ed. To encourage Holiness women to apply Scripture to their daily lives. Bimonthly mag; 20 pgs; circ 3,500-4,000. Subscription $13.95. 50% freelance. Complete ms. Pays $25-50 on publication for 1st or reprint rts. Articles

900-1,800 wds (7/yr). Responds in 4-6 wks. Seasonal 4 mos ahead. Accepts reprints. Some sidebars. No disk. Guidelines/theme list; copy for 9x12 SAE/4 stamps.

Poetry: Buys 0-3/yr. Traditional, $10-40. Submit max. 3.

Fillers: Buys 0-1/yr. Cartoons, jokes, short humor.

Columns/Departments: Buys 6/yr. Senior Savvy (for older women); 900-1,200 wds; $15-40.

Tips: "We look for articles that draw women into a deeper spiritual life—articles on surrender, prayer, Bible study—yet written with personal illustrations."

WOMEN OF SPIRIT, 55 W. Oak Ridge Dr., Hagerstown MD 21740-7390. (301)790-9737. Fax (301)790-9734. E-mail: 74617.4104@compuserve.com. Overstocked this year. (Ads)

WRITER'S MARKETS

+THE ADVANCED CHRISTIAN WRITER, 9731 N. Fox Glen Dr., #6F, Niles IL 60714-5861. (847)296-3964. Fax (847)296-0754. E-mail: linjohnson@compuserve. com. American Christian Writers. Lin Johnson, ed. A professional newsletter for published writers. Bimonthly newsletter; 8 pgs; circ 1,000. Subscription $19. 75% freelance. Complete ms; fax/e-mail query OK. Pays $20 on publication for 1st or reprint rts. Articles 600-1,500 wds (30/yr); book reviews 300-400 wds, $15. Responds in 6-8 wks. Seasonal 6 mos ahead. Accepts simultaneous submissions & reprints (tell when/where appeared). Sidebars OK. Requires disk or e-mail. Prefers NIV. Guidelines; copy for #10 SAE/1 stamp (order from ACW, PO Box 110390, Nashville TN 37222). (Ads)

Tips: "We're new and hungry for manuscripts. We accept articles only from professional, well-published writers. We need manuscripts about all aspects of being a published freelance writer and how to increase sales and professionalism; on the advanced level; looking for depth beyond the basics."

BYLINE, Box 130596, Edmond OK 73013-0001. Phone/fax (405)348-5591. E-mail: ByLineMP@aol.com. Website: http://www.BylineMag.com. Secular. Kathryn Fanning, mng. ed. Offers practical tips, motivation and encouragement to freelance writers and poets. Monthly (11X) mag; 32 pgs; circ 3,000+. Subscription $22. 80% freelance. Query or complete ms; no phone/fax/e-mail query; no electronic submissions. Pays $50 ($100 for fiction) on acceptance for 1st rts. Articles 1,500-1,800 wds (100/yr); personal experiences 800 wds; fiction 2,000-4,000 wds (10/yr). Responds in 6 wks. Seasonal 6 mos ahead. Accepts simultaneous submissions. Accepts disk. Encourages sidebars. Guidelines; copy $4. (Ads)

Poetry: Betty Shipley. Buys 50-100/yr. Any type; to 30 lines; $5-10. Writing themes. Submit max. 3 poems.

Fillers: Anecdotes, prose, short humor for humor page, 200-400 wds, pays $15-20.

Columns/Departments: Buys 50-60/yr. End Piece (personal essay on writing theme), 750 wds; First Sale accounts, 200-400 wds; Only When I Laugh (writing humor), 100-500 wds; End Piece; $15-35. Complete ms.

Contests: Sponsors many year round; details included in magazine.

Tips: "Most open to First Sale account; be upbeat about writing. Need articles, essays and poetry on writing topics; general interest short stories (no religious)."

CANADIAN WRITER'S JOURNAL, White Mountain Publications, Box 5180, New Liskeard ON P0J 1P0 Canada. (705)647-5424. Fax (705)647-8366. E-mail: cwj@ntl.sympatico.ca. Deborah Ramchuk, ed. How-to articles for writers. Quarterly digest; 64 pgs; circ 385. Subscription $15. 95% freelance. Complete ms/cover letter; e-mail query OK. Pays $5 CAN/published pg on publication for 1st or one-time rts. Articles to 2,000 wds (45-50/yr); book reviews to 1,000 wds/$5. Responds in 12 wks. Seasonal 6 mos ahead. Accepts simultaneous submissions & reprints (tell when/where appeared). Prefers e-mail submissions. Sidebars OK. Guidelines; copy $5. (Ads)

> **Poetry:** Elizabeth St. Jacques (406 Elizabeth St., Saulte St. Marie ON P6B 3H4 Canada). Buys 16-20/yr. Free verse, haiku: on writing; to 8 lines. Pays $1. Send 5 poems max.
>
> **Fillers:** Anecdotes, cartoons, quotes; 20-50 wds. Pays $3-5.
>
> **Contest:** Sponsors annual poetry contest (June 30 deadline). Also a fall fiction contest.

THE CHRISTIAN COMMUNICATOR, 3133 Puente St., Fullerton CA 92835-1952. (714)990-1532. Fax (714)990-0310. E-mail: Susanosb@aol.com. American Christian Writers/Reg Forder, Box 110390, Nashville TN 37222, (800)21-WRITE (for advertising or subscriptions). Susan Titus Osborn, ed. For Christian writers/speakers who want to polish writing skills, develop public-speaking techniques, and sell their mss. Monthly mag; 24 pgs; circ 4,000. Subscription $25. 50% freelance. Complete ms/cover letter; phone/fax/e-mail query OK. Pays $5-10 on publication for 1st, one-time or reprint rts. Articles 600-1,200 wds (62/yr). Responds in 6-8 wks. Seasonal 6 mos ahead. Accepts reprints. Free guidelines/copy.

> **Poetry:** Accepts 12/yr. Poems on writing; $5. Submit max. 4 poems.
>
> **Columns/Departments:** Buys 12/yr. Communicator Interview (published author), 800-1,200 wds; Publisher's Profile, 800-1,200 wds; Speaker's Corner (techniques for speakers), 600-1,000 wds; Book Reviews (writing/speaking books), 300-400 wds; $5-10.
>
> **Tips:** "Most in need of publisher profiles."

*THE CHRISTIAN RESPONSE, PO Box 125, Staples MN 56479-0125. (218)894-1165. Christian Writers of America. Hap Corbett, ed. Exposes anti-Christian bias in America & encourages readers to write letters in defense of such bias. Bimonthly newsletter; 6 pgs; circ 400. Subscription $15. Est. 1993. 10% freelance. Complete ms/cover letter; phone query OK. Pays $2.50-20 on acceptance for 1st or simultaneous rts. Articles 50-300 wds (6/yr). Responds in 2 wks. Seasonal 6 mos ahead. Accepts simultaneous submissions & reprints. No sidebars. Guidelines; copy for $1 or 3 stamps.

> **Fillers:** Anecdotes, facts, quotes; 25-100 wds; $2.50-10.
>
> **Special Needs:** Articles on anti-Christian bias; tips on writing effective letters to the editor; pieces on outstanding accomplishments of Christians in the secular media.
>
> **Tips:** "We are looking for news/articles about anti-Christian bias in the media, and how you, as a writer, responded to such incidents."

CROSS & QUILL, Rt. 3 Box 1635, Jefferson Davis Rd., Clinton SC 29325-9542. (864)697-6035. E-mail: cwfi@aol.com. (cwfi@juno.com). Christian Writers Fellowship Intl. Sandy Brooks, ed/pub. For Christian writers, editors, agents, conference directors. Bimonthly newsletter; 12 pgs; circ 1,000+. Subscription $20; CWFI membership $40. 75% freelance. Complete ms; e-mail query OK; query for electronic submissions. Pays small honorarium for feature articles on publication for 1st or reprint rts. Articles 800-1,000 wds (24/yr); book reviews 100 wds (pays copies). Responds in 2 wks. Seasonal 6 mos ahead. Accepts reprints (tell when/where appeared). Sidebars OK. Accepts disk. Guidelines; copy $2/9x12 SAE/2 stamps. (Ads)

> **Poetry:** Accepts 12/yr. Any type; to 12 lines. Submit max. 3 poems. Must pertain to writing/publishing. Currently overstocked.

> **Fillers:** Accepts 12/yr. Anecdotes, cartoons, prayers; to 100 wds. Pays in copies.

> **Columns/Departments:** Accepts 36/yr. Writing Rainbows! (devotional), 600 wds; Writer to Writer (how-to), 900 wds; Editor's Roundtable (interview with editor), 200-800 wds; Tots, Teens & In-Betweens (juvenile market), 200-800 wds; BusinessWise (business side of writing), 200-800 wds; Connecting Points (how-to on critique group), 200-800 wds.

> **Special Needs:** Articles on screenwriting, poetry writing, news writing, greeting cards, and gift books.

> **Tips:** "Most open to feature articles, devotions for writers or book reviews on writing books. We want informative articles, not first-person viewpoint."

EXCHANGE, 15 Torrance Rd. #104, Scarborough ON M1J 3K2 Canada. (416)439-4320. (416)439-5089. E-mail: exchange@ica.net. Audrey Dorsch, ed. A forum for Christian writers to share information and ideas. Quarterly newsletter; 8 pgs; circ 185. Subscription $11.50 US/$16 CAN. 75% freelance. Complete ms/cover letter; fax/e-mail query OK. Pays .08/wd (CAN) on publication for one-time rts. Not copyrighted. Articles 400-600 wds (20/yr). Responds in 4-6 wks. Accepts reprints (.06/wd—tell when/where appeared). Accepts disk. No sidebars. Guidelines/copy for #10 SAE/2 Canadian stamps (.52). (Ads—classified)

> **Columns/Departments:** Buys 4/yr. Did You Know Your Computer Can Do This? (software features), 300 wds. Query.

> **Special Needs:** Material geared to experienced, professional writers.

> **Tips:** "Take a very deliberate approach to the 'how' of good writing."

+FELLOWSCRIPT, 121 Morin Maze, Edmonton AB T6K 1V1 Canada. Fax (403)430-0139. E-mail: nathan_harms@enabel.ab.ca. Alberta Christian Writers' Fellowship-CanadaWide. Nathan Harms, ed. To provide encouragement, instruction and news to Christians who write. Quarterly newsletter; 28-36 pgs; circ 200. Subscription $30 (includes membership). 100% freelance. Complete ms/cover letter; fax/e-mail query OK. Pays $10-30 (.02-.05/wd) on publication for 1st, one-time, reprint or simultaneous rts. Not copyrighted. Articles 350-1,000 wds (6/yr); book reviews, 300-350 wds, $5. Responds in 12 wks. Seasonal 4 mos ahead. Accepts simultaneous submissions & reprints (tell when/where appeared). Accepts disk. Sidebars OK. Prefers KJV. Guidelines; copy $1. (Ads)

> **Fillers:** Anecdotes, cartoons, facts, ideas, quotes, market updates; to 140 wds. Buys 8-25/yr. Pays $2-7.

Columns/Departments: Open to ideas for columns.

Special Needs: Articles of practical help to writers; how to put together a promotional package for the writer.

Contest: Sponsors two a year, one in March for members, one in August that is open. Send #10 SAE/$1 to "Contest Info."

Tips: "Most open to writer's tips and market information, personal experiences with writing, first sales, submitting via the Internet, etc. Appreciate submissions by e-mail, marked 'Attention Fellowscript.'"

#GOTTA WRITE NETWORK LITMAG, 515 E. Thacker St., Hoffman Estates IL 60194-1957. E-mail: netera@aol.com. Secular/Maren Publications. Denise Fleischer, ed. A support system for writers, beginner to well established. Semiannual mag; circ 200. Subscription $12.75. 80% freelance. Query or complete ms/cover letter; e-mail query OK. Pays $5 ($10 for fiction) after publication for 1st rts. Articles 3-5 pgs (25/yr); fiction to 5-10 pgs (10+/yr) on writing techniques; book reviews 2.5 pgs. Responds in 18 wks. Seasonal 6 mos ahead. Guidelines; copy $5.

> **Poetry:** Accepts 75+/yr. Avant-garde, free verse, haiku, experimental; 4 lines to 1 pg. Submit max. 5 poems.
>
> **Fillers:** Accepts 100/yr. Anecdotes, facts, newsbreaks, tips; 100-250 wds; pays in copies.
>
> **Tips:** "Most open to articles on writing techniques. Give me something different and in-depth. No I-love-writing, how-I-did-it."

HEAVEN, HCR-13 Box 21AA, Artemas PA 17211. (814)458-3102. Kay Weems, ed. Published for Easter. New publication. $5/copy. Annual booklet. Est. 1995. 100% freelance. **NO PAYMENT.** Short stories to 2,500 wds. Responds in 4-12 wks. Accepts simultaneous submissions & reprints.

> **Poetry:** All types of poetry on heaven, to 36 lines. Submit max. 10 poems.
>
> **Tips:** "Does different themes throughout the year. Currently the theme is prayers."

*HOUSEWIFE-WRITER, Box 780, Lyman WY 82937-0780. (307)782-7003. Secular. Emma Bluemel, ed; Edward Wahl, fiction ed. For new and unpublished writers who are home-based. Bimonthly magazine; 48 pgs; circ 2,000. Subscription $18. 80-90% freelance. Complete ms; phone query OK. Pays .01/wd on acceptance for 1st rts. Articles (60-100/yr) and fiction (6-12/yr) to 2,000 wds. Responds in 4-12 wks. Seasonal 6 mos ahead. Accepts simultaneous submissions & reprints. Sidebars OK. Guidelines; copy $4/#10 SAE.

> **Poetry:** Maria Reed. Buys 36/yr. Any type; to 45 lines; $1-5. Submit max. 5 poems.
>
> **Fillers:** Buys 24-30/yr. Anecdotes, cartoons, ideas, jokes, short humor; hints (on writing/running a home); 25-200 wds; $1-4.
>
> **Columns/Departments:** Buys 30-40/yr. Confessions of a Housewife-Writer, 250-750 wds; or various writing tips, 150-250 wds; $3. Complete ms.
>
> **Contests:** Sponsors annual contests with a June 1 deadline. Prizes are $30, $20 & $10, plus publication. Send SASE for rules.
>
> **Tips:** "Need how-tos on juggling home, children and writing. We rank verse and emotion ahead of linguistic gymnastics."

INKLINGS, Threads of Truth from Art and Story, 1650 Washington St., Denver CO 80203-1407. (303)861-8191. Fax (303)861-0659. E-mail: inkhick@aol.com.

Website: http://www.inkspot.com. Paradox Publishing. Brad Hicks, pub.; Laura Robinson, fiction ed. For thinking Christians and seekers interested in the arts and literature. Quarterly mag.; 32-48 pgs; circ 10,000. Subscription $15. 50-75% freelance. Query or complete ms/cover letter; phone/fax/e-mail query OK. Pays $100 for fiction (nothing for others) on publication for 1st rts. Articles 250-3,000 wds (8/yr); fiction 250-3,000 wds (4/yr); book/music/film reviews, 300 wds (pays in copies). Responds in 3 wks. Seasonal 6 mos ahead. Prefers disk. Some sidebars. Guidelines/theme list; copy $4. (Ads)

Poetry: Susan Kauffman. Accepts 16-24/yr. All types, 2-100 lines. Submit max. 10 poems. No payment.

Tips: "We will never publish a submission which refuses to acknowledge the legitimate human needs of all individuals and cultures."

*INSPIRATIONAL MARKET NEWS, 1132 - 21st St. SE, Cedar Rapids IA 52403. Helen Hunt, ed.

*MERLYN'S PEN, The National Magazine of Student Writing, Box 1058, East Greenwich RI 02818. Secular. R. James Stahl, ed. Written by students in grades 7-12 only. Mag. printed in 2 editions: Intermediate, 6th-9th grades; Senior, 9th-12th grades. Fiction to 3,500 wds; reviews and travel pieces to 1,000 wds. Pays $5-25, plus copies. Not in topical listings. Students send for guidelines.

Poetry: To 200 lines.

#MY LEGACY, HCR-13 Box 21AA, Artemas PA 17211. (814)458-3102. Kay Weems, ed. For young adults and up. Quarterly booklet; 70-80 pgs; circ 200+. 100% freelance. **NO PAYMENT.** No articles; fiction to 2,500 wds (100/yr). Responds in 14-16 wks. Accepts simultaneous submissions & reprints. Guidelines; copy for 6x9 SAE/4 stamps & $3.50.

Poetry: Accepts 200+/yr. Any type; to 36 lines.

NORTHWEST CHRISTIAN AUTHOR, 10663 NE 133rd Pl., Kirkland WA 98034-2030. (425)821-6647. Fax (206)823-8590. E-mail: newton@integrityol.com. Website: http://www.integrityol.com/newton/ncwa.htm. Northwest Christian Writers' Assn. Lorinda Newton, ed. To encourage Christian authors to share the gospel through the written word and to promote excellence in writing. Bimonthly newsletter; 8 pgs; circ. 60. Subscription $10. 70% freelance. Complete ms/cover letter; e-mail query OK. Query for electronic submissions. **PAYS 3 COPIES** for 1st, one-time, reprint or simultaneous rts. Not copyrighted. Articles 600-1,000 wds (18/yr). Responds in 4 wks. Accepts simultaneous submissions & reprints (tell when/where appeared). Prefers disk. Sidebars OK. Guidelines (also on Website); copy for 6x9 SAE/2 stamps.

Fillers: Accepts 1-2 cartoons/yr.

Tips: "Looking for how-to articles on fiction and nonfiction. Choose a specific aspect of the topic, instead of a general article. Stay within word count."

#OMNIFIC, HCR-13 Box 21AA, Artemas PA 17211. (814)458-3102. Kay Weems, ed. Family-type publication for writers/adults. Quarterly booklet; 100+ pgs; circ 300+. Subscription $16. 100% freelance. **SMALL AWARDS GIVEN.** Accepts simultaneous submissions & reprints. No articles; poetry only. Guidelines; copy for 6x9 SAE/4 stamps & $4.

Poetry: Any type; to 36 lines. Submit max. 4-8 poems.

ONCE UPON A TIME . . . , 553 Winston Ct., St. Paul MN 55118. (612)457-6223.

Fax (612)457-9565. E-mail: AUDREYOUAT@aol.com. Audrey B. Baird, ed/pub. A support publication for children's writers and illustrators. Quarterly mag; 32 pgs; circ 1,000. Subscription $22. 50% freelance. Complete ms/cover letter; phone/fax/e-mail query OK. **PAYS IN COPIES** for one-time rts. Articles to 800 wds (80-100/yr). Responds in 4-5 wks. Seasonal 6 mos ahead. Accepts simultaneous submissions & reprints (tell when/where appeared). Prefers disk or e-mail. Some sidebars. Guidelines; copy $4.50. (Ads)

Poetry: Buys 25/yr. Free verse, haiku, light verse, traditional; any length. Writing/illustrating related. Submit max. 6 poems.

Fillers: Buys 50/yr. Anecdotes, cartoons, prose, quizzes, short humor (all writing/illustrating related); to 100 wds.

Special Needs: How-to articles on writing & illustrating up to 800 wds; short pieces on writing & illustrating, 100-400 wds.

Tips: "Emphasis is on children's writing, but we take general writing pieces too. I don't get enough humor. Half our magazine is open to freelancers. I like how-to pieces. Overstocked on rejection pieces. Looking for articles on viewpoint, collaboration, figures of speech, or avoiding clichés."

*THE POETRY CONNECTION, 13455 SW 16th Ct. #F-405, Pembroke Pines FL 33027. (954)431-3016. Sylvia Shichman, ed/pub. Information for poets, writers and song writers; also greeting card markets. Monthly newsletter; circ. 200. Subscription $20. Phone query OK. Not copyrighted. Guidelines; copy $7/10x13 SAE/$2 postage.

Poetry: Free verse.

Contests: Lists contests in newsletter.

Note: Also offers membership in the Magic Circle, a reading network service for poetry and lyrics. Membership $20. Poems and lyrics will be read over a Florida radio station, WLRN. In addition, rents a mailing list that includes poets, writers, song writers, professional artists, sound recorders, and demotape organizations.

SOUTHWESTERN WRITERS NEWSLETTER, PO Box 331509, Ft. Worth TX 76163-1509. (817)346-6188. Fax (817)292-9525. Protestant. Tillie Read, pub. Writing helps for seniors. Quarterly newsletter; 8-12 pgs; circ. 42. Subscription $10. 75% freelance. Query; fax query OK. **PAYS IN COPIES** for one-time rts. Not copyrighted. Articles 1-2 pgs(4/yr); short book reviews. Responds in 2 wks. Accepts reprints (tell when/where appeared). No disk. Sidebars OK. Guidelines; copy $2.50/6x9 SAE/2 stamps.

Poetry: Accepts 4/yr. Free verse, haiku, light verse, traditional. Submit max. 4 poems.

Fillers: Accepts 4/yr. Anecdotes, prayers, quotes, word puzzles.

Columns/Departments: Accepts 4/yr., 1/2 page. Writing tips.

TEACHERS & WRITERS, 5 Union Square W, New York NY 10003. (212)691-6590. Fax (212)675-0171. Website: http://www.twc.org. Ron Padgett & Chris Edgar, eds. On teaching creative and imaginative writing for children. Mag published 5X/yr; circ 1,500-2,000. Query. **PAYS IN COPIES**. Articles 3,000-6,000 wds. Copy $2.50.

TICKLED BY THUNDER, 7385 - 129 St., Surrey BC V3W 7B8 Canada. Phone/fax

(604)591-6095. E-mail: larry-lindner@mindlink.bc.ca. Larry Lindner, ed. Helps writers get published. Quarterly chapbook; 24 pgs; circ 1,000. Subscription $12 (or $10 US). 95% freelance. Complete ms/cover letter; e-mail query OK. Pays $2-5 (in Canadian or US stamps) on publication for 1st rts. Articles 1,500 wds (5/yr); fiction 2,000 wds (20/yr); book reviews 500 wds. Responds in 12 wks. Seasonal 4 mos ahead. Accepts simultaneous submissions. Prefers disk. Sidebars OK. Guidelines; copy $2.50/9x12 SAE/2 US stamps or $1.00 CAN (unattached). (Ads)

> **Poetry:** Accepts 20-40/yr. Free verse, light verse, traditional; to 40 lines. Submit max. 7 poems.
>
> **Contest:** For fiction, articles and poetry. For subscribers only. Send SASE for guidelines.
>
> **Tips:** "Participate in contests. If writing a religious story, it must do more than push religious buttons. It must stand on its own and not be dragged down by the 'moral' at the end. Looking for articles about writing and writer's groups."

TODAY'S $85,000 FREELANCE WRITER, PO Box 543, Oradell NJ 07648. (201)262-3277. Fax (201)599-2635. E-mail: bskcom@tiac.net. Website: http://www.tiac.net/users/bskcom. BSK Communications & Assoc. Brian Konradt, ed. Focuses on the business and marketing side of freelance writing. Bimonthly mag; 40 pgs; circ 3,000. Subscription $23.70. 95% freelance. Query/clips; phone/fax query OK. Pays .05/wd on publication for 1st rts. Articles 200-2,500 wds. Responds in 4-9 wks. Seasonal 4 mos ahead. Requires disk. Kill fee. Requires sidebars. Guidelines (also at Website); copy $5.

> **Poetry:** To 24 lines.
>
> **Fillers:** Buys 20/yr. Prose, 100-500 wds; newsbreaks, 50-300 wds. Pays $5-15.

W.I.N. INFORMER (Writers' Information Network), Box 11337, Bainbridge Island WA 98110. (206)842-9103. Fax (206)842-0536. E-mail: writersinfonetwork@ juno.com. Professional Christian writers marketing news. Elaine Wright Colvin, ed. Bimonthly mag; 32-36 pgs; circ 1,000+. Subscription $29.95 ($35 Canada/foreign). 30% freelance. Complete ms/cover letter; phone/fax/e-mail query OK. Pays $10-50 (copies or subscription) on publication for 1st rts. Articles 50-300 wds (30/yr); book reviews, 300 wds. Guidelines; copy $5/9x12 SAE/$1.47 postage. (Ads—members and writing-related)

> **Poetry:** Any type.
>
> **Fillers:** Anecdotes, facts, ideas, newsbreaks, quizzes, quotes, prayers, short humor; 50-300 wds; $10-50.
>
> **Columns/Departments:** Buys 42/yr. Industry News, Market News, Bulletin Board, Computer Corner, Speakers Platform, Poetry News, and Readers Q & A; $10-25.
>
> **Tips:** "Be on the cutting edge of what's happening in the religious publishing industry; talk to agents, professional writers and editors."

*THE WRITE TOUCH, PO Box 695, Selah WA 98942. (509)966-3524. Tim Anderson, ed. For writers trying to get published. Monthly newsletter; 12 pgs; circ 40. Subscription $15/yr. Est. 1994. 100% freelance. Complete ms/cover letter. **PAYS 3 COPIES**, for one-time rts. Essays on various subjects (120/yr) & fiction for all ages (120/yr), 100-500 wds. Responds in 2-4 wks. Seasonal 2 mos ahead. Discourages simultaneous submissions & reprints. Accepts disk. Guidelines; copy $1.

Poetry: Any type; 4-30 lines. Submit maximum 3 poems.

Fillers: Anecdotes, facts, ideas, prose, short humor; 15-50 wds.

THE WRITER, 120 Boylston St., Boston MA 02116-4615. (617)423-3157. Fax (617)423-2168. E-mail: writer@user1.channel1.com. Secular. Sylvia Burack, ed/pub. How-to for writers; lists religious markets in December. Monthly mag; 48 pgs; circ 50,000. Subscription $28. 75% freelance. Query. Pays $100 (varies) on acceptance for 1st rts. Articles to 2,000 wds (60/yr). Responds in 3 wks. No disks. No sidebars. No guidelines; copy $3.50. (Ads)

Poetry: Accepts poetry for critiques in "Poet to Poet" column; to 30 lines; no payment. No religious poetry. Submit max. 3 poems.

Fillers: Prose.

Columns/Departments: Buys 24+/yr. Rostrum (shorter pcs. on the craft of writing), 1,000 wds; Off the Cuff (somewhat more personal tone), 1,000-1,200 wds; $75.

Special Needs: How-to on the craft of writing only.

*WRITERS CONNECTION, PO Box 24770, San Jose CA 95154-4770. (408)554-2090. Fax (408)554-2099. Jan Stiles, ed. Nuts and bolts information on writing and publishing in all fields (except poetry). Monthly newsletter; circ 1,500. Subscription/membership $45. Also distributed electronically. 60% freelance. Complete ms; query/clips for profiles. Pays $25-75 on publication for 1st or reprint rts. Articles 800-2,200 wds (25-32/yr); book reviews, 200-300 wds (pays 2 copies). Responds in 9 wks. Seasonal 4 mos ahead. Accepts reprints. Guidelines; copy $3.

Fillers: Accepts 4-10/yr. Facts, newsbreaks, tips, resources; 50-350 wds.

Columns/Departments: Profiles (useful info/insights from professional editors/agents), 725-800 wds; Business & Technical Writing (hard info on how to write), 750-825 wds; $25-50.

Special Needs: In-depth articles on how to write or market your writing (technique). No religious slant or tone.

Tips: "Most open to short features or columns; shorter articles that offer specific, in-depth help for writers."

WRITER'S DIGEST, 1507 Dana Ave., Cincinnati OH 45207. (513)531-2222. Fax (513)531-1843. E-mail: writersdig@juno.com. Secular/F & W Publications. Amanda Boyd, asst. ed. To inform, instruct or inspire the freelancer. Monthly mag; 76 pgs; circ 225,000. Subscription $27. 90% freelance. Query/clips; e-mail query OK. Pays .15-.40/wd on acceptance for 1st and reprint rts. Articles 500-3,000 wds (100/yr). Responds in 9 wks. Seasonal 8 mos ahead. Accepts reprints (tell when/where appeared). Prefers disk. Kill fee 20%. Sidebars OK. Guidelines; copy $3.50 ($3.70 in OH). (Ads—Call Joan Wright, 800-234-0963)

Poetry: Buys 10-15/yr. Light verse on writing; 2-20 lines; $10-50. Submit max. 8 poems.

Fillers: Buys to 50/yr. Anecdotes & short humor on writing; 50-250 wds; .10-.15/wd.

Columns/Departments: Buys 100-150/yr. The Writing Life (anecdotes about writing life & short profiles), 50-800 wds; Tip Sheet (short solutions to writer/business-related problems), 50-600 wds; Chronicle (1st-person narrative about writing life), 1,200-1,500 wds. Pays .10-.15/wd.

Contests: Sponsors annual contest for articles, short stories, poetry and scripts. Also The National Self-Publishing Book Awards. Send SASE for rules.

Tips: "Always in the market for technique pieces. Writing Life and Tip sheet items are great ways to break in."

WRITER'S EXCHANGE, Box 394, Society Hill SC 29593. E-mail: Eboone@ aol.com. R.S.V.P. Press. Eugene Boone, ed. Features writings and small press markets for writers and poets at all levels. Quarterly mag; 36-40 pgs; circ 350. Subscription $12. 100% freelance. Complete ms/cover letter; query for electronic submissions. **PAYS IN COPIES** for one-time rts. Articles 350-5,000 wds (20-30/yr); book reviews 500 wds. Responds in 2-4 wks. Seasonal 6-12 mos ahead. Accepts reprints (tell when/where appeared). Accepts disk. Sidebars OK. Guidelines; copy for 6x9 SAE/3 stamps. (Ads)

Poetry: Accepts 100-150/yr. Any type; 3-35 lines. Submit max. 8 poems.

Fillers: Accepts 300/yr. Various; 10-750 wds.

Special Needs: Poetry how-to; writing techniques; personal experiences with writing groups, conferences, writing courses, using computers, etc. What worked and what didn't.

Contest: Quarterly poetry contest; send SASE for rules.

WRITER'S FORUM, Writer's Digest School, 1507 Dana Ave., Cincinnati OH 45207. (513)531-2222. Fax (513)531-1843. E-mail: writersdig@juno.com. Secular F&W Publications. Amanda Boyd, ed. Writing techniques, marketing and inspiration for Writer's Digest correspondence school students. Quarterly newsletter; 16 pgs; circ 13,000. Subscription $10. 100% freelance. Complete ms/cover letter; e-mail query OK. Pays $10-25 on acceptance for reprint rts. Articles 500-1,000 wds (20/yr). Responds in 6 wks. Seasonal 4 mos ahead. Accepts reprints (tell when/where appeared). Accepts disk. Free guidelines/copy for #10 SAE/3 stamps.

Tips: "A great market for reprints. How-to pieces geared toward beginning writers always stand a good chance. Articles must have a how-to slant; focus on writing technique."

*WRITER'S INK, PO Box 93156, Henderson NV 89009-3156. (800)974-8465. Panabaker Publications. Darla R. Panabaker, ed. Supplies writers with information on writing and selling. Monthly newsletter; 12 pgs; circ. 100. Subscription $24. Est. 1995. 90-95% freelance. Query or complete ms. **PAYS IN COPIES** for 1st, one-time or simultaneous rts. Articles 50-1,000 wds (200/yr); book reviews, 500 wds. Responds within 4 wks. Seasonal 3-6 mos ahead. Accepts simultaneous submissions & reprints. Sidebars OK. Guidelines; copy for 9x12 SAE/2 stamps.

Poetry: All types; on writing topics; to 50 lines. Send any number.

Fillers: Ideas, newsbreaks, quizzes, quotes; to 50 wds.

Columns/Departments: Looking for freelancers to write columns. Topics and subject matter open. Please inquire.

Contest: 1998 Poetry Competition. $100 grand prize. Deadline November 15. Send SASE for rules.

Tips: "Send article with letter describing your previous experience. All areas open. We use a different writer for each cover article. "

+WRITERS' INTERNATIONAL FORUM, PO Box 516, Tracyton WA 98393. Bristol Services Intl. Sandra E. Haven, ed. For those who write to sell. Monthly (10X) newsletter; 6-8 pgs. Subscription $24. 25% freelance. Complete ms/cover letter; no phone/fax/e-mail query. Pays $20-30 (essays), $30 for fiction, on acceptance for 1st rts. Essays to 1,000 wds (4/yr); fiction to 1,000 wds (8/yr). Responds in 6 wks. Seasonal 4 mos ahead. No disk. Guidelines; copy for $3/#10 SAE/1 stamp.

Contest: Sponsors two contests a year for adult writers. Send SASE for details.

Tips: "We use well-crafted essays or short stories only. Rarely use writing-related essays and no slices-of-life or vignettes."

*WRITER'S JOURNAL, PO Box 25376, St. Paul MN 55125-0376. (612)730-4280. Fax (612)730-4356. Secular. Valerie Hockert, ed. Bimonthly journal; circ 52,000. 40% freelance. Complete ms. Pays to $50, 60 days after publication, for 1st rts. Articles 700-1,000 wds (30-40/yr). Responds in 4-6 wks. Seasonal 6 mos ahead. Accepts simultaneous query. Not in topical listings. Guidelines; copy $4.

Poetry: Esther M. Leiper. Buys 20-30/yr. All types; to 25 lines; .25/line. Submit max. 5 poems.

Contest: Runs 2 poetry contests each year, spring and fall. Prizes $15-50. Reading fee $5/entry (4 max.).

*WRITER'S LIFELINE, Box 1641, Cornwall ON K6H 5V6 Canada. (613)932-2135. Stephen Gill, mng. ed. For professional freelancers and beginning writers. Bimonthly mag; 16-35 pgs; circ 1,500. Needs articles of interest to writers, news items of national and international interest, letters to the editor, poetry, interviews. Needs book reviewers; **PAYS IN BOOK REVIEWED & COPIES**. Not in topical listings.

*THE WRITER'S NOOK NEWS, 38114 3rd St. #181, Willoughby OH 44094-6140. (216)953-9292. Fax (216)354-6403. Secular. Eugene Ortiz, ed./pub. Dedicated to giving freelance writers specific information for their immediate practical use in getting published and staying published. Quarterly newsletter; circ 2,000. Subscription $18. 100% freelance. Complete ms. Pays .06/wd on acceptance for 1st rts. Not copyrighted. Articles 100-400 wds (80/yr); book reviews 50-100 wds (.06/wd). Responds in 26 wks. Guidelines; copy $5.

Fillers: Buys 20/yr. Facts, newsbreaks; 20-100 wds.

Tips: "Most open to tips and suggestions about the process of writing and publishing."

*WRITING & SURFING, The Writer's & Journalist's Guide to Making the Most Out of Online Services, 223 Wall St., Huntington NY 11743-2060. (516)421-1682. Write Way Communications. Debra A. Velsmid, ed. Monthly newsletter; 8 pgs. Subscription $18. Est. 1996. Query or complete ms. **PAYS 2 COPIES.** Articles 500 wds. Guidelines; copy $1.50, free 4-pg introductory issue.

+WRITING WORLD, 44 Tarleton Rd., Newton MA 02159. Submit to The Editor.

Bimonthly newsletter; 8 pgs. Subscription $39. Little freelance. Copy for $5/#10 SAE. Not in topical listings.

Contest: Occasionally; see sample issues.

Tips: "Look at back issues and send a fantastic query that shows you've read us."

MARKET ANALYSIS

PERIODICALS IN ORDER BY CIRCULATION

ADULT/GENERAL
Guideposts 3,800,000
Focus on the Family
   2,500,000
Decision 1,800,000
Columbia 1,500,000
Plus 600,000
Catholic Digest 503,500
Marion Helpers 500,000
Oblates 500,000
St. Anthony Messenger
   359,000
Mature Living 350,000
Miraculous Medal 340,000
Lutheran Witness 325,000
Liguorian 300,000
War Cry 300,000
Anglican Journal 272,000
Liberty 250,000
Pentecostal Evangel 250,000
Power for Living 250,000
Signs of the Times 245,000
Upscale Magazine 242,000
Christian Reader 225,000
Charisma & Christian Life
   220,000
Voice (CA) 200,000
Episcopal Life 180,000
Ideals 180,000
Christianity Today 172,500
Lutheran Digest 155,000
The Family Digest 150,000
The Lutheran 150,000
Standard 150,000
Celebrate Life 145,000
Smart Families 140,000
The Plain Truth 135,000
Live 130,000
Lutheran Journal 127,000
Our Sunday Visitor 120,000
United Church Observer
   120,000
Christian Parenting Today
   118,000
Moody 115,000
ParentLife 115,000
Discipleship Journal 110,000

The Lookout 105,000
Presbyterian Survey 105,000
Catholic Forester 100,000+
Christian Entertainment
   100,000
Computing Today 100,000
Kaleidoscope 100,000
Real FamilyLife 100,000
Foursquare World Advance
   98,000
Christian Computing 90,000
Living (tabloid) 90,000
Total Health 90,000
Herald of Holiness 76,000
Spirit of Revival 74,000
Christian History 70,000
Mature Years 70,000
Message 70,000
Physician 68,820
alive now! 65,000
Good News (KY)65,000
Christian Single 63,000
Christian Home & School
   62,000
Catholic Answer 60,000
Christian Standard 59,000
Conquest 55,000
Marriage Partnership 55,000
Northwestern Lutheran 55,000
Presbyterian Record 55,000
Church of God Evangel
   51,000
Gospel Today 50,000
Pursuit 50,000
Single-Parent Family 50,000
Sports Spectrum 50,000
Today's Christian Senior
   50,000
Trumpeter, The 50,000
Who Cares 50,000
Annals of St. Anne 45,000
Seek 45,000
Living with Teenagers 42,000
Catholic Parent 40,000
Christian Motorsports 40,000
Christmas 40,000
A Positive Approach 40,000

Stand Firm 40,000
Vibrant Life 40,000
Weavings 40,000
Cornerstone 38,000
America 36,000
Christian Research Journal
   35,000
Good News Journal 35,000
Highway News 35,000
U.S. Catholic 35,000
Church & State 33,000
The Banner 32,000
Cathedral Age 32,000
First Things 31,500
Catholic Twin Circle 30,000
Evangelical Beacon 30,000
Lifeglow 30,000
Progress 30,000
ProLife News Canada 30,000
At Ease 28,000
The Messenger 27,000
Common Boundary 26,000
African-American Heritage
   25,000
Catholic Heritage 25,000
Interim 25,000
Pray! 25,000
Sojourners 24,000
Light and Life 23,000
Canada Lutheran 23,000
Pentecostal Testimony 21,700
Homeschooling Today 21,000
Accent on Living 20,000
Canadian Mennonite 20,000
Covenant Companion 20,000
The Evangel 20,000
God's Revivalist 20,000
Messenger of St. Anthony
   20,000
New Covenant 20,000
Visitation 20,000
Evangel 19,000-20,000
Commonweal 19,000
Faith Today 18,000
Gadfly Magazine 18,000
SCP Journal 18,000
Experiencing God 17,000

The Door 16,000
Visitation 16,000
AXIOS 15,670
St. Joseph's Messenger 15,500
Christian Edge 15,000
Mennonite Brethren Herald
 15,000
Poet's Park 15,000
Wesleyan Advocate 15,000
Our Family 14,300
Gems of Truth 14,000
Messenger/Sacred Heart
 14,000
New Oxford Review 14,000
Purpose 13,800
Insights 13,500
Emphasis on Faith & Living
 13,000
Island Christian Info 13,000
Bible Advocate 12,500
Books & Culture 12,000
New Horizons 12,000
Table Talk 12,000
Today's Christian Doctor
 12,000
Presbyterian Outlook 11,900
CBA Frontline 11,000
E Street 11,000
Spiritual Life 11,000
The Standard 11,000
Review for Religious 10,200
Disciple's Journal 10,000
Immaculate Heart Messenger
 10,000
Rosebud 10,000
Sacred Journey 10,000
Smart Dads 10,000
The Vision 10,000
The Christian Leader 9,800
Montana Catholic 9,300
Canadian Baptist 9,000
Celebration (Catholic) 9,000
Journal of Christian Nursing
 9,000
Living Church 9,000
Religious Broadcasting 9,000
Sharing 9,000
Prairie Messenger 8,600
CBA Marketplace 8,000
Companions 8,000
The Family 8,000
The Mennonite 8,000
Brethren Evangelist 7,950
Atlantic Baptist 7,500
Plough 7,500
Lutheran Parent 7,300
The Bible Today 7,000
The Gem 7,000

Master's Community 7,000
MN Christian Chronicle 7,000
MovieGuide 7,000
2 Soar 7,000
Christian Courier (CAN)
 6,000
Heartlight Internet 6,000
Impact 6,000
Prism 6,000
General Baptist Messenger
 5,600
Bread of Life 5,200
Contact 5,200
AGAIN 5,000
Companion 5,000
The Evangelical Advocate
 5,000
Green Cross 5,000
Hallelujah! 5,000
Healing Inn 5,000
A New Heart 5,000
The Plowman 5,000
Way of St. Francis 5,000
The Lutheran Ambassador
 4,800
Social Justice Review 4,750
Cresset 4,700
Christian Civic League/ME
 4,600
Chesapeake Citizen 4,500
Christian Living 4,500
Evangelical Visitor 4,500
Message/Open Bible 4,300
ADVOCATE 4,000
Christian Renewal 4,000
Evangelical Baptist 4,000
The Kansas Christian 4,000
Preserving Christian Homes
 4,000
The Witness 4,000
Fellowship Today 3,900
Compass 3,700
Cross Currents 3,500
Culture Wars 3,500
Servant Life 3,500
Perspectives on Science 3,300
Advent Christian Witness
 3,200
Catholilc Insight 3,100
Alive! 3,000
Christianity & the Arts 3,000
Chrysalis Reader 3,000
North American Voice 3,000
Perspectives 3,000
Poets' Paper 3,000
Quiet Revolution 3,000
Rural Landscapes 3,000
Queen of All Hearts 2,800

Mennonite Historian 2,600
The Inspirer 2,500
The Messenger (NC) 2,500
Railroad Evangelist 2,500
Gospel Tidings 2,300
Apocalypse Chronicles 2-
 3,000
Answers in Action 2,000
Baptist History & Heritage
 2,000
Christian Chronicle 2,000
Christian Social Action 2,000
Fellowship Link 2,000
Religious Education 2,000
Touchstone 1,800
Church Herald/Holiness
 Banner 1,700
Journal/Church & State 1,700
Christian Arts Review 1,500
Dovetail 1,500
Jewel Among Jewels 1,500
Grail 1,300
Comments From the Friends
 1,200
The New Trumpet 1,200
Bible Reflections 1,100
Canadian Catholic Review
 1,000
Connecting Point 1,000
Head to Head 1,000
Methodist History 1,000
Moonletters 1,000
No-Debt Living 1,000
Pourastan 1,000
The RIVER 1,000
Broken Streets 500
Hearing Hearts 500
St. Willibrord Journal 500
The Voice 500
Heavenly Thoughts 430
Burning Light 400
Poetry Forum 400
Explorer 300+
Lighthouse Fiction 300
Silver Wings 300
Time of Singing 300
Remembrance 250
Smile 230
Dreams & Visions 200
TEAK Roundup 200
Family Network 150
Pegasus Review 130
Keys to Living 125
Ratio 100
Upsouth 75
New Creation 64

CHILDREN

God's World Today 301,000
Guideposts for Kids 200,000+
Venture 140,000
FOF Clubhouse 100,000
Pockets 93,000
High Adventure 86,000
FOF Clubhouse Jr. 80,000
Crusader (TN) 60,000
R-A-D-A-R 56,000
Junior Trails 50,000
Our Little Friend 45-50,000
Courage 40,000
Live Wire 40,000
Power & Light 40,000
Wonder Time 40,000
Primary Treasure 35,000
GUIDE 33,000
Together Time 19,000
Club Connection 18,000-
  20,000
Venture 18,000
Touch 14,000
My Friend 12,000
Crusader (MI) 12,300
BREAD for God's Children
  10,000
CLUBHOUSE 8,000
Nature Friend 7,600
Listen 7,500
Story Friends 7,000
On the Line 6,000
Partners 5,800
Story Mates 5,500
Junior Companion 3,500
Primary Pal 2,900
Beginner's Friend 2,700
Skipping Stones 2,500
Discovery 2,060

CHRISTIAN
EDUCATION/LIBRARY

Children's Ministry 65,000
GROUP 55,000
Catechist 50,000
Parish Teacher 50,000
Today's Catholic Teacher
  50,000
Religion Teacher's Journal
  40,000
Teachers in Focus 35,000
Church Media Library 30,000
Group's Jr. High Ministry
  25,000
Perspective 24,000
CE Counselor 20,000
Lollipops 20,000

Evangelizing Today's Child
  15,000
Teachers Interaction 14,000
Shining Star 12,000
CE Leadership 9,800
Leader/Church School Today
  9,000
Resource 9,000
Journal/Adventist Ed 7,400
Kids' Ministry Ideas 7,500
CE Connection 6,600
Vision (CA) 6,000
Church Educator 4,500
Christian Educator's Journal
  4,200
Leader 3,500
Church & Synagogue Librar-
  ies 3,000
The Youth Leader 2,800
Insight into CE 2,200
Team 2,000
Changing Lives 1,800
Caravan 1,500
CE Connection Communique
  1,350
Christian Library Journal
  1,000
Church Libraries 600
Christian Librarian 500

MISSIONS

Catholic Near East 100,000
Worldwide Challenge 100,000
Quiet Hour Echoes 80,000
World Vision 78,000
World Christian 40,000
American Horizon 39,200
American Baptist in Mission
  39,000
New World Outlook 30,000
P.I.M.E. World 26,000
Heartbeat 20,000
Latin America Evangelist
  17,000
Wherever 17,000
Message of the Cross 10,000
Evangelical Missions 7,000
World Mission People 7,000
Leaders for Today 6,500
World Pulse 5,000
PFI World Report 4,750
Missiology 2,000
Urban Mission 1,300
Areopagus 1,000
Intl. Journal/Frontier 600
East-West Church 430

MUSIC

Music Makers 105,000
CCM Magazine 85,000
Glory Songs 85,000
Music Time 60,000
7 Ball 50,000
Church Pianist 35,000
Plans & Pluses 35,000
Senior Musician 32,000
Church Musician 16,000
Church Music Report 6,200
Creator 6,000
Gospel Industry Today 3,500
The Hymn 3,000
Tradition 2,500
Christian Composer 2,000-
  6,000
Christian Country 300-1,200

NEWSPAPERS

Presbyterian Layman 520,000
Christian American 400,000
Inside Journal 375,000
Anglican Journal 272,000
Living 250,000
Episcopal Life 170,000
Together 150,000
Catholic New York 130,000
Our Sunday Visitor 125,000
The Alabama Baptist 117,000
Pulpit Helps 106,000
Save Our World 97,000
Something Better News
  75,000
Arlington Catholic Herald
  53,000
Good News Journal 50,000
Catholic Courier 48,000
National Catholic Reporter
  48,000
Dallas/Ft Worth Heritage
  45,000
Good News Etc. 40,000
Indian Life 38,000
Metro Voice 35,000
Catholic Twin Circle 30,000
Single Connection 30,000
Christian Ranchman 28,000
Catholic Telegraph 27,000
NW Christian Journal 26,000
Christian Crusade 25,000
Discovery 25,000
The Interim 25,000
Oblate World 25,000
United Voice 25,000
Catholic Servant 24,000
Life Gate 23,000

The Family Journal 22,000
B.C. Catholic 20,000
Catholic Peace Voice 20,000
Christian News Northwest
20,000
Good News (AL) 20,000
Harvest Press 20,000
The Shantyman 17,000
Christian Advocate 16,000
The Revelation Post 15,000-
45,000
Catholic Sentinel 15,000
Expression Christian Newspa-
per 15,000
Messenger (KY) 15,000
Network 15,000
Island Christian Info 14,000
Church Advocate 13,000
Interchange 12,600
Michigan Christian Advocate
12,000
Mennonite Weekly Review
11,000
Awareness Tennessee 10,000
Baptist Informer 10,000
Christian Courier (WI) 10,000
Disciple's Journal 10,000
Living Light News 10,000
Montana Catholic 8,300
Star of Zion 8,000
Arkansas Catholic 7,000
Minnesota Chr. Chronicle
7,000
John Milton 5,285
Christian Courier (Canada)
5,000
The Parent Paper 5,000
Christian Renewal 4,500
Home Times 4,000
Harvest Times 3,000
Inland NW Christian 2,500
Christian Media 2-6,000
Christian Observer 2,000
Christian Edge 1,500
Diocesan Dialogue 750
Prayerworks 600
Fatted Calf Forum 100

PASTORS/LEADERS

Your Church 150,000
Pulpit Helps 105,000
Leadership Journal 70,000
Eucharistic Minister 50,000
Plugged In 50,000
Worship Leader 43,000
Voice of the Vineyard 40,000
Enrichment 32,000
Christian Century 30,000

Pastor's Family 28,500
Today's Christian Preacher
25,000
Vital Ministry 25,000
Parish Liturgy 22,000
Christian Counseling Today
20,000
Lutheran Partners 20,000
Ministry 20,000
Modern Liturgy 20,000
Preacher's Magazine 18,000
Christian Recreation 17,000
Current Thoughts & Trends
17,000
Proclaim 15,000
Today's Parish 14,800
Ministry Now Profiles 13,500
Youthworker 13,200
Theology Today 13,000+
Cell Church 12,000
Church Administration 12,000
Preaching 10,000-12,000
Christian Sentinel 10,000
Church Bytes 10,000
Clergy Journal 10,000
Jour/Pastoral Care 10,000
Joyful Noiseletter 10,000
Resource 10,000
Technologies/Worship 10,000
Celebration 9,000
Review for Religious 9,000
Bibliotheca Sacra 8,500
Church Growth Network
8,000
Faith & Renewal 8,000
Student Leadership Journal
8,000
The Priest 7,800
Christian Camp & Confer-
ence 7,500
Christian Ministry 6,600
Journal/Christian Camping
6,000
Pastor's Tax & Money 6,000
WCA Monthly 6,000
Catechumenate 5,600
Baptist Leader 5,000
Brigade Leader 5,000
Cross Currents 5,000
National Drama Service 5,000
Single Adult Min Jour 5,000
The Preacher 4,500
Emmanuel 4,000+
Reformed Worship 4,000
Lutheran Forum 3,200
Word & World 3,100
Art+Plus 3,000
Issachar File 3,000

Sermon Notes 3,000
Environment & Art 2,500
Christian Management Report
2,300
Liturgy 2,300
Pastoral Life 1,800
Networks 1,700
Quarterly Review 1,500
Church Worship 1,200
Five Stones 1,200
Jour/Christian Healing 1,200
Ivy Jungle Report 800
Cell Life 300+
Jour/Amer Soc/Chur Growth
300

TEEN/YOUNG ADULT

Brio 170,000
Visions 140,000
The Rock 125,000
Campus Life 100,000
Breakaway 90,000
Listen 65,000
Sharing the Victory 60,000
Devo'Zine 58,000
Alive! 50,000+
Teen Life 50,000
Young Salvationist 48,000
Youth 98 40,000
Today's Christian Teen 39,800
Cross Walk 35,000
You! 35,000
Spirit 30,000
Straight 30,000
Take Five 30,000
Young & Alive 26,000
Challenge (GA) 21,000
Insight 20,000
Certainty 18,000
Youth Update 18,000
Challenge (IL) 16,000
Teenage Christian 10,500
Student Leadership 8,500
Young Adult Today 7,500
Teens on Target 7,000
The Conqueror 6,000
With 6,000
Youth Challenge 5,500
Beautiful Christian Teen 5,000
Youth Compass 4,800
Young Christian 1,500

WOMEN

Today's Christian Woman
351,000
Lutheran Woman Today
230,000

Lutheran Woman's Quarterly 200,000
Journey 150,000
Virtue 110,000
Aspire 50,000
Horizons 25,000
Women of Spirit 17,000
Woman's Touch 16,000+
Welcome Home 15,000
CoLaborer 11,000
Church Woman 10,000
Conscience 10,000
Journal/Women's Ministries 10,000
Esprit 7,000
Joyful Woman 7,000
Just Between Us 5,000
Link & Visitor 4,500
Women Alive 3,500-4,000
Sisters Today 3,500
Wesleyan Woman 3,500
Helping Hand 3,000
Probe 3,000
The Handmaiden 2,500

Proverbs 31 Homemaker 2,000
Virtuous Woman 350
Salt & Light 300
Domestique 200
Anna's Journal 40

WRITERS
Writer's Digest 225,000
Writer's Journal 52,000
The Writer 50,000
Writer's Forum (OH) 13,000
Inklings 10,000
Christian Communicator 4,000
Byline 3,000+
Today's $85,000 Freelance Writer 3,000
Housewife-Writers Forum 2,000
Writer's Nook News 2,000
Teachers & Writers 1,500-2,000
Writers Connection 1,500

Writer's Lifeline 1,500
Cross & Quill 1,000+
Writers Information Network 1,000+
Advanced Christian Writer 1,000
New Writing 1,000
Once Upon a Time 1,000
Tickled By Thunder 1,000
Christian Response 400
Canadian Writer's Journal 385
Writer's Exchange 350
Omnific 300+
My Legacy 200+
Fellowscript 200
Gotta Write Network 200
The Poetry Connection 200
Exchange 185
Writer's Ink 100
Northwest Christian Author 60
Southwestern Writers 42
The Write Touch 40

PERIODICAL TOPICS IN ORDER OF POPULARITY

NOTE: Following is a list of topics in order by popularity. To find the list of publishers interested in each of these topics, go to the Topical Listings for periodicals and find the topic you are interested in. The numbers indicate how many periodical editors said they were interested in seeing something of that type or topic. There are 296 photography markets this year. (*—new topic this year)

Non-topics:
 -Photographs 296
 -Newspapers 79
 -Contests 66
 -Canadian/Foreign 60
 -Take-home Papers 47
 *On-Line Magazines 11

1. Personal Experience 264
2. Christian Living 260
3. Family Life 257
4. Current Social Issues 249
5. Inspirational 249
6. Prayer 246
7. Poetry 245
8. Holiday/Seasonal 244
9. Interviews/Profiles 240
10. Evangelism/Witnessing 229
11. Spirituality 208
12. Marriage 194
13. True Stories 193
14. Humor 188
15. Devotionals/Meditations 186

16. Worship 185
17. Book Reviews 183
18. Discipleship 180
19. Christian Education 177
20. Relationships 177
21. Women's Issues 172
22. Missions 170
23. Fillers: Cartoons 167
24. Parenting 166
25. Youth Issues 166
26. Church Outreach 160
27. How-To 157
28. Controversial Issues 155
29. Leadership 144
30. Ethics 142
31. Theological 141
32. Bible Studies 136
33. Think Pieces 133
34. World Issues 132
35. Men's Issues 130
36. Short Story: Adult/Religious 129
37. Historical 123
38. Fillers: Anecdotes 122

39. Health 119
40. Money Management 117
41. Opinion Pieces 116
42. Ethnic/Cultural Issues 115
43. Fillers: Short Humor 115
44. Divorce 112
45. Environmental Issues 111
46. Religious Freedom 110
47. Essays 106
48. Singles Issues 105
49. Celebrity Pieces 104
50. Salvation Testimonies 104
51. Senior-Adult Issues 103
52. Short Story: Humorous 102
53. Doctrinal 100
54. Stewardship 99
55. Healing 98
56. Church Life 94
57. Social Justice 94
58. Short Story: Contemporary 92
59. Fillers: Ideas 91
60. Church Growth 88

61. Fillers: Facts 87
62. Book Excerpts 85
63. Cults/Occult 85
64. Short Story: Biblical 85
65. Liturgical 84
66. Sports/Recreation 83
67. Christian Business 80
68. Home Schooling 80
69. Miracles 80
70. Church Management 77
71. Fillers: Quotes 77
72. Short Story: Parables 77
73. Death/Dying 73
74. Economics 73
75. Music Reviews 73
76. Political 70
77. Short Story: Adventure 69
78. Spiritual Warfare 69
79. Fillers: Quizzes 68
80. Fillers: Prose 67
81. Fillers: Word Puzzles 67

82. Nature 64
83. Short Story: Historical 63
84. Fillers: Games 62
85. Fillers: Newsbreaks 62
86. How-To Activities (Juv.) 60
87. Fillers: Jokes 59
88. Fillers: Prayers 57
89. Short Story: Teen/Young Adult 56
90. Short Story: Juvenile 55
91. Travel 54
92. Psychology 51
93. Food/Recipes 50
94. Self-Help 49
95. Short Story: Allegory 49
96. Prophecy 48
97. Science 48
98. Sociology 43
99. Sermons 40
100. Short Story: Literary 39

101. Short Story: Mystery 39
102. Writing How-To 39
103. Creation Science 35
104. Short Story: Fantasy 35
105. Video Reviews 34
106. Short Story: Romance 28
107. Fillers: Party Ideas 27
108. Short Story: Frontier 26
109. Short Story: Plays 26
110. Short Story: Science Fiction 25
111. Short Story: Skits 20
112. Short Story: Ethnic 17
113. Puppet Plays 16
114. Short Story: Frontier Romance 12
115. Short Story: Mystery Romance 12
116. Short Story: Historical Romance 10

Comments:

If you are a short story writer, the biggest market is for adult fiction (129 markets—up 2 from last year), then teen, holding second place (56 markets—same as last year), followed closely by juvenile (55 markets—4 more than last year). The most popular genres (in order) are Humorous, Contemporary, Biblical, Parables, Adventure, Historical, and Allegory. Compared to last year, they are in the same order, except for Allegory which fell behind Historical again. The least popular are still the genre romances.

After leveling off last year, this year poetry started to drop slightly in the ratings, going from 260 markets last year to 246 this year. It also dropped from the fourth most popular topic last year to the seventh most popular this year. Nevertheless the poetry market remains strong with a total number of poems expected to be bought or accepted by those markets at about 7,655—over 200 more than last year. The book market for poetry dropped from 33 to 30 this year, so I still recommend that the serious poet pursue the periodical markets and establish a good reputation as a poet before every attempting to sell a book of poetry.

This year the same topics are in the top 11, although every one is in a different position than last year. Personal Experience moved from third to first, Christian Living dropped from first to second, and Family life from second to third. Except for poetry which dropped three places, the others only moved up or down one position. In fiction, Humorous, Historical, Juvenile, Literary, Mystery, Ethnic, and Frontier-Romance went up some; Adult, Contemporary, Biblical, Parables, Adventure, Teen, Allegory, Fantasy, Frontier, Plays, Mystery-Romance, and Historical-Romance went down (Allegory, Parables, Biblical and Adventure the most); and the others stayed the same. The biggest drop was in Allegory which dropped 11 places in the ratings; the biggest gains in Juvenile and Mystery which each moved up 4 places.

Following is a list of topics that either increased or decreased in demand the most since last year. The number following the topic indicates how many positions that particular topic moved up or down in the ratings. An asterisk (*) before a topic indicates that this is at least the second year in a row that it has increased or decreased.

DECREASED IN INTEREST:
Travel—down 15
Book Excerpts—down 12

How-To—down 11
Short Story: Allegory— down 11
Essays—down 10
*Political—down 10

Short Story: Parables— down 8
Economics—down 7
Fillers: Newsbreaks—down 7
Writing How-to—down 7

Church Outreach—down 6
Fillers: Word Puzzles—
    down 6
*Psychology—down 6
Short Story: Adventure—
    down 6
Short Story: Biblical—down 6
Theological—down 6

INCREASED IN INTEREST:
Church Life—up 21
Death/Dying—up 19
Youth Issues—up 13
*Church Growth—up 12
Fillers: Quotes—up 10
Christian Education—
    up 9
Women's Issues—up 9
Divorce—up 7

Fillers: Prose—up 7
*Men's Issues—up 7
Self-Help—up 7
Christian Business—up 6
Devotionals/Meditations—
    up 6
Money Management—up 6
Singles Issues—up 6
Social Justice—up 6

SUMMARY OF INFORMATION ON CHRISTIAN PERIODICAL PUBLISHERS FOUND IN THE ALPHABETICAL LISTINGS

NOTE: *The following numbers are based on the maximum total estimate for each periodical. For example, if they gave a range of 4-6, the average was based on the higher number, 6. These figures were all calculated from those periodicals that reported information in each category.*

WANTS QUERY OR COMPLETE MANUSCRIPT:
Of those periodicals that indicated a preference, 49% will accept a complete manuscript (up 4% from last year), and 37% require or will accept a query (up 3% from last year). Fourteen percent of all reporting will accept either (up 1% from last year).

ACCEPTS PHONE QUERY:
This year, 153 periodical publishers are accepting phone queries—down from 168 last year. Many seem to now prefer fax or e-mail to phone queries. It is suggested that you reserve phone queries for timely material that won't wait for the regular mailed query. If you phone in a query, be sure you have your idea well thought out and can present it succinctly and articulately.

ACCEPTS FAX QUERY:
More and more publishers have fax numbers and a good many are willing (and even prefer) to accept fax queries, but some are also beginning to say No to them. Last year, over 42% of all the periodical publishers accepted fax queries. This year, 226 publishers (40%) will accept them. Since a fax query will not have an SASE, it is suggested that you make fax queries only if you have your own fax machine to accept their response.

ACCEPTS E-MAIL QUERY:
This is the third year we have asked about e-mail queries, and as expected, the number of publishers with e-mail addresses has jumped dramatically. Last year only 135 publishers were open to receiving messages or submissions by e-mail. This year 363 publications have e-mail, and 183 publishers (50%) are open to e-mail queries. In addition, 145 publishers have Websites.

SUBMISSIONS ON DISK:
Of the 368 periodicals that responded to the question about whether or not they accepted, preferred, or required submissions on disk, 123 (33%) said they accepted disks, 145 (39%) preferred disks, only 40 (11%) required disk, and 60 (16%) do not want disks.

PAYS ON ACCEPTANCE OR PUBLICATION:
Thirty-nine percent of the publishers pay on acceptance (down 4 1/2 % from last year), while 61% pay on publication.

PERCENTAGE OF FREELANCE:
Most of the publishers responded to the question about how much freelance material they use.

The average indicates that 54 1/2% of material used is from freelancers (up 1/2% from last year). As to the question of whether the amount of freelance used is going up or down, of those who responded this year, 51% are using the same amount of freelance material, 27% are using less, and 22% are using more than last year (down 4%).

CIRCULATION:

In dividing the list of periodicals into three groups, according to size of circulation, the list comes out as follows: Publications with a circulation of 100,000 or more (up to 3,900,000), 12% (14% last year); publications with circulations between 50,000 and 100,000, only 10% (10% last year); the remaining 78% have circulations of 50,000 or less (76% last year). If we break that last group into three more groups by circulation, we come out with 8% of those from 33,000-50,000 (down 1% from last year); 19% from 17,000-32,000 (up 3% from last year); and the remaining 73% with less than 17,000. That means that nearly 57% of all the periodicals that reported their circulation are at a circulation of 17,000 or less.

Looking at just those periodicals that completed questionnaires this year and indicated their circulation, for 27% their circulation went up (same as last year), for 29% their circulation went down (a decrease of 13%), and the remaining 44% stayed the same.

RESPONSE TIME:

Although according to the 520 publishers who indicated response time, the average response has dropped below 7 weeks, those who are writing and submitting regularly generally believe that most publishers are taking longer than they used to to respond to submissions.

REPRINTS:

Just under 55% of the periodicals reporting accept reprints, that's about the same as last year. Although in the past it has not been necessary to tell a publisher where a piece has been published previously, that seems to be changing. Most Christian publishers are now wanting a tear sheet of the original publication and a cover letter telling when and where it appeared originally. Be sure to check the listings to see if a publisher wants to know when and where a piece has appeared previously. Many are also paying less for reprints than for original material.

PREFERRED BIBLE VERSION:

Again this year, the most preferred Bible version is the NIV, the preference of 53% of the publishers (up 6% from last year). Other preferred versions are the KJV with 17%, the New Revised Standard Version at 14%, the NAB with 6%, New American Standard and Revised Standard Version with 3%, and the NKJV with 2 %. The NIV seems a good choice for those that didn't indicate a preference, although the more conservative groups seem to favor the KJV.

PERIODICALS THAT HAVE CHANGED NAMES OR CEASED PUBLICATION

This information is now included in the General Index. See introduction to that section.

PERIODICALS NOT INTERESTED IN FREELANCE SUBMISSIONS, OR WHO ASKED NOT TO BE LISTED

This information is now included in the General Index. See introduction to that section.

GREETING CARD/GIFT/SPECIALTY MARKETS

PLEASE NOTE: This listing contains both Christian/religious card publishers and secular publishers who have religious lines or produce some religious or inspirational cards. Keep in mind that the secular companies may produce other lines of cards that are not consistent with your beliefs, and that for a secular company, inspirational cards usually do not include religious imagery.

(*) Indicates that publisher did not return questionnaire.
(#) Indicates that listing was updated from guidelines or other sources.
(+) Indicates new listing.

NOTE: See the end of this listing for specialty product lists.

#ALLPORT EDITIONS, INC., 532 NW 12th, Portland OR 97209. (503)223-7268. Fax (503)223-9182. E-mail: info@allport.com. Michael & Victoria Allport, eds. General card publisher that does inspirational cards. 5% freelance. Buys all rts. Pays on publication. Responds in 1 mo. Seasonal/holiday 16 mos ahead. Submit 10 ideas. Guidelines.

BLUE MOUNTAIN ARTS, PO Box 1007, Boulder CO 80306. (303)449-0536. Fax (303)447-0939. E-mail: mail@bluemountainarts.com. Web site: http://www. bluemountainarts.com. Submit to Editorial Department. General card publisher with a religious line. Open to freelance. Prefers outright submissions. Pays $200 for all rts, or $25 for one-time use in a book, on publication. No royalties. Responds in 8-12 wks. Uses unrhymed or traditional poetry; usually longer than 15 lines. Produces inspirational and sensitivity. Needs anniversary, birthday, Christmas, congratulations, Easter, friendship, get well, graduation, keep in touch, love, miss you, new baby, please write, relatives, sympathy, thank you, Valentines, wedding. Holiday/seasonal 4 mos. ahead. Open to ideas for new card lines. Send any number of ideas. Open to ideas for calendars, gift books, mugs, and posters (prints). Guidelines; no catalog.

> **Tips:** "We are interested in reviewing poetry and writings for greeting cards, and expanding our field of freelance poetry writers." They sponsor a tri-annual poetry contest (last one was September 1997).

BOB SIEMON DESIGNS INC., 3501 W. Segerstrom Ave., Santa Ana CA 92704-6497. (714)549-0678. Fax (714)979-2627. Web site: http://www.bobsiemon.com. Colleen Welch, marketing coord. Christian card publisher/specialty products. 20-25% freelance. Buys 5-10 ideas/yr. Query. Pays variable royalty and advance, on acceptance, based on artist and product. Responds in 4-6 wks. Prefers traditional or light verse; 1-2 verses. Produces humorous, inspirational, religious, sensitivity and soft line. Needs anniversary, birthday, Christmas, congratulations, Easter, friendship, get well, graduation, keep in touch, love, miss you, new baby, please write, sympathy, thank you, Valentines, wedding. Seasonal 6 mos ahead. Open to ideas for new card lines. Send any number. Also open to ideas for gift books, gift/novelty items, magnets, mugs, plaques. No guidelines; catalog available.

#THE BRANCHES, INC., 16163 Fillmore Ave. SE, Prior Lake MN 55372-2515. (612)474-0924. Ronald Olson, marketing mngr. General card publisher/religious line. 5% freelance; 9 ideas/yr. Pays $240/camera-ready design, on publication. Royalties 2-5%. Responds in 6 mos. Prefers unrhymed. Produces traditional, inspirational, juvenile and sensitivity. Holiday/seasonal 1 yr ahead. Open to ideas for greeting books, plaques, postcards, mugs, coaster magnets, bookmarks. Catalog.

CATHEDRAL ART METAL CO., 250 Esten Ave., Pawtucket RI 02915. (401)726-2100x27. Fax (401)728-5666. Fritzi Frey, art. dir. Producer of specialty products. 10% freelance; buys 6-12 ideas/yr. Outright submissions. Pays $50-150 on acceptance for all rights. Royalties 5%. Responds in 1-4 wks. Open to ideas for figurines, pins, bookmarks, gift/novelty items and plaques. No guidelines; catalog for 9x12 SAE/$3.

CELEBRATION GREETINGS (A div. of Leanin' Tree), Box 9500, Boulder CO 80301. (303)530-1442. Fax (303)530-2152. Nancy Trumble Fox, V.P. Product. Christian/religious card publisher & specialty products. 50% freelance. Buys 30 ideas/yr. Query. Pays $100 on publication for all rts. No royalties. Responds in 12 wks. Any type of verse, including humorous; to 8 lines. Produces conventional, humorous, informal, inspirational, religious. Needs anniversary, birthday, Christmas, friendship, get well, keep in touch, love, miss you, new baby, sympathy, thank you, wedding, and encouragement. Christmas ideas 12 mos ahead. Not open to new card lines. Prefers 12-20 ideas. Open to ideas for magnets, mugs, and posters. Guidelines; no catalog.

*CREATIVE CHRISTIAN MINISTRIES, PO Box 12624, Roanoke VA 24027. Phone/fax (540)342-7511. Barbara Shaffer; mkg. dir. Christian/religious card publisher. 50% freelance. Outright submissions. Pays $5-10 on acceptance for reproduction rts. No royalties. Responds in 6 wks. Rhymed, unrhymed & traditional. Produces inspirational, religious and sensitivity. Needs birthday, Christmas, friendship, get well, new baby, sympathy, thank you, wedding, and thinking of you. Seasonal 6 mos ahead. Open to ideas for new card lines. Submit any number. Also open to ideas for magnets, plaques, and post cards. Guidelines; catalog available in mid 1996.

    Special Needs: Cards for older adults, caregivers, adult children of aging parents facing role reversal.

CREATIVE GRAPHICS, 785 Grant, Eugene OR 97402. (541)484-2726. Fax (541)345-2550. Terry Dusseault, corp. sec. General card publisher/religious lines and specialty products. 10% freelance. Query. Usage rights on designs. Pays on acceptance. No royalties. Responds in 4 wks. Uses rhymed and light verse; short. Produces inspirational, religious, and soft line. Needs Christmas, friendship, Valentines, and Mother's Day. Seasonal 10 mos ahead. Open to ideas for new card lines. Send 5 ideas. Open to ideas for magnets & post cards. No guidelines/catalog.

+CURRENT, INC., PO Box 2559, Colorado Springs CO 80901. (719)594-4100. Fax (719)534-6259. Mar Porter, freelance coordinator. General card publisher with a few inspirational & religious cards, and specialty products. 30-40% freelance (100+ ideas/yr). Follow guidelines for submissions. Pays $100 on acceptance for all rts. Royalties only on licensed property. Responds in 2-4 wks. Uses rhymed, unrhymed, traditional, light verse; open length (but uses a lot of short copy). Produces announcements, conventional, humorous, informal, inspirational, invitations, juvenile, novelty, religious, sensitivity, and soft line. Needs all types except relative & St. Patrick's Day. Needs "additional copy" ideas—plaque copy, "What is Easter?" format or "What is a Friend?" Holiday/seasonal 4-6 mos ahead. Open to ideas for new card lines. Send 4 ideas. Open to ideas for banners, calendars, coloring books, gift books, gift/novelty items, greeting books, magnets, mugs, plaques, post cards, posters, puzzles, T-shirts. Guidelines/needs list; catalog for 9x12 SAE/2 stamps.

DAYSPRING GREETING CARDS, Box 1010, 20984 Oak Ridge Rd., Siloam Springs AR 72761. (501)549-6303. Fax (501)524-8959. E-mail: annw@dayspring.com. Ann Woodruff, ed. Christian/religious card publisher. 20% freelance; buys up to 1,000 ideas/yr. Query or outright submission. Pays from $50/idea on acceptance for all rts. No royalty. Responds in 4-8 wks. Uses unrhymed, traditional, light verse, conversational, contemporary; various lengths. Produces announcements, humorous, informal, inspirational, invitations, juvenile, novelty, religious, soft line. Needs anniversary, birthday, Christmas, congratulations, Easter, friendship, get well, graduation, keep in touch, love, miss you, new baby, please write, relatives, sympathy, Thanksgiving, thank you, Valentines, wedding, and all major sending seasons and everyday occasions. Also needs pastor and Christian service appreciation and encouragement. Seasonal 1 yr ahead. Open to new card lines. Send 20 ideas or less. Open to ideas for calendars and post cards. Guidelines; no catalog.

#DIVINE INSPIRATION, 2110 Hobson Rd., #C101, Fort Wayne IN 46805-4873. Lori George, pres. Christian/religious card publisher. Does inspirational and religious cards. All need to contain scriptures. Open to ideas for new card lines. Open to ideas for calendars, post cards, posters, bookmarks, wallet cards, note cards and spiral-bound booklets. No guidelines or catalog.

*FREEDOM GREETING CARDS, Box 715, Bristol PA 19007. (215)945-3300. J. Levitt, pres. General card publisher/religious and inspirational lines. Currently has all the freelancers they need. Let them know the kind of work you can do and they will put your name in their file.

#GALLANT GREETINGS, PO Box 308, Franklin Park IL 60131. (708)671-6500. Fax (708)671-7500. E-mail: gallant-greetings@worldnet.att.net. Website: http://gallant-greetings.com. General card publisher/a few inspirational/religious cards. Chris Allen, VP-Sales & Marketing. 90% freelance. Query. Responds in 1 month. Pays 60-90 days after acceptance for world greeting card rts. Pays royalties. Uses rhymed, unrhymed, traditional and light verse; 4-6 lines. Produces announcements, conventional, humorous, informal, inspirational, invitations, juvenile, religious. Needs all types of greetings. Holiday/seasonal 6 months ahead. Open to new card lines. Prefers 20 ideas/submission. Guidelines/needs list; no catalog.

*GENESIS MARKETING GROUP, 16 Wellington Ave., Greenville SC 29609. (803)233-2651. Fax (803)232-0059. Peter Sullivan, pres. Christian/religious card publisher. 100% freelance. Buys 10 ideas/yr. Outright submission. Royalty 5%. Traditional & light verse. Produces inspirational, religious, sensitivity. Needs anniversary, birthday, Christmas, congratulations, Easter, friendship, get well, graduation, keep in touch, love, miss you, new baby, please write, relatives, sympathy, thank you, valentines, wedding. Also produces calendars, gift books, magnets, mugs, plaques, posters, T-shirts.

HEART IMPRESSIONS, PO Box 12624, Roanoke VA 24027. Phone/fax (703)342-7511. E-mail: ccmbbr@juno.com. Creative Christian Ministries. Betty Robertson, ed. Christian card publisher. 25% freelance. Pays $5-10/idea on acceptance for all rts. Prefers outright submissions. Responds in 6 wks. Prefers rhymed, unrhymed, or traditional; variable length. Produces inspirational and religious. Does friendship, new baby, sympathy, thank you, and wedding. Seasonal 9 mos ahead. Open to ideas for new card lines. Submit any number. Also open to ideas for audio tapes, magnets, plaques and post cards. Guidelines; no catalog.

*HEART STEPS, INC., PO Box 307, King WI 54946. (715)258-8141. Fax (715)256-9170. General card publisher with a religious line. Open to freelance art; beginning to review copy. Bought 1 idea in 1996. Query. Pays variable rates on acceptance. No royalties. Responds in 4 wks. Unrhymed verse, 3-5 lines. Produces conventional, inspirational, juvenile, religious and sensitivity. Needs Christmas, sympathy and Valentines. Seasonal 1 yr ahead. Send any number. Also open to ideas for gift/novelty items, magnets, and T-shirts. No guidelines; catalog for 10x13 SAE/3 stamps.

+THE HERITAGE COLLECTION, 79 - 5TH Ave., 4th Floor, New York NY 10003. (212)647-1000. Fax (212)647-0188. Allison Powe, creative dir. General card publisher with a religious line. 20% freelance; buys 50-60 ideas/yr. Outright submission. Pays $35 on publication for domestic rights. No royalties. Responds in 4 wks. Prefers unrhymed; to 3 paragraphs. Produces announcements, inspirational, religious, and sensitivity. Needs anniversary, birthday, congratulations, friendship, get well, keep in touch, love, miss you, new baby, sympathy, thank you, and wedding. Also open to ideas for mugs. Guidelines/needs list; free catalog.

IMAGE CRAFT, INC. and **LAWSON FALLE LTD.**, 1245 Franklin Blvd., Box 814, Cambridge ON N1R 5X9 Canada. (519)622-4310. Fax (519)621-6774. Jeanette W. Gilmour or Manny Dutra, Product Dev. Dept.. Christian/religious card publisher and general card publisher with a religious line. Open to freelance. Query. Pays on acceptance. No royalties. Responds in 4-6 wks. Prefers unrhymed, traditional and humorous, 6-12 lines. Produces announcements, conventional, humorous, informal, inspirational, invitations, juvenile, religious, sensitivity and studio cards. Needs anniversary, birthday, Christmas, congratulations, Easter, friendship, get well, graduation, Halloween, keep in touch, love, miss you, new baby, Mother's Day/Father's Day, new baby, relatives/St. Patrick's Day, all occasion, sympathy, Thanksgiving, thank you, Valentines, wedding, confirmation, and First Communion. Seasonal 8 mos ahead. Not open to new card lines. Send 6-8 ideas.

Tips: "We need good, but clean humor."

J-MAR, PO Box 23149, Waco TX 76702-3149. (254)751-0100. Fax (254)751-0054. Kelly Shivers, marketing mngr. Producer of cards & specialty products. 25% freelance; buys 50 ideas/yr. Outright submission. Pays variable rates on acceptance for all rts; no royalties. Responds in 6 wks. Prefers unrhymed (short, focused submissions receive the most attention). Produces humorous, informal, inspirational, novelty, softline. Needs friendship, love, and thank you cards. Seasonal 9 mos ahead. Open to new card lines. Send 5-10 ideas. Open to ideas for calendars, 2"x3" inspirational cards, gift/novelty items, magnets, post cards, posters, & stationery. Guidelines; no catalog.

Tips: "We appreciate writing submissions that are focused on inspirational Christian themes. These themes can include biblical references or verses, poems and/or text."

*LIFE GREETINGS, Box 468, Little Compton RI 02837. (401)635-8535. Kathy Brennan, ed. Christian/religious card publisher. Open to freelance. Outright purchases. Pays $10 on acceptance for all rts. No royalties. Responds in 6 wks. Uses rhymed, unrhymed, traditional; 6-8 lines. Produces announcements, conventional, humorous, inspirational, and religious. Needs congratulations, friendship, get well, new baby, sympathy, thank you and wedding. Also clergy reassignment, ordination, anniversary of ordination, and pro-life Christmas. Seasonal 6 mos ahead. Open to new card lines. Prefers 6 ideas/submission. Guidelines; no catalog.

*MANHATTAN GREETING CARD CO., 150 E 52 St. c/o Platzer/Fineberg, New York NY 10022. (718)894-7600. Paula Haley, ed. General card publisher/inspirational line. 100% freelance. Pays $5-250. Responds in 3 wks. Produces announcements, conventional, humorous, informal, inspirational, invitations, juvenile, sensitivity, soft line, studio, Christmas (85% of the line). Holiday/seasonal 18 months ahead. Also open to ideas for bumper stickers, calendars, gift books, greeting books, post cards, and promotions. Free guidelines.

#NOVO CARD PUBLISHERS, INC., 4513 N Lincoln Ave., Chicago IL 60625. (312)769-6000. Fax (312)769-6769. Thomas Benjamin/Sheri Cline, art dirs. General card publisher that does a few inspirational and religious cards. 95% freelance; buys 200-500 ideas/yr. Prefers query for writers and outright submissions for art samples. Pays $2/line on publication for greeting card rts. No royalties. Responds in 9 wks. Uses any type verse, variable lengths. Produces all types of cards. Needs birthday, congratulations, friendship, graduation, keep in touch, relatives (all occasions), sympathy, thank you. Seasonal 8 mos ahead. Open to ideas for new card lines. Submit enough ideas to show style. Guidelines/needs list; samples for 9x12 SAE/5 stamps.

Tips: "Sympathy cards need to be a bit more inspirational than just 'my deepest sympathy'."

*PACIFIC PAPER GREETINGS, INC., Box 2249, Sidney BC V8L 3S8 Canada. (604)656-0504. Louise Rytter, ed. Inspirational cards. 50% freelance; buys 20 ideas/yr. Pays on acceptance for all rts. Responds in 3 wks. Produces conventional, inspirational, romantic, sensitivity, soft line. Holiday/seasonal 12 months ahead. Guidelines for SAE/1 IRC.

#PAINTED HEARTS & FRIENDS, 1222 N. Fair Oaks Ave., Pasadena CA 91103-3614. (818)798-3633, Fax (818)798-7385. E-mail: teri@paintedhearts.com. Teri Willis, ed. General card publisher that does a few inspirational and religious cards. 20% freelance. Query or outright submission (copies only, no original artwork). Pays $25/message on acceptance. 5% royalty on artwork only. Responds in 1-2 wks. Uses unrhymed, traditional, light verse; 2-3 liners. Produces announcements, inspirational, invitations. Needs most types of greetings (no Please Write), plus graduation and Jewish holidays. Holiday/seasonal 3 mos ahead. See guidelines for submission schedule. Open to ideas for new card lines.

Submit 12 art designs max, or 24 messages. Open to ideas for banners, gift books, invitations, postcards, posters and stationery. Guidelines/marketlist for #10 SASE.

#RED FARM STUDIO, 1135 Roosevelt Ave., Pawtucket RI 02862-0347. (401)728-9300. Fax (401)728-0350. Submit to Production Coordinator. General card publisher with a religious line. 100% freelance; buys 100 ideas/yr. Outright submission. Pays variable rates within 1 mo. of acceptance for exclusive rts. No royalties. Responds in 2 mos. Use traditional and light verse; 1-4 lines. Produces announcements, invitations, religious. Needs anniversary, birthday, Christmas, friendship, get well, new baby, sympathy, wedding. Holiday 6 months ahead. Not open to ideas for new card lines. Submit any number of ideas. Guidelines/needs list for SASE.

#SUNRISE PUBLICATIONS, INC., 1145 Sunrise Greeting Ct., Box 4699, Bloomington IN 47402-4699. (812)336-9900. Fax (812)336-8712. Website: http://www.interart.com. Angeline R. Larimer, creative writer. General card publisher that does inspirational cards. 5% freelance; buys 15 ideas/yr. Outright submission. Pays $50 on acceptance for worldwide exclusive rts. No royalties. Responds in 3 mos. Prefers unrhymed, traditional; 2 stanzas max. Produces conventional, humorous, inspirational. Needs anniversary, birthday, belated birthday, Christmas, congratulations, Easter, friendship, get well, graduation, Halloween, keep in touch, love, miss you, new baby, please write, relatives, St. Patrick's Day, sympathy, Thanksgiving, thank you, Valentines, wedding; also baptism, confirmation, bar and bat mitzvah. Holiday/seasonal 6 mos ahead. Open to ideas for new card lines. Up to 15 ideas/submission. Also open to ideas for gift/novelty items, greeting books, magnets and posters. Guidelines/marketlist.

> **Tips:** "We use very little religious imagery or verse. However, it is sometimes used in sympathy, Easter and Christmas captions."

WARNER PRESS INC., 1200 E 5th St., PO Box 2499, Anderson IN 46018-9988. (765)644-7721. Fax (765)649-3664. Robin Fogle, product ed. Producer of specialty products. 30% freelance; buys 30-50 ideas/yr. Query for guidelines. Pays $35 on acceptance for all rts. No royalties. Responds in 4-6 wks. Uses rhymed, unrhymed, traditional verse for bulletins; 16-32 lines. Holiday/seasonal 6 months ahead. Accepts 10 ideas/submission. Also open to ideas for coloring books, novelty items, and post cards. Guidelines (must send for before submitting); no catalog.

> **Tips:** "Most of our present purchases are for church bulletins. Verses may be general inspirational as well as specifically for holiday seasons. Verses should try to inspire worshippers before the church service begins."

ADDITIONAL CARD PUBLISHERS

The following greeting card publishers did not complete a questionnaire, but are included for reference or to contact on your own. Do not submit to them before you send for guidelines or ascertain their needs. Card publishers who do not accept freelance submissions are now listed in the General Index.

ABUNDANT TREASURES, PO Box 605, Calimesa CA 92320-0605.

APPALACHIAN BIBLE CO. INC., 506 Princeton Rd, Johnson City TN 37601.

ART BEATS, 33 River Rd., Cos Cob CT 06807-2717.

BERG CHRISTIAN ENTERPRISES, 4525 SE 63rd Ave., Portland OR 97206.

BLACK FAMILY GREETING CARDS, 20 Cortlandt Ave., New Rochelle NY 10801. Bill Harte, pres.

CAROLE JOY CREATIONS, INC., 107 Mill Plain Rd., Danbury CT 06811. (203)798-2060. African-American greetings cards.

CAROLYN BEAN PUBLISHING, 1700 Corporate Cir., Petaluma CA 94954-6924.

CD GREETING CARDS, PO Box 5084, Brentwood TN 37024-5084.

EARTH CARE PAPER, INC., PO Box 8507, Ukiah CA 95482.

FREDERICK SINGER AND SONS, INC., 2-15 Borden Ave., Long Island City NJ 11101.

FRIENDLY SALES, PO Box 755, Quakertown PA 18951.

FRIENDS OF ISREAL GOSPEL MINISTRIES, PO Box 908, Bellmawr NJ 08099-9900.

GREENLEAF, INC., 200 Wending Way, Spartanburg SC 29306.

THE HERMITAGE ART COMPANY INC., 5151 N. Ravenswood Ave., Chicago IL 60640.

HIGHER HORIZONS, Box 78399, Los Angeles CA 90016.

IDESIGN, 12020 W. Ripley, Milwaukee WI 53226. (414)475-7176.

JONATHAN & DAVID INC, Box 1194, Grand Rapids MI 49501.

KIMBERLY ENTERPRISES INC., 15029 S. Figueroa St., Gardena CA 90248. Inspirational cards.

KRISTEN ELLIOTT, INC., 6 Opportunity Way, Newburyport MA 01950.

+LAURA LEIDEN CALLIGRAPHY, INC., PO Box 141, Watkinsville GA 30677. (706)769-6989. Inspirational cards.

LAWSON FALLE LTD., Eden Hall, 3330 Griswold Rd., Port Huron MI 48060.

THE LORENZ COMPANY, 1208 Cimmaron Dr., Waco TX 76712-8174.

MCBETH CORP., PO Box 400, Chambersburg PA 17201.

MERI MERI, 11 Vista Ave., San Mateo CA 94403-4612.

MORE THAN A CARD, 5010 Baltimore Ave., Bethesda MD 20816.

OAKSPRINGS IMPRESSIONS, Box 572, Woodacre CA 94973.

OATMEAL STUDIOS, PO Box 138, Rochester VT 05767. Helene Lehrer, creative dir.

PS GREETINGS/FANTUS PAPER PRODUCTS, 5060 N. Kimberly Ave., Chicago IL 60630-1744.

RANDALL WILCOX PUBLISHING, 826 Orange Ave. #544, Coronado CA 92118. (619)437-1321.

SENDJOY GREETING CARDS, Laurel Park, Wappingers Falls NY 12590.

+SOUL-SEARCHER GREETING CARDS, PO Box 3462, ManKato MN 56002-3462. Inspirational cards.

THESE THREE, INC., 2105 N. Scott St #79, Arlington VA 22209-1023. Jean Bridgers, ed.

THINGS GRAPHIC & FINE ARTS, 1522 - 14th St. NW, Washington DC 20005.

T.S. DENISON GREETING CARDS, PO Box 1650, Grand Rapids MI 49501.

WEST GRAPHICS, 1117 California Dr., Burlingame CA 94010-3505. Carol West, ed.

NOTE: Most of the markets listed below for games, gift items and videos have not indicated their interest in receiving freelance submissions. Contact these markets on your own for information on submission procedures before sending them anything.

GAME MARKETS

*BIBLE GAMES CO., 14389 Cassell Rd., Fredericktown OH 43019. Kelly Vozar, asst. Produces Bible games. 10% freelance. Buys 1-2 ideas/yr. Query. Pays on publication for all rts (negotiable). Royalties 8%. Responds in 6-8 wks. Open to new ideas. One game per submission. Guidelines; catalog for 9x12 SAE/6 stamps.

> **Tips:** "Send developed and tested game play; target market and audience. Must be totally non-sectarian and fully biblical—no fictionalized scenarios." Board games, CD-roms, computer games and video games.

BIBLE WALK GOSPEL EDUCATION GAMES, (800)829-1883. Board games.

CACTUS GAME DESIGN, INC., 8845 Stevens Chase Ct., Las Vegas NV 89129. Games.

GOOD STEWARD GAME CO., 6412 Sunnyfield Way., Sacramento CA 95823-5781. (916)393-4263. William Parker, ed. Board games.

*LATE FOR THE SKY PRODUCTION COMPANY, 561 Reading Rd., Cincinnati OH 45202. Fax (513)721-5757. Board games.

MARTIN LEVY INC., 1405 Brewester Dr., El Cerrito CA 94530. (510)234-8888. Board games.

M.J.N. ENTERPRISES, 1624 McMillan, Memphis TN 38106. (901)946-8185. Board games.

TALICOR, 4741 Murietta St., Chino CA 91710-5156. (909)517-0076. Fax (909)517-1962. E-mail: webmaster@Talicor.com. Lew Herndon, pres. Produces board games & puzzles. 100% freelance; buys 10 ideas/yr. Outright submissions. Pays variable rates on publication for all rts. Variable royalty. Responds in 2 wks. Seasonal 4 mos ahead. Open to new ideas. Submit 1-4 ideas. Free catalog for.

WISDOM TREE, 16701 N. Oracle Rd. #264, Tucson AZ 85739-9102. (520)825-5702. Fax (520)825-5710. Web site: Http://www.christianlink.com/media/wisdom. Brenda Huff, owner. Produces Bible-based computer games. 30% freelance (Beta versions). Query. Negotiable rights. Pays variable rates on acceptance or publication. Variable royalties. Responds in 1-6 wks. Seasonal 8 mos ahead. Open to ideas for computer games or computer software. No guidelines; catalog on request.

GIFT/SPECIALTY ITEM MARKETS

ARGUS COMMUNICATIONS, 400 W. Bethany, Allen TX 75013. (972)396-6500. Fax (972)396-6789. Amy Craft, ed.; submit to Beth Davis. Primarily interested in Christian posters. 90% freelance. Query. Outright purchase. Pays $75 on acceptance for all rts. Royalty 5-8%. Responds in 6-8 wks. Uses unrhymed, traditional, light verse; 1-2 lines. Produces humorous and inspirational (one line of sweet, light bear cards). Needs birthday, congratulations, friendship, get well, keep in touch, love, miss you, sympathy, thank you, and wedding. Submit maximum 20 ideas. Also open to calendars & postcards appropriate for Christian schools and Sunday school classrooms. Guidelines; no catalog .

> **Special Needs:** "We need Christian posters for teens and adults that are

positive, inspirational and motivational."

#THE CALLIGRAPHY COLLECTION, 2604 NW 74th Pl., Gainesville FL 32653. (352)375-8530. Fax (352)374-9957. Katy Fischer, ed. General publisher/inspirational line of framed prints. 40% freelance; 20 ideas/yr. Outright submission. Pays $75-150 for framed print idea on publication for all rts; no royalties. Responds in 6 months. Uses rhymed, unrhymed (preferred), traditional, light verse; under 50 words. Produces inspirational (not too specific or overly religious), framed prints for friends, family, teachers, etc. Holiday/seasonal 6 months ahead. Send 3 ideas/batch. Also open to ideas for gift books, plaques, and musical framed pieces. Guidelines; no catalog.

#CONTENOVA GIFTS, 16052 SW Westminster Dr., Portland OR 97224-1395. Vicki Boynton, dir. of marketing. Specializes in personalized gifts & novelties. Accepts outside submissions for mug sayings and artwork, but currently has no religious designs; mainly humorous birthday. Guidelines; no catalog.

*DICKSONS, INC., 709 B Ave. E., PO Box 368, Seymour IN 47274. (812)522-1308. Fax (812)522-1319. Vice President of Product Development. Produces specialty products; no greeting cards. 1% freelance; open. Submit cover letter/sample. Outright purchases. Responds ASAP. Uses religious/inspirational verses for bookmarks, Quik Notes, plaques, etc. Seasonal 1 yr ahead. Open to ideas for specialty items. Send any number. Produces banners, board games, calendars, coloring books, computer software, gift/novelty items, magnets, mugs, plaques, puzzles and T-shirts. No guidelines or catalog.

+FIRST HOUSE PUBLISHING, 2209 Hand Blvd., Orlando FL 32806. (407)895-3547. Posters.

+GARBORG'S, 2060 W. 98th St., Bloomington MN 55431. (612)888-5727. Fax (612)888-4775. E-mail: garborgbf@aol.com. Barbara Farmer, ed. Producer of specialty products. 2% freelance. Query. Pays negotiable rates on acceptance. Negotiable royalties. Responds in 4-6 wks. Seasonal 9 mos ahead. Open to ideas for calendars, bookmarks, gift books, journals. Guidelines; catalog for 9x12 SAE/2 stamps.

> **Tips:** "Our main product is a page-a-day perpetual calendar with inspirational thoughts, quotes and scripture (see guidelines)."

+IN CELEBRATION, a division of Instructional Fair/TS Denison, 2400 Turner NW, Grand Rapids MI 49501. (616)363-1290. Fax (616)363-8243. Alyson Kieda, prod. mgr. Producer of specialty products, including cards and books. 90% freelance. Query or outright submission. Pays varying amounts on acceptance for all rts. Rarely pays royalties. Responds in 4-8 wks. Does a few inspirational or religious cards (doesn't need cards, but will look at ideas). Open to ideas for new card lines or specialty products. Send 1-2 ideas. Open to ideas for audio tapes, banners, clip-art books, coloring books, computer software, craft/activity books, post cards, posters, puzzles, stickers, note pads, award certificates, parent/teacher resources, children's books for church/home. Guidelines; free catalog.

> **Tips:** "Open to new book ideas. Looking for authors/artists to produce books to match our ideas."

*INSPIRATIONS, Thomas Nelson Gifts, 506 Nelson Pl., Nashville TN 37214. (800)251-4000. Fax (800)448-8403. Stationery, journals, monthly planners, note pads, and gift collection.

*MARYCANA, 23 Great Oaks Blvd., Ste. S, San Jose CA 95119. (800)869-3733. Gift items, including: gift dolls, note paper, bookmarks, etc.

#NEW VENTURES, RR 1 Box 2091, Moretown VT 05660-9511. (802)229-1020. Fax (802)229-1020. Action figures.

*PEELE ENTERPRISES SHIRT PRINTS, LTD., 3401 Hwy 25N, Hodges SC 29653. (803)374-7339. Christian T-shirts and sweatshirts.

#QUALITY ARTWORKS, INC., 2262 N. Penn Rd., Hatfield PA 19440-0369. (215)822-0125. Fax (215)822-2619. A bookmark and scroll publisher with inspirational/religious lines. Linda Tomezsko Morris, creative dir. 10% freelance; buys 0-10 ideas/yr. Query. Pays $50-300 on acceptance for all rts; no royalties. Responds in 9 wks. Uses rhymed, unrhymed, traditional, light verse; medium length. Produces bookmarks, decorative scrolls, blank journals, stationery, blank note card sets and notepads. Anniversary, congratulations, friendship, love, new baby, relative and thank you. Not open to ideas for new products. Guidelines/market list for #10 SASE.

*RAYS OF SONSHINE, 910 Ave. E/Box 736, Wisner NE 68791. (402)529-6531. Marlene Colligan, owner. Christian/religious card publisher. New company. Open to freelance. Needs anniversary, birthday, get well, new baby, sympathy. Open to ideas for new card lines. Current line mostly designed for seniors.

*SCANDECOR, 430 Pike Rd., Southampton PA 18966. (215)355-2410. Fax (215)364-8737. Lauren Harris Karp, product mngr. A general poster publisher that does a few inspirational posters for children, teens and adults. 40% freelance; buys 50 ideas/yr. Makes outright purchase, for world-wide, exclusive rts. Pays $100 on publication, depends on size of poster. No royalties. Responds in 9 wks. Uses rhymed, unrhymed and light verse; one line up to 20 lines. Produces humorous, inspirational, juvenile, novelty and soft line. No holiday posters. Submit several ideas. Open to ideas for calendars, posters and novelty products/copy. Guidelines; no catalog.

*SWANSON CHRISTIAN SUPPLIES, 1200 Park Ave., Murfreesboro TN 37133-1257. (615)896-4114. Fax (615)898-1313. E-mail: swanson@hotcc.com. Website: http://www.hotcc.com/swanson. Carmel S. Tritschler, adver. dir. Produces specialty products. Just opening up to freelancers. Query. Pays on publication. No royalties. Responds in 4-8 wks. Uses rhymed, unrhymed, traditional and light verse; short. Inspirational/Christian. Open to new ideas. Send any number. Open to ideas for coloring books, gift/novelty items, magnets, mugs, plaques, post cards. No guidelines or catalog.

*YOUTH LIFE CREATIONS, 2004 Carrolton, Muncie IN 47304. (800)784-0078. Action cards.

SOFTWARE DEVELOPERS

BAKER BOOK HOUSE, see book section.

BIBLESOFT, 22014 17TH Ave. S., Seattle WA 98198. (206)824-0647.

EPIPHANY SOFTWARE, 15897 Alta Bista Way, San Jose CA 95127. (408)251-9788.

EXEGESES (exeGeses), PO Box 1776, Orange CA 92668. (714)835-1705. (714)835-1705.

KIRKBRIDE TECHNOLOGIES, PO Box 606, Indianapolis IN 46206. (317)633-1900.

LOGOS RESEARCH SYSTEMS, 2117 200th Ave. W., Oak Harbor WA 98277. (360)679-6575. (360)679-6575.

LOIZEAUX BROTHERS, see book listing.

NAVPRESS SOFTWARE, 16002 Pool Canyon Rd., Austin TX 78734. (512)266-1700.

PARSONS TECHNOLOGY, 1 Parsons Dr., Hiawatha IA 52233. (319)378-7006.

SAGE SOFTWARE, PO Box 1926, Albany OR 97321-0509. (541)967-8337.

ZONDERVAN CORP., see book listing.

VIDEO/CD MARKETS

CHRISTIAN DUPLICATIONS INTL., INC., 1710 Lee Reed Rd., Orlando FL 32810. (800)327-9332. Videos.

CITY ALIVE, PO Box 4952, Chicago IL 60680-4952. (312)433-3838. Fax (312)433-3839. Music and teaching videos.

DALLAS CHRISTIAN VIDEO, 1878 Firman, Richardson TX 75081. (800)231-0095.

EDDE ENTERTAINMENT, 21822 Lassen St., Ste. J, Chatsworth CA 91311-3680. (800)727-2229. Videos.

+HEARTSONG, PO Box 2455, Glenview IL 60025. (800)648-0755. Videos.

MARK IV PICTURES VIDEO, 5907 Meredith Dr., Des Moines IA 50322. (800)247-3456. Videos.

PROPHECY PARTNERS, PO Box 2204, Niagara Falls NY 14302. (905)684-5561. Videos.

PROPHECY PUBLICATIONS, PO Box 7000, Oklahoma City OK 73153. (800)475-1111. Religious education videos.

RANDOLF PRODUCTIONS, 23181 Verdugo Dr., Laguna Hills CA 92653. (800)266-7741. Videos.

RUSS DOUGHTEN FILMS, INC., 5907 Meredith Dr., Des Moines IA 50322. (515)278-4737. Fax (515)278-4738. E-mail: doughten@mustardseed-rdfilms. com. Submit to Production Dept. Produces dramatic Christian videos. Open to ideas. Guidelines; free catalog.

SOLDIERS OF LIGHT PRODUCTIONS, PO Box 16354, Encino CA 91416-6354. (813)345-3866. Fax (818)345-1162. Videos.

THIS WEEK IN BIBLE PROPHECY, PO Box 1440, Niagara Falls NY 14302. (905)684-7700. Videos.

VISUAL PROGRESSIONS, PO Box 1327, Melbourne FL 32902. (800)922-1985. Videos.

PUBLISHERS PRODUCING SPECIALTY PRODUCTS

NOTE: Most of the following publishers are greeting card publishers, but some will be found in the book publisher listings.

ACTIVITY/COLORING BOOKS
Current
Dicksons
In Celebration
Rainbow Books

Chariot (Rainfall)
Regina Press
Shining Star
Standard
Swanson
Warner Press

AUDIO TAPES
Eldridge Publishing
Heart Impressions
In Celebration
Liguori Publications
Success Publishers

Tyndale House
Word
World Publishing
Zondervan

BANNERS

Argus Communications
Current
Dicksons
In Celebration
Painted Hearts & Friends

BOARD GAMES

Bethel Publishing
Bible Games Co.
Chariot (Rainfall Inc.)
Dicksons
Good Steward Game Co.
Late for the Sky
Lightwave Publishing
Master Books
Joshua Morris Publishing
M.J.N.Enterprises
Shining Star
Standard Publishing
Talicor
Tyndale House

CALENDARS/DAILY JOURNALS

Abingdon
American Tract Society
Argus Communications
Barbour & Co.
Blue Mountain Arts
Current
DaySpring
Dicksons
Divine Inspiration
Garborg's
Genesis
Group Publishing
J-Mar
Manhattan Greeting Card
Neibauer Press
Pilgrim Press
Read 'N Run Books
Scandecor
Tyndale House
Women of the Promise

CD-ROMS

Bible Games Co.
Chariot
GROUP Publishing
Image Books/Doubleday

Lydia Press
NavPress
Our Sunday Visitor
World Publishing

CHARTS

Rose Publishing

COMIC BOOKS

Dicksons
Kaleidoscope Press
Thomas Nelson

COMPUTER GAMES

Bible Games Co.
Brown-ROA
Master Books
NavPress Software
Wisdom Tree
Wood Lake Books

COMPUTER SOFTWARE

Baker (BakerBytes)
Biblesoft
Concordia
Dicksons
Epiphany Software
exeGeses
Gospel Light
In Celebration
Kirkbride Technology
Logos Research Systems
Loizeaux Brothers
NavPress Software
Parsons Technology
Resource Publications
Sage Software
Wisdom Tree
Zondervan

GIFT BOOKS

(See listing under Book Topics)
Blue Mountain Arts
Current
Garborg's
Genesis
Image Craft
Painted Hearts & Friends
Review and Herald
Bob Siemon Designs

GIFT/NOVELTY ITEMS

Abingdon
Cathedral Art
Contenova Gifts

Current
Dicksons
Garborg's
Heartsteps
In Celebration
J-Mar
Manhattan Greeting Card
New Boundary Designs
Scandecor
Bob Siemon Designs
Swanson
Sunrise Publications
Zondervan

GREETING BOOKS

Calligraphy Collection
Current
Joshua Morris (novelty books)
Manhattan Greeting Card
New Boundary Designs
Sunrise Publications

MAGNETS

Celebration Greetings
Creative Christian
Creative Graphics
Current
Dicksons
Genesis
Heart Impressions
Heartsteps
J-Mar
New Boundary Designs
Bob Siemon Designs
Sunrise Publications
Swanson

MUGS

Blue Mountain Arts
Celebration Greetings
Contenova Gifts
Current
Dicksons
Genesis
Heritage Collection
Bob Siemon Designs
Swanson

PLAQUES

Dicksons
Calligraphy Collection
Cathedral Art
Creative Christian
Current
Dicksons
Genesis

Heart Impressions
New Boundary Designs
Bob Siemon Designs
Swanson

POST CARDS
Abingdon
Argus Communications
Creative Christian
Creative Graphics
Current
Dayspring
Divine Inspiration
Heart Impressions
In Celebration
J-Mar
Manhattan Greeting Card
New Boundary Designs
Read 'N Run Books
Swanson
Warner Press
Zondervan

POSTERS
Argus Communications
Blue Mountain Arts
Celebration Greetings
Current
Divine Inspiration
Eldridge Publishing
First House
Genesis
In Celebration

J-Mar
Read 'N Run Books
Scandecor
Standard Publishing
Sunrise Publications

PUZZLES
Current
Dicksons
Talicor

STATIONERY
Dicksons
In Celebration
J-Mar
Painted Hearts & Friends

SUNDAY BULLETINS
Warner Press

T-SHIRTS
Current
Dicksons
Eldridge Publishing
Genesis
Heartsteps
Peele Enterprises
Women of the Promise

VIDEOS/VIDEO GAMES
Abingdon

Augsburg
Bible Games Co.
Brentwood Music
Broadman & Holman
Brown-ROA
Chariot (Rainfall)
Church Street Press
City Alive
Destiny Image
Diamante
Russ Doughten Films
Editorial Unilit
Focus on the Family
Gospel Light/Regal
Group Publishing
Howard Publishing
Integrity Music
InterVarsity
Liguori Publications
Moody Press
Paraclete Press
Pauline Video
Prophecy Publications
Star Song
Tyndale Family Video
Vermont Story Works
Victor Books
Vision Video
Wisdom Tree
Word
Zondervan

CHRISTIAN WRITERS' CONFERENCES AND WORKSHOPS

(*) Asterisk before a listing means the information was not verified or updated by the group leader.
(+) A plus sign before a listing indicates a new listing.

ALABAMA

CHRISTIAN LEADERS AND SPEAKERS SEMINARS (The CLASSeminar). Montgomery (334-274-8912); August 31-September 2, 1998. For anyone who wants to improve their communication skills for either the spoken or written word, for professional or personal reasons. Speakers: Florence Littauer and Marita Littauer. Contact: Marita Littauer, PO Box 66810, Albuquerque NM 87193. (800)433-6633. Fax (505)899-4283. E-mail: mlittauer@aol.com. Attendance: 100.

SOUTHERN CHRISTIAN WRITERS CONFERENCE. Birmingham/Samford University, June 12-13,1998 Contact: Joanne Sloan, SCWC, PO Box 1106, Northport AL 35476. (205)333-8603. Fax (205)339-4528. E-mail: Visionslo@ aol.com. Attendance: 150-200.

ARIZONA

AMERICAN CHRISTIAN WRITERS PHOENIX CONFERENCES. April 3-4, 1998 & October 22-24, 1998. Contact: Reg A. Forder, Box 110390, Nashville TN 37222. 1-800-21-WRITE. Attendance: 50-150.

MINI WRITING WORKSHOPS. Held in various U.S. locations, throughout the year. Contact and speaker: Donna Goodrich, 648 S. Pima St., Mesa AZ 85210. (602)962-6694. One to three-day-long workshops on various topics. Attendance: 20-30.

*SOUTH-EASTERN ARIZONA CHRISTIAN WRITERS SEMINAR. Tucson; September 1998. Contact: Bea Carlton, HCR 1 Box 153C, Willcox AZ 85643. (520)384-9232.

ARKANSAS

AMERICAN CHRISTIAN WRITERS LITTLE ROCK CONFERENCE. August 28-29, 1998. Contact: Reg A. Forder, Box 110390, Nashville TN 37222. 1-800-21-WRITE. Attendance: 35-50.

*ARKANSAS WRITERS' CONFERENCE. Little Rock; June 1998. Contact: Peggy Vining, 6817 Gingerbread Ln., Little Rock AR 72204. (501)565-8889. Attendance: 200.

CALIFORNIA

AMERICAN CHRISTIAN WRITERS FULLERTON CONFERENCE. March 27-28, 1998. Contact: Reg Forder, Box 110390, Nashville TN 37222. 1-800-21-WRITE. Attendance: 35-50.

+AMERICAN CHRISTIAN WRITERS LOS ANGELES CONFERENCE. October 15-17, 1998. Contact: Reg Forder, Box 110390, Nashville TN 37222. 1-800-21-WRITE. Attendance: 50-150.

AMERICAN CHRISTIAN WRITERS SAN DIEGO CONFERENCE. March 20-21, 1998. Contact: Reg Forder, Box 110390, Nashville TN 37222. 1-800-21-WRITE. Attendance: 35-50.

CASTRO VALLEY CHRISTIAN WRITERS SEMINAR. Castro Valley, February 27-28, 1998. Speaker: Lissa Halls Johnson. Contact: Pastor Jon Drury, 19300 Redwood Rd., Castro Valley CA 94546-3465. (510)886-6300. Fax (510)581-5022. Attendance: 170.

*CEHUC SPANISH CHRISTIAN WRITERS SEMINAR . Los Angeles, San Diego or Tijuana; April 1998. Contact: Magdalena Latorre, 9802 Quail Canyon Rd., El Cajon CA 92021-6000. Phone/fax (619)390-3747. New.

CHRISTIAN LEADERS AND SPEAKERS SEMINARS (The CLASSeminar). Fresno (209-435-2200); February 9-11, 1998. For anyone who wants to improve their communication skills for either the spoken or written word, for professional or personal reasons. Speakers: Florence Littauer and Marita Littauer. Contact: Marita Littauer, PO Box 66810, Albuquerque NM 87193. (800)433-6633. Fax (505)899-4283. E-mail: mlittauer@aol.com. Attendance: 100

+CHRISTIAN WRITERS CONFERENCE OF SANTA BARBARA. Westmont College; October 10-11, 1998. Contact: Rev. Opal Mae Dailey, PO Box 42429, Santa Barbara CA 93140. (805)563-9230. Offers track for advanced writers.

*CHRISTIAN WRITERS FELLOWSHIP OF ORANGE COUNTY WRITER'S DAYS. Santa Ana, April and October 1998. Contact: Carol Hutchins, PO Box 538, Lake Forest CA 92630. (310)379-5646. Attendance: 100.

LODI ALL-DAY WRITERS SEMINAR. Stockton, July 1998. General writing conference; not just Christian writers. Contact: Dee Porter, 103 Koni Ct., Lodi CA 95240. Phone/fax (209)334-0603. E-mail: crcomm@lodinet.com. Write and ask to be put on mailing list.

+MASTER CLASS. Pine Valley Bible Conference Center, Pine Valley, March 19-21, 1998. A creative writing workshop co-sponsored by San Diego Co. Christian Writers Guild and AD LIB Christian Arts. Speakers include: Jim Schaap (fiction) and Jean Janzen (poetry). Contact: Judith Deem Dupree, PO Box 365, Pine Valley CA 91962. Phone/fax (619)473-8683. E-mail: 755-5321@mcimail.com. New.

MOUNT HERMON CHRISTIAN WRITERS CONFERENCE. Mount Hermon (near Santa Cruz), April 3-7, 1998. Keynote speaker: John Fischer. Advanced track with Sally Stuart. Contact: David R. Talbott, Box 413, Mount Hermon CA 95041-0413. (408)335-4466. Fax (408)335-9218. E-mail: MHSherry@aol.com. Attendance: 200-250.

SAN DIEGO CHRISTIAN WRITERS GUILD ONE-DAY SEMINAR. San Diego, September 1998. Contact: Robert Gillespie, 17041 Palacio Pl., San Diego CA 92027. (619)487-7929. E-mail: riters@adnc.com. Web Page: www.globalwebs.com/writers. Attendance: 150.

*SAN DIEGO STATE UNIVERSITY WRITERS CONFERENCE. SDSU Aztec Center, January 1998. To advanced writers offers a read and critique by editors and agents. Contact: Jan Wahl, Gateway Center, College of Extended Studies, 5250 Campanile Dr., San Diego CA 92182. (619)594-2514. Attendance: 350.

WRITE TO BE READ WORKSHOP. Hume Lake; July 1998, call for date. Speakers: Norm Rohrer and Jeff Lilley. Contact: Norman B. Rohrer, 260 Fern Ln., Hume CA 93628-9999. (209)335-2333. Fax (209)335-2770. E-mail: NVRohrer @juno.com. Attendance: 50.

COLORADO

AD LIB CHRISTIAN WRITERS RETREAT. Black Forest/Colorado Springs, September 23-27, 1998. Speakers: Jean Janzen, Marci Whitney-Schenck, and Leonard Goss. Contact: Judith Deem Dupree, PO Box 365, Pine Valley CA 91962. Phone/fax (619)473-8683. E-mail: 755-5321@mcimail.com. Designed as a forum and format for renewal. Solitude, issues and ideas, critiquing. Attendance: 50.

#CHRISTIAN ARTISTS' SEMINAR IN THE ROCKIES. Estes Park, July/August 1998. For anyone interested in Christian music industry and ministry. Has classes in song writing and sketch writing. Contact: Cam Floria, 475 W 115th Ave #6, Denver CO 80234-3048. (303)452-1313. Attendance: 1,000-1,300.

COLORADO CHRISTIAN WRITERS CONFERENCE. Estes Park; May 14-16, 1998. Director: Marlene Bagnull, 316 Blanchard Rd., Drexel Hill PA 19026-3507. Phone/fax (610)626-6833. E-mail: mbagnull@aol.com. Website: http://nancepub.com/cwf/co/. Offers track for advanced writers. Attendance: 250.

GLEN WRITERS' WORKSHOPS. Colorado Springs; August 9-14, 1998. Contact: Virginia Stem Owens, The Milton Center, Kansas Newman College, 3100 McCormick, Wichita KS 67213. (316)942-4291, ext. 326. Fax (316)942-9658. E-mail: miltonc@ksnewman.edu. Includes advanced track; beginning and advanced fiction and poetry workshops. Attendance: 70.

CONNECTICUT

***WESLEYAN WRITERS CONFERENCE.** Middletown, June 1998. Contact: Anne Green, c/o Wesleyan University, Middletown CT 06459. (203)347-9411, ext. 2448. Attendance: 100.

FLORIDA

+AMERICAN CHRISTIAN WRITERS FT. LAUDERDALE CONFERENCE. November 12-13, 1998. Contact: Reg A. Forder, Box 110390, Nashville TN 37222. 1-800-21-WRITE. Attendance: 35-50.

FLORIDA CHRISTIAN WRITERS CONFERENCE. Park Avenue Retreat Center/Titusville; January 29-February 2, 1998; February 18-22, 1999. Offers advanced track by application only. 1998 keynoters: Custer & Hoose (drama team). Contact: Billie Wilson, 2600 Park Avenue, Titusville FL 32780. (407)269-6702x202. Fax (407)383-1741. E-mail: writer@digital.net. Attendance: 200.

WRITING STRATEGIES FOR THE CHRISTIAN MARKET. Classes for basics, intermediate marketing & business; Building the Novel, October-November, March & May 1998. Also material available for an independent studies program by mail. Contact: Rosemary J. Upton, 2712 S. Peninsula Dr., Daytona Beach FL 32118. (904)322-1111. Write to be put on mailing list. Attendance: 10-20.

GEORGIA

AMERICAN CHRISTIAN WRITERS ATLANTA CONFERENCE. February 21, 1998 (Impact Day) & September 18-19, 1998. Contact: Reg Forder, Box 110390, Nashville TN 37222. 1-800-21-WRITE. Attendance: 35-50.

*NORTHEAST GEORGIA WRITERS CONFERENCE. Gainesville, October 1998 (biennial/even-numbered years). Contact: Elouise Whitten, 660 Crestview Terrace, Gainesville GA 30501-3110. (770)532-3007. Attendance: 50-60.

SOUTHEASTERN WRITERS CONFERENCE. St. Simons Island; June 21-26, 1998. Contact: Nelle McFather, 5952 Alma Hwy., Waycross GA 31503. (912)285-9159. E-mail: nellemc@almatel.net. Includes advanced track & teen track. Attendance: 100 (limited). Awards cash prizes in every genre.

HAWAII

*YWAM WRITERS SEMINAR. Kona, July 1998. Speakers: Janice Rogers & Beverly Caruso. Contact: Beverly Caruso, 1621 Baldwin Ave., Orange CA 92665. (714)637-1733. Fax (714)282-0496. Attendance: 30-40.

IDAHO

*INTERNATIONAL NETWORK OF COMMUNICATORS & THE ARTS CONFERENCE. Coeur d'Alene; September/October 1998. Contact: Sheri Stone, Box 1754, Post Falls ID 83854-1754. Phone/fax (208)667-9730. Attendance: 300.

ILLINOIS

AMERICAN CHRISTIAN WRITERS/CHRISTIAN WRITERS INSTITUTE CHICAGO CONFERENCE. August 21-22, 1998. Contact: Reg Forder, Box 110390, Nashville TN 37222. 1-800-21-WRITE. Attendance: 50-100.

CHRISTIAN LEADERS AND SPEAKERS SEMINARS (The CLASSeminar). Decatur (217-428-4557); May 11-13, 1998. For anyone who wants to improve their communication skills for either the spoken or written word, for professional or personal reasons. Speakers: Florence Littauer and Marita Littauer. Contact: Marita Littauer, PO Box 66810, Albuquerque NM 87193. (800)433-6633. Fax (505)899-4283. E-mail: mlittauer@aol.com. Attendance: 100

EVANGELICAL PRESS ASSOCIATION CONVENTION. Chicago; April 26-29,1998 (held in different location each year). 1998 speakers: Michael Medved, Kay Cole James, Joseph Stowell, and Ravi Zacharias. 1999 convention will be held in Orlando FL (Sheraton World Resort), May 2-5. 1999.Contact: Ron Wilson, dir., 314 Dover Rd., Charlottesville VA 22901. (804)973-5941. Fax (804)973-2710. E-mail: 74473.272@compuserve.com. Attendance: 300-400. Annual convention; freelance communicators welcome.

*ILLINOIS PRAIRIE WRITER'S CONFERENCE. Wyanet; June 1998. Contact: Illinois Prairie Writer's Assn., PO Box 372, Wyanet IL 61379.

*INTERNATIONAL BLACK WRITERS CONFERENCE. Chicago, June 1998. Contact: Mable Terrell, PO Box 1030, Chicago IL 60690-1030. (312)409-2292.

*MISSISSIPPI VALLEY WRITERS CONFERENCE. (24th) Augustana College/Rock Island, June 1998. Contact: David R. Collins, 3403 45th St., Moline IL

61265. (309)762-8985. Offers advanced novel track. Attendance: 80.

*THE SALVATION ARMY CHRISTIAN WRITERS' CONFERENCE. Des Plaines IL, April 1998 (held every other year). Contact: Elizabeth Kinzie, 10 W. Algonquin Rd., Des Plaines IL 60016-6006. (847)294-2050. Attendance: 60. For S.A. officers, laymen, and employee staff.

WRITE-TO-PUBLISH CONFERENCE. Wheaton (Chicago area); June 1-5, 1998. Keynoter: Bill Myers. Contact: Lin Johnson, 9731 Fox Glen Dr., #6F, Niles IL 60714-5861. (847)296-3964. Fax (847)296-0754. E-mail: linjohnson@compuserve. com. Offers advanced track. Attendance: 150.

INDIANA

+AMERICAN CHRISTIAN WRITERS INDIANAPOLIS CONFERENECE. JUNE 5-6, 1998. Contact: Reg Forder, Box 110390, Nashville TN 37222. 1-800-21-WRITE. Attendance: 35-50.

*BETHEL COLLEGE CHRISTIAN WRITERS' WORKSHOP. Mishawaka; July 1998. Contact: Carol Gravelyn, 1001 W. McKinley Ave., Mishawaka IN 46545-5509. (219)257-3352. Attendance: 120.

IMAGE FESTIVAL OF LITERATURE AND THE ARTS. Location & date undecided. Contact: Gregory Wolfe, IMAGE, PO Box 674, Kennett Square PA 19348, (800)526-7022x115, (610)444-8065 (evenings & weekends), fax (302)652-1760, e-mail: gwolfe@isi.org.

MIDWEST WRITERS WORKSHOP. Muncie, July 29-August 1, 1998. Speakers: James Alexander Thom, William Brasheer, and Linda Tomblin. Contact: Dr. Earl Conn, Dept. of Journalism, Ball State University, Muncie IN 47306-0675. (765)285-6000. Fax (765)285-6001. E-mail: 00ELCONN@bsu.edu. Attendance: 120.

OPEN DOOR CHRISTIAN WRITERS SEMINAR. Westport; April or May 1998. Contact: Janet Teitsort, PO Box 129, Westport IN 47283-0129. Phone/fax (812)591-2210. Attendance: 50-60.

"WRITE HIS ANSWER" SEMINAR. Evansville; January 30-31, 1998. Contact: Marlene Bagnull, 316 Blanchard Rd., Drexel Hill PA 19026-3507. Phone/fax (610)626-6833. E-mail: mbagnull@aol.com. Website: http://nancepub.com/ cwf/wha/. Attendance: 30-100. Two-day seminar by the author of *Write His Answer—Encouragement for Christian Writers*.

KANSAS

*BCCC CREATIVE WRITING WORKSHOP. Butler County Community College, El Dorado; Fall 1998. Contact: Vivien Minshull-Ford, 901 S. Haverhill Rd., El Dorado KS 67042. (316)321-5083, ext. 233. Attendance: 200.

*BOONDOCKS RETREAT. Dodge City; possibly June, date not set. Contact: Linda Fergerson, 2500 Memory Ln., Dodge City KS 67801. (316)225-1126. Attendance: 25-40. Offers a spiritual retreat for writers, rather than a nuts & bolts conference.

KANSAS CITY CHRISTIAN WRITERS' NETWORK FALL CONFERENCE. Kansas City area; October 23-24, 1998. Speaker: Don Hawkins. Contact: Teresa Vining, 1438 N. Lucy Montgomery Way, Olathe KS 66061-6706. Phone/fax: (913)764-4610. E-mail: KCCWN@aol.com. Offers classes for teens. Attendance:

150. Also offers a spring writing retreat, May 1-2, 1998; attendance: 40.
PITTSBURG CHRISTIAN WRITERS' CONFERENCE. Pittsburg; April 1998. Contact: LeAnn Campbell, 267 SW 1st Ln., Lamar MO 64759. (417)682-2713. Attendance: 20-25.

KENTUCKY

AMERICAN CHRISTIAN WRITERS LOUISVILLE CONFERENCE. February 6-7, 1998. Contact: Reg A. Forder, Box 110390, Nashville TN 37222. 1-800-21-WRITE. Attendance: 35-50.

"WRITE HIS ANSWER" SEMINAR. Elizabethtown; June 19-20, 1998. Contact: Marlene Bagnull, 316 Blanchard Rd., Drexel Hill PA 19026-3507. Phone/fax (610)626-6833. E-mail: mbagnull@aol.com. Website: http://nancepub.com/cwf/wha/. Attendance: 30-100. Two-day seminar by the author of *Write His Answer—Encouragement for Christian Writers*.

+WRITERS WORKSHOP AT LOUISVILLE PRESBYTERIAN SEMINARY. Louisville; March 22-25, 1998. Co-directors/keynote speakers: Cec Murphy & Perry Biddle. Contact: Dr. James Andrews, Louisville Presbyterian Seminary, 1044 Alta Vista Rd., Louisville KY 40205. (800)264-1839. Fax (502)895-1096. Attendance: 40.

LOUISIANA

+AMERICAN CHRISTIAN WRITERS NEW ORLEANS CONFERENCE. May 1-2, 1998. Contact: Reg A. Forder, Box 110390, Nashville TN 37222. 1-800-21-WRITE. Attendance: 35-50.

MAINE

*FIFTH ANNUAL (98) CHRISTIAN WRITERS' CONFERENCE. China Lake Conference Center, August 1998. Contact: Dr. Ken Parker, Minister of Conferencing & Camping, China Lake Conference Center, PO Box 149, China ME 04926. (207)968-2101, Fax (207)968-2434. Attendance: 35-50.

STATE OF MAINE WRITERS' CONFERENCE. Ocean Park; August 18-21,1998. Contact: Richard F. Burns, PO Box 7146, Ocean Park ME 04063-7146. (207)934-9806. E-mail: rburnsO@wnec.edu. Attendance: 25-40. Contest announcement available March 1; brochure available June 1. Half-price tuition for teens.

MARYLAND

CHRISTIAN LEADERS AND SPEAKERS SEMINARS (The CLASSeminar). Baltimore (800-287-4843); October 26-28, 1998. For anyone who wants to improve their communication skills for either the spoken or written word, for professional or personal reasons. Speakers: Florence Littauer and Marita Littauer. Contact: Marita Littauer, PO Box 66810, Albuquerque NM 87193. (800)433-6633. Fax (505)899-4283. E-mail: mlittauer@aol.com. Attendance: 100

SANDY COVE CHRISTIAN WRITERS CONFERENCE. Sandy Cove/North East, October 4-8, 1998. Offers Advanced Track. Contact: Jeff Vogan, Director of Ministries, Sandy Cove Ministries, Box B, North East MD 21901. Attendance: 150.

SPAN '98: JUMP-START YOUR BOOK SALES. Baltimore; September 1998. Sponsored by the Small Publishers Assn. of North America. Speakers: Tom & Marilyn Ross, John Kremer. For pro-active authors who seek creative & proven ways to promote & sell their books, self-publishers and small presses. Contact: Marilyn Ross, PO Box 1306, Buena Vista CO 81211-1306. (719)395-4790. Fax (719)395-8374. E-mail: SPAN@SPAN-net.org. Attendance: 150.

*REVIEW AND HERALD WRITERS' WEEK. Review & Herald Publishing Assn., Hagerstown; July 1998. Contact: Penny E. Wheeler, 55 W. Oak Ridge Dr., Hagerstown MD 21740. (301)790-9731. Attendance: 50.

MASSACHUSETTS

*CAPE COD WRITERS' CONFERENCE. Craigville Conference Center, August 1998. Contact: Joseph Ryan, c/o Cape Cod Conservatory, Rt. 132, West Barnstable MA 02668. (508)375-0516. Attendance: 125. Also offers **CAPE LITERARY ARTS WORKSHOPS**: 6 simultaneous week-long workshops (poetry, romance novels, juvenile writing, children's book illustrating, and play writing), August 1998. Limited to 10 in each workshop.

MICHIGAN

+AMERICAN CHRISTIAN WRITERS GRAND RAPIDS CONFERENCE. JUNE 12-13, 1998. Contact: Reg Forder, Box 110390, Nashville TN 37222. 1-800-21-WRITE. Attendance: 35-50.

+JOURNEY WRITING WORKSHOPS/LIFELINE: A SPIRITUAL JOURNEY FOR WRITERS. Leelanau Center for Education. Glen Arbor MI. Held every 6 weeks. Contact: Elizabeth Hawkins, 1049 Floral Dr. SE, East Grand Rapids MI 49506. (616)245-9245. Classes limited to 20.

MARANATHA CHRISTIAN WRITERS SEMINAR. Maranatha Bible & Missionary Conference/Muskegon, August 24-28, 1998. Contact: Leona Hertel, 4759 Lake Harbor Rd., Muskegon MI 49441-5299. (616)798-2161. Attendance: limited to 50.

"SPEAK UP WITH CONFIDENCE" SEMINARS. Hillsdale/Michindoh Ministries Conference Center, July 23-25,1998. Contact: Carol Kent, 1614 Edison Shores Pl., Port Huron MI 48060. (810)982-0898. Fax (810)987-4163. E-mail: speakupinc@aol.com. Speaker: Carol Kent. Speaking seminar. Offers advanced training. Attendance: 110.

+WRITERS CONFERENCE AT SKYLINE. Skyline Conference Center/Calumet; November 1998. Contact: Nancy A. Regensburger, 615 Wightman St., Vassar MI 48768. Attendance: 50.

MINNESOTA

AMERICAN CHRISTIAN WRITERS MINNEAPOLIS CONFERENCE. August 14-15, 1998. Contact: Reg Forder, Box 110390, Nashville TN 37222. 1-800-21-WRITE. Attendance: 35-50.

MINNESOTA CHRISTIAN WRITERS GUILD SPRING SEMINAR. Minneapolis/St. Paul, May 8-9, 1998. Speakers: Elizabeth & John Sherrill. Followed by a 2-day, limited enrollment session. Contact: Charette Barta, 5344 Ewing Ave. S., Minneapolis MN 55410. (612)922-4609. E-mail: CBartcc@aol.com. Attendance: 80-100.

MISSISSIPPI
+AMERICAN CHRISTIAN WRITERS JACKSON IMPACT DAY. January 31, 1998. Contact: Reg Forder, Box 110390, Nashville TN 37222. 1-800-21-WRITE. Attendance: 35-50.

MISSOURI
AMERICAN CHRISTIAN WRITERS ST. LOUIS CONFERENCE. September 11-12, 1998. Contact: Reg Forder, Box 110390, Nashville TN 37222. 1-800-21-WRITE. Attendance: 35-50.

*MARK TWAIN WRITERS CONFERENCE. Hannibal, Heartland Lodge, four separate weeks in June, July, August & September, 1998. Contact: Cyndi Allison, 921 Center St., Hannibal MO 63401. (800)747-0738. (573)221-2462. Fax (573)221-6409. Attendance: 25 per conference. Note: This is a general conference under the direction of evangelical Christians.

NEW MEXICO
CHRISTIAN LEADERS AND SPEAKERS SEMINARS (The CLASSeminar). Santa Fe (800-797-4242); March 2-4, 1998. For anyone who wants to improve their communication skills for either the spoken or written word, for professional or personal reasons. Speakers: Florence Littauer and Marita Littauer. Contact: Marita Littauer, PO Box 66810, Albuquerque NM 87193. (800)433-6633. Fax (505)899-4283. E-mail: mlittauer@aol.com. Attendance: 100

*GHOST RANCH WRITING WORKSHOPS. Abiquiu; October 1998. Contact: Ghost Ranch, HC 77 Box 11, Abiquiu NM 87510-9601.

GLORIETA CHRISTIAN WRITERS' CONFERENCE. Glorieta (18 mile N. of Santa Fe); November 11-15, 1998. Contact: Mona Hodgson, PO Box 999, Cottonwood AZ 86326-0999. (800)797-4222. Fax (520)634-3145. E-mail: mona@ sedona.net. Offering classes for pastor/writers, children's writers dramatists & puppet programs, and poets. Attendance 150.

*SOUTHWEST CHRISTIAN WRITERS ASSN. SEMINAR. Farmington, September 1998 (19th Annual). Contact: Tom Walmsley, PO Box 1008, Flora Vista NM 87415. (505)334-0617. Attendance: 30.

SOUTHWEST WRITERS WORKSHOP. Albuquerque, August 17-20, 1998. Speaker: David Guterson. Contact: Carol Bruce-Fritz, 1338 Wyoming Blvd. NE, Ste. B, Albuquerque NM 87112-5067. (505)293-0303. Fax (505)237-2665. E-mail: swriters@aol.com. Attendance: 400.

*WRITERS' CONFERENCE AT SANTA FE. Santa Fe, February 1998. Contact: Michele Lis, Program Coordinator, Dept. of Continuing Education, Santa Fe Community College, Box 4187, Santa Fe NM 87502-4187. (505)438-1251. Attendance: 100-120.

NORTH CAROLINA
+AMERICAN CHRISTIAN WRITERS CHARLOTTE IMPACT DAY. January 24, 1998. Contact: Reg Forder, Box 110390, Nashville TN 37222. 1-800-21-WRITE. Attendance: 35-50.

ASSOCIATED CHURCH PRESS 1998 ANNUAL CONVENTION. Hendersonville; April 19-22, 1998. Contact: John Stapert, The Associated Church Press, PO Box 30215, Phoenix AZ 85046-0215. E-mail: John_Stapert@Ecunet.org. Workshops, individual critique, meet editors, discuss potential assignments, etc.

OHIO

+AMERICAN CHRISTIAN WRITERS AKRON CONFERENCE. May 15-16, 1998. Contact: Reg Forder, Box 110390, Nashville TN 37222. 1-800-21-WRITE. Attendance: 35-50.

*CINCINNATI BIBLE COLLEGE CHRISTIAN WRITERS WORKSHOP. Cincinnati, September 1998. Contact: Dr. Ward Patterson, 2852 McKinley Ave., Cincinnati OH 45211. (513)244-8445. Attendance: 80-100.

COLUMBUS CHRISTIAN WRITERS CONFERENCE. Columbus, fall 1998 (tentative). Contact: Brenda Custodio, 3069 Bocastle Ct., Reynoldsburg OH 43068. (614)861-1011. E-mail: custodiob1@aol.com. Attendance: 60.

*HEIGHTS WRITERS CONFERENCE. Beechwood, May 1998 (always 1st Saturday of May). Contact: Lavern Hall, Writer's World Press, PO Box 24684, Cleveland OH 44124-0684. (216)481-1974.

NORTHWEST OHIO CHRISTIAN WRITERS SEMINAR. Toledo; September 19, 1998. Speaker: Holly Miller. Contact: Linda Tippett, 4221 Woodmont Rd., Toledo OH 43613. (419)475-9169. Attendance: 75-100.

*SET FORTH CHRISTIAN WRITERS GUILD SEMINAR. North Central OH/Mansfield area; July 1998. Contact: Donna Caudill, 836 Delph Ave., Mansfield OH 44906. (419)747-1755.

*STATELINE CHRISTIAN WRITER'S CLUB PEOPLE IN PRINT SEMINAR. Celina, October 1998. Contact: Shirley Knox, 54106 Club Island Rd., Celina OH 45822. (419)268-2040.

WEST-DAYTON CHRISTIAN WRITERS SEMINAR. Dayton; August 1998. Speaker: Donna Goodrich. Contact: Tina V. Toles, PO Box 251, Englewood OH 45322-0251. (937)832-0541.

OKLAHOMA

AMERICAN CHRISTIAN WRITERS OKLAHOMA CITY CONFERENCE. April 17-18, 1998. Contact: Reg Forder, Box 110390, Nashville TN 37222. 1-800-21-WRITE. Attendance: 35-50.

*WRITING WORKSHOPS. Various locations and dates. Contact: Kathryn Fanning, PO Box 18472, Oklahoma City OK 73154-0472.

OREGON

OREGON CHRISTIAN WRITERS COACHING CONFERENCE. Salem, July 20-23, 1998. Contact: Sandy Cathcart, 341 Flounce Rock Rd., Prospect OR 97536-9726. (541)560-2367. E-mail: 75222.3643@compuserve.com. Attendance: 125-150.

PENNSYLVANIA

GREATER PHILADELPHIA CHRISTIAN WRITERS' CONFERENCE. Dresher (N. of Philadelphia), April 16-18, 1998 (10th anniversary). Especially encourages

African-American writers. Contact: Marlene Bagnull, 316 Blanchard Rd., Drexel Hill PA 19026-3507. Phone/fax (610)626-6833. E-mail: mbagnull@aol.com. Website: http://nancepub.com/cwf/cwf/. Attendance: 270.

MONTROSE CHRISTIAN WRITERS CONFERENCE. Montrose, July 1998. Contact: Patti Souder, c/o Montrose Bible Conference, 5 Locust St., Montrose PA 18801-1112. (800)598-5030. (717)278-1001. Fax (717)278-3061. E-mail: mbc@epix.net. Includes advanced track. Attendance: 70.

ST. DAVIDS CHRISTIAN WRITERS' CONFERENCE. Geneva College/Beaver Falls, near Pittsburgh, June 21-26, 1998. Keynote speaker: Linda Tomblin (Guideposts). Offers advanced track. Susan Swan, director. Contact: Audrey Stallsmith, registrar, 87 Pines Rd. E., Hadley PA 16130. (412)253-2738. E-mail: cygnet@ penn.com. Attendance: 60-80.

***WEST BRANCH CHRISTIAN WRITERS SEMINAR.** Williamsport, October 1998. Contact: Eileen Berger, RR 2 Box 378, Hughesville PA 17737. (717)584-2280.

***WRITING FOR PUBLICATION.** Pittsburgh Theological Seminary, April 1998. Speaker: Dr. Roland Tapp. Contact: The Rev. Mary Lee Talbot, 616 N. Highland Ave., Pittsburgh PA 15206. (412)362-5610x296. Attendance: 25.

SOUTH CAROLINA
SOUTH CAROLINA CHRISTIAN WRITERS CONFERENCE. Greenville; September 12, 1998. Contact: Betty Robertson, PO Box 12624, Roanoke VA 24027. Phone/fax (540)342-7511. E-mail: ccmbbr@juno.com. Attendance: 50.

TENNESSEE
+AMERICAN CHRISTIAN WRITERS KNOXVILLE IMPACT DAY. February 14, 1998. Contact: Reg Forder, Box 110390, Nashville TN 37222. 1-800-21-WRITE. Attendance: 35-50.

AMERICAN CHRISTIAN WRITERS MEMPHIS CONFERENCE. May 22-23, 1998. Contact: Reg Forder, Box 110390, Nashville TN 37222. 1-800-21-WRITE. Attendance: 35-50.

TEXAS
AMERICAN CHRISTIAN WRITERS AUSTIN CONFERENCE. March 13-14, 1998. Contact: Reg Forder, Box 110390, Nashville TN 37222. 1-800-21-WRITE. Attendance: 35-50.

AMERICAN CHRISTIAN WRITERS DALLAS CONFERENCE. July 9-11, 1998. Contact: Reg Forder, Box 110390, Nashville TN 37222. 1-800-21-WRITE. Attendance: 35-50.

+CHRISTIAN WRITERS' FELLOWSHIP OF HUNT COUNTY SEMINAR. Greenville; October 1998. Speaker: Becky Freeman, Christian humorist. Contact: Jim Pence, 1551 Hunt Co. Rd. 4109, Campbell TX 75422-1201. (903)450-4944. E-mail: jhpence@flash.net.

***FRONTIERS IN WRITING.** Amarillo College, August 1998. Sponsored by Panhandle Professional Writers. Contact: Doris R. Meredith, Box 19303, Amarillo TX 79114. (806)352-3889. Attendance: 100. Write for contest information.

INSPIRATIONAL WRITERS ALIVE!/AMARILLO SEMINAR. April 4, 1998.

Speaker: Susan Titus Osborn. Contact: Helen Luecke, 2921 S. Dallas, Amarillo TX 79103-6713. (806)376-9671.

TEXAS CHRISTIAN WRITERS FORUM. Houston; August 1, 1988 (first Saturday in August in even numbered years). Speakers: Holly Miller, Pam Zollman & Sally Stuart. Contact: Maxine E. Holder, Rt. 4 Box 81-H, Rusk TX 75785-9410. (903)795-3986. Attendance: 70.

*YWAM HANDS-ON WRITERS TRAINING WORKSHOPS. Lindale; various dates. Contact: Pamela Warren, PO Box 1380, Lindale TX 75771-1380. (903)882-5591x288. Send SASE for list of workshops.

VIRGINIA

AMERICAN CHRISTIAN WRITERS VIRGINIA BEACH CONFERENCE. June 26-27, 1998. Contact: Reg Forder, Box 110390, Nashville TN 37222. 1-800-21-WRITE. Attendance: 35-50.

+HELP! I'M A CHRISTIAN WRITER OR I'D LIKE TO BE ONE. Held in various locations by invitation. Contact: Betty B. Robertson, PO Box 12624, Roanoke VA 24027-2624. Phone/fax:(540)342-7511. E-mail: ccmbbR@juno.com.

NORTHERN VIRGINIA CHRISTIAN WRITERS CONFERENCE. Springfield; March 14, 1998. Keynote speaker: Cal Thomas. Contact: Jennifer Ferranti, dir., PO Box 12390, Burke VA 22009. Phone/fax (703)503-5366. E-mail: JenniferF@compuserve.com. Attendance: 150.

PRESBYTERIAN WRITER'S GUILD WORKSHOP. Richmond; date to be determined. Contact: Jack Purdy, director, 209 Rendon Rd., Santa Fe NM 87501. (615)370-4008.

VIRGINIA CHRISTIAN WRITERS SEMINAR. Hampton; April 25, 1998. Contact: Betty B. Robertson, PO Box 12624, Roanoke VA 24027-2624. (540)342-7511. Fax (540)342-7511. E-mail: ccmbbr@juno.com. Attendance: 75.

WASHINGTON

AMERICAN CHRISTIAN WRITERS SEATTLE CONFERENCE. October 2-3, 1998. Contact: Reg Forder, Box 110390, Nashville TN 37222. 1-800-21-WRITE. Attendance: 35-50.

*DOMINION COLLEGE WRITERS' CONFERENCE. Seattle area; November 1998. Contact: Geoff Pope, 20833 Highway 99S, Seattle Washington 98198. (206)870-3492. Fax (206)870-3553. E-mail: Geoffish@aol.com. Attendance: 75-160.

SDA CAMP MEETING WRITING CLASS. Auburn, June 22-27, 1998. Open to non-Adventists; free. Contact: Marian Forschler, PO Box 58785, Renton WA 98058-1785. (425)235-1435. Fax (425)204-2070. E-mail: marian-forschler@compuserve.com. Attendance: 50.

+YAKIMA WRITERS WORKSHOP. Yakima, May 3, 1998. Contact: Helen Haverland, PO Box 146, College Place WA 99324. (509)938-3838. Attendance: 35.

*SEATTLE PACIFIC CHRISTIAN WRITERS CONFERENCE. Seattle. Contact for new schedule. Offers Mentoring Program, Process Sessions, Issues Forums, & Marketing Update Sessions. Contact: Linda Wagner, Humanities Dept., Seattle Pacific University, Seattle WA 98119. (206)281-2109.

WENATCHEE CHRISTIAN WRITERS MINI-SEMINAR. Wenatchee, September 1998/1999 (tentative). Contact: Shirley Pease, 1818 Skyline Dr. #31,

Wenatchee WA 98801-2302. (509)662-8392. Attendance: 35-40.

WRITERS HELPING WRITERS. Spokane; March 19-21, 1998. This is not a conference, but a booth offering manuscript evaluation and help to writers during the annual Christian Workers Conference. Contact: Pat Pfeiffer, PO Box 104, Otis Orchards WA 97027-0140. (509)927-7671 or 226-3532 (evenings).

WRITERS INFORMATION NETWORK (W.I.N.) SEMINARS. Seattle; 3 times a year. Contact: Elaine Colvin, Box 11337, Bainbridge Island WA 98110. (206)842-9103. Fax (206)842-0536. E-mail: WritersInfoNetwork@juno.com. Website: http://www.bluejaypub.com/win/. Attendance: 75-100. Write or call to be put on mailing list for conference brochure.

WRITER'S WEEKEND AT THE BEACH. Ocean Park, February 27-March 1, 1998. Contact: Pat Rushford, 3600 Edgewood Dr., Vancouver WA 98661. (206)695-2263 or Birdie Etchison, PO Box 877, Ocean Park WA 98640. (206)665-6576. Attendance: Limited to 45-50.

WISCONSIN

GREEN LAKE CHRISTIAN WRITER'S CONFERENCE. Green Lake, July 4-11, 1998. Contact: Jan DeWitt, Program Dept., American Baptist Assembly, W2511 State Hwy 23, Green Lake WI 54941-9300. (800)558-8898 or (920)294-7364. Fax (920)294-3848. E-mail for information: glcc@worldnet.att.net. Website: http://www.abc-usa.org. Attendance: 80. Also provides Christian Writer's Weeks when you can stay at the conference center for writing time. Contact for dates.

*TIMBER-LEE CHRISTIAN WRITER'S CONFERENCE. Timber-Lee Christian Center/East Troy, February or April 1998. Contact: Mary Kay Meeker, N8705 Scout Rd., East Troy WI 53120. (414)642-7345. Attendance: 30-40.

WORD & PEN CHRISTIAN WRITERS CONFERENCE. Oshkosh, next conference 2000. Contact: Beth A. Ziarnik, 1963 Indian Point Rd., Oshkosh WI 54901. (920)235-0664. Attendance: 75.

CANADA

ALBERTA CHRISTIAN WRITERS' SEMINARS. Sponsored by Alberta Christian Writers Fellowship—CanadaWide. Last week-end of April (Rocky Mountain College, Calgary AB) & last Friday/Saturday of September 1998 (King's University College in Edmonton AB). September Speaker: Luci Shaw. Contact: Elsie Montgomery, pres., 34 - 1130 Falconer Rd., Edmonton AB T6R 2J6, Canada. (403)988-5622. Fax (403)430-0139. E-mail: emongom@compusmart.ab.ca

GOD USES INK WRITERS CONFERENCE AT BRIERCREST SCHOOLS. Caronport, SK, June 4-6, 1998. Speaker: Dr. John Stackhouse. Contact: Shirley Klassen, 510 College Dr., Caronport SK S0H 0S0 Canada. (306)756-3306. Fax (306)756-3366. E-mail: Sklassen@briercrest.ca. Speaker: John Stackhouse. Attendance: 75.

GOD USES INK WRITERS CONFERENCE/ON. Guelph, Ontario; June 18-20, 1998. Speaker: Sigmund Brouwer. Contact: Marianne Meed Ward, c/o Faith Today, M.I.P. Box 3745, Markham ON L3R 0Y4 Canada. (905)479-6071x245. Fax (905)479-4742. E-mail: ft@efc-canada.com. Attendance: 80. Offering a special track in song writing.

*WORDPOWER. Clearbrook, schedule for 1998 unknown. Contact: MB Herald, 3-169 Riverton Ave., Winnipeg MB R2L 2E5 Canada. (204)669-6575. Offers workshops for advanced and young writers. Attendance: 100-150.

FOREIGN COUNTRIES

AMERICAN CHRISTIAN WRITERS CARIBBEAN CRUISE. November 14-21, 1998. Open to non-writers & spouses. Contact: Reg A. Forder, Box 110390, Nashville TN 37222. 1-800-21-WRITE. Attendance: 40-50.

ASSOCIATION OF CHRISTIAN WRITERS SEMINARS. London & Leeds, England. Contact: Warren Crawford, 73 Lodge Hill Rd., Farnham, Surrey, UK GU10 3RB. Phone/fax: 01252 715746. Sponsors 3 writer's days a year: March 1998 (London), May 1998 (Leeds), October 1998 (London), and March & October 1999 (London).

CHRISTIAN COMICS TRAINING COURSES. Austrailia; second week of September, 1998. Contact: Graham Wade at Pilgrim International; fax 02 99062112; e-mail: 100036.700@compuserve.com. Another 1998 conference in Japan is under discussion. For more information on these conferences held around the world, visit the ROX35Media, Inc. Website at: http://members.aol.com/ROX35Media/.

+LITT-WORLD '98. Hoddesdon, Hertfordshire, England; September 28-October 2, 1998. Contact: John D. Maust, 130 N. Bloomingdale Rd., Bloomingdale IL 60108. (630)893-1977. Fax (630)893-1141. E-mail: MAI_LittWorld@compuserve. com. Attendance 140.

WRITERS' SUMMER SCHOOL. Swanwick, Derbyshire, England; August 8-14, 1998. Contact: Brenda Courtie, The New Vicarage, Parsons St., Woodford Halse, Daventry, Northants, NN11 3RE, England, United Kingdom. Phone/fax: +44-1327-261477. E-mail: bcourtie@aol.com. A secular conference attended by many Christians. Attendance: 300.

*YWAM WRITING SEMINARS. Seminars pending in Egypt, Israel, Great Britain, Chile, Guatemala during 1998. Open to invitations. Contact: Beverly Caruso, 1621 Baldwin Ave., Orange CA 92665. (714)282-0496. Attendance 15-50.

CONFERENCES THAT CHANGE LOCATIONS

ASSOCIATED CHURCH PRESS 1998 ANNUAL CONVENTION. Hendersonville, North Carolina, April 19-22, 1998. Contact: John Stapert, The Associated Church Press, PO Box 30215, Phoenix AZ 85046-0215. E-mail: John_Stapert@ Ecunet.org. Workshops, individual critique, meet editors, discuss potential assignments, etc.

CATHOLIC PRESS ASSOCIATION ANNUAL CONVENTION. New Orleans, June 3-5, 1998. Contact: Owen McGovern, exec. dir., 3555 Veterans Memorial Hwy Ste. O, Ronkonkoma NY 11779-7636. (516)471-4730. Fax (516)471-4804. E-mail: CathJourn@aol.com. For media professionals. Attendance: 400.

CHRISTIAN BOOKSELLERS ASSN. CONVENTION. (held in a different location each year), July 13-16, 1998, Dallas TX. Contact: CBA, Box 200, Colorado Springs CO 80901. (719)576-7880. Entrance badges available through book publishers.

CHRISTIAN LEADERS AND SPEAKERS SEMINARS (The CLASSeminar). Various dates & locations across the country. For anyone who wants to improve their communication skills for either the spoken or written word, for professional or personal reasons. Speakers: Florence Littauer and Marita Littauer. Contact: Marita Littauer, PO Box 66810, Albuquerque NM 87193. (800)433-6633. Fax (505)899-4283. E-mail: mlittauer@aol.com. Attendance: 100.

EVANGELICAL PRESS ASSOCIATION CONVENTION. Chicago; April 26-29, 1998 (held in different location each year). Contact: Ron Wilson, dir., 314 Dover Rd., Charlottesville VA 22901. (804)973-5941. Fax (804)973-2710. E-mail: 74473.272@compuserve.com. Attendance: 300-400. Annual convention; freelance communicators welcome.

"WRITE HIS ANSWER" SEMINARS. Various locations around U.S.; dates throughout the year; choice of article writing or books (includes self-publishing). Contact: Marlene Bagnull, 316 Blanchard Rd., Drexel Hill PA 19026-3507. Phone/fax (610)626-6833. E-mail: mbagnull@aol.com. Website: http://nancepub. com/cwf/wha/. Attendance: 30-100. One and two-day seminars by the author of *Write His Answer—Encouragement for Christian Writers.*

*THE WRITING ACADEMY SEMINAR. Changes location every year; summer conference. Contact: Nora Buys, 11534 Hillpark Ln., Los Altos CA 94024.

*YWAM CHRISTIAN WRITERS SEMINARS. Various states, Africa, Middle East, and South America; various dates. Contact: Registrar, YWAM Writer's Seminars, Box 3464, Orange CA 92665. (714)637-1733. Fax (714)282-0496.

AREA CHRISTIAN WRITERS' CLUBS, FELLOWSHIP GROUPS, AND CRITIQUE GROUPS

Note: See end of list for on-line writers' groups.

(*) An asterisk before a listing means the information was not verified or updated by the group leader.
(+) A plus sign before a listing indicates a new listing.

ALABAMA

CHRISTIAN FREELANCERS, Tuscaloosa. Contact: Joanne Sloan, 3230 Mystic Lake Way, Northport AL 35476. (205)333-8603. Fax (205)339-4528. Membership (25) open.

+CHRISTIAN WRITERS' GROUP, Birmingham/Hoover area. Contact: Jackie Britton, 2281 Old Tyler Rd., Birmingham AL 35226. (205)978-6008. Membership (25+) open.

ARIZONA

FOUNTAIN HILLS CHRISTIAN WRITERS. Contact: Nelia Greer, 15929 E. Cholla Dr., Fountain Hills AZ 85268. (602)837-2913. Membership (24) open.

MESA CHRISTIAN WRITERS CLUB. Contact: Donna Goodrich, 648 S. Pima St., Mesa AZ 85210. (602)962-6694. Membership (15-20) open.

*PHOENIX CHRISTIAN WRITERS' FELLOWSHIP. Contact: Victor J. Kelly Sr., 2135 W. Cactus Wren Dr., Phoenix AZ 85021. (602)864-1390. E-mail: Vkelly@getnet.com. Membership (20) open.

*SOUTH-EASTERN ARIZONA CHRISTIAN WRITERS GROUP. Benson. Contact: Bea Carlton, HCR 1 Box 153C, Willcox AZ 85643. (520)384-9232. Membership (18) open. Sponsoring a September 1998 seminar.

TEMPE CHRISTIAN WRITERS CLUB. Contact: Kitty Bucholtz, 1025 N. 48 St., #240, Phoenix AZ 85008-7306. (602)267-8529. E-mail: jkbuch@primenet.com. Membership (30) open.

TEMPE CHRISTIAN WRITERS GROUP. Contact: Andrea Huelsenbeck, 6510 S. Alder Dr., Tempe AZ 85283-3907. (602)730-0052. Membership (60) open.

TUCSON CHRISTIAN WRITERS FELLOWSHIP. Contact: Marianne Matthews, 7887 N. LaCholla Blvd. Box 3191, Tucson AZ 85741-4360. Phone/fax: (520)797-2298. E-mail: Matthewsaz@aol.com. Membership (35) open.

CALIFORNIA

CASTRO VALLEY CHRISTIAN WRITERS GROUP. Contact: Pastor Jon Drury, 19300 Redwood Rd., Castro Valley CA 94546-3465. (510)886-6300. Fax (510)581-5022. Membership (10) open. Sponsoring a Christian Writers Seminar, February 27-28, 1998.

CEHUC SPANISH CHRISTIAN WRITERS GROUP. El Cajon. Contact: Magdalena Latorre, 9802 Quail Canyon Rd., El Cajon CA 92021-6000. Phone/fax

(619)390-3747. Fax (619)561-6172. Membership (34) open. Sponsors a contest open to non-members. Planning a Spanish conference for February 1998 in Tijuana, Mexico.

*CHILDREN'S WRITERS GROUP. Lake Forest. Contact: Eileen Reinoehl, 24902 Winterwood Dr., Lake Forest CA 92630. (714)859-6294. For serious children's writers.

*CHRISTIAN WRITERS FELLOWSHIP OF ORANGE COUNTY. Santa Ana. Contact: Carolyn Hutchins, PO Box 538, Lake Forest CA 92630. (310)379-5646. Membership (100) open. Monthly newsletter. Sponsors critique groups throughout southern California (contact critique group coordinator, Jessica Shaver, 186 E. Cameron Pl., Long Beach CA 90807-3851, (562)595-4162). Sponsors two annual Writers' Days: April and October 1998.

DIABLO VALLEY CHRISTIAN WRITERS GROUP. Danville. Contact: Marcy Weydemuller, 3623 Corte Segundo, Concord CA 94519. (510)676-6555. Fax (510)681-1771. E-mail: meweyde@hotcoco.infi.net. Membership (12) open.

HAYWARD AREA CHRISTIAN WRITERS GROUP. Contact: Launa Herrmann, 21555 Eden Canyon Rd., Castro Valley CA 94552-9721. (510)889-7564. Membership (10) open.

HIGH DESERT CHRISTIAN WRITERS GUILD. Lancaster. Contact: Ellen Bergh, 3600 Brabham Ave., Rosamond CA 93560-6891. (805)256-1266. E-mail: mastermedia@hughes.net. Membership (8-10) open.

INLAND EMPIRE CHRISTIAN WRITERS GUILD. Moreno Valley. Contact: Bill and Carole Gift Page, 10653 Ridgefield Terr., Moreno Valley CA 92557. (909)924-0610. Membership (46) open.

LODI WRITERS ASSOCIATION. (General membership, not just Christian). Contact: Dee Porter, 103 Koni Ct., Lodi CA 95240. Phone/fax (209)334-0603. E-mail: crcomm@lodinet.com. Membership (70) open. Sponsors one-day workshop, July 1998.

*NATIONAL WRITER'S ASSN./SOUTHERN CALIFORNIA CHAPTER. Fountain Valley. Liaison: Shirl Thomas, 9379 Tanager Ave., Fountain Valley CA 92708-6557. (714)968-5726. Membership (142) open. Secular group/many Christians.

SACRAMENTO CHRISTIAN WRITER'S CLUB. Contact: Jan Roach, 8304 Bellsbrae Dr., Antelope CA 95843-5145. Phone/fax (916)729-3858. Membership (30) open.

SAN DIEGO COUNTY CHRISTIAN WRITERS' GUILD. Contact: Robert Gillespie, 17041 Palacio Pl., San Diego CA 92027. (619)487-7929. Fax (619)673-3921. E-mail: riters@adnc.com. Membership (250+) open. Sponsors fall seminar and March awards banquet. Contest for members.

SIERRA VALLEY AREA CHRISTIAN WRITERS' GROUP. Loyalton. Contact: Janet McHenry, PO Box 750, Loyalton CA 96118-0750. Phone/fax (916)993-4019. Membership (6) open.

COLORADO

+CHRISTIAN WRITERS OF SOUTHERN COLORADO. Colorado Springs. Contact: Sue Sutherland or Sharon McAllister, 4605 Splendid Cir. S., Colorado Springs CO 80917. (719)591-0370. Membership (8) open.

CHRISTIAN WRITERS IN TOUCH. Denver. Contact: Christine Adams, 1257 Logan St., Apt. 204, Denver CO 80203-2442. (303)595-5857. Membership (6) open.

DELAWARE
DELMARVA CHRISTIAN WRITERS' FELLOWSHIP. Georgetown. Contact: Candy Abbott, PO Box 777, Georgetown DE 19947-0777. Phone/fax (302)856-6649. E-mail: cabbott@outland.dtcc.edu. Membership (12) open.

FLORIDA
ADVENTURES IN CHRISTIAN WRITING. Orlando. Contact: Mary Shaw, 350 E. Jackson St. #811, Orlando FL 32801. (407)841-4866. Membership (20-25) open.

CHRISTIAN WRITERS CRITIQUE GROUP. Miami Area. Contact: Eva Sartorio at (305)234-7378 or Karen Whiting at (305)388-8656. E-mail: eva@cs.miami.edu. Membership (7-12) open.

+FAMU CHRISTIAN WRITERS GROUP. Tallahassee. Contact: Rev. Larry Hunt, BSM Director, Baptist Student Ministries Center, Florida A&M University, Tallahassee FL 32307. (850)224-7151. E-mail: ethomas@famu.edu. Ebony Thomas, 1998 Chairperson. Membership (15+) open.

SUNCOAST CHRISTIAN WRITERS GROUP. Largo. Contact: Elaine Creasman, 13014 - 106th Ave. N., Largo FL 34644-5602. (813)595-8963. Membership (30+) open.

TITUSVILLE CHRISTIAN WRITERS' FELLOWSHIP. Contact: Nancy Otto Boffo, 2625 Riviera Dr., Titusville FL 32780-5144. (407)267-7604. Membership (10) open.

WRITING STRATEGIES CRITIQUESHOP. Daytona Beach. Meets monthly (10X). Sponsors seminars the 2nd Tuesday of each month (except July & August) for working authors who have completed one course of Writing Strategies (see conference listing). Speakers: Rosemary Upton & Kistler London. Send SASE for brochure. Contact: Rosemary J. Upton, 2712 S. Peninsula Dr., Daytona Beach FL 32118. Phone/fax (904)322-1111. Membership (20) open.

GEORGIA
+LAMBLIGHTER'S CRITIQUE GROUP. Lilburn. Contact: Cisi Morrow-Smith, 1056 Sawgrass Ct., Lilburn GA 30047. (770)978-9129. Membership (4-6) open.

IDAHO
+EAGLE ROCK CHRISTIAN WRITER'S GROUP. Idaho Falls. Contact; Steve or Kathy Sanders, PO Box 606, Ucon ID 83454. (208)528-8595. Critique group only. Membership (10+) open.

INTERNATIONAL NETWORK OF COMMUNICATORS & THE ARTS. Couer d Alene. Contact: Sheri Stone, Box 1754, Post Falls ID 83854-1754. Phone/fax (208)667-9730. Membership (25) open. Sponsors a contest and an annual fall seminar.

ILLINOIS

*INTERNATIONAL BLACK WRITERS. Chicago & New York. Contact: Mable Terrell, PO Box 1030, Chicago IL 60690-1030. (312)409-2292. Membership (2,000) open. Sponsors a contest open to nonmembers. Conference in Chicago, June 1998.

*JUVENILE FORUM. Moline. Contact: David R. Collins, 3403 45th St., Moline IL 61265. (309)762-8985. Membership (6-12) open to those writing for children or youth.

INDIANA

BLOOMINGTON AREA CHRISTIAN WRITERS. Bloomington & Ellettsville. Contact: Kathi Adams, 9576 W. St. Rd. 48, Bloomington IN 47404-9737. (812)876-8265. Membership (10) open.

EVANSVILLE-AREA CHRISTIAN WRITERS' FELLOWSHIP. Contact: Cynthia Bezek, 1820 E. Boonville-New Harmony Rd., Evansville IN 47711-9220. (812)867-9211. E-mail: db36@evansville.edu. Membership (20) open.

FORT WAYNE CHRISTIAN WRITERS CLUB. Fort Wayne. Contact: Linda R. Wade, 739 W. Fourth St., Fort Wayne IN 46808-2613. (219)422-2772. E-mail: linda_wade@juno.com. Membership (32) open. Also publishes a bimonthly newsletter called Fort and Field (editor: Phyllis Posey, PO Box 127, Hicksville OH 43526).

OPEN DOOR CHRISTIAN WRITERS. Westport. Contact: Janet Teitsort, PO Box 129, Westport IN 47283-0129. Phone/fax (812)591-2210. Membership (20-25) open. Sponsors a seminar about every two years in April or May.

IOWA

CEDAR RAPIDS CHRISTIAN WRITER'S CRITIQUE GROUP. Contact: Billie Parr, 2222 - 1st Ave. NE, Cedar Rapids IA 52402. (319)363-0039. Membership (12) open. A day and a night group.

*RIVER CITY WRITERS. Council Bluffs. Contact: Dee Barrett, 16 Susan Lane, Council Bluffs IA 51503. (712)322-7692. Membership (10+) open.

SIOUXLAND CHRISTIAN WRITERS. Sioux City. Contact: William B. Tucker, 4881 Bradford Ln., Sioux City IA 51106-9519. (712)943-1412. Membership (12) open.

KANSAS

*CHRISTIAN WRITERS GROUP OF TOPEKA. Contact: Charles White, 4102 NW Dondee Ln., Topeka KS 66618. (913)286-0388. Membership (14) open.

KANSAS CITY CHRISTIAN WRITERS' NETWORK. Overland Park. Contact: Teresa Vining, 1438 N Lucy Montgomery Way, Olathe KS 66061-6706. Phone/fax: (913)764-4610. E-mail: KCCWN@aol.com. Membership (200) open. Sponsors a spring retreat (May 1-2, 1998) and a fall writers' conference (October 23-24,1998). Contest for those who attend conference.

*LEARNERS CHRISTIAN WRITING CLUB. Medicine Lodge. Contact: Ruth E. Montgomery, PO Box 308, Medicine Lodge KS 67104-0308. (316)886-9863. Membership (10) open.

*PITTSBURG CHRISTIAN WRITERS FELLOWSHIP. Pittsburg. Contact: LeAnn Campbell, 267 SW 1st Ln., Lamar MO 64759. (417)682-2713. Membership (20) open. Sponsors an April seminar.

KENTUCKY

JACKSON CHRISTIAN WRITERS' CLUB. Vancleve. Contact: Donna J. Woodring, PO Box 10, Vancleve KY 41385-0010. (606)666-5000. Fax 606-666-7744. Membership (7) open.

LOUISIANA

SCRIBES OF NEW ORLEANS. Contact: Jack Cunningham, PO Box 55601, Metairie LA 70055-5601. (504)837-4397. E-mail: 72440.1623@compuserve.com. Membership (10) not open.

MAINE

MAINE FELLOWSHIP OF CHRISTIAN WRITERS. China Lake. Contact: Vicki Schad, RR 1 Box 540, N. Vassalboro ME 04962-9709. (207)923-3956. E-mail: vschad@pivot.net. Membership (12) open. Sponsors contest open to non-members. Conference, April 13-15, 1998.

MARYLAND

ANNAPOLIS FELLOWSHIP OF CHRISTIAN WRITERS. Annapolis. Contact: Mark Littleton, 5350 Eliot's Oak Rd., Columbia MD 21044. Phone/Fax (410)995-0831 or Jeri Sweany (410)267-0924. E-mail: MarkLitt@aol.com. Membership (15-20) open. Sponsors occasional seminars.

MASSACHUSETTS

WESTERN MASSACHUSETTS CHRISTIAN WRITERS FELLOWSHIP. Springfield. Contact: Barbara A. Robidoux, 127 Gelinas Dr., Chicopee MA 01020-4813. (413)592-4386. Fax 594-8375. Membership (50) open.

MINNESOTA

MINNESOTA CHRISTIAN WRITERS GUILD. Minneapolis. Contact: Jane Kise, 5504 Grove St., Edina MN 55436. (612)926-4343. E-mail: JAGKISE@aol.com. Membership (100) open. Sponsors a contest (open to non-members) and an annual spring seminar in April or May (May 8-9, 1998).

MISSOURI

CHRISTIAN WRITERS WORKSHOP. St. Louis. Contact: Ruth McDaniel, 15233 Country Ridge Dr., Chesterfield MO 63017-7432. (314)532-7584. Membership (25) open.

KANSAS CITY CHRISTIAN WRITERS' NETWORK. Independence. Contact: Teresa Vining, 1438 N Lucy Montgomery Way, Olathe KS 66061-6706. Phone/fax: (913)764-4610. E-mail: KCCWN@aol.com. Membership (200) open. Sponsors a spring retreat (May 1-2, 1998) and a fall writers' conference (October

23-24,1998). Contest for those who attend conference.

*NORTHLAND CHRISTIAN WRITERS. Kansas City. Contact: Margaret Owen, 207 NW 67th St., Gladstone MO 64118. (816)436-5240.

SPRINGFIELD CHRISTIAN WRITERS CLUB. Contact: Owen Wilkie, 4909 Old Wire Rd., Brookline MO 65619-9655. (417)882-5185. Fax (417)862-4382. E-mail: owilkie@publish.ag.org. Membership (7) open.

MONTANA

*HELENA CHRISTIAN WRITERS. Contact: Lenore Puhek, 1215 Hudson, Helena MT 59601. (406)443-2552. Membership (12) open as space allows. Has one-day writers' retreat for members.

*MONTANA CHRISTIAN WRITERS. Contact: Margaret Wilkison, 2007 Sweet Grass Rd., Helena MT 59061. (406)442-9939.

NEBRASKA

+MY THOUGHTS EXACTLY WRITERS GROUP. Fremont. Contact: Cheryl Paden, 1959 E. 10th St., Fremont NE 68025. (402)727-6508. Membership (4) open. Periodically sponsors a writers' retreat, October 1998 and/or April 1999.

NEW HAMPSHIRE

+LIVING WORD WRITERS FELLOWSHIP. Lebanon. Contact: James A. Blaine, 80 1/2 Mascoma St., Lebanon NH 03766-2646. (603)448-4609. Membership (20) open.

WORDSMITHS' CHRISTIAN WRITERS' FELLOWSHIP. Nashua. Contact: Cynthia Vlatas, 5 Jeremy Ln., Hudson NH 03051. (603)882-2851. Fax (603)883-7518. E-mail: sasacindy@aol.com. Website: http://members.aol.com/nh4jesus/wrdsmith.htm. Membership (26) open. Sponsors occasional workshop.

NEW JERSEY

+CENTRAL JERSEY CHRISTIAN WRITERS' FELLOWSHIP. Somerset. Contact: Catherine J. Barrier, 13 Oliver St., Somerset NJ 08873-2142. (712)545-5168. Membership open. New group. Morning and evening meetings.

*SOUTH JERSEY CHRISTIAN WRITERS FELLOWSHIP. Atlantic City. Contact: Sandi Cleary, 308 Clark Pl., Northfield NJ 08225. (609)646-5694.

NEW MEXICO

*SOUTHWEST CHRISTIAN WRITERS ASSOCIATION. Farmington. Contact: Patti Cordell, #74 RD 3535, Flora Vista NM 87415. (505)334-2258. Membership (18) open. Sponsors annual one-day seminar the third Saturday in September.

SOUTHWEST WRITERS WORKSHOP. Albuquerque. Contact: Carol Bruce-Fritz, 1338 Wyoming Blvd. NE, Ste. B, Albuquerque NM 87112-5067. (505)293-0303. Fax (505)237-2665. SWRITERS@aol.com. Membership (1,200) open. Sponsors a contest (open to non-members)and a conference in Albuquerque, September 17-20, 1998.

NEW YORK
*BROOKLYN WRITER'S CLUB. Contact: Ann Dellarocco, Box 184, Bath Beach Station, Brooklyn NY 11214. (718)837-3484. Membership (500) open.

*INTERNATIONAL BLACK WRITERS. New York & Chicago. Contact: Mable Terrell, PO Box 1030, Chicago IL 60690-1030. (312)409-2292. Membership (2,000) open. Sponsors a contest open to nonmembers. Conference in Chicago, June 1998.

NEW YORK CHRISTIAN WRITERS GROUP. New York City. Contact: Zoe Blake, 361 Clinton Ave., #7H, Brooklyn 11238. (718)430-5898 or (718)636-5547. Membership (25) open.

SOUTHERN TIER CHRISTIAN WRITERS' FELLOWSHIP. Binghamton/ Johnson City area. Contact: Kenneth Cetton, 20 Pine St., Port Crane NY 13833-1512. (607)648-7249. E-mail: KC1933@juno.com. Membership (6) open.

NORTH CAROLINA
COVENANT WRITERS. Lincolnton. Contact: Janice Stroup, 403 S. Cedar St., Lincolnton NC 28092-3342. (704)735-8851. Membership (7) open.

OHIO
*AKRON MANUSCRIPT CLUB. Contact: Tom Raber, Box 966, Cuyahoga Falls OH 44223. (216)928-7268. Membership open. Sponsors annual writers' conference in May.

*CHRISTIAN WRITERS GUILD. Youngstown area. Contact: Susan K. Virgalitte, 240 Sawmill Run Dr., Canfield OH 44406. Phone/fax (330)533-5833. E-mail: TOVIR@aol.com. Membership (30) open.

COLUMBUS CHRISTIAN WRITERS ASSN. Contact: Brenda Custodio, 3069 Bocastle Ct., Reynoldsburg OH 43068. (614)861-1011. E-mail: custodiob1@ aol.com. Membership (40) open. Sometimes sponsors a fall workshop and a contest open to non-members.

DAYTON CHRISTIAN SCRIBES. Kettering. Contact: Lois Pecce (secretary), Box 41613, Dayton OH 45441-0613. (937)433-6470. Fax (937)435-2175. Membership (36) open.

GREATER CINCINNATI CHRISTIAN WRITERS' FELLOWSHIP. Contact: Teresa Cleary, 895 Garnoa St., Cincinnati OH 45231-2618. Phone/fax (513)521-1913. E-mail: tcwriter@aol.com. Membership (25) open. Dues $15.

NORTHWESTERN OHIO CHRISTIAN WRITERS. Bowling Green. Contact: Linda R. Tippett, 4221 Woodmont Rd., Toledo OH 43613. (419)475-9169. Membership (25) open. Sponsors a Saturday seminar, September 19, 1998.

*OHIO FELLOWSHIP OF CHRISTIAN WRITERS. Contact: John G. Hoffman, 233 W. Church St., Marion OH 43302. (614)387-6683. Membership open. Sponsors annual writers' conference.

PATASKALA CHRISTIAN WRITERS. Contact: Melissa Morgan, PO Box 667, Pataskala OH 43062. (614)927-7773. Membership (6-20) open.

*SET FORTH WRITERS GUILD. North Central OH/Mansfield area. Contact: Donna Caudill, 836 Delph Ave., Mansfield OH 44906. (419)747-1755. Membership (35) open. Planning seminar for July 1998.

STATELINE CHRISTIAN WRITER'S CLUB. Celina. Contact: Shirley Knox,

54106 Club Island Rd., Celina OH 45822. (419)268-2040. Membership (20) open. Sponsors a People in Print Seminar, October 1998 (tentative).

WEST-DAYTON CHRISTIAN WRITERS GUILD. Contact: Tina V. Toles, PO Box 251, Englewood OH 45322-0251. (937)832-0541. Membership (50) open. Sponsoring an August 1998 seminar.

*WESTERN OHIO CHRISTIAN WRITERS. Sidney. Contact: Alice Linsley, 231 N. Miami Ave., Sidney OH 45365. (513)663-4131/492-8584. Membership (43) open.

OKLAHOMA

TULSA CHRISTIAN WRITERS. Contact: Eugene C. Scott, PO Box 35625, Tulsa OK 74135. (918)459-0004. E-mail: 104676.1742@compuserve.com. Membership (50) open.

WORDWRIGHTS. Oklahoma City. Contact: Mary Murphy, 428 Brookside, Guthrie OK 73044. (405)354-5042. Membership (40-50) open. Hosting an American Christian Writers Seminar, April 24-25, 1998, in Oklahoma City; send SASE for information.

OREGON

+BEAVERTON CHRISTIAN WRITERS GROUP. Contact: Lucibel Van Atta, 12925 SW Morgan Ct., Beaverton OR 97008. (503)671-0865. Serious group; must write regularly. Waiting list.

CHRISTIAN WRITERS SUPPORT GROUP. Portland area. Contact: Karen Taylor, 5530 NW Osprey Pl., Portland OR 97229-1089. (503)645-4906. Membership (6) open.

EUGENE CHRISTIAN WRITERS GROUP. Contact: Dorothy A. Grant, PO Box 502, Eugene OR 97440. (541)343-2187. Or Lois Erickson, (541)342-6896. Membership (11) may be open.

HOCKETT CRITIQUE GROUP. Contact: Betty Hockett, 1100 N. Meridian #38, Newberg OR 97132-1187. (503)538-9871. E-mail: hocketgb@open.org. Membership (8-10) not currently open.

+MILWAUKIE CHRISTIAN WRITERS GROUP. Contact: Geneva Iijima, (503)656-3632. Serious group; must write regularly. Waiting list available.

OREGON CHRISTIAN SCRIBES. Portland. Contact: Blanche B. Butler, 11351 Corvallis Rd., Independence OR 97351-9748. (503)838-2470. Membership (12+) open. Annual conference in Yakima WA, May 3, 1998.

OREGON CHRISTIAN WRITERS. Contact: Debbie Hedstrom, pres., 5490 - 8th Ave. SE, Salem OR 97306. (503)370-9153. Fax (503)365-1801. E-mail: 74361.452@compuserve.com. Meets three times annually: February in Salem, May in Eugene, and October in Portland. All-day Saturday conferences. Membership (250) open. Sponsors annual conference in July or August (in Salem). Newsletter & critique groups.

+OREGON CITY CHRISTIAN WRITERS GROUP. Contact: Geneva Iijima, (503)656-3632. Serious group; must write regularly. Waiting list available.

+ORTHODOX AUTHOR'S ASSN. Eugene, Ashland, perhaps Bend. Contact: Sarah Cowie, 25372 Eldale Dr., Eugene OR 97402. Phone/fax (541)935-6763. Membership (15) open. May sponsor a spring writer's retreat in Forestville, CA.

+PORTLAND CHRISTIAN WRITERS GROUP. Contact: Stan Baldwin,

(503)659-2974. Serious group; must write regularly. Waiting list available.

+SALEM I CHRISTIAN WRITERS GROUP. Contact: Marcia Mitchell, (503)588-0372. Membership (7) open.

+SALEM II CHRISTIAN WRITERS GROUP. Contact: Diane Hopper, (503)378-7974. Membership (6) open.

SMITH ROCK CHRISTIAN WRITERS. Redmond. Contact: Josephine Manes, 2135 NE O'Neil Way, Redmond OR 97756. (541)548-8872. Membership (5) open.

WORDSMITHS. Gresham/Vancouver/Battle Ground. Contact: Susan Thogerson Maas, 27526 SE Carl St., Gresham OR 97080-8215. Phone/fax (503)663-7834. E-mail: STM663@aol.com. Membership (8) open. Christian and secular writers.

PENNSYLVANIA

*BETHEL WORDSPINNERS. Bethlehem. Contact: Wanda Dean, 4100 Birch Dr., Bethlehem PA 18017-4512. Membership (7) open. Monthly meetings and critique by mail.

THE FIRST WORD. Sewickley. Contact: Shirley Stevens, 326 B Glaser Ave., Pittsburgh PA 15202-2910. (412)761-2618. Membership (12) open.

GREATER JOHNSTOWN CHRISTIAN WRITERS' GUILD. Contact: Betty Rosian, 108 Deerfield Ln., Johnstown PA 15905-5703. (814)255-4351. E-mail: RayRosian@aol.com. Membership (20) open.

GREATER PHILADELPHIA CHRISTIAN WRITERS' FELLOWSHIP. Broomall. Contact: Marlene Bagnull, 316 Blanchard Rd., Drexel Hill PA 19026. Phone/fax (610)626-6833. E-mail: mbagnull@aol.com. Website: http://nancepub.com/cwf/cwf/. Membership (40) open. Sponsors contest (open to non-members) and annual writers' conference (April 16-18, 1998).

LANCASTER AREA CHRISTIAN WRITERS FELLOWSHIP. Contact: John Brenneman, 258 Brenneman Rd., Lancaster PA 17603-9623. (717)872-5183. Membership (8-13) open.

MONTROSE CHRISTIAN WRITERS FELLOWSHIP. Contact: Patti Souder, PO Box 159, Montrose PA 18801-1059. (800)598-5030. Membership (13) open. Holding a conference July 26-30, 1998.

+PUNXSUTAWNEY AREA CHRISTIAN WRITERS FELLOWSHIP. Contact: Michele T. Huey, RD 1 Box 112, Glen Campbell PA 15742-9604. (814)845-7683. Membership (12) open.

WEST BRANCH CHRISTIAN WRITERS. Williamsport. Contact: Eileen Berger, RR 2 Box 378, Hughesville PA 17737. (717)584-2280. Membership (15) open. Sponsors occasional workshop.

SOUTH CAROLINA

CHRISTIAN WRITERS GROUP. Greenville. Contact: Nancy Parker, 2530 E North St. Apt. 6A, Greenville SC 29615-1448. (864)322-5594. Fax (864)322-5596. E-mail: NKPediting@aol.com. Membership (6-8) open.

SOUTH DAKOTA

BLACK HILLS CHRISTIAN WRITERS. Rapid City. Contact: Loma Davies Silcott, 1777 Zinnia St., Rapid City SD 57701-6280. Phone/fax (605)393-2246.

E-mail: 73500.3633@compuserve.com. Membership (8) open. Instruction at each meeting.

TENNESSEE
CHATTANOOGA CHRISTIAN WRITERS WORKSHOP. Chattanooga Bible Institute. Contact: Peter Snyder, 181 Lovella Dr., Ringgold GA 30736. (706)891-0858. Fax (706)891-3931. E-mail: PFSnyder3@compuserve.com. Membership (10) open.

TEXAS
*****AUSTIN CHRISTIAN WRITERS' GUILD.** Contact: Bob Rose, 12218 Ranch Rd. 620, Ste 101, Austin TX 78750-1074. Phone/fax (512)219-5444. E-mail: HRHbob @juno.com. Membership (50) open. Seminar February 1998.
+CHRISTIAN WRITERS' FELLOWSHIP OF HUNT COUNTY. Greenville. Contact: Jim Pence, 1551 Hunt Co. Rd. 4109, Campbell TX 75422-1201. (903)450-4944. E-mail: jhpence@flash.net. Membership (12) open. Sponsoring an October 1998 seminar.
INSPIRATIONAL WRITERS ALIVE! Pasadena. Contact: Sharon O'Maley (713)460-8374, or Pat Vance (713)477-4968. Membership (90-100) open. Sponsors summer seminar on even years, monthly newsletter, and annual contest (November 1-April 1).
INSPIRATIONAL WRITERS ALIVE!/AMARILLO CHAPTER. Contact: Helen Luecke, 2921 S. Dallas, Amarillo TX 79103-6713. (806)376-9671. Or Doris Crandall (806)355-0533. Membership (30) open. Seminar April 4, 1998 in Amarillo.
INSPIRATIONAL WRITERS ALIVE!/CENTRAL TX CHAPTER. Buffalo. Contact: Juanice Teer (903)322-4701.
INSPIRATIONAL WRITERS ALIVE!/HOUSTON CHAPTER. Houston. Contact: Martha Rogers (713)686-7209 or Wanda Shadle (713)862-1115. Membership (30) open.
INSPIRATIONAL WRITERS ALIVE!/NORTHWEST HOUSTON CHAPTER. Spring. Contact: Lynn Grice (713)370-7111. Membership open.
INSPIRATIONAL WRITERS ALIVE!/JACKSONVILLE CHAPTER. Contact: Maxine Holder, Rt. 4 Box 81H, Rusk TX 75785. (903)795-3986. Or, Debra Smith (903)586-6423. Membership open.
INSPIRATIONAL WRITERS ALIVE!/TRINITY CHAPTER. Anahuac. Contact: Mary Ann Evans, PO Box 1027, Anahuac TX 77514. (409)267-3284. Membership (13) open.

UTAH
UTAH CHRISTIAN WRITERS FELLOWSHIP. Salt Lake City & suburbs. Contact: Kimberly Malkogainnis, 117 W Park St., Bingham Canyon UT 84006-1134. (801)568-7761. Membership (12) open.

VERMONT
PROFESSIONAL WRITERS GROUP. Central Vermont and Eastern New York.

Contact: Celeste Perrino Walker, RR #3 Box 4913, Rutland VT 05701. (802)773-0535. Membership open. Instruction given at monthly meetings. Secular group with Christian members.

VIRGINIA

NEW COVENANT WRITER'S GROUP. Hampton. Contact: Mary Tatem, 451 Summer Dr., Newport News VA 23606-2515. Phone/fax (757)930-1700. Membership (12) open. Sponsors an annual writers seminar, April 25, 1998.

NORTHERN VIRGINIA CHRISTIAN WRITERS FELLOWSHIP. Burke. Contact: Jennifer Ferranti, dir., PO Box 12390, Burke VA 22009. Phone/fax (703)503-5366. E-mail: JenniferF@compuserve.com. Membership (200+) open. Sponsors a spring seminar (March 14, 1998).

S.O.N. WRITERS. Alexandria. Contact: Susan Lyttek, 2434 Temple Ct., Alexandria VA 23307-1524. Phone/fax (703)768-5582. E-mail: SusanAJL@aol.com. Membership (100/3-7 attend meetings) open. May sponsor a contest in September 1998.

WINCHESTER CHRISTIAN SCRIBES. Contact: Traci Noe, 208 Hackberry Dr., Stephens City VA 22655-2131. (540)869-0446. E-mail: SHYAN@visuallink. com. Membership (7) open.

WASHINGTON

ADVENTIST WRITERS ASSOCIATION OF WESTERN WASHINGTON. Auburn. Contact: Marian Forschler, PO Box 58785, Renton WA 98058-1785. (425)235-1435. Fax (425)204-2070. E-mail: marian-forschler@compuserve.com. Membership (40) open. Newsletter $10/yr. Sponsors annual writers' conference in late June.

*CAPITOL CHRISTIAN WRITERS ASSN. Olympia. Contact: Teresa Graham, 7030 Tolmie Ct. NE, Olympia WA 98516-3131. Membership (19) open.

CHILDREN'S WRITERS CRITIQUE GROUP. Spokane. Contact: Christine Tangvald, S. 5219 Pittsburg, Spokane WA 99223. (509)448-0593. Membership open.

CHRISTIAN WRITERS. Walla Walla. Contact: Dolores Walker, 904 Ankeny, Walla Walla WA 99362-3705. (509)529-2974. Membership (6) open.

*NORTHWEST CHRISTIAN WRITERS ASSN. Bellevue. Contact: Beth Harris, 14313 - 130th Ave. NE, Kirkland WA 98034. (206)821-5672. Membership (90) open.

*SPOKANE CHRISTIAN WRITERS. Contact: Niki Anderson, 1405 E 54th Ave., Spokane WA 99223-6374. (509)448-6622. Membership (12+) open.

SPOKANE NOVELISTS. Contact: Joan Mochel, 12229 N. Ruby Rd., Spokane WA 99218-1924.(509)466-2938. E-mail: MOCHEL@aol.com. Membership (18) open. Secular group with mostly Christian members.

WASHINGTON CHRISTIAN WRITERS. Seattle. Contact: Elaine Wright Colvin, Box 11337, Bainbridge Island WA 98110. (206)842-9103. Fax (206)842-0536. E-mail: writersinfonetwork@juno.com. Membership (400) open. Holds four annual meetings.

*WENATCHEE CHRISTIAN WRITERS' FELLOWSHIP. East Wenatchee. Contact: Shirley R. Pease, 1818 Skyline Dr. #31, Wenatchee WA 98801. (509)662-

8392. Membership (35-50) open. Holds one-day seminar in September.

WHATCOM CHRISTIAN WRITERS CLUB. Group does not meet regularly. Area contact: Judy Slotemaker, 840 E. Pole Rd., Lynden WA 98264. (206)354-2636.

WISCONSIN

WORD & PEN CHRISTIAN WRITERS CLUB. Menasha. Contact: Linda DeVries, W4897 Escarpment Terrace, Sherwood WI 54169-9760. (920)989-2844. E-mail: devries@fox.tds.net. Membership (14) open: Holds a seminar every few years.

CANADA

ALBERTA CHRISTIAN WRITERS' FELLOWSHIP—CANADAWIDE. Calgary & Edmonton. Contact: Elsie Montgomery, pres., 34 - 1130 Falconer Rd., Edmonton AB T6R 2J6, Canada. (403)988-5622. Fax (403)430-0139. E-mail: emongom@compusmart.ab.ca. Membership (150) open. Newsletter. Membership fee $30. Sponsors seminars the last week-end of April & September. See conference listing. Sponsors 2 contests, spring & fall (fall open to non-members).

ARTISTIC LICENSE. Langley, BC. Contact: Christy Bowler, Box 56040, Valley Center PO, Langley BC V3A 8B3 Canada. (604)532-0401. Membership (20) open.

*CHRISTIAN WRITERS CLUB. Montreal, Quebec. Contact: Mary Ann Lipscombe , 7428 Stuart (Park Extension District), Montreal QB H3N 2R4 Canada. (514)273-5356. Annual membership fee, $15. Membership (18) open. Holds occasional writers' seminar.

*FRASER VALLEY CHRISTIAN WRITERS GROUP. Abbotsford. Contact: Ingrid Shelton, 2082 Geneva Ct., Clearbrook BC V2T 3Z2 Canada (Box 783, Sumas WA 98295). (604)859-7530. Membership (30) open.

MANITOBA CHRISTIAN WRITERS ASSN. Winnipeg. Contact: Edward D. Hughes, 39 Valleyview Dr., Winnipeg MB R2Y 0R5 Canada. (204)890-0460. E-mail: hughes@aecc.escape.ca. Membership (15) open.

SOUTHERN MANITOBA FELLOWSHIP OF CHRISTIAN WRITERS. Winkler, Roland or Carman. Contact: Ellie Reimer, 173 - 10th St., Winkler MB R6W 1W8 Canada. (204)325-7701. Membership (4) open.

*SPIRITWOOD SCRIBES. Meets 19X/yr. Contact: Elmer Bowes, Spiritwood SK, S0J 2M0. (306)883-2003. Annual dues $5. Membership open.

*SWAN VALLEY WRITERS GUILD. Swan River, Manitoba. Contact: Julie Bell, Box 2115, Swan River MB R0L 1Z0 Canada. (204)734-7890. Membership (7-8) open. Sponsors a seminar.

FOREIGN

ASSOCIATION OF CHRISTIAN WRITERS. London & Venves, England. Contact: Warren Crawford, 73 Lodge Hill Rd., Farnham, Surrey, UK GU10 3RB. Phone/fax: 01252 715746. Membership (750) open. Sponsors a contest (open to non-members) and 3 writer's days a year: March 1998 (London), May 1998 (Leeds), October 1998 (London), and March & October 1999 (London).

NATIONAL/INTERNATIONAL GROUPS (no state location)

AMERICAN CHRISTIAN WRITERS SEMINARS. Sponsors conferences in various locations around the country (see individual states for dates and places). Call for dates and locations. Sponsoring a Caribbean cruise, November 15-22, 1998. Contact: Reg Forder, Box 110390, Nashville TN 37222. 1-800-21-WRITE.

CHRISTIAN WRITERS FELLOWSHIP INTL. Contact: Sandy Brooks, Rt. 3 Box 1635, Jefferson Davis Rd., Clinton SC 29325-9542. (864)697-6035. E-mail: cwfi@aol.com or cwfi@juno.com. Website: http://members.aol.com/cwfi/writers. htm. No meetings, but offers market consultations, critique service, writers books and conference workshop tapes. Connects writers living in the same area, and helps start writer's groups.

*NAZARENE CHRISTIAN WRITERS CLUBS. Puts out a quarterly newsletter to encourage writers and would-be writers. Contact: Bonnie Perry, ed, %Communications division, 6401 The Paseo, Kansas City MO 64131.

THE PRESBYTERIAN WRITERS GUILD. No regular meetings. National writers' organization with a quarterly newsletter. Dues $15 per year. Contact: Vic Jameson, PO Box 6551, Hendersonville NC 28793. (314)725-6290. Membership (220) open. Sponsors contests for members each year. Sponsors annual conference.

*THE WRITING ACADEMY. Contact: Nora Buys, 11534 Hillpark Ln., Los Altos CA 94024. Website: http://www.wams.org. Membership (56) open. Sponsors year-round correspondence writing program and annual seminar in August (held in various locations).

ON-LINE WRITER'S GROUPS

+KINGDOM WRITERS. Leader: Marilyn Phemister. An e-mail critique group and fellowship for Christian writers. You may submit work for critique, and critique the works of others in return. To sign up, write to: owner-kingwrit@netside.com. Leave subject blank (AOL members type *). In body of message type: subscribe kingwrit Your Name. Website: http://www.angelfire.com/ks/kingwrit/index.html. Membership (60 & growing) open.

+THE WISE STEWARD'S CLUB. Website: http://home.sprynet.com/sprynet/ WiseStewards/writers.htm. Leader: Melissa Morgan.

Note: If your group is not listed here, please send information to Sally Stuart, 1647 SW Pheasant Dr., Aloha OR 97006. November 1 is deadline for the next year's edition.

EDITORIAL SERVICES

The following listing is included because so many writers contact me looking for experienced/qualified editors who can critique or evaluate their manuscripts. These people from all over the country offer this kind of service. I cannot personally guarantee the work of any of those listed, so you may want to ask for references or samples of their work.

The following abbreviations indicate what kinds of work they are qualified to do: GE indicates general editing/manuscript evaluation; LC—line editing or copy editing; GH—ghostwriting; CA—co-authoring; B—brochures; NL—newsletters; SP—special projects; and BC—book contract evaluation. The following abbreviations indicate the types of material they evaluate: A—articles, SS—short stories, P—poetry, F—fillers, N—novels, NB—nonfiction books, BP—book proposals, JN—juvenile novels, PB—picture books, BS—Bible studies, TM—technical material, E—essays, D—devotionals, S—scripts.

Always send a copy they can write on and an SASE for return of your material.

(*) Indicates that editorial service did not return questionnaire.
(+) Indicates new listing.

ALABAMA
*ELLA ROBINSON, 735 - 7th Pl., Pleasant Grove AL 35127. Phone/fax (205)744-4925. Send $18 deposit. LC/N/SP. Does NB/BS/D. Charges $18 (estimates for longer projects).

ARIZONA
CARLA'S MANUSCRIPT SERVICE/CARLA BRUCE, 4326 N. 50th Ave., Phoenix AZ 85031-2031. Phone/fax (602)247-0174. Call. GE/LC/GH/CA. Does A/SS/NB/BS. Charges by the page or gives project estimate after evaluation. Does ghostwriting for pastors & teachers; professional typesetting.

JOY P. GAGE, 2370 S. Rio Verde Dr., Cottonwood AZ 86326-5923. (520)646-6534. Send material with $25 deposit. GE. Does A/N/NB/BP/BS/D. Charges $25/hr.

DONNA GOODRICH, 648 S. Pima St., Mesa AZ 85210. (602)962-6694. Call/write. GE/LC. Does A/SS/P/F/N/NB/BP/D. Also types ($1/pg) and proof-reads ($15/hr) manuscripts. Editing $1.50/pg.

'LEEN POLLINGER, 14805 W. Ravenswood Dr., Sun City West AZ 85375-5705. (602)546-4757. E-mail: FRALEEN@worldnet.att.net. Write. GE/LC. Does SS/F/N/NB/BP/JN/BS/D. Charges $12-35/hr depending on work done. Fee schedule available for SASE.

CALIFORNIA
CHRISTIAN COMMUNICATOR MANUSCRIPT CRITIQUE SERVICE/SUSAN TITUS OSBORN, 3133 Puente St., Fullerton CA 92835-1952. (714) 990-1532. Fax (714) 990-0310. E-mail: Susanosb@aol.com. Website:

http://www.christiancommunicator.com. Call/write. For book, send material with $90 deposit. Staff of 14 editors. GE/LC/SP book contract evaluation. Edits all types of material. Articles/stories/picture books $65. Three chapter-book proposal $90. Additional editing $25/hr.

DIANE FILLMORE PUBLISHING SERVICES, PO Box 489., La Habra CA 90633-0489. (562)697-1541. E-mail: DianeFillmore@compuserve.com. Call. GE/LC/GH/CA/B/NL/SP. Does A/SS/N/NB/BP/JN/BS/E/D/small group or SS curriculum. Charges $15/hr. Member of Assn. of Professional Writing Consultants.

*VICKI HESTERMAN, Ph.D., PO Box 6788, San Diego CA 92166. (619)224-4549. Call/write. GE/LC/CA/SP. Does A/NB/BP/TM/E/D. Specializes in helping people tell their personal stories. Charges standard rates.

*DARLENE HOFFA, 512 Juniper St., Brea CA 92621. (714)990-5980. Write. GE. Does A/F/NB/BP/BS/D. Charges $35/article or short piece; $65 for book ms up to 52 pgs, plus $1.25/pg; or $15/hr.

MAIN ENTRY EDITIONS/REBECCA JONES, 1057 Chestnut Dr., Escondido CA 92025. (619)741-3750. Fax (619)480-0252. E-mail: Perejone@mailhost2. csusm.edu. Call/e-mail. GE/LC/GH/B/NL/basic formatting. Does A/SS/P/F/N/ NB/BP/JN/PB/BS/E/D. Send payment and SASE. Content $20-25/hr; copy-editing $15-20/hr; rewriting $25-30/hr, formatting/indexing $25/hr. Graduate writing instructor, Westminster Theological Seminary in California.

KIMURA CREATIONS/DENELLA KIMURA, PO Box 785, Benicia CA 94510-0785. (707)746-8421. E-mail: dkimura@juno.com. Write/$30 deposit. GE/LC. Does P/F/E/D/poetry book proposals & chapbooks. Charges $30 initial fee, plus $10/hr; 3-5 poems only.

LIGHTHOUSE EDITING/DR. LON ACKELSON, 13326 Community Rd., #11, Poway CA 92064. Phone/fax: (619)748-9258. E-mail: JER333@aol.com. Write, or call first if faxing. GE/LC/BC. Does A/SS/NB/BP/BS/D. Charges $25 for article/short story critique; $35 for book proposal; $25-35 + $4/pg for critique and revision.

LONNIE HULL DUPONT & ASSOCIATES, 21 Columbus Ave. Ste 210, San Francisco CA 94111. (415)296-8944. Fax (415)296-8854. E-mail: Lonniehd@ aol.com. Call/write. GE/GH/B/NL/SP/condensing. Does N/NB/BP. Charges by the hour with a $100 deposit.

MARY CARPENTER REID, 925 Larchwood Dr., Brea CA 92821. (714)529-3755. E-mail: MARYCREID@aol.com. Call/write. GE. Does A/SS/N/BP/JN/PB/E. Charges $25/hr., $75 minimum.

JANE RUMPH, 1130 Leonard Ave., Pasadena CA 91107-1746. (626)351-8703. Fax (626)822-1022. E-mail: rumph@alumni.caltech.edu. Write. GE/LC. Does A/F/ NB/BS/TM/E/D/theses/dissertations. Charges $15-20/hr.

+SHIRL'S EDITING SERVICE/SHIRL THOMAS, 9379 Tanager Ave., Fountain Valley CA 92708-6557. (714)968-5726. E-mail: ShirlTH@aol.com. Call or write, or send material with $50 deposit. GE/LC/GH/CA/Rewriting. Does A/SS/P/F/ N/NB/BP/TM/greeting cards. Consultation/evaluation, $30/hr; copy editing $35/hr; content editing/rewriting, $50/hr. Teaches a 5-week class, three times a year, "Stepping Stones to Getting Published."

LAURAINE SNELLING, 19872 Highline Rd., Tehachapi CA 93561-7796.

(805)823-0669. E-mail: TLSnelling@aol.com. Call/write. GE. Does N/BP/JN. Charges $50/hr ($50 minimum), or by the project after discussion with client.

COLORADO

ARIEL COMMUNICATIONS/DEBBIE BARKER, 67 Seminole Ct., Lyons CO 80540. Phone/Fax (970)532-0950. E-mail: dkbarker@cris.com. Call or e-mail. GE/LC. Does A/SS/N/NB/BP/JN/PB/E/TM. Negotiable rates on a project basis. Temporarily living in Canada: 99 Bristol Rd. E. #176, Mississauga ON L4Z 3P4 Canada. (905)502-0928. Fax (905)502-0929.

ECLIPSE EDITORIAL SERVICES/TRACI MULLINS, 901 N. El Paso St., Colorado Springs CO 80903. (719)578-1201. Fax (719)578-0230. E-mail: tmullins@ compuserve.com. Write. GE/LC/GH/CA/SP/book proposal preparation and/or critique, or book-concept shaping. Does NB/BP/BS/D. Charges $40/hr or flat fee by project.

CONNECTICUT

KAREN ORFITELLI, 105 Shepard Dr., Manchester CT 06040. (860)645-1100. E-mail: KarenOrf@aol.com. Write. GE/LC/GH. Does A/F/BS/E/D. Charges $25/hr. Estimates given.

FLORIDA

JULIA LEE DULFER, 705 Hibiscus Trail, Melbourne Beach FL 32951. (407)727-8192. Call. GE/LC. Does A/SS/F/N/NB/BP/JN/PB/BS/TM/E/D. Charges $20/hr for all functions.

KNUTH EDITORIAL SERVICES/DEBORAH L. KNUTH, 3965 Magnolia Lake Ln., Orlando FL 32810. (407)293-2029. Write. GE/LC/BC. Does SS/N/BP/JN. Send SASE for price sheet. Specializes in historical fiction.

LESLIE SANTAMARIA, PO Box 780066, Orlando FL 32878-0066. E-mail: santamar@magicnet.net. E-mail inquiry or send material (3-chapter book proposal, article up to 2,500 words, or poems to 5 pages) with $30 deposit. GE/LC/GH/CA/SP. Does A/SS/N/NB/BP/JN/BS/TM/E/D/S/query & cover letters/resumes. Charges $30 for initial review; $20/hour for all additional work.

GEORGIA

+LAMBLIGHTER'S/CISI MORROW-SMITH, 1056 Sawgrass Ct., Lilburn GA 30047. (770)978-9129. Call/Write; send non-book material with $35 deposit. GE/LC/GH/CA/B/NL/SP/BCE/tutoring writing (child or adult). Does A/SS/P/F/N/NB/JN/PB/BS/TM/E/D/S/Query or other letters. Charges $15-75/hr (negotiable).

+POSITIVE DIFFERENCE COMMUNICATIONS/ROSS WEST, 100 Martha Dr., Rome GA 30165-4138. (706)232-9325. Fax (706)235-2716. E-mail: drrwest@aol.com. Write, call or e-mail before sending material. GE/LC/GH/CA/SP. Does A/NF/BP/BS/E/D. Charges by the page or provides a project cost estimate.

SANDRA A. HUTCHESON, 210 Montrose Dr., McDonough GA 30253. (770)474-8880. Fax (770)389-9662. Call. GE/LC/CA/B/NL/SP. Does A/SS/F/N/NB/BP/

JN/PB/BS/TM/E/D. Charges $25/hr ($25 min.), plus expenses (telephone, research, postage).

ILLINOIS

DEBORAH CHRISTENSEN, PO Box 354, Addison IL 60101. (630)665-3044. Send with $20 deposit. GE/LC/B/NL. Does A/SS/F/N/NB/JN/D. Charges $20/hour.

*EDITECH/DOUGLAS C. SCHMIDT, 872 S. Milwaukee Ave., Ste. 272, Libertyville IL 60048. Write. GE/LC/SP. Does A/SS/F/BS/D; Sunday school curriculum. Charges $25/hr or negotiated flat fee.

+JOY LITERARY AGENCY, 3 Golf Center, Ste. 141, Hoffman Estates IL 60195. (847)310-0003. Fax (847)310-0893. Write. GE/LC. Does A/SS/N/NB/JN. Charges $1.50/pg for line editing; $15/hr for reading & critique.

*VIRGINIA J. MUIR EDITORIAL SERVICES, 130 Windsor Park Dr. #C205, Carol Stream IL 60188. (708)665-2994. Write. GE/LC/CA. Does A/SS/N/NB/JN/BS/TM/E/D. Charges $30/hr; $30 minimum, plus telephone, research expenses and postage.

THE WRITER'S EDGE, PO Box 1266, Wheaton IL 60189. No phone calls. A manuscript screening service for 45 cooperating Christian publishers. Charges $45 to evaluate a book proposal and if publishable, they will send a synopsis of it to 45 publishers who might be interested. If not publishable they will tell how to improve it. If interested, send an SASE for guidelines and a Book Information Form, or request a Form via e-mail: writersedge@usa.net. Beginning in 1998, The Writer's Edge will also handle previously published books now out of print and available for reprint. Cost will be the same.

INDIANA

DENEHEN, INC./DR. DENNIS E. HENSLEY, 6824 Kanata Ct., Fort Wayne IN 46815-6388. Phone/Fax (219)485-9891 (Fax 10 a.m-6 p.m., M-F). E-mail: DENEHEN@juno.com. Call/write. GE/LC/GH. Does A/SS/F/N/NB/JN/E/D/academic articles/editorials/op-ed pieces. Rate sheet for SASE.

*PMN PUBLISHING/GEORGE ALLEN, Box 47024, Indianapolis IN 46247. (317) 888-7156. Fax (317)791-8113. Write. Various editorial services and newsletters. Call or write for services available and charges.

+JAMES N. WATKINS, PO Box 117, LaOtto IN 46763-0117. (219)897-4121. (219)897-3700. E-mail: watkins@noblecan.org. Send with $25 deposit. GE/CA. Does A/SS/NB/BP/E/D. Charges $25 to critique up to 2,000 wds; book proposals with one sample chapter. Awarded four Evangelical Press Assn. awards for editing. American Christian Writers Assn. consultant.

KANSAS

ESTHER L. VOGT, 113 S. Ash, Hillsboro KS 67063. (316)947-3796. Write. GE/LC/CO/GH. Does SS/N/JN. $15 for first chapter (to 20 pgs); $12 for each chapter thereafter.

LOUISIANA

BLUE-PENCIL SPECIALISTS/JOHN M. CUNNINGHAM, JR., Box 55601, Metairie LA 70055-5601. (504)837-4397. E-mail: 72440.1623@compuserve. com. Send material with $10 deposit. GE/LC. Does A/SS/F/BS/D. Charges according to word count; rate sheet for SASE.

*GLORY ARTS/BARBARA NAUER, 1808 Brightside Dr., Apt.11-A, Baton Rogue LA 70820-4710. (504)673-6481. Fax (504)673-6330. Does editing, re-writing, ghosting, graphics, radio promo, and author advising. Charges by the hour. Send SASE for price list.

*SHILOH REVISIONS/MELINDA JOY LEMMON, 4635 Baccich St., New Orleans LA 70122-6115. (504)282-9464. Call, write or send with $20 deposit. GE/LC/CA. Does A/SS/F/N/NB/BP/JN/PB/BS/TM/E/D/S. Articles/stories $25-$75; books $175-450.

MARYLAND

NEE EDITORIAL SERVICES/KATHIE NEE, 7115 Varnum St., Landover Hills MD 20784. (301)577-9072. Call/write. GE/LC/B/SP. Does A/F/NB/BP/BS/E/D/tracts/pamphlets/resumes/job application letters/biographical sketches. Charges $10-12/hr. Brochure available for SASE.

MASSACHUSETTS

MARION VUILLEUMIER, 579 Buck Island Rd. #147, West Yarmouth MA 02673-3225. (508)775-4811. Call or write. GE (readies mss for presentation to publishers). Does A/N/NB/BP. Contact for estimate on projects (about $30/hour); consultations $75; ten-session writing classes $100.

WORD PRO/BARBARA ROBIDOUX, 127 Gelinas Dr., Chicopee MA 01020-4813. (413)592-4386. Fax (413)594-8375. Call. GE/LC/GH/B/NL. Does A/SS/F/NB/BP/BS/TM/E/D. Fee negotiable; estimate given.

MICHIGAN

+PRATT COMMUNICATIONS, 518 W. Nepessing, Ste. 201, Lapeer MI 48446. (810)664-1267. Fax (810)664-4610. E-mail: lcollpr@tir.com. Call. GE/CA/B/SP/BCE/publicist. Does A/NB/BP/BS/E/D. Charges $10/pg.

WORD FOR WORD/SHAUNNA HOWAT and LINDA WACYK, 9523 Riverside Dr., Grand Ledge MI 48837. (517)626-2419. E-mail: discipler1@aol.com. Call/write. GE/LC/GH/CA/B/NL/SP/curriculum/educational materials. Does A/SS/F/N/NB/BS/TM/E/D. Charge $25/hour or call for a quote.

MINNESOTA

PTL SECRETARIAL SERVICES/CONNIE PETTERSEN, R 4 Box 289, Aitkin MN 56431. (218)927-6176. E-mail: Pett289@mlecmn.net. Call/write. Manuscript typing; edit for punctuation, spelling/grammar. Published freelance writer; 24 years secretarial/Dictaphone experience. IBM compatible computer, WordPerfect 6.1, Corel 7.0 and Microsoft Office 97 software; microcassette transcriber. Fees: $1.25/page + postage, for legible writing or microcassette. Internet/e-mail/fax access. Confidentiality guaranteed.

MISSOURI

*TIM PATRICK MILLER, 4131 Manchester Blvd., St. Louis MO 63110. Line edit, $1/pg; copy edit, $2/pg; structural edit, $7/hr; proofing, .95/pg. literary consultations/new writers, $10/hr; literary consultations/published writers, $25-150/hr.

PRO WORD WRITING & EDITORIAL SERVICES/MARY R. RUTH, PO Box 155, Labadie MO 63055-0155. (314)742-3663. Call/write. GE/LC/SP/manuscript or script typing, scan hard copy to disk, proofreading, indexing. Does A/SS/N/ NB/BP/JN/BS/TM/E/D/S/biographies/textbooks. Call to discuss your project. Reasonable rates/professional results. MC/Visa available.

DEBI STACK, Box 11805, Kansas City MO 64138-0305. Phone/fax: (816)763-5743. E-mail: Stackedits@aol.com. Call/write. GE/LC/GH/customized marketing analysis. Does A/SS/N/NB/BP/JN/BS/E/D. Speaks to groups. Send for rate sheet.

NEW HAMPSHIRE

*SALLY WILKINS, Box 393, Amherst NH 03031-0393. (603)673-9331. Write. GE/LC. Does A/F/JN/PB/ BS/TM. Rate sheet for SASE.

NEW JERSEY

BURNING LIGHT PRESS/CARL SIMMONS, 4 Robin Ln., West Milford NJ 07480-4037. (201)283-9516. Call/write. GE/LC/B/NL/SP. Does A/SS/P/N/NB/ JN/PB/BS/E/D. Charges $15-20/hr.

DAYSTAR COMMUNICATIONS/DR. MARY ANN DIORIO, Box 405, Millville NJ 08332-0405. (609)327-1231. Fax (609)327-0291. E-mail: 72602.1027@compuserve.com or madiorio@aol.com. Call/write. GE/LC. Does A/SS/P/F/E/D/copy for ads and PR material/resumes/business letters; also translations in French, Italian, and Spanish. Rate sheet for SASE.

NEW MEXICO

*K.C. MASON, 1882 Conejo Dr., Santa Fe NM 87501. Write for information, fees, and availability.

NEW YORK

*STERLING DIMMICK, 86 Route 34, Waverly NY 14892-9793. (607)565-4470. Write. GE/GH/CA. Does A/SS/P/F/N/NB/BP/JN/PB/BS/TM/E/D/S. Charges $15-20/hour or by the project.

*SWANSON EDITYPE SERVICES/NANCY SWANSON, PO Box 946, Elizabethtown NY 12932-0946. (518)873-3405, days; (518)962-8702, eves. GE/LC/ GH/CA/NL/SP. Does A/SS/N/NB/JN/BS/TM/E/D/S. Charges negotiable, according to project; $10 minimum.

NORTH CAROLINA

*ANNA FISHEL, 3416 Hunting Creek Dr., Pfafftown NC 27040. (910)924-5880. Call. GE/CA/SP. Does A/SS/N/JN. Charges variable rates depending on job.

OHIO

BOB HOSTETLER, 2336 Gardner Rd., Hamilton OH 45013-9317. Phone/fax

(513)737-1102. E-mail: BobHoss@compuserve.com. Call/write. GE/LC/GH/ CA/B/N. Does A/SS/P/N/NB/BP/JN/PB. Rate sheet available for SASE.

+ADRIENNE MIKLOVIC, 5741 Acres Rd., Sylvania OH 43560. (419)882-0278.

A WRITE IMPRESSION/KELLY BOYER SAGERT, PO Box 3181, Lorain OH 44052. (440)245-1569. Fax (440)245-1569. E-mail: DarkPrint@aol.com. Call/ write/e-mail. GE/LC/GH/CA/B/NL/SP. Does A/SS/F/N/NB/BP/JN/E. Charges contract price or $25/hr.

OKLAHOMA

*KATHRYN FANNING, Critique Service, PO Box 18472, Oklahoma City OK 73154-0472. N/NB; no poetry. Charges $3.50/page.

*THE WRITE WORD/IRENE MARTIN, PO Box 300332, Midwest City OK 73140. (800)799-9424. Write. GE/LC/GH. Does A/SS/N/JN/PB. For fee schedule send SASE/query letter detailing project. Charges $3/pg or $15/hr.

OREGON

*NASIRA ALMA, 8851-A SE 11th Ave #2, Portland OR 97202-7050. Call. GE/GH. Does A/SS/P/N/NB/BP/BS/E/D. For an initial overview, which includes a single-spaced report of not less than 10 pgs, charges $400 (for book of average size). Sometimes negotiates a flat fee for the project.

+DICK BOHRER, PO Box 624, West Linn OR 97068. Offers a writing course based on his 228-page text, *How to Write What YOU Think.* Cost of book $25. Then you pay him $1 per page as you write the assignments in the text. To enroll, send $25 with a short Christian testimony.

BESTSELLER CONSULTANTS/URSULA BACON, PO Box 922, Wilsonville OR 97070. (503)682-3235. Fax (503)682-8684. Write. GE/LC/GH. Does A/SS/N/NB/ BP. Fees are quoted on a per project basis. Ms evaluation for 250-325 pgs starts at $550. Full report and chapter-by-chapter recommendations included. Secular, but handles Christian books.

*CHRISTIAN WRITING SERVICES/ED STEWART, 3540 SE Spring Dr., Hillsboro OR 97123. (503)640-2522. Call. LC/GH/CA. Does NB/BP. Charges by the project based on $35/hr.

GAIL DENHAM, Box 89, Newberg OR 97132. (503)538-4691. Call. GE. Does A/SS/P/F/JN/PB/E/D/brochures/newsletters. Has photos to go with articles or books. Charges $20/hour; $25 minimum.

MARION DUCKWORTH, 2495 Maple NE, Salem OR 97303. (503)364-9570. Call/write. GE. Does A/SS/F/NB/BP/PB/BS/D. Charges $20/hr. Consultations or private lessons, $25/hr.

LIT.DOC/KRISTEN JOHNSON INGRAM, 955 S. 59TH St., Springfield OR 97478. (503)726-8320. Fax (503)988-9126. E-mail: kris64@worldnet.att.net. Call. GE/LC/CA/B. Does A/SS/P/F/N/NB/BP/E/D. Charges $25/hr, or negotiates on longer manuscripts.

*LYON'S LITERARY SERVICES/ELIZABETH LYON, 2123 Marlow Ln., Eugene OR 97401-6431. (541)344-9118. Fax (541)485-2216. Call/write. GE/LC/ SP. Does A/SS/N/NB/BP/JN/PB/TM/E/D. Charges $45/hr or $75, plus $3/pg. for longer projects.

*PRIMA FACIE PUBLISHERS/BEN RIGALL, 13002 SE Alder St., Portland OR

97233-1629. (503)255-2199. Write or call. GE/LC. Contact for information and fees.

CONNIE'S EASY WRITER SERVICE/CONNIE SOTH, 4890 SW Menlo Dr., Beaverton OR 97005-2612. (503)644-4972. Call/Write. GE/LC/SP/book doctoring & guidance. Does A/N/NB/BP/JN/PB/E/D. Charges $10/hour.

*ANNA LLOYD STONE, PO Box 2251, Lake Oswego OR 97035. (503)638-3705. Fax (503)638-3811. Call. LC/special projects/word processing. Does A/SS/P/ F/N/NB/BP/JN/PB/BS/TM/E/D/S. Charges $20/hr for copyediting or word processing; $30/hr for both.

SALLY STUART, 1647 SW Pheasant Dr., Aloha OR 97006. (503)642-9844. Fax (503)848-3658. E-mail: stuartcwmg@aol.com. Website: http://www.stuartmarket. com. Call/write. GE. Does A/SS/N/NB/ BP/JN/PB/E. Charges $25/hr. for critique; $35/hr. for consultations. Comprehensive publishing contract evaluation $50-80.

PENNSYLVANIA

*VAL CINDRIC EDITING & PUBLISHING SERVICES, 536 Monticello Dr., Delmont PA 15626. Phone/Fax (412)468-6185. Call/write. GE/GH/CA. Does NB. Charges $20/hr.

IMPACT COMMUNICATIONS/DEBRA PETROSKY, 11331 Tioga Rd., N. Huntingdon PA 15642-2445. Phone/fax (412)863-5906. E-mail: Editing 4U@aol.com. Call/e-mail. GE/LC. Does NB/BP. Charges $20/hr. Satisfied self-publishers endorse our typesetting services. Very reasonable rates.

SPREAD THE WORD/MAURCIA DELEAN HOUCK, 1618 Rockwell Rd., Abington PA 19001. Phone/fax (215)659-2912. Write/send deposit of 50%. GE/LC/B/SP/BC. Does A/SS/F/N/NB/BP/JN/BS. Charges $1.75/pg., or as quoted. Discount for over 250 pgs.

WRITE HIS ANSWER MINISTRIES/MARLENE BAGNULL, 316 Blanchard Rd., Drexel Hill PA 19026-3507. Phone/fax: (610)626-6833. E-mail: mbagnull@ aol.com. Website: http://nancepub.com/cwf/wha/. Call/write. GE/LC/typesetting. Does A/SS/N/NB/BP/JN/BS/D. Charges $25/hr; estimates given. Call or write for information on At-Home Writing Workshops, a correspondence study program.

SOUTH CAROLINA

+NANCY KOESY PARKER WRITING & EDITING SERVICES, 2530 E. North St., Ste. 6A, Greenville SC 29615. (864)322-5594. Fax (864)322-5596. E-mail: NKPediting@aol.com. Send SASE for resume, services and references.

TENNESSEE

CHRISTIAN WRITERS INSTITUTE MANUSCRIPT CRITIQUE SERVICE, PO Box 110390, Nashville TN 37222. (800)21-WRITE. Call/write. GE/LC/GH/CA/SP/BCE. Does A/SS/P/F/N/NB/BP/JN/PB/BS/TM/E/D/S. Send SASE for rate sheet and submission slip.

JOHNSON LITERARY AND TALENT SERVICES/JOSEPH S. JOHNSON JR., 2915 Walnut Crest Dr., Antioch TN 37013-1337. Phone/fax (615)361-8627. Send $20 deposit. GE/LC/GH/CA/SP/BCE/consultations. Does A/SS/P/F/N/NB/BP/ JN/BS/E/D/S/advice on song writing. Reasonable rates; negotiable.

*WILLIAM PENS/WILLIAM D. WATKINS, 342 Alden Cove Dr., Smyrna TN 37167. (615)355-4455. Fax (615)355-9977. Write. GE/CA/B/NL/SP/BC/consulting, contract negotiations, book proposal evaluations & creations, market analysis of book ideas. Does A/SS/N/NB/BP/BS/ TM/E/D. Send SASE for rate sheet.

TEXAS

SYLVIA BRISKEY, PO Box 9053, Dallas TX 75209-9053. (214)521-7507. Call. GE/LC. Does SS/P/N/JN/PB/children's stories/secular articles. Poetry, charges $5.60 plus $1/line; fiction $30 to 2,000 wds, $2.50/page thereafter.

JAN E. KILBY, Ph.D. , PO Box 171390, San Antonio TX 78217-8390. (210)657-0171. Fax (210)657-0173. Call. GE/LC. Does A/SS/P/F/N/NB/BP/JN/PB/TM/E/D/S/speeches. Charges by the hour; call for prices/information.

VIRGINIA

+ADVOCATE MEDIA GROUP, 908 Ventures Wy., Chesapeake VA 23320. (800)439-5055. Fax (757)547-5544. Contact: Shelly Simone. AMG is an all-inclusive media marketing company that promotes authors, musicians, and other product producers through their nationally syndicated TV & radio show, Interviews & Reviews, as well as their nationally circulated Interviews & Reviews magazine and their Web site at http://www.advocate-media.com. Specializes in generating TV and radio exposure in the Christian marketplace.

CREATIVE CHRISTIAN MINISTRIES/BETTY ROBERTSON, PO Box 12624, Roanoke VA 24027-2624. Phone/fax (540)342-7511. E-mail: ccmbbr@juno.com. Send with full payment. GE/LC. Does A/SS/F/NB/BP/BS/D/S. Charges $2/page for everything.

*IRENE BOYER, 8836 Burbank Rd., Annandale VA 22003-3859. (703)425-1080. Fax (703)425-1090. E-mail: caboyer@mnsinc.com. Write. LC/GH/CA/B/NL/SP. Does A/F/NB/BS/E/D. Word processing, typesetting, hard copy, electronic. Charge depends on type/scope. Brochure for SASE.

HCI EDITORIAL SERVICES/DAVID HAZARD, PO Box 568, Round Hill VA 20142-0568. Write. GE. Does N/NB/BP. Works with agents and self-publishers. Fees on request.

PUBLICATIONS MANAGEMENT, INC./JANETTE G. BLACKWELL, 1507 N. Amelia St., Sterling VA 20164-3612. Write. GE/LC/GH/CA/B/ NL/SP. Does A/SS/N/NB/TM/E/D/biographies; design and production of brochures, newsletters, books. Charges $25/hr. for writing/editing, or as negotiated.

WASHINGTON

DUE NORTH PUBLISHING/SCOTT R. ANDERSON, 7372 Guide Meridian, Lynden WA 98264. Phone/fax (360)354-0234 (call first for fax). Write. GE/LC/GH/CA/B/NL/SP. Does A/NB/BP/E. Charges $25/hr for copy and content editing or by the project (estimate given). Offers wide range of editorial & pre-press (design/layout) services, including layout and design for brochures.

MARY ARMSTRONG LITERARY SERVICES, 8018 - 38TH Dr. NE, Marysville WA 98270. (360)653-6548. Call. GE/LC. Does A/SS/F/N/NB/BP/BS/E/D. No picture books. Line-editing $1.50/pg.; evaluations $25/hr.

BIRDIE ETCHISON, Box 877, Ocean Park WA 98640. (206)665-6576. Write.

GE/LC. Does A/SS/F/N/BP/PB. Charges according to length, $15 minimum.

JAN GREEN, 1616 SW Henderson St., Seattle WA 98106. (206)763-2760. E-mail: janmgreen@juno.com. Call/write. GE/LC/GH/CA/B/NL/SP. Does A/SS/P/F/N /NB/JN/BS/TM/E/D. Negotiable rates.

KALEIDOSCOPE PRESS/PENNY LENT, 2507 - 94th Ave. E., Puyallup WA 98371-2203. Phone/Fax (206)848-1116. Call/write. GE/LC/GH/CA/B/NL/ SP/BC. Does A/SS/F/N/NB/BP/JN/PB/E/D. Also market analysis. Line item editing $3/pg; other projects negotiated individually.

GLORIA KEMPTON, 2139 - 52nd Ave. SW #B, Seattle WA 98116-1803. Phone/fax: (206)935-3075. Call/write. GE. Does A/SS/F/N/NB/BP/JN/E. Free estimates; generally $25-50 for article/short story, $100-250 for book proposal.

AGNES C. LAWLESS, 17462 NE 11th St., Bellevue WA 98008-3814. (425)644-5012. E-mail: AGNESLAW@aol.com. Write. GE/LC/CA. Does A/SS/P/F/NB/ BP/BS/E/D. Articles/stories $60; book proposal (3 chapters) $80; additional $20/hr.

MOODY LITERARY AGENCY/VIRGINIA A. MOODY, 17402 - 114th Pl. NE, Granite Falls WA 98252-9667. (360)691-5402. Call/write. GE/LC/GH/CA/BC. Does A/SS/F/N/NB/BP/JN/BS/D/S. Charges $2/pg or as agreed.

PATRICIA H. RUSHFORD, 3600 Edgewood Dr., Vancouver WA 98661. (360)695-2263. E-mail: PRushford@aol.com. Call. GE/personal consultation and conference; Weekend With a Writer. Does A/SS/N/NB/BP. Fee $15-35/hr (negotiable). Offers private week-end workshop for $300, plus expenses.

PAULINE SHEEHAN, Box 801, Lake Stevens WA 98258. (425)334-7049. Fax (425)397-0854. E-mail: DAT1johns@aol.com. Write/$25 deposit. GE. Does BP/S. Book proposals. Charges $25 minimum for up to 10 pages; bid on further work.

WRITERS INFORMATION NETWORK/ELAINE WRIGHT COLVIN, Box 11337, Bainbridge Island WA 98110. (206)842-9103. Fax (206)842-0536. E-mail: writersinfonetwork@juno.com. Send material/ $100 deposit. GE/LC/GH/ CA/B/NL/SP/BC. Does A/SS/P/N/NB/BP/JN/PB/BS/TM/E/D/S. Send SASE for rate sheet & list of all services.

WISCONSIN

BETHESDA LITERARY SERVICE/MARGARET L. BEEN, South 63 West 35530 Piper Rd., Eagle WI 53119-9726. (414)392-9761. Fax (414)547-8871. E-mail: MLJBeen@aol.com. Write. GE/LC. Does A/SS/P/F/NB/BS/E/D. Charges $15/hr. Also does devotional & inspirational readings. Teaches writers' classes/poetry seminars for all ages, with emphasis on classical literature.

+MARCIA HOEHNE, 609 Walter St., Kaukauna WI 54130. (920)766-5028. Call/write. GE/LC/proofreading. Does A/SS/N/NB/JN/E/D. Charges $20/hr or $2.50/page for GE/LC ($20 min.); $10/hr or $1.25/page for proofreading ($10 min.)

MARGARET HOUK, 514 S Buchanan, Appleton WI 54915. Phone/fax (920)739-4997. E-mail: marghouk@juno.com. Call/write. GE/LC. Does A/NB/BP/BS. Charges *Writer's Market* rates, or will negotiate.

CANADA

*A. BIENERT, Box 1358, Three Hills AB T0M 2A0 Canada. 443-2491. GE/LC.

Does N/NB. Charges negotiable.

*BERYL HENNE, 541 - 56 Street, Delta BC V4L 1Z5 Canada (U.S. address: Box 40, Pt. Roberts WA 98281-0040). (604)943-9676. Fax (604)943-9651. Write. GE/LC/ B/NL/SP. Does A/SS/NB/E/D. Charges $20/hr.

DANIEL YORDY, Box 6855, Fort St. John BC V1J 4J3 Canada. (250)774-1020. GE/LC. Does A/SS/P/N/NB/BS/E/D. Charges $25/hr. Call/write for fee/services list. Estimates given.

*WINDFLOWER COMMUNICATIONS/THE WRITER'S EDGE, 844-K McLeod Ave., Winnipeg MB R2G 2T7, Canada. (204)668-7475. Fax (204)661-8530. Write first. Charges $100.

WRITING SERVICES INSTITUTE (WSI)/MARSHA L. DRAKE, Collingwood PO Box 27113, Vancouver BC V5R 6A8, Canada. Phone/fax (604)438-7507. E-mail: 103270.2051@compuserve.com. Call/write. GE/LC/GH/CA; also biographies, resumes, or company history. Does A/SS/N/NB/BP/D. Offers correspondence course: Write for Fun and Profit. Charges $20/hr. for critique; $30/hr for consultation. Write for details and information on correspondence course.

CHRISTIAN LITERARY AGENTS

(*) Indicates that publisher did not return questionnaire.
(#) Indicates that listing was updated from guidelines or other sources.
(+) Indicates new listing.

ALIVE COMMUNICATIONS, 1465 Kelly Johnson Blvd. #320, Colorado Springs CO 80920-3955. (719)260-7080. Fax (719)260-8223. E-mail: 103753.1116@ compuserve.com. Agents: Rick Christian/ Greg Johnson/Jeff Tikson/Kathryn Yanni. Well known in the industry. Est. 1989. Represents over 50 clients. Open to unpublished authors occasionally. Occasionally open to new clients. Handles any material except poetry, for all ages. Deals in both Christian (80%) and general market (20%). Also runs a speaker's bureau.
> **Contact:** Query with letter, previous history and future ideas (no calls)/ SASE.
> **Commission:** 15%
> **Fees:** Only extraordinary costs with client's pre-approval; no review/reading fee.

*ALLEGRA LITERARY AGENCY, 2806 Pine Hill Dr., Kennesaw GA 30144-2834. Phone/fax (770)795-8318. Agent: Cynthia Lambert. Est. 1994. Establishing reputation. Represents 4 clients. Open to unpublished authors. Handles adult & teen (rarely) novels, adult nonfiction, scripts (rarely). Interested in Christian science fiction, romance and mainstream novels. Books only.
> **Contact:** By mail, phone, or fax.
> **Commission:** 12%.
> **Fees:** Requires a $150 retainer for postage and copying: 100% refundable when manuscript sells.
> **Tips:** "We're interested in fictional manuscripts that are spiritually uplifting as well as educational."

#AUTHOR AID ASSOCIATES, 7542 Bear Canyon Rd. NE, Albuquerque NM 87109-3847. Agent: Arthur Orrmont. Not known in industry but expanding Christian/religious client list. Est. 1967. Represents 10 Christian clients. Open to unpublished authors. Handles novels for all ages, nonfiction for all ages, and scripts.
> **Contact:** By mail or phone.
> **Commission:** 15%.
> **Fees:** Evaluation fees for new/unpublished authors.

+AVATAR LITERARY AGENCY, 3389 Sheridan St. #308, Hollywood FL 33021. Agent: Karen Weiss.

BK NELSON LITERARY AGENCY, 84 Woodland Rd., Pleasantville NY 10570. (914)741-1322. E-mail: bknelson@compuserve.com. Internet: http://www. CMONLINR.Com/bknelson. Agent: Jennifer. Recognized in the industry. Est. 1979. Represents 3 clients. Open to unpublished authors & new clients. Handles adult & teen fiction, adult nonfiction, TV/movie scripts, screenplays, gift books, business, self-help, how-to. Also CD-ROM, audio tapes and lecturers.

Contact: Letter or e-mail.

Commission: 20%, foreign 25%.

Fees: $350 reading fee for complete mss or $2/pg for proposals with sample chapters.

Comments: "Our success with first-book authors is outstanding. We work with you if you work with us to get published. If we suggest an edit, we expect you will have it done. After all, we share a common interest which is getting your book published."

BRANDENBURGH & ASSOCIATES LITERARY AGENCY, 24555 Corte Jaramillo, Murrieta CA 92562. (909)698-5200. Agent: Don Brandenburgh. Recognized in industry. Est. 1986. Represents 5 clients. No unpublished authors. No new clients at this time. Handles adult novels (limited) and nonfiction. Specializes in nonfiction for the religious market only. Books only.

Contact: Query/SASE (or no response).

Commission: 10%; 20% for foreign or dramatic rights.

Fees: $35 for mailing/materials when contract is signed.

PEMA BROWNE LTD., Pine Rd., HCR Box 104B, Neversink NY 12765. (914)985-2936. Fax (914)985-7635. Agent: Perry Browne. Recognized in industry. Est. 1966. Represents 4 clients. Open to unpublished authors and to new clients. Handles novels and nonfiction (preferred) for all ages; picture books & screenplays. Only wishes mss not sent previously to publishers.

Contact: Letter query with credentials & SASE.

Commission: 15%; 20% foreign

Fees: None.

Tips: Check at the library in reference section, in Books in Print, for books similar to yours.

*CISKE & DIETZ LITERARY AGENCY, 10605 W. Wabash, Milwaukee WI 53224. (414)355-8915. Agent: Andrea Boeshaar. Recognized in industry. Open to unpublished authors and new clients at this time. Handles romance novels only, contemporary and historical.

Contact: One-two page query letter, with an SASE.

Commission: 15%.

Fees: None.

Tips: We prefer query letters that sum up the book in one paragraph, giving word length and whether contemporary or historical. If historical, give date. Additional info on the author is important if it pertains to their writing or the manuscript.

*CREATIVE CONCEPTS LITERARY AGENCY, PO Box 128, Troy MI 48083. (810)524-0864. Agent: Michele Glance. Recognized in the industry. Est. 1987. Open to unpublished authors and new clients. Handles Adult/teen/children's novels, adult/children's nonfiction, poetry books, and gift books.

Contact: Send brief description of book in letter, plus sample chapters.

Commission: Negotiable.

Fees: Charges $95 to critique a full manuscript.

Tips: Write from the heart, that's how the best books always start. Persist in your efforts to be published. Having the right attitude is 95% of the key to success.

*LOIS CURLEY ENTERPRISES, 18755 W. Bernardo Dr., Suite 1039, San Diego

CA 92127-3010. (619)675-2031. Fax (619)675-2026. Agent: Lois L. Curley. Recognized in industry. Est. 1979. Represents 24 clients. May be open to unpublished authors. Handles adult fiction and nonfiction. Books only. Currently has a waiting list of new clients.

> **Contact:** Query, fax, or call. Send SASE for submission guidelines.
> **Commission:** 15% on first 35,000 copies, 10% thereafter.
> **Fees:** Charges normal office expenses.
> **Comments:** "We have a waiting list of writers from which we select one or two new clients each quarter for representation."

*CVK INTERNATIONAL, 277 Smith St., New York NY 11231. (718)237-4570. Fax (718)237-4571. Agent: Cynthia Neeseman. Handles adult fiction and nonfiction; screenplays; and seeks foreign sales for translations of books published in the US.

> **Contact:** Query.

+DANAN LITERARY SERVICES, 10605 W. Wabash Ave., Milwaukee WI 53224-2315. (414)355-8930. Agent: Andrea Boeshaar. Recognized in the industry. Est. 1997. Represents only Christian authors. Open to unpublished authors. Handles adult novels (primarily women's fiction and inspirational romance).

> **Contact:** Query letter, brief bio, synopsis and first three chapters (up to 50 pages). Send SASE for submission guidelines first.
> **Commission:** 15%.
> **Fees:** Charges $30 reading fee; $25 marketing fee (upon a signed, non-binding terms agreement).
> **Comments:** "Read books already published and be analytical. Figure out how and why they work (plot, characterization, etc.)."

JOYCE FARRELL AND ASSOCIATES, 669 Grove St., Upper Montclair NJ 07043. (973)746-6248. Fax (973)746-7348. Agent: Joyce Farrell. Recognized in the industry. Est. 1985. Represents 20-25 clients. Open to unpublished authors; selectively open to new clients. Handles fiction and nonfiction for children and adults. No fantasy novels. In nonfiction, prefers issue books, or books with historical, scientific, psychological or theological orientation.

> **Contact:** Prefers phone or fax. If by mail, send query letter, author bio, synopsis and SASE.
> **Commission:** 15%
> **Fees:** Reading fee: up to 50 pgs, $35; complete manuscript $65 additional. Author provides copies for multiple submissions.
> **Tips:** "Check the marketplace to see what is currently available, and whether your treatment of a subject presents a fresh, somewhat different angle than books already published. If not, choose another subject."

SARA A. FORTENBERRY LITERARY AGENCY, PO Box 8177, Hermitage TN 37076-8177. (615)902-9471. Fax (615)902-9479. E-mail: safberry@aol.com. Recognized in the industry. Est. 1995. Represents 32 clients. Open to unpublished authors or new clients only by referral. Handles nonfiction and novels for all ages, picture books, and gift books.

> **Contact:** Query with overview of work in progress and brief bio, including publishing and writing history.
> **Commission:** 15%.
> **Fees:** Standard expenses (printing, mailing, phone, supplies, etc.) are charged

back to the client.

Tips: "I don't represent science fiction or fantasy. Rarely do I accept unpublished authors who write children's books or young adult."

+THE FRANKLIN LITERARY AGENCY, 310 Pine Burr St., Vidor TX 77662-6527. (409)769-7938. Agent: Larry V. Franklin. Est. 1996. Represents 12 clients. Handles adult fiction and nonfiction; children's and young adult books; stage and screen plays; short story collections.

Contact: Query with 2-7 page synopsis.

Commission: 15%.

Fees: Requires a $35 reading fee for each manuscript for unpublished authors unless previous arrangements are made with the agency. No fee for published authors. .

*GOOD NEWS LITERARY SERVICE, Box 587, Visalia CA 93279. Phone/fax (209)627-6241 (call first for fax). Agent: Cynthia A. Wachner. Recognized in industry. Est. 1986. Not accepting mss at this time.

*STEPHEN GRIFFITH, PO Box 939, Leicester NC 28748. Unlisted phone. Fax (704)683-2851. Recognized in industry. Est. 1990. Not open to unpublished authors. Open only to referrals from existing clients. Handles novels for all ages and adult nonfiction.

Contact: By mail or fax.

Commission: 15% (10% on reprinted books).

Fees: None.

*HARTLINE LITERARY AGENCY, 123 Queenston Dr., Pittsburgh PA 15235. (412)829-2483. Fax (412)829-2450. Agent: Joyce Hart. Recognized in industry. Est. 1992. Represents 14 clients. Published authors preferred. Open to new clients. Handles adult or teen novels (no science fiction) and adult or teen nonfiction. Handles books only.

Contact: Phone or query.

Commission: 15%.

Fees: Fee schedule available on request.

Tips: "Send your manuscript as professionally done as possible; on disk and the hard copy printed on a laser or inkjet printer is best."

*HOLUB & ASSOCIATES, 24 Old Colony Rd., North Stonington CT 06359. (203)535-0689. Agent: William Holub. Recognized by Catholic publishers. Est. 1966. Open to unpublished authors. Handles adult nonfiction; possibly picture books; Christian living in secular society.

Contact: Query with outline, 2 sample chapters, intended audience, and bio.

Commission: 15%.

Fees: Postage and photocopying.

+JOY LITERARY AGENCY, 3 Golf Center, Ste. 141, Hoffman Estates IL 60195. (847)310-0003. Fax (847)310-0893. Agent: Carol Joy. Gaining recognition in industry. Est. 1996. Represents 3 clients. Open to unpublished authors and new clients. Handles adult novels and nonfiction, articles, short stories and children's fiction.

Contact: Letter or fax.

Commission: 15%.

Fees: Charges only for extra editorial services.

+NANCY LOVE LITERARY AGENCY, 250 E. 65th St., New York NY 10021. Agent: Nancy Love. Open to unpublished authors. Handles adult nonfiction (including inspirational and spiritual books), some fiction (mysteries and thrillers only).

>   **Contact:** Query letter; no multiple submissions on fiction.
>   **Commission:** 15%.
>   **Fees:** Photocopying.

*JEAN V. NAGGAR LITERARY AGENCY, 216 E. 75th St., New York NY 11201. (212)794-1082. Agent: Jean Naggar. Not recognized in industry. Est. 1978. Represents 5 clients. Open to unpublished authors. Handles adult/teen/children's novels and nonfiction, picture books. Handles articles/short stories only if handling book-length as well.

>   **Contact:** Query letter/1-2 pg. synopsis.
>   **Commission:** 15%; 20% foreign.
>   **Fees:** No reading fee, but Xerox, telephone & overseas mailing for clients.

+PRATT COMMUNICATIONS, 518 W. Nepessing, Ste. 201, Lapeer MI 48446. Phone/fax (810)664-4610. E-mail: lcollpr@tir.com. Agent: Lonni Collins Pratt. No overtly evangelical themes; their market is religious books for secular publishers, mainline and Catholic. Considers full-length adult fiction, art books with text, sophisticated young-adult fiction, and nonfiction on spirituality. Considers first-time authors if they have a track record with newspapers and magazines, and the project is outstanding.

*THE SHEPARD AGENCY, Pawling Savings Bank Bldg., Brewster (Rt. 22) NY 10509. (914)279-2900/3236. Fax (914)279-3239. Agents: Jean or Lance Shepard. Recognized in the industry. Est. 1986. Represents 8 clients. Open to unpublished authors. Handles fiction and nonfiction for all ages; no picture books; especially business, reference, professional, self-help, cooking and crafts. Books only.

>   **Contact:** Query letter and sample material.
>   **Commission:** 15%
>   **Fees:** None except long-distance calls and copying.

+SCOTT WAXMAN AGENCY, INC., 1650 Broadway, New York NY 10019. (212)262-2388. Fax (212)262-0119. E-mail: waxman@interport.net. Agent: Scott Waxman. Recognized in the industry. Est. 1996 (5 years experience). Represents 11 clients. Open to unpublished authors and new clients. Handles adult fiction and nonfiction ; children's nonfiction.

>   **Contact:** Query letter or e-mail.
>   **Commission:** 15%
>   **Fees:** Copy/shipping if unable to sell book.

*WOLGEMUTH & HYATT, INC., 8012 Brooks Chapel Rd., Ste. 243, Brentwood TN 37027. (615)370-9937. Fax (615)370-9939. Agents: Michael S. Hyatt and Robert D. Wolgemuth. Well recognized in the industry. Est. 1992. Represents 30 clients. No unpublished authors. Handles only adult nonfiction.

>   **Contact:** By letter, phone or CompuServe.
>   **Commission:** 15%
>   **Fees:** Charges fees.
>   **Other Services:** Offers a manuscript evaluation service for unpublished authors to assist them in increasing their chances of getting published.

Comments: "We work with authors who are either best-selling authors or potentially best-selling authors. Consequently, we want to represent clients with broad market appeal."

*THE WRITER'S EDGE—See listing under Editorial Services—Illinois.

ADDITIONAL AGENTS

NOTE: The following agents did not return a questionnaire, but have been identified as agents who handle religious manuscripts. Be sure to send queries first if you wish to submit to them.

(*) Indicates they are known in the industry.

Bonnie Crown
B R Crown Intl. Literary & Arts Agency
50 E. 10th St.
New York NY 10003
(212)475-1999
nonfiction/fiction

Al Hart
Fox Chase Agency Inc.
5 Radnor Corporate Ctr. Ste. 441
Radnor PA 19087-4526
nonfiction

Ned Leavitt
The Ned Leavitt Agency
70 Wooster St. #4F
New York NY 10012
(212)334-0999
nonfiction/fiction

DENOMINATIONAL LISTING OF BOOK PUBLISHERS AND PERIODICALS

An attempt has been made to divide publishers into appropriate denominational groups. However, due to the extensive number of denominations included, and sometimes incomplete denominational information, some publishers may have inadvertently been included in the wrong list. Additions and corrections are welcome.

ASSEMBLIES OF GOD

Book Publishers:
Gospel Publishing House
Logion Press

Periodicals:
American Horizon
At Ease
CE Counselor
Club Connection
Enrichment
High Adventure
Junior Trails
Live
Paraclete
Pentecostal Evangel
Pentecostal Testimony (Canada)
Resource (Canada)
Teen Life
Take Five
Woman's Touch
Youth Leader

BAPTIST, SOUTHERN

Book Publishers:
Baylor Univ. Press
Broadman & Holman
New Hope Publishers
Southern Baptist Press
Woman's Missionary Union

Periodicals:
Baptist History & Heritage
Challenge
Christian Recreation
Christian Single
Church Administration
Church Media Library
Church Musician
Crusader
Experiencing God
Glory Songs
Journey

Let's Worship
Living With Teenagers
Mature Living
Minister's Family
Music Makers
Music Time
National Drama Service
ParentLife
Plans & Pluses
Proclaim
Senior Musician
Stand Firm

BAPTIST, OTHER

Book Publishers:
Judson Press (American)
National Baptist (Missionary)
Sword of the Lord Publishers (Independent)

Periodicals:
American Baptist in Missions
Atlantic Baptist
Baptist Informer (General)
Baptist Leader (American)
Beautiful Christian Teen
The Canadian Baptist
Certainty (Regular)
Challenge (Regular)
Co-Laborer (Free Will)
Conquest
Courage (Regular)
E Street (GA Baptist)
Fundamentalist Journal
God's Special People (Independent)
Heartbeat (Free Will)
LIGHT...For/Christian Walk (Independent)
The Link (Fellowship/Canada)
Link & Visitor
Messenger, The (Pentecostal Free Will)
Messenger, The (Regular)

Friends Journal
Moments with God (North American)
Primary Pal (Regular)
Secret Place (American)
Standard, The (General)
Writer's Forum

CATHOLIC

Book Publishers:
ACTA Publications
Alba House
American Catholic Press
Brown Publishing
Catholic Book Publishing
Catholic University of America Press
Christendom Press
Cistercian Publications
Dimension Books
Faith Publishing Co.
Franciscan University Press
Harper SF (Cath. bks)
Hi-Time Publishing
ICS Publications
Libros Liguori
Liguori Publications
Liturgical Press
Loyola Press
Thomas More Press
Orbis Books
Our Sunday Visitor
Pastoral Press
Pauline Books
Paulist Press
Regina Press
Regnery Publishing
Resurrection Press
St. Anthony Messenger
St. Bede's Publications
Sheed & Ward
Tabor Publishing

Periodicals:
America
Annals of St. Anne
Arkansas Catholic
Arlington Catholic Herald
Bible Today
Bread of Life
Canadian Catholic Review
Caravan
Catechist
Catechumenate
Catholic Answer
Catholic Courier
Catholic Digest
Catholic Forester
Catholic Heritage
Catholic Insight
Catholic Near East
Catholic New York
Catholic Parent
Catholic Peace Voice
Catholic Rural Life
Catholic Sentinel
Catholic Servant
Catholic Telegraph
Catholic Twin Circle
Celebration
Columbia
Commonweal
Companion
Compass
Conscience
Culture Wars
Diocesan Dialogue
Environment & Art
Emmanuel
Eucharistic Minister
Family Digest, The
Good News for Children
Immaculate Heart Messenger
Interim, The
Liguorian
Living Words
Marian Helpers Bulletin
Messenger/Sacred Heart
Messenger (KY)
Messenger/St. Anthony
Miraculous Medal
Montana Catholic
My Friend
National Catholic Reporter
New Covenant
New Oxford Review
N.A. Voice of Fatima
Oblates
Oblate World
Our Family
Our Sunday Visitor

Parish Liturgy
Pastoral Life
Prairie Messenger
Priest, The
Queen of All Hearts
Religion Teacher's Journal
Review for Religious
St. Anthony Messenger
St. Joseph's Messenger
St. Willibrord Journal
Seeds
Sisters Today
Social Justice Review
Spirit
Spiritual Life
Sursum Corda!
This Rock
Today's Catholic Teacher
Today's Parish
U.S. Catholic
Visions
Way of St. Francis
YOU! Magazine
Youth Update

CHRISTIAN CHURCH/CHURCH OF CHRIST

Book Publishers:
CBP Press (Disciples of
   Christ)
Chalice Press (Disciples of
   Christ)
College Press (Church of
   Christ)
Pilgrim Press, The (United
   Church of Christ)

Periodicals:
Christian Standard
Disciple, The (Disciples of
   Christ)
Four and Five
Lookout, The
R-A-D-A-R
Straight
Teenage Christian (Church of
   Christ)
Weekly Bible Reader

CHURCH OF GOD (Anderson, IN)

Book Publisher:
Warner Press

Periodicals:
Pathways to God

CHURCH OF GOD (Cleveland, TN)

Book Publisher:
Editorial Evangelica

Periodicals:
Church of God EVANGEL
Save Our World
Youth and CE Leadership

CHURCH OF GOD (holiness)

Beginner's Friend
Church Herald and Holiness
   Banner
Gems of Truth
Junior Companion
Primary Pal (KS)
Youth Compass

CHURCH OF GOD, OTHER

Periodicals:
Bible Advocate (Seventh-day)
Bible Advocate Online (Sev-
   enth-day)
Church Advocate
Gem, The
2 Soar (Church of God in
   Christ)

CHURCH OF THE NAZARENE

Book Publishers:
Lillenas (music)
Beacon Hill Press

Periodicals:
Children's Church Exch.
Discoveries
Herald of Holiness
Listen
Power and Light
Preacher's Magazine
Resource
Standard
Table Talk
Teens Today
Together Time
Wonder Time

EPISCOPAL/ANGLICAN

Book Publishers:
Alban Institute
Forward Movement
Morehouse Publishing

Periodicals:
Cathedral Age
Episcopal Life
Interchange
Living Church

FREE METHODIST

Book Publishers:
Light and Life Communications

Periodicals:
Evangel
Light and Life
Light From the Word
World Mission People

FREE WILL BAPTIST

Periodicals:
CoLaborer
Heartbeat

LUTHERAN

Book Publishers:
Concordia
Langmarc Publishing

Periodicals:
Canada Lutheran (ELCC)
Christmas (ELCA)
Cresset
Esprit (ELCC)
Evangelism (MO Synod)
Lutheran, The (ELCA)
Lutheran Digest
Lutheran Educ. (MO Synod)
Lutheran Forum
Lutheran Journal
Lutheran Parent
Lutheran Parent's Wellspring
LutheranPartners (ELCA)
Lutheran Witness (MO
    Synod)
Lutheran Woman's Quarterly
    (MO Synod)
Lutheran Woman Today
    (ELCA)
Northwestern Lutheran
Parenting Treasures (MO
    Synod)
Parish Teacher (ELCA)
Word & World (ELCA)
Teachers Inter. (MO Synod)

MENNONITE

Book Publishers:
Kindred Press

Periodicals:
Canadian Mennonite
Christian Leader, The
Christian Living
Companions
Mennonite Brethren Herald
Mennonite Historian
Mennonite Weekly Review
The Messenger
On the Line
Partners
Purpose
Story Friends
Story Mates
With

MISSIONARY CHURCH

Book Publisher:
Bethel Publishing

Periodicals:
Emphasis/Faith & Living

PENTECOSTAL HOLINESS CHURCH

Periodicals:
CE Connection
Helping Hand, The
Evangelism USA
Worldorama

PRESBYTERIAN

Book Publishers:
Presbyterian & Reformed
Westminster John Knox

Periodicals:
Covenanter Witness
Horizons (USA)
PCA Messenger
Presbyterian Layman (USA)
Presbyterian Outlook (USA)
Presbyterian Record
Presbyterian Today

QUAKER/FRIENDS

Book Publishers:
Barclay Press
Friends United Press

REFORMED CHURCHES

Periodicals:
Perspectives
Reformed Worship
Vision (MI)

SEVENTH-DAY ADVENTIST

Book Publishers:
Pacific Press
Review and Herald

Periodicals:
GUIDE Magazine
Insight (MD)
Journal/Adventist Ed
Kids' Ministry Ideas
Liberty
Listen
Message
Ministry
Our Little Friend
Primary Treasure
Sabbath School Leadership
Signs of the Times
Vibrant Life
Young and Alive

UNITED METHODIST

Book Publishers:
United Methodist Publishing
    House
Imprints: Abingdon Press
Cokesbury
Upper Room Books

Periodicals:
alive now!
Christian Social Action
Good News
Kaleidoscope
Leader/Church School Today
Magazine/Christian Youth!
Mature Years
Methodist History
Michigan Christian Advocate
New World Outlook
Pockets
Quarterly Review
Upper Room

UNITED PENTECOSTAL

Periodicals:
Conqueror, The
Preserving Christian Homes
Teen Life
Vision
Youth World

WESLEYAN CHURCH

Book Publishers:
Wesleyan Publishing House

Periodicals:
Changing Lives
Friend
In Touch
Wesleyan Advocate
Wesleyan World

MISCELLANEOUS DENOMINATIONS
Armenian Holy Apostolic
Pourastan
Brethren Church
Brethren Evangelist
Christian Reformed
The Banner
Brethren in Christ

Evangel Publishing House
Christian & Missionary Alliance
Christian Publications
Evangelical Covenant Church
Cornerstone
Covenant Companion
Evangelical Free Church
Evangelical Beacon
Pursuit
Fellowship of Christian Assemblies
Fellowship Today
Fellowship of Evangelical Bible Churches
Gospel Tidings

Foursquare Gospel Church
Foursquare World Advance
Greek Orthodox
Holy Cross Orthodox Press
Open Bible Standard Churches
MESSAGE of the Open Bible
Orthodox
The Handmaiden
United Church of Canada
United Church Publishing House
United Church Observer
United Church of Christ
United Church Press

LIST OF BOOK PUBLISHERS AND PERIODICALS BY CORPORATE GROUP

In the second year of including this list, we are expanding the listing of book publishers and periodicals that belong to the same group or family of publications.

CCM COMMUNICATIONS
Aspire
CCM (Contemporary Christian Music)
Worship Leader
Youthworker
The CCM Update

CHRISTIAN BOOKSELLERS ASSN.
CBA Frontline
CBA Marketplace

CHRISTIANITY TODAY, INC.
Books & Culture
Campus Life
Christian Computing
Christian History
Christianity Today
Christian Reader
Computing Today
Leadership Journal
Marriage Partnership
Today's Christian Woman
Your Church

CHRISTIAN MEDIA
Christian Media (books)
The Apocalypse Chronicles
Christian Composer
Christian Media

COOK COMMUNICATIONS MINISTRIES
Accent Bible Curriculum
Accent Publications (books)
Chariot Victor Books
Chariot Family Publishing (books)
Lion Publishing (books)
Christian Parenting Today
Counselor
I.D.
Power for Living
Primary Days
Quiet Hour, The
The Rock
Single Adult Ministries Journal
Teen Power
Virtue

FOCUS ON THE FAMILY
Focus on the Family (books)
Breakaway
Brio
Citizen
Clubhouse
Clubhouse Jr.
Focus on the Family
Pastor's Family
Physician
Plugged-In
Single-Parent Family
Teachers in Focus

GROUP PUBLICATIONS, INC.
Children's Ministry
Group Publishing, Inc. (books)
Group Magazine
Group's Jr High Ministry
Group's Hands-On Bible Curriculum
Vital Ministry

GUIDEPOSTS
Guideposts Books
Angels on Earth
Guideposts
Guideposts for Kids

THOMAS NELSON PUBLISHERS
Thomas Nelson Publishers (books)
Tommy Nelson (books)
Word (books)

STANDARD PUBLISHING
Standard Publishing (books)
Christian Standard
The Lookout
R-A-D-A-R
Seek
Straight

STRANG COMMUNICATIONS
Creation House (books)
Charisma & Christian Life
Christian Retailing
Ministries Today
New Man
Vida Cristiana

THE UPPER ROOM
Upper Room Books
alive now!
Devo'Zine
The Upper Room
Weavings

GLOSSARY OF TERMS

NOTE: This is not intended to be an exhaustive glossary of terms. It includes primarily those terms you will find within the context of this market guide.

Advance. Amount of money a publisher pays to an author up front, against future royalties.

All rights. An outright sale of your material. Author has no further control over it.

Anecdote. A short, poignant, real-life story, usually used to illustrate a single thought.

Assignment. When an editor asks a writer to write a specific piece for an agreed-upon price.

Avant-garde. Experimental; ahead of the times.

Bible Versions. KJV—King James Version; NAS—New American Standard; NIV—New International Version; NKJV—New King James Version; NRSV—New Revised Standard Version; RSV—Revised Standard Version.

Bimonthly. Every two months.

Biweekly. Every two weeks.

Book proposal. Submission of a book idea to an editor, usually includes a cover letter, thesis statement, chapter-by-chapter synopsis, market survey, and 1-3 sample chapters.

Byline. Author's name printed just below the title of a story, article, etc.

Circulation. The number of copies sold or distributed of each issue of a publication.

Clips. See "Published Clips."

Column. A regularly appearing feature, section, or department in a periodical using the same heading; written by the same person or a different freelancer each time.

Contributor's copy. Copy of an issue of a periodical sent to the author whose work appears in it.

Copyright. Legal protection of an author's work.

Cover letter. A letter that accompanies some manuscript submissions. Usually needed only if you have to tell the editor something specific, or to give your credentials for writing a piece of a technical nature.

Critique. An evaluation of a piece of writing.

Devotional. A short piece which shares a personal spiritual discovery, inspires to worship, challenges to commitment or action, or encourages.

Editorial guidelines. See "Writer's guidelines."

EPA/Evangelical Press Assn. A professional, trade organization for periodical publishers and associate members.

Essay. A short composition usually expressing the author's opinion on a specific subject.

Evangelical. A person who believes that one receives God's forgiveness for sins through Jesus Christ, and believes the Bible is an authoritative guide for daily living.

Feature article. In-depth coverage of a subject, usually focusing on a person, event, process, organization, movement, trend or issue; written to explain, encourage, help, analyze, challenge, motivate, warn, or entertain—as well as to inform.

Filler. A short item used to "fill" out the page of a periodical. It could be a timeless news item, joke, anecdote, light verse or short humor, puzzle, game, etc.

First rights. Editor buys the right to publish your piece for the first time.

Freelance. As in 50% freelance: means that 50% of the material printed in the publication is supplied by freelance writers.

Freelancer or freelance writer. A writer who is not on salary, but sells his material to a number of different publishers.

Free verse. Poetry that flows without any set pattern.

Genre. Refers to type or classification, as in fiction or poetry. In fiction, such types as westerns, romances, mysteries, etc., are referred to as genre fiction.

Glossy. A black and white photo with a shiny, rather than matte finish.

Go-ahead. When a publisher tells you to go ahead and write up or send your article idea.

Haiku. A Japanese lyric poem of a fixed 17-syllable form.

Holiday/seasonal. A story, article, filler, etc. that has to do with a specific holiday or season. This material must reach the publisher the stated number of months prior to the holiday/season.

Humor. The amusing or comical aspects of life that add warmth and color to an article or story.

Interdenominational. Distributed to a number of different denominations.

International Postal Reply Coupon. See "IRC."

Interview article. An article based on an interview with a person of interest to a specific readership.

IRC or IPRC. International Postal Reply Coupon: can be purchased at your local post office and should be enclosed with a manuscript sent to a foreign publisher.

Journal. A periodical presenting news in a particular area.

Kill fee. A fee paid for a completed article done on assignment that is subsequently not published.

Light verse. Simple, light-hearted poetry.

Mainstream fiction. Other than genre fiction, such as romance, mystery or science fiction. Stories of people and their conflicts handled on a deeper level.

Ms. Abbreviation for manuscript.

Mss. Abbreviation for more than one manuscript.

NASR. Abbreviation for North American serial rights.

Newsbreak. A newsworthy event or item sent to a publisher who might be interested in publishing it because it would be of interest to his particular readership.

Nondenominational. Not associated with a particular denomination.

Not copyrighted. Publication of your piece in such a publication will put it into public domain and it is not then protected. Ask that the publisher carry your copyright notice on your piece when it is printed.

On acceptance. Periodical pays a writer at the time an article is accepted for publication.

On assignment. Writing something at the specific request of an editor.

On publication. Periodical pays a writer when his/her article is published.

On speculation. Writing something for an editor with the agreement that he will buy it only if he likes it.

One-time rights. Selling the right to publish a story one-time to any number of publications (usually refers to publishing for a non-overlapping readership).

Payment on acceptance. See "On acceptance."

Payment on publication. See "On publication."

Pen Name. Using a name other than your legal name on an article in order to protect your identity or the identity of people included in the article. Put the pen name in the byline under the title, and your real name in the upper, left-hand corner.

Personal experience story. A story based on a real-life experience.

Personality profile. A feature article that highlights a specific person's life or accomplishments.

Photocopied submission. Sending an editor a photocopy of your manuscript, rather than an original. Some editors prefer an original.

Published clips. Copies of actual articles you have had published.

Quarterly. Every three months.

Query letter. A letter sent to an editor telling about an article you propose to write and asking if he or she is interested in seeing it.

Reporting time. The number of weeks or months it takes an editor to get back to you about a query or manuscript you have sent in.

Reprint rights. Selling the right to reprint an article that has already been published elsewhere. You must have sold only first or one-time rights originally, and wait until it has been published the first time.

Royalty. The percentage an author is paid by a publisher on the sale of each copy of a book.

SAE. Self-addressed envelope (without stamps).

SASE. Self-addressed, stamped envelope. Should always be sent with a manuscript or query letter.

Satire. Ridicule that aims at reform.

Second serial rights. See "Reprint rights."

Semiannual. Issued twice a year.

Serial. Refers to publication in a periodical (such as first serial rights).

Sidebar. A short feature that accompanies an article and either elaborates on the human interest side of the story or gives additional information on the topic. It is often set apart by appearing within a box or border.

Simultaneous rights. Selling the rights to the same piece to several publishers simultaneously. Be sure everyone is aware that you are doing so.

Simultaneous submissions. Sending the same manuscript to more than one publisher at the same time. Usually done with non-overlapping markets (such as denominational) or when you are writing on a timely subject. Be sure to state in a cover letter that it is a simultaneous submission and why.

Speculation. See "On speculation."

Staff-written material. Material written by the members of a magazine staff.

Subsidiary rights. All those rights, other than book rights, included in a book contract—such as paperback, book club, movie, etc.

Subsidy publisher. A book publisher who charges the author to publish his book, as opposed to a royalty publisher who pays the author.

Tabloid. A newspaper-format publication about half the size of a regular newspaper.

Take-home paper. A periodical sent home from Sunday School each week (usually) with Sunday School students, children through adults.

Think piece. A magazine article that has an intellectual, philosophical, or provocative approach to a subject.

Third World. Reference to underdeveloped countries of Asia and Africa.

Transparencies. Positive color slides, not color prints.

Trade magazine. A magazine whose audience is in a particular trade or business.

Traditional verse. One or more verses with an established pattern that is repeated throughout the poem.

Unsolicited manuscripts. A manuscript an editor did not specifically ask to see.

Vanity publisher. See "Subsidy publisher."

Vitae/Vita. An outline of one's personal history and experience.

Work-for-hire assignment. Signing a written contract with a publisher stating that a particular piece of writing you are doing for him is "work for hire." In the agreement you give the publisher full ownership and control of the material.

Writers' guidelines. An information sheet provided by a publisher which gives specific guidelines for writing for the publication. Always send an SASE with your request for guidelines.

GENERAL INDEX

This index includes only periodicals, books, and greeting cards. Conferences, groups, and editorial services are listed alphabetically by state; agents are listed alphabetically by the name of the agency. Check the Table of Contents for the location of these supplementary listings.

Note: Due to the many changes in the market, and to help you determine the current status of any publisher you might be looking for, this year all markets will be listed in this index. If they are not viable markets, their current status will be indicated here, rather than in separate listings as they have been in prior years. The following codes will be used: (ABD) - asked to be deleted, (BA) - bad address or phone numbers, (ED) - editorial decision, (NF) - no freelance, (NR) - no recent response, (OB) - out of business. These changes will be noted in this listing for 5 years before being dropped altogether.